June 17–21, 2013
New York, NY, USA

Association for Computing Machinery

Advancing Computing as a Science & Profession

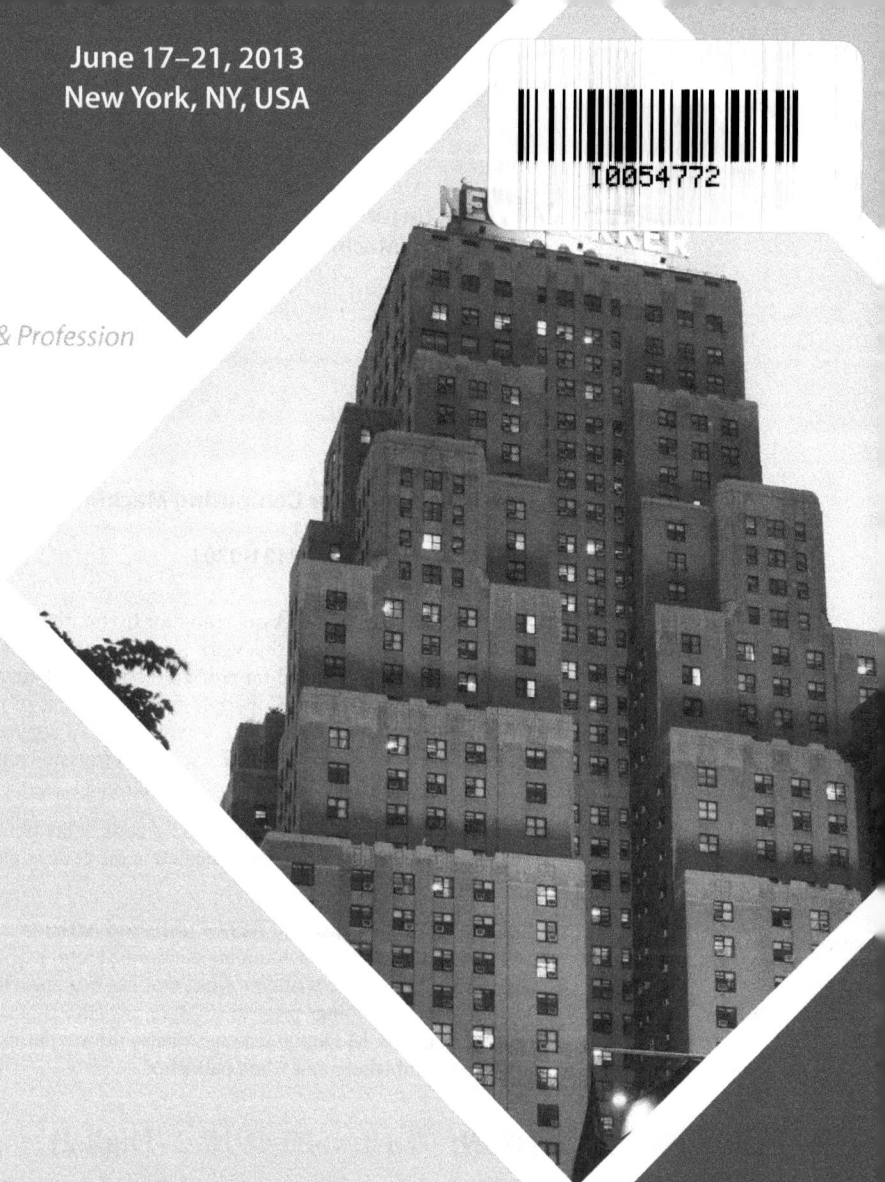

HPDC'13

Proceedings of the 22nd ACM International Symposium on
High-Performance Parallel and Distributed Computing

Sponsored by:

ACM SIGARCH and University of Arizona

Supported by:

NVIDIA, CloudStack, VMWare, IBM Research, and NSF

Association for Computing Machinery

Advancing Computing as a Science & Profession

The Association for Computing Machinery
2 Penn Plaza, Suite 701
New York, New York 10121-0701

ISBN: 978-1-4503-1910-2 (Digital)

ISBN: 978-1-4503-2286-7 (Print)

Additional copies may be ordered prepaid from:

ACM Order Department
PO Box 30777
New York, NY 10087-0777, USA

Phone: 1-800-342-6626 (USA and Canada)
+1-212-626-0500 (Global)
Fax: +1-212-944-1318
E-mail: acmhelp@acm.org
Hours of Operation: 8:30 am – 4:30 pm ET

Printed in the USA

Welcome from the General and Program Co-Chairs

Welcome to the *22nd ACM Symposium on High-Performance Parallel and Distributed Computing* (HPDC'13). HPDC'13 follows the tradition of previous versions of the conference by providing a high-quality, single-track forum for presenting new research results on all aspects of the design, the implementation, the evaluation, and the use of parallel and distributed systems for high-end computing. The HPDC'13 program features six paper sessions on I/O- and Data-Intensive Computing, Networks, Communication, Checkpointing, Bugs and Errors, Multicore and GPUs, and Virtualization and Clouds, and keynotes by Garth Gibson of Carnegie Mellon University and by David Shaw of D.E. Shaw Research. This program is complemented by an interesting set of workshops on a range of timely and related infrastructure and application topics.

The conference once again features the presentation of the HPDC Annual Achievement Award, which was started in 2012. The purpose of this award is to recognize individuals who have made long-lasting, influential contributions to the foundations or practice of the field of high-performance parallel and distributed computing, to raise the awareness of these contributions, especially among the younger generation of researchers, and to improve the image and the public relations of the HPDC community. The process of selecting the winner of the award was formalized this year with an open call for nominations. The recipient of the 2013 HPDC Achievement Award is Miron Livny of the University of Wisconsin, who will give an Achievement Award Talk as a keynote at the conference.

The HPDC'13 call for papers attracted 131 paper submissions. In the review process this year, we retained the two innovations that were introduced in 2012, i.e., the two-round reviewing process and author rebuttals. In the first round, all papers received three reviews, and based on these reviews, 72 papers went to the second round in which virtually all of them received another three reviews (six in total). In total, 592 reviews were provided by the 50-member Program Committee along with a number of external reviewers. For many of the 72 second-round papers, the authors submitted rebuttals. Rebuttals were carefully taken into consideration during the Program Committee deliberations as part of the selection process. In March, the Program Committee met at Rutgers University, and decided on the acceptance of 20 full papers resulting in an acceptance rate of 15.3%. The committee also accepted 14 papers for posters, of which 11 appear in the proceedings. We are very grateful to the members of the Program Committee for their hard work and for providing their reviews on time, in what was a very tight review schedule and a very rigorous review process.

There are a large number of people whom we want to thank for their help in making HPDC'13 a success. We thank the Posters Chair, Ivan Rodero, for putting together the Poster Session. In addition to posters that were accepted based on submitted papers, the poster session also includes posters for accepted full papers, which will be on display throughout the conference, as well as posters submitted in response to a separate call enabling attendees to showcase their ongoing work. We do hope that these additional posters will foster lively discussions.

We greatly appreciate the work of the Workshops Chair, Abhishek Chandra, who has assembled a set of seven very interesting workshops, viz., Scientific Cloud Computing, Energy Efficient High Performance Parallel and Distributed Computing, High Performance and Programmable Networking, Optimization Techniques for Resource Management in Clouds, Fault-Tolerance for HPC at Extreme Scale, Changing Landscapes in HPC Security, and Virtualization Technologies in Distributed Computing.

We acknowledge the help of Dean Hildebrand, who did an excellent job as the Sponsorship Chair, the help of the Publicity Chairs, Alexandru Iosup, Ioan Raicu, Bruno Schulze, and Kenjiro Taura, for diligently disseminating the different calls related to the conference, and the help of Daniele Scarpazza, who took care of all the local arrangements, respectively. We thank our sponsors, ACM

SIGARCH and the University of Arizona, and our supporters, the National Science Foundation, the Department of Energy, Nvidia, IBM, Citrix, and VMware.

We hope that you will enjoy the conference and your stay in New York City!

Manish Parashar
Rutgers University, USA

Jon Weissman
University of Minnesota, USA

General Co-Chairs

Dick Epema
Delft University of Technology
& Eindhoven University of Technology, The Netherlands

Renato Figueiredo
University of Florida, USA & Vrije Universiteit Amsterdam, The Netherlands

Program Co-Chairs

Table of Contents

Session 5: Keynote

Session 6: Checkpointing, Bugs and Errors

Session 7: Multicore and GPUs

Session 8: Virtualization and Clouds

Author Index

2013 International ACM Symposium on High Performance Parallel and Distributed Computing

General Chairs: Manish Parashar *(Rutgers University, USA)*
Jon Weissman *(University of Minnesota, USA)*

Program Chairs: Dick Epema *(Delft University of Technology and Eindhoven University of Technology, The Netherlands)*
Renato Figueiredo *(University of Florida, USA and Vrije Universiteit, The Netherlands)*

Workshops Chair: Abhishek Chandra *(University of Minnesota, USA)*

Posters Chair: Ivan Rodero *(Rutgers University, USA)*

Local Arrangements Chair: Daniele Scarpazza *(D.E. Shaw Research, USA)*

Sponsorship Chair: Dean Hildebrand *(IBM Research, USA)*

Publicity Chairs: Alexandru Iosup *(Delft University of Technology, the Netherlands)*
Ioan Raicu *(Illinois Institute of Technology, USA)*
Kenjiro Taura *(University of Tokyo, Japan)*
Bruno Schulze *(National Laboratory for Scientific Computing, Brazil)*

Steering Committee Chair: Jon Weissman *(University of Minnesota, USA)*

Steering Committee: Henri Bal *(Vrije Universiteit, the Netherlands)*
Andrew A. Chien *(University of Chicago and Argonne National Laboratory, USA)*
Peter Dinda *(Northwestern University, USA)*
Dick Epema *(Delft University of Technology and Eindhoven University of Technology, the Netherlands)*
Renato Figueiredo *(University of Florida, USA and Vrije Universiteit, The Netherlands)*
Ian Foster *(University of Chicago and Argonne National Laboratory, USA)*
Salim Hariri *(University of Arizona, USA)*
Thilo Kielmann *(Vrije Universiteit, the Netherlands)*
Arthur "Barney" Maccabe *(Oak Ridge National Laboratory, USA)*
Manish Parashar *(Rutgers University, USA)*
Matei Ripeanu *(University of British Columbia, Canada)*
Karsten Schwan *(Georgia Institute of Technology, USA)*
Douglas Thain *(University of Notre Dame, USA)*

Program Committee: David Abramson *(Monash University, Australia)*
Kento Aida *(National Institute of Informatics, Japan)*
Gabriel Antoniu *(INRIA, France)*
Henri Bal *(Vrije Universiteit, the Netherlands)*
Adam Barker *(University of St Andrews, UK)*
Michela Becchi *(University of Missouri - Columbia, USA)*
John Bent *(EMC, USA)*
Ali Butt *(Virginia Tech, USA)*
Kirk Cameron *(Virginia Tech, USA)*
Franck Cappello *(INRIA, France & University of Illinois at Urbana-Champaign, USA)*
Henri Casanova *(University of Hawaii, USA)*
Abhishek Chandra *(University of Minnesota, USA)*
Andrew Chien *(University of Chicago & Argonne National Laboratory, USA)*
Paolo Costa *(Microsoft Research Cambridge, UK)*
Peter Dinda *(Northwestern University, USA)*
Gilles Fedak *(INRIA, France)*
Ian Foster *(University of Chicago and Argonne National Laboratory, USA)*
Clemens Grelck *(University of Amsterdam, the Netherlands)*
Dean Hildebrand *(IBM Research, USA)*
Fabrice Huet *(INRIA-University of Nice, France)*
Adriana Iamnitchi *(University of South Florida, USA)*
Alexandru Iosup *(Delft University of Technology, the Netherlands)*
Kate Keahey *(Argonne National Laboratory, USA)*
Thilo Kielmann *(Vrije Universiteit, the Netherlands)*
Charles Killian *(Google, USA)*
Zhiling Lan *(Illinois Institute of Technology, USA)*
John Lange *(University of Pittsburgh, USA)*
Barney Maccabe *(Oak Ridge National Laboratory, USA)*
Carlos Maltzahn *(University of California, Santa Cruz, USA)*
Naoya Maruyama *(RIKEN Advanced Institute for Computational Science, Japan)*
Satoshi Matsuoka *(Tokyo Institute of Technology, Japan)*
Manish Parashar *(Rutgers University, USA)*
Judy Qiu *(Indiana University, USA)*
Ioan Raicu *(Illinois Institute of Technology, USA)*
Philip Rhodes *(University of Mississippi, USA)*
Matei Ripeanu *(University of British Columbia, Canada)*
Prasenjit Sarkar *(IBM Research, USA)*
Daniele Scarpazza *(D. E. Shaw Research, USA)*
Karsten Schwan *(Georgia Institute of Technology, USA)*
Martin Swany *(Indiana University, USA)*
Michela Taufer *(University of Delaware, USA)*
Kenjiro Taura *(University of Tokyo, Japan)*
Douglas Thain *(University of Notre Dame, USA)*
Cristian Ungureanu *(NEC Labs, USA)*
Ana Varbanescu *(Delft University of Technology, the Netherlands)*

HPDC 2013 Sponsors & Supporters

Sponsors:

Supporters:

Scalable In Situ Scientific Data Encoding for Analytical Query Processing

Sriram Lakshminarasimhan [1,2,+], David A. Boyuka II [1,2,+], Saurabh V. Pendse [1,2], Xiaocheng Zou [1,2], John Jenkins [1,2], Venkatram Vishwanath [3], Michael E. Papka [3,4], Nagiza F. Samatova [1,2,*]

[1] North Carolina State University, Raleigh, NC 27695, USA
[2] Oak Ridge National Laboratory, Oak Ridge, TN 37830, USA
[3] Argonne National Laboratory, Argonne, IL 60439, USA
[4] Northern Illinois University, DeKalb, IL 60115, USA
* Corresponding author: samatova@csc.ncsu.edu   + Authors contributed equally

ABSTRACT

The process of scientific data analysis in high-performance computing environments has been evolving along with the advancement of computing capabilities. With the onset of exascale computing, the increasing gap between compute performance and I/O bandwidth has rendered the traditional method of post-simulation processing a tedious process. Despite the challenges due to increased data production, there exists an opportunity to benefit from "cheap" computing power to perform query-driven exploration and visualization during simulation time. To accelerate such analyses, applications traditionally augment raw data with large indexes, post-simulation, which are then repeatedly utilized for data exploration. However, the generation of current state-of-the-art indexes involve a compute- and memory-intensive processing, thus rendering them inapplicable in an *in situ* context.

In this paper we propose DIRAQ, a parallel *in situ, in network* data encoding and reorganization technique that enables the transformation of simulation output into a query-efficient form, with negligible runtime overhead to the simulation run. DIRAQ begins with an effective core-local, precision-based encoding approach, which incorporates an embedded compressed index that is $3 - 6x$ smaller than current state-of-the-art indexing schemes. DIRAQ then applies an *in network* index merging strategy, enabling the creation of aggregated indexes ideally suited for spatial-context querying that speed up query responses by up to 10x versus alternative techniques. We also employ a novel aggregation strategy that is topology-, data-, and memory-aware, resulting in efficient I/O and yielding overall end-to-end encoding and I/O time that is less than that required to write the raw data with MPI collective I/O.

Categories and Subject Descriptors

H.3.1 [**Content Analysis and Indexing**]: Indexing Methods— *inverted index, aggregation*; D.4.2 [**Storage Management**]: Secondary storage—*data compression, parallel storage*

Keywords

exascale computing; indexing; query processing; compression;

1. INTRODUCTION

In high-performance computing (HPC), the concept of *in situ* processing, or processing data at application run time and in application memory, is one of increasing importance. The traditional approach of performing data processing, analysis, etc. as a post-processing step is becoming a rate-limiting factor as application data sizes increase faster than I/O capabilities. Recent research has been investigating the design space and implications of *in situ* processing and data staging frameworks to facilitate this model [1–3, 25, 33]

While the concept of *in situ* processing has been realized in such areas as visualization [19, 24, 31] and analysis frameworks [33], in this paper we focus specifically on index generation. Such indexing enables the acceleration of tasks, such as exploratory and query-driven analysis, that may not themselves be amenable to *in situ* processing, thus indirectly reducing time-to-analysis. This approach to supporting *query-driven analytics* for large-scale data has only just begun to be studied. Recently, the bitmap indexing technique Fast-Bit [21, 28] has been applied in parallel with FastQuery [5, 8, 9] and extended to demonstrate indexing in an *in situ* context [17].

However, in order to extend *in situ* indexing to the production context of high core count application runs, several challenges must first be overcome. Most index generation processes are both computationally expensive and storage intensive, incurring significant processing and I/O overhead. These are opposed to one of the central goals of *in situ* computation: to minimally disturb application run time. Furthermore, as indexing in a global context is prohibitively expensive due to the need for global coordination, current methods of index generation produce *fragmented* indexes across compute resources, which significantly increases query response time. Related to these overheads is the memory-intensive nature of indexing, placing hard constraints on the memory overhead of indexing and limiting the degree of aggregation that can take place.

To address these challenges, we propose a methodology for Data Indexing and Reorganizing for Analytics-induced Query processing (DIRAQ). The following contributions enable us to make inroads towards a storage-lightweight, resource-aware data encoding technique that incorporates a query-efficient index:

Storage-lightweight, Query-optimized Data Encoding We describe an encoding technique that converts raw floating-point data into a compressed representation, which incorporates a *compressed inverted index* to enable optimized query access, while also exhibiting a total storage footprint *less than* that of the original data. We exploit the spatio-temporal properties of the data by leveraging our previous work with ALACRITY [16], augmenting it with a highly-compressed inverted index using a modified version of the PForDelta compression [34] algorithm.

Scalable, Parallel Data Reorganization For fixed-size groups of processes, we "defragment" indexes to optimize query performance by developing an *in network* aggregation and merge technique tailored to our encoding, which distributes the computation equally among all compute cores in the group and allows arbitrary selection of aggregator cores to gather/write the resulting data. This way, we avoid the pitfalls of serializing the encoding process at various stages.

Resource-aware Aggregation We additionally make our group-wise indexing *resource-aware*, dynamically learning optimal data paths and choices of aggregators through per-group neural network modeling that supports online feedback. The optimization space for the model is constrained by the available memory, ensuring memory constraints are not violated.

Our proposed method shows promising results on 9 datasets from the FLASH astrophysics simulation [11] and 4 datasets from S3D combustion simulation [7]. Our encoding reduces the overall storage footprint versus the raw data by a factor of 1.1–1.8x, and versus FastQuery-indexed data by 3–6x. Our scalable reorganization and aggregation method combined with our encoding allows up to 6x to-disk throughput improvement compared to MPI-IO on the raw data. Finally, query performance on our defragmented indexes is improved by up to 10x versus FastQuery-generated bitmap indexes.

2. RELATED WORK

In this section we cover previous work related to *in situ* processing, *in situ* indexing and aggregation strategies for I/O.

The onset of petascale and exascale computation has seen a significant growth in works that encompass simulation-time processing relating to *in situ* and *in network* processing [4, 19, 31], along with several data staging systems such as JITStaging [1], DataStager [3], DataTap [2], PreDatA [33] and GLEAN [25] that explore movement of simulation data to co-located clusters for processing. The DIRAQ pipeline has been carefully designed to complement staging-driven approaches for generating indexes; parts of the index merging process can be offset to staging routines, but is not the focus of this paper.

Distributed and parallel indexing itself has been well researched in the database community. The majority of the indexing techniques are variants of the commonly used B-Tree indexing technique, which have been shown to have sub-optimal performance for many workloads over read-only scientific datasets, when compared to other techniques such as bitmap indexing [27]. The parallel indexing scheme FastQuery [5,8,9] and subsequent *in situ* work [17], which extend the WAH-compressed bitmap indexing method FastBit [21,28], share the same overarching goal as DIRAQ. However, DIRAQ differs in that it utilizes *in situ* index aggregation over a larger spatial context, instead of concatenating indexes from each core, making it more suitable for analytics, and because it explicitly addresses issues such as including network aggregation and limited I/O throughput.

In contrast to a post-processing context, performing indexing *in situ* demands special attention to scalable I/O, an area with much prior work. MPI collective I/O is the canonical approach to this problem, which typically incorporates a two-phase I/O technique [23] to *aggregate* data into fewer, larger requests to the filesystem. This principle has been refined in various ways, including a 3-phase collective I/O technique with hierarchical Z-order encoding [18], and pipelined aggregation enabling the overlap of computation and threaded I/O [12, 13]. However, while these approaches are well-suited to a variety of common I/O patterns, indexing introduces an irregular access pattern. To overcome this, we opt for a customized I/O aggregation strategy that includes *in network* merging of core-local encoded data.

As for optimizing the I/O aggregation process, recent work has been performed on auto-tuning the number of aggregators involved in MPI collective I/O [6]. Depending on the amount of data written out with each group, they either merge or split process groups (indirectly changing the aggregator ratio) to better utilize the available I/O bandwidth. In this paper, we group compute processes that belong to the same processor set (*pset*) since I/O forwarding is done on a per-*pset* level. While they use process mapping based on topology, we employ the aggregator placement to be topology-aware as well. Additionally, our method tunes aggregators within a group, rather than changing the underlying group size.

3. BACKGROUND

3.1 ALACRITY - Indexing for Scientific Data

We use our previous work with ALACRITY [16] as the starting point for indexing in DIRAQ. ALACRITY is a storage-lightweight indexing and data reduction method for floating-point scientific data that enables efficient range query with position and value retrieval. Specifically, ALACRITY is optimized to identify positions satisfying range conditions (e.g. "temperature > 2500") and efficiently retrieves the values associated with those points. It achieves this by utilizing a byte-level binning technique to simultaneously compress and index scientific data. Because ALACRITY integrates data reduction with indexing, it exhibits a much lower storage footprint relative to existing indexing methods. For instance, while ALACRITY's total footprint (data + index) is consistently about 125% of the raw data for double-precision datasets, a typical FastBit [26] encoding over the same data requires $\approx 200\%$, and a B+-Tree may require more than 300% [27].

The key observation in ALACRITY is that, while floating-point datasets have a large number of unique values, the values are still clustered and do not span the entire floating point domain. If we examine the most significant k bytes of these floating point values (typically $k = 2$), this value clustering translates into a list with much lower cardinality. This is because the IEEE floating point format defines the highest k bytes (which we denote as *high-order bytes*) to contain the sign bit, exponent bits, and most significant mantissa bits of the value. The high-order bytes will therefore exhibit lower cardinality than the *low-order bytes*, which typically contain much more variation and noise.

ALACRITY leverages this observation by binning on the high-order bytes of the data. Because the exact high-order bytes are stored as bin "header values," this information does not need to be repeated for each value, and so the data is substantially reduced by storing only the low-order bytes for each datapoint. As a property of the floating-point format, each bin contains points belonging to a single, contiguous value range. Therefore, by properly ordering the bins, range queries can be answered by reading a contiguous range of bins in a single, contiguous read operation, significantly reducing the number of seeks necessary to support value retrieval.

However, because the binning operation rearranges the values, an index is required to maintain the original ordering. In the original paper, we explore two alternatives: a "compression index" and an inverted index. The compression index was shown to be effective in providing data compression, but is not appropriate for querying, and so we do not consider it in this paper. The inverted index, while larger, is still lightweight, with a storage requirement of only 50% of the original data size for double-precision data, and is effective for querying.

While ALACRITY works well in the context of serial indexing, we must develop additional methods in order to support parallel indexing in DIRAQ. In particular, although ALACRITY's total storage size is notably smaller than previous methods, it still represents a non-trivial I/O overhead beyond raw data, and would be expensive if applied as-is for *in situ* indexing. Additionally, index merging was not previously considered, as ALACRITY operated using full-context data. However, in this paper, we analyze the end-to-end performance of indexing, starting from core-local data generation to data capture on storage devices.

3.2 PForDelta - Inverted Index Compression

PForDelta [34] (standing for Patched Frame-of-reference Delta) is a method for efficiently compressing inverted indexes, and is frequently used in the context of indexing and search over unstructured data, such as documents and webpages [29,32]. As ALACRITY presents a viable inverted index-based method for encoding scientific data, it presents a perfect opportunity to further reduce storage overhead by applying PForDelta.

PForDelta encoding operates on a stream of sorted integer values, divided into fixed-size chunks. Each chunk is transformed to encode the first value (the frame of reference) and the differences between consecutive values. A fixed bit width b is then selected to encode the majority of deltas – those remaining are stored as *exceptions* in a separate *exception list*. The majority of deltas typically require a far fewer number of bits to encode than the original data, and a relatively small chunk size (128 elements in the original work) enables a highly adaptive, per-chunk selection of b.

4. METHOD

4.1 Overview

Figure 1 illustrates the logical flow behind DIRAQ *in situ* indexing. Our method consists of the following components:

1. **Storage-lightweight, query-optimized data encoding** that produces a compressed form of the data with an integrated index, combining both data *and* index compression. By achieving a low storage requirement while also supporting optimized range queries, this encoding approach enables us to surmount the obstacle that the HPC I/O bottleneck represents to *in situ* indexing. This component is explained in Section 4.2.

2. **Scalable, parallel data reorganization**, which reduces I/O time and improves post-simulation query performance by aggregating encoded data, without incurring unacceptable global communication costs. For comparison, existing indexing methods produce either a single, global index, or a highly-fragmented set of per-core indexes. Unfortunately, the former can only be accomplished with post-processing or expensive global communication, and the latter results in degraded query performance (as demonstrated in Section 5.2). In contrast, our group-level index aggregation technique largely avoids both

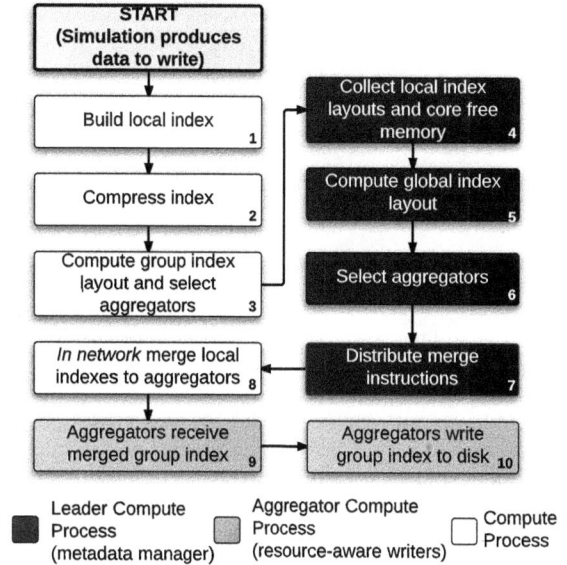

Figure 1: Overview of the DIRAQ indexing methodology, with lightweight encoding[1,2], scalable index aggregation[8,9] and resource-aware dynamic aggregator selection [6].

of these drawbacks. We also leverage the hardware-level RMA support in modern HPC clusters to perform fast *in network* merging. These aspects of DIRAQ are discussed in Section 4.3.

3. **Resource-aware dynamic aggregator selection**, which incorporates the inherent *network topology* and *available memory* constraints of a running system to improve the choice of aggregator cores at runtime. Leveraging this information helps to achieve improved performance over MPI-IO two-phase I/O [10]. More detail is given in Section 4.4.

4.2 Lightweight, Query-optimized Data Encoding

The first step for DIRAQ is to address the fundamental challenge of *in situ* processing, and indexing in particular: because simulation I/O blocking time is already a serious concern today, any *in situ* process must ensure this metric is not substantially impacted. However, while there exist parallel indexing methods for scientific data, no current method has addressed this issue sufficiently to operate within the context of a running simulation. The root of the problem is two-fold. First, current indexing methods inherently *increase* total storage footprint (data + index), commensurately increasing I/O times. Second, computation time for current indexing methods dominates even the I/O time.

We address this problem in DIRAQ by extending ALACRITY, a storage-lightweight indexing method with integrated *data compression*, by augmenting it with *index compression* to achieve even higher overall compression. By thus reducing both components of the output, we reduce the storage footprint to **55%-90%** (a compression ratio of 1.1-1.8x) for 9 variables from FLASH [11] simulation data (Table 1). Note that these compression ratios include both index *and* data; this implies the data encoding can simultaneously support efficient range queries *while also reducing total simulation I/O*, a win-win scenario.

As with ALACRITY, the DIRAQ query-optimized encoding format enables two-sided range queries of the form $a < var < b$ to be evaluated efficiently (a or b may also be $-\infty$ or $+\infty$, respectively, allowing one-sided range queries, as well). Given such a constraint, DIRAQ can retrieve the matching values (value retrieval) and/or the matching dataset positions (position retrieval). Additionally, DIRAQ supports an approximate query mode that accepts a bounded per-point error in order to perform an index-only query, which has benefits to query performance. These query types are discussed in more detail in a previous paper [16]. In pseudo-SQL syntax, the index supports queries of the forms:

SELECT *var* [and/or] *position* WHERE $a < var < b$
SELECT $\sim$*var* [and/or] *position* WHERE $a < \sim var < b$

An overview of the encoding format produced by DIRAQ is depicted in Figure 2. The process of binning is largely similar to that presented in the ALACRITY paper [16], as reviewed in Section 3.1, although some modifications have been made (including a generalization to support bit-level, rather than byte-level, adjustment of the high/low-order division point). However, the major extension that enables this encoding methodology to be used for in situ indexing is the incorporation of index compression, and thus this component is described in detail next.

4.2.1 Inverted Index Compression

In DIRAQ, an inverted index is used to map binned values to their (linearized) positions in the original dataset, referred as "record IDs," or "RIDs." Within each bin, we keep the low-order byte elements sorted by ascending RID, which enables us to apply PForDelta to the inverted index of each bin. Thus, the problem of index compression in DIRAQ can be reframed as compressing sorted lists of unique integers; the chosen method can then be applied to each bin's inverted index independently to achieve overall index compression.

Instead of using general-purpose compression routines, we use a modified version of PForDelta to leverage the specific properties of our inverted index. As stated in Section 3.2, PForDelta operates on a sorted list of integers, which matches the nature of DIRAQ's inverted indexes. Furthermore, PForDelta achieves high compression ratios for clustered elements; in DIRAQ, the inverted index RIDs typically exhibit good clustering, as these spatial identifiers are grouped by bin, and thus correspond to similar-valued points, which tend to cluster spatially.

We make modifications to PForDelta to achieve higher compression ratios for our application. The first difference is in the method for specifying the positions of exceptions in the delta list for patching. As opposed to the original approach, which uses a linked list of relative offsets embedded in the delta list, we instead leverage the fact that all RIDs are unique, implying that all deltas are strictly positive. This permits us to place 0's in the delta list to mark exception positions, as they do not normally appear, thus eliminating the need for an embedded linked list and forced exceptions. These 0's have low overhead, as they are bit-packed along with the deltas.

The second modification we implement is to deal with overhead when compressing small chunks. While our implementation maintains the fixed 128-element chunk sizes used in the original PForDelta work, the last chunk may have fewer elements. If the original input stream (inverted index bin, in our case) has far fewer elements than one chunk (128), PForDelta's chunk metadata may become dominant, reducing compression ratios or even slightly *inflating* the index. This situation occurs for datasets with high variability (when modeling turbulence for example), which leads to a large number of small bins. To prevent this issue from unduly harming overall compression, we add a dynamic capability in PForDelta to selectively disable compression of chunks that are not successfully reduced in size.

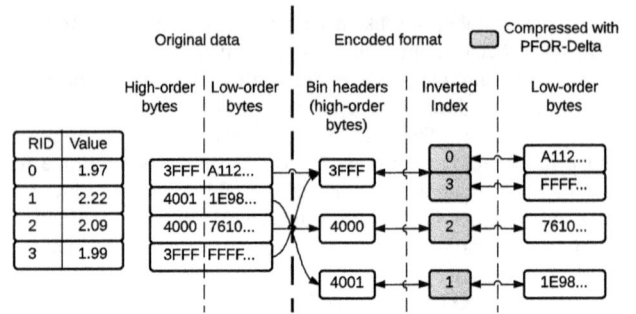

Figure 2: An overview of how raw floating-point data is encoded by DIRAQ for compact storage and query-optimized access. CII stands for compressed inverted index.

4.2.2 Effectiveness of Index Compression

As a preliminary microbenchmark, we evaluate the overall throughput and compression ratios of DIRAQ's encoding on 6 single-precision and 3 double-precision datasets from the FLASH [11] simulation. The test platform is the Intrepid BlueGene/P supercomputer. For each dataset, we take 256 compute cores worth of data, and encode each independently (simulating the core-local indexing that will be used in the next section), reporting the mean statistics in Table 1.

Compression Ratio: In our microbenchmarks, we observed index compression ratios from 3x to 20x across different variables and different refinement levels in the FLASH dataset. We observe that the compression ratio directly correlates with the number of bins in the dataset encoding, as shown in Table 1. With fewer bins, each bin's inverted index contains a larger portion of the RIDs for the dataset. This yields a denser increasing sequence of RIDs per bin, and thus smaller delta values, which ultimately results in a high compression ratio due to PForDelta bitpacking with 1 or 2 bits per element. Even with less compressible datasets like *vely, velz*, we observe ≈ 2.5x compression of the index.

Overall, this level of compression results in substantial I/O reduction, and also improves aggregation performance (as discussed in Section 4.3). For comparison, when encoding these same datasets using the original ALACRITY method, total storage footprints (data + index) are all around 150% for the single-precision datasets, and 125% for those with double-precision. Over the datasets we evaluate, we observe effective I/O throughput to be increased by a factor of $1.5 - 2.5$x based on this data encoding method

Throughput: The indexing throughput is also dependent on the number of bin values, but to a lesser degree as compared to the compression ratio (max-over-min variation of about 1.4x vs. about 10x). This is primarily due to the use of fixed-size chunks during index compression, each of which is processed independently. However, since the compression is considerably faster than I/O access and has the net result of reducing the data footprint, the variation in indexing throughputs of DIRAQ do not contribute to a noticeable variation in end-to-end times , unlike with other compute-intensive indexing techniques [8, 9].

4.3 Scalable, Parallel, In Situ Index Aggregation

In the simplest case, we can parallelize our indexing method by applying it to all compute cores simultaneously, generating *core-local* indexes, similar to FastQuery. However, this method of parallelization produces *fragmented* indexes, which are poor for query performance. Queries must necessarily process each core-local in-

Table 1: Effect of dataset entropy (number of bins) on index compression ratio and total size on 256 processes each indexing 1 MB of data on BG/P.

Dataset	Average Bins	Index Compression Ratio	Total Size (% of Raw)	Encoding Throughput (MB/s)
flam	8	19.8	55	18.7
pres	1	20.6	54	18.7
temp	7	17.1	55	18.7
velx	339	4.3	78	17.6
vely	1927	2.4	90	14.0
velz	1852	2.5	89	14.1
accx*	172	3.3	88	15.1
accy*	166	3.3	88	15.0
accz*	176	3.3	88	15.0

* double-precision datasets.
+ total data written out as a % of original raw data.

dex in turn, incurring numerous disk seek costs and other overheads. Thus, it is desirable to build an index over aggregated data. However, performing global data aggregation is not scalable due to expensive global communication, so we instead consider *group-level* index aggregation, where compute nodes are partitioned into fixed-size groups, balancing the degree of index fragmentation (and thus query performance) with I/O blocking time (and thus simulation performance).

A particular challenge in building an index over a group of processes is the distribution of computation over the group. Forwarding per-core data to a small number of "aggregator cores" to be indexed poorly utilizes compute resources. Instead, we make the observation that core-local DIRAQ indexes can be merged efficiently. However, merging the indexes solely using aggregator cores again underutilizes the remaining compute cores, which sit idle during that time.

Given these challenges, we opt for a third option, shown in Figure 3, that eliminates compute bottlenecks at the aggregator cores. After each core in the group locally encodes its data, a group "leader" core collects the local index metadata and computes the group index metadata. The group index metadata is then used by each compute core to implicitly merge the indexes *in network* by using Remote Memory Access (RMA), thereby materializing the group index fully formed across any number of chosen aggregator cores. Using this method, aggregators and all the other group cores perform the same degree of computation, as well as avoid per-core file writing, at the small cost of a metadata swap (which would be necessary, regardless).

Having given an overview of the aggregation method in DIRAQ, we now examine each step in more detail. Note that, while we focus on *index aggregation* this section, because DIRAQ's encoding tightly integrates the index and low-order bytes, an equivalent aggregation and merging process is also applied to the low-order bytes. Thus, unless specifically noted, every step in the follow procedure is applied to both the index and low-order bytes simultaneously, but we discuss in terms of the index for brevity.

4.3.1 Building the group index

The DIRAQ encoding technique is especially suited for *in situ* index aggregation, as it enables efficient determination of the group index layout before any actual data or index is transferred. Recall that our encoding bins data according to values that share the same most significant bits (called the bin's "header value"). Because this number of significant bits is fixed across all cores, if bins with the same header value appear on multiple cores, all these bins will have

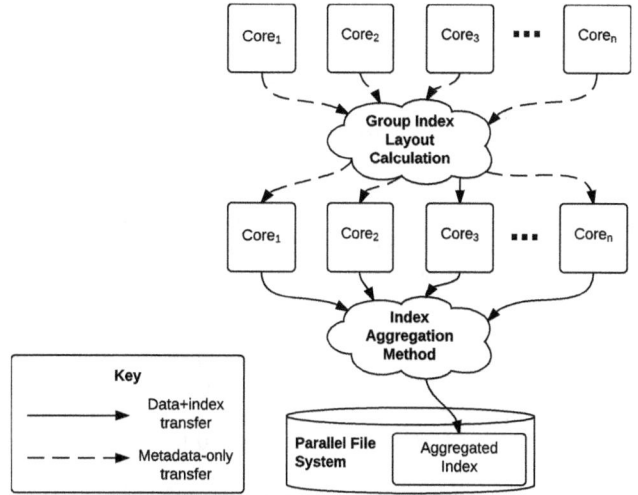

Figure 3: A logical view of group index aggregation and writing.

equivalent value boundaries, and will furthermore be part of the same bin in the group index, greatly simplifying the index merge operation. Furthermore, because the data within a bin is ordered by RID, and we assign a contiguous range of RIDs to each core, merging several local bins into a group bin is a simple matter of concatenation. Note that "bin" here refers to both the bin's low-order bytes and its associated inverted index.

The process for building the group layout on the leader core is shown in Figure 4. First, the layouts for all core-local indexes within the group are collected to a "group leader" core. Next, the leader takes the union of all bin header values for the group, and then determines the offset of each local index bin within the corresponding group index bin, with bins from cores with lower RID ranges being filled first. Finally, the newly-constructed group layout is disseminated back to the compute cores, along with the set of bin offsets specific to each core (referred to as "bin placements"). Note that indexes could also be aggregated across groups, by exchanging bin metadata between group leaders. We expect to study this possibility in future work.

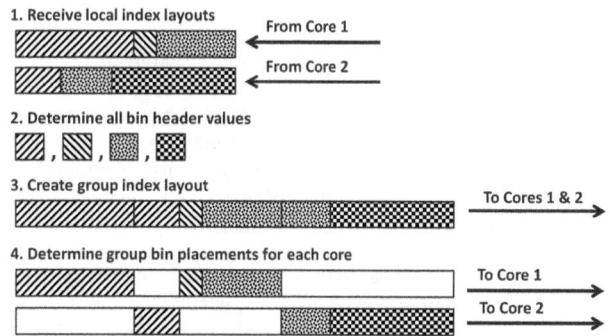

Figure 4: Steps for building a group index layout on the leader core (shown for a group size of 2, generalizable for more cores).

The end result is that each core obtains a complete view of the group index to build, as well as precise locations for its local index bins within that group index. In other words, the cores now collectively have a logical view of how the aggregation should proceed. It is important to note that this cooperative layout construction process constitutes only a small part of the overall end-to-end indexing time, and so we focus the bulk of our optimization efforts on the more time-intensive aggregation and write phases next.

4.3.2 *Index aggregation via* in network *memory reorganization*

After all cores in the group receive the group index layout and core-specific bin placements, the cores proceed to transfer their local bins to the appropriate locations within the group index. This mapping is straightforward at this point; the bin placements include an offset and length within the group index for each local bin. However, simply writing at these offsets to a shared file will result in $N \cdot B$ qualitatively random write operations hitting the parallel file system servers at once (where N is cores per group, and B is average local index bins per core). With $N \approx 64$ and $B \approx 4,000+$, typical in our experiments with FLASH, the resultant $250,000+$ I/O requests *per group* would be prohibitively expensive, and an alternative approach must be sought. Furthermore, the straightforward usage of MPI-IO would necessarily require numerous, small writes and high communication overhead, corresponding to the highly interleaved mapping between core-local and group indexes.

Our solution leverages a cooperative *in network memory reorganization* technique to utilize the RMA capabilities of modern network infrastructure to perform index merging during network transfer. Using this method, the system can materialize the group index fully-formed across the memory of a subset of the compute cores in the group, called the "aggregator cores." The process proceeds as follows:

1. A set of aggregator cores with sufficient memory to collectively accommodate the group index is selected. This is done by piggybacking available memory statistics from each core on the existing local layout messages sent to the group leader, and having the leader disseminate the selection along with the group index layout and bin placements. We examine the importance of selecting topologically-separated and memory-balanced aggregators in Section 4.4; for now, the specific selection criteria are not pertinent.

2. After this selection, the memory commitment needed for the group index is balanced as evenly as possible across the aggregators, which then expose the required memory to all the compute cores for RMA operations.

3. Finally, all compute cores treat the exposed memory on the aggregators as a single, contiguous memory buffer, and use their bin placements and knowledge of the group index layout to inject their local index bins onto the proper aggregators at the right offsets. These data transfers utilize MPI one-sided RMA operations, using relaxed consistency and reduced-locking hints to achieve increased performance.

4. After RMA synchronization is completed, the group index is fully formed on the aggregators, which then simply write out the entire contents of their exposed memory window in sequential chunks on disk, completing the process.

By circumventing the need for an in-memory index merge, the computational load on the aggregators is reduced (which is important because there are few of them relative to the number of cores in the group). Furthermore, this approach also eliminates the need for temporary swap buffers required during an in-memory merge, and so is more robust in the face of limited spare memory available under many real-world simulations.

4.4 Optimizing index aggregation using memory- and topology-awareness

---

Algorithm 1: Topology-aware aggregator assignment on group leader processes

---

Input : n: Number of processes in the group.
Input : $M[1,...,n]$: Free memory size of each process in the group.
Input : d: Average amount of data per-core.
Input : b: Average number of bins per-core.
Output: a: Estimated ideal number of aggregators.
Output: t: Estimated neural-net time.
Output: $R[1,...,a]$: Ranks of aggregators.
Output: O: Start and end offsets associated with each aggregator.

1   $minAggs = getMinAggregators(M,n,d)$
2   $maxAggs = getMaxAggregators(M,n,d)$
3   $t = \infty$

4   // Estimate the optimal number of
5   // aggregators using trained model
6   **for** $numAggs = \{minAggs, ..., maxAggs\}$ **do**
7      $estimatedTime = NNEstimate(numAggs, d, b)$
8   **if** $t > estimatedTime$ **then**
9         $t = estimatedTime$
10         $a = numAggrs$
11   **end**
12 **end**

13 // Try placing aggregators using
14 // topology-aware settings
15 **for** $aggSet \in \{topologyAwareAggregatorSetList\}$ **do**
16   **if** $fit(a, aggSet, M) == TRUE$ **then**
17         $R = \text{assign}(a, aggSet)$
18         $O = \text{generateOffsets}(a, R, d)$
19   **return** $\{a, t, R, O\}$
20   **end**
21 **end**

22 // Generate a valid random placement
23 $R = \text{generateRandomAggregators}(a, M)$
24 $O = \text{generateOffsets}(a, R, d)$
25 **return** $\{a, t, R, O\}$

One of the most common techniques employed for I/O is two-phase MPI collective I/O, which performs a data aggregation phase prior to writing. However, the number and placement of aggregators within MPI, which can be tuned using "hints," does not take topology considerations into account, leading to network hotspots and other performance degradations [25]. Hence, recent works have explored topology-aware mapping for BlueGene/P [25] and tuning the aggregation ratio [6, 25].

However, these static techniques are not directly applicable within DIRAQ for the following reasons. First, the use of index compression results in varying data sizes written out by process groups. Second, with DIRAQ, the aggregation phase not only includes a simple data transfer, but also an *in network* index merging strategy. Thus, the *in network* aggregation performance is based on a number of changing parameters, such as differing bin layouts across write phases, and so requires a more dynamic approach.

To account for these *time-variant* characteristics in DIRAQ, as well as the highly interleaved (core-local) I/O access patterns DIRAQ produces, data aggregation requires a strategy in which the number of aggregators/writers evolve according to simulation data characteristics. In DIRAQ, the group leaders are a natural fit for driving this process, as they have a complete view of the aggregated index and are responsible for distributing aggregator information to the other cores in the group.

We build an optimization framework that can dynamically select the number of aggregators, given the group index and low-order byte layout, while leveraging the work done in GLEAN [25] to contol aggregator placement. Since this layout has numerous, interacting characteristics, our initial study found that rigid, linear models insufficiently captured the relationship between group layout and I/O. Hence, we train a neural network, bootstrapping offline to model and optimize DIRAQ aggregation parameters. Our choice of using neural-network-based learning is based on the fact that it is suitable to learn representations of the input parameters that capture the characteristics of the input distribution and subsequently carry out function approximation, especially when modeling non-linear functions [14, 30]. The topology- and memory-aware strategy is described in the Algorithm 1. The details of the performance modeling are explained in the following section.

Both the neural network and the list of topology-aware aggregator sets are determined simultaneously using a set of offline microbenchmarks. The usage of the neural network warrants further discussion (See Section 4.4.1). We estimate the execution time of the aggregation process as a function of the number of aggregators. Then, after pruning the possible number of aggregators based on memory constraints, we run the neural network over each possible number of aggregators, and choose the number that is predicted to have the minimal completion time. By estimating the completion time, the leader can perform error propagation based on the actual time taken. Furthermore, we observed negligible computational overhead (on the order of milliseconds), even when running multiple iterations of the neural network estimation.

4.4.1 Performance Model

The goal of the neural network-based performance model is to accurately predict the performance of three components: the index and low-order byte aggregation times as well as the I/O times for DIRAQ, both with and without inverted index compression. Given these predictions, we can apply the model on each group to determine at run-time a well-performing set of aggregators. Furthermore, we focus on the BlueGene/P architecture, though our methods can be applied to other cluster architectures. Table 2 gives the necessary parameters.

Given the BlueGene/P architecture, the DIRAQ indexing framework consists of three components, namely the compute cores, the aggregators, and the BlueGene I/O pipeline, which consists of the I/O forwarding cores and a Myrinet switch which provides connectivity to file server cores of a cluster-wide file system [25]. We assume an aggregation group of size ρ. An aggregation group is defined as a logical group of ρ compute cores (with one of them also as the group leader) and corresponding a aggregator cores. Each aggregation group forms an MPI communicator in our implementation. We model the aggregation and I/O process taking place in a single aggregation group.

In order to build an accurate model, we must take into account the RMA contention at the aggregators. To do so, we ran a set of microbenchmarks to measure the aggregation and I/O times, for varying parameters ρ, B, d, and a (refer to Table 2). Linear regression is not suitable for modeling the non-linear relationship $t_{agg\_io} = f(\rho, d, b, a)$. Therefore, we used a 3-layered neural network with ρ, B, d, and a as inputs, 40 neurons in the hidden layer and the t_{agg_io} as the output. This is further used to determine the

Table 2: Parameters for the performance model.

Fixed Input Parameters	
ρ	Number of compute cores per MPI communicator
e	Unit element size (e.g. 32 bits for single-precision)
s	Number of significant bits used in DIRAQ encoding
γ	Data reduction due to indexing $(= s/(8 \cdot e))$
Run-time Input Parameters	
a^*	Number of aggregators per MPI communicator
d	Average size of core-local data
B	Average number of core-local bins
l	Average local inverted index size
σ	Average inverted index compression ratio
Bootstrapped Input Parameters	
μ_w	Disk write throughput per aggregator (determined using microbenchmarks)
Output Parameters	
$t_{agg\_io\_index}$	Index aggregation and I/O time (sec)
$t_{agg\_io\_LOB}$	Low-order byte aggregation and I/O time (sec)

* Iterated over by leader node for optimization.

optimal number of aggregators in Algorithm 1.

We collected measurements for the aggregation and I/O times for various combinations of ρ, d, B, and a. We then trained the neural network using the FANN neural network library [20] with a total of 630 such samples. We used a $85 - 15\%$ division into the training and testing subsets. With this configuration, we obtained a mean squared error of $1.15e^{-4}$ and an R^2 statistic of 0.9812 on the test data using the iRPROP training algorithm [15] and the symmetric sigmoid (tanh) activation function. On the contrary, a simple linear regression model resulted in a R^2 statistic of 0.553.

4.4.1.1 Case 1 : Without compression.

In this case, the local layout of the index corresponding to the target variable is first built on every compute core. Then, the local index generation takes place which is followed by the process of building the global index layout and transferring the index metadata. Note that the former is purely a computation step, while the latter primarily involves communication between the compute cores. The index and low-order bytes are then aggregated followed by the initiation of the index and low-order bytes I/O operations. During I/O, the compute cores produce the data for the next time step and initiate the corresponding local layout generation.

The index and low-order byte aggregation steps involve the compute cores writing at known offsets in the aggregator core's memory via one-sided RMA calls. The indexing scheme reduces the data by about $\gamma = \frac{s}{8 \cdot e}$ of its original size. Thus,

$$t_{agg\_io\_index} = f(\rho, l, B, a) \qquad (1)$$

$$t_{agg\_io\_LOB} = f(\rho, (1-\gamma)d, B, a) \qquad (2)$$

4.4.1.2 Case 2 : With compression.

This scenario includes an additional index compression stage. In this case, we add the index compression phase after the local index generation at every compute core. The low-order byte aggregation and I/O remains the same. However, the index aggregation and I/O take place over the compressed index. Thus,

$$t_{agg\_io\_index} = f\left(\rho, \frac{l}{\sigma}, B, a\right) \qquad (3)$$

Using the above equations for index and low-order byte aggre-

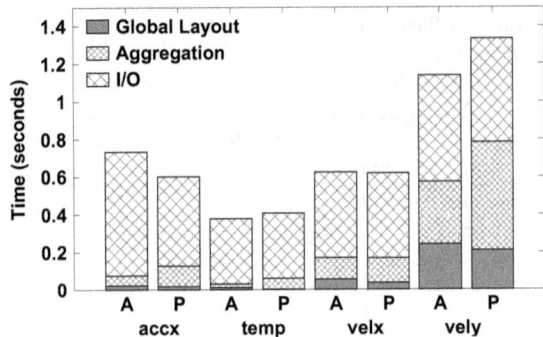

Figure 5: Accuracy of the performance model prediction on Group Layout, Aggregation, and I/O timings with compression for a fixed compute to aggregator ratio of 8:1. A, P stand for actual and predicted timings, respectively.

gation, and the values of ρ, d, and B as input, we determine the optimal number of aggregators for both the index and low-order bytes as the one which results in the minimum t_{agg_io} times :

$$\hat{a}_{LOB} = \underset{a}{\text{argmin}} \ t_{agg\_io\_LOB}(a) \qquad (4)$$

$$\hat{a}_{index} = \underset{a}{\text{argmin}} \ t_{agg\_io\_index}(a) \qquad (5)$$

4.4.2 Accuracy of Performance Model

In this section, we analyse the accuracy of the trained neural network in two scenarios. One, where the model predicts the aggregation and I/O times when the aggregation ratio is fixed, and the other when model picks the aggregation ratio. This is done at the group leader nodes, which has the necessary parameters like the number of bins, compression ratios and access to the trained neural network to make smart decisions. Figure 5 shows the predicted accuracy on component timings when the aggregation ratio is fixed for 4 variables from FLASH simulation, with 1 MB of data indexed and compressed at each core.

5. EXPERIMENTAL EVALUATION

With regards to our parallel, *in situ* indexing methodology, there are three primary performance metrics we evaluate. The first, query performance, serves two purposes: it gives a comparison between DIRAQ and FastQuery indexes, and it underscores the need for defragmented indexes to accelerate query-driven analytics. The second, index performance, evaluates our group-wise index aggregation methodology, looking at index size, generation speed, and scalability. The final metric, end-to-end time (which is broken down stage-by-stage for better insight), evaluates the effectiveness of our memory- and topology-aware optimizations, as based on dynamic neural network application, as well as our methodology as a whole.

5.1 Experimental Setup

Our experiments were conducted on the "Intrepid" system at the Argonne Leadership Computing Facility (ALCF). It is a 40K node quad-core BlueGene/P cluster consisting of 80 TB memory delivering a peak performance of 557 TFlops. Unless otherwise specified, evaluations were done on the General Purpose Filesystem (GPFS) [22] with the default striping parameters. Each experiment below was repeated 5 times and the reported numbers correspond to the median times for each of the results below. All experiments were performed in the "VN" mode in which one MPI process is launched on every core on the chosen set of nodes.

Before we describe the results, we would like to point out that the GPFS storage utilization was over 96%, at the time of our evalution. As a result, the practically observed I/O throughput (Figure 9) is only a fraction of the theoretical maximum throughput.

We execute DIRAQ with the Sedov white-dwarf FLASH simulation [11] and analyze its *in situ* performance on 9 different datasets (6 single-precision and 3 double precision). However, for the sake of brevity, we present the results on 4 datasets. Based on the dataset entropy (Table 1), the chosen single-precision variables *temp, velx, vely* can be considered representative samples of all the datasets used in this paper. Since, the number of unique values (bins) in the index directly relates to the compression ratio we take datasets that have low $(100 - 200)$, medium $(1000 - 5000)$ and high (> 10000) number of *global* bins, which correspond to *temp, velx,* and *vely*, respectively. Additionally, we choose one double precision dataset *accx* as well.

Additionally, to analyze the performance of index compression and querying across simulations, we show results on 4 datasets from S3D combustion simulation as well. We do not include scaling results from S3D in this paper, since S3D does not run on Intrepid, and our optimizations related to topology-aware aggregations exploit BlueGene/P-specific hardware. We analyze the serial query performance over S3D datasets on the Lens Analysis Cluster at Oak Ridge National Laboratory. Each node of Lens consists of four 2.23 GHz AMD Opteron quad-core processors and is equipped with 64 GB of RAM. We run the queries over the Lustre File System with the default striping parameters.

5.2 Query Performance

We first demonstrate the importance of aggregation for postsimulation query performance. Figure 6 depicts the serial query performance of DIRAQ and FastQuery with full-precision value retrieval (meaning exact values are returned). We use single-sided range queries of the form $var < b$, where b is selected to induce a particular query selectivity. We perform this experiment using multiple partition sizes (that is, amounts of data indexed as a unit), ranging from 1 MB to 1024 MB on a 2 GB dataset, while fixing query selectivity (i.e., the fraction of data satisfying the query) at 0.1%. Note that FastQuery is constrainted to a partition size equal to the amount of data available per variable per core, as the algorithm produces a local index for on core (though all such indexes are stored contiguously on disk). In contrast, DIRAQ can produce larger partition sizes by increasing its aggregation ratio, even when per-core data is low.

The figures show two trends. First, the DIRAQ indexing scheme, being lightweight in both computation and storage, outperforms FastQuery's method given a particular partition size. Second, for both methods, query performance is directly proportional to index partition size, presumably because the number of seeks induced is inversely proportional to the partition size, while the sizes of any contiguous reads are reduced. This performance characteristic of indexing in general is precisely our motivation for opting to perform index aggregation, rather than core-local indexing.

5.3 Indexing Performance

The performance of an indexing methodology can be considered in numerous contexts: a *storage* context, a *computational* context, and a *scalability* context. The following sections explore these contexts, providing a finer grain performance measure and analysis of individual tasks in DIRAQ.

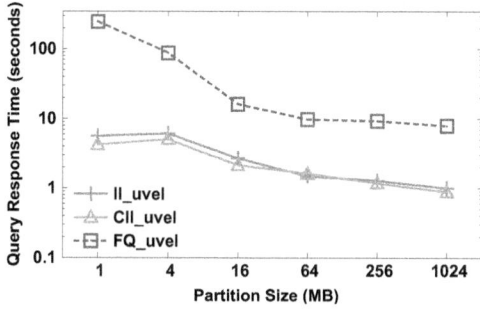

(a) uvel from S3D simulation.

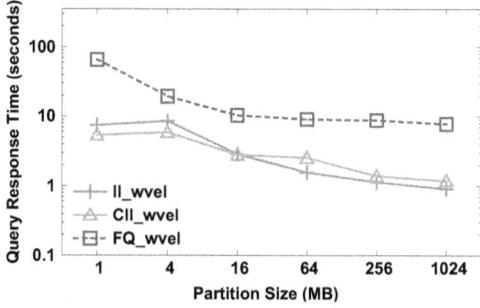

(b) wvel from S3D simulation.

Figure 6: Comparison of response times of DIRAQ compressed (CII) and uncompressed (II) indexes with FastQuery, over various aggregation sizes, on queries of fixed-selectivities.

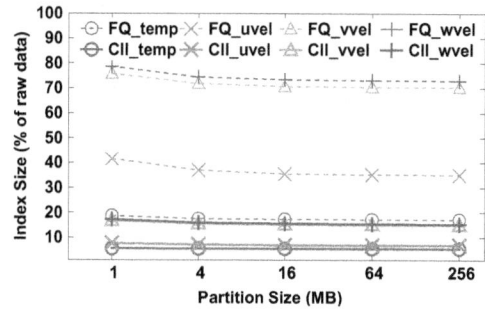

(a) Double-precision datasets from S3D simulation.

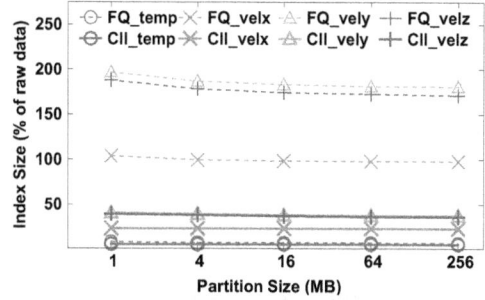

(b) Single-precision datasets from FLASH simulation.

Figure 7: Resulting index sizes (as a % of raw data) on varying amount of data aggregated per-core with FastQuery (FQ) and DIRAQ (CII) indexing techniques.

5.3.1 Index Size

Figure 7 shows the index size generated for both single-precision FLASH variables as well as double-precision S3D variables over 256 MB of raw data. As with the query processing results, we experiment with multiple partition sizes to ascertain the effect of index fragmentation on index size. FastQuery's index size, as a proportion of the raw data, slightly increases for smaller partition sizes, and the difference in resulting index sizes using DIRAQ is near imperceptible. While the index metadata size increases in proportion to decreasing partition sizes, the overall effect is negligible. This means that, when considering the size of aggregation groups in DIRAQ, overall index size can be disregarded as an optimization parameter.

5.3.2 Indexing Speed

The core-local indexing throughput was shown in Table 1. In this section, we instead look at end-to-end indexing performance through scalability metrics, as well as study the stage-by-stage timing breakdown of DIRAQ with and without compression.

5.3.2.1 Scalability.

It is crucial that DIRAQ exhibit favorable scalability properties, as it aims to index large-scale data. To this end, we have performed both strong and weak scalability benchmarks, simulating the indexing of one variable during one timestep. In both benchmarks, we keep the aggregator group size constant. In the strong scalability experiment, the overall data size is kept constant at 2 GB, whereas in the weak scalability experiment, the data size per core is kept constant at 1 MB per core.

The weak scaling results vary as shown in the Figure 9. We observe that the throughput for DIRAQ with compression increases almost linearly with the number of cores in the simulation for all the variables, due to increasing utilization of I/O resources. We

compare DIRAQ with the baseline case of writing the raw simulation output using MPI-I/O and POSIX file-per-process approaches, both evaluated using the IOR benchmark. With DIRAQ we observe throughput gains of approximately 5x and 6x on the *velx* and *temp* variables respectively, and close to a 2x improvement for the least compressible *vely* variable. On the other hand, DIRAQ without compression yields a similar performance as these baseline approaches. Note that, without index compression, DIRAQ writes out 1.5x more than the original raw output, but performs comparably to the other write schemes, likely due to our topology-aware aggregation.

The strong scaling results vary as shown in the Figure 8. Under strong scaling, the amount of data indexed per core reduces at larger scales. While the index size generated by DIRAQ is proportional to the input data size (Figure 7), and so remains constant, the data movement stage now generates smaller message sizes per bin. This slightly increases the network contention at larger scales, but since the available I/O throughput increases as we request more cores, and this is the dominant component, we see improvements in the end-to-end times.

5.3.2.2 Performance Breakdown.

We breakdown the performance of DIRAQ by analyzing the execution time of each stage in the pipeline for the 4 datasets, namely *temp*, *velx*, *vely*, and *accx*, with and without compression. We componentize the stages of DIRAQ into *Encoding, Group Layout, Aggregation*, and *I/O*.

The *Encoding* stage gives the total time involved in encoding the core-local data, including the optional PForDelta compression of the inverted index. The *Group Layout* involves sending the core-local layout to the group leader, which constructs the global layout and assigns aggregators in charge of performing I/O. The *Aggregation* component includes the time taken to send both the index and

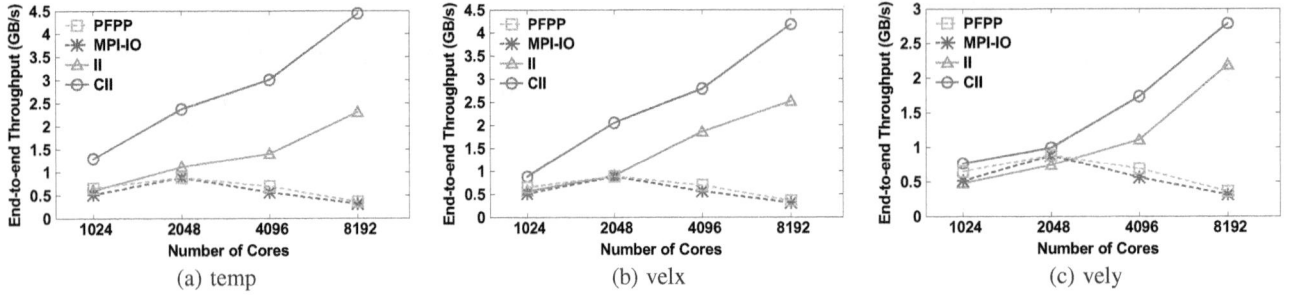

(a) temp

(b) velx

(c) vely

Figure 8: Strong scaling on the effective end-to-end throughput (original data size / end-to-end encoding time) on 3 FLASH simulation datasets indexing a total of 2 GB, on Intrepid. PFPP (POSIX file-per-process) and MPI-IO (two-phase collective) perform raw data writes with no overhead of indexing.

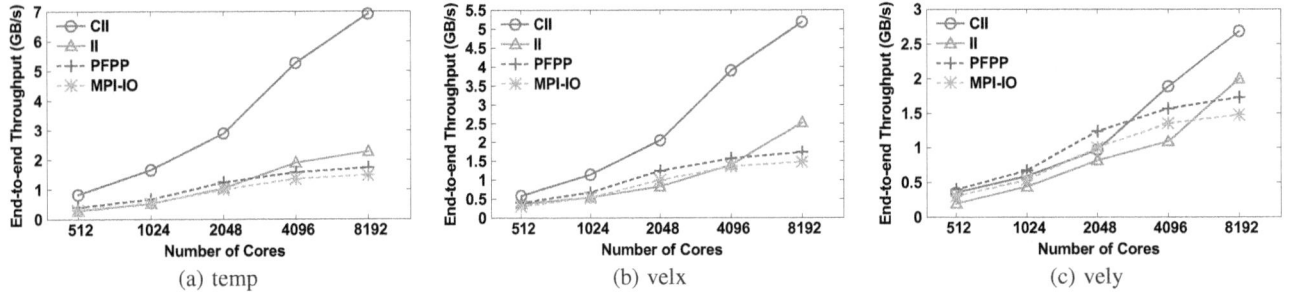

(a) temp

(b) velx

(c) vely

Figure 9: Weak scaling on the effective throughput (original data size / end-to-end indexing time) for 3 FLASH simulation datasets indexing 1 MB on each core on Intrepid. PFPP, MPI-IO performs raw data writes with no overhead of indexing.

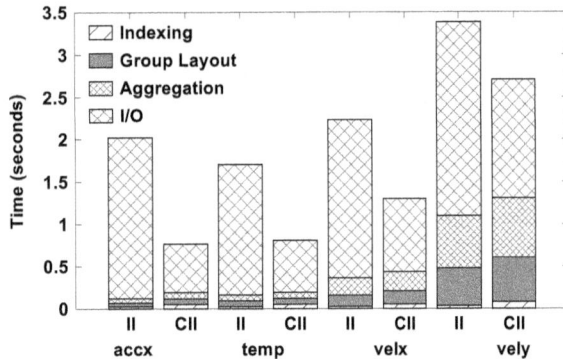

Figure 10: Cumulative time spent on each stage of DIRAQ for 4 datasets from FLASH simulation on Intrepid, with each process indexing 1 MB of data using an uncompressed index (II), and a compressed inverted index (CII).

low-order bytes to its corresponding aggregator, and the *I/O* component includes the time taken to perform the I/O operation on the aggregators, and the waiting-time on the non-aggregator processes.

Figure 10 shows the total time involved in creating aggregated indexes for the chosen datasets, with and without compression. Each process operates on 1 MB of data and a group, consisting of 256 processes uses 32 aggregators (writers). In almost all the cases, compression has a positive impact by reducing the amount of data moved within the network and I/O. However, the time spent in each stage of the pipeline varies with the entropy of the candidate dataset. For example, the time spent in the aggregation and group layout phases of the *temp* variable (highly compressible) is significantly less than the same for the *vely* variable (least com-

pressible). We further discuss the breakdown results for the *temp* and *vely* variables since they are representative of the dataset entropy spectrum. We observe an average case performance for the *velx* and *accx* variables.

- *Encoding*: The encoding time at local cores is affected by the number of unique bin values present in the data. The dataset *vely*, which has 100x more unique bins than *temp*, requires around 2x more time to complete the encoding process. Even with the application of compression, which roughly doubles the amount of encoding time, this stage consumes less than 5% of the total execution time.

- *Group Layout*: Unlike the encoding process, which is local to each core, the group layout stage requires M:1 communication within each group for merging the bin layouts from each process. However, the group-leader performs more work when the dataset has a larger number of unique bins, since calculating the offsets for each core in the group-aggregated layout requires M-way list-merge-like operations that induce loop branching and semi-random access. This explains why *vely* has a pronounced *Group Layout* stage compared to the other datasets. Activating index compression adds another 10% to the group layout time, since additional index compression metadata must be communicated and merged.

- *Aggregation*: This step essentially converts a set of distributed, non-contiguous, core-local views of the index/low-order bytes into a smaller set of aggregated, contiguous segments of the index/low-order bytes on the aggregators. To achieve this, each process would need to make B_{local} RMA calls, where B_{local} is the number of local bins at that process. For datasets with few unique bins, very few RMA calls are required to

10

cluster the index and low-order bytes by bin, which occurs quickly on the 3D torus network.

- *I/O and end-to-end times*: The number of bins, and the clustering factor of values determine the final compression ratio. For example, the variable *pres*, and to a lesser extent *flam*, possesses little variation in the indexed values on a single core. These datasets have indexes that are compressed by as much 20x, and thus have $\approx$ 22% and 35% less data to write to disk when compared with *velx* and *vely*, respectively. When compared with using an uncompressed inverted index, the amount of data written is reduced by as much as 2.7x, leading to end-to-end completion times that are up to 2.2x faster.

5.4 Resource Awareness

Figure 11 shows the performance of the aggregator selection mechanism on the dataset *vely* at 4096 cores. The resource-aware aggregation algorithm chooses a well-performing number of aggregators. On the hard-to-compress dataset *vely*, for example, the neural network predicts within a group, 8 aggregators for the index aggregation, and 16 for the low-order bytes aggregation, as opposed to a single, fixed aggregation ratio. Compared with static aggregation strategies, this results in 10-25% improvement in average throughput when writing to disk. The additional benefit from this scheme is that the variation in end-to-end times across groups is reduced as well, thereby reducing the idle time on some groups waiting to synchronize after I/O.

The neural net is inclined to pick a higher number of aggregators when indexes are less compressible. For other variables such as *temp*, which are highly compressible, an aggregation ratio of 64:1 (4 aggregators) enables aggregator writers to avoid making very small I/O requests to the filesystem. Because of topology-aware aggregator placement along with an aggressive compression scheme, aggregation times generally do not present a bottleneck when compared with I/O times.

6. CONCLUSION

This paper describes DIRAQ, an effective parallel, *in situ* method for compressing and indexing scientific data for analysis purposes during simulation runtime. DIRAQ produces a compressed index that is significantly smaller than state-of-the-art indexes. The combination of index compression and data reduction results in an encoding that, in many cases, is actually smaller than the original, unindexed data. By using a high-throughput local indexing and compression scheme followed by an effective *in network* index merging and aggregation strategy, DIRAQ is able to generate group-level indexes with minimal overhead to the simulation. For our application, a custom aggregation scheme, along with an adaptive approach to choosing aggregator ratios, results in better performance compared to MPI collective I/O routines. Overall, DIRAQ presents an analysis-efficient data encoding that is smaller than the raw data in majority of the cases, offers faster query processing time than current indexing schemes, and can be generated *in situ* with little-to-no overhead (and possibly an I/O performance improvement) for simulation applications.

7. ACKNOWLEDGMENT

We would like to thank the FLASH Center for Computational Science at the University of Chicago for providing access to the FLASH simulation code and both the FLASH and S3D teams for providing access to the related datasets. We would like to acknowledge the use of resources at the Leadership Computing Facilities at Argonne National Laboratory and Oak Ridge National Laboratory, ALCF and OLCF respectively. Oak Ridge National Laboratory is managed by UT-Battelle for the LLC U.S. D.O.E. under Contract DE-AC05-00OR22725. This work was supported in part by the U.S. Department of Energy, Office of Science, Advanced Scientific Computing Research and the U.S. National Science Foundation (Expeditions in Computing and EAGER programs). The work of MEP and VV was supported by the DOE Contract DE-AC02-06CH11357.

8. REFERENCES

[1] H. Abbasi, G. Eisenhauer, M. Wolf, K. Schwan, and S. Klasky. Just in time: adding value to the IO pipelines of high performance applications with JITStaging. In *Proc. Symp. High Performance Distributed Computing (HPDC)*, 2011.

[2] H. Abbasi, J. Lofstead, F. Zheng, K. Schwan, M. Wolf, and S. Klasky. Extending I/O through high performance data services. In *Proc. Conf. Cluster Computing (CLUSTER)*, Sep 2009.

[3] H. Abbasi, M. Wolf, G. Eisenhauer, S. Klasky, K. Schwan, and F. Zheng. DataStager: scalable data staging services for petascale applications. In *Proc. Symp. High Performance Distributed Computing (HPDC)*, 2009.

[4] J. C. Bennett, H. Abbasi, P.-T. Bremer, R. Grout, A. Gyulassy, T. Jin, S. Klasky, H. Kolla, M. Parashar, V. Pascucci, P. Pebay, D. Thompson, H. Yu, F. Zhang, and J. Chen. Combining in-situ and in-transit processing to enable extreme-scale scientific analysis. In *Proc. Conf. High Performance Computing, Networking, Storage and Analysis (SC)*, 2012.

[5] S. Byna, J. Chou, O. Rübel, Prabhat, H. Karimabadi, W. S. Daughton, V. Roytershteyn, E. W. Bethel, M. Howison, K.-J. Hsu, K.-W. Lin, A. Shoshani, A. Uselton, and K. Wu. Parallel I/O, analysis, and visualization of a trillion particle simulation. In *Proc. Conf. High Performance Computing, Networking, Storage and Analysis (SC)*, 2012.

[6] M. Chaarawi and E. Gabriel. Automatically selecting the number of aggregators for collective I/O operations. In *Proc. Conf. Cluster Computing (CLUSTER)*, 2011.

[7] J. H. Chen, A. Choudhary, B. de Supinski, M. DeVries, E. R. Hawkes, S. Klasky, W.-K. Liao, K.-L. Ma, J. Mellor-Crummey, N. Podhorszki, R. Sankaran, S. Shende, and C. S. Yoo. Terascale direct numerical simulations of turbulent combustion using S3D. *Journal of Computational Science & Discovery (CSD)*, 2(1), 2009.

[8] J. Chou, K. Wu, and Prabhat. FastQuery: a parallel indexing system for scientific data. In *Proc. Conf. Cluster Computing (CLUSTER)*, 2011.

[9] J. Chou, K. Wu, O. Rübel, M. Howison, J. Qiang, Prabhat, B. Austin, E. W. Bethel, R. D. Ryne, and A. Shoshani. Parallel index and query for large scale data analysis. In *Proc. Conf. High Performance Computing, Networking, Storage and Analysis (SC)*, Nov 2011.

[10] J. M. del Rosario, R. Bordawekar, and A. Choudhary. Improved parallel I/O via a two-phase run-time access strategy. *ACM SIGARCH Computer Architecture News*, 21(5):31–38, Dec 1993.

[11] B. Fryxell, K. Olson, P. Ricker, F. X. Timmes, M. Zingale, D. Q. Lamb, P. MacNeice, R. Rosner, J. W. Truran, and H. Tufo. FLASH: an adaptive mesh hydrodynamics code for modeling astrophysical thermonuclear flashes. *Astrophysical Journal Supplement Series*, 131:273–334, Nov 2000.

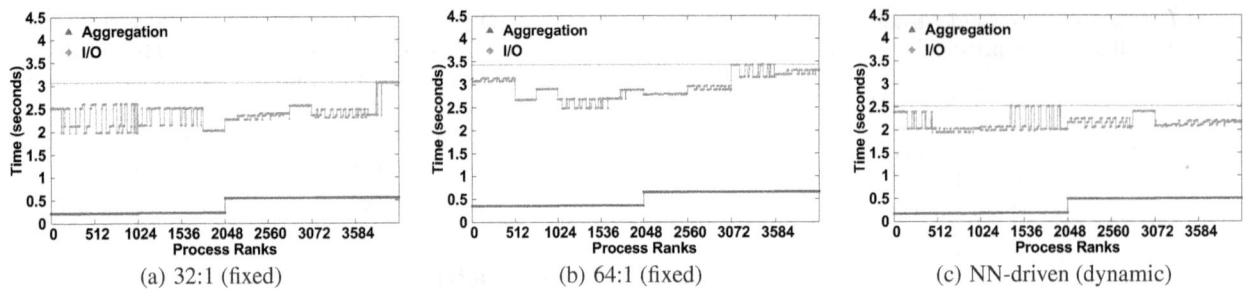

(a) 32:1 (fixed)	(b) 64:1 (fixed)	(c) NN-driven (dynamic)

Figure 11: Comparison of different aggregation strategies (number of compute to aggregator process) on I/O and aggregation timings, with process ranks sorted by aggregation times. 1 MB of the dataset *vely* is indexed by each of the 4096 processes.

[12] J. Fu, R. Latham, M. Min, and C. D. Carothers. I/O threads to reduce checkpoint blocking for an electromagnetics solver on Blue Gene/P and Cray XK6. In *Proc. Workshop on Runtime and Operating Systems for Supercomputers (ROSS)*, 2012.

[13] J. Fu, M. Min, R. Latham, and C. D. Carothers. Parallel I/O performance for application-level checkpointing on the Blue Gene/P system. In *Proc. Conf. Cluster Computing (CLUSTER)*, 2011.

[14] K. Hornik, M. Stinchcombe, and H. White. Multilayer feedforward networks are universal approximators. *Proc. Conf. Neural Networks*, Jul 1989.

[15] C. Igel and M. Hüsken. Empirical evaluation of the improved Rprop learning algorithm. *Journal of Neurocomputing*, 50:2003, 2003.

[16] J. Jenkins, I. Arkatkar, S. Lakshminarasimhan, N. Shah, E. R. Schendel, S. Ethier, C.-S. Chang, J. H. Chen, H. Kolla, S. Klasky, R. B. Ross, and N. F. Samatova. Analytics-driven lossless data compression for rapid in-situ indexing, storing, and querying. In *Proc. Conf. Database and Expert Systems Applications, Part II (DEXA)*, 2012.

[17] J. Kim, H. Abbasi, L. Chacon, C. Docan, S. Klasky, Q. Liu, N. Podhorszki, A. Shoshani, and K. Wu. Parallel in situ indexing for data-intensive computing. In *Proc. Symp. Large Data Analysis and Visualization (LDAV)*, Oct 2011.

[18] S. Kumar, V. Vishwanath, P. Carns, J. A. Levine, R. Latham, G. Scorzelli, H. Kolla, R. Grout, R. Ross, M. E. Papka, J. Chen, and V. Pascucci. Efficient data restructuring and aggregation for I/O acceleration in PIDX. In *Proc. Conf. High Performance Computing, Networking, Storage and Analysis (SC)*, 2012.

[19] K. L. Ma. In situ visualization at extreme scale: challenges and opportunities. *Journal of Computer Graphics and Application (CG&A)*, pages 14–19, 2009.

[20] S. Nissen. Implementation of a fast artificial neural network library (fann). Technical report, Department of Computer Science University of Copenhagen (DIKU), Oct 2003. http://fann.sf.net.

[21] O. Rübel, Prabhat, K. Wu, H. Childs, J. Meredith, C. G. R. Geddes, E. Cormier-Michel, S. Ahern, G. H. Weber, P. Messmer, H. Hagen, B. Hamann, and E. W. Bethel. High performance multivariate visual data exploration for extremely large data. In *Proc. Conf. High Performance Computing, Networking, Storage and Analysis (SC)*, 2008.

[22] F. Schmuck and R. Haskin. GPFS: a shared-disk file system for large computing clusters. In *Proc. Conf. File and Storage Technologies (FAST)*, Jan 2002.

[23] R. Thakur and A. Choudhary. An extended two-phase

[24] method for accessing sections of out-of-core arrays. *Journal of Scientific Programming*, 5(4):301–317, Dec 1996.

[24] T. Tu, H. Yu, J. Bielak, O. Ghattas, J. C. Lopez, K.-L. Ma, D. R. O'Hallaron, L. Ramirez-Guzman, N. Stone, R. Taborda-Rios, and J. Urbanic. Remote runtime steering of integrated terascale simulation and visualization. In *Proc. Conf. High Performance Computing, Networking, Storage and Analysis (SC)*, 2006.

[25] V. Vishwanath, M. Hereld, V. Morozov, and M. E. Papka. Topology-aware data movement and staging for I/O acceleration on Blue Gene/P supercomputing systems. In *Proc. Conf. High Performance Computing, Networking, Storage and Analysis (SC)*, pages 1–11, 2011.

[26] K. Wu. FastBit: an efficient indexing technology for accelerating data-intensive science. In *Journal of Physics: Conference Series (JPCS)*, volume 16, page 556, 2005.

[27] K. Wu, E. Otoo, and A. Shoshani. On the performance of bitmap indices for high cardinality attributes. In *Proc. Conf Very Large Data Bases (VLDB)*, 2004.

[28] K. Wu, R. R. Sinha, C. Jones, S. Ethier, S. Klasky, K.-L. Ma, A. Shoshani, and M. Winslett. Finding regions of interest on toroidal meshes. *Journal Computational Science & Discovery (CSD)*, 4(1), 2011.

[29] H. Yan, S. Ding, and T. Suel. Inverted index compression and query processing with optimized document ordering. In *Proc. Conf. World Wide Web (WWW)*, 2009.

[30] R. M. Yoo, H. Lee, K. Chow, and H.-H. S. Lee. Constructing a non-linear model with neural networks for workload characterization. In *Proc. Symp. Workload Characterization (IISWC)*, Oct 2006.

[31] H. Yu, C. Wang, R. W. Grout, J. H. Chen, and K.-L. Ma. In situ visualization for large-scale combustion simulations. *Journal of Computer Graphics and Applications (CG&A)*, 30(3):45 –57, May-Jun 2010.

[32] J. Zhang, X. Long, and S. Torsten. Performance of compressed inverted list caching in search engines. In *Proc. Conf. World Wide Web (WWW)*, 2008.

[33] F. Zheng, H. Abbasi, C. Docan, J. Lofstead, Q. Liu, S. Klasky, M. Parashar, N. Podhorszki, K. Schwan, and M. Wolf. PreDatA: preparatory data analytics on peta-scale machines. In *Proc. Symp. Parallel Distributed Processing (IPDPS)*, Apr 2010.

[34] M. Zukowski, S. Heman, N. Nes, and P. Boncz. Super-scalar RAM-CPU cache compression. In *Proc. Conf. Data Engineering (ICDE)*, 2006.

Taming Massive Distributed Datasets: Data Sampling Using Bitmap Indices

Yu Su
Computer Science and
Engineering
The Ohio State University
Columbus, OH 43210
su1@cse.ohio-state.edu

Gagan Agrawal
Computer Science and
Engineering
The Ohio State University
Columbus, OH 43210
agrawal@cse.ohio-
state.edu

Jonathan Woodring
Los Alamos National
Laboratory
Los Alamos, NM 87544
woodring@lanl.gov

Kary Myers
Los Alamos National
Laboratory
Los Alamos, NM 87544
kary@lanl.gov

Joanne Wendelberger
Los Alamos National
Laboratory
Los Alamos, NM 87544
joanne@lanl.gov

James Ahrens
Los Alamos National
Laboratory
Los Alamos, NM 87544
ahrens@lanl.gov

ABSTRACT

With growing computational capabilities of parallel machines, scientific simulations are being performed at finer spatial and temporal scales, leading to a data explosion. The growing sizes are making it extremely hard to store, manage, disseminate, analyze, and visualize these datasets, especially as neither the memory capacity of parallel machines, memory access speeds, nor disk bandwidths are increasing at the same rate as the computing power. Sampling can be an effective technique to address the above challenges, but it is extremely important to ensure that dataset characteristics are preserved, and the loss of accuracy is within acceptable levels.

In this paper, we address the data explosion problems by developing a novel sampling approach, and implementing it in a flexible system that supports server-side sampling and data subsetting. We observe that to allow subsetting over scientific datasets, data repositories are likely to use an indexing technique. Among these techniques, we see that bitmap indexing can not only effectively support subsetting over scientific datasets, but can also help create samples that preserve both value and spatial distributions over scientific datasets. We have developed algorithms for using bitmap indices to sample datasets. We have also shown how only a small amount of additional metadata stored with bitvectors can help assess loss of accuracy with a particular subsampling level. Some of the other properties of this novel approach include: 1) sampling can be flexibly applied to a subset of the original dataset, which may be specified using a value-based and/or a dimension-based subsetting predicate, and 2) no data reorganization is needed, once bitmap indices have been generated. We have extensively evaluated our method with different types of datasets and applications, and demonstrated the effectiveness of our approach.

Categories and Subject Descriptors

H.2.8 [**Information Systems**]: DATABASE MANAGEMENT—*Database Applications*

General Terms

Performance

Keywords

big data, bitmap indexing, data sampling

1. INTRODUCTION

Many of the 'big-data' challenges today are arising from increasing computing ability, as data collected from simulations has become extremely valuable for a variety of scientific endeavors. With growing computational capabilities of parallel machines, scientific simulations are being performed at finer spatial and temporal scales, leading to a data explosion. As a specific example, the Global Cloud-Resolving Model (GCRM) [24] currently has a grid-cell size of 4 km, and already produces 1 petabyte of data for a 10 day simulation. Future plans include simulations with a grid-cell size of 1 km, which will increase the data generation 64 fold.

Finer granularity of simulation data offers both an opportunity and a challenge. On one hand, it can allow understanding of underlying phenomena and features in a way that would not be possible with coarser granularity. On the other hand, larger datasets are extremely difficult to store, manage, disseminate, analyze, and visualize. Neither the memory capacity of parallel machines, memory access speeds, nor disk bandwidths are increasing at the same rate as the computing power, contributing to the difficulty in storing, managing, and analyzing these datasets. Simulation data is often disseminated widely, through portals like the Earth System Grid (ESG) [6], and downloaded by researchers all over the world. Such dissemination efforts are hampered by dataset size growth, as wide area data transfer bandwidths are growing at a much slower pace. Finally, while visualizing datasets, human perception is inherently limited relative to dataset sizes.

The above trends are leading to the following three problems:

1. Creating subsampled (lower-resolution) datasets from a high resolution simulation dataset, on demand and efficiently, while maintaining the characteristics of the original dataset.

2. Assessing the loss of quality (with respect to the key statistical measures) incurred with a particular level of resolution, on the given dataset, without having to take a pass through the entire high resolution dataset.

3. Providing the above functionality in a flexible system, which can support sampling at the server-side in response to requests from the client-side, and combine sampling with data subsetting.

1.1 Existing Sampling Techniques, Limitations, and Big Data Needs

Though, to the best of our knowledge, no system provides all of the above functionality, sampling itself has been extensively studied. Broadly, different statistical sampling methods [12, 30, 42, 44] have been proposed to find a representative subset of the entire dataset. Some popular techniques include *simple random sampling*, where we select a certain percent of elements randomly out of original dataset, and *stratified random sampling*, where we first divide the dataset into strata and then perform random sampling within each stratum. The latter method maintains certain spatial properties of the original dataset. To compare the accuracy between the sampled dataset and the original dataset, different error metrics [27, 43, 21] have also been used.

However, as we argue below, the existing work does not meet all the requirements, especially in the context of growing dataset sizes and the need for data dissemination and analysis in a distributed environment.

Sampling Accuracy: Two factors are extremely important while creating samples of scientific datasets so as to facilitate accurate analysis. The first is *value distribution*, i.e., the value distribution of the sampled dataset should be as close to the original dataset as possible. The second is *spatial distribution*, i.e., the data accuracy should be maintained not only for the entire dataset but also for various spatial sub-blocks. Most of the sampling methods [33, 43] developed in the context of scientific data management are focused on the second factor, but ignore the first one. On the other hand, value distribution based sampling is well studied and has been proven to be a good method in the database area [18, 35]. These methods, however, are not developed for scientific datasets, and do not even consider spatial distribution. Consideration of both value distribution and spatial locality is necessary for scientific datasets, and unfortunately, none of the existing work has included both.

Error Calculation without High Overheads: After sampling, it is also important to know how accurately the current sample is able to represent the original dataset. Different error metrics, such as mean, variance, histogram[1] and Q-Q plot[2] are used as diagnostics of the accuracy. With increasing dataset sizes and the distributed nature of analysis, there are several challenges in applying these methods. In particular, when the goal is to find the smallest sample that can achieve a satisfactory accuracy, the traditional sampling process involves the following (possibly iterative) process: 1) sample generation, and 2) error metrics calculation. If the error is too high, repeat with a larger sample, starting from step 1. The entire process can be extremely time consuming, especially if one needs to iterate multiple times. In particular, with the current methods, there is no way to know in advance what may be the smallest sample size at which acceptable accuracy levels can be achieved.

Flexible Data Analysis over Any Subset: In many cases, users are only interested in data analysis or visualization over a subset of the data. For example, only certain timestamps may be of interest, and/or only a particular spatial subarea needs to be analyzed. Even if server-side subsetting is available, the resulting dataset size may

---

[1]http://en.wikipedia.org/wiki/Histogram
[2]http://en.wikipedia.org/wiki/Q-Q_plot

be very large. Thus, the sampling method should be such that it can be applied to any specified subset. Unfortunately, existing sampling methods cannot support such flexible data subset sampling.

Data Sampling without Data Reorganization: Certain sampling methods, such as KDTree-based stratified sampling[44], have been shown to be effective for scientific datasets. However, before sampling can be performed, data reorganization is necessary. This imposes huge memory and disk I/O costs. Moreover, it is not possible to maintain multiple copies of a massive dataset, and sampling is not the only operation to be performed at server-side. After reorganization, other data features that are necessary for other tasks could be lost. Thus, we need sampling methods which operate while maintaining the data in the original format.

1.2 Our Contributions

In this paper, we address the above limitations of existing work by developing a novel sampling approach. We observe that to allow subsetting over scientific datasets, data repositories are likely to use an indexing technique [39]. Among these techniques, we see that bitmap indexing can not only effectively support subsetting over scientific datasets, but can also help create samples that preserve both value and spatial distributions over scientific datasets. We have developed algorithms for using bitmap indices to sample datasets. We have also shown how only a small amount of additional metadata stored with bitvectors can help assess loss of accuracy with a particular subsampling level, i.e., we do not need to take a pass over the entire sampled dataset to calculate accuracy based on these metrics. Some of the other properties of this novel approach include: 1) value distribution as well as spatial distribution of the original dataset are preserved, 2) sampling can be flexibly applied to a subset of the dataset, which may be specified using a value-based and/or a dimension-based subsetting predicate, and 3) no data reorganization is needed, once bitmap indices have been generated.

We have extensively evaluated our method with different types of datasets and applications. First, considering two applications - visualization and clustering, we show that server-side sampling can drastically improve the efficiency of remote datasets analysis. Next, we show that our method has much better accuracy than simple random sampling and stratified random sampling methods, and with respect to different metrics, either better or comparable performance to KDTree-based sampling (which requires expensive data reorganization). Next, we show that our error pre-calculation methodology, a unique characteristic of our approach, gives very accurate estimation of error in sampled datasets. We also analyze the sample generation time with our approach, and show that when error calculation time and possibility of resampling to meet desired accuracy is included, our method outperforms other approaches. Finally, we show that we can combine our sampling method with value-based and/or dimension-based subsetting effectively.

2. SYSTEM OVERVIEW

This section gives an overview of the system we have developed to support flexible server-side sampling of large datasets. Technical details of the sampling method will be given in the next Section.

Figure 1 shows a high-level overview of our system. In our previous work we designed a system to support flexible data subsetting (including both value-based and dimension-based predicates) using a standard SQL-like interface [38, 39]. The advantage of this approach is that a simplified *virtual* or high-level view of the dataset is presented to users. Thus, users downloading the data do not need to be familiar with the details of the data format. Instead, they can specify subsetting (and now sampling) requests with the high-level view.

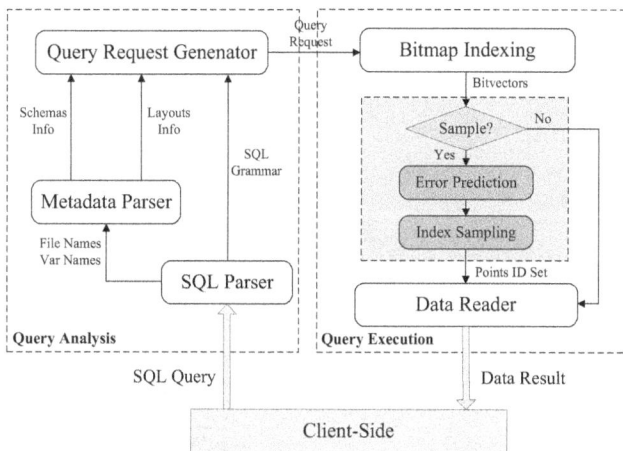

Figure 1: System Architecture

There are two main modules in the system, the *Query Analysis Module* and *Query Execution Module*. The *Query Analysis Module* takes an SQL query and corresponding metadata as input and generates a query request (in a specific format internal to the system) as the output. The *SQL Parser* is responsible for parsing the SQL query and generating a parse tree. We have implemented the parser by making certain modifications to the parser from SQLite[3], which is a lightweight open-source database engine. After the parse tree is generated, the *Metadata Parser* will take the data file names and variable names as input, look up the metadata files, find the data schema and data layout information, and load them into memory.

The second major module, *Query Execution Module*, takes the query request as input, performs data subsetting and sampling based on bitmap indices, and sends the data result back to the client. The *Bitmap Indexing* performs different indexing operations based on the query request and generates a collection of bitvectors which satisfies the current query as output. After that, we check to see if sampling is needed for the current query. If data sampling is not required here, the *Data Reader* will query the data subset based on the indexing information and return the result to the client. Otherwise, the *Data Sampling* sub-module will generate data samples based on bitmap indices.

There are two main components in the *Data Sampling* sub-module: *Error Prediction* and *Index-based Sampling*. Our approach includes a novel error prediction mechanism based on bitmap indices. With the help of this mechanism, we are able to pre-calculate approximation errors before actually sampling the data. Moreover, the error estimation can be performed based on indices instead of scanning through the entire sample. While the latter also reduces the error calculation time, our pre-calculation method allows a user to choose a sampling level which maintains a desired level of accuracy. Moreover, this alleviates the need for extracting a sample, calculating the error, and then resampling (likely with a different subsampling level), which can be very expensive in practice.

After error estimation, the *Index-based Sampling* component performs data sampling directly over bitmap indices and generates a set of data record identifiers as the result. Then the *Data Reader* will take the data record identifiers as the input, extract the data records, and return the results.

Besides error pre-calculation, which can improve the overall sampling efficiency significantly, and the overall effectiveness of our method, there are at least three other advantages for our system.

---

[3]http://www.sqlite.org

Small Preprocessing Costs: If the data repository already uses bitmap indices, or will like to use bitmap indices to efficiently obtain subsets of the original dataset, we can directly apply our sampling method without any preprocessing. For those applications without bitmap indexing support, the computational complexity of index generation is only $O(n \log(m))$ where n is the number of total elements and m is the number of bitvectors [47]. With the help of binning, m can be much smaller than n, so $\log(m)$ can be considered a constant number. Thus, our method is much faster compared with sampling methods with $O(n \log(n))$ preprocessing time, such as the KDTree-based method [44]. Another advantage of our method is that we do not need any modifications or reorganization of the original dataset. All sampling operations are performed using data in the original format and the bitmap indices.

Tradeoff between Accuracy and Sampling/Memory Costs: The bitmap indexing allows flexible multi-level indices over a given dataset. The *low-level* bitmap indices are able to reflect data features at a fine granularity, whereas the high-level indices improve the efficiency by binning a group of low-level bitmap indices together. By choosing to perform sampling using high-level or low-level bins, and even choosing the bin size at one or both levels, one can achieve the desired tradeoff between accuracy of sampling and time/memory costs of the sampling process.

Combining Sampling and Subsetting: Since our system is built on top of a data subsetting system, users can combine sampling with subsetting. Moreover, such queries can be executed efficiently because of the properties of bitmap indices.

3. SAMPLING USING BITMAP INDICES

This section first provides background on bitmap indexing and then introduces our data sampling method using bitmap indices. We also describe three enhancements of our sampling method, which are error prediction, sampling over a data subset, and sampling to support multi-attributes data analysis.

3.1 Background - Bitmap Indexing

Indexing provides an efficient way to support value-based queries and has been extensively researched and used in the context of relational databases. Bitmap indexing, which utilizes the fast bitwise operations supported by the computer hardware, has been shown to be an efficient approach, and has been widely used in scientific data management [32, 47]. In particular, recent work has shown that bitmap indexing can help support efficient querying of scientific datasets stored in native formats [11, 39].

Figure 2 shows an example of a bitmap index. In this simple example, the dataset contains a total of 8 elements with 4 distinct values. The *low-level* bitmap indices contain 4 bitvectors, where each bitvector corresponds to one value. The number of bits within each bitvector is the same as total number of elements in the dataset. In each bitvector, a bit is set to 1 if the value for the corresponding data element's attribute is equal to the *bitvector value*, i.e. the particular distinct value for which this vector is created. The *high-level* indices can be generated based on either the value intervals or value ranges. From Figure 2, we can see two *high-level* indices are built based on value intervals.

This simple example only contains integer values. Bitmap indexing also has been shown to be an efficient method for floating-point values [46]. For such datasets, instead of building a bitvector for each distinct value, we can first group a set of values together (*binning*) and build bitvectors for these bins. This way, the total number of bitvectors is kept at a manageable level.

From the example we can also see that the number of bits within each level of bitmap indices is $n \times m$, where n is the total number of elements and m is the total number of bitvectors. This can result in sizes even greater than the size of the original dataset,

ID	Value	e_0	e_1	e_2	e_3	i_0	i_1
		=1	=2	=3	=4	[1, 2]	[3, 4]
0	4	0	0	0	1	0	1
1	1	1	0	0	0	1	0
2	2	0	1	0	0	1	0
3	2	0	1	0	0	1	0
4	3	0	0	1	0	0	1
5	4	0	0	0	1	0	1
6	3	0	0	1	0	0	1
7	1	1	0	0	0	1	0
Dataset		Low Level Indices				High Level Indices	

Figure 2: An Example of Bitmap Indexing

causing high time and space overheads for index creation, storage, and query processing. To solve this problem, *run-length compression* algorithms such as Byte-aligned Bitmap Code (BBC) [4] and Word-Aligned Hybrid (WAH) [45] have been developed to reduce the bitmap size. The main idea of these approaches is that for long sequences of 0s and 1s within each bitvector, an encoding is used to count the number of continuous 0s or 1s. Such encoded counts are stored, requiring less space. Another property of the run-length compression methods is that it supports fast bitwise operations without decompressing the data.

3.2 Stratified Random Sampling over Bitvectors

Consider data storage in a large-scale scientific repository. If we are using bitvectors to be able to retrieve subsets of the original dataset [11, 39], the question we want to focus on is "can the same bitvector be used to obtain accurate and representative samples, while also assessing the loss of accuracy with a particular sampling level". It turns out that bitvectors can not only be used in this fashion, but they also provide several advantages over existing and popularly used sampling techniques.

We now describe the bitvector based sampling method we have developed. The basic idea in our method is to perform *random stratified sampling* over each bitvector, which corresponds to a particular value or, more likely, a bin of values. Specifically, we extract the same percent of samples out of each bitvector. By sampling over bins with equal probability, we are able to keep value distribution in the sampled dataset close to that of the original dataset. In fact, as we will show below, this approach preserves *entropy* of the original dataset, a highly desired property of samples in many applications.

Within each bitvector, we first divide the bitvector into *sectors* of a certain size, and choose the same percent of samples out of each sector. This way, we can also preserve the value distribution within each spatial region. Furthermore, when multi-level bitvectors are created (such as the example earlier in Figure 2) this method can be applied to either the low-level or the high-level index. This choice allows a tradeoff between efficiency and accuracy.

We now explain the steps of our method in more detail, using an example in Figure 3. There are three main steps:
Building bitmap indices: In this example, the small dataset contains 32 elements, so each bitvector has 32 bits. The number of distinct values is 4. The low-level bitmap indices contain 4 bitvectors: $e_0(= 1)$, $e_1(= 2)$, $e_2(= 3)$, $e_3(= 4)$, and the high-level bitmap indices include 2 bitvectors: $i_0([1, 2])$, $i_1([3, 4])$. In this simple example, all values are integers, though as we mentioned in Section 3.1, bitmap indices can be (and have been) used for floating-point values by generating bins with value ranges.
Dividing bitvectors into sectors: In order to preserve distribution of values in each spatial region, bitmap indices should be logically

Sampling over Low Level Indices:

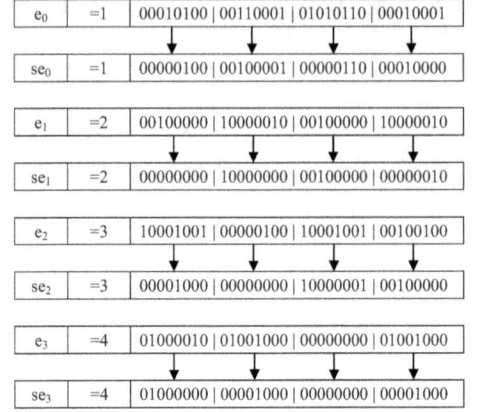

e_0	=1	00010100 | 00110001 | 01010110 | 00010001
se_0	=1	00000100 | 00100001 | 00000110 | 00010000

e_1	=2	00100000 | 10000010 | 00100000 | 10000010
se_1	=2	00000000 | 10000000 | 00100000 | 00000010

e_2	=3	10001001 | 00000100 | 10001001 | 00100100
se_2	=3	00001000 | 00000000 | 10000001 | 00100000

e_3	=4	01000010 | 01001000 | 00000000 | 01001000
se_3	=4	01000000 | 00001000 | 00000000 | 00001000

Sampling over High Level Indices:

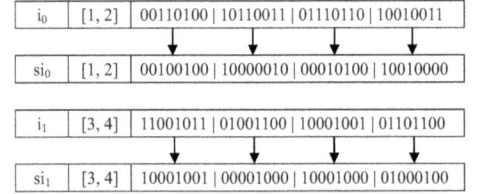

i_0	[1, 2]	00110100 | 10110011 | 01110110 | 10010011
si_0	[1, 2]	00100100 | 10000010 | 00010100 | 10010000

i_1	[3, 4]	11001011 | 01001100 | 10001001 | 01101100
si_1	[3, 4]	10001001 | 00001000 | 10001000 | 01000100

Figure 3: Our Proposed Sampling Method: Stratified Random Sampling over Bitmap Indices

divided into spatial sectors. In the figure, we can see that for both the low-level and the high-level bitmap indices, every bitvector is divided into 4 sectors, and there are 8 bits within each sector.
Random sampling over each sector: After creating sectors, random sampling can be performed within each sector, and for each bitvector, to generate data samples. Within each bitvector, random sampling is only applied to 1-bits. To preserve value distribution within each region, we need to make sure sample percentages over each sector are the same. One advantage of using bitmap indexing is that its implementations help us locate all 1-bits efficiently. In Figure 3, we are generating 50% samples out of the original dataset. We can see that se_0, se_1, se_2, se_3 are identifiers of data records that are in the sample generated using the low-level bitvectors, whereas si_0, si_1 are the data records for the sample using the high-level bitvectors. For both low-level and high-level bitmap indices, within each sector, only half of the 1-bits are picked. For example, after sampling, the number of 1-bits in the sample bitvector se_0 is 6, which is only half of that in original bitvector e_0.

From the figure, we can also see that although low-level bitmap indices have more bitvectors, each bitvector has fewer 1-bits. On the other hand, the number of bitvectors in the high-level bitmap indices is smaller, but more 1-bits exist in each bitvector. Hence, both methods generate sampled datasets of the same size. Low-level bitmap indexing is able to achieve better accuracy because it reflects the value distribution at a finer granularity. However, it also has an additional time cost, because of higher indices loading time and bitvector striding time.

Finally, we point out the property of this method with respect to preserving entropy. Information theory and *entropy* have been extensively used while sampling data (or even selecting angles, streamlines, or other features) in graphics and visualization, as also summarized by Xu *et al.* [48].

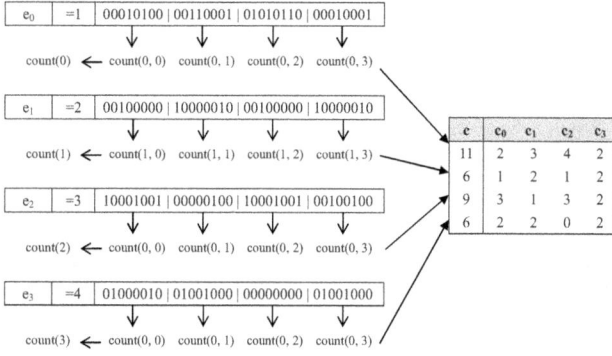

Figure 4: Metadata Generation for Error Prediction

Formally, if X is a random variable with a series of possible outcomes x, where $x \in \{x_1, x_2, \ldots, x_n\}$, and if the probability for the random variable to have the outcome x_i is $p(x_i)$, then Shannon's entropy is defined as

$$H(X) = \sum_i p(x_i) \times \log(1/p(x_i)).$$

Assuming no binning is performed, and sector sizes are large enough that precisely the same fraction of values can be chosen, we can see that the sampled dataset using bitvectors will have the same distribution of values, or the same entropy.

3.3 Error Prediction

After sampling, it is also important to know how accurate the sampled dataset is compared with the original dataset. Traditional sampling methods can only calculate error metrics after samples are generated, and if the error is too high, the entire sampling process has to be repeated with another sample percentage. As we will show now, with bitvectors we are able to pre-calculate error metrics based on bins. Thus, we can perform error predictions analysis to find a sample percentage which will give desired accuracy levels, and then can perform data sampling only once. This is a significant advantage, since the error calculation method only takes at most $O(m)$ time, where m is the number of bitvectors. In comparison, sample generation normally takes $O(n)$ time, where n is the number of data records in the original dataset, and $n >> m$.

As we stated earlier, while evaluating quality of a sampled dataset, different error metrics, like mean, variance, histogram and Q-Q plot are used. In particular, for our discussion we consider error metrics of two types: 1) mean, variance, histogram, and Q-Q plot for each variable, and 2) mean and variance for each sector.

We need to calculate and store some additional information during bitmap index generation. Figure 4 shows the metadata generation over bitmap indices. For dataset or variable level error calculation, the only additional information we need is the total number of 1-bits within each bitvector. From the figure, we can see that $count(0)$, $count(1)$, $count(2)$ and $count(3)$ record the total number of 1-bits for each bitvector. The results are stored in the first column of the 2-dimensional count matrix c. The metadata we need for sector-level mean and variance calculation is the number of 1-bits within each sector. From the figure, we can see that for bitvector $e0(= 1)$, $count(0,0)$, $count(0,1)$, $count(0,2)$ and $count(0,3)$ record the number of 1-bits within each sector. The result is stored in columns $c0$, $c1$, $c2$ and $c3$ of the count matrix.

Now we elaborate on calculation of specific metrics. Our approach can also be referred to as *error pre-calculation*, which is in contrast to *error post-calculation* normally done with the traditional sampling methods.

Mean, Variance, Sector Means, and Sector Variances: We now show how to pre-calculate *mean* and *variance* of the sampled dataset based on bins and the count matrix. The input is the representative value ($value$) of each bin, which we determined at the time of index generation, and the total number of elements ($count$) within each bin, which we can find from the count matrix. Besides that, each time we also set a sample percentage to decide the size of the sample result, denoted as $SamplePercent$. Equation 1 computes the number of samples selected from each bitvector($scount_i$) based on $count_i$ and $SamplePercent$:

$$scount_i = count_i \times SamplePercent. \qquad (1)$$

Our method fetches the same percent samples out of each bitvector, which is equal to $SamplePercent$. Hence, by multiplying $count_i$ with $SamplePercent$, we are able to compute the approximate number of samples within each bitvector. Now, Equation 2 calculates the mean value of the sampled dataset:

$$Mean = \frac{\sum_{i=1}^{m}(scount_i \times value_i)}{\sum_{i=1}^{m}(scount_i)}. \qquad (2)$$

Within each bitvector, we know both the representative $value_i$ and sample size $scount_i$. By multiplying these two factors together, we can get the sum value of samples in the current bitvector. Based on that, we can calculate the total value by adding the sum value of each bitvector together. We are also able to count the total number of sample elements by adding $scount_i$ of each bitvector together. Based on the sum value and total sample elements count, we can get the *mean* value.

Equation 3 calculates the *variance* of the sampled dataset. We first compute the value differences within each bitvector based on *mean* and $value_i$, then add all value differences together and finally divide by the total number of sample elements:

$$Variance = \frac{\sum_{i=1}^{m}\left(scount_i \times (Mean - value_i)^2\right)}{\sum_{i=1}^{m}(scount_i)}. \qquad (3)$$

The method of calculating *sector means* and *sector variances* is similar. We simply need to apply the Equations 2 and 3 for each sector.

We can see that our approach, error pre-calculation, can calculate *mean* and *variance* within $O(m)$ where m is the total number of bitvectors. Note that in contrast, the error post-calculation method will have to scan the entire sampled dataset twice to compute the mean and the variance. The time complexity is $O(s)$, where s is the sample size.

Histogram: The input is still $value$, $count$ and $SamplePercent$. Based on Equation 1, we can obtain the number of sampled elements for each bitvector ($scount_i$). Now,

$$Prob_i = \frac{scount_i}{\sum_{i=1}^{m}(scount_i)}. \qquad (4)$$

Equation 4 calculates each value $Prob_i$ in the histogram by simply dividing the sample size of each bitvector $scount_i$ by the total sample size. This way, we obtain the element probability of each bitvector. By calculating probabilities over all bitvectors, we are able to generate a histogram.

This method can compute the *histogram* within $O(m)$, where m is the number of bitvectors. In comparison, error post-calculation has to first perform a *Radix Sort*[4] over the entire sampled dataset. After that, it needs to count the number of elements within each bucket and then divide this number by the total sample size. The time complexity is $O(s)$ where s is the sample size.

---
[4] http://en.wikipedia.org/wiki/Radix_sort

Q-Q Plot: We first recap the definition of a Q-Q plot. Viewing the original dataset and the sampled dataset as two distributions, we compare them by plotting their quantiles against each other.

Algorithm 1 shows how to calculate a Q-Q plot using bitvectors. The input is s, which indicates the total number of sample elements; m, the total number of bitvectors; q, the total number of quantiles; *count*, the number of elements within each bitvector; and *value*, the *representative value* of each bitvector (calculation described below). In line 1, we define a variable *curCount* to record the total number of elements that are smaller than the value of the current bitvector. The variable *pos* indicates each quantile position identifier in the sampled dataset. It can be computed based on total sample size(s), multiplying it with the quantile percentage, as shown in line 8. Lines 3 to 12 compute the quantile value based on each quantile position. We iterate from the bitvector with the smallest value to the bitvector with the largest value. If the current quantile position *pos* is larger than *curCount*, we update the *curCount* and go to the next bitvector, as shown in line 4 and line 10. If *pos* becomes smaller than *curCount*, it means the current quantile is located within the current bitvector. Then we can record the representative value of the current bitvector as the quantile value and go to the next quantile, as captured by lines 5 through 8. We keep performing this calculation until we find the value of all the desired quantile positions.

Algorithm 1: Compute_QQPlot(s, m, q, *count*, *value*)

```
1:  curCount ← 0, pos ← 0
2:  i ← 0, j ← 0
3:  while i < m && j < q do
4:      curCount ← curCount + count_i
5:      if curCount > pos then
6:          QQPlotArray_j ← value_i
7:          j ← j + 1
8:          pos ← s * j / 100
9:      else
10:         i ← i + 1
11:     end if
12: end while
```

Our method is able to calculate the Q-Q plot with $O(q)$ in the best case and $O(q+m)$ in the worst case, where q is the total number of selected quantiles. In comparison, the error post-calculation method has to first perform a quick sort over the entire sampled dataset to calculate the Q-Q plot. After that, certain quantiles need to be selected out of the sorted dataset as Q-Q plot values. For example, we can fetch the data elements located at 1%, 2%, ... ,100% positions out of the sorted sample dataset as the result. The time complexity is $O(s \times \log(s))$ where s is the sample size.

Now, we describe how we calculate *value*, the representative value of a bitvector, when we have multi-level bitmap indices. For low-level bitmap indices, we can simply use the mean or the median value as the representative value of each bin. For high-level bitmap indices, each bitvector indicates a relatively larger value range. In our work, we use three indicators to predict errors for high-level bitmap indices. In high-level bitmap indices, each bin indicates a value range which has both a lower-bound and an upper-bound. By using lower-bound and upper-bound values during the error prediction process, we are able to calculate a boundary on the actual error metric results. Besides, each high-level bin is built by combining a group of low-level bins together. Hence, we are able to calculate the value distribution of each high-level bin by looking at corresponding low-level bins and finding an estimated value to represent each high-level bin. This way, we are able to find the actual error boundaries and also generate a relatively accurate error prediction. In some cases, when the data range of the dataset is

large, the bin size of low-level bitmap indices can be big. We can also apply this three indicators method to low-level bitmap indices.

3.4 Sampling Only a Subset of Data

When a data repository is disseminating data, a particular user might only be interested in a certain subset of data, based on spatio-temporal ranges (*dimension subsetting*) and/or specific values for attributes (*value-based subsetting*). However, as the dataset size for the subset may still be too large, sampling may still be needed.

Traditional sampling methods cannot efficiently support data sampling over a user-specified subset of data that includes value-based subsetting. For example, simple random sampling, stratified random sampling and KDTree stratified random sampling methods can all handle dimension-based subsetting, but when value-based subsetting is involved, they have to first generate data samples over the entire dataset and then perform post-filtering, which is clearly not efficient.

Suppose we need to sample datasets at a certain level, in conjunction with a subsetting condition, which includes both dimension-based and value-based subsetting conditions. We will proceed as follows. We first focus on the value subsetting conditions and search the (possibly) multi-level bitmap indices to find corresponding bitvectors. Only these bitvectors need to be loaded. Next we perform dimension subsetting over the retrieved bitvectors. Finally, we apply the stratified sampling only over this bitset.

3.5 Data Subsetting and Sampling over Multiple Attributes

In a typical scientific dataset, certain attributes can be *stand-alone*, i.e., can be analyzed separately. On the other hand, certain attributes can be closely connected with each other, and it is better to study them together. Suppose we consider the output from the cosmology data described in Section 4 below. Each record in the dataset corresponds to one particle and includes multiple attributes. For example, the attribute *mass* indicates the field value related to the current particle, and *VX*, *VY*, *VZ* indicate the particle velocity in each of the three spatial dimensions. *mass* can be analyzed separately, as it does not have a strong connection with the other attributes. For *VX*, *VY*, *VZ*, however, scientists prefer to analyze them together to find the relationships among them.

The techniques we have described so far build indices over each attribute separately, which does not fit the second scenario very well. We now describe an extension to support sampling to ensure a preserved distribution over multiple attributes.

Suppose we need to sample with respect to two attributes, X and Y. The entire process can be divided into 3 steps: (1) Divide the value range of each attribute into *one-attribute* bins, say, $(X_1, X_2, \ldots, X_{m1})$ and $(Y_1, Y_2, \ldots, Y_{m2})$. (2) Form *multiple attributes bins* (or *mbins*) $(X_1, Y_1), (X_1, Y_2), \ldots, (X_{m1}, Y_{m2})$ based on the one-attribute bins generated in the previous step. For each *mbin*, generate a bitvector and initially set all bits to 0. (3) Scan through the dataset. For each record, find its X and Y value, classify it into the corresponding *mbin* and set the corresponding bit to 1. Repeat this process until all records are mapped to related *mbins*.

4. EXPERIMENTAL RESULTS

In this section, we report results from a number of experiments conducted to evaluate our sampling approach. We designed experiments with the following goals: (1) To show how data sampling is able to improve data analysis efficiency in a distributed environment (where data source and resources for data analysis are geographically separated), (2) To examine the accuracy of our bitmap indices sampling method and compare it with a number of other sampling methods, (3) To evaluate the accuracy of error precalculation, by comparing predicted errors with the actual errors,

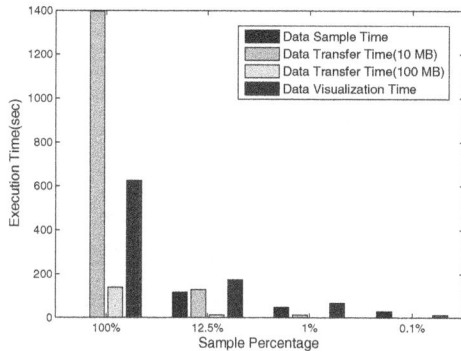

Figure 5: Visualizing a Remote Dataset: Execution Time with and without Sampling

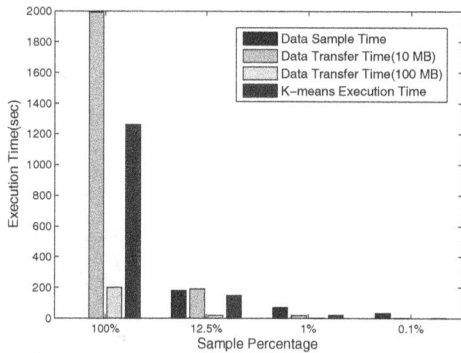

Figure 6: Clustering a Remote Dataset: Execution Time with and without sampling

(4) To compare the efficiency of our method against other sampling methods, in particular in view of error pre-calculation, and (5) To show how sampling over data subsets improves the efficiency.

We used two different scientific datasets. The *ocean* dataset is generated by the Parallel Ocean Program (POP) [22], which is an ocean circulation model. The execution we used has a grid resolution of approximately 10 km (horizontally), and vertically it has a grid spacing close to 10 m near the surface, increasing up to 250 m in the deep ocean. POP generates 1.4 GB output for each variable per time-slice, and each variable is modeled with three dimensions: longitude, latitude, and depth. The data is stored in the NetCDF format. The *cosmology* dataset is generated by the Road-Runner Universe MC^3, which is a large N-body cosmology simulation of dark matter physics. An MC^3 time step of 4000^3 (64 billion) particles with 36 bytes per particle takes 2.3 TB per time-slice. The particles generated per time-slice are split into a collection of data files based on the spatial information. Each particle within the file corresponds to one record, which is formed by 8 attributes (X, Y, Z, VX, VY, VZ, MASS, TAG). The data is stored in binary format.

In our experiments, the data repository and the server-side data sampling are on the Darwin Cluster at Los Alamos National Laboratory. Darwin consists of 120 compute nodes with 48 core(12-core by 4 socket) 2GHz AMD Opteron 6168 and 64 GB memory. The client-side data analysis is performed on one compute node which has 8 cores Intel(R) Xeon(R) CPU 2.53GHz and 32 GB memory.

4.1 Improving Efficiency of Distributed Data Analysis with Sampling

In this experiment, we consider the following scenario. The entire dataset is located on a remote server, and any analysis must be done after the data is downloaded to the client-side. We consider two distinct applications: data visualization and data mining. In the data visualization scenario, we visualize the sampled dataset using Paraview [2], a widely used data analysis and visualization application. In the data mining scenario, we take data samples as input and perform K-means clustering using MATE [20], a map-reduce like system. With these two applications, we compare the efficiency of data analysis (including data downloading time), when using the original dataset against the cases where different subsampling levels are used. In particular, we divide the data processing time into three parts: 1) Server-side data sampling time, 2) Data transfer time between the server and the client, and 3) Client-side data analysis time. The second factor above varies with the wide-area data transfer bandwidths one might have. For our experiments, we used two different networks, one with 10 MB/s bandwidth and the other with 100 MB/s bandwidth.

Figure 5 compares the efficiency of the data visualization using different subsampling levels: 100%, which means that we are using the original dataset without sampling, 12.5%, 1%, and 0.1%. The dataset without sampling is 11.2 GB in size and is from the POP application. From the figure, we can see that although our method incurs extra sampling costs compared to the case when the original dataset is analyzed, both the data transfer and analysis time is much lower, and more than compensates for the sampling time. Specifically, we find that compared to visualization over the original dataset, if network bandwidth is 10 MB/s, the speedup with 12.5% sampling rate, 1% sampling rate, and 0.1% sampling rate is 4.82, 15.91, and 47.59, respectively. If network bandwidth is 100 MB/s, the corresponding speedups are 2.61, 6.72, and 19.02, respectively. Another consideration with sampling is the accuracy of the analysis, which we will focus on in the next subsection.

Figure 6 compares the efficiency of K-means clustering (data mining) execution, using the original dataset and the three sampling levels (12.5%, 1%, and 0.1%). The dataset is from cosmology, and is 16 GB in size. The number of K-means cluster centers is 10 and the number of iterations is 50. The number of threads is 4. From the figure, we can see that, similar to data visualization, with the help of sampling, the speedup with 10 MB/s network bandwidth ranges from 5.25 to 84.24, and the speedup with 100 MB/s network bandwidth ranges from 3.26 to 39.8. Again, accuracy is another consideration, which we will analyze next.

4.2 Accuracy Comparison with Different Sampling Methods

As we stated above, besides efficiency, accuracy is a very important consideration for a sampling method. Using visualization and clustering as representative data analysis applications, we not only evaluate the absolute accuracy of our method, but also compare the accuracy against three other methods.

The sampling methods we compare against are as follows. Simple random sampling involves randomly selecting a data subset out of the original dataset without focusing on any features. Stratified random sampling [12] performs random sampling within each *stratum*. Normally, the way these strata are formed can preserve spatial distribution of samples, but not the value distribution. KDTree-based sampling [44] has been proven to be a good method for visualization, and has also been applied to the cosmology dataset. It divides data into strata by building a k-dimensional tree over the dataset. The tree construction method is primarily based on spatial dimension(s) but can also consider data values as one dimension. Random sampling is performed within each stratum to generate a data sample. Because both data values and spatial distribution are considered in forming the strata, KDTree-based sampling has led to better accuracy than stratified random sampling.

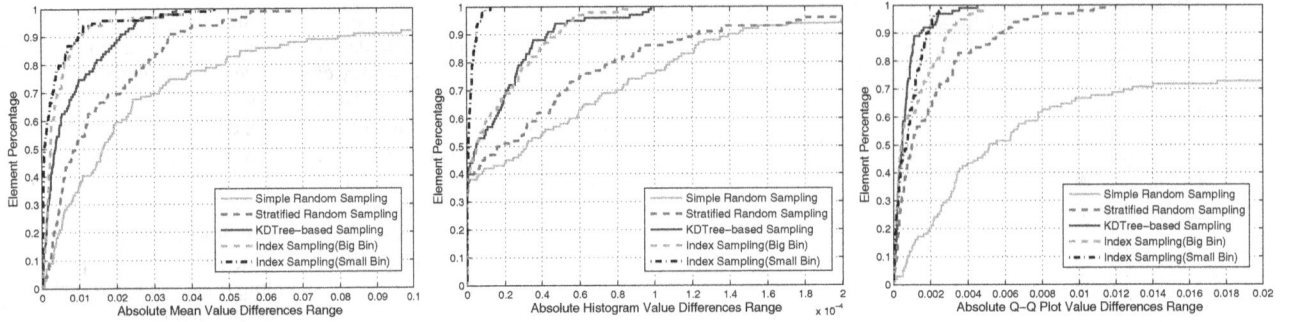

Figure 7: Error (Means, Histogram, and Q-Q Plot) Comparison Using Cumulative Frequency Plots: TEMP from POP Dataset

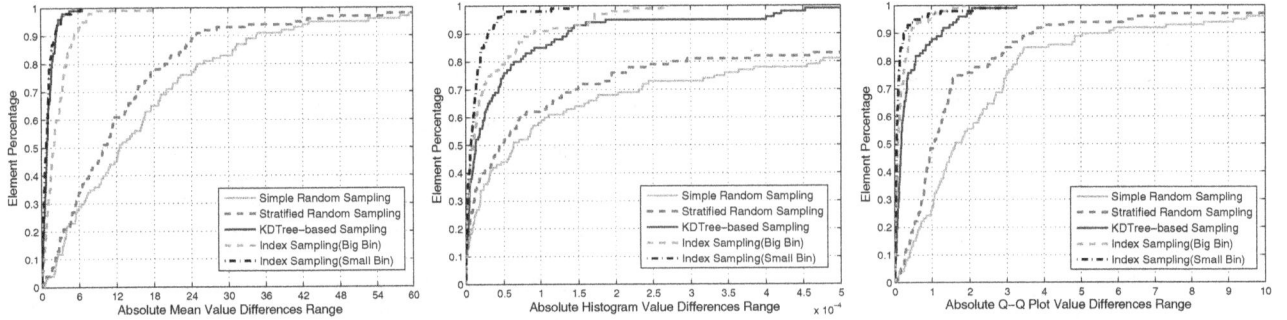

Figure 8: Error (Means, Histogram, and Q-Q Plot) Comparison Using Cumulative Frequency Plots: VX from Cosmology Dataset

In our method, which we will refer to as *index sampling*, we chose two bitmap indexing levels. The method we will denote as *small bin* corresponds to the use of low-level bitmap indices, which indicates fine-grained value distribution. The method we will denote as *big bin* corresponds to the use of high-level bitmap indices. Here, we groups 10 small bins into a big bin, and thus, value distributions are preserved only at a coarser level. The datasets and the variables used here are the same as the previous experiment: *TEMP* from the POP dataset and (*VX, VY, VZ*) from the cosmology dataset. The sample percentage is 0.1% of the original dataset.

It turns out that the appropriate error metrics for visualization and clustering are very distinct. Now we discuss the accuracy of the two applications separately.

4.2.1 Accuracy for Visualization

Characterizing the impact of sampling on visualization is hard, since human perception plays a role in how a dataset is viewed. Based on the existing literature from visualization [44], we used the following metrics: means of the value over 200 separate sectors, histogram using 200 value intervals, and Q-Q plot with 200 quantiles. To make the results more obvious, we calculated the sector means, histogram, and Q-Q plot value of both the original dataset and each sample dataset, and computed the absolute value differences between the original dataset and the sample dataset. To represent these charts, we use a *Cumulative Frequency Plot*(CFP). In our plots (Figure 7 for example), a point (x, y) indicates that the fraction y of all calculated absolute value differences are less than x. Since the error metric value differences should be as small as possible, it implies that a method with the curve to the left has a better accuracy than the method with the curve to the right. For the bitmap index sampling method, the total number of small bins

of *TEMP* is 442, and the total number of small bins of *VX* is 670. Each 10 small bins are grouped into a big bin.

The left subfigures of Figures 7 and 8 show the absolute value differences of sector means using the five sampling methods (including two versions of our approach). The simple random sampling shows the worst accuracy. The stratified random sampling, which considers spatial distribution, achieves better accuracy than simple random sampling. However, as it does not consider value distribution, the results are still worse than KDTree-based sampling and index sampling. If we compare KDTree-based sampling with index sampling, we can see that for POP data, index sampling(both small bin and big bin) achieves better accuracy than KDTree-based sampling. For cosmology data, KDTree-based sampling shows better accuracy than index sampling(big bin). However, index sampling(small bin) method still achieves the best accuracy.

The middle subfigures of Figures 7 and 8 show the absolute value differences for histogram entries, comparing the five sampling methods. KDTree-based sampling considers value distribution by treating variable value as one dimension during the KDTree sorting process. This method is more focused on spatial partitions and only considers value distribution at a very coarse level. Thus, as we can also see from the figures, for the cosmology dataset, the histogram results with KDTree-based sampling are not as good as our method. For the POP dataset, KDTree-based sampling and index sampling with big bin achieve a similar accuracy. Index sampling with small bin achieves a better accuracy than all the other methods.

The right subfigures of Figures 7 and 8 show the absolute value differences of Q-Q plot values among the five sampling methods. If we compare KDTree-based sampling with index sampling, we can see that for the POP dataset, KDTree-based sampling achieves the

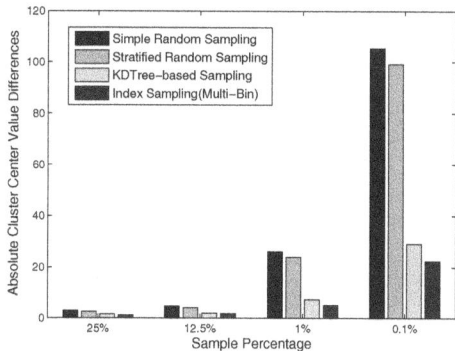

Figure 9: K-means: Accuracy Differences with Different Sampling Levels and Sampling Methods

best accuracy, but for the cosmology dataset, index sampling(both small bin and big bin) shows better accuracy. On the whole, the Q-Q plot value differences between KDTree-based sampling and index sampling are small.

4.2.2 Accuracy for Clustering

The error metric here is the difference between cluster centers, using the original and the sampled dataset. Specifically, we first calculate cluster center values for the original dataset, then calculate cluster center values for the sampled dataset, and finally compute the Euclidean distance between cluster centers in the the original dataset and the sampled dataset. The dataset we used here is the cosmology data and the indices are built over the three attributes VX, VY and VZ, i.e., the multiple attribute sampling method summarized in Section 3.5 is used here. The total number of multiple bins for VX, VY, VZ is 2000.

Figure 9 shows the accuracy using four sampling methods. The X axis shows different sampling percentages (25%, 12.5%, 1%, 0.1%), and Y axis shows the average cluster center value differences. KDTree-based sampling considers sorting based on spatial information first and then values. In this case, this method sorts the data based on X, Y, Z and then VX, VY and VZ. It achieves better accuracy compared with simple random sampling and stratified random sampling. Indices sampling, which considers binning over VX, VY and VZ first and then spatial locality, achieves better accuracy than all the other methods. As sampling percentage decreases, the advantage of our method becomes even more prominent.

To summarize our discussion, we can observe the following. Traditional methods from statistics, i.e., simple random and stratified random sampling, cannot get accurate samples as they are not considering enough features of the data. KDTree-based sampling, which is more focused on spatial locality, achieves good accuracy on sector means and Q-Q plots. However, the histogram result is not as good as for bitmap index sampling. Our method, which considers the value distribution first and then spatial locality, is able to generate a better histogram, while at the same time achieving good accuracy for sector means and Q-Q plots compared to KDTree-based sampling. It also achieves a better result than all the other methods when multiple attributes need to be considered while sampling. Furthermore, our method allows flexibility in choosing bin levels, and thus, users can adjust the bin size and level to get the desired tradeoff between accuracy and efficiency. Finally, as we will elaborate later, another advantage of our method lies in its ability to pre-calculate error levels.

4.3 Error Prediction Accuracy

As we have stated throughout, an important and distinct feature of our approach is the ability to pre-calculate error levels. However,

we need to verify if the predicted error results are close to the actual error results. We now describe results from an experiment designed for this purpose using the POP dataset. The sampling percentage is 0.1%.

In this experiment, we first calculate predicted error metrics with the methods described earlier in Section 3.3, then compute the actual error metrics by scanning over the entire sample dataset and compare the two sets of results. Figure 10 compares the predicted and actual errors for sector mean values, histogram and Q-Q plots, using the index sampling(small bin) method. The two sets of lines are either always or almost always identical, which shows that for index sampling(small bin) method, our error pre-calculation is able to accurately reflect actual error results.

Figure 11 compares the predicted and actual errors for sector mean values, histogram, and Q-Q plots, now using the index sampling(big bin) method. Here, we use the mean value as the representative value for each big bin. In the left figure (means), if we compare the predicted errors with the actual errors, we can see that there are only small value differences between the 60th sector and the 85th sector. In most cases, these two lines are identical. In the middle figure (histogram), we can see that there is some variation. This is because the index sampling with big bin method represents value distributions at a relatively coarse granularity. Each big bin can only be classified into one value interval in a histogram, but each bin contains a value range and some values may belong to the neighboring intervals. In the right figure (Q-Q Plot), again the differences are very small.

4.4 Efficiency Comparison with Different Sampling Methods

Earlier we have shown the benefits of sampling for improving the execution time when datasets are remote. However, so far we have not compared efficiency of our method against other methods. We now report such a comparison. Since a key feature of our approach is error pre-calculation, we focus on a scenario where the samples must be generated so as to meet certain accuracy requirements. Thus, the total sampling time can be divided into two components: *sample generation time* and *error calculation time*. Moreover, with other methods, one may need to sample multiple times to obtain the right accuracy levels. The variable we use here is *TEMP* from the POP simulation, and the data size is 1.4 GB.

Figure 12(a) compares the sample generation time among the five sampling methods. The X axis shows different sampling percentages, (3.13%, 6.25%, 12.5%, 25%), and the Y axis shows the execution time in seconds. We can see that simple random sampling takes the least time, which is not surprising. Stratified random sampling and KDTree-based sampling have similar sample generation time, each being somewhat slower than simple random sampling because of the time needed for generating strata. Another difference between stratified random sampling and KDTree-based sampling is that the latter requires $n \log(n)$ preprocessing time, which is not included here. In our method, the random sampling must be applied to each bitvector, which leads to higher time cost than the other three methods. This time depends upon the number of bins used. We can see that with the big bin method, which has one-tenth the number of bins compared to the small bin method, the time cost is only marginally higher than other methods. However, the index sampling(small bin) method has 1.19 to 3.98 times slowdown over KDTree-based sampling.

Figure 12(b) compares the error calculation time among the five sampling methods. With simple random sampling, stratified random sampling, and KDTree-based methods, we have to take a pass over the entire sampled dataset to perform error calculations. This is not only a high cost, but one that also increases with the size of the sampled dataset. In comparison, our method is able to pre-

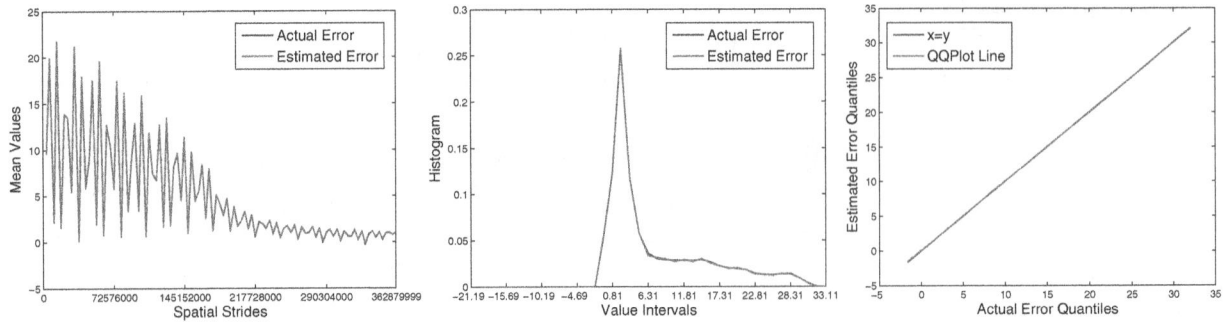

Figure 10: Predicted and Actual Errors (Means, Histogram, and Q-QPlot): Small Bin Method

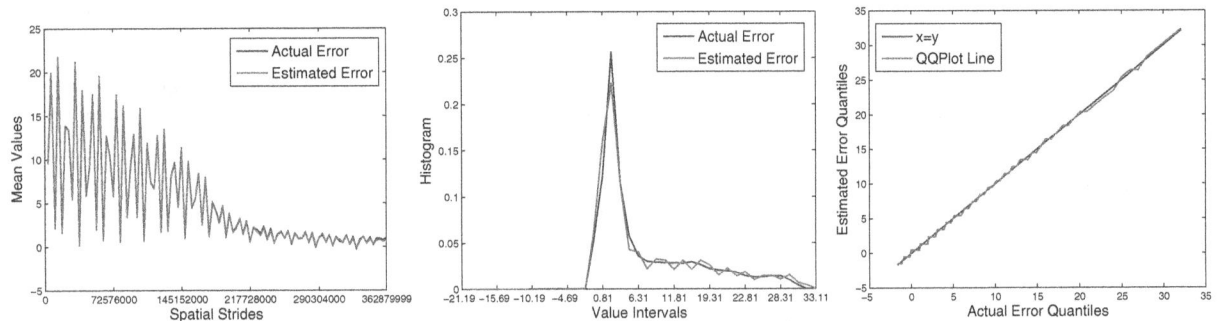

Figure 11: Predicted and Actual Errors (Means, Histogram, and Q-QPlot): Big Bin Method

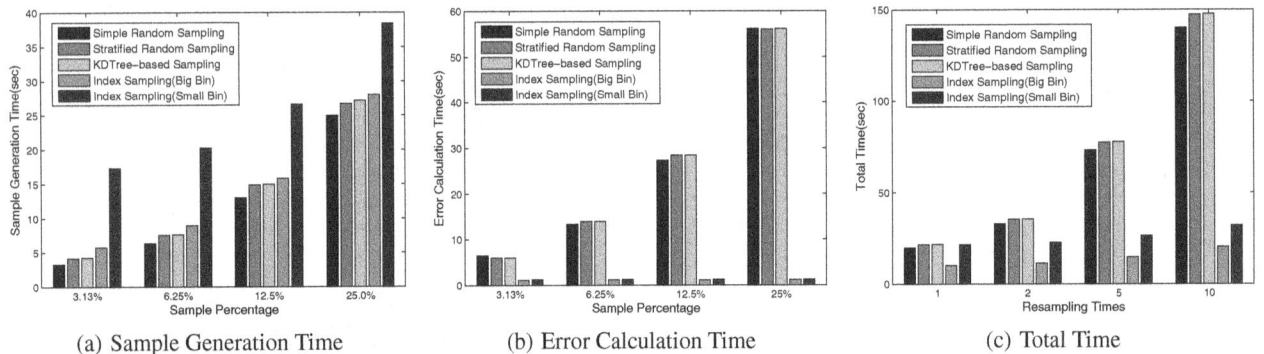

(a) Sample Generation Time   (b) Error Calculation Time   (c) Total Time

Figure 12: Time Cost Comparison across Sampling Methods

calculate error metrics based on bins(quite accurately, as we established earlier) before sampling. And the cost of performing the pre-calculation is not related to the sample size. From the figure, we can see that our method achieves at least 28x speedup compared with the other three methods while creating a 25% sample of the dataset. Note that these results are for a 1.4 GB dataset, and the advantage of our method will increase for larger sized datasets.

Figure 12(c) compares the overall efficiency among the five sampling methods. The X axis shows the resampling times, and the Y axis shows the total time cost in seconds. The sampling percentage is 6.25%. Because the first three methods cannot support error prediction, the sample generation and error calculation process may have to be repeated multiple times until a satisfactory accuracy level is found. However, using index sampling, we can perform multiple error pre-calculations first (with different sampling levels) and then need only one round of sample generation. If we look at the first set of bars which correspond to the case where we sample only once, we can see that index sampling(small bin) method has a similar total cost compared with the other three methods, whereas the index sampling(big bin) method is significantly faster. However, if the sampling process needs to be repeated, both big bin and small bin methods are much faster than any of the other methods.

4.5 Data Sampling over Data Subsets

Another advantage of bitmap indexing is that it supports efficient subsetting over subsets of the original dataset, where these subsets

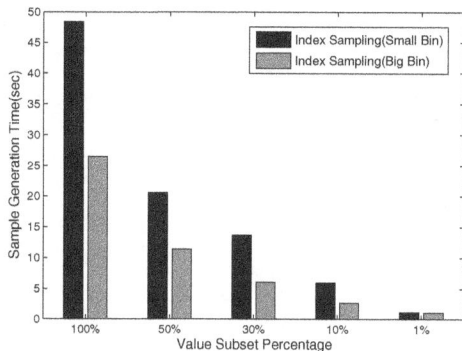

Figure 13: Sampling over Value Subsets

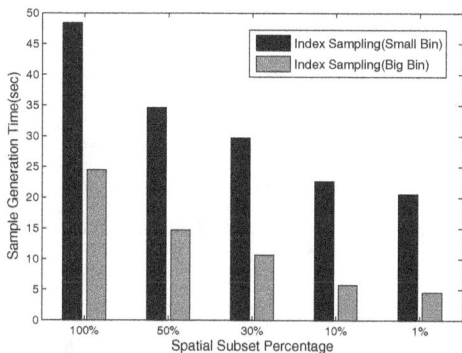

Figure 14: Sampling over Spatial Subsets

may involve spatial (dimension-based) and/or value-based conditions. In this subsection, we show how our method is effective, i.e. data sampling efficiency improves if sampling is performed over a subset of values or spaces. Here we discuss value subsetting and spatial subsetting separately, although our method is able to support a combination of the two.

Figure 13 shows the time incurred while sampling over different value-based subsets. The X axis shows the subsetting percentage, i.e. the fraction of the original dataset that meet the conditional predicate. The Y axis shows the sampling time, which includes both the index loading time and the sample generation time. The sampling rate is 25% in all cases, i.e. 25% of the data records that meet the conditional predicate are returned. From the figure, we can see that for both the small bin and big bin methods, the efficiency improves as the subsetting percentage decreases. Smaller value-based subset implies not only smaller index loading time but also smaller sample generation time. Take the index sampling(small bin) method for example, sampling over 10% of the data takes 6.95 times less time than sampling over 100% of the data.

Figure 14 shows the time cost of sampling with different spatial subsets. The X axis shows the spatial subsetting percentage and the Y axis shows the indices sampling time. The sampling percentage is still 25%. From the figure, we can see that the time cost decreases as the spatial subsetting percentage decreases, though the improvement is not as obvious as in the case of value subsetting. This is because for spatial subsetting, all indices still have to be loaded, so the only speedups are on the sample generation time.

5. RELATED WORK

Sampling of datasets has been widely studied, including work specific to scientific datasets and/or visualization.

Traditional statistical sampling methods [12], including simple random sampling and stratified random sampling, have been used often. We have performed a detailed comparison against these methods and demonstrated how our approach is more effective. KDTree-based sampling [44] uses a KDTree to divide data into sub-blocks and performs random sampling within each block. It needs to reorganize the entire dataset, with a time complexity of $O(n \log(n))$. We have also compared our method with this method, and shown that our approach outperforms this method in several aspects, and is comparable in other ways. The Z-curve order sampling method [33] involves a hierarchical indexing framework that uses a Z-order curve. However, it can only be applied to regular array-based datasets. Among the datasets we have used, this method will not even be applicable to the cosmology dataset. The WTSP Tree method [43] builds a wavelet-based time-space partitioning tree over large-scale time-varying datasets and supports multi-level data sampling on that. The entire dataset has to be reorganized and the WTSP Tree building process is time consuming.

Sampling has also been studied in the context of databases. One area of emphasis has been online aggregation, with initial work by Hellerstein et al [17]. Jermaine et al [19] proposed an online aggregation method for the DBO engine. Histograms [34] and wavelets [8] can be pre-computed and used. Chaudhuri et al [9] have conducted extensive studies on executing approximate aggregation queries using workload information and biased samples. More recent work in the database community has been in the context of speeding up map-reduce jobs with sampling. One initial study [16] proposed a framework to support incremental data sampling. EARL [28] involves a new sampling strategy with support for early error approximation based on bootstrapping, which has been widely employed in statistics and can be applied to arbitrary functions and data distributions. This method is able to decrease the resampling times and achieve good efficiency and accuracy. However, resampling is still needed to generate a satisfying sampling result.

Dissemination and analysis of large-scale and distributed datasets has been the focus of other studies as well. Some of the popular directions have been replica services [7, 10], reliable and predictable data transfers [3, 41], and constructing workflows [1, 13]. Chimera is a system for supporting virtual data views and demand-driven data derivation [15]. Metadata cataloging and metadata services have also been developed [14, 36]. The Metadata Catalog Service (MCS) [37] and Artemis [40] are collaborative components used to access and query repositories based on metadata attributes. Many middleware efforts have specifically focused on the needs of data-driven sciences [5], and enhancing and optimizing data transfer frameworks has been a popular topic [3, 25, 26, 29, 31, 23]. Our sampling techniques can work in conjunction with these efforts to make it feasible to analyze large-scale datasets.

6. CONCLUSIONS

This paper has described a novel sampling method for massive scientific simulation datasets. We utilize the value distribution and spatial locality features of bitmap indices and have developed an accurate sampling method over multi-level bitmap indices. We also developed an error prediction mechanism to pre-calculate error metrics before sampling the data. Moreover, with the help of bitmap indexing, our method is able to support data sampling over any combination of value subset and dimension subset.

7. ACKNOWLEDGMENTS

This work was supported by the Department of Energy (DOE) Office of Science (OSC) Advanced Scientific Computing Research (ASCR) and NSF award IIS-0916196 to the Ohio State University.

8. REFERENCES

[1] David Abramson and Jagan Kommineni. A Flexible IO Scheme for Grid Workflows . In *Proceedings of the International Parallel and Distributed Processing Symposium (IPDPS)*, April 2004.

[2] James Ahrens, Berk Geveci, and Charles Law. Paraview: An end user tool for large data visualization. *the Visualization Handbook. Edited by CD Hansen and CR Johnson. Elsevier*, 2005.

[3] W. E. Allcock, I. Foster, and R. Madduri. Reliable Data Transport: A Critical Service for the Grid. In *Proceedings of the Workshop on Building Service Based Grids*, 2004.

[4] G. Antoshenkov. Byte-aligned bitmap compression. In *Data Compression Conference, 1995. DCC'95. Proceedings*, page 476. IEEE, 1995.

[5] Andrew Baranovski, Keith Beattie, Shishir Bharathi, Joshua Boverhof, John Bresnahan, Ann Chervenak, Ian Foster, Tim Freeman, Dan Gunter, Kate Keahey, Carl Kesselman, Rajkumar Kettimuthu, Nick Leroy, Michael Link, Miron Livny, Ravi Madduri, Gene Oleynik, Laura Pearlman, Robert Schuler, and Brian Tierney. Enabling petascale science: Data management, troubleshooting, and scalable science services. *Journal of Physics: Conference Series*, 125, 2008.

[6] D. Bernholdt, S. Bharathi, D. Brown, K. Chanchio, M. Chen, A. Chervenak, L. Cinquini, B. Drach, I. Foster, P. Fox, et al. The earth system grid: Supporting the next generation of climate modeling research. *Proceedings of the IEEE*, 93(3):485–495, 2005.

[7] M. Cai, A. Chervenak, and M. Frank. A Peer-to-Peer Replica Location Service Based on A Distributed Hash Table. In *Proceedings of SC 2004*, November 2004.

[8] Kaushik Chakrabarti, Minos Garofalakis, Rajeev Rastogi, and Kyuseok Shim. Approximate query processing using wavelets. *VLDB Journal*, 10:199–223, 2001.

[9] Surajit Chaudhuri, Gautam Das, Mayur Datar, Rajeev Motwani, and Vivek Narasayya. Overcoming limitations of sampling for aggregation queries. In *Proceedings of ICDE 1999*, pages 534–542, 1999.

[10] A.L. Chervenak, N. Palavalli, S. Bharathi, C. Kesselman, and R. Schwartzkopf. Performance and Scalability of a Replica Location Service. In *Proceedings of the Conference on High Performance Distributed Computing (HPDC)*, June 2004.

[11] J. Chou, K. Wu, O. Rübel, M.H.J.Q. Prabhat, B. Austin, E.W. Bethel, R.D. Ryne, and A. Shoshani. Parallel index and query for large scale data analysis. In *SC*, 2011.

[12] W.G. Cochran. *Sampling techniques*. Wiley-India, 2007.

[13] Ewa Deelman, Jim Blythe, Yolanda Gil, Carl Kesselman, Gaurang Mehta, Karan Vahi, Albert Lazzarini, Adam Arbree, Richard Cavanaugh, and Scott Koranda. Mapping Abstract Complex Workflows onto Grid Environments. In *Journal of Grid Computing*, pages 9–23, 2003.

[14] Ewa Deelman, G. Singh, M.P. Atkinson, A. Chervenak, N.P. Chue Hong, C. Kesselman, S. Patil, L. Pearlman, and M. Su. Grid-Based Metadata Services. In *Proceedings of the 16th International Conference on Scientific and Statistical Database Management (SSDBM04)*, 2004.

[15] I. Foster, J. Voeckler, M. Wilde, and Y. Zhao. Chimera: A Virtual Data System for Representing, Querying and Automating Data Derivation. In *Proceedings of the Conference on Scientific and Statistical Data Management*, July 2002.

[16] R. Grover and M.J. Carey. Extending map-reduce for efficient predicate-based sampling. In *Data Engineering (ICDE), 2012 IEEE 28th International Conference on*, pages 486–497. IEEE, 2012.

[17] Joseph M. Hellerstein, Peter J. Haas, and Helen J. Wang. Online aggregation. In *Proceedings of SIGMOD 1997*, 1997.

[18] Y. Ioannidis and V. Poosala. Histogram-based approximation of set-valued query-answers. In *Proceedings of the International Conference on Very Large Data Bases*, pages 174–185, 1999.

[19] Christopher Jermaine, Subramaniam Arumugam, Abhijit Pol, and Alin Dobra. Scalable approximate query processing with the dbo engine. In *Proceedings of SIGMOD 2007*, pages 725–736, 2007.

[20] W. Jiang, V.T. Ravi, and G. Agrawal. A map-reduce system with an alternate api for multi-core environments. In *Proceedings of the 2010 10th IEEE/ACM International Conference on Cluster, Cloud and Grid Computing*, pages 84–93. IEEE Computer Society, 2010.

[21] C.R. Johnson and A.R. Sanderson. A next step: Visualizing errors and uncertainty. *Computer Graphics and Applications, IEEE*, 23(5):6–10, 2003.

[22] PW Jones, PH Worley, Y. Yoshida, JB White III, and J. Levesque. Practical performance portability in the parallel ocean program (pop). *Concurrency and Computation: Practice and Experience*, 17(10):1317–1327, 2005.

[23] Rajkumar Kettimuthu, Alex Sim, Dan Gunter, Bill Allcock, Peer-Timo Bremer, John Bresnahan, Andrew Cherry, Lisa Childers, Eli Dart, Ian Foster, Kevin Harms, Jason Hick, Jason Lee, Michael Link, Jeff Long, Keith Miller, Vijaya Natarajan, Valerio Pascucci, Ken Raffenetti, David Ressman, Dean Williams, Loren Wilson, and Linda Winkler. Lessons learned from moving earth system grid data sets over a 20 gbps wide-area network. In *Proceedings of the 19th ACM International Symposium on High Performance Distributed Computing (HPDC 2010)*, Jun 2010.

[24] M.F. Khairoutdinov and D.A. Randall. A cloud resolving model as a cloud parameterization in the ncar community climate system model: Preliminary results. *Geophys. Res. Lett*, 28(18):36173620, 2001.

[25] Ezra Kissel, D. Martin Swany, and Aaron Brown. Improving GridFTP performance using the Phoebus session layer. In *Proceedings of SC*, November 2009.

[26] T. Kosar and M. Livny. Stork: Making Data Placement a First Class Citizen in the Grid. In *Proceedings of International Conference on Distributed Computing Systems (ICDCS)*, 2004.

[27] E.C. LaMar, B. Hamann, and K.I. Joy. Efficient error calculation for multiresolution texture-based volume visualization. *Hierachical and Geometrical Methods in Scientific Visualization*, pages 51–62, 2003.

[28] N. Laptev. K. Zeng, and C. Zaniolo. Early accurate results for advanced analytics on mapreduce. *Proceedings of the VLDB Endowment*, 5(10):1028–1039, 2012.

[29] Wantao Liu, Brian Tieman, Rajkumar Kettimuthu, and Ian Foster. A data transfer framework for large-scale science experiments. In *3rd International Workshop on Data Intensive Distributed Computing (DIDC 2010) in conjunction with 19th International Symposium on High Performance Distributed Computing (HPDC 2010*, 2010.

[30] S.L. Lohr. *Sampling: design and analysis*. Thomson, 2009.

[31] D. Lu, Y. Qiao, P. A. Dinda, and F. E. Bustamante. Modeling and Taming Parallel TCP on Wide Area Networks. In *Proceedings of the 12th International Parallel and Distributed Processing Symposium (IPDPS)*, April 2005.

[32] P. O'Neil and D. Quass. Improved query performance with variant indexes. In *ACM Sigmod Record*, volume 26, pages 38–49. ACM, 1997.

[33] V. Pascucci and R.J. Frank. Global static indexing for real-time exploration of very large regular grids. In *Supercomputing, ACM/IEEE 2001 Conference*, pages 45–45. IEEE, 2001.

[34] V. Poosala and V. Ganti. Fast approximate query answering using precomputed statistics. In *Proceedings of ICDE 1999*, page 252, 1999.

[35] V. Poosala, P.J. Haas, Y.E. Ioannidis, and E.J. Shekita. Improved histograms for selectivity estimation of range predicates. *ACM SIGMOD Record*, 25(2):294–305, 1996.

[36] G. Singh, S. Bharathi, A. Chervenak, E. Deelman, C. Kesselman, M. Mahohar, S. Pail, and L. Pearlman. A Metadata Catalog Service for Data Intensive Applications. In *Proceedings of Supercomputing 2003 (SC2003)*, November 2003.

[37] Gurmeet Singh, Shishir Bharathi, Ann Chervenak, Ewa Deelman, Carl Kesselman, Mary Manohar, Sonal Patil, and Laura Pearlman. A metadata catalog service for data intensive applications. In *SC '03: Proceedings of the 2003 ACM/IEEE Conference on Supercomputing*, page 33, Washington, DC, USA, 2003. IEEE Computer Society.

[38] Y. Su and G. Agrawal. Supporting user-defined subsetting and aggregation over parallel netcdf datasets. In *2012 12th IEEE/ACM International Symposium on Cluster, Cloud and Grid Computing*, pages 212–219. IEEE, 2012.

[39] Y. Su, G. Agrawal, and J. Woodring. Indexing and parallel query processing support for visualizing climate datasets. In *2012 41th IEEE/ACM International Conference on Parallel Processing (ICPP)*, pages 249–258. IEEE, 2012.

[40] Rattapoom Tuchinda, Snehal Thakkar, A Gil, and Ewa Deelman. Artemis: Integrating scientific data on the grid. In *Proceedings of the 16th Conference on Innovative Applications of Artificial Intelligence (IAAI*, pages 25–29, 2004.

[41] S. Vazhkudai and J. Schopf. Using disk throughput data in predictions of end-to-end grid transfers. In *Proceedings of the Third Workshop on Grid Computing (Grid 2002)*, November 2002.

[42] J.S. Vitter. An efficient algorithm for sequential random sampling. *ACM transactions on mathematical software (TOMS)*, 13(1):58–67, 1987.

[43] C. Wang, A. Garcia, and H.W. Shen. Interactive level-of-detail selection using image-based quality metric for large volume visualization. *Visualization and Computer Graphics, IEEE Transactions on*, 13(1):122–134, 2007.

[44] J. Woodring, J. Ahrens, J. Figg, J. Wendelberger, S. Habib, and K. Heitmann. In-situ sampling of a large-scale particle simulation for interactive visualization and analysis. In *Computer Graphics Forum*, volume 30, pages 1151–1160. Wiley Online Library, 2011.

[45] K. Wu, E.J. Otoo, and A. Shoshani. Compressing bitmap indexes for faster search operations. In *Scientific and Statistical Database Management, 2002. Proceedings. 14th International Conference on*, pages 99–108. IEEE, 2002.

[46] K. Wu, K. Stockinger, and A. Shoshani. Breaking the curse of cardinality on bitmap indexes. In *Scientific and Statistical Database Management*, pages 348–365. Springer, 2008.

[47] Kesheng Wu, W. Koegler, J. Chen, and A. Shoshani. Using bitmap index for interactive exploration of large datasets. In *15th International Conference on Scientific and Statistical Database Management, 2003*, pages 65–74. IEEE, July 2003.

[48] L. Xu, T.Y. Lee, and H.W. Shen. An information-theoretic framework for flow visualization. *Visualization and Computer Graphics, IEEE Transactions on*, 16(6):1216–1224, 2010.

I/O Acceleration with Pattern Detection

Jun He*, John Bent‡, Aaron Torres⋈, Gary Grider⋈,
Garth Gibson◇, Carlos Maltzahn△, Xian-He Sun†
*University of Wisconsin, Madison ‡EMC ⋈Los Alamos National Laboratory
◇Carnegie Mellon University and Panasas △University of California, Santa Cruz †Illinois Institute of Technology

ABSTRACT

The I/O bottleneck in high-performance computing is becoming worse as application data continues to grow. In this work, we explore how patterns of I/O within these applications can significantly affect the effectiveness of the underlying storage systems and how these same patterns can be utilized to improve many aspects of the I/O stack and mitigate the I/O bottleneck. We offer three main contributions in this paper. First, we develop and evaluate algorithms by which I/O patterns can be efficiently discovered and described. Second, we implement one such algorithm to reduce the metadata quantity in a virtual parallel file system by up to several orders of magnitude, thereby increasing the performance of writes and reads by up to 40 and 480 percent respectively. Third, we build a prototype file system with pattern-aware prefetching and evaluate it to show a 46 percent reduction in I/O latency. Finally, we believe that efficient pattern discovery and description, coupled with the observed predictability of complex patterns within many high-performance applications, offers significant potential to enable many additional I/O optimizations.

Categories and Subject Descriptors

D.4.2 [**Operating Systems**]: Storage Management—*Secondary storage*; D.4.3 [**Operating Systems**]: File Systems Management—*Access methods*

General Terms

Algorithms, Design, Performance

Keywords

I/O; pattern; large-scale storage systems; high performance computing; PLFS; prefetching

1. INTRODUCTION

As scientific applications strive to explore new frontiers with increasingly fine granularities of simulation, high performance computing infrastructure must continue to scale. However, the ability to scale processing greatly exceeds the ability to scale storage

I/O and it is increasingly important to extract all available performance from the storage hardware. Our earlier work with PLFS [12] has shown that some patterns of I/O are much more amenable to high performance than others. Therefore, understanding I/O behaviors and taking advantage of their characteristics become a natural direction of optimizations. Much of the application I/O in this domain is structured as in checkpoint-restart, which transfers distributed data structures such as multi-dimensional arrays between compute node memory and parallel file systems.

However, a typical I/O stack ignores I/O structures as data flows between these layers. I/O libraries like HDF5 [19], NetCDF [3] and MPI-IO [40] do store descriptive metadata alongside data, such as dimension information and data types. But eventually distributed data structures resolve into simple offset and length pairs in the storage system, regardless of what initial information was available. In this study, we propose techniques to rediscover structures in unstructured I/O and represent them in a lossless and compact way. We recognize great potential in applying these techniques to many scenarios and demonstrate that with metadata compaction within the PLFS virtual file system and within a prefetching FUSE [1] file system we built to help evaluate our ideas. Additionally, we describe a few other potential usages briefly in Section 6.

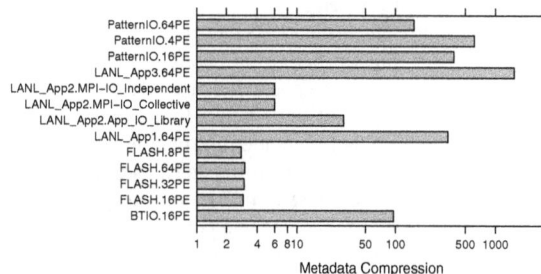

Figure 1: **Compression rates for indices of real applications and benchmarks obtained by discovering patterns and representing them in a compact way. The compression rate is represented as** ($Uncompressed\ Size$)/($Compressed\ Size$). **Higher is better.**

Recent projections by the United States' Department of Energy have predicted extremely challenging storage requirements for exaflop supercomputers. The primary storage driver is checkpointing and the current projections specify that checkpoints of up to 64 petabytes in size should complete in 300 seconds. The bulk of computational scientists seem to prefer checkpointing into a single checkpoint file over checkpointing into a directory containing tens of thousands of checkpoint fragments [17]. Therefore, the performance of shared file writing is critical for effective HPC.

Unfortunately, many otherwise scalable file systems suffer poor performance when many concurrent processes write to the same file [12]. The most powerful way to fix this problem is to transparently transform the representation of a concurrently written file into many exclusively written file fragments, as is done by ADIOS [26] and PLFS. However, recent PLFS development has hit a performance wall as the amount of internal metadata required to reconstruct the file fragments grows with the number of writers. Current petascale size checkpoints are challenging and exascale will be impossible without a more compact representation of the metadata.

In this study, we achieve metadata reduction using a gray-box technique [10] of rediscovering valuable information that was lost as data moved across the POSIX interface. In this case, we rediscover the structure of the checkpoint using pattern detection. Checkpoints are typically the conversion of a distributed data structure into a linear array of bytes. High-level middleware abstractions, such as views within MPI and the data types within HDF and NetCDF, allow the user to describe the structure of their data (e.g. the number and size of the dimensions in a mesh). The middleware then will use the restrictive interface of POSIX to store the data structure using a sequence of writes. Since these writes are storing a structured data set, they will typically follow a regular pattern. By discovering this pattern, PLFS can replace its index entry (metadata) per write with a single pattern entry describing all the writes thereby converting the size of the index from O(n) to a small constant value. An alternative approach to reduce the metadata would be to *clean* the logfiles into a single *flat* file. However, this cleaning is expensive and notoriously difficult; additionally, earlier work [35] has shown, somewhat counter-intuitively, that flattening files can lead to slower read performance.

As shown in Figure 1, we are able to reduce the size of the PLFS index by up to several orders of magnitude for various applications and benchmarks. As we will see in Section 3, this structure discovery also results in performance improvements in PLFS of up to 40 percent for writes and up to 480 percent for reads. We also present a visualization of the access patterns of the MILC code [7] and Pagoda [4] application to illustrate the inherent structure which our algorithms successfully detect.

In addition to improvements in PLFS metadata, we also evaluate our idea by implementing a pattern aware prefetching file system. Prefetching is an important technique to hide I/O latency dependent on the ability of the storage system to predict future requests. High layers in I/O stack have richer semantic information which can be used to raise prediction accuracy. Unfortunately, as described earlier, most of the I/O interfaces lose information as they descend in the I/O stack. Hints [34] can also enable consequential improvement. However, hints require extra, perhaps significant, effort from the users and this foreknowledge may not always be available.

Since our techniques can discover patterns at a low level without requiring the semantic information available at higher levels, they can be used to predict future requests at a file and block level. To evaluate this, we have designed and implemented a FUSE based prefetch system with the pattern detection algorithm proposed in this paper and tested it with a trace from the real application called Pagoda. Our results show that the I/O cost is reduced by up to 46%.

Our main contribution is to propose and evaluate effective algorithms and representations to discover and describe pattern in unstructured I/O. Although we note that this technique is further useful in a variety of cases such as block pre-allocation, metadata reduction within systems such as SciHadoop [14], as well as I/O trace reduction in large scale systems, we demonstrate its value in this paper exclusively with evaluations of the compressibility of the PLFS index and the predictability in a prefetching file system.

The rest of the paper is organized as follows. Section 2 describes the implementation of a pattern structured PLFS in detail. The key pattern detection algorithms, pattern representations of this paper, as well as pattern unfolding techniques, are described. Section 3 evaluates the pattern structured PLFS extensively. Section 4 describes the design details of a pattern prefetching system, which is evaluated in Section 5. Several other potential uses of the proposed patterns are discussed in Section 6 and we conclude in Section 8.

2. PATTERN STRUCTURED PLFS

PLFS, a virtual parallel file system, is a powerful transformative I/O middleware layer. By transparently reorganizing shared-file writing into a separate log-structured file for each process, PLFS has been shown to improve the performance of many important HPC applications by several orders of magnitude. In PLFS, we refer to the file that the user writes (and later reads) as the *logical* file and the set of files which PLFS creates to store the data within the logical file as *physical* files. The user accesses their logical files through PLFS and PLFS in turn accesses its physical files from a set of *backend* file systems such as Lustre, GPFS, PanFS, or Ceph.

2.1 PLFS Index

As each process writes to the shared logical file, PLFS appends that data to a unique physical logfile (*data dropping*) for that process and creates an index entry in a unique physical index file (*index dropping*) which maintains a mapping between the bytes within the logical file and their physical location within the data droppings. When a read request (e.g. *read(fd, off, len)*) is performed, PLFS queries the index to find where that actual data resides within the data dropping files. The key variables of a current index entry are:

- *logical offset*: where the data is, from the application's perspective in a single logical file;

- *length*: number of bytes written;

- *physical offset*: this is the physical offset within a contiguous data dropping file;

- *chunk id*: the ID of the dropping file where the data resides.

Figure 2 is an example of how PLFS works today. As applications grow in size, the number of the physical index files, and the number of index entries within them, grows correspondingly. This growth introduces overhead in several different ways. The performance overhead of the index creation is slight, but noticeable, during writes. Performance overhead for reading however is much larger; since a reader might read from any portion of the file, every index file and every index entry must be read. Also, the sheer quantity of the index entries results in a large footprint in both memory and on disk. For example, an anonymous application at Los Alamos National Laboratory (referred to here as LANL App 3) writes a file of 4 GB and creates an index size of 192 MB for each process [11]. In this case, when reading the file with 64 processes, the total memory index footprint is 12 GB since each process has to hold a copy of the whole index. To use less memory, an alternate option is to not cache entire index data but to access them on disk whenever it is necessary. However, this will be very slow since PLFS has to conduct I/O for each index access. Earlier work [28] addresses the latency of reading the complete index entries from disk and building the in-memory index structure by exploiting parallelism within the MPI library. This paper extends that

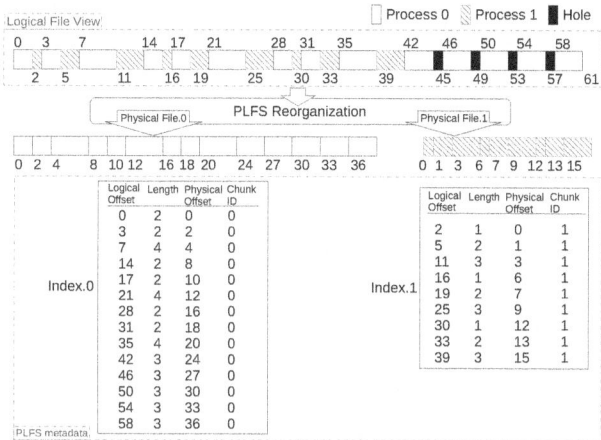

Figure 2: An example of two processes writing to a traditional PLFS file. If the application writes a lot of data in small extents, the indices shown can become very large.

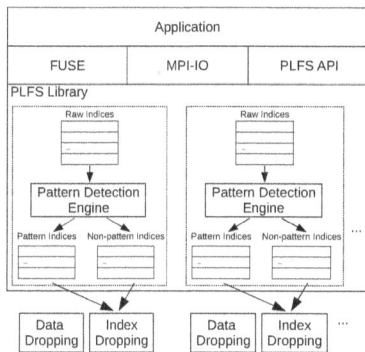

Figure 3: Pattern PLFS index framework

work by further reducing the latency as well as the other overheads by using efficient pattern detection and compact pattern descriptions to reduce the amount of PLFS index information. As shown in Figure 1, this results in a compression factor of several orders of magnitude for LANL App 3.

2.2 Architecture

The design goal of Pattern Structured PLFS (Pattern PLFS) [5] is to discover pattern structures in indices (which can be considered as I/O traces) and represent the mapping in a compact way, so that reading takes less time and uses less space for processing indices. We demonstrate the effectiveness of Pattern PLFS here. First, we show how we reduce the per-process metadata (indices) size by discovering local patterns, and then we further demonstrate how to achieve even better compression by merging local indices into a single global one per PLFS file.

In our design illustrated in Figure 3, when writing, Pattern PLFS buffers traditional indices in raw index buffers for each process. After the buffer is full or at the time of closing, a pattern discovering engine starts processing the raw indices and puts the generated pattern structure entries to pattern index buffer and non-pattern ones to non-pattern indices. At the end, the entries will be written to pattern index files. The file format is illustrated in Figure 4. The header stores what type the entries are and the length of them.

Figure 4: Pattern PLFS index file format. The headers indicate the type and size of the entries following them.

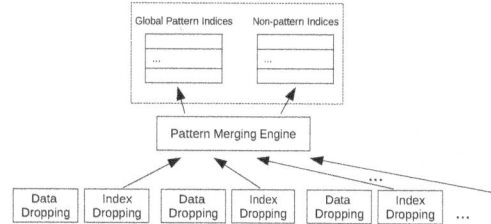

Figure 5: Read and merge indices to form global indices

When an application reads a file (Figure 5), Pattern PLFS reads indices from files, merges pattern entries into global ones whenever possible, and stores the global pattern entries and non-pattern entries in separate buffers. The contents of the buffers are broadcast to other processes that are reading the PLFS file.

We chose the design described above based on efficiency and feasibility. One of the other options is to compress using both local and global patterns at the time of writing in ADIO layer. This approach requires communication and synchronization when writing, which may ruin the biggest advantage of PLFS - fast writing. It becomes worse when the application has more write requests and smaller write extents. Another possibility is to use existing compression libraries, such as zlib [9], to compress indices in memory, write compressed data to files, read them into memory and decompress them. The problem of this is that the eventual memory footprint is still big, although the I/O time of reading indices is reduced due to the compression.

2.3 Local Pattern Structure

The local pattern structure describes the access behaviors of a single process. For example, a process may write to a file with a *(offset, length)* pair sequence such as: *(0, 4), (5, 4), (10, 4), (15, 4)*. This is an example of a typical fixed-stride pattern and can easily be described in some form (e.g. saying start offset is 0; stride is 5; length is 4) of smaller size by checking if the stride is constant. Strided patterns occur when accessing parts of regular data structure (e.g. odd columns of a 2-d matrix). A more complex pattern would occur when accessing discrete parts of an array consisting of complex data types (e.g. MPI file view with complex data types or high-dimension data with complex types). To compress complex patterns, we need an algorithm to identify the repeating sequences and a structure to represent them in a compact way. The structure should also allow fast random accesses without decoding. The algorithm proposed in this section can discover complex pattern structures and compress them. Figure 2 shows an example in which two processes write into one PLFS file with traditional indices. This section uses this example to demonstrate how local pattern structure discovering works.

Figure 6 is the structure of one pattern entry. Chunk *id* is used to find the data dropping file for which the pattern is. One logical offset pattern may map to many length and physical offset patterns. But if you expand patterns to their original sequences, the num-

id: chunk id used to locate the corresponding data dropping file
logical: logical offset pattern unit (See Figure 7)
length[ ]: an array of pattern units representing lengths
physical[ ]: an array of pattern units representing physical offsets

Figure 6: Structure of a pattern index entry.

$$[i, (d[0], d[1], ...)^\wedge r]$$

Figure 7: Pattern unit notation. i **is the first element of the original sequence.** $d[]$ **(***delta***) is the repeating part of an array containing the distances of any two consecutive elements in the original sequence.** r **is the number of repetitions. For example,** $(5, 7, 10, 12, 15)$ **can be represented as** $[5, (2, 3)^\wedge 2]$**.**

ber of logical offsets, lengths and physical offsets represented by a pattern entry should be exactly the same.

Based on the sliding window algorithm in LZ77 [44], we propose a new algorithm to discover common patterns in data accesses and store them in a data structure that allows PLFS to conduct lookups without decompressing the index. The algorithm is described in Algorithm 1. There are three major steps. The first one is to retrieve the distances ($delta[]$) of consecutive numbers. The second one is to move two sliding windows along the $delta[]$ to find any consecutive repeating subsequences, and place them on a stack (p). The third one is to put the original starting numbers of each repeating subsequence back on the pattern stack in order to form the final patterns. By using the original starting number and the deltas, any number in the original sequence can be recovered. To demonstrate the algorithm, Figure 8 gives an example for discovering patterns in logical offsets of Process 0 in Figure 2. The sequence of logical offsets $(0, 3, 7, 14, 17, 21, 28, ...)$ are preprocessed to deltas $(3, 4, 7, 3, 4, 7, ...)$. Two windows move along the deltas to find repeating subsequences. To represent a pattern of a sequence of numbers in a compact way, we introduced a structure called *pattern unit*, described in Figure 7. The eventual pattern output in Figure 8 is $[0, (3, 4, 7)^\wedge 3], [42, (4)^\wedge 4]$.

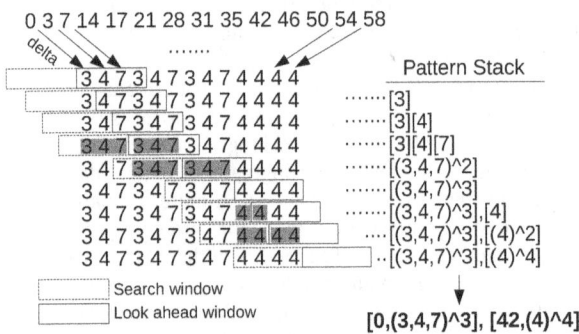

Figure 8: An example of local pattern structure discovering.

Suppose w is the window size in the algorithm demonstrated in Algorithm 1 and Figure 8, the time complexity of finding repeating parts between the search window and lookahead window is $O(w)$, since it is essentially a string searching problem and can be solved using the KMP algorithm [24] or other, similar, algorithms. According to the *while* loop of Algorithm 1, two windows move forward by at least one position in an iteration. The overall time

---

Algorithm 1: Pattern Detection

Data: A sequence of numbers: q
Result: Pattern of q
```
/* delta is the distance between
   consecutive numbers in q          */
```
for $i=0; i<q.length-1; i++$ **do**
  $\mid$ $delta[i] = q[i + 1] - q[i]$
end
```
/* container of pattern units        */
```
initialize pattern stack ps;

initialize lookahead window lw on $delta[0]$;
initialize search window sw in front of $delta[]$;
while lw *is NOT empty* **do**
  if $\forall k, lw[1:k]==sw[sw.size-k+1:sw.size]$
  AND lw[1:k] can be merged with the last elements in ps
  then
    $\mid$ `/* merge lw[1:k] to ps.top()   */`
    $\mid$ update ps.top();
    $\mid$
    $\mid$ lw.moveforwardby(k);
    $\mid$ sw.moveforwardby(k);
  else
    $\mid$ initialize pattern unit p;
    $\mid$ $p.d = lw.first()$;
    $\mid$ ps.push(p);
    $\mid$ lw.moveforwardby(1);
    $\mid$ sw.moveforwardby(1);
  end
end
foreach p *in ps* **do**
  $\mid$ $p.init = p.d[0]$'s corresponding number in q
end

---

complexity of this pattern recognition algorithm is $O(wn)$. n is the length of the input sequence.

To compress PLFS mappings, given a sequence of tuples (i.e. raw index entries) *(logical offset, length, physical offset)*, they are separated into three arrays by their types: $logical\_offset[]$, $length[]$, $physical\_offset[]$. First, patterns in $logical\_offset[]$ are found using a pattern detection engine based on Algorithm1. Then, elements in $length[]$ are grouped according to patterns found in $logical\_offset[]$, and their patterns are discovered separately by group. Later, $physical\_offset[]$ is processed in the same way. This procedure is illustrated by an example in Figure 9. Two patterns are found in $logical\_offset[]$. $length[]$ is separated into two groups, and patterns are detected within each group. Also, elements in $physical\_offset[]$ are grouped and patterns are detected.

Since data has been reorganized, when I/O read requests come to PLFS, PLFS needs to look up the requested offsets in associated indices to decide the corresponding physical offsets. The lookup algorithm is described in Algorithm 2. The basic idea is to find the position of the biggest logical offset that is not larger than the request offset, *off*, in the logical offset pattern, find the corresponding length, *len*, by the position, check if *off* falls in (off, len) and return the corresponding physical offset. For example, when a request of *read(off=29, len=1)* comes, suppose we have the patterns in Figure 9. Because $0 < 29 < 42$, the request can only fall within the pattern starting with 0 (Pattern A). Then:

$$row = (29 - 0)/(3 + 4 + 7) = 2$$
$$rem = (29 - 0) \bmod (3 + 4 + 7) = 1$$

Logical Offset	Length	Physical Offsets
0	2	0
3	2	2
7	4	4
14	2	8
17	2	10
21	4	12
28	2	16
31	2	18
35	4	20
42	3	24
46	3	27
50	3	30
54	3	33
58	3	36

$[0,(3,4,7)^3]$ $[2,(0,2,-2)^3]$ $[0,(2,2,4)^3]$

$[42,(4)^4]$ $[3,(0)^4]$ $[24,(3)^4]$

↓ Final Index Pattern

	Logical Offset	Length	Physical Offset
Pattern A	$[0,(3,4,7)^3]$	$[2,(0,2,-2)^3]$	$[0,(2,2,4)^3]$
Pattern B	$[42,(4)^4]$	$[3,(0)^4]$	$[24,(3)^4]$

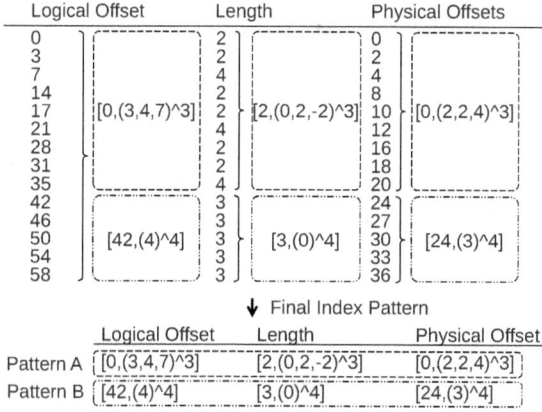

Figure 9: Compressing mapping from logical positions to physical positions. In this particular example, two patterns are found in logical offsets. Then the corresponding raw lengths of the two patterns are fed into pattern recognition engine and length patterns are found. Physical offsets are processed the same way as lengths. Finally, patterns for the same raw entries are grouped together.

Because $0 < rem \leq 3, rem$ falls in the $1st$ delta in Pattern A's logical offsets ($[0, (\mathbf{3}, 4, 7)^\wedge 3]$). So the position that $off = 29$ falls into is $pos = 2 \times 3 + 1 = 7$ (3 is the number of deltas in the pattern). We can use pos to find out the logical offset (29), length (2) and physical offset (16). Then we can check if the requested data is within the segment and decide the physical offset.

Suppose n is the total number of index entries, the time complexity of traditional PLFS lookup is $O(logn)$ if binary search is used. The time complexity of the lookup in Algorithm 2 is $O(e.logical.d.size())$, since it has to calculate $stride$ and go through $e.logical.d[]$ to find pos. Fortunately, $e.logical.d.size()$ is usually not big from what we have seen and the constant factor in $O(e.logical.d.size())$ is small (2). If m is the number of total entries, the time complexity of looking up an offset in all indices is $O(logm * delta.size())$ when the entries have already been sorted by their initial offsets. The worst case scenario is that the request offset is in a hole and PLFS has to check every pattern index entry to find out. Fortunately, if patterns present, m is very small. To simplify lookup, special cases such as overlaps and negative strides should be avoided by sorting and merging entries.

2.4 Global Pattern Structure

Global pattern is constructed using local pattern structures. To merge local patterns into global patterns, Pattern PLFS first sorts all local patterns by their initial logical offsets. Then it goes through every pattern to check if neighbor patterns abuts one another. Figure 10 is an example of a global pattern. At the beginning of it, a group of three processes (PID: 4,7,6) write with a local strided pattern (We call the size of data shared by the same group of processes a *global stride*). After that, (2,8,9) writes the following global stride. Then (4,7,6) repeats the pattern. Global pattern is essentially consecutive repeating local patterns. Since local patterns are repeating, only one local pattern is stored in global pattern structure and the difference between global and local pattern is that global pattern maintains a list of chunk IDs instead of only one chunk id.

Assuming each local pattern repeats twice and physical offset starts at 0, the global pattern structure in Figure 10 can be described

---

Algorithm 2: Lookup offset in an pattern index entry.

Data: Requested offset: off, a pattern entry (Figure 6): e
Result: if off is inside e, return the corresponding physical offset and length of a contiguous piece of data

if $off < e.logical.init$ OR $off > e.logical.last$ **then**
  | return $false$;   /* out of range */
end
$roff = off - e.logical.init$; /* relative offset */
/* stride of the pattern   */
$stride = sum(e.logical.d[])$;
/* remainder   */
$rem = roff \% stride$
/* num of strides the offset passed */
$row = roff / stride$;
/* Find the delta that roff fails in */
$sum = 0$;
for $col\_pos = 0$; $sum <= rem$;col_pos++ **do**
  | $sum+ = e.logical.d[col\_pos]$;
end
$col\_pos = col\_pos - 1$;
$pos = col\_pos + row * e.logical.d.size()$;
$o\_offset = e.logical[pos]$;   /* posth offset */
$o\_length = e.length[pos]$;   /* posth length */
if off falls in (o_offset, o_length) **then**
  | $shift = off - o\_offset$;
  | $o\_length = o\_length - shift$;
  | $o\_physical = e.physical[pos] + shift$;
  | $o\_chunk\_id = e.chunkid$;
  | return (o_length, $o\_physical$, o_chunk_id);
else
  | return false;
end

---

by Figure 12. For many MPI applications, rank numbers are related to data processing and its data layout, so id's can be further compressed by patterns if it is necessary.

Of course, there are some more complicated global patterns that the global pattern structure cannot describe. However, in practice, this simple structure is effective enough and it favors fast lookups.

To look up an offset in a global pattern, Pattern PLFS uses Algorithm 3. The basic idea is to locate which row and column the requested offset is in the imaginary global pattern matrix (e.g. Figure 10). To find the physical offset within a data dropping file, Pattern PLFS needs to figure out how much data has been written to file before the piece of data requested. For example, the global stride ($gs.size$) of Figure 10 is 120. Stride (s) is 30. If the request off is 1250, r is 250. Global stride id ($gs.id$) is $250/120 = 2$, which indicates off falls in the Global Stride 2. Global stride remainder ($gs.rem$) is 10, $row = 10/30 = 0$, $col = (10 \mod 30)/10 = 1$. The logical offset of the data is $1000 + 120 * 2 + 30 * 0 + 10 = 1250$; $length = 10$. Because:

$$s/length * gs.id + col = (30/10) * 2 + 1 = 7,$$

so the chunk id is $g.id[7] = 7$. Physical offset is

$$0 + 10 * 4 * 1 + 10 * 0 = 40.$$

The most time consuming part of Algorithm 3 is $cnt=g.id[1:p].count(chunkid)$, where Pattern PLFS has to go from the first id to the pth and find out how many $chunkid$ there is in $g.id[1 : p]$. Fortunately, this can be calculated once with time complexity $O(n)$ (n is the number of local patterns) and cached in the

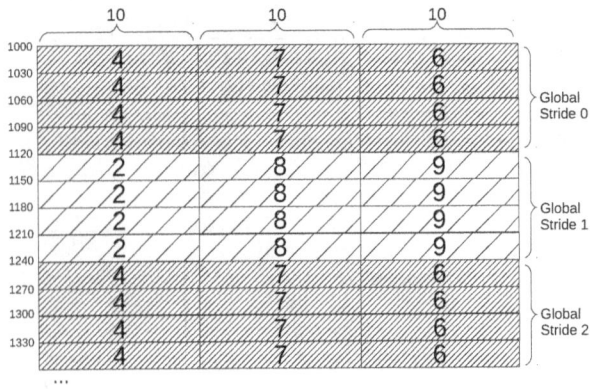

Figure 10: An example of global pattern. 4,7,6,2 and so on are PIDs. Blocks of same texture represent data area that is shared by a group of processes, i.e. *global strides.*

id[]: an array of chunk id indicating the positions of processes inside the global pattern

logical: a logical offset pattern unit

length: a length pattern unit

physical: a physical offset pattern unit

Figure 11: Global pattern structure

pattern structure (This can be even faster if $g.id[]$ can be described by patterns). So the later lookups do not need to calculate it again and the time complexity becomes $O(1)$. The time complexity of looking an offset in p global pattern entries in memory is $O(logp)$, since it has to locate an entry in p entries.

3. PLFS EVALUATION

For a holistic test, several benchmarks and real applications were used to test Pattern PLFS. *FS-TEST* [8] is a synthetic checkpoint tool from LANL. It can be configured to write or read with N-N (N processes write N files) or N-1 (N processes write N files) pattern with many parameters. In addition, we developed a benchmark tool called MapReplayer [20], which can replay traces previously collected by PLFS and show the performance. In order to test pattern structure discovering from unstructured I/O, several real applications were ran on top of Pattern PLFS. The experiments were conducted on LANL's RRZ testbed, which has eight cores/16GB RAM per node. PanFS was used as the underlying parallel file system.

3.1 FS-TEST

FS-TEST has very similar write patterns to many real checkpoint systems. In this experiment, each FS-TEST process writes data stridely, which leads to many index entries in Traditional PLFS (PLFS 2.2.1). The write sizes of all tests are fixed at 4KB. Large amount of indices take lots of space in both disks and memory, resulting in poor I/O performance. Pattern PLFS is expected to reduce index sizes and therefore improve performance.

As shown in Figure 13(A), write open times of Pattern PLFS and PLFS 2.2.1 are very close. Since there are little differences between the implementations of Pattern PLFS and PLFS 2.2.1, the result serves as a sanity check and shows the system's stability. As we can see, the results are reasonable and the system is stable. In Figure 13(B), we can observe that write bandwidth of Pattern PLFS is consistently better than that of Traditional PLFS. The reason for this is that Pattern PLFS writes much less metadata (pattern struc-

id[]: [4,7,6,2,8,9,4,7,6,2,8,9]

logical: $1000,(30)^{\wedge}4$

length: $10,(0)^{\wedge}4$

physical: $0,(10)^{\wedge}4$

Figure 12: Global Pattern of Figure 10

Algorithm 3: Lookup offset in an global index pattern entry.

Data: Requested offset: *off*, a global pattern entry (Figure 11): g

Result: if *off* is inside g, return the corresponding physical offset and length of the contiguous piece of data

```
/* check if off falls in the range of the
   global pattern                          */
```
if $off < g.logical.init$ OR $off > g.logical.last$ **then**
  | return *false*
end

$r = off - g.logical.i$;   /* relative offset */
$s = g.logical.d[0]$;   /* stride */
```
/* global stride, r is the number of
   repetitions in the pattern unit         */
```
$gs.size = s * g.logical.r$;
```
/* which global stride r falls in          */
```
$gs.id = r/gs.size$

$gs.rem = rmodgs.size$;
```
/* row inside a global stride              */
```
$row = gs.rem/s$;
```
/* column inside a stride                  */
```
$col = (gs.rem\%s)/g.length.i$;
if $g.logical[gs.id][row][col]$ *is out of the range of g* **then**
  | return false;
end
$p = (s/g.length.i) * gs.id + col - 1$;
$chunkid = g.id[p]$;   /* pth local pattern id */
$shift = off - g.logical[gs.id][row][col]$;
```
/* Num of chunkid in the 1~p id's          */
```
$cnt = g.id[1 : p].count(chunkid)$

$o\_physical\_offset = g.physical.i + g.physical.d[0]$
  $* g.physical.r * cnt + g.physical.d[0] * row$;
return $gs[gs.id][row][col].length - shift$,
  $o\_physical\_offset + shift, chunkid$;

---

ture index entries in Pattern PLFS), which are much smaller than traditional unstructured index entries, to disks. It is worth noticing that Pattern PLFS is about 1.5 GB/s faster than Traditional PLFS with 512 processes and 16K writes per process. As shown in Figure 13(C), Pattern PLFS and Traditional PLFS have very similar performance on close, when PLFS flushes data/indices and closes all opened files. Overall, Pattern PLFS has better write performance than Traditional PLFS. In addition, from the experiments we have conducted, we also see a trend towards growing gap between performance of Pattern PLFS and Traditional PLFS as the scale becomes larger.

The read performance is shown in Figure 14. Uniform read uses the same number of processes as the originating write, while non-uniform read uses a different number. As shown in Figure 14, Pattern PLFS has much shorter open time than Traditional PLFS for both uniform and non-uniform reads, since indices are read and processed at read open time and Pattern PLFS is able to significantly reduce index size by discovering patterns and representing

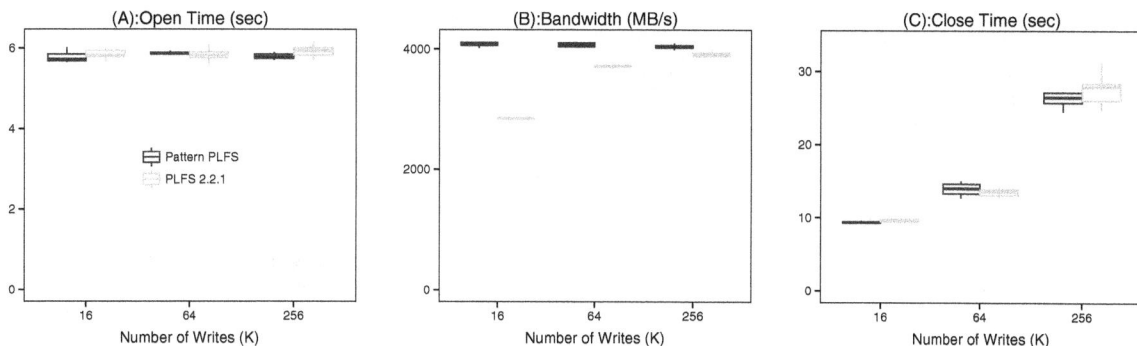

Figure 13: Write performance of 512 processes with write size of 4K. Write Open/Close Time: lower is better. Write Bandwidth: higher is better. Please note that the scale of X axis is K. So 16 represents $16 \times 1024 = 16384$ writes.

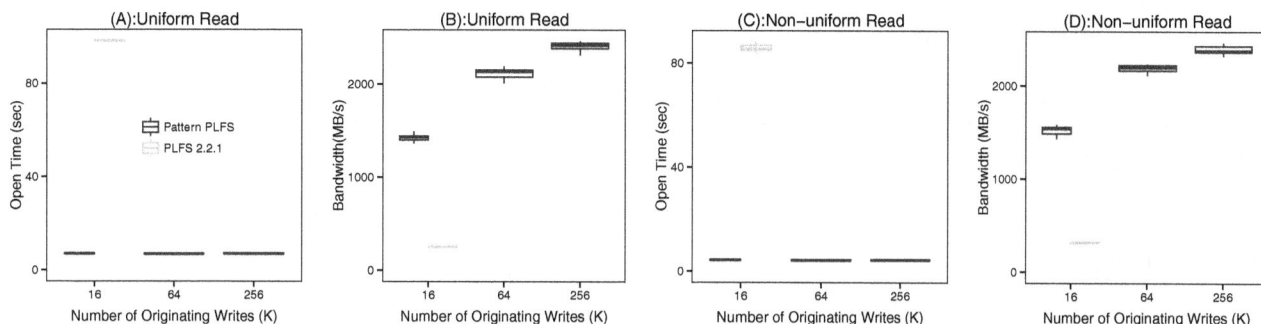

Figure 14: Performance of uniform read (512 processes) and non-uniform read (256 processes) with originating write size of 4K. Some of the PLFS 2.2.1 data points are missing because large index took too much memory and PLFS crashed when allocating memory. (Read Open Time: lower is better. Read Bandwidth: higher is better.)

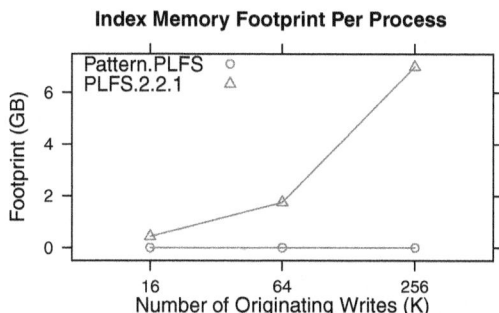

Figure 15: Index memory footprint of 512 processes. Note that Y axis shows the per-process memory footprint. For example, an eight-core node needs more than 48 GB memory to hold index for PLFS 2.2.1 if the number of originating writes is 256 K.

indices as compact pattern structures. Please note that the unit of X-axis is "K". For example, *256* represents *256 × 1024 = 262144* writes per process. One entry of index is 56 bytes. One copy of the whole index is *256 × 1024 × 512PE × 56bytes = 7GB*. If there are *8* processes per node, the node needs to hold *7 × 8 = 56 GB* of indices in memory. The combined metadata from all processes takes large memories and prevents PLFS 2.2.1 from functioning, which is the reason why its data points are missing. Figure 15 shows the comparison between index memory footprint of

Pattern PLFS and PLFS 2.2.1. The overall index size of PLFS 2.2.1 on disk is the same as the size per process on memory, since each process has to hold the whole index. The overall index size of Pattern PLFS on disk is bigger than its index size on memory. This is because the indices on memory have been compressed with global patterns. The on-disk index size of Pattern PLFS is 3MB and on-memory one is 6KB, both of which are significantly smaller than the sizes of PLFS 2.2.1. The reduction of index leads to up to 80 percent and 480 percent higher bandwidth for write (Figure 13) and read (Figure 14), respectively. The improvement is asymmetrical because index write is more parallelized than read in PLFS.

3.2 Real Applications

We explored writes of several real applications to see if there are any patterns and if Pattern PLFS can discover them. In addition, it is really nice that PLFS indices are essentially write traces, by which we can plot and see the patterns if they exist.

3.2.1 The MILC Code

The MILC code is an implementation of LQCD (lattice quantum chromodynamics) and it is widely used to solve real physics problems and to benchmark supercomputers [7, 21, 6]. Figure 16 shows the write patterns of three I/O configurations for saving the same data. All of them are N-1 writes, which are ideal cases for PLFS. In Figure 16 *(A)*, each MILC process writes small fix-size pieces of data with a 2-d strided pattern (stride sizes vary). In *(B)*, each process writes to one contiguous portion of the file. The difference between *(C)* and *(B)* is that in *(C)* each process also writes a header at the beginning of the file. The compression rates of *(A)*, *(B)* and *(C)* are 37.0, 3.0 and 3.6, respectively. *(A)* has a better compression rate since it has more writes and they have patterns. Pattern PLFS was able to compress by discovering local and global patterns. The other two are both simple and most of the compressions came from using global pattern.

3.2.2 Pagoda

Pagoda [4] stands for Parallel Analysis of GeOscience DAta. It is a set of PnetCDF-based tools and APIs that have been developed to mitigate the I/O bottleneck of GCRM (Global Cloud Resolving Model) data analysis, whose scale can be PB's per year. Pagoda conducts N-1 write stridely, which generates a great amount of index entries. By discovering patterns out of unstructured writes, Pattern PLFS achieved a compression rate of 2.9 in a typical run.

3.3 Replay

By using MapReplayer, we were able to replay the I/O behaviors of various benchmarks and real applications. The compression rates are already shown in Figure 1. NERSC Pattern I/O [2] is a benchmark in which each process writes with a single fixed-stride pattern. By the local and global pattern structure discovering techniques described in this paper, they can be represented as one global pattern and index size is significantly reduced. Each process of LANL App 3 writes with a 2-D strided pattern. Pattern PLFS was able to represent them by one single pattern entry in memory. In LANL App 2 MPI I/O collective and LANL App 2 Independent, each process writes with different strides in different periods of time. The compression was achieved by the local pattern compression. Pattern PLFS has better compression rate for LANL App 2 I/O library since the application's own I/O library arranged data to be written with fixed-stride pattern, which made global pattern compression possible. LANL App 1 writes with 2-D strided pattern and global pattern was found. The FLASH traces used were collected by FUSE-based PLFS. For FUSE's own performance concerns, it may split large requests to smaller requests, which breaks the pattern of FLASH and makes it hard to find patterns. Actually, I/O requests of FLASH have patterns and we believe the patterns can be detected by our techniques. Each BTIO process writes with a 2-d strided pattern and they are combined to a single global pattern in memory. To sum up, traditional PLFS does not handle these applications very well, while Pattern PLFS can discover structures and be able to shrink their index sizes.

4. PATTERN-AWARE PREFETCHING

Typical applications involve both I/O and computation; they read data from file systems into memory and then manipulate that data. For example, scientific applications need to read data generated by simulations for subsequent analysis, or read checkpoints to resume after interruptions. Visualization applications need to read large amounts of saved data structures, process them, and render them visually for analysis in a timely manner. In these cases, large read latency can result in intolerable delays. Prefetching is an effective way of reducing the I/O latency. This technique predicts future data that will be used by the application and makes it available in memory before it is requested by the application. The process of prefetching can overlap computation with I/O so that the I/O latency, while unchanged, does not affect the users' experience.

The accuracy of prediction is important for prefetching. Inaccurate predictions will introduce overhead without any corresponding benefit. Accurate predictions which are not made quickly enough also do not provide benefit. Even more challenging is that prefetching the right data too early can also degrade performance since the

data occupies memory and prevents it from being used for other purposes. Even though it is challenging, prefetching with simple readahead [25, 37] is implemented in almost all storage systems and has been shown to provide large benefits for applications which do sequential reading. Unfortunately, many applications, especially scientific ones, present I/O patterns [31, 16, 13] that do not appear sequential at the storage system.

For example, Pagoda and MILC read data with patterns of varying strides as is shown for Pagoda in Figure 20. This is due to the fact that they read from different segments of their files where each segment contains data of different types. These patterns are regular, but not sequential, so simple readahead prefetch algorithms cannot provide benefit. However, the pattern detection algorithm proposed in this paper can discover the patterns and predict their future I/O requests.

4.1 System Overview

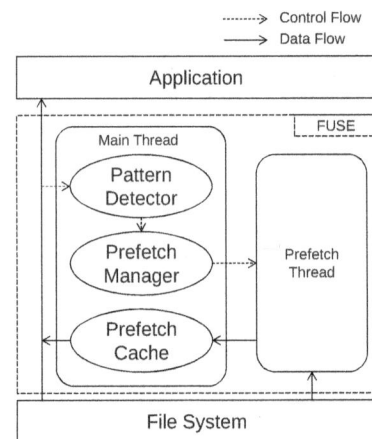

Figure 17: Prefetch Framework

To test the ability of patterns to allow prefetching for nonsequential, but regular, I/O patterns, we have designed and implemented a pattern-aware prefetching file system using FUSE. This provides a simple mechanism by which we can intercept, inspect, and forward I/O requests to another file system. In our case, as we observe the requests, we attempt to detect patterns, and use any detected patterns to prefetch data for predicted future reads.

The framework of our pattern-aware file system is shown in Figure 17. It is a simple layer between applications and a standard *underlying* file system such as ext3. For write workloads, our layer merely forwards all writes to the underlying file system. For read workloads, however, our layer will attempt pattern-aware prefetching; reads which were correctly predicted and prefetched will be satisfied from the cache of our layer but reads which were not predicted will necessarily be forwarded to the underlying file system.

Our layer is comprised of several main components. The *Pattern Detector* records read requests and detects their patterns. It is modularized so that any pattern detection algorithm may be plugged into it. The *Prefetch Manager* receives pattern information from the Pattern Detector and predicts future requests based on these patterns. It sends requests for predicted future requests to our *Prefetch Thread*, which is in charge of fetching data from file systems into our *Prefetch Cache*. When read requests are received from the application, our pattern-aware FUSE file system will check the Prefetch Cache. If the data is not in the cache, it will issue I/O calls to

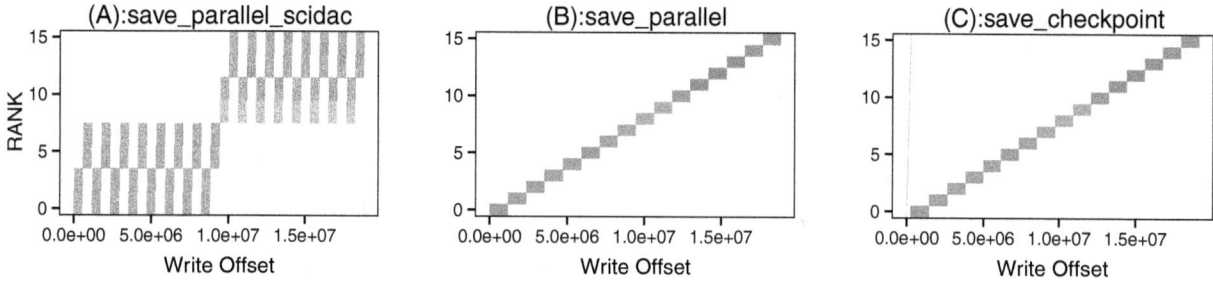

Figure 16: MILC write patterns. In-memory index compression rates by Pattern PLFS (higher is better): (A):37.0;(B):3.0;(C):3.6

the underlying file system and wait for the data. Otherwise, it will return data to the application from the Prefetch Cache immediately without again fetching data from the file system. Since moving data within memory is much faster than moving from disk to memory, I/O latency is reduced.

4.2 Pattern Detection and Prediction

To discover patterns for prefetching, the Pattern Detector periodically tries to find patterns from the recent request history using the algorithm described in Algorithm 1 and Figure 8. Then, the prefetch is conducted using prediction based on current pattern. For example, if the current offset pattern detected is $[0, (3, 4, 7)^\wedge 2]$ (pattern unit, Figure 7), the Prefetch Manager can predict future requests that may follow it. In this example, the next three request offsets predicted should be $31, 35, 42$, as explained below.

$$0 + (3 + 4 + 7) \times 2 + 3 = 31$$
$$0 + (3 + 4 + 7) \times 2 + 3 + 4 = 35$$
$$0 + (3 + 4 + 7) \times 2 + 3 + 4 + 7 = 42$$

For more advanced predictions, the patterns can be organized as nodes of a tree structure as shown by the example in Figure 18. This multi-level pattern tree can be built by using Algorithm 1 multiple times. For the first time, the input is a sequence of numbers. Starting from the second time, the input is the sequence of patterns found from the previous time. In the tree structure, child patterns are represented as pattern unit (Figure 7) without i. The parent pattern has a full pattern unit describing the pattern of i of its children. I/O libraries using multi-level data layout or I/O operations in complex embedded loops may produce recursive patterns. The tree structured pattern is suitable for these cases.

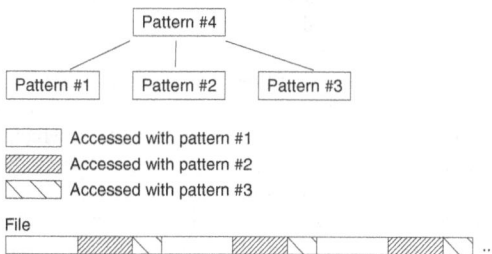

Figure 18: Pattern Tree. Pattern #1, #2 and #3 repeat as a whole and they form the bigger pattern #4.

4.3 Markov Model Prediction Algorithm

Since Markov model prediction [31] is an important related work to the pattern detection proposed in this paper, we briefly describe it here and compare its performance with the pattern detection algorithm of this paper in Section 5.

A Markov model can be represented as an $N \times N$ matrix M. $M_{i,j}$ is the probability of transition from state i to state j. The probability of transition from state i to any states is determined only by state i. To build a Markov model for read requests, a file should be divided to data blocks of equal size and each block is assigned a block number. The block numbers are used to represent the states in the Markov matrix. For example, if blocks $2, 3, 6, 7, 10, 11$ are read by an application, the corresponding Markov matrix will be the one in Figure 19. To predict by the model, when a read request for block 3 comes, the Markov model will predict the next request to be block 6 because $M_{3,6} = 1$.

Figure 19: Markov Matrix

5. PREFETCH EVALUATION

The evaluation of our prefetch system is based on a trace-driven approach. We developed FUSE-Tracer and Trace-Replayer, which are publicly available with our pattern-aware prefetching FUSE file system [20]. FUSE-Tracer records fine-granularity I/O requests with information such as hostname, offset, length, PID, operation start time, operation end time. It is very easy to use and it does not require recompilation of the application to be traced or any libraries. To use FUSE-Tracer, all you need to do is mount FUSE-Tracer on a directory and file operations performed on the mount will be recorded to a file. Trace-Replayer then is a tool that replays the traces collected by FUSE-Trace; it also provides some extra functionality such as adding fixed computational delays between I/O operations. This allows us to easily vary the ratio of I/O to computation to study how much latency is required in order for pre-fetching to be beneficial.

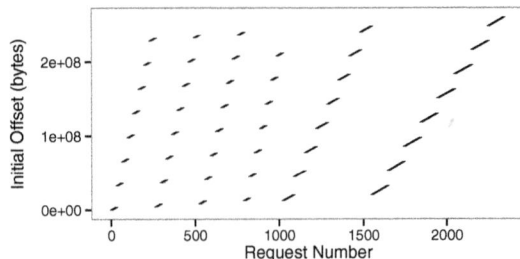

Figure 20: Pagoda I/O Requests. Only initial offsets of the requests are plotted. The graph shows the requests may have more complex patterns than simple strided ones.

5.1 Trace-Driven Simulation

To evaluate the prefetch system, we collected traces of Pagoda by FUSE-Tracer and replayed them using Trace-Replayer on the mount point of the prefetch system. Figure 20 shows the I/O requests of one Pagoda process. We replayed the Pagoda trace and the results are shown in Figure 21.

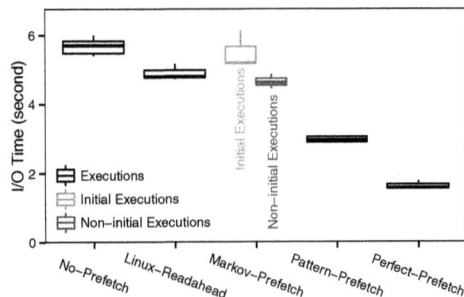

Figure 21: Pagoda I/O cost from the user's perspective.

To compare the performance of prefetching, we replayed Pagoda traces on different types of FUSE prefetching systems. The X axis in Figure 21 indicates the type of the FUSE application. No-Prefetch is basic vanilla FUSE that does not have any prefetch capabilities enabled. Linux-Readahead has the Linux built-in readahead functionality enabled. Markov-Prefetch uses Markov prediction proposed by Oly and Reed [31]. Since the Markov prediction [31] cannot work on the parts of the file that have not been read, we had to run the replayer more than once to build the model and then use it for prefetching. In the initial execution, the Markov pattern detector collects read requests and builds the Markov model with no prefetch being conducted. In the non-initial executions, the Markov model was used to predict future requests and prefetching was then conducted.

Pattern-Prefetch uses the pattern detection algorithm proposed in this paper. Since the prediction is not limited to the regions that have been read, prefetching in Pattern-Prefetch works with all reads. As a result, there is only one box showing its performance in Figure 21. In Perfect-Prefetch, the Prefetch Manager loads the I/O trace that is also used by the replayer and uses it for prediction, which means the prefetch manager knows exactly what will be read by the replayer. In this case, the prediction accuracy is 100 percent.

The Y axis in Figure 21 is the I/O time that users observe and less is better. It includes the time spent on I/O by the application, pattern detection, and prefetch management (e.g. communicating with prefetch helper thread), but does not include the time spent on the Prefetch Thread, since it is overlapped with the computation of the replayer or main thread of FUSE. Because the interfere from prefetching to computation is ignorable in this test case, the reduction of I/O time leads to the reduction of the overall execution time.

5.2 Discussion

Linux-Readahead is slightly better than No-Prefetch, because the read offsets were increasing most of the time. Reading several KBs ahead had positive effects. However, it is limited. The initial executions of Markov-Prefetch do not have prefetch, so the results are very close to the No-Prefetch ones. The Markov-Prefetch non-initial executions, which are with prefetching, have shorter I/O time than the initial tests. In the Markov model, there are several key parameters that need to be tuned in order to achieve good performance. Inappropriate parameters may degrade performance. For example, if block size is too small, the Markov matrix will use too much memory and disk space. When the block size is reduced to one byte, the Markov model is essentially equal to records of every single requests. Loading and storing the model can be slow. In addition, the prediction speed can be negatively affected. If the block size is too large, many read requests can fall into one block, which makes prediction inaccurate. We picked the optimal 8KB as the blocking for Markov model after inspecting the trace. On average, the non-initial executions of Markov-Prefetch reduces No-Prefetch I/O time by 18%.

Pattern-Prefetch can reduce I/O latency regardless of whether it is the initial execution or non-initial execution, since it is based on latest patterns detected. The patterns are mostly related to strides, not positions within the file. In addition, according to the evaluation on PLFS metadata, it is already proved that the pattern representation proposed in this paper is compact. So less memory is taken for the purpose of prefetching. The pattern information stored in memory for prefetching is less than 1 KB, while the Markov model for the 250 MB file is 0.6 MB both on memory and disk. The Markov model will also be larger when the file is larger. In addition to the advantage of compact pattern representation, the future read requests predicted by Pattern-Prefetch are *(offset, length)* pairs, which allows it to prefetch the exact data requested without any unnecessary data. On average, Pattern-Prefetch reduces No-Prefetch I/O time by 46%.

6. OTHER POSSIBLE USE CASES

Discovering patterns within unstructured I/O and representing them compactly and losslessly are promising techniques and can be applied in other systems. One such example is pre-allocation of blocks in file systems. This eager technique, similar to prefetching, uses predictions of future accesses to optimistically perform expensive operations ahead of time. Our pattern detection of complex access patterns can improve these predictive abilities. Another example, in SciHadoop, the ratio of metadata (keys, which are dimensional information) to data can be very high, thereby incurring tremendous latency when it is transferred [15]. Our technique can be applied to shrink the size of these keys and eventually reduce overhead by using these discovered structures to represent keys. Finally, as HPC continues to grow to extreme scales, tracing I/O is increasingly challenging due to the size of the traces. Lossy techniques such as sampling are one way to reduce the size of the traces; our patterns could do so without loss and make it feasible to understand I/O behaviors at very large scale with fine granularity.

7. RELATED WORK

Our study in this paper involves data compression and pattern recognition. A related work is LZ77 [44], which compresses by describing repeating occurrences of data with the uncompressed single copy. It uses sliding windows to discover repeating data and uses length-distance pairs to encode the data. The drawback of LZ77 is that it does not allow random accesses to input. To decode, it has to start from the beginning of the input. In addition, it does not address the special characteristics I/O requests. Our approach takes advantage of repeating strides of I/O requests with patterns and builds patterns locally (intra-process) and globally (inter-process). The compact representation of pattern allows fast random accesses without decoding.

I/O access patterns have been studied for decades [17, 32, 39, 38, 33, 29, 16, 43]. By various approaches, these studies record and analyze I/O behaviors by statistics, such as the counts of I/O request sizes in different ranges, number of files, I/O interface/library usage, bandwidth over time and so on. However, the majority of studies are of coarse granularity or they do not provide effective ways to recognize fine patterns.

Madhyastha et al. use feedforward neural network and hidden Markov models separately to classify I/O accesses patterns [27]. The classifications are used to guide file system policies. Both of the methods used are based on statistics models. These models are not lossless and cannot serve our need for recovering exact mapping for PLFS. In reference [31], in order to prefetch, Markov model is built to predict future accesses. Again, Markov model is based on statistics and not accurate for storing mappings. It cannot serve as index in PLFS. As a prefetch approach, Markov model proposed in [31] cannot predict in the file regions that have not been accessed. In addition, for the regions that are accessed many times, the predict accuracy decreases. More details are discussed in Section 4 and Section 5.

ScalaTrace [30] allows very concise tracing of MPI applications by intra- and inter-node compression techniques. It compresses MPI events with identical parameters in loops. However, the techniques only focus on communications and do not provide a way to deal with I/O. ScalaIOTrace [42] extends ScalaTrace to I/O. But it inherits most of ScalaTrace techniques and does not provide any techniques to detect I/O patterns either.

Byna et al. proposed an access pattern notation, *I/O Signature*, to guide prefetching [16]. Although the notation is general to represent a broad categories of patterns, the paper fails to present any effective algorithm to discover access patterns or any practical implementation of the notation. Application-level hints can be used to guide prefetching. The hints are provided by users [34], generated by speculative execution [18] or special programming toolkits [41, 36]. They may put significant burden on the users in some cases. In addition, they are not sophisticated enough to recognize the I/O patterns and are not as universal as our approach.

In previous work [22], He et al. proposed an approach to reorganize data to make data accesses larger and more sequential. To locate the reorganized data, a simple remapping index was used. However, it is not able to describe sophisticated mapping and pattern recognition algorithm is not studied. In [23], high-level usage patterns are used to conduct prefetching. However, high-level I/O libraries are required.

8. CONCLUSION

The era of big data and exascale is nigh and is pushing I/O to its limits. Knowledge of I/O's structure can improve performance but its discovery is not trivial. In this paper, we have developed efficient and practical techniques to discover structures from seemingly unstructured I/O operations, thereby enabling powerful I/O optimizations. We applied these techniques within a virtual parallel file system, PLFS, to compress its internal metadata by up to several orders of magnitude with corresponding improvements in write and read performance of up to 40% and 480% respectively. We also applied the techniques to implement a prefetch system using pattern detection to predict future I/O requests. The evaluation with a trace of a real application shows it can reduce I/O latency by 46%, more than doubling the increase shown in prior work which used Markov modeling. We hope, and expect, that these techniques will enable many further I/O optimizations to extend HPC computing into the exascale era and beyond.

Acknowledgments

The authors are thankful to Michael Lang (Los Alamos National Laboratory) and Adam Manzanares (California State University, Chico) for their help toward this study. The authors are also grateful to all the anonymous reviewers for their constructive comments and suggestions, which improve the quality of this paper. This work was performed at the Ultrascale Systems Research Center (USRC) at Los Alamos National Laboratory, supported by the U.S. Department of Energy DE-FC02-06ER25750. The publication has been assigned the LANL identifier LA-UR-13-22371.

9. REFERENCES

[1] Filesystem in Userspace. http://fuse.sourceforge.net/.

[2] National Energy Research Scientific Computing Center. https://outreach.scidac.gov/.

[3] NetCDF website. http://www.unidata.ucar.edu/software/netcdf/.

[4] Pagoda website. https://svn.pnl.gov/gcrm/wiki/Pagoda.

[5] Pattern PLFS. https://github.com/junhe/plfs/tree/complexindex.

[6] SPEC MPI2007 Benchmark Description. http://www.spec.org/auto/mpi2007/Docs/104.milc.html.

[7] The MIMD Lattice Computation (MILC) Collaboration. http://www.physics.utah.edu/ detar/milc/.

[8] LANL FS-TEST, 2012. http://institutes.lanl.gov/data/software/.

[9] zlib, 2012. http://zlib.net/.

[10] A. C. Arpaci-Dusseau and R. H. Arpaci-Dusseau. Information and control in gray-box systems. In *Proceedings of the 18th ACM Symposium on Operating Systems Principles (SOSP '01)*, pages 43–56, Banff, Canada, October 2001.

[11] J. Bent. PLFS maps, 2012. http://www.institutes.lanl.gov/plfs/maps.

[12] J. Bent, G. Gibson, G. Grider, B. McClelland, P. Nowoczynski, J. Nunez, M. Polte, and M. Wingate. PLFS: A checkpoint filesystem for parallel applications. In *Proceedings of the 2009 ACM/IEEE conference on Supercomputing*, page 21. ACM, 2009.

[13] M. Bhadkamkar, J. Guerra, L. Useche, S. Burnett, J. Liptak, R. Rangaswami, and V. Hristidis. BORG: block-reORGanization for self-optimizing storage systems.

In *Proccedings of the 7th conference on File and storage technologies*, pages 183–196. USENIX Association, 2009.

[14] J. Buck, N. Watkins, J. LeFevre, K. Ioannidou, C. Maltzahn, N. Polyzotis, and S. Brandt. Scihadoop: Array-based query processing in hadoop. In *Proceedings of 2011 International Conference for High Performance Computing, Networking, Storage and Analysis*, page 66. ACM, 2011.

[15] J. Buck, N. Watkins, G. Levin, A. Crume, K. Ioannidou, S. Brandt, C. Maltzahn, and N. Polyzotis. Sidr: Efficient structure-aware intelligent data routing in scihadoop. Technical report, UCSC.

[16] S. Byna, Y. Chen, X. Sun, R. Thakur, and W. Gropp. Parallel I/O prefetching using MPI file caching and I/O signatures. In *Proceedings of the 2008 ACM/IEEE conference on Supercomputing*, page 44. IEEE Press, 2008.

[17] P. Carns, K. Harms, W. Allcock, C. Bacon, S. Lang, R. Latham, and R. Ross. Understanding and improving computational science storage access through continuous characterization. *ACM Transactions on Storage (TOS)*, 7(3):8, 2011.

[18] F. Chang and G. Gibson. Automatic i/o hint generation through speculative execution. *Operating systems review*, 33:1–14, 1998.

[19] HDF5. http://www.hdfgroup.org/HDF5/.

[20] J. He. JIOPAT: I/O Pattern Study Toolkit. http://junhe.github.io/jiopat/.

[21] J. He, J. Kowalkowski, M. Paterno, D. Holmgren, J. Simone, and X.-H. Sun. Layout-aware scientific computing: a case study using milc. In *Proceedings of the Workshop on Latest Advances in Scalable Algorithms for Large-Scale Systems in conjunction with ACM/IEEE SuperComputing 2011*, 2011.

[22] J. He, H. Song, X. Sun, Y. Yin, and R. Thakur. Pattern-aware file reorganization in mpi-io. In *Proceedings of the sixth workshop on Parallel Data Storage*, pages 43–48. ACM, 2011.

[23] J. He, X.-H. Sun, and R. Thakur. Knowac: I/o prefetch via accumulated knowledge. In *Proceedings of the IEEE International Conference on Cluster Computing*, pages 429–437, Beijing, China, September 2012.

[24] D. Knuth, J. Morris, and V. Pratt. Fast pattern matching in strings. *SIAM Journal on Computing*, 6(2):323–350, 1977.

[25] Linux. http://www.kernel.org/.

[26] J. Lofstead, S. Klasky, K. Schwan, N. Podhorszki, and C. Jin. Flexible io and integration for scientific codes through the adaptable io system (adios). In *Proceedings of the 6th international workshop on Challenges of large applications in distributed environments*, pages 15–24. ACM, 2008.

[27] T. Madhyastha and D. Reed. Learning to classify parallel input/output access patterns. *Parallel and Distributed Systems, IEEE Transactions on*, 13(8):802–813, 2002.

[28] A. Manzanares, J. Bent, M. Wingate, and G. Gibson. The power and challenges of transformative i/o. In *IEEE Cluster 2012*, Beijing, China, September 2012.

[29] N. Nieuwejaar, D. Kotz, A. Purakayastha, C. Ellis, and M. Best. File-Access Characteristics of Parallel Scientific Workloads. 1995.

[30] M. Noeth, P. Ratn, F. Mueller, M. Schulz, and B. R. de Supinski. Scalatrace: Scalable compression and replay of communication traces for high-performance computing. *Journal of Parallel and Distributed Computing*, 69(8):696–710, 2009.

[31] J. Oly and D. Reed. Markov model prediction of i/o requests for scientific applications. In *Proceedings of the 16th international conference on Supercomputing*, pages 147–155. ACM, 2002.

[32] B. Pasquale and G. Polyzos. A static analysis of i/o characteristics of scientific applications in a production workload. In *Proceedings of the 1993 ACM/IEEE conference on Supercomputing*, pages 388–397. ACM, 1993.

[33] B. Pasquale and G. Polyzos. Dynamic i/o characterization of i/o intensive scientific applications. In *Proceedings of the 1994 ACM/IEEE conference on Supercomputing*, pages 660–669. ACM, 1994.

[34] R. H. Patterson, G. A. Gibson, E. Ginting, D. Stodolsky, and J. Zelenka. Informed prefetching and caching. In *SOSP*, pages 79–95, 1995.

[35] M. Polte, J. Lofstead, J. Bent, G. Gibson, S. Klasky, Q. Liu, M. Parashar, N. Podhorszki, K. Schwan, M. Wingate, et al. ... and eat it too: high read performance in write-optimized hpc i/o middleware file formats. In *Proceedings of the 4th Annual Workshop on Petascale Data Storage*, pages 21–25. ACM, 2009.

[36] P. J. Rhodes, X. Tang, R. D. Bergeron, and T. M. Sparr. Iteration aware prefetching for large multidimensional scientific datasets. In *Proc. of the 17th international conference on Scientific and statistical database management (SSDBM)*, pages 45–54, 2005.

[37] E. Shriver, C. Small, and K. Smith. Why does file system prefetching work. In *Proceedings of the 1999 USENIX Annual Technical Conference*, volume 27, 1999.

[38] H. Simitci and D. A. Reed. A comparison of logical and physical parallel i/o patterns. *International Journal of High Performance Computing Applications*, 12(3):364–380, 1998.

[39] E. Smirni and D. Reed. Lessons from characterizing the input/output behavior of parallel scientific applications. *Performance Evaluation*, 33(1):27–44, 1998.

[40] R. Thakur, W. Gropp, and E. Lusk. On implementing mpi-io portably and with high performance. In *Proceedings of the sixth workshop on I/O in parallel and distributed systems*, pages 23–32. ACM, 1999.

[41] S. VanDeBogart, C. Frost, and E. Kohler. Reducing seek overhead with application-directed prefetching. In *Proceedings of USENIX Annual Technical Conference*, 2009.

[42] K. Vijayakumar, F. Mueller, X. Ma, and P. C. Roth. Scalable i/o tracing and analysis. In *Proceedings of the 4th Annual Workshop on Petascale Data Storage*, pages 26–31. ACM, 2009.

[43] Y. Yin, J. Li, J. He, X.-H. Sun, and R. Thakur. Pattern-direct and layout-aware replication scheme for parallel i/o systems. In *Proceeding of the 27th IEEE International Parallel & Distributed Processing Symposium (IPDPS'2013)*. IEEE, 2013.

[44] J. Ziv and A. Lempel. A universal algorithm for sequential data compression. *Information Theory, IEEE Transactions on*, 23(3):337–343, 1977.

MTC Envelope: Defining the Capability of Large Scale Computers in the Context of Parallel Scripting Applications

Zhao Zhang
Department of Computer
Science
University of Chicago
zhaozhang@uchicago.edu

Daniel S. Katz
Computation Institute
University of Chicago &
Argonne National Laboratory
d.katz@ieee.org

Michael Wilde
Computation Institute
University of Chicago &
Argonne National Laboratory
wilde@mcs.anl.gov

Justin M. Wozniak
Mathematics and Computer
Science Division
Argonne National Laboratory
wozniak@mcs.anl.gov

Ian Foster
Computation Institute
University of Chicago &
Argonne National Laboratory
foster@anl.gov

ABSTRACT

Many scientific applications can be efficiently expressed with the parallel scripting (many-task computing, MTC) paradigm. These applications are typically composed of several stages of computation, with tasks in different stages coupled by a shared file system abstraction. However, we often see poor performance when running these applications on large scale computers due to the applications' frequency and volume of filesystem I/O and the absence of appropriate optimizations in the context of parallel scripting applications.

In this paper, we show the capability of existing large scale computers to run parallel scripting applications by first defining the MTC envelope and then evaluating the envelope by benchmarking a suite of shared filesystem performance metrics. We also seek to determine the origin of the performance bottleneck by profiling the parallel scripting applications' I/O behavior and mapping the I/O operations to the MTC envelope. We show an example shared filesystem envelope and present a method to predict the I/O performance given the applications' level of I/O concurrency and I/O amount. This work is instrumental in guiding the development of parallel scripting applications to make efficient use of existing large scale computers, and to evaluate performance improvements in the hardware/software stack that will better facilitate parallel scripting applications.

Categories and Subject Descriptors

D.4.8 [**Operating systems**]: Performance—*Measurements, Modeling and prediction*

General Terms

Design; Performance

Keywords

Many-task computing, Parallel scripting, Shared file system

1. INTRODUCTION

Many-task computing applications [25] link existing parallel or sequential programs via a filesystem abstraction. Task dependencies are represented by file production and consumption. Parallel scripting is a powerful and convenient tool to construct such applications without modifying the original programs and can naturally maximize execution parallelism. Such parallel scripting applications have been widely used by scientists in fields of astronomy [24, 14, 15], biological science [26, 22, 2, 18], chemistry [12], earth science [17, 11], economics [10], material science [9] and many others. And researchers have enabled such applications on many types of platforms such as clusters, clouds, supercomputers, and grids [37, 1, 3, 19, 34, 36, 35].

On the platforms where there is shared file system that can be used for inter-task communication, a task reads one or several files as input, executes for a while, then writes several files as output. Tasks in later stages might consume the files produced in previous stages as input files. Parallel scripting applications usually have a large number of tasks, and both filesystem access frequency and I/O amount are not well addressed by existing shared file systems and I/O modules. To make good use of a large scale computer, a programmer should have a picture of how the machine facilitates his application, or how his application fits the machine. For example, parallel scripting programmers should know how many times a task could read a file within unit time and how many bytes a task could write to shared filesystem given the concurrency. Unfortunately, we don't have a well-defined shared filesystem benchmark suite that shows the capacity of parallel scripting applications.

This paper's goal is to define and quantitatively evaluate such large scale computers' capacity of parallel scripting applications, which we call the envelope. Our approach is to first understand the applications' I/O behavior and identify the performance metrics that characterize the application I/O performance on large scale computers. Second, we measure those performance metrics on existing large scale system with scales to define the MTC envelope on each scale

Table 1: Basic Application Stage Statistics

stage	Montage				BLAST			CyberShake		
	mProject	mDiff	mFit	mBack	formatdb	blastall	merge	extract	seis	peakGM
tasks	1319	3883	3883	1297	63	1008	16	393	11868	11868
input files	2638	7766	7766	1297	63	4032	1008	1179	35604	11868
output files	2594	3883	7746	1297	252	1008	16	786	11868	11868
input amount (GB)	3.2	2.2	35.8	5.8	4.0	64.5	0.9	41.3	2655.2	0.4
output amount (GB)	10.9	0.001	3.6	5.4	4.7	0.9	0.06	40.1	0.3	0.03

as well as the scalability of existing shared file systems. The third step is to map the applications' behavior on the measured envelope. By doing this, we can classify the application by the factor(s) that bound its I/O performance. The last step is to deliver an guide to show the estimated I/O time consumption given the application's I/O concurrency and I/O amount.

More specifically, we pick three typical parallel scripting applications: Montage [14], BLAST [2] and CyberShake PostProcessing [17]. We run all stages of those applications and trace the filesystem related system calls, then align the trace of the tasks in any one stage with the system call sequence from the profile of that stage. We identify four common concurrent filesystem accesses from those application profiles: file open, file create, read, and write. The parallel scripting applications feature a multi-read-single-write I/O pattern, where a file can be read many times, but only written once. Within the multi-read pattern, we further classify read access as 1-to-1 read and N-to-1 read. The 1-to-1 read refers to the case where each task reads one distinct file, while the N-to-1 read refers to the cases where many tasks read one common file.

We therefore define the MTC envelope as eight curves, showing

- file open operation throughput,
- file creation operation throughput,
- 1-to-1 read data throughput,
- 1-to-1 read data bandwidth,
- N-to-1 read data throughput,
- N-to-1 read data bandwidth,
- write data throughput, and
- write data bandwidth

on the y axis, versus the number of GPFS clients on the x axis.

With these eight curves measured on the GPFS system of the Intrepid BG/P supercomputer, we are able to classify those application stages by the factors that bound them. An application can be metadata bound or I/O bound. In the I/O bound case, they can further be classified as operation throughput bound, data bandwidth bound or concurrency bound. To guide users programming parallel scripting applications on systems with shared filesystems, we compile benchmark performance data on operation concurrency and I/O amount into two heat maps of projected I/O throughput and bandwidth for each filesystem. This allows the programmer to tell if the application can run efficiently on a given computer, what is an efficient scale for the application, and how much time the I/O operations will take.

In this first attempt to characterize the MTC envelope of large-scale systems we assume two realistic constraints: we evaluate a set of existing, unmodified application scripts as they are currently implemented by their science communities (but transcribed into Swift for ease of testing); similarly we measure the behavior of the current production BG/P filesystem with its current configuration, typical background workload, and performance limitations. Note that we run many of our performance measurements on the I/O nodes (referred to as GPFS clients). The reader should consider that each of these I/O nodes is associated with 64 compute nodes, or 256 compute cores.

Regarding definitions, throughout the paper, we refer to the entire parallel script used to execute a scientific task as the *application*, and examine in detail the various stages of processing within these application scripts. A *task* within these stages refers to the invocation of a single application *program* by the parallel script. Further, we model and examine the *throughput* of the application script in terms of the rate at which it performs I/O *operations*, and the *bandwidth* in terms of the rate of data transfer in units of (scaled) bytes per second.

The contributions of this work include a novel approach to understand the concurrency of parallel scripting applications I/O behavior, a suite of performance metrics that characterize parallel scripting applications' I/O behavior and measure later system improvements, and a guide for parallel scripting application writers to make better use of existing hardware-software stack.

2. APPLICATION I/O PROFILE

We profile the I/O behavior of the parallel stages of Montage, BLAST, and CyberShake (ten stages total). Table 1 shows basic statistics: number of tasks, number of input/output files, and total input/output amounts. Note that the ratio between the input amounts and the number of input files denotes how many bytes are read from each input file, while a file or part of a file can be read many times.

2.1 Application Configuration

For Montage, we run a 6x6 degree mosaic centered at galaxy m101. Montage has four parallel stages: mProject, MDiff, mFit, and mBackground (referred to as mBack in this paper for reasons of space.) For BLAST, we search the first 256 sequences in the NCBI nr database against the database itself. BLAST has three parallel stages: formatdb, blastall, and merge. For CyberShake, we run the post-processing workload against the geographic site TEST. CyberShake has three parallel stages: extract, seis, and peak (referred to as peakGM in this paper for reasons of clarity.)

2.2 Application Profiling Methodology

For each application stage, we run all tasks in parallel and trace all system calls during execution. We initially attempted to align the execution trace with the absolute time, as shown in Figure 1, and found two problems. First, run time is dependent on the machine where the application stage is run, so the profile on Machine A is not necessarily valid on Machine B. Second, the filesystem is usually shared by multiple users, so if we align the execution trace by time, the shared filesystem access delay from other users will add noise, and we won't be able to observe the spike of operations that would otherwise be concurrent. Note that we aggregated file creation and file open over one second intervals. Most of the time, the frequency of open is identical to the frequency of create, as in most of the traces for peakGM, the open and creation occur in the same second.

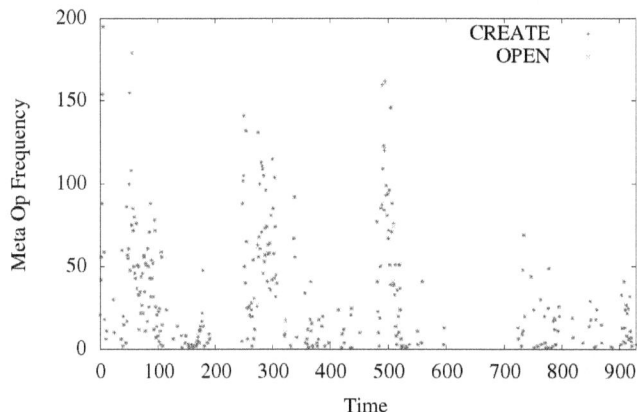

Figure 1: peakGM metadata operations vs. time

We therefore decided to align the system call trace with the order of the system call sequence, rather than with time. The significant benefit of this is that the profile represents the characteristics of the application, independent of any machine, and the time can be projected when we map the filesystem operation onto specific machines. We are thus able to see spikes of concurrent metadata operations in reads and writes.

2.3 Metadata Operation Distribution

Among the ten application stages, we see two major patterns of metadata operation distribution. Figure 2 shows file creation and open distribution over the system call sequence: file creation and file open accesses are two spikes. When those two sets of operations are executed on a system with a shared file system, they will first be limited by the concurrency bound, then they will be limited by throughput at a particular scale. A second pattern is shown in Figure 3, where the file creations are spread across a time range, which mean that at any given time, the concurrency bound of file creation in mProjectPP is 303, though there are 2,594 file creations in total.

In those reads, we see three access patterns for input files: some files are read by only one task in a stage, some files are read by all tasks in a stage, and some files are read by a number of tasks less than the total number of tasks in a stage. We refer those three cases as 1-to-1, N-to-1, and Few-to-1 respectively. Table 2 shows the detailed statistics of the metadata operation spikes as well as the maximum concurrency. Those access patterns suggestion opportunities for potential read optimization in I/O middleware. For

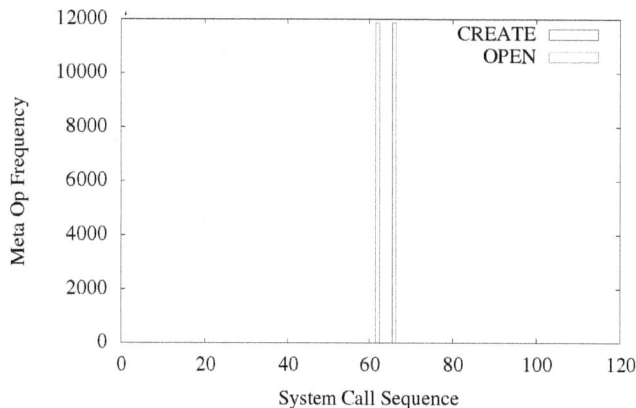

Figure 2: peakGM metadata operations vs. system call sequence

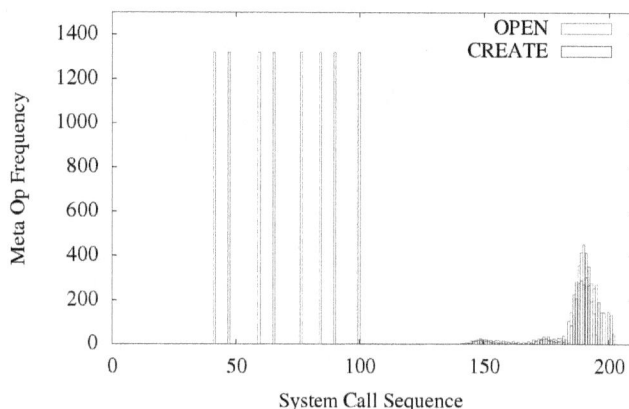

Figure 3: mProjectPP metadata operations vs. system call sequence

example, the N-to-1 reads can be replaced by a single read by one of the tasks, followed by a broadcast to all other tasks with a parallel algorithm. MPI-collective functions [32] can apply such optimizations, but this breaks the independent MTC paradigm.

2.4 I/O Distribution

To show the I/O traffic of each application stage, we record the number of bytes of each read() and write() system call. Then we align this I/O traffic to the system call sequence to determine its concurrency. In Figures 4-9, the vertical lines show the total number of bytes read/written at any given system call, and the points show the average I/O amount. Table 3 shows the trace length (number of system calls), the maximum read/write concurrency, and the maximum I/O traffic.

One interesting I/O pattern in the mProjectPP, mFit, and mBack stages is shown in Figures 4, 5, and 6, where the reads and writes tend to transfer the same amount of I/O traffic per system call, and the number is close to 64 KBytes. It is likely that a buffer of size 64 KBytes is used for file access. We see the same pattern for reads in the formatdb, blastall, and merge stages, shown in Figures 7, 8, and 9. However, the write traffic in formatdb and blastall comprises

	Montage				BLAST			CyberShake		
stage	mProject	mDiff	mFit	mBack	formatdb	blastall	merge	extract	seis	peakGM
open spikes	8	1	10	4	1	4	63	1	1	1
Max. open concurrency	1319	3883	3883	1297	63	1008	16	393	11868	11868
create spikes	0	1	0	0	3	1	1	0	0	1
Max. create concurrency	303	3883	445	113	63	1008	16	81	768	11868
1-to-1 read spikes	4	1	6	4	1	0	63	1	0	1
N-to-1 read spikes	4	0	4	0	0	1	0	0	0	0
Few-to-1 read spikes	0	0	0	0	0	3	0	0	1	0

Table 3: Application I/O Stats

	Montage				BLAST			CyberShake		
stage	mProject	mDiff	mFit	mBack	formatdb	blastall	merge	extract	seis	peakGM
trace length	388	80	328	201	488145	17977	3206	35048	393	11868
Max. read concurrency	1319	3883	3883	1297	63	1008	63	16	393	11868
Max. write concurrency	1246	913	1931	1216	63	1008	16	16	183	768
Max. bytes read/call (MB)	86.4	250.3	254.5	84.9	4.1	6.6	1	1.0	129.0	777.8
Max. bytes written/call (MB)	81.5	0.3	110.2	79.6	2.6	0.2	16	1.0	6.0	18.4

many small writes of hundreds of bytes. The reason is that these two stages process the protein sequence in a sequential order, and each sequence has hundreds of bytes. The I/O traffic patterns in the extract, seis and peakGM stages are all unique, yet they feature high concurrency and are data-intensive.

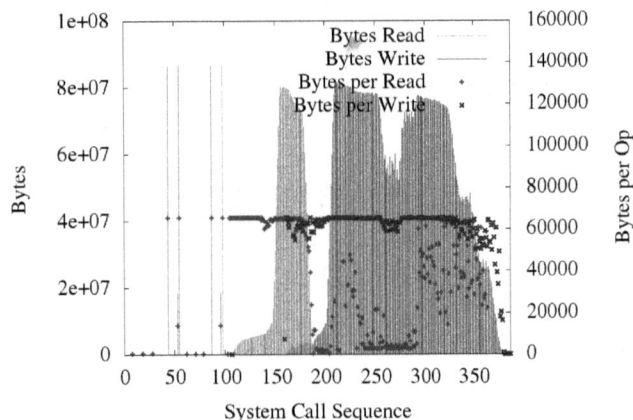

Figure 4: mProjectPP I/O traffic profile

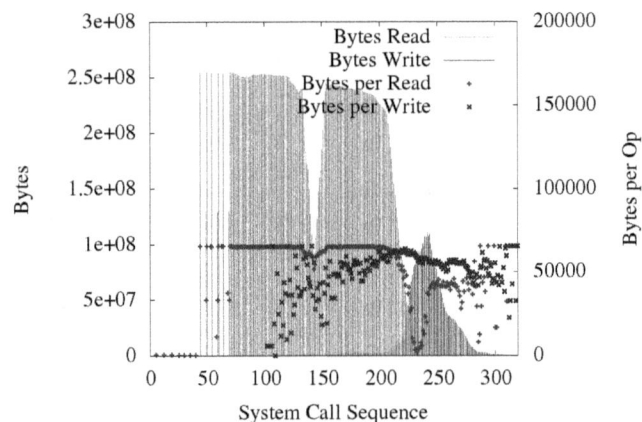

Figure 5: mFit I/O traffic profile

cation of the actual files or create entries in metadata server if the files do not exist in the write case. Finally, the I/O performance is bound by I/O throughput for small files and by I/O bandwidth for large files.

3. MTC ENVELOPE

The goal of the MTC envelope is to show the capacity of large scale computers in the context of parallel scripting applications. Section 2 showed us that the I/O performance of an application stage is first bound by concurrency, which determines the metadata throughput, I/O throughput and bandwidth at a certain scale. Then the I/O performance is bound by metadata throughput. For either read or write traffic, the stage will query the metadata to find out the lo-

3.1 Definition

We define the MTC envelope for a fixed number of computing resources as a set of eight performance metrics:

- file open operation throughput,
- file creation operation throughput,
- 1-to-1 read data throughput,
- 1-to-1 read data bandwidth,
- N-to-1 read data throughput,
- N-to-1 read data bandwidth,
- write data throughput, and
- write data bandwidth

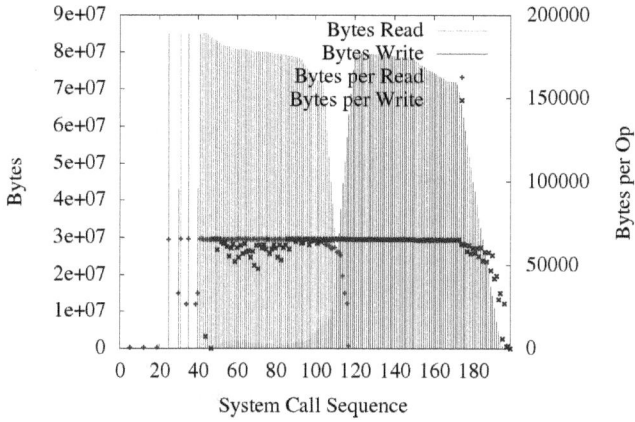

Figure 6: mBack I/O traffic profile

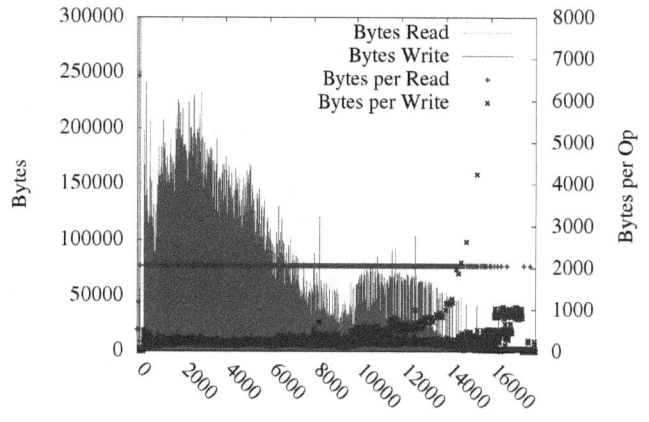

Figure 8: blastall I/O traffic profile

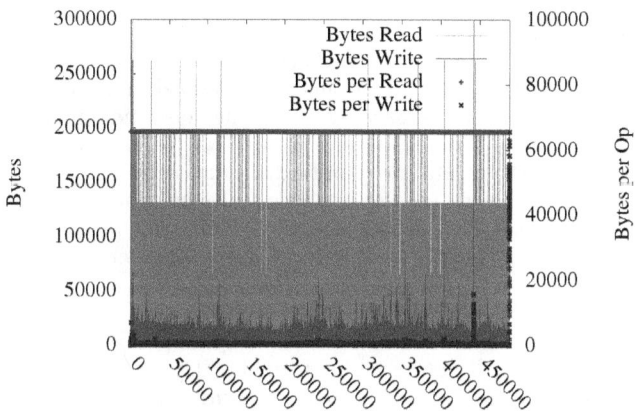

Figure 7: formatdb I/O traffic profile

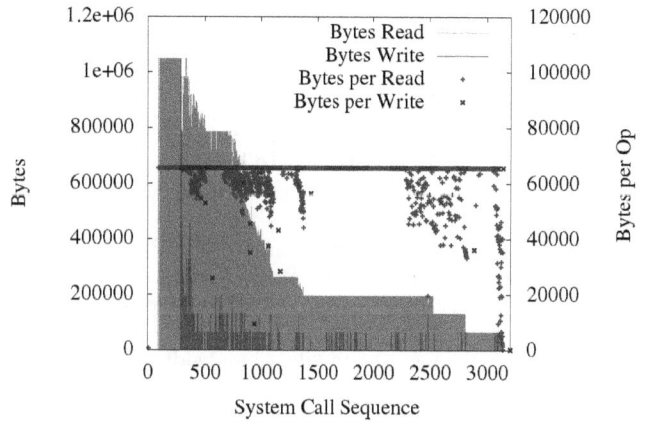

Figure 9: merge I/O traffic profile

In §2, we also discussed the Few-to-1 case, but here we simplify this by merging Few-to-1 into 1-to-1.

A system will exhibit different MTC envelopes at different scales. Its throughput and bandwidth will change as the level of I/O concurrency changes. Therefore, we further define the MTC envelope for a given large scale system as eight curves (rather than eight points), where each curve reflects the change of one of the performance metric along the scales.

3.2 Measurements

In this paper, we measure the GPFS deployment on the Intrepid BG/P at Argonne National Laboratory as an example. This GPFS deployment has one metadata server and 128 IBM x3545 file servers, each with two 2.6-GHx Dual Core CPU and 8 GB RAM. The compute nodes reach the shared file system through I/O nodes, where each I/O node is associated with 64 compute nodes. In this paper, we run our envelope measurements directly on the I/O nodes.

We run our I/O benchmark workloads on the I/O nodes, where each I/O node is a GPFS client. The performance test space for metadata operations is {create, open}×{1, 2, 4, 8, 16, 32, 64, 128, 256} clients, while the performance test space for I/O is {read, write}×{1 KB, 128 KB, 1 MB,

16 MB}×{1, 2, 4, 8, 16, 32, 64, 128, 256} clients. The total number of performance test jobs is 630, and the whole test takes about 2.2 million core hours on the BG/P. Note that we used a shell script as our test framework to represent a typical parallel scripting application, and that we ran on a multiuser system, not a dedicated system. Therefore, we are not measuring the peak performance of the I/O system, but rather the performance that parallel scripting applications experience when sharing the filesystem with other users.

3.3 Metadata Operation Throughput

We measure file creation throughput by asking all GPFS clients to create independent files in one single directory. In all test cases, the total number of file creations is 8,192. Using a similar strategy, we measure file open throughput by creating 8,192 files in one directory, then ask all GPFS clients to query the files, with each file only queried once.

Figure 10 shows the scaling of throughput of file creation and open in a single directory. Both creation and open throughput increase linearly to eight GPFS clients. Then the rate of increase slows down from eight clients to 32 clients. Above 32 clients, throughput starts to slow down. The reason for the creation slowdown is that the GPFS metadata server uses a locking mechanism to resolve concurrent create operations in one directory, and 64 and more clients triggers the concurrency bottleneck of the locking mechanism. The query slowdown is due to a concurrency bottleneck of the tested GPFS deployment.

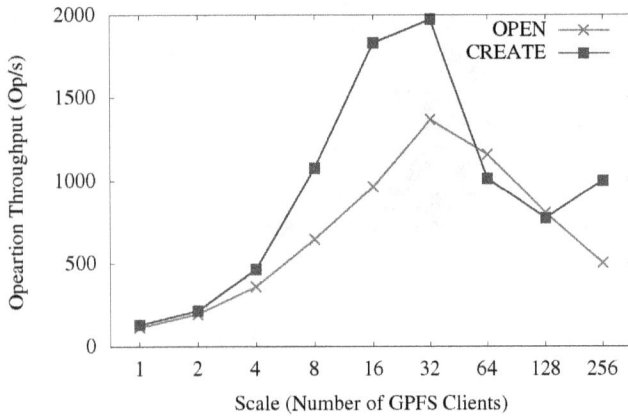

Figure 10: Metadata Operation Throughput

3.4 1-to-1 Read Performance

In the 1-to-1 read benchmark measurement, we first create 8,192 files with size of {1 KB, 128 KB, 1 MB, 16 MB} in one directory. Then we start a number of GPFS clients to simultaneously read those files. With N clients, each client reads $8,192/N$ distinct files by copying the file from GPFS to its local RAM disk. Figures 11 and 12 show the 1-to-1 read operation throughput and data bandwidth respectively.

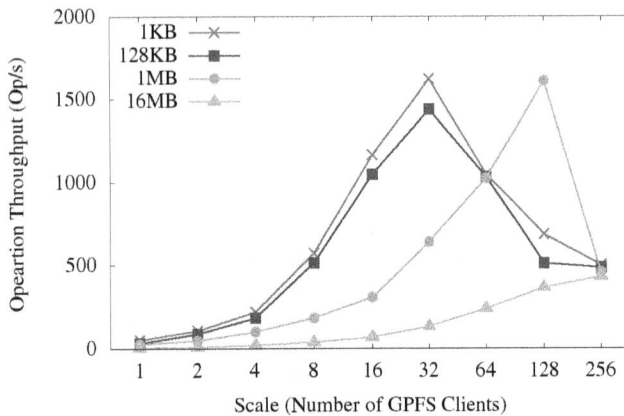

Figure 11: 1-to-1 Read Operation Throughput

In Figure 11, the 1 KB and 128 KB 1-to-1 reads are dominated by latency, as seen by the closeness of the two curves. For these two reads, the throughput increases up to 32 GPFS clients, then starts to slow down. This slowdown is similar to that of the open operation in §3.3, and is likely due to the same cause. As the cost of the small file read is mostly that of determining the file's location by querying the metadata server, the throughput of read is about 25% lower than that of open due to the extra overhead that comes from the actual data transfer. 1 MB reads reach the throughput bound at a larger scale than 1 KB and 128 KB reads because the data transfer has less traffic congestion than open

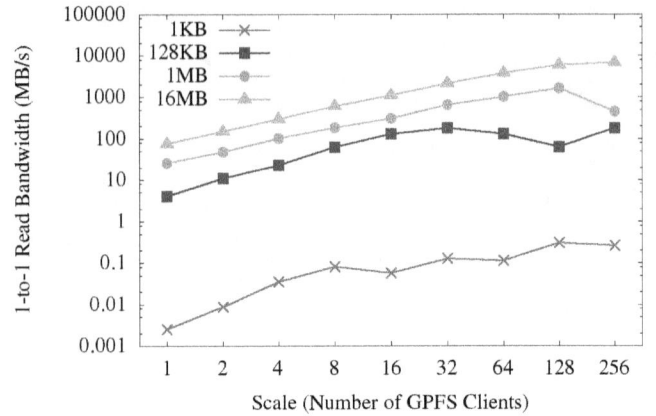

Figure 12: 1-to-1 Read Data Bandwidth

does. With larger file size, the 16 MB reads have not become throughput bound with 256 clients.

Peak GPFS read performance has been documented at 62,000 MB/s [4]. Figure 12 (log scale) does not manage to reach this limit; the peak bandwidth for 16 MB read is 6,880 MB/s. For the bandwidth dominated 1 MB and 16 MB read tests, the performance scales up nearly linearly from one to 128 clients, then the 1 MB read reaches its ceiling, while 16 MB read performance is still increasing.

3.5 N-to-1 Read Performance

Here, we first create a single file with size {1 KB, 128 KB, 1 MB, 16 MB}. Then we let a number {1, 2, 4, 8, 16, 32, 64, 128, and 256} of GPFS clients concurrently read the file. With N clients, each client will read the same file $8,192/N$ times.

Figures 13 and 14 show the N-to-1 read operation throughput and data bandwidth respectively. 1 KB and 128 KB reads reach peak throughput with 64 clients, which is twice as many clients as where the 1-to-1 read throughput peaks. One potential explanation of the improvement is metadata caching in the GPFS client, where when file is read multiple times, the client does not have to re-query the metadata server. However, with 128 clients, the performance is bound by the read concurrency of the shared file system.

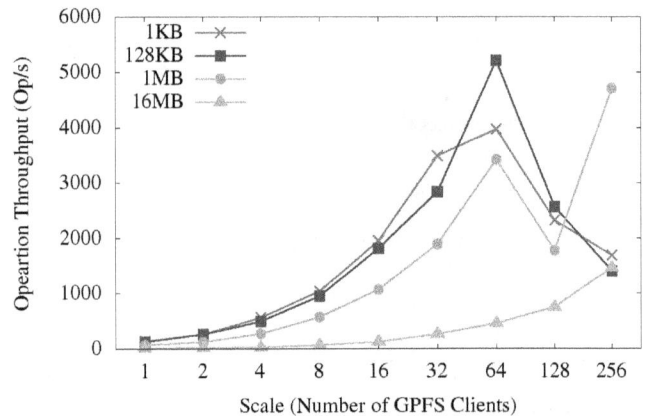

Figure 13: N-to-1 Read Operation Throughput

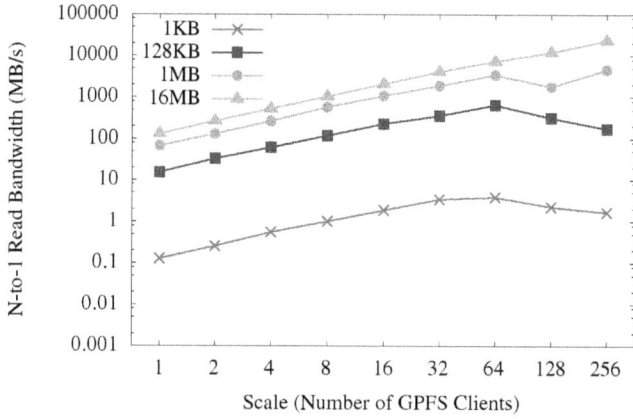

Figure 14: N-to-1 Read Data Bandwidth

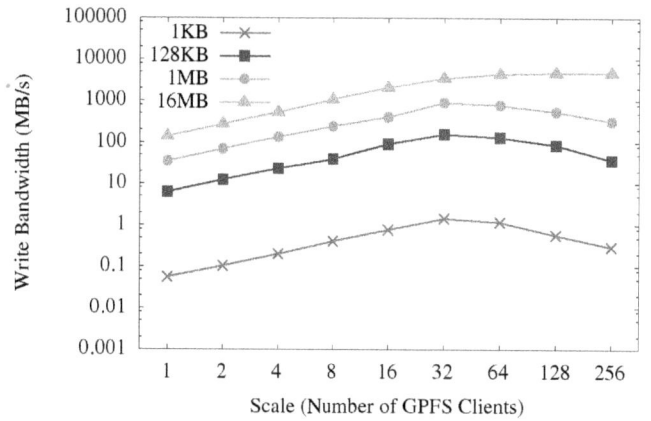

Figure 16: Write Data Bandwidth

3.6 Write Performance

We run the write performance benchmark in the space of {1 KB, 128 KB, 1 MB, 16 MB}×{1, 2, 4, 8, 16, 32, 64, 128, 256} clients. To focus only on write performance, we initially create 8,192 empty files in one directory, and then each client writes to a mutually exclusive group of the files. With N clients, each client writes to $8,192/N$ distinct files.

As shown in Figure 15, the 1 KB, 128 KB, and 1 MB writes reach the operations throughput bound at 32 clients, which is identical to the peak of 1-to-1 reads. In Figure 16, the 16 MB write reaches the data bandwidth bound at 64 clients, yielding a data bandwidth of 3,497 MB/s.

One interesting observation of Figures 11 and 15 is that the operations throughput is independent of the file size. This suggests that 256 clients limit the throughput of GPFS to approximately 470 Op/s for read and 180 Op/s for write. This is a significant characteristic and a limiting factor of the envelope.

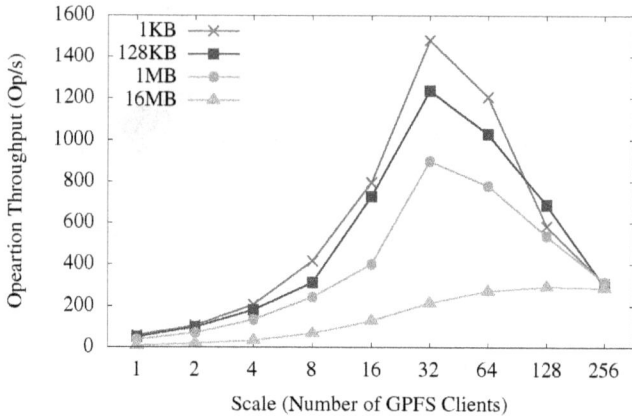

Figure 15: Write Operation Throughput

3.7 Envelope Summary

We have defined the MTC envelope as eight performance metrics of file open throughput, file creation throughput, 1-to-1 read throughput, 1-to-1 read bandwidth, N-to-1 read throughput, N-to-1 read bandwidth, write throughput, and write bandwidth. We show the envelope on 1, 2, 4, 8, 16, 32, 64, 128, and 256 clients as a Kiviat diagram in Figure 17.

This shows the performance on each metric relative to that on one client.

Scaling up to 16 clients shows generally good performance. Overall, most of the metrics reach a peak at some number of clients and then decrease, with the exception of N-to-1 read bandwidth, which has not yet reached a peak using 256 clients. The throughput metrics, for both metadata and transfer, appear to have the worst scalability. 1-to-1 read bandwidth and write bandwidth appear to have reached their peak with 256 clients. Our characterization of the MTC envelope indicates that while the BG/P I/O system can sustain a very large I/O data bandwidth, its peaks in operation throughput per second remain a limiter of MTC application performance.

4. PUTTING THE APPLICATION IN THE ENVELOPE

So far, we have measured the performance metric suite at multiple scales, which is enough to characterize the I/O performance of the system for running parallel scripting applications. Now, we examine predicting I/O time consumption and I/O performance bounding factors for the parallel scripting applications themselves.

4.1 I/O Time Consumption

To ease the work of predicting I/O time consumption of parallel scripting applications on the shared filesystem, we first example write on GPFS.

Assume one stage of an application has N tasks, with each writing one output file of size D bytes at the same time, and that the stage runs on a group of computing resources that has C shared filesystem clients. To evaluate the I/O consumption of this stage, we first find the I/O bandwidth B, throughput T_w, and metadata creation throughput T_m at scale C. All writes will come as $\lceil N/C \rceil$ rounds. In each round, metadata creation takes C/T_m time, and the write time consumption is C/T when throughput dominates or $C * D/B$ when bandwidth dominates. So the write time consumption can be approximately expressed as

$$Time = \lceil N/C \rceil * (C/T_m + C * D/B) \tag{1}$$

when the write is bandwidth bound, or as

$$Time = \lceil N/C \rceil * (C/T_m + C/T_w) \tag{2}$$

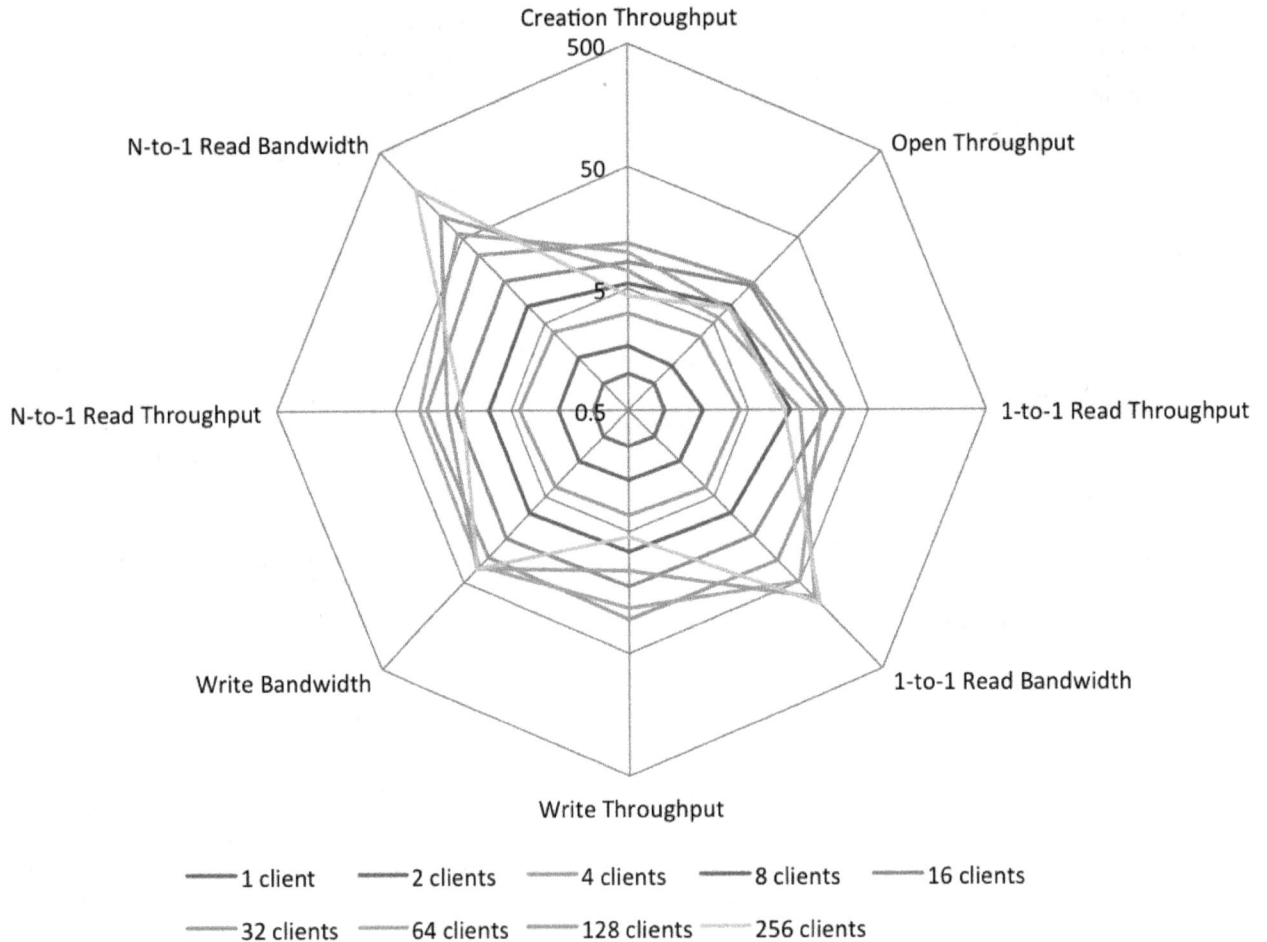

Figure 17: MTC Envelope (log scale). The performance on each metric (0.5 - 500) is relative to that on one client.

when the write is throughput bound. Higher throughput and bandwidth are desired for parallel scripting applications in order to reduce runtime.

We plot two heat maps of concurrent write bandwidth and throughput with our benchmark numbers and Equations 1 and 2. Figure 18 shows the bandwidth distribution with various file size on multiple scales, while Figure 19 shows the throughput distribution with the same input as Figure 18. When used to predict write performance, the two heat maps yield the same predictions, however, in Figure 18, the difference among the file size of 1 KB, 128 KB and 1 MB is barely discernible.

For a read workload, we denote N as the number of tasks, with each reading a file of size D_1 bytes at the same time and a common input file of size D_N shared among all tasks. On a group of computing resources that has C shared filesystem clients, the MTC envelope delivers 1-to-1 read bandwidth of B_1, throughput of T_1, N-to-1 read bandwidth of B_N and throughput of T_N. The read time consumption can be approximately expressed as

$$Time = \lceil N/C \rceil * (\max(C/T_1, C * D_1/B_1) + \max(C/T_N, C * D_N/B_N)) \quad (3)$$

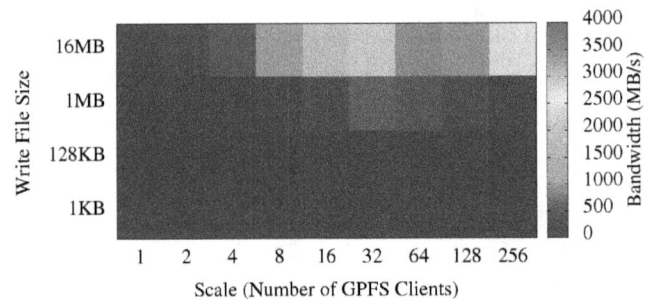

Figure 18: Heat map of write bandwidth

We do not compile the 1-to-1 read and N-to-1 read performance into heat maps because the benchmark numbers are measured directly. Users can refer to Figures 11, 12, 13, 14 for numbers to project read time consumption.

Using such information, a parallel scripting application programmer could obtain a rough picture of how much time was taken by I/O in the execution. For example, assuming we have an application stage with 8,192 tasks, each writing one output file of size 16 MB, and running on 64 GPFS

44

Table 4: Application I/O Performance Decomposition and Bounding Factor(s) Classification (bw=bandwidth, tput=throughput) on 32 GPFS Clients

		Montage				BLAST			CyberShake		
		mProject	mDiff	mFit	mBack	formatdb	blastall	merge	extract	seis	peakGM
Read	Metadata	**69.7%**	**82.0%**	23.3%	24.1%	1.7%	6.0%	1.9%	3.1%	1.4%	**82.4%**
	I/O	30.3%	18.0%	**76.7%**	**75.9%**	**98.3%**	**94.0%**	**98.1%**	**96.9%**	**98.6%**	17.6%
	Bound. Fact.	bw	tput	bw	bw	bw	bw	bw	bw	bw	tput
Write	Metadata	37.4%	**52.0%**	**52.0%**	37.7%	11.9%	**52.0%**	40.8%	4.7%	**52.0%**	**52.0%**
	I/O	**62.6%**	48.0%	48.0%	**62.3%**	**88.1%**	48.0%	**59.2%**	**95.3%**	48.0%	48.0%
	Bound. Fact.	bw	tput	tput	bw	bw	tput	bw	bw	tput	tput

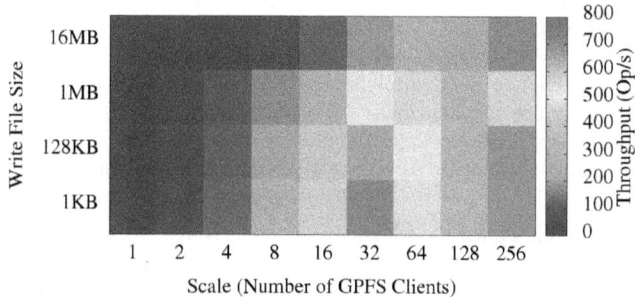

Figure 19: Heat map of write throughput

clients, then the write consumption can be estimated by the following steps. 16 MB writes are bandwidth dominated, so we look at the bandwidth heat map, and find that the bandwidth is about 3500 MB/s. The write has 8,192*16 MB of data to write, so it will take 8,192*16/3,500 = 37 seconds. Alternatively, if a programmer with a requirement for the I/O time might first determine what file size and scale combinations for the I/O time are valid on the shared file system, and then could choose from the candidate combinations.

4.2 I/O Performance Bounding Factors

To begin to investigate the I/O performance bounding factor(s) of the example applications, we map the applications' I/O behavior to the MTC envelope that we measured on GPFS on 32 clients. Table 4 illustrates the time consumption decomposition and bounding factors for each applications stage. The calculations were done based on the profile of each application and Equations 1 and 2. The MTC envelope on 32 GPFS clients shows file creation throughput of 1,367 Op/s, file open throughput of 1,974 Op/s, 1-to-1 read performance of 1,624 reads/s and 2,123 MB/s, N-to-1 read performance of 3,489 reads/s and 4,118 MB/s, and write performance of 1,481 writes/s and 3,429 MB/s.

Given an application stage profile, we compute the the read I/O consumption as the difference between the time consumption of reads and metadata operations. Write I/O consumption can be measured directly as shown in §3.6. We also compute the time consumption numbers from Equations 1 and 2 and determine which is larger to decide if an operation is bandwidth bound or throughput bound.

We see from the read time distribution for mProject and mDiff in Table 4 that for small file I/O, even though the metadata processing takes more time than the I/O, we can

determine if the I/O is bandwidth-bound or throughput-bound. If we perform the same calculation on the MTC envelope on 64 clients, we would see a dramatical decrease of metadata and I/O throughput, which is the concurrency bounding factor of the applications' I/O behavior.

We will continue analysis of application performance within the constraints of the envelope in our future work.

4.3 I/O Performance Prediction

To predict the I/O performance of a given application or a stage of the application, we define two models.

- Coarse model: The coarse model maps the I/O traffic of an application stage to the **peak** metadata operation throughput and read/write bandwidth (MB/s) and operation throughput (Op/s) at a given scale.

- Fine model: Instead of just looking at the peak measured performance in the MTC envelope, the fine model takes into account the impact of the I/O file sizes on I/O bandwidth and throughput. We assume the bandwidth and throughput distribution along files sizes are linear. For example, Figure 12 shows the bandwidth of 1-to-1 read for file sizes of 1 KB, 128 KB, 1 MB, and 16 MB. The 1-to-1 read bandwidth for a file size of 8.5 MB is calculated as the average of the bandwidth of 1 MB and 16 MB. For multiple input and output files, we only compute the metadata operation time once, as the subsequent metadata operation congestion will be reduced by the diffusion of operations in those rounds, due to delays in the earlier round(s). The bandwidth factor is computed as the sum of time used for each file.

We compare the coarse model, the fine model, and the measured application I/O performance for three sample stages: Montage:mBack, CyberShake:peakGM and Montage:mProjectPP. These represent an I/O bandwidth-bound workload, a metadata throughput-bound workload, and a mixed bounding factor workload. We run 1024 tasks of each stage on 32 GPFS clients.

Table 5 shows the errors predicted by the coarse and fine models. We show the average of five runs of each application on 32 GPFS clients. Both the coarse and fine prediction of mProjectPP and mBack are based on the file access bandwidth, while the predictions of peakGM are based on the file access throughput because the file sizes in this stage are small.

We observe that the fine model predicts the stages with bandwidth-dominant read performance (mProjectPP and

Table 5: Application I/O Performance Prediction Error on 32 GPFS Clients

Stage	Phase	Time (secs)	Coarse Model Error	Fine Model Error
mProjectPP	Input	83.0	-60.9%	**+0.4%**
	Output	87.8	**+18.7%**	+45.7%
mBack	Input	116	-29.7%	**+17.5%**
	Output	48.6	**+32.0%**	+86.6%
peakGM	Input	12.2	+65.9%	+69.5%
	Output	42.7	+8.0%	+8.0%

mBack) well, while the coarse model predicts bandwidth-dominant write well. So our assumption in the fine model that the read bandwidth is linear with file size appears correct. The similar assumption in the fine model for write bandwidth fails. But the assumption in the coarse model of rounding the file size to the closest bandwidth of file size of {1 KB, 16 KB, 1 MB, 16 MB} seems to work well.

We also observe that the fine model predicts read better than write for bandwidth-dominant I/O. The reason is that in our runs, the first round of reads starts at the same time and the model correctly predicts that. On the other hand, write concurrency overhead is somewhat neutralized by the preceding reads, so we have more concurrency overhead in our models than actually exists.

A third observation is that for throughput-dominant reads in peakGM, neither model works well, as this stage is metadata operation bound, and it is more sensitive to the current workload of the machine. While the models seem to reasonably predict the throughput-dominant write in peakGM, the measured performance's standard deviation is 11.7 seconds with the average time consumption of 42.7 seconds.

5. RELATED WORK

Examples of alternative approaches to profiling the I/O performance of applications on specific systems include work on general HPC applications [30] and on FLASH [28]. In comparison, our approach can be used to predict I/O performance on different systems.

Previous benchmark include MADbench2 [6], which originated from the cosmic microwave background application MADCAP [5]. It measures the system's unique (one-file-per-process) and shared file (one-file-for-all-processes) access performance. It could also measure the improvement of the asynchronous I/O with computation and I/O overlapped on the timeline. However, it does not work well for applications that are metadata-intensive. The Effective I/O Benchmark [23] is a purely synthetic benchmark with predefined configurations that runs for a limited time to output a score as the performance metric. It is difficult to understand real application performance using the Effective I/O Benchmark. The SPIObench [31] and PIORAW [33] benchmarks are synthetic benchmarks to measure the concurrent read/write operations on unique files. They can measure the 1-to-1 read performance, but similarly to MADbench2, they overlook metadata-intensive applications. The IOR [13] benchmark is a highly-parameterized HPC storage benchmark, and previous work [29] has used it to model and predict the HPC application I/O performance with specified parameters com-

binations. With slightly modification, the IOR benchmark can be used a standard test framework for MTC envelope. It also comes with a limitation of MPI-dependency.

Many research groups have observed that metadata throughput is a bottleneck in today's shared file system. GIGA+ [21, 20] explores the idea of scalable directories in a hierarchical layout, and the work has been migrated in OrangeFS (PVFS) [8]. ZHT [16] distributes the metadata storage fully over storage servers, which could significantly improve the metadata operation throughput. Our previous AME work [36] has a similar metadata server design, but it is has a simplified implementation without the notion of directories. The work of Data Diffusion [27] and AMFS [35] explore the benefit of addressing data locality in parallel scripting applications. In the context of file system benchmarking, Data Diffusion [27] and AMFS [35] enhance the read/write bandwidth by redirecting the I/O to local storage. A similar approach has been implemented in HDFS [7] to facilitate MapReduce applications. The performance improvements to the applications from scalable metadata access and locality can be quantitatively profiled with the MTC envelope.

6. CONCLUSION

In this paper, we first studied the I/O behavior of parallel scripting applications that use a shared filesystem abstraction for inter-task communication on large scale computers. Then we defined the MTC envelope as a set of eight performance metrics: metadata query throughput, metadata creation throughput, 1-to-1 read throughput, 1-to-1 read bandwidth, N-to-1 read throughput, N-to-1 read bandwidth, write throughput, and write bandwidth. We also showed that the MTC envelope is sufficient to characterize the I/O behavior of parallel scripting application. Taking GPFS on BG/P as an example, we benchmarked the MTC envelope of GPFS at multiple scales, and studied its scalability. We believe the envelope model may be useful as a guide for aggregating many smaller operations into fewer larger ones, replacing shared filesystem accesses with scalable local filesystem usage, and spreading shared filesystem accesses in a manner that reduces locking and other forms of resource contention. Finally, we presented a way to convert performance measurements into heat maps that can guide programmers to make better use of existing shared filesystems for parallel scripting applications.

We believe this work can also benefit other types of applications such as HPC and MapReduce, as the same approach can be applied to those applications and hardware-software stacks. We are in the era of Big Data where many interesting applications are inevitably data-intensive, so such shared filesystem studies in other communities will help them use the current I/O and storage in a more efficient way.

Acknowledgements

This work was supported in part by the U.S. Department of Energy under the ASCR X-Stack program (contract DE-SC0005380) and contract DE-AC02-06CH11357. Computing resources were provided by the Argonne Leadership Computing Facility. We thank the ZeptoOS team in Argonne's MCS Division for their effective and timely support. We also thank the ALCF support team at Argonne. Some work by DSK was supported by the National Science Foundation, while working at the Foundation. Any opinion, finding, and conclusions or recommendations expressed in this material are those of the authors and do not necessarily reflect the views of the National Science Foundation.

7. REFERENCES

[1] M. Albrecht, P. Donnelly, P. Bui, and D. Thain. Makeflow: A portable abstraction for data intensive computing on clusters, clouds, and grids. In *Workshop on Scalable Workflow Enactment Engines and Technologies (SWEET) at ACM SIGMOD*, 2012.

[2] S. F. Altschul, W. Gish, W. Miller, E. W. Myers, and D. J. Lipman. Basic local alignment search tool. *Journal of Molecular Biology*, 215:403–410, 1990.

[3] Amazon simple workflow service. http://aws.amazon.com/swf/.

[4] Argonne Leadership Computing Facility. Intrepid file system information. https://www.alcf.anl.gov/resource-guides/intrepid-file-systems.

[5] J. Borrill. MADCAP: The microwave anisotropy dataset computational analysis package. In *Proceedings of the 5th European SGI/Cray MPP Workshop*, 1999.

[6] J. Borrill, L. Oliker, J. Shalf, and H. Shan. Investigation of leading HPC I/O performance using a scientific-application derived benchmark. In *Supercomputing, 2007. SC '07. Proceedings of the 2007 ACM/IEEE Conference on*, pages 1 –12, nov. 2007.

[7] D. Borthakur. HDFS architecture. http://hadoop.apache.org/hdfs/docs/current/hdfs_design.pdf.

[8] P. H. Carns, W. B. Ligon, III, R. B. Ross, and R. Thakur. PVFS: a parallel file system for linux clusters. In *Proc. of the 4th annual Linux Showcase & Conf. - Volume 4*, pages 28–28. USENIX Association, 2000.

[9] M. W. Deem, R. Pophale, P. A. Cheeseman, and D. J. Earl. Computational discovery of new zeolite-like materials. *J. of Phys. Chem. C*, 113:21353–21360, 2009.

[10] J. Elliott, I. Foster, K. Judd, E. Moyer, and T. Munson. CIM-EARTH: Philosophy, Models, and Case Studies. Technical Report ANL/MCS-P1710-1209, Argonne National Laboratory, Mathematics and Computer Science Division, Feb 2010.

[11] R. Graves, T. Jordan, S. Callaghan, E. Deelman, E. Field, G. Juve, C. Kesselman, P. Maechling, G. Mehta, K. Milner, D. Okaya, P. Small, and K. Vahi. CyberShake: A physics-based seismic hazard model for southern California. *Pure and Applied Geophysics*, Online Fir:1–15, May 2010.

[12] G. Hocky, M. Wilde, J. Debartolo, M. Hategan, I. Foster, T. Sosnick, and K. Freed. Towards petascale ab initio protein folding through parallel scripting. argonne. Technical Report ANL/MCS-P1612-0409, Argonne National Laboratory, Mathematics and Computer Science Division, April 2009.

[13] The ASCI I/O stress benchmark. http://www.llnl.gov/asci/purple/benchmarks/limited/ior/.

[14] J. C. Jacob, D. S. Katz, G. B. Berriman, J. C. Good, A. C. Laity, E. Deelman, C. Kesselman, G. Singh, M.-H. Su, T. A. Prince, and R. Williams. Montage: a grid portal and software toolkit for science-grade astronomical image mosaicking. *Intl. J. of Comp. Sci. and Eng.*, 4(2):73–87, 2009.

[15] D. S. Katz, J. C. Jacob, G. B. Berriman, J. Good, A. C. Laity, E. Deelman, C. Kesselman, and G. Singh. A comparison of two methods for building astronomical image mosaics on a grid. In *Proc. 2005 Intl. Conf. on Par. Proc. Works.*, pages 85–94, 2005.

[16] T. Li, X. Zhou, K. Brandstatter, D. Zhao, K. Wang, A. Rajendran, Z. Zhang, and I. Raicu. ZHT: A light-weight reliable persistent dynamic scalable zero-hop distributed hash table. In *to appear in Parallel & Distributed Processing Symposium (IPDPS), 2013 IEEE 27th International*. IEEE, 2013.

[17] P. Maechling, E. Deelman, L. Zhao, R. Graves, G. Mehta, N. Gupta, J. Mehringer, C. Kesselman, S. Callaghãn, D. Okaya, H. Francoeur, V. Gupta, Y. Cui, K. Vahi, T. Jordan, and E. Field. SCEC CyberShake workflows – automating probabilistic seismic hazard analysis calculations. In I. J. Taylor, E. Deelman, D. B. Gannon, and M. Shields, editors, *Workflows for e-Science*, pages 143–163. Springer, 2007.

[18] D. R. Mathog. Parallel blast on split databases. *Bioinformatics*, 19(14):1865–1866, 2003.

[19] A. Matsunaga, M. Tsugawa, and J. Fortes. Cloudblast: Combining mapreduce and virtualization on distributed resources for bioinformatics applications. In *eScience, 2008. eScience '08. IEEE Fourth International Conference on*, pages 222 –229, dec. 2008.

[20] S. Patil and G. Gibson. Scale and concurrency of giga+: file system directories with millions of files. In *Proceedings of the 9th USENIX conference on File and stroage technologies*, FAST'11, pages 13–13, Berkeley, CA, USA, 2011. USENIX Association.

[21] S. V. Patil, G. A. Gibson, S. Lang, and M. Polte. Giga+: scalable directories for shared file systems. In *Proceedings of the 2nd international workshop on Petascale data storage: held in conjunction with Supercomputing '07*, PDSW '07, pages 26–29, New York, NY, USA, 2007. ACM.

[22] A. Peters, M. E. Lundberg, P. T. Lang, and C. P. Sosa. High throughput computing validation for drug discovery using the DOCK program on a massively parallel system. In *Proc. 1st Annual Midwest Symposium on Computational Biology and Bioinformatics*, September 2007.

[23] R. Rabenseifner and A. Koniges. Effective file-I/O bandwidth benchmark. In *Euro-Par 2000 Parallel Processing*, volume 1900, pages 1273–1283. Springer Berlin / Heidelberg, 2000. 10.1007/3-540-44520-X_179.

[24] I. Raicu, I. Foster, A. Szalay, and G. Turcu. Astroportal: A science gateway for large-scale astronomy data analysis. In *Proc. TeraGrid Conf. 2006*, 2006.

[25] I. Raicu, I. Foster, and Y. Zhao. Many-task computing for grids and supercomputers. In *Proc. of Many-Task Comp. on Grids and Supercomputers, 2008*, 2008.

[26] I. Raicu, Z. Zhang, M. Wilde, I. Foster, P. Beckman, K. Iskra, and B. Clifford. Toward loosely coupled programming on petascale systems. In *Proc. IEEE/ACM Supercomputing 2008*, November 2008.

[27] I. Raicu, Y. Zhao, I. T. Foster, and A. Szalay. Accelerating large-scale data exploration through data diffusion. In *Proc. of 2008 Intl. Work. on Data-Aware Dist. Comp.*, DADC '08, pages 9–18. ACM, 2008.

[28] R. Ross, D. Nurmi, A. Cheng, and M. Zingale. A case study in application I/O on Linux clusters. In *Proceedings of the 2001 ACM/IEEE conference on Supercomputing (CDROM)*, pages 11–11. ACM, 2001.

[29] H. Shan, K. Antypas, and J. Shalf. Characterizing and predicting the I/O performance of HPC applications using a parameterized synthetic benchmark. In *Proceedings of the 2008 ACM/IEEE conference on Supercomputing*, SC '08, pages 42:1–42:12, Piscataway, NJ, USA, 2008. IEEE Press.

[30] E. Smirni and D. Reed. Lessons from characterizing the input/output behavior of parallel scientific applications. *Performance Evaluation*, 33(1):27–44, 1998.

[31] Streaming parallel I/O benchmark. http://www.nsf.gov/pubs/2006/nsf0605/spiobench.tar.gz.

[32] R. Thakur and R. Rabenseifner. Optimization of collective communication operations in MPICH. *Intl. J. of High Perf. Comp. Applications*, 19:49–66, 2005.

[33] The PIORAW Test. http://cbcg.lbl.gov/nusers/systems/bassi/code_profiles.php.

[34] M. Wilde, I. Foster, K. Iskra, P. Beckman, Z. Zhang, A. Espinosa, M. Hategan, B. Clifford, and I. Raicu. Parallel scripting for applications at the petascale and beyond. *Computer*, 42:50–60, 2009.

[35] Z. Zhang, D. Katz, J. Wozniak, A. Espinosa, and I. Foster. Design and analysis of data management in scalable parallel scripting. In *Proceedings of the International Conference on High Performance Computing, Networking, Storage and Analysis*, page 85. IEEE Computer Society Press, 2012.

[36] Z. Zhang, D. S. Katz, M. Ripeanu, M. Wilde, and I. Foster. AME: An anyscale many-task computing engine. In *6th Work. on Workflows in Support of Large-Scale Science (WORKS11)*, 2011.

[37] Y. Zhao, M. Hategan, B. Clifford, I. Foster, G. Von Laszewski, V. Nefedova, I. Raicu, T. Stef-Praun, and M. Wilde. Swift: Fast, reliable, loosely coupled parallel computation. In *Services, 2007 IEEE Congress on*, pages 199–206. IEEE, 2007.

Virtual TCP Offload: Optimizing Ethernet Overlay Performance on Advanced Interconnects

Zheng Cui[†]   Patrick G. Bridges[†]   John R. Lange[*]   Peter A. Dinda[‡]

[†]Department of CS
University of New Mexico
Albuquerque, NM 87131, USA
{cuizheng,bridges}@cs.unm.edu

[*]Department of CS
University of Pittsburgh
Pittsburgh, PA 15260 USA
jacklange@cs.pitt.edu

[‡]Department of EECS
Northwestern University
Evanston, IL 60208 USA
pdinda@northwestern.edu

ABSTRACT

Ethernet overlay networks are a powerful tool for virtualizing networked applications. Their performance suffers on advanced interconnects such as Infiniband, however, because of differences between the semantics of Ethernet and the underlying network. In this paper, we demonstrate that providing a virtual TCP offload Ethernet device to the guest operating system dramatically improves overlay network performance on advanced interconnects like Infiniband. The virtual offload device enables the overlay system to leverage the semantics and performance characteristics of the underlying network to maximize overlay performance. Our evaluation shows that this approach allows applications to achieve near-native microbenchmark bandwidth and dramatically improved application performance compared to alternative overlay approaches when running on an Ethernet virtual overlay on a QDR Infiniband fabric.

Categories and Subject Descriptors

D.4.4 [**Software**]: OPERATING SYSTEMS

Keywords

Overlay Networks; Virtualization; HPC; InfiniBand

1. INTRODUCTION

Data centers and scientific clouds require clusters and supercomputers interconnected with advanced networks, such as InfiniBand, SeaStar, and Gemini interconnects. Such hardware resources are increasingly being integrated with virtualization as a means of deploying and managing large-scale computing systems with the "Infrastructure as a Service" (IaaS) cloud computing model. The combination of

This project is made possible by support from the United States National Science Foundation (NSF) via grants CNS-0707365 and CNS-0709168, and by the Department of Energy (DOE) via grants DE-SC0005050 and DE-SC0005343.

virtual machines and virtual overlay networking provides a powerful model to realize virtual distributed and parallel computing with strong isolation, portability, and recoverability properties.

A virtual *Ethernet overlay network* supports broad classes of applications and software stacks by presenting a uniform Ethernet communication environment. This simple, yet powerful abstraction is provided regardless of the underlying networking hardware, which may be quite different from Ethernet, and which may span multiple different data center and supercomputer networks. The abstraction is a form of software-defined networking (SDN), albeit the implementation is accomplished purely in end-system software via tunneling. This has the benefit that it does not require hardware support (e.g., OpenFlow), nor cooperation among data center/supercomputer networks, and can extend anywhere where IP networking is available.

Past work has shown that this model can provide near-native performance on high-speed Ethernet networks [6,17]. Providing the same Ethernet abstraction on high-end data center, cluster, and supercomputer networks provides a number of additional advantages, such as reducing the effort porting applications designed for Ethernet to other heterogeneous networks.

Current virtual overlay networks, however, are unable to deliver near-native network performance on advanced interconnects such as Infiniband due to the *semantic gap* between the Ethernet overlay network and underlying physical network. Such a semantic gap [8] is inevitable in virtual overlays whenever the semantics of the underlying physical network are different from that of the overlay network. In the case of an Ethernet overlay on top of Infiniband, for example, performance problems from the semantic gap arise from differences in overlay and network MTUs, or unnecessary protocol overheads from providing reliability semantics in both the guest protocol stack and in the host network adapter. While substantial work has been done bridging the semantic gap between the VM and the VMM in general [12–15,21,23], comparatively little work has been done on bridging this gap for virtual overlay networks.

This paper proposes enhancing the Ethernet virtual overlay network with virtual TCP offload support to bridge the semantic gap between the guest application, the overlay network, and the underlying interconnect. TCP offload capabilities in the virtual Ethernet device allow the guest to better communicate its desired network semantics to the overlay, improving its ability to meet guest network demands. We demonstrate the viability of this approach by enhancing the VNET/P virtual network overlay with offload device capabilities and running it on top of a high-performance Infiniband network fabric. Our results show that adding offload capabilities to the Ethernet overlay network substantially increases network performance on sophisticated data center networks while preserving the advantages of Ethernet overlay networks.

The remainder of this paper is organized as follows. In Section 2, we provide basic background on virtual overlay networks in general, the VNET overlay we use in this paper, and the Infiniband interconnect on which we evaluate our proposed overlay enhancement. Section 3 then follows with a discussion of the challenges the semantic gap presents when running an Ethernet overlay on top of an advanced interconnect such as Infiniband. Section 4 describes our proposed mechanism for spanning this semantic gap, Virtual TCP Offload Engines (VTOEs), and Section 5 provides details of the implementation of this mechanism for Infiniband networks with Linux guests. Sections 6 and 7 then provide microbenchmark and application benchmarks demonstrating the advantages of this approach. Finally, Section 8 concludes and describes directions for future work.

2. BACKGROUND AND RELATED WORK

In this section, we provide a brief introduction to virtual overlay networks. The implementation and evaluation of our approach to optimizing overlay performance for advanced interconnects was conducted using the VNET/P high-performance virtual overlay on an InfiniBand network. Because of this we also provide key architectural details of VNET/P and the Infiniband network architecture.

2.1 Virtual Overlay Networks

Current adaptive cloud computing systems use software-based overlay networks to carry inter-VM traffic. For example, the user-level VNET/U system [18, 24, 25] combines a simple networking abstraction within VMs with location-independence, hardware-independence, and traffic control. Specifically, it exposes a layer 2 abstraction that lets the user treat his VMs as being on a simple LAN, while allowing the VMs to be migrated seamlessly across resources by routing their traffic through the overlay. By controlling the overlay, the cloud provider or adaptation agent can control the bandwidth and the paths between VMs over which traffic flows. Such systems [22, 24] and others that expose different abstractions to the VMs [26] have been under continuous research and development for several years.

2.2 VNET/P Implementation

VNET/P [17] is an in-VMM, overlay-based layer-2 virtual networking system for the Palacios VMM [19]. VNET/P consists of a virtual NIC in each guest OS, an extension to the VMM (the VNET/P Core) that handles packet routing and interfacing to virtual NICs, and a Linux kernel module (the VNET/P Bridge) for interacting with the host's network interfaces and remote systems. For high performance applications, as in this paper, the virtual NIC conforms to the virtio interface, but several virtual NICs with hardware interfaces are also available in Palacios.

In operation, the virtual NIC moves Ethernet packets between the application VM and Palacios, and includes receive and transmit rings. Interrupts are injected into the guest via a virtual IOAPIC/APIC interrupt controller structure. Routing and packet forwarding occur in the VNET/P Core. Routing is based on MAC addresses with a hash-based cache system that allows for constant time lookups in the common case. A packet routed by the VNET/P Core to a guest is handed to a virtual NIC, while a packet routed to an external network or machine is routed to the VNET/P bridge. The VNET/P bridge, which is embedded in the host kernel, encapsulates guest Ethernet packets into UDP datagrams and sends them out through host Ethernet devices.

Our experiments in this paper include portions of the VNET/P+ (note the "+") optimizations that improve the performance of VNET/P for high speed networks [6]. They allow VNET/P to achieve near-native performance for a wide range of microbenchmarks and MPI application benchmarks on high-speed Ethernet networks, including 10 Gigabit/second Ethernet networks. In particular, we utilize zero-copy data overlay data movement techniques, but have not yet merged in support for optimistic interrupt techniques.

2.3 InfiniBand

InfiniBand [1] is a standard switched fabric that supports high bandwidth (up to 120Gb/s) and low latency. Processor nodes connect to the fabric through Host Channel Adapters (HCA). High-performance connections on these devices, particularly Reliable Connected (RC) modes, provide zero-copy RDMA data transfer which bypasses OS involvement in data movement. Infiniband NICs also provide other network interfaces, for example the Unreliable Datagram (UD) mode, whose semantics are similar to that of traditional Ethernet and are generally used for administrative tasks.

The InfiniBand specification defines an HCA interface called Verbs. Upper layer protocols are implemented on top of Verbs. This interface is asynchronous: a consumer posts Work Requests (Send, Receive, RDMA Write, RDMA Read and Atomic operations) to the HCA. The HCA optionally signals their completion and can schedule a completion notification (through event queues or interrupt).

In addition, Infiniband implementations generally provide IP-over-Infiniband support (IPoIB) [16]. The IPoIB functionality of the device driver allows the TCP/IP stack of the host to use the NIC to transport IP packets. Network overlay systems such as VNET/P can use IPoIB functionality to get basic overlay functionality on Infiniband networks. For reasons discussed later in Section 3, this approach has significant performance problems.

2.4 InfiniBand Virtualization

Currently two approaches are very popular in virtualizing InfiniBand with high performance: VMM-bypass [20] and Passthrough [2, 6, 19]. VMM-bypass I/O extends the idea of OS-bypass originated from user-level communication, and allows time-critical I/O operations to be carried out directly in guest VMs without involvement of the VMM and/or a privileged VM. However, the user-space application in the guest has the direct access to the physical IB device resources. In the Passthrough model, the VM has direct access to the InfiniBand devices via VMM's passthrough mechanism.

Both of these approaches can significantly improve I/O and communication performance for VMs, in some cases even without sacrificing safety or isolation. However, they lock the VM to the specific InfiniBand infrastructure, los-ing the portability of virtual networks. This makes check-pointing and migration more difficult because when a VM is restored from a previous checkpoint or migrated to another node, the corresponding state information on the device needs to be restored also, which requires a similar or identical device.

3. CHALLENGES

Virtual Ethernet overlay mechanisms like VNET effectively support high-performance applications on physical networks with semantics similar to Ethernet. On more advanced interconnects, however, the semantic gap between overlay features and physical interconnect features presents difficult performance challenges. In particular, guest OSes see only a relatively simple Ethernet interface and so do not provide the overlay with higher-level semantic information about desired network semantics. This lack of knowledge about the guest-level communications can lead to performance degradation.

When deploying a virtual Ethernet overlay on top of advanced interconnects, there are two straightforward approaches to addressing the semantic gap between the virtual overlay and underlying networks, like Infiniband, with more advanced features: (1) Using minimal interconnect features to minimize the semantic gap, or (2) using more advanced features without guest knowledge. Each has significant performance problems as we describe below.

3.1 Using Minimal Features

The first alternative is to use minimal interconnect features to transport guests' traffic. The interconnect may be able to provide reliability to applications on demand, while the overlay delivers packets without any guarantees.

As an example, overlays could use the InfiniBand Unreliable Datagram (UD) transport service to minimize the gap between overlay semantics and physical network semantics. Unfortunately, datagram-based transport services in most advanced interconnect implementations are limited to Maximum Transmission Unit (MTU) sizes which are usually less than 4KB. The Infiniband MLX4 NICs used in this paper, for example, impose a 2KB MTU. Small MTUs dramatically reduce network throughput on high-speed networks by increasing the required number of network headers, routing decisions in the routers, protocol processing and device interrupts [5].

In addition, minimal-feature interconnect modes generally do not bypass the OS and require significant interrupt processing. Such interrupts are even more expensive in virtualized operating systems than in non-virtualized hosts [6]. For example, virtual interrupt emulation introduces overhead for virtual device register handling (such as APIC, IOAPIC, and NIC), guest context switches, and the VM/guest stack switch. Moreover, the virtual machine monitor (VMM) has to maintain the emulation state for each trap, which significantly increases virtual network latency and decreases throughput by more than 30%.

3.2 Translating to Advanced Features

Alternatively, the overlay system can use advanced interconnect features that provide more complex semantics (e.g., connected reliable streams) while hiding these features from the guest. However, guests cannot assume these semantics will be provided since the overlay exports a simple Ether-net interface to VMs. As a result, guests must provide such semantics themselves when they are necessary. This can introduce duplicated guest/overlay protocol processing overheads.

For example, using a Linux guest and Infiniband RC connections in the overlay causes the guest to unnecessarily send TCP connection establishment requests and acknowledgments over the reliable Infiniband connection. The guest also unnecessarily checksums the incoming packets and performs congestion and flow control activities. These increase packet latency and guest CPU processing requirements, reducing application performance.

4. VIRTUAL TCP OFFLOAD

To address these semantic gap issues, we supplement the virtual Ethernet NIC exported to the guest by the overlay with a Virtual TCP Offload Engine (VTOE). In this section, we give an overview of our the general VTOE approach, show the architecture of VNET/P as enhanced with VTOE capabilities, and describe the overall architecture of the VNET VTOE NIC.

4.1 Overview

TCP Offload Engine (TOE) Ethernet devices offload the processing of the entire kernel TCP/IP stack to the network controller. They are primarily used with high-speed network interfaces such as 10 Gbps Ethernet, where the processing overheads of the network stack are significant [4]. Most modern operating systems support TCP offload engines, though Linux has no generic support for TCP offload.

By exporting a virtual TCP offload engine to the guest, the overlay enables guests that support TCP offload to designate both reliable and unreliable traffic at the Ethernet level. This reduces the semantic gap between the guest and overlay. For connections that span only interconnects that guarantee reliable transport, this results in lower virtualization overhead and achieves better network performance, as shown in Section 7. For connections that cross networks that do not guarantee reliable transport, the overlay itself provides reliability using TCP; existing overlays such as VNET already support overlay-level TCP tunneling. By exposing VTOE to the guest, the overlay promises to either run TCP itself or to use a network that obviates the need for it.

4.2 Virtual TCP Offload in VNET/P

Figure 1 shows the overall architecture of VNET/P supplemented with a Virtual TCP Offload Engine, which we denote VNET+VTOE. In this system, guests run in application VMs. The VMM provides a *virtual (Ethernet) NIC* with an offload engine to each guest. Basic Ethernet virtual NIC functionality is used to transport non-TCP Ethernet packets between the application VM and the overlay implementation inside the VMM, while the VTOE carries TCP traffic.

Inside the virtual machine monitor, the VNET Core and Host Connection Agents (*VNET_Core_CA* and *VNET_Host_-CA*) are respectively responsible for interacting with the guest VNIC and the host physical NIC. Specifically, the VNET_Core_CA supplies the guest with a VNET Socket ID for each connection it creates to use to make requests to the overlay. The VNET_Host_CA creates and manages shadow connections over the underlying high performance

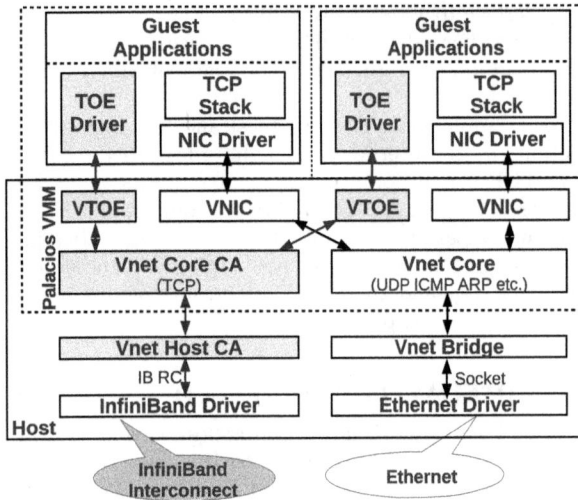

Figure 1: VNET+VTOE architecture with Linux VM and Palacios VMM.

fabric, which the VNET_Core_CA references using a shadow connection ID (shadow CID).

More specifically, VNET_Core_CA:

1. Maps between guest VNET Socket IDs (SIDs) and host shadow Connection IDs (CIDs),

2. Provides receive buffers to the VNET_Host_CA based on buffers supplied by the guest, and

3. Translates events and interrupts from the underlying physical device to VTOE events and interrupts as necessary.

For example, when the guest requests the creation of a new offload TCP connection through the VTOE NIC, the VNET_Core_CA allocates a unique Socket ID for the guest and returns this to the guest using the VTOE NIC. When a connection is later established between two VNET sockets, the VNET_Host_CAs on each hosts create a unique shadow Connection ID. Each guest uses its local Socket ID when enqueuing buffers to the overlay, and VNET_Core_CAs maps between the VNET Socket ID and the shadow Connection ID when interacting with the VNET_Host_CA.

The VNET_Core_CA memory allocator manages direct memory access (DMA) from buffers posted to the guest SID to the underlying shadow CID, and the VNET_Core_CA event dispatcher handles virtual interrupt and asynchronous event delivery to virtual offload engines based on the physical interrupts raised by local devices and events signaled by the underlying physical device. These components are also responsible for handling the memory mapping and interrupt processing for zero-copy cut-through forwarding.

4.3 VTOE NIC Architecture

The VTOE NIC provides a simple offload interface between the guest and the VNET_Core_CA. It supports two main classes of operations between the guest and the overlay in the virtual machine monitor. Specifically, I/O ports and an event queue are used for managing connection creation and state changes, while interrupts and send and receive

work queues are used to manage data movement between the guest, the overlay, and the network.

The guest and overlay manage connection creation and state management using I/O ports and a memory-mapped event queue. Guests request the creation of new connections by programming VTOE I/O ports, and the overlay communicates connection state information back to the guest using the event queue. All event queue entries are tagged with the corresponding socket ID, and event queue includes events for all TCP-relevant state changes, including CONNECT_-REQUEST, CONNECT_ESTABLISHED, DISCONNECTED, ADDRESS_ERROR, UNREACHABLE, and CONNECT_-REJECTED,

Likewise, the guest uses send and receive work queues (SWQ and RWQ) to enqueue data buffers to the overlay for transmission or receiving incoming data. Each queue entry is tagged with the relevant SID, enabling the VNET_Host_-CA to map to the relevant underlying shadow connection. Once data has arrived into a guest buffer, the overlay raises a virtual interrupt into the guest at the appropriate time, either eagerly or using more complex optimization such as optimistic interrupts [6].

5. IMPLEMENTATION

Our initial implementation of VTOE support in VNET/P has focused on Infiniband networks, but VTOE could also be used to support overlay functionality on other high-performance network fabrics such as Cray SeaStar or Gemini systems. In addition, we have implemented VTOE NIC support for Linux guests; because general Linux support for TCP offload is somewhat lacking, this required special measures on Linux guests. We detail the specific work done to support VNET+VTOE on Infiniband with Linux guests in the remainder of this section.

5.1 Infiniband Support

VNET+VTOE Infiniband support has two main elements: connection management and data movement. Connections are established in a multistep handshake process before entering the data transfer phase. After data transmission is completed, the connection termination closes established virtual circuits and releases all allocated resources. In the remainder of this subsection, we describe the mapping between TCP and Infiniband RC connection states, and detail management of data movement for Infiniband and VNET+-VTOE.

5.1.1 Connection Management

For connection management, the VNET_Core_CA must manage three different sets of states: the guest TCP state, the Infiniband connection state as per the IB Connection Management standard, and the underlying Infiniband queue pair state. To do this, it makes requests to the VNET_Host_-CA in response to guest connection changes, maps event notifications from the VNET_Host_CA to TCP event notifications to the guest, and communicates with the local Infiniband connection manager. We use Active/Passive (also referred as client/server) mode to establish a connection. In the client/server model, the shadow server side listens for connection requests with a service ID; the client shadow side initiates a connection request with a matching service ID.

Connection Establishment: Figure 2(a) shows the TCP state machine of the VNET socket and the IB state of the

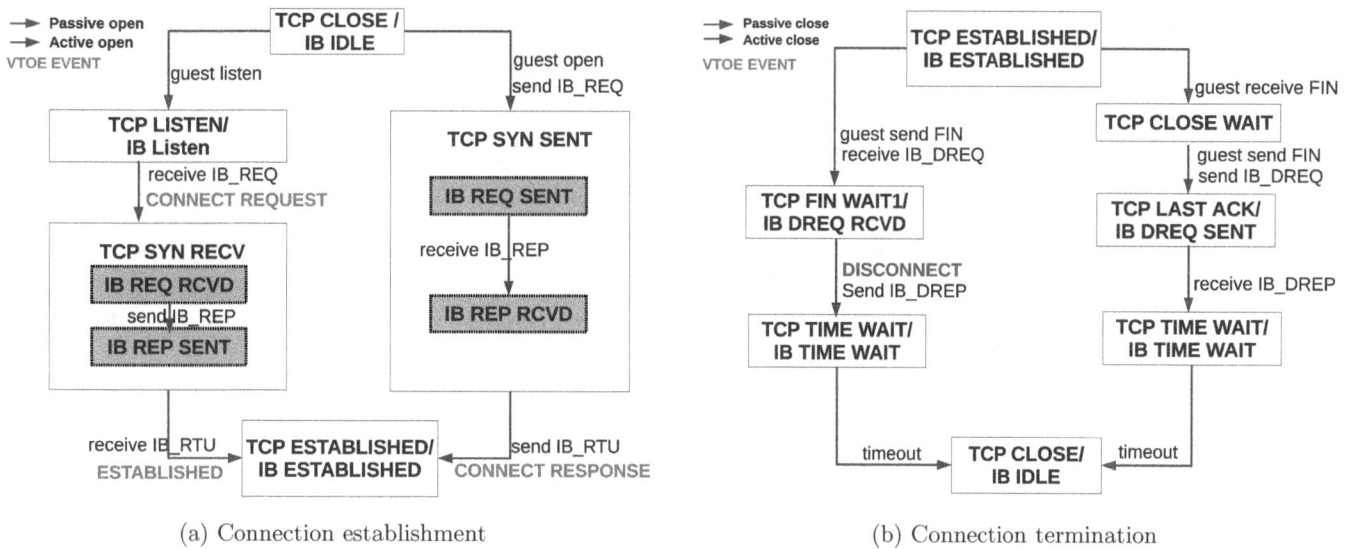

(a) Connection establishment   (b) Connection termination

Figure 2: State machines for both frontend VNET sockets and shadow CIDs, during connection establishment and termination.

shadow connection during connection establishment. The right half of figure Figure 2(a) corresponds to an active open by the guest (i.e. a `connect()` system call), while the left half of the figure corresponds to a passive open by the guest (i.e. a **listen()** system call). Note the close, but not exact, correspondence between the TCP and IB connection state machines.

When the guest performs an active open on the VNET socket and changes its socket state to TCP_SYN_SENT, the overlay sends of an IB_REQ (request) packet which includes the Socket ID and number of available receive buffers. It also changes the IB connection state changes to IB_REQ_-SENT and changes the underlying queue pair (not shown) to the READY_TO_RECEIVE state.

Note that during this process, overlay routing tables and existing IB infrastructure are used to handle address resolution mapping guest Ethernet addresses to underlying Infiniband addresses in the overlay. As part of this process, the overlay delivers ROUTE_RESOLVED events to the guest as necessary.

When the remote side responds with an IB_REP (reply) message, the VNET Core Connection Agent changes the shadow connection state to IB_REP_RECEIVED, sets the queue pair to READY_TO_SEND state, sends an IB_RTU (ready-to-use) message, and transitions to IB_ESTABLISHED state. It then notifies the guest of the response to its connection request. The guest transitions the guest socket to the TCP_ESTABLISHED state in response.

The process is similar on passive opens. The overlay sends CONNECT_REQUEST events to the guest upon receipt of an IB_REQ packet, initializes the underlying queue pair (not shown), and sends IB_REP message. Similarly, it sets the queue pair to READY_TO_SEND and delivers the guest an ESTABLISHED event on the receipt of an IB_RTU message.

Connection Termination: Figure 2(b) illustrates the procedure for connection teardown. When a guest wishes to stop its half of the connection, it send a TCP FIN packet

to its peer and changes state from TCP_ESTABLISHED to TCP_FIN_WAIT1.

On receiving the FIN message, the peer changes state from TCP_ESTABLISHED to TCP_CLOSE_WAIT. It continues sending any outstanding data, however, before notifying the overlay to close its half of the connection. After sending out all the outstanding packets, the peer sends a FIN packet to its peer, sends a disconnect command to the overlay, and transitions to state TCP_LAST_ACK. In the overlay, the shadow CID sends a disconnection request message to the peer host and changes IB connection state to IB_DREQ_-SENT. Upon receiving IB_DREP from the active-closing host, the shadow CID changes queue pair state to ERROR, and transitions to state IB_TIME_WAIT.

When the active-closing shadow CID receives the disconnection request from the passive-closing host, it transits to state DREQ_RCVD. It delivers all the incoming packets to the guest VTOE buffers, and raises a DISCONNECT event to the guest. It then changes queue pair state to ERROR, sends an IB disconnection reply message to the peer host, and changes IB connection state to IB_TIME_WAIT. When the guest either gets the FIN packet from the peer, or the DISCONNECT event from the overlay, it processes all the incoming data and transitions to state TCP_TIME_WAIT. Finally, timeouts are used to transition from time wait to idle connection states.

5.1.2 Data Transfer

Data transfers leverage two optimization techniques.

Transmission with Zero Overlay Copies: The guest OS in the VM includes the device driver for the virtual NIC and the VTOE. The socket initiates packet transmission by posting a SEND request with Socket ID and data source to the send work queue in the VTOE NIC. In the overlay, the packet dispatcher sends the packet of type TCP_OFFLOAD to the VNET Core Connection Agent. The VNET_Core_-CA maps the packet Socket ID to the appropriate shadow

CID and posts the packet to the appropriate Infiniband RC queue pair.

While the packet is handed off multiple times, there is no copy from the guest's socket buffer to the host's NIC. We adopt the zero-copy data forwarding technique to avoid any data copies in the overlay. Note, however, that the guest may include a copy from the application's data buffers to the VNET socket's private buffer.

Reception with Zero Overlay Copies: As in the transmit case, guests use the receive work queue in the VTOE NIC to post receive buffers to different connections. The VNET_Core_CA and VNET_Host_CA work together to post these buffers to the queue pair associated with the shadow connection. As in the send case, the receive datapath to the guest OS does not require any copies, using the zero-copy data forwarding technique. Also note that the receive path does not need to route packets in the overlay, since each shadow CID is associated with a unique guest socket ID.

5.2 Interfacing With Linux Guests

Interfacing VNET+VTOE with Linux is somewhat complicated due to the lack of general TCP offload support in Linux. We worked around this problem similarly to how Infiniband and other Linux TCP offload implementations do. In particular, we use the Infiniband SDP [3] approach to dynamically change the application address family into AF_INET_VNET using a preload library. This address family then redirects to new offload drivers in the guest. This code has two elements, the *VNET socket provider* and the *VTOE socket module.*

The VNET socket provider is user-mode shared library code that provides socket direct extensions to the TCP/IP stack and determines which connections to redirect, based on protocol type, to the AF_INET_VNET address family. These socket direct extensions are completely transparent to the higher-layer protocols and applications that run on top of them. Applications interact in the same way with a VNET+VTOE stack as they would with a standard TCP/IP stack.

For the connection establishment calls, the provider makes a routing and policy decision and decides whether a TCP or VNET socket should be created. If a TCP socket is required, all calls on the socket are redirected to the Linux socket chain. If a VNET socket is required, the calls are redirected to the kernel VNET socket module.

The VNET socket module handles the socket operations redirected from the TCP socket by the VNET socket provider, updating kernel socket state and interfacing the VTOE device as necessary. and responding asynchronous events.

Although in this work the user is responsible for inserting the kernel module into the guest, and for assuring that the application uses the preload library, this not strictly necessary. In related work, we have shown how both of these steps can be done without user or guest cooperation through VMM-based code injection [9].

6. MICROBENCHMARKS

We first studied the effects of VTOE on a set of simple TCP and MPI throughput and latency microbenchmarks. Application benchmarks are described in Section 7.

6.1 Testbed

Our testbed, which is used both here and in the next section, consists of 6 physical machines each with dual quad core 2.3 GHz 2376 AMD Opteron "Shanghai" processors (8 cores total), 32 GB RAM, and a Mellanox MT26428 InfiniBand NIC in a PCI-e slot. The Infiniband NICs were connected via a Mellanox MTS 3600 36-port 20/40 Gbps InfiniBand switch.

We compared the performance of four different configurations, all mapped to underlying Infiniband RC connections:

- **Native+SDP/Uverbs:** Infiniband Socket Direct Protocol to offload TCP connections or MPI directly using Infiniband user-level verbs.

- **Native+IPoIB:** In-kernel TCP over the Infiniband in-kernel IP-over-IB implementation.

- **VNET+VTOE:** VNET Ethernet overlay with virtual TCP offload support.

- **VNET+IPoIB:** In-kernel TCP over VNET on top of the host IP-over-IB implementation.

For VNET+VTOE and VNET+IPoIB measurements, we ran a simple Linux 2.6.32 host with a minimal BusyBox configuration, and the Palacios VMM. The guest used was a Linux 2.6.30 kernel also with a minimal BusyBox running on a virtual machine with a single virtio network interface, 4 cores, and 2.5 GB of memory. In the VNET+VTOE configuration, the guest is provided with a single virtual TOE. Unless otherwise specified, the virtio NIC provided to the guest was configured to use 9000 byte MTUs. For native measurement, we ran a Linux 2.6.30 kernel also with a minimal BusyBox. For Native+IPoIB and VNET+IPoIB configurations, MTUs are set to 65520.

Performance measurements were made between identically configured machines. To assure accurate time measurements in the virtualized case, each guest was configured to use the CPU's cycle counter, and Palacios was configured to allow the guest direct access to the underlying hardware cycle counter.

The CPU utilization is reported by TTCP by dividing the total of user mode time + guest OS kernel time by real used wall-clock time, so it includes both the guest OS and VMM CPU costs, and is not averaged for single-thread TTCP.

6.2 Microbenchmarks

We used simple two-node TCP and MPI benchmarks to provide an initial characterization of the impact of our proposed VTOE infrastructure. TCP throughput was measured using *ttcp-1.10*. For simple MPI tests, we used the Intel MPI Benchmark Suite (IMB 3.2.2) [11] running on OpenMPI 1.3 [7], focusing on the point-to-point messaging performance. For each test case, we ran 10 times and report the average as the result.

6.2.1 TCP Uni-stream Bandwidth

Figure 3(a) shows uni-stream bandwidth performance for VNET+VTOE running over a single connection along with CPU utilization.

VNET+VTOE achieves near-native micro-benchmark performance of 9.4 Gbps, compared to the 10 Gbps in the Native+SDP case. This is higher bandwidth than Native+IPoIB performance, and Virtual TCP offload offers nearly 2.7 times the performance of VNET using IP-over-IB.

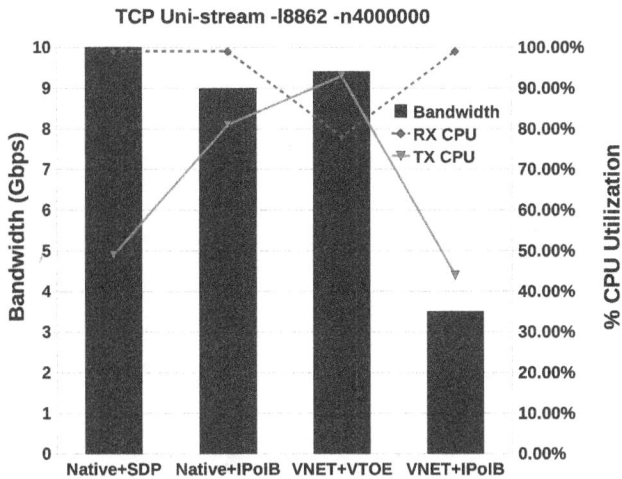

(a) TCP Uni-stream Bandwidth
(b) TCP Bi-stream Bandwidth

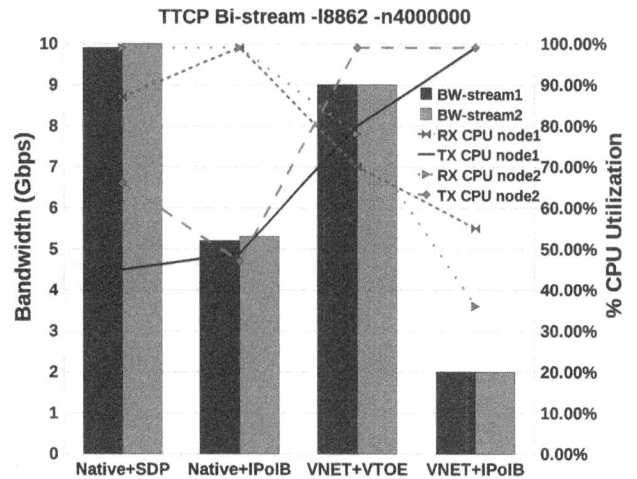

Figure 3: End-to-end TCP throughput and CPU utilization of Native+SDP, Native+IPoIB, VNET+VTOE, and VNET+IPoIB on InfiniBand Interconnect. VNET+VTOE performs more than 2.5 times better then VNET+IPoIB on the InfiniBand Interconnect

In terms of CPU usage, Native+IPoIB and Native+SDP have the same receive-side CPU usage, while Native+IPoIB has more transmit-side CPU utilization than Native+SDP. In the virtualization cases, VNET+VTOE has 76% receive-side usage compared to 99% for VNET+IPoIB. On the transmit side, VNET+IPoIB has less CPU usage than VNET+VTOE.

Analysis: First, in the native cases, the more transmit-side CPU utilization in Native+IPoIB, mainly comes from the interrupt processing triggered by large amount of ACKs generated in the receive-side TCP stack.

Second, in the virtualization cases, on the receive side, the higher CPU usage in VNET+IPoIB comes from two-level overheads: 1) On the first level, sender's TCP processing, and overlay's data copies, encapsulation, de-encapsulation, and routing all slower down the packet delivering rate (virtual link speed), and thus more virtual interrupts are generated to the receive side, which have the receive side spend more time on virtual interrupt processing; and 2) on the second level, each incoming packet goes through the whole guest TCP stack, which makes the receive side busier.

On the transmit side, in VNET+IPoIB, each incoming packet has to go through the TCP stack, so the receive-side TCP is slower in generating ACKs to the sender; moreover, the virtual link is slower in delivering ACKs, and virtual interrupt handling takes time, thus the flow control window in the sender is exhausted faster, and therefore the sender slows down.

6.2.2 TCP Bi-Stream Bandwidth

In addition to unidirectional TCP performance, we also examined bi-stream bandwidth performance to measure the duplex capability of VNET+VTOE. In this test, we use two machines and two threads on each machine. Each thread connects to its partner on the other machine, thus two connections are established between the machines. On each

connection, the basic TTCP bandwidth test is performed. The throughput and CPU usage are shown in Figure 3(b).

Native+SDP shows good duplex performance, delivering 10 Gbps bandwidth for each stream. In contrast, Native+IPoIB hits a bottleneck on bi-directional data transfer, with each stream dropping to half of the wire capacity. This is due to the TCP acknowledgment processing, which increases CPU interrupt processing overhead.

In the virtual overlay configurations, VNET+VTOE also fully utilizes the physical interconnect's full duplex features. Similar to the native case, VNET+IPoIB does not utilize the interconnect's full-duplex capabilities. This again mainly comes from the guest-level duplicated reliability processing and virtual interrupts triggered by ACKs from the TCP stack.

The CPU utilization is also presented for each test configuration. The benchmark reveals that Native+SDP and VNET+VTOE can not only achieve high aggregated bandwidth, they also show reduced overall CPU utilization. Specifically, Native+SDP reduces receive-side average CPU utilization compared with Native+IPoIB, and VNET+VTOE reduces the transmit-side average CPU usages compared to VNET+IPoIB.

6.2.3 CPU Utilization

There are two important observations regarding the measurements shown in Figure 3.

1. Receive-side CPU utilization in the virtualized configurations is lower than for the native configurations, while the opposite is true for the transmit-side.

2. In both native cases, receive-side CPU utilization higher than transmit-side CPU utilization, while the opposite is true for both virtualized configurations.

In the native cases, the real physical link is fast enough to keep the receive-side CPU busy with incoming packets, and the NIC speed is faster than the CPU, thus the application

55

cannot consume data from the buffer as fast as it is filled. The receive-side flow control window is quickly exhausted and the sender has to slow down. In the native cases, the network performance is bound to the receive-side CPU utilization.

In contrast, in the virtualized cases, the virtual link provided by the overlay is slower, reducing load on the receiver. The receiver now buffers data slower than the application can consume it. The receive window is open, the sender delivers data as fast as possible, and thus the network performance is bound to the overlay virtual link data-transfer rate.

6.2.4 MPI

Figure 4 shows the IMB MPI point-to-point performance with VNET+VTOE. For small messages, VNET+VTOE has more than two times lower message delay than VNET+-IPoIB, but two times higher message delay than Native+-IPoIB. For medium-sized messages, VNET+VTOE approaches Native+IPoIB performance. For large messages, Native+-IPoIB achieves about 47% of Native+Uverbs throughput, while VNET+VTOE achieves 60% of Native+Uverbs performance. VNET+IPoIB delivers about 28% of Native+-Uverbs bandwidth.

7. APPLICATION BENCHMARKS

Beyond the microbenchmarks we described in the previous section, we also evaluated VNET+VTOE using the HPC Challenge benchmarks, with the goal of characterizing the performance impact of the VTOE optimization on communication-intensive applications.

7.1 HPC Challenge Benchmarks

The HPC Challenge (HPCC) benchmarks [10] are a set of macro and application benchmarks for evaluating various aspects of the performance of high performance computing systems. We used the communication-oriented macro-benchmarks and application benchmarks to compare the performance of VNET+VTOE with Native+Verbs, Native+-IPoIB, and VNET+IPoIB. For these tests, each VM was configured with 4 virtual cores, 2.5 GB RAM, and a virtio NIC. For VNET+VTOE, each VM is also configured with a virtual TOE. For VNET testing, each host had one VM running on it. We ran tests with 2, 3, 4, 5, and 6 VMs with 4 HPCC processes started on each VM. Thus our performance results are based on HPCC with 8, 12, 16, 20, and 24 processes. In the native cases, no VMs are used and the processes ran directly on the host.

7.1.1 Latency-Bandwidth Benchmark

This benchmark consists of the ping-pong test and the ring-based tests, where the former measures the latency and bandwidth between all distinct pairs of processes. The ring based tests arrange the processes in a ring topology and then engage in collective communication among neighbors in the ring, measuring bandwidth and latency. The ring-based tests model the communication behavior of multi-dimensional domain-decomposition applications. Both naturally ordered rings and randomly ordered rings are evaluated. Communication is done with MPI non-blocking sends and receives, and MPI SendRecv. Here, the bandwidth per process is defined as total amount of message data divided

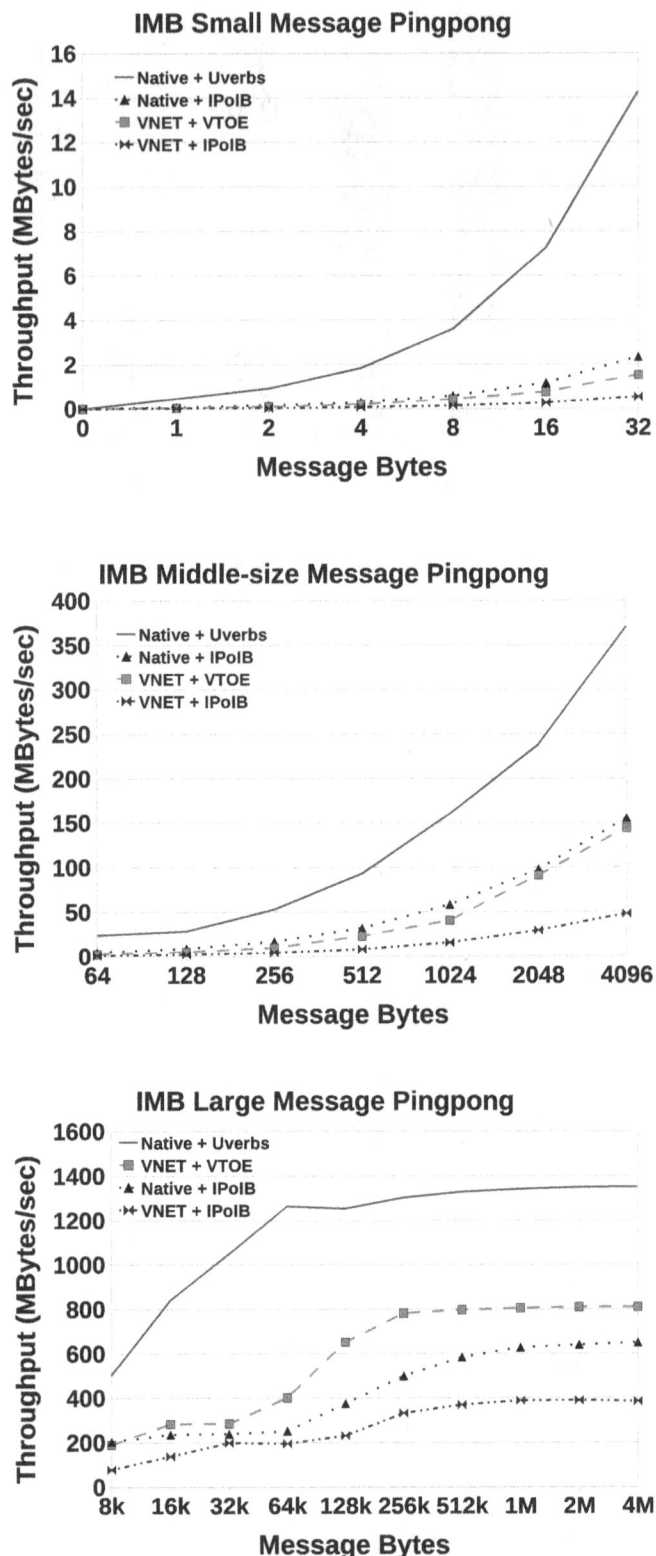

Figure 4: Intel MPI PingPong microbenchmark showing bidirectional throughput as a function of message size on InfiniBand Interconnect

by the number of processes and the maximum time needed in all processes.

Figure 5 shows the results of the HPCC Latency-Bandwidth benchmark for different numbers of test processes. Ping-Pong Latency and Ping-Pong Bandwidth results are consistent with the previous microbenchmarks: Native+IPoIB generally has 5–12 times higher latency than Native+Uverbs, and 40–60% bandwidth of Native+Uverbs. In VNET+-VTOE, bandwidths are within 60% of Native+Uverbs, and latencies are about 2 times that of Native+IPoIB. In VNET+-IPoIB, bandwidths are within 20–30% of Native+Uverbs, and latencies are about 4 times that of Native+IPoIB latencies. The results show that our VTOE can substantially enhance the performance of a software-based overlay virtual network like VNET/P on InfiniBand.

7.1.2 HPCC application benchmarks

We considered the three application benchmarks from the HPCC suite that exhibit the largest volume and complexity of communication: MPIRandomAcceess, PTRANS, and MPIFFT.

In MPIRandomAccess, random numbers are generated and written to a distributed table, with local buffering. Performance is measured in billions of updates per second (GUPs) that are performed. Figure 6(a) shows the results of MPI-RandomAccess, comparing the Native+Uverbs, Native+-IPoIB, VNET+VTOE, and VNET+IPoIB cases. Native+-IPoIB achieves 90–100% of Native+Uverbs performance in cases of 8 and 12 processes. However, when the scale increases, Native+IPoIB only delivers 40–75% of Uverbs performance. For the overlay, VNET+VTOE delivers full Native+-IPoIB performance at 8 and 12 processes and 60% of Native+-Uverbs performance as the scale increases. VNET+IPoIB achieves 60–70% of Native+Uverbs performance at scale of 8 and 12 processes, while delivers 40–45% of Native+Uverbs performance at greater scales.

PTRANS does a parallel matrix transpose, exercising the simultaneous communications between pairs of processors. The performance is measured in the total communication capacity (GB/s) of the network. Figure 6(b) shows the result of PTRANS for the Native+Uverbs, Native+IPoIB, VNET+VTOE, and VNET+IPoIB cases. Native+IPoIB achieves 63–80% of Native+Uverbs performance. VNET+-VTOE achieves 100% of Native+IPoIB performance and outperforms Native+IPoIB performance as the scale of the application gets bigger, while VNET+IPoIB frequently delivers 5–10% of the Native+IPoIB performance.

MPIFFT implements a double precision complex one-dimensional Discrete Fourier Transform (DFT). Its performance is measured in Gflop/s. Figure 6(c) shows the result of MPIFFT for the Native+Uverbs, Native+IPoIB, VNET+-VTOE, and VNET+IPoIB cases. Native+IPoIB achieves 65–85% of Native+Uverbs performance. VNET+VTOE achieves near Native+IPoIB performance, while VNET+IPoIB delivers around 19–50% of Native+IPoIB performance.

7.2 Discussion

As shown in the evaluation results, VTOE significantly improves bandwidth and reduces CPU utilization for bandwidth-intensive codes. For large messages and throughput-sensitive applications, VTOE outperforms Native+IPoIB. On the other hand, for the application benchmarks, the network communication consisted of a mixture of small and large packets,

and so their performance was determined both by throughput and latency. Recall small-message latency in VNET+-VTOE is still high, about twice Native+IPoIB latency and 10–14x higher than Native+Uverbs, although it has been improved compared with that in VNET+IPoIB by more than 50%. This may explain why some application benchmarks cannot achieve native performance despite VNET+VTOE achieving native throughput in the microbenchmarks.

The long latency mainly comes from the virtual interrupt emulation overhead, and the virtualization overhead is more expansive than TCP kernel stack processing. From the results of application MPIRandomAccess, we can see the high latency has negative impacts on the overall performance. We expect that the optimistic interrupt techniques described elsewhere will reduce this overhead, but have not yet implemented these techniques in VNET+VTOE.

Considering the tradeoff between CPU overhead and network performance, it is again true that MPI applications mix communication and computation, and thus reduced CPU availability and thus more CPU-intensive communication handling may affect computation. However, when the communication is slow, the application cannot make progress even if sufficient CPU time is available. This is of particular concern for MPI applications that do significant collective communication and synchronization.

8. CONCLUSION AND FUTURE WORK

We analyzed the challenges in deploying virtual Ethernet overlays on advanced heterogeneous interconnects such as InfiniBand. The difficulties come from the semantic gap generated by virtualization. To reduce the semantic gap, we proposed, designed, and implemented a virtual TCP offload model to improve virtual Ethernet overlay performance, in terms of throughput, latency, and CPU utilization. This approach improves virtual Ethernet overlay TCP throughput by more than 2.5 times, cuts TCP latency by 50%, and improves TCP application performance.

Although VTOE has reduced VNET+IPoIB latency on InfiniBand by 50%, its latency is still high. Our previous work [6] did a quantitative analysis of virtual overlay overhead. The high overlay latency is due to the *delayed* virtual interrupt delivery into the guests. Optimistic interrupt allows the overlay delivers virtual interrupts to the guest prior to the overlay data processing, overlaps the overlay's processing with the virtual interrupt emulation. Merging this technique into the virtual TCP offload model should reduce latency. Additionally, current VTOE overhead still includes a memory copy between guest kernel space and application buffers. Since advanced interconnects have RDMA features, it should be possible enable remote user space memory copiess without the intervention of either guest kernels or VTOE modules, avoiding all data copies. We are currently implementing such functionality in the VTOE.

9. REFERENCES

[1] The InfiniBand architecture specification, release 1.2. www.infinibandta.org/specs.
[2] RDMA performance in virtual machines using QDR Infiniband on VMware vSphere 5. http://www.mellanox.com/pdf/whitepapers/RDMA_-Performance_in_Virtual_Machines_using_QDR_-InfiniBand_on_VMware_vSphere5.pdf.

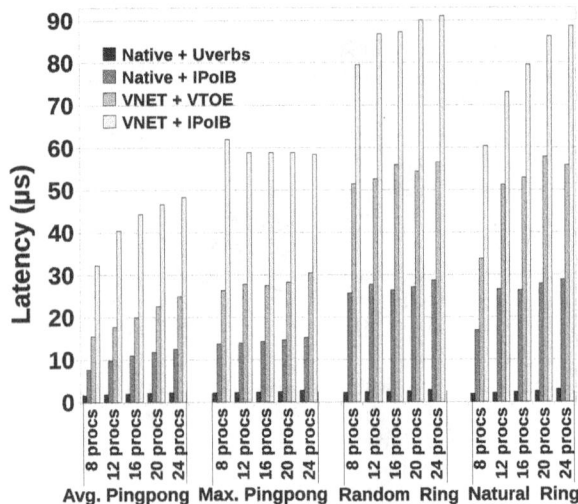

(a) HPCC Latency on InfiniBand

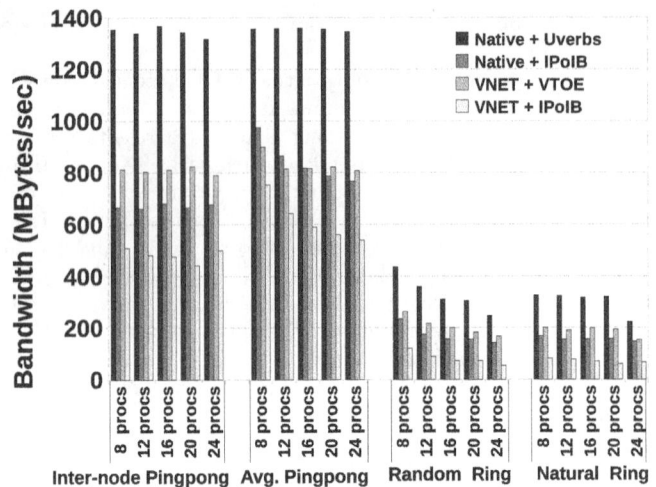

(b) HPCC Bandwidth on InfiniBand

Figure 5: HPCC Latency-Bandwidth benchmark for all of Native+Uverb, Native+IPoIB, VNET+VTOE, and VNET+IPoIB. The results are generally consistent with the previous microbenchmarks, while the ring-based tests show that latency and bandwidth of VNET+VTOE scale and perform better than VNET+IPoIB.

[3] Socket Direct Protocol. en.wikipedia.org/wiki/Sockets_Direct_Protocol.

[4] TCP offload engine. www.networkworld.com/details/653.html.

[5] CLARK, D., JACOBSON, V., ROMKEY, J., AND SALWEN, H. An analysis of TCP processing overhead. *Communications Magazine, IEEE 27*, 6 (june 1989), 23 –29.

[6] CUI, Z., XIA, L., BRIDGES, P. G., DINDA, P. A., AND LANGE, J. R. Optimizing overlay-based virtual networking through optimistic interrupts and cut-through forwarding. In *Proceedings of the International Conference on High Performance Computing, Networking, Storage and Analysis* (Los Alamitos, CA, USA, 2012), SC '12, IEEE Computer Society Press, pp. 99:1–99:11.

[7] GABRIEL, E., FAGG, G. E., BOSILCA, G., ANGSKUN, T., DONGARRA, J. J., SQUYRES, J. M., SAHAY, V., KAMBADUR, P., BARRETT, B., LUMSDAINE, A., CASTAIN, R. H., DANIEL, D. J., GRAHAM, R. L., AND WOODALL, T. S. Open MPI: Goals, concept, and design of a next generation MPI implementation. In *Proceedings of the 11th European PVM/MPI Users' Group Meeting* (September 2004).

[8] GARFINKEL, T., AND ROSENBLUM, M. When virtual is harder than real: security challenges in virtual machine based computing environments. In *Proceedings of the 10th conference on Hot Topics in Operating Systems - Volume 10* (Berkeley, CA, USA, 2005), HOTOS'05, USENIX Association, pp. 20–20.

[9] HALE, K., XIA, L., AND DINDA, P. Shifting GEARS to enable guest-context virtual services. In *Proceedings of the 9th International Conference on Autonomic Computing (ICAC 2012)* (September 2012).

[10] INNOVATIVE COMPUTING LABORATORY. HPC challenge benchmark. http://icl.cs.utk.edu/hpcc/.

[11] INTEL. Intel Cluster Toolkit 3.0 for Linux. http://software.intel.com/en-us/articles/intel-mpi-benchmarks/.

[12] JONES, S. T. Implicit operating system awareness in a virtual machine monitor. http://citeseerx.ist.psu.edu/viewdoc/download?rep=-rep1&type=pdf&doi=10.1.1.143.6999, 2007.

[13] JONES, S. T., ARPACI-DUSSEAU, A. C., AND ARPACI-DUSSEAU, R. H. Antfarm: Tracking processes in a virtual machine environment. In *Proceedings of the USENIX Annual Technical Conf* (2006).

[14] JONES, S. T., ARPACI-DUSSEAU, A. C., AND ARPACI-DUSSEAU, R. H. Geiger: monitoring the buffer cache in a virtual machine environment. *SIGARCH Comput. Archit. News 34*, 5 (Oct. 2006), 14–24.

[15] JONES, S. T., ARPACI-DUSSEAU, A. C., AND ARPACI-DUSSEAU, R. H. VMM-based hidden process detection and identification using Lycosid. In *Proceedings of the fourth ACM SIGPLAN/SIGOPS international conference on Virtual execution environments* (New York, NY, USA, 2008), VEE '08, ACM, pp. 91–100.

[16] KASHYAP, V. IP over InfiniBand (IPoIB) architecture. IETF Network Working Group Request for Comments RFC 4392, April 2006.

[17] L. XIA AND Z. CUI AND J. LANGE AND Y. TANG AND P. DINDA AND P. BRIDGES. VNET/P: Bridging the cloud and high performance computing through fast overlay networking. In *Proceedings of the 21st ACM International Symposium on High-performance Parallel and Distributed Computing (HPDC)* (June 2012).

[18] LANGE, J., AND DINDA, P. Transparent network services via a virtual traffic layer for virtual machines.

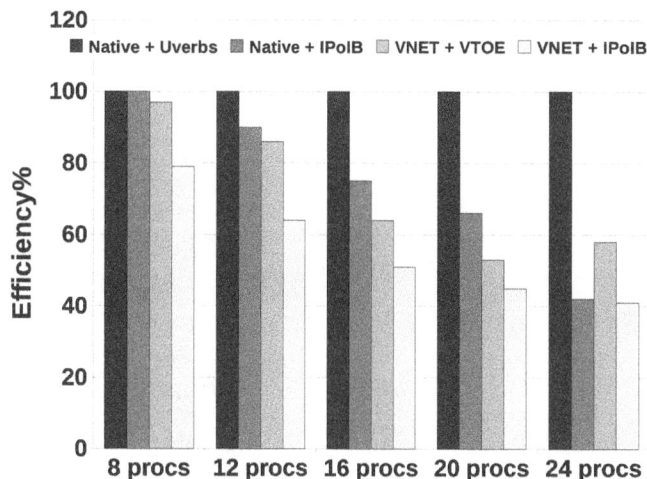

(a) HPCC MPIRandomAccess

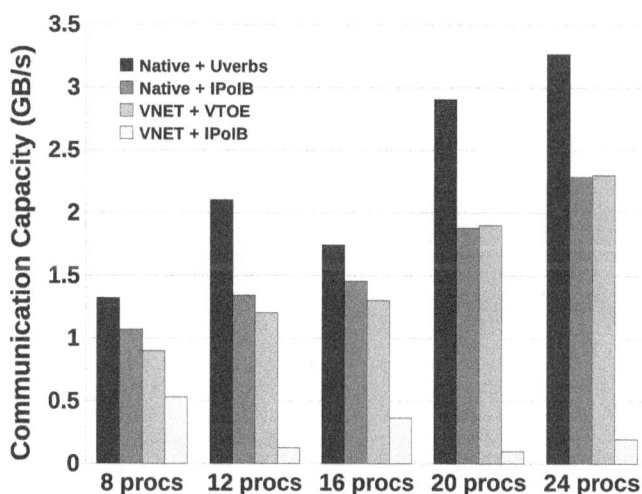

(b) HPCC PTRANS

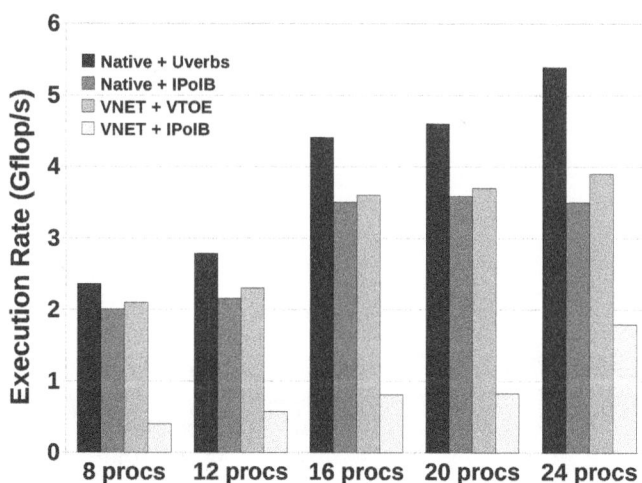

(c) HPCC MPIFFT

Figure 6: HPCC application benchmark results. VNET+VTOE approaches Native+IPoIB performance and scalable application performance when supporting parallel application workloads on Infiniband with rigorous network communication.

In *Proceedings of the 16th IEEE International Symposium on High Performance Distributed Computing (HPDC)* (June 2007).

[19] LANGE, J., PEDRETTI, K., HUDSON, T., DINDA, P., CUI, Z., XIA, L., BRIDGES, P., GOCKE, A., JACONETTE, S., LEVENHAGEN, M., AND BRIGHTWELL, R. Palacios and Kitten: New high performance operating systems for scalable virtualized and native supercomputing. In *Proceedings of the 2010 IEEE International Symposium on Parallel Distributed Processing (IPDPS)* (April 2010), pp. 1 –12.

[20] LIU, J., HUANG, W., ABALI, B., AND PANDA, D. K. High performance VMM-bypass I/O in virtual machines. In *Proceedings of the annual conference on USENIX '06 Annual Technical Conference* (Berkeley, CA, USA, 2006), ATC '06, USENIX Association, pp. 3–3.

[21] MENON, A., COX, A. L., AND ZWAENEPOEL, W. Optimizing network virtualization in Xen. In *Proceedings of the annual conference on USENIX '06 Annual Technical Conference* (Berkeley, CA, USA, 2006), ATC '06, USENIX Association, pp. 2–2.

[22] RUTH, P., JIANG, X., XU, D., AND GOASGUEN, S. Towards virtual distributed environments in a shared infrastructure. *IEEE Computer* (May 2005).

[23] SANTOS, J. R., TURNER, Y., JANAKIRAMAN, G., AND PRATT, I. Bridging the gap between software and hardware techniques for I/O virtualization. In *Proceedings of USENIX 2008 Annual Technical Conference* (Berkeley, CA, USA, 2008), ATC'08, USENIX Association, pp. 29–42.

[24] SUNDARARAJ, A., AND DINDA, P. Towards virtual networks for virtual machine grid computing. In *Proceedings of the 3rd USENIX Virtual Machine Research And Technology Symposium (VM 2004)* (May 2004). Earlier version available as Technical Report NWU-CS-03-27, Department of Computer Science, Northwestern University.

[25] SUNDARARAJ, A., GUPTA, A., AND DINDA, P. Increasing application performance in virtual environments through run-time inference and adaptation. In *Proceedings of the 14th IEEE International Symposium on High Performance Distributed Computing (HPDC)* (July 2005).

[26] WOLINSKY, D., LIU, Y., JUSTE, P. S., VENKATASUBRAMANIAN, G., AND FIGUEIREDO, R. On the design of scalable, self-configuring virtual networks. In *Proceedings of 21st ACM/IEEE International Conference of High Performance Computing, Networking, Storage, and Analysis (Supercomputing 2009)* (November 2009).

Scalanytics: A Declarative Multi-core Platform for Scalable Composable Traffic Analytics

Harjot Gill, Dong Lin, Xianglong Han, Cam Nguyen, Tanveer Gill, Boon Thau Loo
University of Pennsylvania
{gillh,lindong,hanxiang,camng,tgill,boonloo}@cis.upenn.edu

ABSTRACT

This paper presents SCALANYTICS, a declarative platform that supports high-performance application layer analysis of network traffic. SCALANYTICS uses (1) stateful network packet processing techniques for extracting application-layer data from network packets, (2) a declarative rule-based language called ANALOG for compactly specifying analysis pipelines from reusable modules, and (3) a task-stealing architecture for processing network packets at high throughput within these pipelines, by leveraging multi-core processing capabilities in a load-balanced manner without the need for explicit performance profiling. We have developed a prototype of SCALANYTICS that enhances a declarative networking engine with support for ANALOG and various stateful components, integrated with a parallel task-stealing execution model. We evaluate our SCALANYTICS prototype on a wide range of pipelines for analyzing SMTP and SIP traffic, and for detecting malicious traffic flows. Our evaluation on a 16-core machine demonstrate that SCALANYTICS achieves up to $11.4\times$ improvement in throughput compared with the best uniprocessor implementation. Moreover, SCALANYTICS outperforms the Bro intrusion detection system by an order of magnitude when used for analyzing SMTP traffic.

Categories and Subject Descriptors

C.2.3 [**Computer-Communication Networks**]: Network Operations—*Network monitoring*; D.3.2 [**Programming Languages**]: Language Classifications—*Concurrent, distributed, and parallel languages, Constraint and logic languages, Data-flow languages*; D.1.3 [**Programming Techniques**]: Concurrent Programming—*Parallel programming*

Keywords

Applications of parallel and distributed computing; Data-intensive computing; Programming languages and environments

1. INTRODUCTION

As networked applications become increasingly complex and heterogeneous, there is an increasing need for extensibility at the data

plane, in order to carry out sophisticated operations such as traffic flow management, traffic filtering, and content-based networking. Central to several of these operations is the ability to perform content-based analysis of network traffic, in order to determine how traffic should be shaped, transformed, or filtered. These analysis tasks are often times compute and memory intensive, since multiple packets need to be buffered and correlated in order to extract application-layer semantics. If deployed at routers, such analysis can potentially slow down packet forwarding, which needs to occur at "line-speed".

In order to speed up packet processing, one promising direction is the use of multicore machines in software-based routers [9, 27]. While these solutions scale as the number of cores/machines increases, they suffer from three limitations: (1) the lack of programming tools to rapidly customize different forms of traffic analysis specific to individual applications, (2) require explicit performance profiling to determine how the packet processing workload should be partitioned across cores, or (3) are not capable of performing complex operations beyond stateless per-packet processing, such as basic IP routing and packet encryption. To address these limitations, we present SCALANYTICS (stands for *Scalable Analytics*), a software-based traffic analysis platform deployed at the network layer, that aims to provide high-performance analysis of packets, capable of extracting and assembling application-layer information from individual packets for analysis.

SCALANYTICS makes the following contributions:

- **Component-based stateful processing.** SCALANYTICS uses a component-based dataflow architecture [11] that allows for rapid assembly of packet processing functionalities from components into *dataflow pipelines* that perform tasks such as assembling packets into application-layer content, operations such as aggregating traffic statistics, or deep-packet inspections into specific application traffic.

- **Declarative configuration language.** SCALANYTICS uses a declarative rule-based language called ANALOG for compactly specifying pipelines that are assembled from existing packet processing components. SCALANYTICS extends prior declarative networking [12] languages with constructs for modularization and components, interoperability with legacy code, and runtime support for parallelism. To illustrate the flexibility of ANALOG, we provide four example pipelines: (1) analyzing SMTP message content using regular expression, (2) analyzing SMTP message content using a machine-learning based spam filter [19], (3) tracking VoIP (SIP [20] protocol) sessions, and (4) detecting Denial of Service (DoS) attack [13], using support vector machines [5] on actual datasets [8]. These pipelines require only 7, 7, 7, and 5 ANALOG rules respectively, and reuse some common components shared across these pipelines.

- **High-performance fine-grained parallelization.** In order to execute these pipelines efficiently, SCALANYTICS provides fine-grained parallelism at the level of individual components within the pipelines. This is achieved through the use of a threading library based on the task-stealing model [18], that achieves both automatic load-balancing and high throughput processing. In addition to stateless per-packet processing (e.g. packet routing, IPSec etc.), SCALANYTICS can analyze the semantics of stateful protocols (e.g. SIP) with high degrees of parallelism. To ensure correct packet ordering in the presence of parallel processing, SCALANYTICS allows packets to be ordered based on its specified *context* attribute, defined in terms of application specific semantics (for instance, SIP session is uniquely identified by its call ID).

- **Implementation and evaluation.** We have developed a prototype of SCALANYTICS, by enhancing an open-source declarative networking engine [17] with the task-stealing model of parallelism and support for various stateful processing components. Using pipelines compactly expressed in ANALOG, we demonstrate the use of SCALANYTICS for performing high-throughput analysis of SMTP, SIP, and detection of malicious flows. In data intensive workloads such as SMTP and SIP, we achieve up to $11.4\times$ speedup on a 16-core machine and a throughput of 1.89 Gbps for analyzing SMTP emails. SCALANYTICS incurs low per-packet latency ranging from 0.1 ms to 2.3 ms. Even under a heavy workload that saturates the system with significant queueing delays, SCALANYTICS's per-packet latency ranges from 0.5 ms to 6.0 ms. We further compared with the Bro Intrusion Detection System (IDS) [14], and observe an order of magnitude performance improvement for SCALANYTICS in analyzing SMTP traffic.

2. DATAFLOW ARCHITECTURE

Figure 1 shows the architecture of SCALANYTICS. The system is deployed at core routers, capturing IP packets for analysis as they arrive. In a typical deployment, SCALANYTICS is used as a non-intrusive network monitoring tool through a network tap. SCALANYTICS can also be deployed inline for making decisions on packet forwarding/filtering and packet transformation.

A network operator provides a ANALOG program that specifies a linear pipeline of components, where each component corresponds to a specific *stage* in the analysis pipelines. Each component can be implemented from scratch or as wrappers over existing libraries. Multiple ANALOG programs corresponding to different analysis pipelines can be installed at the same time. As input to each pipeline, SCALANYTICS accepts events that could either be external, e.g. packet capture from the network, or internal, e.g. local periodic events. The events are queued and scheduled by the *platform thread*, which generates a continuous stream of tuples from the incoming events and inserts them into the pipelines for execution. In this paper, we refer to events processed within the pipeline as *tuples*.

The SCALANYTICS utilizes a *token-based* scheduling mechanism, whereby each incoming tuple is assigned a token number by the *token-dispenser*, and then scheduled for running within the dataflow pipeline. Each pipeline has its own token dispenser. At any time, only a pre-specified number of tokens are allocated for each pipeline, hence limiting the number of in-flight tuples in the pipeline.

Once tuples are assigned a token number, they are then processed within the dataflow pipeline. The first stage in the pipeline

is an input component. All components are executed using a *task-stealing* framework (Section 2.2). As input tuples traverse each component at every processing stage, output tuples are generated and buffered for processing in the next component. Based on the ordering semantics of each component, each buffered tuple ready for processing is designated a ready *task*, and enqueued into task queues. Each task queue is assigned to a *task stealing thread* running on a processing core, which dequeues the task from its assigned task queue for processing. In a multicore system, these threads can run in parallel, hence allowing multiple tuples to be processed in parallel within the pipelines. This enables concurrent processing within each component (for different incoming tuples), or processing stages within a pipeline to run in parallel.

In the event of overload due to high traffic load, incoming packets are dropped by the packet capture thread. However, once a packet is accepted into the event queue, SCALANYTICS ensures that this packet will be processed by the system.

At the final stage of the pipeline, output *action tuples* are generated and are used to perform specific actions, including (1) shipping the tuples into another pipeline (at the same or remote node) for further processing, (2) redirecting tuples to a router controller for making traffic management decisions (e.g. rate limit or block a particular flow), (3) materializing into tables as traffic statistics, or (4) raising alarms for the user.

2.1 Dataflow Pipeline

Figure 2 shows an example dataflow pipeline that illustrates the execution model of SCALANYTICS. Each dataflow pipeline consists of several components connected in a linear chain. Briefly, this pipeline receives packets from the network (Packet Capture), assembles packets into complete IP packets and TCP segments (IP Assembler and TCP Assembler, filters out packets related to emails (by recognizing the SMTP protocol from the packet payloads using the Protocol Detector component), assembles complete emails (SMTP Processor), before finally filtering out emails that match a given regular expression (Regex Matcher).

Each SCALANYTICS pipeline can be specified as a ANALOG program (described in Section 3). SCALANYTICS compiles the program into a pipeline, which is installed into the runtime system. To support different forms of serial and parallel execution, SCALANYTICS has three types of components:

- **Serial.** Packets are processed in strict FIFO order. This is typically done for operations where total order is essential. For instance, in our example, Packet Capture is a serial component, since the initial stream of packets obtained from the network should be first processed in the order in which they arrive.

- **Parallel.** Incoming packets to a parallel component can be processed by multiple concurrent threads in a manner where ordering does not matter. For instance, once SMTP messages are assembled, regular expression matches on individual email messages can be parallelized, and the order in which these emails are processed is not essential. IP Assembler and Regex Match are parallel components.

- **Parallel context-ordered.** These components are processed in a partial order. A *context-key* is specified, in which all packets that have the same key should be processed in an order based on their arrival into the system. However, the ordering of packet processing for packets with different keys is not required. For instance, when assembling email messages from TCP segments, messages have to be assembled in partial order (based on TCP flows). Likewise, TCP Assembler processes incoming packets

62

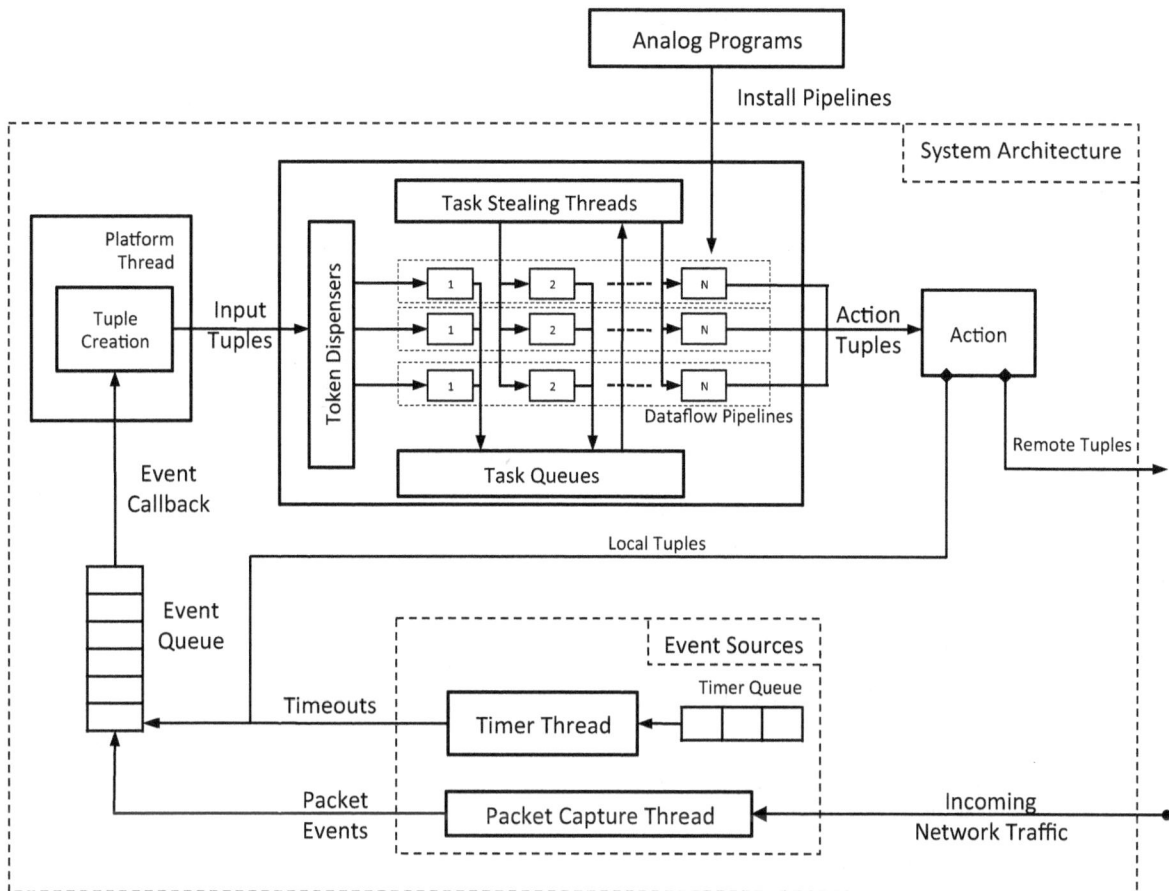

Figure 1: System architecture.

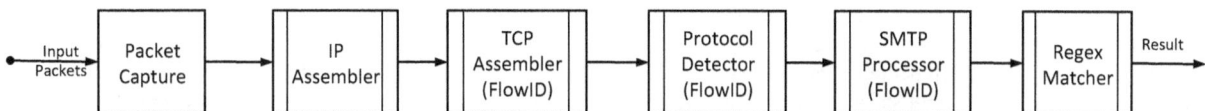

Figure 2: A SCALANYTICS pipeline for SMTP analysis. Parallel components have double lines, and context-ordered component additionally have their context-keys shown in (...).

belonging to the same flow in the order of their arrival, but the ordering of packets across flows is not enforced. `TCP Assembler`, `Protocol Detector`, and `SMTP Processor` are parallel context-ordered components. Note that flow ID is not the only form of context-key supported by SCALANYTICS. As we will later show in our examples, other forms of context-keys are easily supported, e.g. the call ID for a VoIP session.

SMTP pipeline details. Given the above component types, we describe the SMTP pipeline in greater detail. This SMTP pipeline assembles SMTP emails from IP packets, and then filters out emails whose content matches a specified regular expression. The pipeline receives a stream of incoming IP packets that are captured via the `Packet Capture` component. Since the incoming IP packets may be fragmented, they are sent to the `IP Assembler` component for assembling the packets. This component is *stateful*, since previous packet fragments must be kept in-memory at the component until assembled.

After IP assembly, the packets are filtered based on their protocol types (TCP or UDP). Further processing is done to the TCP stream to assemble TCP segments based on the TCP sequence numbers in the incoming packets. The `TCP Assembler` component is also stateful and *context ordered* based on flow ID. This means that the TCP messages with the same flow ID are processed serially and each unique flow is processed in parallel. The flow ID is extracted from a 4-tuple consisting of source and destination IP addresses and port numbers.

Each assembled TCP flow (consisting of TCP segments in the form of tuples) is then sent to the `Protocol Detector` component, which is stateful and context ordered by flow ID as its context key. The detection component monitors the flow and tries to detect its application layer protocol. For example, the detection component looks for the initial handshake of the SMTP protocol and marks the flow as SMTP if handshake is detected. All the subsequent TCP segments in the SMTP flow would bypass the detector and be marked as SMTP segments.

The detected SMTP segments are sent to the `SMTP Processor` component for message assembly, which is stateful with the flow ID as its context key. The SMTP component tracks the state machine of the active SMTP session. When the data portion of the email is detected, it assembles the complete email message, which may arrive in several TCP segments.

The assembled message is then sent to a parallel regular expression matcher component to look for patterns in the emails. Regex matcher is a stateless component. If there is a match, a positive result is generated. All of the above components are decoupled and run in parallel with respect to each other. This allows flexibility to insert compatible components in between any two components. e.g. an `IP filter` can be inserted between `IP assembler` and `TCP assembler` components to process packets which are destined to specific destination address and port number.

Note that in all of the above components, they can be extracted from existing libraries, rather than be implemented from scratch. We will describe in Section 4 more details on the extraction process. Once extracted into pipeline components, pipeline can be constructed using ANALOG specifications.

2.2 Parallel Execution

SCALANYTICS aims to minimize latency when the system is under light load and maximize the throughput when the system is under heavy load. To achieve this goal, SCALANYTICS uses a task stealing [18, 10] framework to enable adaptive fine-grained parallel processing of individual components within each pipeline.

Figure 3 shows an example SMTP pipeline similar to the one described in Section 2.1. Here, all emails that match the given regular expression are stored in a serial `Logger` component. For ease of exposition, we defer the discussion on context ordered components to Section 2.4, and focus on serial and parallel components here.

Token-based task scheduling. SCALANYTICS utilizes token-based task scheduling mechanism as follows. Each pipeline is assigned its own *token dispenser* component (that is situated just outside the pipeline), as shown in Figure 3. All incoming tuples are first assigned a monotonically increasing token number by its token dispenser component before entering pipeline. Tuples outputted from each component retain the token number of the tuple that triggers its generation. If multiple output tuples are generated from a single input tuple (possibly from multiple rules within one component), these tuples will be processed as a single batch with a common token number. Conversely, if one output tuple is generated from multiple input tuples (a common occurrence when doing application level data assembly), the tuple will be tagged with the token number of the final input tuple that generates this output. In addition, for each input tuple that comes before the final input tuple, a dummy tuple is generated with the corresponding token number of the input tuple. This ensures that the next component sees tokens in increasing order. Hence, token numbers do not disappear. These dummy tokens add minimal processing overhead since each subsequent component simply passes them along.

The token dispenser implements flow control, by allowing only a limited number of in-flight tokens in the pipeline. There is a memory vs. speedup tradeoff in the number of tokens allowed. Having more tokens potentially increases the degree of parallelism, since in-flight tuples can be processed by multiple cores simultaneously. However, this comes at the expense of requiring larger buffer sizes.

Once tuples are assigned tokens, they enter the pipeline for processing. These tuples are processed within components as *tasks*. Each task is hence associated with a component and a set of tuples for execution. Once a tuple is ready for processing within a component, it is inserted into one of the *task queues* for execution. Each task queue is assigned to a task stealing thread, which can process any task on its designated queue. Once a task is executed, any output tuples generated from the component are reinserted into the input buffer for the next component. When these tuples are again ready for execution (for instance, in a serial or parallel context-ordered component, they are next in line for processing based on token numbers), they are placed into a task queue for execution in the next component

Serial components process tuples in strict FIFO order based on token numbers. Since tuples can arrive out of order when a parallel component precedes a serial component, an input buffer is used internally at the beginning of each serial component, to ensure that tuples are processed in-order. This requires each component to maintain the token number for the last tuple processed (*lastToken*), and only allow the next tuple whose token number is one larger than *lastToken* to be processed. Once a tuple is ready for processing within a component (i.e. reaches the head of the input queue), it is then inserted into one of the *task queues* for execution. On the other hand, since *Parallel* components have no ordering constraints, they can process tuples in completely parallel fashion. As a result, no input buffer is necessary. Tuples arriving at the parallel component are directly inserted into task queue for execution and are never deferred.

2.3 Task Stealing

SCALANYTICS provides dynamic load balancing through the use of a task stealing architecture [18], also known as *work stealing* [10]. A task stealing framework achieves parallelism by using multiple cores at the same time. Each core on a multicore machine can run one or more task stealing thread with hyper-threading. Each task stealing thread is assigned a task queue, where tasks can be dequeued in any order by the thread for processing.

In SCALANYTICS, a task is denoted by the processing of a tuple (or group of tuples with the same token number) within a component. Whenever a tuple is ready for processing, it is inserted into one of the task queues. By default, the task is inserted into the task queue of the currently executing thread, in order to minimize CPU cache misses. A thread that has completed a task can then dequeue from its corresponding task queue. However, if a thread is idle and has no outstanding tasks, it can *steal* tasks designated for other threads that are currently busy, hence achieving dynamic load balancing. This is unlike other prior approaches used in scaling software-based routers, which either utilize a static partitioning approach [9], or require pre-creation of multiple component instances based on performance profiling [27].

In SCALANYTICS, task stealing is particularly useful when not all flows are arriving at the same rate. For instance, when the rate of SIP messages is higher than SMTP messages, SCALANYTICS's use of task stealing would naturally adapt to use more threads for processing SIP components. A task stealing thread (referred to as thread below) is responsible for executing tasks (in this case, tuples or sets of tuples designated for each component to be processed). Each thread attempts to steal tasks from another randomly chosen thread (the victim) when there are no pending tasks in its local task queue. An unsuccessful attempt to steal, in case of an empty victim task queue, leads the thread to back off for a predetermined amount of time and try again. A point to be noted is that components do not map to any particular thread. However, SCALANYTICS optimizes CPU cache locality, by using the same thread whenever possible to process the same tuple across components. This vastly reduces the cache-misses (associated with transfer/stealing of a task to another core) as most tuples would be recycled into being processed by the next component on the same core. A task is transferred only when

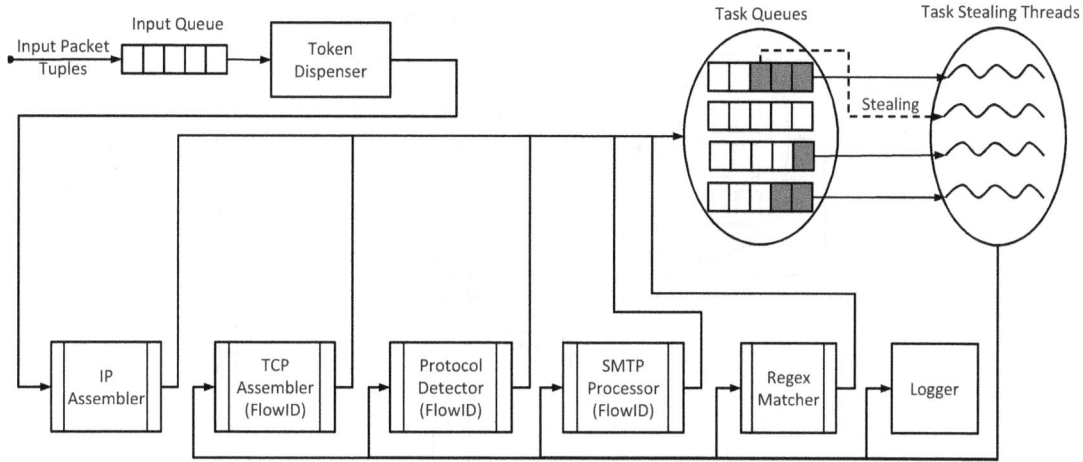

Figure 3: SCALANYTICS's pipeline architecture showing task stealing in action.

a thread is busy processing a component and some idle thread is able to steal that task.

2.4 Enforcing Context-Order

Figure 4 shows the internals of a parallel context-ordered component. Unlike an unordered parallel component, all tuples within this component have to be processed in a partially ordered fashion based on user-specified context key(s). The context keys can be specified when defining each component in ANALOG (Section 3).

An *Input Buffer* is required here, in order to process event tuples in FIFO order based on their token numbers. A key difference here compared with the serial component is the use of *context keys*, where tuples from the *Input Buffer* are further divided into sub-buffers, one for each key. To ensure correct ordering within each sub-buffer, a *Context Designator* is used to classify incoming tuples based on their context keys, and then insert them into their respective sub-buffers. Note that a tuple may have multiple context keys, in which case, it will be placed in multiple buffers, and dequeued for processing when it reaches the front in all its buffers. Once a tuple is ready for processing, it will be inserted into the task queue, at which point, its corresponding ANALOG execution rules becomes eligible for execution by one of the task stealing threads.

In order to ensure that outgoing tuples (corresponding to the same context key) are processed in order of their token numbers, at any point in time, only the topmost outgoing tuple from each sub-buffer is inserted into task queues. Upon executing this tuple, the next tuple from the same sub-buffer is inserted into the task queues for execution.

3. ANALOG LANGUAGE

Each pipeline component in SCALANYTICS is specified using the ANALOG language. We extend this language based on prior work on declarative networking [12]. Declarative networking enables specification of networking protocols as a set of queries in a high-level language, primarily based on Datalog [16]. A Datalog program is a set of *rules*, which are of the form q :- p1, p2, ..., pn. Here, q is the *head* of the rule and p1, p2, ..., pn is a set of *literals* that constitute the *body* of the rule. Literals are either *predicates* (e.g. relations or streaming tuples) with *attributes* or boolean expressions that involve function symbols (e.g. arithmetic) applied to attributes. A Datalog program is said to be

recursive if a *cycle* exists through any predicate, i.e. predicate appearing in a rule's body appears in the head of the same rule. Body predicates are evaluated in a left-to-right order. Like prior declarative networking languages, we adopt the use of a location specifier attribute @ that is used to denote the location (physical network address) of each tuple. Though not an emphasis in this paper, location specifiers will make distributed extensions natural to realize in future, hence further improving the scalability of our system.

3.1 Components

Our ANALOG language extends traditional Datalog by allowing the specification of a processing pipeline as a linear chain of components. These components are executed in parallel to each other by the run-time, thus exhibiting pipelined parallelism. A component is essentially a set of rules, and its syntax is as follows:

```
component comp-name(type, context_keys(pA1(k1, ..., kn), ...,
                                        pNn(k1, ...,kn))) {
    rA qA :- pA1, pA2, ..., pAn.
    rB qB :- pB1, pB2, ..., pBn.
    ..
}
```

The component specification is labeled by the keyword `component`, followed by the component name, `comp-name`. In the component specification, `type` can be `serial`, `parallel` or `parallel_context_ordered`. `context_keys(...)` specifies the *context-keys* for parallel context ordered components.

To ensure deterministic behavior, we constrain the ANALOG language specification to only allow pipelines that can be represented as a linear chain of components. This technique is logically similar to *stratification* restrictions (e.g. on the use of negation operator) in Datalog [15], where the next component is not executed until the previous component has completed its execution.

Within each component, a set of rules is executed to a *fixpoint*, upon the arrival of an input tuple that triggers the execution of the component. Typically, a component is triggered for execution only if the incoming tuple matches the body predicates in one of the rules. The execution of one of these rules may generate new tuples that will trigger other rules within a component. A fixpoint is reached when no new facts are derived locally, at which point, all output tuples are batched, tagged with the token number of the initial input tuple, and sent to the next component for further processing. If a newly derived or an input tuple does not invoke any

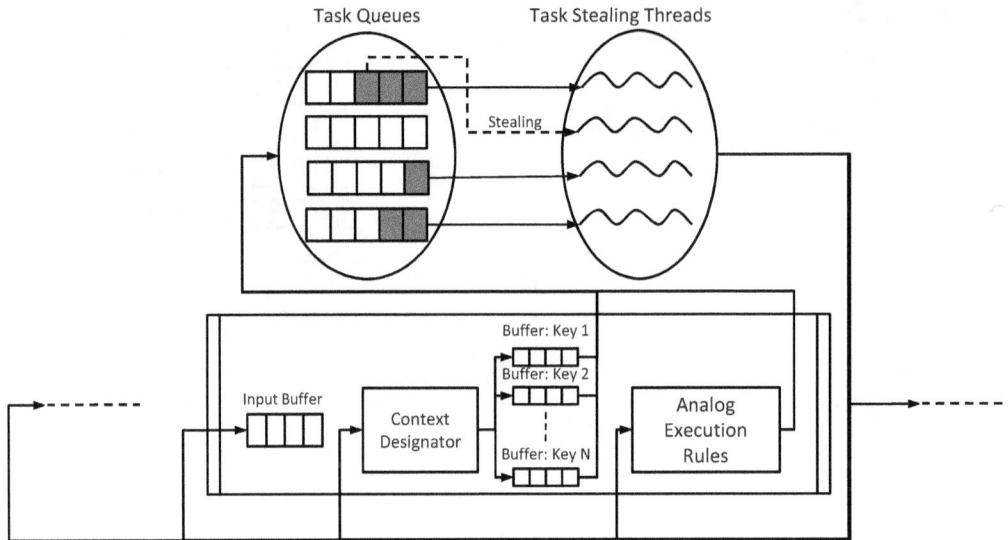

Figure 4: Parallel context-ordered component.

rule within a component, it is simply used as an output tuple of the component without any rule executions.

3.2 Example Pipeline in ANALOG

To better illustrate ANALOG language, we provide an example program of three components that corresponds to the pipeline in Figure 2.The compete ANALOG program is shown in Appendix A. In our example, ANALOG is used as a wrapper for gluing together various components. Within each component, user-defined functions are used to invoke external libraries implementing various processing capabilities (Section 4). These components are connected into a linear chain, since the output of one component is used as input to the next component.

```
component tcp_protocol_detector(parallel_context_order,
        context_keys(tcp_stream(5))) {
det1 detected_tcp_protocol(@N, PKT, SRC_IP, DST_IP,
                        FLOW_ID, TCP_MESSAGE, PROTOCOL) :-
    tcp_stream(@N, PKT, SRC_IP,
                DST_IP, FLOW_ID, TCP_MESSAGE),
    PROTOCOL = f_processTCPDetector(TCP_MESSAGE, FLOW_ID).

det2 smtp_segment(@N, PKT, SRC_IP, DST_IP,
            FLOW_ID, TCP_MESSAGE) :-
    detected_tcp_protocol(@N, PKT, SRC_IP, DST_IP,
                        FLOW_ID, TCP_MESSAGE, PROTOCOL),
    PROTOCOL = "SMTP".
}

component smtp_processor(parallel_context_order,
        context_keys(smtp_segment(5))) {
smtp1 smtp_mail(@N, PKT, SRC_IP, DST_IP, FLOW_ID, MAIL) :-
    smtp_segment(@N, PKT, SRC_IP, DST_IP,
                FLOW_ID, TCP_MESSAGE),
    MAIL = f_processSMTPSegment(TCP_MESSAGE, FLOW_ID),
    MAIL != "".
}

component regex_match(parallel) {
regex1 positive_match(@N, PKT, SRC_IP, DST_IP,
                FLOW_ID, MAIL, MATCH) :-
    smtp_mail(@N, PKT, SRC_IP, DST_IP, FLOW_ID, MAIL),
    MATCH = f_match(MAIL, "hello"),
    MATCH = "true".
}
```

`tcp_protocol_detector` and `smtp_processor` are parallel

context-ordered components, since they are both declared to be of type `parallel_context_order`. The `context_keys` parameter is only applicable to parallel context-ordered components. Both components are parameterized by `context_keys(tcp_stream(5))` and `context_keys(smtp_segment(5))`, which means that they use the 5th attribute (FLOW_ID)[1] of their respective `tcp_stream` and `smtp_segment` input tuples as their context key.

Hence, tuples carrying packets (PKT) with different FLOW_ID are allowed to be assembled and processed in parallel. Component `regex_match` on the other hand is a `parallel` component. The `tcp_protocol_detector` component is triggered upon the arrival of an input `tcp_stream` tuple. Each input tuple carries the assembled TCP payload as its TCP_MESSAGE attribute as well as the FLOW_ID attribute. Upon its arrival, rule `det1` is triggered, which then results in the invocation of a protocol detection module implemented by the `f_processTCPDetector` function call (which returns a PROTOCOL type, e.g. "SMTP" or "SIP").

The firing of `det1` results in the generation of a `detected_tcp_protocol` tuple, which is then used to execute rule `det2`. The rule `det2` checks if the PROTOCOL is "SMTP" and generates `smtp_segment` tuple if true. Since the resulting `smtp_segment` tuple does not occur in any rule body, a fixpoint is reached, and this tuple is added to the list of output tuples to be sent to the next component. When there are no tuples pending evaluation in any rules within the component, a local fixpoint is reached, and all outgoing tuples are batched and sent to the next component in the pipeline.

The output tuple `tcp_segment` is then used as input to the next component, which in this case, is the `smtp_processor` component (rule `smtp1`). The `smtp_processor` component generates a `smtp_mail` tuple if a mail is successfully assembled. This is then used as input to the `regex_match` component, which generates a `positive_match` tuple if MAIL matches the given regular expression string.

---

[1]The FLOW_ID attribute is a concatenation of the source and destination IP addresses and port numbers, and used to uniquely identify a TCP or SMTP session.

4. IMPLEMENTATION AND USE CASES

We have developed a prototype of SCALANYTICS using the open-source RapidNet declarative networking engine [17], which provides support for Click-like dataflows [11] and a Datalog compiler. We have enhanced the Datalog compiler to support the ANALOG language, and implemented several dataflow pipelines in SCALANYTICS from ANALOG specifications.

We enhanced RapidNet's runtime engine to support the new architecture described in Section 2. The new execution model is designed and implemented to enable local fixed-point computation (i.e. rules are executed till no new facts are derived) within a component before the derived tuples are batched together and sent to the next component in pipeline. The runtime engine is enhanced through task stealing framework (i.e. the task queues and task stealing threads) described in Section 2.2 using Intel's Threading Building Blocks (TBB) library [18]. Using TBB as a basis, we are able to implement SCALANYTICS's serial and parallel components. To enable parallel context-ordered components, we implemented a new feature called *context-filter*. Briefly, the context-filter allows us to create sub-buffers (Figure 4) keyed using context key. This ensures strict ordering of tuples that share the same context key but allows parallel processing of tuples across multiple contexts.

In the rest of this section, we briefly present four example dataflow pipelines that highlight different uses of SCALANYTICS. In all cases, these pipelines are assembled from reusable components that are implemented from existing legacy code.

4.1 SMTP Analysis Pipeline

In our first use case, we implemented the SMTP analysis pipeline as shown in Figure 2. The detailed specification of the pipeline in ANALOG is in Appendix A. The entire pipeline requires only 7 rules in 6 components (including the initial `Packet Capture`). The `IP Assembler` and `TCP Assembler` components are adapted from libnids [26] source code, which in itself is derived from the Linux kernel's TCP/IP stack code.

For the purpose of this project, libnids code is unusable directly as it is designed for single threaded use. The libnid's IP and TCP stacks are decoupled from each other and made thread-safe by adding locks to their internal tables. The locks are added to protect the lookup and insertion of stateful structures in hash tables (e.g. flow table). The context-filter extensions to TBB guarantees safe access to these structures based on TCP flow ID, and thus no fine-grained locks are added. Also, we have made modifications to hashing scheme used by TCP stack so as to map client to server and server to client packets to the same hash bucket. This change allows us to use a single, unique flow ID for identifying TCP packets flowing in either direction. Our changes enable libnids's IP stack to run in completely parallel and the TCP stack to run in parallel context-ordered mode. It takes us just a couple of days to make these changes to the code.

The `SMTP Processor` component is adapted from the SMTP analysis code from Bro IDS [14, 1]. It outputs each assembled email on observing end of DATA for each SMTP session. The assembled email will be used by `Regex Matcher` to search for the given regular expression.

All in all, it takes us a few days to port existing legacy implementations into components usable by our SMTP analysis pipeline. Note that this is a one-time effort, as these components are reusable for other pipelines.

4.2 SMTP Spam Detector Pipeline

In our second use case, we improved upon the basic SMTP analysis pipeline shown above. Rather than do a generic regular expression match on the email body, we instead added a spam detector

module that allows us to filter out unwanted emails. Figure 5 shows the entire pipeline. We reuse earlier components for assembling SMTP messages from incoming traffic. The assembled emails are then classified into spam or regular emails, using a `Naïve Bayes Text Classifier` component. This pipeline requires only 7 rules in 6 components.

Naïve Bayes classification is a well-known machine learning algorithm for performing efficient text classification [19]. The classifier is first trained offline, in our case, using pre-existing emails that have previously been identified as spams. Our `Naïve Bayes Text Classifier` is a generic implementation of the naïve Bayes classification algorithm tailored for text input. The component first tokenizes each incoming text document into individual words. Each input word is then tagged with a number indicating its probability of being a keyword for spam data. This probability is derived from the offline training phase. The classifier then computes a final value from all the input word probabilities, to make a final decision on whether the input text is classified as spam.

Note that this component is implemented in a generic fashion, and can be reused for any other forms of text classification that uses the naïve Bayes classification technique. It is also embarrassingly parallel, meaning that one can implement the classifier as a parallel component within SCALANYTICS.

4.3 SIP Analysis Pipeline

Our third use case is a pipeline that performs VoIP traffic analysis. Figure 6 shows a pipeline that implements an interception of VoIP traffic by monitoring setup and tear-down of VoIP calls based on Session Initiation Protocol. This pipeline reuses the `IP Assembler` component used in our previous example. The entire pipeline requires 7 rules in 5 components. The detailed ANALOG pipeline specification is provided in Appendix B.

In the pipeline, SIP protocol processing is composed of `SIP Parser` and `SIP Transaction Processor` components. The `SIP Parser` component parses the header of each SIP call to extract out relevant information from the call, such as the CallID. This information is then used by the `SIP Transaction Processor` component to track the state of the SIP call. This is a stateful component, since it needs to maintain the state machine corresponding to the SIP session. These two components are extracted from existing implementations of the GNU oSIP library [2], which provides interface for controlling SIP based sessions.

Once the setup or tear-down of a SIP session is detected, this information can be used by other components for further processing. For example, we can add a filter (either by CallID or user) to identify VoIP data streams of interests, and then record the VoIP data stream of these selected calls using a RTP stream interceptor component.

4.4 DoS Attack Detection Pipeline

Our last use case implements a Denial of Service (DoS) attack detection [13] using support vector machines (SVM) [5], a popular algorithm used in machine learning for data classification. Figure 7 shows the pipeline, which reuses earlier components for packet capture, IP and TCP assembly. The `Feature Extractor` component extracts out features for each assembled TCP flow, which are then used by the `SVM Classifier` to detect potentially malicious flows that exhibit DoS behavior. The complete ANALOG specification (in Appendix C) contains 5 rules in 4 components.

The `SVM Classifier` is implemented using libsvm [5], a publicly available SVM implementation. It is written as a component that can be used for other types of traffic analysis beyond our use case. The classifier is first trained using existing traces, a subset of which are tagged as malicious. The classifier depends on fea-

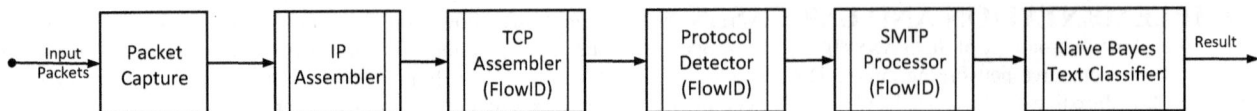

Figure 5: SMTP Spam Detector pipeline

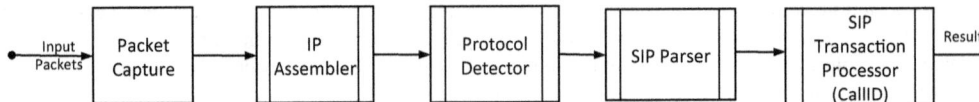

Figure 6: SIP call traffic interception pipeline. Tasks queues and task stealing threads are omitted for brevity.

tures extracted from each TCP flow for determining whether the flow is malicious. This is achieved using the `Feature Extractor` component that maintains features useful for separating malicious from normal TCP flows, such as connection duration, bytes/packets transferred, number of connections in the recent 1 minute to this same port number or IP address. Note that the last feature requires maintaining a global ordered list of TCP connections that is updated by all threads, which potentially limits the scalability of `Feature Extractor` component. We will revisit this issue in 5.2

5. EVALUATION

We perform an experimental evaluation to study SCALANYT-ICS's performance characteristics in extracting fine-grained parallelism. We also validate its capability to correctly implement the packet processing functionality specified in the ANALOG programs.

Our experiments are carried out on a HP ProLiant BL420c machine, that has dual-socket processors. Each processor is an Intel Xeon E5-2450 with 8 cores. In total, the machine has 16 cores, and with hyper-threading support on each core. Each core has a 2 MB L2 cache, and each processor includes a 20 MB L3 cache. The total memory size is 24 GB.

5.1 Experimental Setup

Given 16 cores and support for hyper-threading, all experiments are carried out with up to 32 threads. All experimental results are averaged across 5 runs. Our experiments consist of benchmarking the 4 pipelines described in Section 4.

- **SMTP analysis (Section 4.1)**. As input to this pipeline, we use a packet trace that contains transmission traffic of 50,000 emails with an average size of 150 KB. In this experiment, we assemble and match emails with a simple regular expression, and validate that SCALANYTICS is able to filter out all such emails. This experiment allows us to explore system's throughput when the workload is composed of large packets. (SMTP)

- **SMTP Spam Detector (Section 4.2)**. In this experiment, the input data contains of SMTP traffic traces generated by replaying emails from the *SpamAssassin* dataset [23]. This dataset includes 2155 (3160) emails tagged as spam (non-spam). Each email averages 6.7KB in size. By comparing directly to the original tagged dataset, we observe that our spam detector achieves high accuracy with only 0.3% false positive rate and 4.7% false negative rate in classifying SpamAssassin dataset. (SPAM)

- **SIP analysis (Section 4.3)**. As input, we use a trace file that contains 100,000 SIP sessions, which is generated using SIPp traffic generator [21]. Our analysis pipeline is able to correctly recognize the setup and tear-down of all SIP sessions, decode

and record related information, including duration and URI of each session. (SIP)

- **DoS attack detection (Section 4.4)**. Our final experiment involves the DoS attack traffic. The SVM model used in the pipeline is trained offline using DARPA intrusion detection dataset [8], which contains traces that have been tagged with one of 155 different DoS attacks. We use 5 weeks of traffic traces consisting of 825K TCP connections for training purposes. To validate the model and pipeline, we instantiate the model into the SVM `Classifier` component, and inject 2 weeks of traffic traces into the pipeline. The 2 weeks of traces contain 810K connections, of which 371K are tagged as malicious. Our DoS detection pipeline achieves 95.85% accuracy on 371 thousand attack connections and 99.75% accuracy on 439 thousand non-attack connections. Note the false-positive rate is only 0.25%, which makes the system very useful for deployment in practice. (DOS)

For each pipeline, we execute two load scenarios. Under the *heavy* load scenario, we replay a PCAP file to generate the maximum amount of traffic that can be handled by our pipelines. This saturates our pipelines, maximizes the queueing delays between components, and allows us to explore the limits of our system in terms of its throughput and speedup. Under the *light* load scenario, we rate limit our input traces at 5 Mbps. This allows us to measure response time when the system is not experiencing heavy queueing delays. The response time is hence dominated by just the processing overhead of each component.

In all our experiments, we set the maximum number of in-flight tokens for each pipeline to 1000. We observe that the throughput does not increase significantly beyond 1000 tokens. In addition, the system is able to maintain a reasonably small resident memory footprint.

5.2 Speedup and Throughput

Figure 8 shows the speedup, and Figures 9-12 show the throughput achieved for all pipelines, as the number of threads increases from 1 to 32. Here, we subject all pipelines to the heavy load scenario. The speedup is then compared with the best uniprocessor implementation of each dataflow pipeline, without the added overhead of TBBs. The error bars in Figures 9-12 show the standard deviation obtained across 5 experimental runs.

We make the following observations. First, as the number of threads increases (and hence more cores are utilized), the maximum speedup ranges from 9.0×-11.4× for *SMTP*, *SPAM*, and *SIP*. We observe that linear speedup is not achievable, given that our pipelines have serial as well as parallel context-ordered components, and hence are not embarrassingly parallel. Nevertheless, SCALANYTICS provides a significant speedup over the uniprocessor performance.

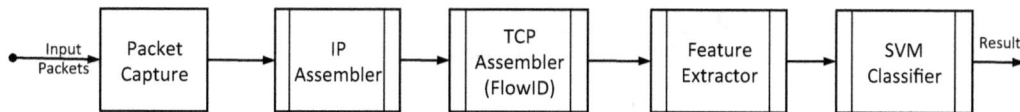

Figure 7: DoS attack detection pipeline

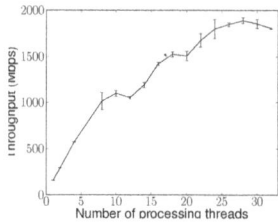

Figure 9: SMTP Analysis Throughput (Mbps).

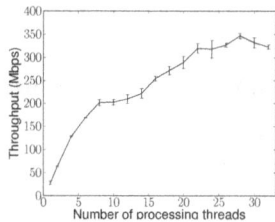

Figure 10: Spam Filter Throughput (Mbps).

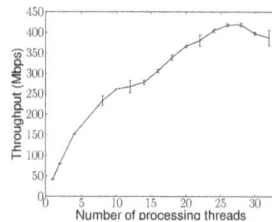

Figure 11: SIP Analysis Throughput (Mbps).

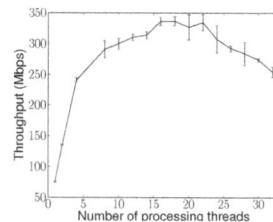

Figure 12: DoS Attack Detection Throughput (Mbps).

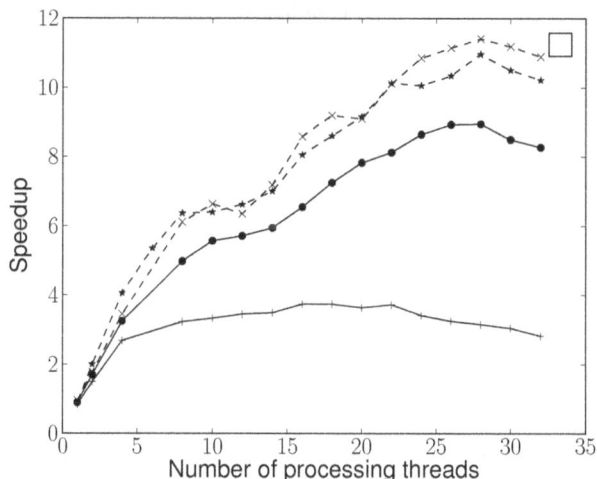

Figure 8: Speedup

The maximum speedup (3.8×) obtained by *DoS* pales in comparison with that of other pipelines. This is because our `Feature Extractor` component in the *DoS* pipeline maintains a global list of all TCP connections within a specified time window. This list is continuously updated for each incoming packet, hence slowing down the entire pipeline.

Table 1 shows the performance statistics for each pipeline execution, under the setting where throughput is maximized for a given number of threads. We observe that the throughput of *SMTP* is as high as 1.89 Gbps (1474 emails per second). The resident memory footprint across all pipelines is below 310 MB, well within the physical memory capacity of the machine. We further observe that dynamic load balancing via task stealing is actively used by our system. On average, between 15.4% and 35.5% of tasks are stolen by idle threads.

To explore the limits of our system, we further experiment with larger number of threads beyond 16 (number of cores). Our Intel processor supports *hyper-threading*, in which two simultaneous execution threads can be maintained by each core sharing the same execution resources. This allows two threads to essentially context-

switch "for free" without involving any heavy-weight kernel operations. In principle, this allows us to parallelize up to 32 threads. We observe that hyper-threading is indeed useful at increasing system throughput in all of our experiments, in particularly the SMTP pipelines that are data-intensive. Pipelines such as *SMTP* benefit more from hyper-threading, given that there is a larger likelihood of L2 cache misses due to the larger payloads and emails assembled. For example, at 28 threads, using the Intel VTune [3] profiler, we observe that on average, the *SMTP* workload incurs 2×-2.5× the number of L2 cache misses as compared to the other pipelines that are processing smaller payloads.

When a L2 cache miss occurs, hyper-threading allows another thread to execute a new task, while the previously executing thread yields the processor to perform out-of-core memory operations. However, beyond 28 threads, we observe that the use of hyper-threading actually backfires due to spin lock contention on the TBB queues by threads running on the same core. Note that such TBB locking contention is not an issue when the number of threads is the same as the number of cores, given that each TBB task stealer owns its own processing core.

Bro comparison. As a basis for comparison, we compare our SMTP analysis throughput against that of the Bro IDS [14]. This allows us to sanity check that SCALANYTICS indeed can outperform an existing Bro deployment on a single core. We use Bro 2.0 [1], and its existing protocol decoder and SMTP module. We configure Bro to use its existing regular expression pattern search operation over the emails. The pattern search operation is similar to our SMTP pipeline. We observe that for the SMTP analysis pipeline, Bro achieves a throughput of 140 Mbps (109 emails/s). Compared to our highest throughput numbers (*SMTP*) in Table 1, SCALANYTICS shows a 13.5× improvements in throughput over Bro. We note that while one can naively scale Bro by running multiple independent instances on a single machine, this approach does not easily support stateful analysis for any of our four applications, since these Bro instances would not be coordinated.

5.3 Latency

Table 2 shows the average per-tuple latency for all pipelines. In addition to the heavy load, we also contrast each pipeline execution to a light load scenario, as described in our experimental setup (Section 5.1). In the table, *Latency* shows the per-tuple latency (in ms), averaged across all tuples that traverse each pipeline.

We further broken down this latency number into the follow-

Pipeline	Threads	Speedup	Throughput	Packets/s	Memory	% TBB steal
SMTP	28	11.4	1892 Mbps (1474 emails/s)	6.2×10^4	310MB	15.4%
SPAM	28	11.0	347 Mbps (4842 emails/s)	1.2×10^5	255MB	20.2%
SIP	28	9.0	419 Mbps (19200 sessions/s)	1.2×10^5	204MB	24.8%
DoS	18	3.8	337 Mbps (1632 flows/s)	1.7×10^6	195MB	35.5%

Table 1: Summary of performance statistics for each pipeline execution with the number of threads where throughput is maximized.

Pipeline	Workload	Latency (ms)	Queueing time (ms)	Processing time (ms)
SMTP	Heavy	6.036	5.227	0.809
	Light	2.338	1.398	0.940
SPAM	Heavy	5.000	3.320	1.680
	Light	1.960	0.275	1.685
SIP	Heavy	0.451	0.246	0.205
	Light	0.236	0.022	0.214
DoS	Heavy	0.520	0.425	0.095
	Light	0.114	0.018	0.096

Table 2: Average per-tuple latency (ms) for each pipeline under the heavy and light load scenarios.

ing components: (1) *Queueing* corresponds to the time each tuple spends in the input buffer of each component; and (2) *Processing* is the actual time spent by each tuple within each component execution.

We observe that under the heavy load scenario, when SCALANYTICS utilizes all cores at or close to 100% for maximum throughput, each tuple incurs on average 0.5 to 6 ms latency across all pipelines. As expected, queueing time dominates the overall latency. Under the light load scenario where queueing time is not a factor, per-tuple latency is modest, requiring only 0.1 to 2.3 ms. Each component typically requires only a fraction of a millisecond to complete execution, demonstrating the overall efficiency of SCALANYTICS. We further observe that for pipelines that are less data intensive (such as SIP and DoS), the per-tuple latency is below 0.5 ms for both heavy and light load scenario.

5.4 Summary of Results

Overall, our SCALANYTICS system is able to implement the SMTP, SPAM, SIP and DoS detection pipelines efficiently. Moreover, SCALANYTICS is able to leverage up to 16 processing cores to achieve speedup ranging from $9.0\times$ to $11.4\times$. Large emails can be processed within 6 ms even under heavy load, at a rate of 1474 emails per second (or 1.89 Gbps) on an inexpensive commodity multi-core machine. Our SMTP analysis throughput outperforms the Bro IDS by up to $13.5\times$. Spam filter assembles and classifies incoming emails at a rate of 4842 emails per second (or 347 Mbps). SIP traffic is similarly identified and analyzed at a rate of $19,200$ SIP calls per second. In the DoS dataflow pipeline, 1632 TCP flows are analyzed per second, and our SVM component exhibits high accuracy on the DARPA dataset. In all our experiments, under the light load scenarios, the per-tuple latency within the pipeline is less than 2.3 ms, and the resident memory footprint of SCALANYTICS is modest (reaching 310 MB for *SMTP*).

6. RELATED WORK

The component-based framework that SCALANYTICS uses is similar to that of the approach taken by Click [11]. We have enhanced Click's dataflow framework to incorporate support for fine-grained parallelism. Our ANALOG language has its root in declarative net-

working [12], which aims to provide a compact domain specific language for implementing network routing protocols. We have extended the original declarative networking language with constructs for specifying and gluing components, as well as invoking existing libraries through the use of user-defined functions. Moreover, our task-stealing framework can be used for executing Datalog programs in parallel, hence exploiting multicore processing capabilities.

Multi-core software router platforms such as RouteBricks [9] similarly leverage multiple processing cores within a cluster environment to scale up packet processing. However, these systems are typically geared towards stateless processing, such as packet forwarding, packet classification, IPSec etc. at the network layer, and are ill-suited for sophisticated workloads such as SPAM and SIP analysis. *Pipeline-parallelism* approaches taken by [27, 6] provide fine-grained parallelism when processing a packet. However, these approaches require run-time system profiling and periodic load-balancing across cores, which is expensive and also susceptible to inaccuracy. Through our use of a task-stealing approach, we are able to achieve dynamic load-balancing and fine-grained parallelism without requiring explicit runtime profiling.

Prior work on multi-core Snort [7] are unable to support stateful processing. Hence, these systems would not be able to support any of our use cases. Gnort [24] uses GPUs for parallelizing packet analysis. However, their approach is only suited for embarrassingly parallel applications, e.g. pattern matching, and is not suited for processing stateful flows. Moreover, the restricted execution model of GPUs (which requires all cores to run the same instructions under the SIMD architecture) limits the flexibility of their system in allowing different cores to perform different processing tasks simultaneously. A recent work[25] uses a hybrid CPU/GPU approach, where GPUs are again limited to embarrassingly parallel pattern matching, while stateful operations are serialized on CPUs on a per-flow basis. This approach lacks the flexibility provided by SCALANYTICS, where pipelines involving a combination of serial, embarrassingly parallel, and parallel context-ordered components can be easily specified. The underlying system automatically load-balances and parallelizes the pipelines, while respecting the semantics of different component types.

Sommer *et al.* [22] proposed a parallelization strategy for Bro. However, the evaluation of this system appears preliminary: most of the results are presented in simulation, and the actual evaluation is smaller in scale compared to our paper (both in scale and use cases). In terms of the execution model, Sommer et al. does a static partitioning of flows across threads, an approach that may result in load imbalance across cores. Scalanytics avoids such load imbalance issues through the use of the task stealing framework, where each task represents an execution instance of a tuple within a component

A key contribution of SCALANYTICS is to provide a programming platform that allows us to assemble component modules out of existing packet analysis platforms for parallel execution, as we have demonstrated in Section 4. We note that intrusion detection systems (IDS) such as Bro and Snort achieves only a subset of the functionality provided by Scalanytics. SCALANYTICS enables traffic analytics to be customized and parallelized, and has applications beyond IDS, for instance, allowing machine-learning based classification of application-layer content at the network layer, performing spam email detection, measuring VoIP usage statistics so as to customize traffic shaping policies, etc.

7. CONCLUSION

This paper presents the design and implementation of SCALANYTICS, a scalable packet processing platform that supports (1) stateful application-layer traffic analytics, (2) high degrees of configuration through reusable components in a dataflow framework and a high-level declarative configuration language, and (3) parallelism and automatic load-balancing through the use of a task-stealing framework integrated into a declarative networking engine. We have developed a prototype of SCALANYTICS, and our evaluations demonstrate its scalability as well as functionality. As ongoing work, we are enhancing our language and runtime system to enable directed acyclic graphs beyond linear pipelines. We are integrating our system with existing software-defined networking platforms such as OpenFlow [4], so that the analysis output from SCALANYTICS can be used to actuate flows in the network. We are also working towards a distributed implementation that allows pipelines to be constructed across components running on different machines.

Acknowledgements. This project is supported in part by NSF grants IIS-0812270, CAREER CNS-0845552, DARPA SAFER award N66001-C-4020, and a AFOSR Young Investigator Award FA9550-12-1-0327.

8. REFERENCES

[1] Bro Intrusion Detection System. http://bro-ids.org.
[2] GNU oSIP library. http://www.gnu.org/software/osip.
[3] Intel VTune Amplifier XE 2013. http://software.intel.com/en-us/intel-vtune-amplifier-xe/.
[4] OpenFlow. http://www.openflow.org/.
[5] CHANG, C.-C., AND LIN, C.-J. LIBSVM: A library for support vector machines. *ACM Transactions on Intelligent Systems and Technology 2* (2011), 27:1–27:27. Software available at http://www.csie.ntu.edu.tw/~cjlin/libsvm.
[6] CHEN, B., AND MORRIS, R. Flexible control of parallelism in a multiprocessor pc router. In *USENIX ATC* (2001).
[7] CHEN, X., WU, Y., XU, L., XUE, Y., AND LI, J. Para-snort: A multi-thread snort on multi-core ia platform. *Proceedings of Parallel and Distributed Computing and Systems (PDCS)* (2009).

[8] DARPA INTRUSION DETECTION DATASET. http://www.ll.mit.edu/mission/communications/ist/corpora/ideval/data/index.html.
[9] DOBRESCU, M., EGI, N., ARGYRAKI, K., CHUN, B.-G., FALL, K., ET AL. RouteBricks: Exploiting Parallelism To Scale Software Routers. In *SOSP* (2009).
[10] FRIGO, M., LEISERSON, C. E., AND RANDALL, K. H. The Implementation of the Cilk-5 Multithreaded Language. In *PLDI* (1998).
[11] KOHLER, E., MORRIS, R., CHEN, B., JANNOTTI, J., AND KAASHOEK, M. F. The Click Modular Router. *ACM Trans. Comput. Syst.* (Aug. 2000).
[12] LOO, B. T., CONDIE, T., GAROFALAKIS, M., GAY, D. E., HELLERSTEIN, J. M., MANIATIS, P., RAMAKRISHNAN, R., ROSCOE, T., AND STOICA, I. Declarative Networking. *CACM* (2009).
[13] MUKKAMALA, S., AND SUNG, A. H. Detecting Denial of Service Attacks Using Support Vector Machines. In *IEEE International Conference on Fuzzy Systems (IEEE FUZZ)* (2003).
[14] PAXSON, V. Bro: a System for Detecting Network Intruders in Real-Time. *Computer Networks 31*, 23-24 (1999), 2435–2463.
[15] PRZYMUSINSKI, T. C. *On the declarative semantics of deductive databases and logic programs.* Morgan Kaufmann Publishers Inc., San Francisco, CA, USA, 1988, pp. 193–216.
[16] RAMAKRISHNAN, R., AND ULLMAN, J. D. A survey of research on deductive database systems. *Journal of Logic Programming 23* (1993), 125–149.
[17] RAPIDNET: A DECLARATIVE TOOLKIT FOR RAPID NETWORK SIMULATION AND EXPERIMENTATION. http://netdb.cis.upenn.edu/rapidnet/.
[18] REINDERS, J. Intel Thread Building Blocks. In *OReilly Associates* (2007).
[19] SAHAMI, M., DUMAIS, S., HECKERMAN, D., AND HORVITZ, E. A bayesian approach to filtering junk e-mail. In *Learning for Text Categorization: Papers from the 1998 workshop* (1998), vol. 62, Madison, Wisconsin: AAAI Technical Report WS-98-05, pp. 98–105.
[20] SIP: SESSION INITIATION PROTOCOL. http://www.ietf.org/rfc/rfc3261.txt.
[21] SIPP OPEN SOURCE TEST TOOL / TRAFFIC GENERATOR FOR THE SIP PROTOCOL. http://sipp.sourceforge.net/.
[22] SOMMER, R., PAXSON, V., AND WEAVER, N. An architecture for exploiting multi-core processors to parallelize network intrusion prevention. *Concurrency and Computation: Practice and Experience* (2009).
[23] SPAMASSASSIN DATASET. http://spamassassin.apache.org/publiccorpus.
[24] VASILIADIS, G., ANTONATOS, S., POLYCHRONAKIS, M., MARKATOS, E. P., AND IOANNIDIS, S. Gnort: High Performance Network Intrusion Detection Using Graphics Processors. In *RAID* (2008).
[25] VASILIADIS, G., POLYCHRONAKIS, M., AND IOANNIDIS, S. Midea: a multi-parallel intrusion detection architecture. In *Proceedings of the 18th ACM conference on Computer and communications security* (New York, NY, USA, 2011), CCS '11, ACM, pp. 297–308.
[26] WOJTCZUK, R. http://libnids.sourceforge.net/.

[27] WOLF, T., WENG, N., AND TAI, C.-H. Runtime support for multicore packet processing systems. *Network, IEEE 21*, 4 (2007), 29 –37.

APPENDIX

A. SMTP EXAMPLE IN ANALOG

```
/* Assemble IP Fragments
   Takes as an input raw IP fragments and emits
   assembled IP payload. */
component ip_assembler(parallel) {
ip1  ip_pkt(@N,PKT, IP_PKT, SRC_IP2,
            DST_IP2, TRANSPORT_PROTOCOL) :-
    input(@N, PKT, SRC_IP, DST_IP),
    IP_PKT = f_processIpFrag(PKT),
    TRANSPORT_PROTOCOL = f_getTransportProtocol(IP_PKT),
    SRC_IP2 = f_getSrcIPAddr(IP_PKT, TRANSPORT_PROTOCOL),
    DST_IP2 = f_getDstIPAddr(IP_PKT, TRANSPORT_PROTOCOL),
    P = f_traffic(PKT, "input").
ip2  tcp_pkt(@N, PKT, IP_PKT, SRC_IP, DST_IP, FLOW_ID) :-
    ip_pkt(@N, PKT, IP_PKT, SRC_IP,
        DST_IP, TRANSPORT_PROTOCOL),
    TRANSPORT_PROTOCOL == "TCP",
    FLOW_ID = f_getTCPFlowId(SRC_IP, DST_IP).  }


/* Assemble TCP payload.
   Takes IP payload as input and emits assembled TCP messages. */
component tcp_process(parallel_context_order,
                      context_keys(tcp_pkt(6))) {
tcp1 tcp_stream(@N, PKT, SRC_IP,
                DST_IP, FLOW_ID, TCP_MESSAGE) :-
    tcp_pkt(@N, PKT, IP_PKT, SRC_IP, DST_IP, FLOW_ID),
    TCP_MESSAGE = f_processTCP(IP_PKT).  }

/* Detect TCP user protocol, e.g. SMTP. */
component tcp_protocol_detector(parallel_context_order,
                      context_keys(tcp_stream(5))) {
det1 detected_tcp_protocol(@N, PKT, SRC_IP, DST_IP,
    FLOW_ID, TCP_MESSAGE, PROTOCOL) :-
    tcp_stream(@N, PKT, SRC_IP, DST_IP, FLOW_ID, TCP_MESSAGE),
    PROTOCOL = f_processTCPDetector(TCP_MESSAGE, FLOW_ID).
det2 smtp_segment(@N, PKT, SRC_IP, DST_IP, FLOW_ID, TCP_MESSAGE) :-
    detected_tcp_protocol(@N, PKT, SRC_IP, DST_IP,
    FLOW_ID, TCP_MESSAGE, PROTOCOL),
    PROTOCOL == "SMTP".  }


/* Process SMTP message.
   Assemble e-mails from multiple SMTP segments. */
component smtp_processor(parallel_context_order,
                      context_keys(smtp_segment(5))) {
smtp1 smtp_mail(@N, PKT, SRC_IP, DST_IP, FLOW_ID, MAIL) :-
    smtp_segment(@N, PKT, SRC_IP, DST_IP, FLOW_ID, TCP_MESSAGE),
    MAIL = f_processSMTPSegment(TCP_MESSAGE, FLOW_ID),
    MAIL != "".  }

/* Match payload with a regular expression */
component regex_match(parallel) {
regex1 positive_match(@N, PKT, SRC_IP,
    DST_IP, FLOW_ID, MAIL, MATCH) :-
    smtp_mail(@N, PKT, SRC_IP, DST_IP, FLOW_ID, MAIL),
    MATCH = f_match(MAIL, "hello"),
    MATCH == "true".  }
```

B. SIP EXAMPLE IN ANALOG

```
/* Assemble IP Fragments
   Takes as an input raw IP fragments and emits
   assembled IP payload. */
component ip_assembler(parallel) {
ip1  ip_pkt(@N, PKT, IP_PKT, SRC_IP2,
        DST_IP2, TRANSPORT_PROTOCOL) :-
    input(@N, PKT, SRC_IP, DST_IP),
    IP_PKT = f_processIpFrag(PKT),
    TRANSPORT_PROTOCOL =
        f_getTransportProtocol(IP_PKT),
    SRC_IP2 = f_getSrcIPAddr(IP_PKT,
        TRANSPORT_PROTOCOL),
    DST_IP2 = f_getDstIPAddr(IP_PKT,
        TRANSPORT_PROTOCOL),
    P = f_traffic(PKT, "input").
ip2 udp_pkt(@N, PKT, IP_PKT, SRC_IP, DST_IP, FLOW_ID) :-
    ip_pkt(@N, PKT, IP_PKT, SRC_IP,
        DST_IP, TRANSPORT_PROTOCOL),
    TRANSPORT_PROTOCOL == "UDP",
    FLOW_ID = f_getUDPFlowId(SRC_IP, DST_IP). }

/* Detect UDP user protocol, e.g. SIP */
component udp_protocol_detector(parallel) {
ud1 detected_udp_protocol(@N, PKT, IP_PKT, SRC_IP,
        DST_IP, FLOW_ID, PROTOCOL) :-
    udp_pkt(@N, PKT, IP_PKT, SRC_IP,
        DST_IP, FLOW_ID),
    PROTOCOL = f_processUDPDetector(IP_PKT).
ud2 sip_segment(@N, PKT, IP_PKT, SRC_IP,
        DST_IP, FLOW_ID) :-
    detected_udp_protocol(@N, PKT, IP_PKT, SRC_IP,
        DST_IP, FLOW_ID, PROTOCOL),
    PROTOCOL == "SIP". }

/* Parse the SIP payload and emit SIP event */
component sip_parse(parallel) {
s1 sip_event(@N, PKT, EVENT, FLOW_ID) :-
        sip_segment(@N, PKT, IP_PKT, SRC_IP,
        DST_IP, FLOW_ID),
        EVENT = f_sipEventParse(IP_PKT).
s2 sip_event_callid(@N, PKT, EVENT, CALLID) :-
        sip_event(@N, PKT, EVENT, FLOW_ID),
        CALLID = f_sipcallid(EVENT).
}

/* Process the parsed SIP message */
component sip_process(parallel_context_order,
            context_keys(sip_event_callid(4))) {
sip1 sip_session_event(@N, PKT, SESSION_EVENT, CALLID):-
        sip_event_callid(@N, PKT, EVENT, CALLID),
        SESSION_EVENT = f_sipEventProcess(EVENT). }
```

C. DOS EXAMPLE IN ANALOG

```
/* Assemble IP Fragments
   Takes as an input raw IP fragments and emits
   assembled IP payload. */
component ip_assemble(parallel) {
ip1  ip_pkt(@N, PKT, IP_PKT, SRC_IP2, DST_IP2, TRANSPORT_PROTOCOL) :-
    input(@N, PKT, SRC_IP, DST_IP), IP_PKT := f_ProcessIpFrag(PKT),
    TRANSPORT_PROTOCOL := f_GetTransportProtocol(IP_PKT),
    SRC_IP2 := f_GetSrcIPAddr(IP_PKT, TRANSPORT_PROTOCOL),
    DST_IP2 := f_GetDstIPAddr(IP_PKT, TRANSPORT_PROTOCOL),
    P := f_Traffic(PKT, "input").
ip2 tcp_pkt(@N, PKT, IP_PKT, SRC_IP, DST_IP, FLOW_ID) :-
    ip_pkt(@N, PKT, IP_PKT, SRC_IP, DST_IP, TRANSPORT_PROTOCOL),
    TRANSPORT_PROTOCOL == "TCP",
    FLOW_ID := f_GetTCPFlowId(SRC_IP, DST_IP). }

/* Assemble TCP payload.
   Takes IP payload as input and emits assembled TCP messages. */
component tcp_process(serial_context_order,
                context_keys(tcp_pkt(6))) {
tcp1 tcp_stream(@N, PKT, SRC_IP, DST_IP, FLOW_ID, TCP_MESSAGE) :-
    tcp_pkt(@N, PKT, IP_PKT, SRC_IP, DST_IP, FLOW_ID),
    TCP_MESSAGE := f_ProcessTCP(IP_PKT). }

/* Detect malicious TCP flows
   Extract features and classify TCP flow using support vector machine*/
component tcp_ddos_detect(parallel) {
ddos1 tcp_stream_feature(@N, SRC_IP, DST_IP, FEATURE) :-
    tcp_stream(@N, PKT, SRC_IP, DST_IP, FLOW_ID, TCP_MESSAGE),
    FEATURE := f_GetTCPFeature(TCP_MESSAGE).
ddos2 tcp_stream_attack(@N, SRC_IPSTR, DST_IPSTR) :-
    tcp_stream_feature(@N, SRC_IP, DST_IP, FEATURE),
    ISATTACK := f_DetectAttack(FEATURE),
    ISATTACK == "true", SRC_IPSTR := f_IPtoSTR(SRC_IP),
    DST_IPSTR := f_IPtoSTR(DST_IP). }
```

CamCubeOS: A Key-based Network Stack for 3D Torus Cluster Topologies

Paolo Costa   Austin Donnelly   Greg O'Shea   Antony Rowstron

Microsoft Research Cambridge, UK
{pcosta,austind,gregos,antr}@microsoft.com

ABSTRACT

Cluster fabric interconnects that use 3D torus topologies are increasingly being deployed in data center clusters. In our prior work, we demonstrated that by using these topologies and letting applications implement custom routing protocols and perform operations on path, it is possible to increase performance and simplify development. However, these benefits cannot be achieved using mainstream point-to-point networking stacks such as TCP/IP or MPI, which hide the underlying topology and do not allow the implementation of any in-network operations.

In this paper we describe CamCubeOS, a novel key-based communication stack, purposely designed from scratch for 3D torus fabric interconnects. We note that many of the applications used in clusters are key-based. Therefore, we designed CamCubeOS to natively support key-based operations. We select a virtual topology that perfectly matches the underlying physical topology and we use the keyspace to expose the physical locality, thus avoiding the typical overhead incurred by overlay-based approaches.

We report on our experience in building several applications on top of CamCubeOS and we evaluate their performance and feasibility using a prototype and large-scale simulations.

Categories and Subject Descriptors

C.2.4 [**Computer Communication Networks**]: Distributed Systems; H.3.4 [**Information Systems**]: Information Storage and Retrieval

General Terms

Algorithms, Design, Performance

Keywords

Data center clusters, 3D torus topologies, key-based routing, in-network processing

1. INTRODUCTION

The recent acquisitions of Cray Interconnect by Intel [45] and SeaMicro by AMD [41] confirmed the increasing trend of deploying HPC-inspired fabric interconnects in general-purpose data center clusters [49]. This trend has been mostly driven by the opportunity of drastically reducing space and power consumption. For instance, the SeaMicro SM10000-XE appliance has three times the density of today's servers and consumes half of the power while providing 12x more bandwidth [46]. An additional feature of these interconnect fabrics is that the switching functionality is distributed across the servers, typically using a 3D torus topology [29], like the one in Figure 1. This provides a tight integration between servers and network.

We explored the opportunities provided by this integration in the context of general purpose data centers [11] and we showed the benefits of implementing custom routing protocols [1] and performing in-network packet processing [10]. Unfortunately, most of these benefits are lost with current platforms, which use traditional networking stacks such as TCP/IP and MPI, which are oriented towards point-to-point server communication and completely hide the underlying topology, thus inhibiting the implementation of any in-network functionality.

To address these shortcomings, we developed CamCubeOS, a novel networking stack for 3D torus topologies. Many of the applications that run in a cluster are key-based, e.g., [6,9,14,15,24,26], using keys to identify data or users. The CamCubeOS API has been designed to make it easier to develop these applications by supporting key-based routing along with traditional point-to-point, server-based, communication. CamCubeOS provides an API similar to the Key-Based Routing API (KBR) [12], which has been successfully used in many distributed hash tables (DHTs) [34,38]. The main benefit of KBR is that the destination of a packet is represented by a key, which is mapped to a reachable server and is re-mapped to another server in case of failure. This means that, unlike for server-based communication in which the packet is dropped if the destination server is unreachable, with key-based routing the packet is *always* delivered because the system ensures that there will always be a valid mapping between keys and servers.

Current data center thinking is dominated by networking technology and abstractions designed to support the Internet and enterprise networking. CamCubeOS challenges these views, and demonstrates that the combination of HPC-inspired fabrics and key-based abstractions makes writing applications easier and achieves higher performance than traditional setups.

A major issue when using key-based routing is how to expose the physical topology through the keyspace so as to minimize path stretch. CamCubeOS addresses this problem by making the physical and virtual topologies the same. The topology defines a keyspace: each server is assigned a coordinate in the 3D space defined by its location and neighbors in the 3D torus.

The workloads generally used in HPC are batch-based and computationally intensive. Normally, HPC clusters are *vertically* partitioned, i.e., applications are allocated on disjoint subsets of nodes. In contrast, CamCubeOS focuses on the workloads typically run in general-purpose data center clusters such as data analytics jobs, web services, and data stores. It uses a *horizontal* partitioning of the services; every server runs an instance of every service. We built a number of services on top of CamCubeOS, including a file distribution service, a `memcached`-inspired key-value cache layer, an extensible persistent key-value store, and Camdoop [10], a MapReduce-like system that, in common scenarios, achieves up to two orders of magnitude higher performance than Hadoop [42] and Dryad [23]. We also implemented a TCP/IP service to support legacy applications.

The CamCubeOS runtime controls when packets are sent on a link and uses fair or weighted-queues to control the number of packets that each service can send on a link. This provides good link bandwidth partitioning between services, which services can exploit to implement their own queuing policies as well as implementing their own transport protocols and routing protocols [1] if needed.

To evaluate the performance of our stack, we built a 27-server (3x3x3) 3D Torus prototype, using commodity servers interconnected through 1 Gbps Ethernet cables. Clearly, our prototype cannot match the performance of dedicated SeaMicro appliances and we use it as a proof-of-concept. We compared the performance of applications built on top of CamCubeOS against the performance of equivalent applications implemented using TCP/IP over the switch. The results demonstrates that the benefits of using CamCubeOS outweighs the overhead of servers participating in packet forwarding. For instance, the key-value store outperforms an equivalent switch-based application by a factor of 1.93 and the file distribution service achieves a throughput per member of 5.66 Gbps, which is more than five times higher than what can be achieved in a traditional, switch-based, setup.

2. BACKGROUND: CAMCUBE

CamCubeOS is part of CamCube, a research project that explores the benefits of using 3D torus topologies to interconnect clusters of servers for general-purpose applications.

2.1 Motivation

A 3D torus (or k-ary 3-cube) [29] can be visualized as a wrapped 3D mesh, with each server connected to six other servers, similar to the one depicted in Figure 1. This is a popular topology, used in high performance computing, e.g., the IBM BlueGene/L and Cray XT3/Red Storm, and in cluster appliances, e.g., the SeaMicro SM10000-XE. Its properties are well understood and it provides a high degree of multi-path, which makes the topology very resilient to link and server failure. There are also well known wiring

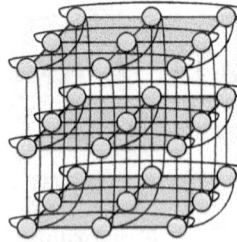

Figure 1: A 3-ary 3-cube (or 3D torus).

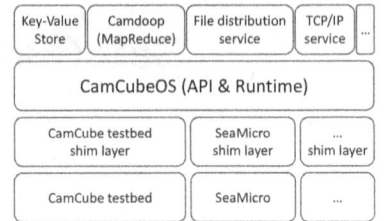

Figure 2: The CamCube software architecture.

techniques that allow efficient inter-connections using only short cables, each cable traversing a single server at most [2].

A key benefit of using a direct-connect topology like the 3D torus is that applications can implement their own custom routing protocols. Typically, both in switched-based network and HPC clusters, only one routing protocol, e.g., the IS-IS link-state protocol [28] for the former and a variant of greedy routing protocols [2,36] for the latter, is available to applications. We demonstrated that in many cases running a custom routing protocol is beneficial both from the application and network perspective [1]. For example, applications that need to exchange large amount of data between two servers may be interested in using as many disjoint paths as possible so as to maximize the throughput between the two servers. In contrast, multicast applications desire to minimize the number of links used by the spanning tree to reduce the impact over network resources. We showed that custom routing protocols enable higher application-level performance, even when used concurrently, and reduce the network link stress.

A further advantage, beside enabling implementing custom *forwarding* decisions at each hop, is the ability of *processing* packets on-path. This means that applications can intercept packets on every server along the path from the source to the destination, inspect the *payload* (as opposed to just the *header*) of the packet and decide whether to drop the packet (possibly after storing its content in memory), to forward as is, to modify part of its payload, or to create a new packet. This functionality is really powerful as it enables sophisticated on-path operations, e.g., opportunistic caching or in-network aggregation [10].

2.2 CamCube Architecture

To simplify building CamCube applications, we developed CamCubeOS, a novel networking stack, which represents the core contribution of this paper. The overall CamCube software architecture is depicted in Figure 2. The top boxes represent the applications and services that we have implemented for CamCube. These include fully-fledged applications, e.g., a key-value store (described in Section 5) and a MapReduce-like system (Section 6.2) but also lower-level services like the file distribution service (Section 6.1) that can be used by other applications to disseminate large files to a subset of the CamCube servers. We also developed a TCP/IP service (Section 6.3) that allows to run *unmodified* TCP/IP applications on top of CamCubeOS.

CamCubeOS consists of two parts: the CamCubeOS API, which exposes a key- and server-based interface, and the runtime, which handles the packet outbound queues and demultiplexes packets among applications and services. We provide more details about both the API and the runtime in the next section.

To communicate between the CamCubeOS runtime and the specific underlying cluster hardware we use a shim layer. We have implemented a shim layer for the prototype 27-server testbed that we used in our evaluation and we are currently developing one for a SeaMicro appliance. The only functionality that we require from the underlying platform is the ability to send and receive packets to/from the six neighbors. No further functionality (e.g., multi-hop routing protocol) is assumed. Therefore, we expect that CamCubeOS be able to support most (if not all) 3D torus-based platforms currently available on the market with limited effort.

3. CamCubeOS OVERVIEW

We first describe the CamCubeOS API and then highlight the main features of the CamCubeOS runtime.

3.1 API

An early choice in the design of the CamCubeOS API was to support multi-hop key-based communication along with the traditional server-based communication. Services provide the reference to the packet (represented as a byte array) to be transmitted and specify whether the final destination is a key or server address. In the former case, the packet is always delivered to the server that is currently responsible for the given key. If, instead, a server address is used as destination, the packet is delivered only if that server is reachable, otherwise it is dropped. The motivation for selecting this model is that we wanted to make it easier to write key-based applications and, in particular, to simplify failure recovery.

One possible approach could have been to just run any structured overlay, e.g., Chord [38] or Pastry [34], over the underlying 3D torus network. This, however, would have created a mismatch between the overlay virtual topology and the physical network topology because each hop in the overlay would correspond to multiple links in the physical network. This would destroy locality, by increasing the physical hop count between two overlay neighbors, and induce fate sharing of links [20]. Typical solutions to this usually reduce failure resilience of the overlay, and still do not fully address the mismatch between the physical and virtual topologies. In contrast, in CamCubeOS we chose a virtual topology that matches the underlying 3D torus physical topology. We selected the virtual topology used by the Content Addressable Network (CAN) [33] structured overlay, a 3D torus topology. Hence, each link in the virtual overlay represents a single link in the physical topology.

In contrast to most structured overlays, node identifiers in CAN are not constant, and change over time as nodes join and fail. Many other structured overlays, like Chord and Pastry, have static node identifiers. This is necessary in CAN because it uses greedy routing over the keyspace, so failures with static identifiers can cause voids in the keyspace, that cause greedy routing to fail. In a structured overlay, non-static node identifiers are not ideal because the applications need to handle the mapping between nodes and keyspace, which usually requires migration of keys, as well as making maintaining consistency harder. In CamCubeOS we want the identifier of servers to be fixed. We assign a server identifier using its location in the initial physical topology. We use the 3D torus to define a 3D coordinate

space. When a CamCube is first commissioned, a bootstrap service assigns each server an (x, y, z) coordinate representing its offset within the 3D torus from an arbitrary origin. The symmetry of the 3D torus means that any server can be the origin: it has no special role other than having the address *(0,0,0)*. The bootstrap service on each server exposes the coordinate and dimensions of the 3D torus to local services. It also provides a mapping between the one-hop neighbors and their coordinates. Intuitively, the coordinates of one-hop neighbors will each differ in only one axis and by +/-1 modulo the axis size. The assigned coordinate is the address of the server and, once assigned, it is never changed.

CamCube services are partitioned horizontally, i.e., all servers run an instance of the service. This means that the services running on all servers on the path to the destination are able to intercept and arbitrarily modify a packet or even drop it and create a new packet. For instance, a cache service can intercept a query packet along the path and, if a cache hit occurs, it can halt its propagation and immediately reply to the originating server.

Although the multi-hop routing functionality can be used to deliver packets end-to-end, in many cases, the key or server address specified is not the final destination of the packet but it is an intermediate destination. This allows services to implement custom routing protocols by leveraging the default routing protocol only between two intermediate destinations (possibly just between 1-hop neighbors). For instance, our key-value store (described in Section 5) uses intermediate destinations as cache locations and adopts a custom routing protocol to ensure that both query and reply packets are routed through them.

Services can also query the CamCubeOS API to retrieve up-to-date information about reachable and unreachable servers, in case they need fine-grained control over routing.

Finally, services can access the custom APIs offered by other services running on the same server. For example, a de-duplication backup service could use in its implementation the functionality offered by the key-value store and the file distribution service in addition to the standard CamCubeOS API.

3.2 Keyspace Management

An important aspect of the CamCubeOS API is the keyspace management, especially in the presence of failures.

By default all keys are considered as 160-bit keys, but only the least significant 64 bits are used when routing a message to a key. Each key is mapped to a *root* server that is responsible for that key. The highest bits[1] of the 64-bit key generate an (x, y, z) coordinate. If the server with this coordinate–hereafter referred to as the *home server*–is reachable then it is the root.

If the home server is unreachable, then a naive solution would be to simply map the failed coordinate onto another single coordinate. Although this would preserve correctness, it would incur significant load skew because a single server would now be responsible for twice the number of keys of the other servers. A more elegant and efficient solution is to distribute the keys that the failed server was root for, over the set of one-hop neighbors. This maintains locality

---

[1]In our deployment, we use 4 bits per dimension, which can encode clusters of up to $(2^4)^3 = 4,096$ servers. If 8 bits per dimension were used, we could support clusters comprising more than 16 million servers.

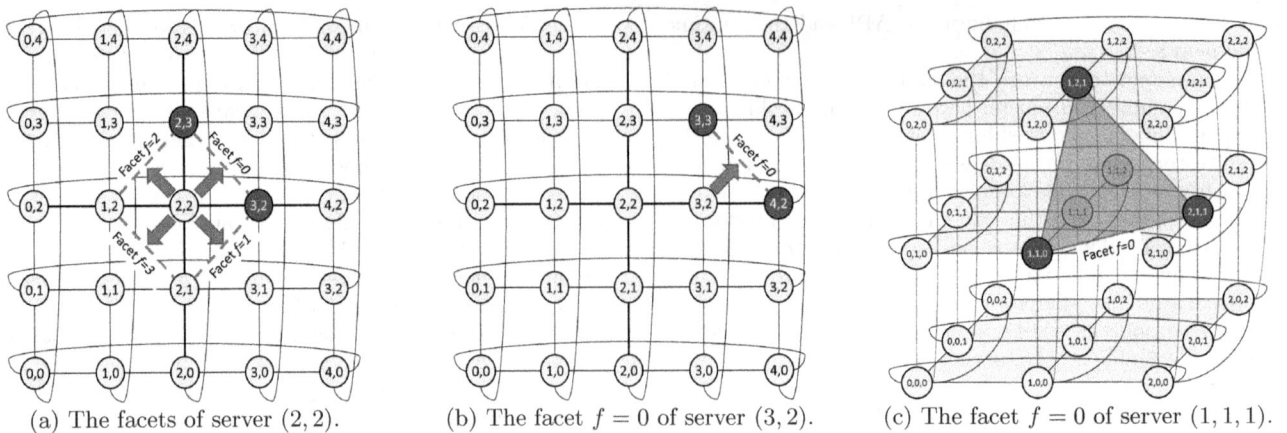

(a) The facets of server $(2,2)$.   (b) The facet $f = 0$ of server $(3,2)$.   (c) The facet $f = 0$ of server $(1,1,1)$.

Figure 3: The facets in the 2D and 3D torus. Dark circles indicates the servers lying on facet 0.

and reduces load skew. To do this, when a root server is unreachable, the remainder of the 64-bit key is used to determine the coordinate of the server which will be the root. Conceptually, the 64-bit key can be thought as an (x, y, z, w) coordinate in a 4D space. The first three dimensions, x, y, and z, identify the home server while the fourth dimension w is used to select the neighbor to remap the key to if the current root server becomes unreachable.

This key-to-server mapping in the presence of failures should achieve the following design goals:

- *G1: Correctness.* If there is at least one server that has not failed, every key must have a valid (i.e., not failed) root server.
- *G2: Efficiency.* In case of failure, the keys of the failed server should be remapped to nearby servers (to achieve *locality*) while minimizing *load skew*.

A straw-man approach would be to simply represent the fourth dimension w as a ring like in Chord [38] and then assign each key range to a different reachable server. While this would satisfy *G1* and would ensure good key distribution, it would completely disregard locality (*G2*), since the keys of a failed server F would end up on all servers, including severs located several hops away from F.

In CamCubeOS, we implemented a novel keyspace management solution that ensures correctness and that achieves high locality with a good load distribution. CamCubeOS provides a function `GetServersForKey(key,r)` that given a `key` and an integer `r` returns an ordered list of *reachable* servers $\mathcal{L} = [S_0, S_1, \ldots, S_{r-1}]$ with the following property. S_0 is the server that is currently responsible for `key`. S_1, is the one that would become responsible for `key` if S_0 failed. Likewise, S_2 would take over the key if both S_0 and S_1 should fail and so on.

If `GetServersForKey` is invoked with `r=1`, it just returns the current root of `key`. Invoking the function with higher values of `r` can be used to implement n-way replication. For example, `GetServersForKey(key,n)` returns the list $\mathcal{L}$ of the n servers that should store a replica of the object indexed by `key`. In this way, if the primary replica becomes unreachable, the new root server for `key` is one of the secondary replicas.

We now explain how we implemented the function `GetServersForKey` in CamCubeOS and how it achieves both design goals *G1* and *G2*. To simplify the exposition, we

start by describing it using a 2D torus and then we extend it to cover the 3D case.

2D torus. We first introduce the notion of a *facet*. Let us consider a home server $S = (x, y)$ and let us divide the coordinate space into four sub-spaces (i.e., squares in the 2D cases), each with a corner located in S. We call facets the lines connecting the neighbors of S in each sub-space. Figure 3(a) shows the four facets of server $(2,2)$. The dark neighbors, $(2,3)$ and $(3,2)$, are the ones belonging to facet $f = 0$.

Given a key $k = (x, y, w)$, we can use some of the bits of w to select one of the four facets. Once we have selected a facet f, e.g., $f = 0$, we need to choose the order o in which the two neighbors should appear in $\mathcal{L}$. We can reuse the remainder bits of w to decide whether to pick first the neighbor on the x axis and then the one on the y axis ($o = xy$) or vice versa ($o = yx$). As an example, consider the scenario depicted in Figure 3(a) and a key $k = (2, 2, w)$ and suppose that the bits in w yield $f = 0$ and $o = xy$. In this case, the home server would be $S_0 = (2, 2)$ and S_1 and S_2 would be, respectively, $(3, 2)$ (i.e., the neighbor on the x axis) and $(2, 3)$ (i.e., the neighbor on the y axis).

The next servers S_i are retrieved by proceeding recursively in a breadth-first fashion. S_1 is taken as home server and its two neighbors on the chosen facet are appended at the end of the list. Next, the two neighbors on S_2's facet are appended to the list, unless they are already part of it. The process terminates when either **r** servers are retrieved or all reachable servers have been visited at least once. In our example, if we consider $S_1 = (3, 2)$ as the new home server and assume again $f = 0$ and $o = xy$, we have $S_3 = (4, 2)$ and then $S_4 = (3, 3)$ (see Figure 3(b)). Therefore, assuming no failures, `GetServersForKey(k,5)` would return the following ordered list of servers: $\mathcal{L} = [(2, 2), (3, 2), (2, 3), (4, 2), (3, 3)]$.

Since the keyspace is wrapped, eventually all servers will be visited at least once, which satisfies *G1*. Further, it is easy to see that this strategy ensures that, in case of failure, all the keys of the failed server are equally distributed among its four 1-hop neighbors (assuming all of them are reachable), which fulfills both the locality and the load-balance requirements of *G2*. This is particularly important if n-way replication is used because the closer the secondary replicas are to the primary, the higher bandwidth would be available.

In the 2D case, we have four facets per server and two possible orderings between the two neighbors of each facet.

Therefore, in total, for a home server $S = (x, y)$ we have eight possible different sequences of r-servers that can be generated, all starting from S. For efficiency, we pre-compute offline a lookup table containing these sequences and then, given a key $k = (x, y, w)$, we use the index $i = (w \mod 8)$ to retrieve the correct sequence for k.

3D torus. The main difference between the 2D and the 3D case is that in the latter the facet is a plane rather than a line. This is depicted in Figure 3(c), which shows the facet $f = 0$ for the home server $(1, 1, 1)$. This means that instead of two neighbors per facet, we now have three neighbors per facet. Therefore, there are six (as opposed to two for the 2D case) possible orderings to select these neighbors, corresponding to the six permutations of xyz. Further, instead of four facets per home server, we now have eight facets, one for each of the equal-size sub-cubes in which the cube can be divided. This yields $8 \times 6 = 48$ (as opposed to eight in the 2D case) possible entries in the lookup table.

3.3 Runtime

The runtime component is responsible for handling packet queuing and forwarding, and sharing the network resources across services. As already mentioned, CamCube services run on every server. Services are independent and can be registered and de-registered. Each service has a unique identifier. The packet header is a service identifier and when the runtime receives a packet it uses this to de-multiplex the packet and deliver it to the correct service. In most cases, services include their own identifier in the packet header but they could also include the identifier of a different service if the packet needs be received by a different service.

The runtime uses a simple link-state routing protocol and shortest paths to support key- and server-based multi-hop routing. Control traffic for maintaining the link-state is negligible, as failures are comparatively rare. When packets need be transmitted, the multi-hop routing protocol returns the set of outbound links that can be used to forward the packet towards a key or server, as required. In general, due to the high-degree of multi-path in the 3D torus, for a given destination the routing protocol is likely to yield multiple outbound links. Instead of arbitrarily selecting one of this, e.g., randomly, the runtime keeps track of the set of valid outbound links and transmits the packet over the link that becomes available first.

Each service maintains its own outbound packet queue. Services are polled, in turn, by the runtime for packets to be sent on each of the six outbound links, when there is capacity on the link. This means there is implicit per-link congestion control; if a link is at capacity then a service will not be polled for packets for that link. A service is able to control link queue sizes, packet drop policy, and packet prioritization. We provide a number of parameterizable default queue implementations, but services are free to implement their own. By default the runtime provides a fair queuing mechanism, meaning that each service is polled at the same frequency, and if s services wish to send packets on the same link then each will get $1/s$th of the link bandwidth. Partitioning the per-link bandwidth, combined with the fact that all packets on a single link are explicitly sourced by only two servers, means that they do not interfere. If services need to be partitioned into foreground and background tasks then a weighting queuing can be used.

4. THE CAMCUBE TESTBED

To evaluate the feasibility and performance of CamCubeOS and the services written on top of it, we built a small-scale testbed using commodity hardware. We now describe its setup and evaluate its base performance.

4.1 Setup

The testbed consists of 27 servers, interconnected in a 3D torus (3x3x3) like the one in Figure 1. We use Dell Precision T3500 servers with quad-core Intel Xeon 5520 2.27 GHz processors and 12 GB RAM, running an unmodified version of Windows Server 2008 R2. Each server has a 32 GB Solid State Drive (Intel X-25E SATA). In the current prototype platform we use a 1 Gbps Intel PRO/1000 PT Quadport NIC and two 1 Gbps Intel PRO/1000 PT Dualport NICs in PCIe slots to provide sufficient per-server ports. This limits the server form factors we can use as this requires three PCIe slots. However, we have started to use Silicom PE2G6I PCIe cards with six 1 Gpbs ports per NIC, requiring only a single PCIe slot. All experimental results are qualitatively and quantitatively the same when using a Silicom card, but as we have only a small number of cards for evaluation, we configured all servers identically using the Intel cards. One port is connected to a dedicated commodity 48-port 1 Gbps NetGear GS748Tv3 switch that uses store-and-forward routing (as opposed to cut-through). This provides the external connectivity to the CamCube. Six of the remaining ports, two per multi-port NIC, provide the 3D torus network. In all the experiments, intra-CamCube traffic is routed using the 3D torus topology, and all inbound and outbound traffic to / from the CamCube uses the switch.

The Intel NICs support jumbo Ethernet frames of 9,014 bytes (including the Ethernet header). In the experiments, unless otherwise stated, we use jumbo frames and use default settings for all other parameters on the Ethernet cards.

Due to space constraints, we omit the full details of the shim layer implementation. However, we used techniques similar to those presented in [16,25]. In particular, we follow a zero-copy approach and use a pool of pre-allocated packet buffers. We also batch multiple asynchronous I/O requests to minimize the number of transfers across the kernel-user boundary. Further, whenever possible, we exploit aggregation at the packet level by concatenating multiple small packets into a single jumbo frame to reduce the overhead of Ethernet headers and the interrupts generated at the receiving server. Finally, we keep the transmit and receive paths separate by using two distinct threads per link to minimize interference between them. We also allow processing of incoming packets on the receive thread, provided the computation performed on the packet is small, to reduce the overhead of context switching on each packet.

In order to demonstrate how our platform scales we also present results using a packet-level discrete event simulator. The simulator allows the same codebase used on the testbed to be compiled for the simulator. It accurately simulates the Ethernet network links, assuming 1 Gbps links and with jumbo frames.

4.2 Benchmarking

This set of experiments benchmark the performance of our CamCube testbed. We also include simulation results to show the impact of server failure and scale.

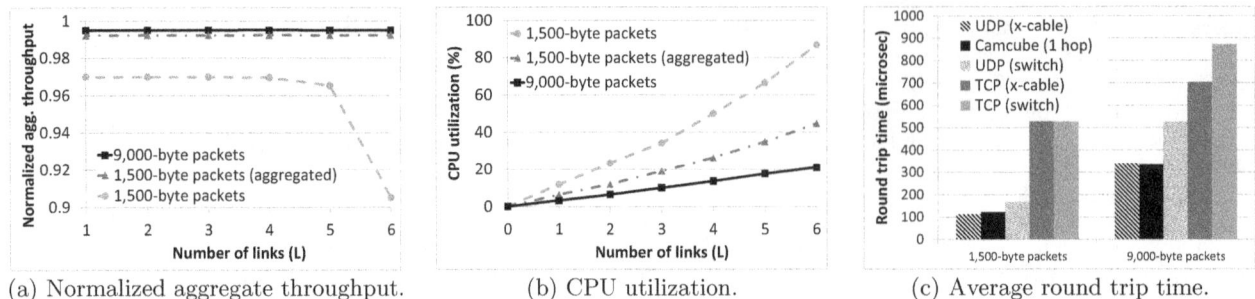

(a) Normalized aggregate throughput.

(b) CPU utilization.

(c) Average round trip time.

Figure 4: Throughput and CPU utilization versus number of links and average round trip time.

4.2.1 Throughput and CPU overhead

For the purpose of performance analysis, we developed a benchmarking service that attempts to saturate $1 \leq L \leq 6$ links with full payload packets, and records the number of packets delivered per second per server across the servers inbound links and the CPU utilization. The benchmarking service ensures that when $L = k$, all servers have k inbound links receiving packets. This service runs the same code used by CamCubeOS to route packets. Therefore, this experiment allows us to quantify the network performance and CPU overhead of using the servers to route packets. We ran the experiments using standard packets (1,500 bytes) and using jumbo frames. We measure the CPU utilization by using Windows performance counters that provide, per core, an estimate of the CPU utilization. As we have a quad core processor, with hyper-threading, we have eight CPU readings per server. The CPU utilization per server is the average of these eight readings. We also confirmed that the per-core CPU utilization is not skewed across the cores.

Figure 4(a) shows the median aggregate throughput per server for $L = 1$ to 6 normalized with respect to the maximum achievable for that value of L. We do not show error bars, but across all experiments the maximum and minimum throughput observed per-server is within 1.28% of the median value. We define the aggregate throughput per server as the total number of packets per second received by the server and the total number of packets received by one-hop neighbors of that server that are sourced by this server. The maximum aggregate throughput for a server, when $L = 6$, is 12 Gbps. Passing packets across the kernel user-space boundary induces overhead, and intuitively, using larger packets is more efficient. Figure 4(a) shows that for jumbo frames all servers are able to sustain close to the maximum aggregate throughput. At 1500-byte packets the results show CamCubeOS is able to achieve about 0.97 of the maximum aggregate throughput for up to $L = 5$. This is less than the jumbo frames as we are not including the Ethernet header overhead, and at 1500-byte packets this overhead is higher and accounts for the difference. When $L = 6$ the 1500-byte packet experiment achieves approximately 0.91. If we use the packet-level aggregation optimization described above, where multiple packets are aggregated into a single jumbo frame, the throughput increases, as the Ethernet headers are removed, and close to maximum aggregate throughput is achieved for all values of L.

With servers using CPU resources to handle packets, we next look at the CPU load during the experiment. Figure 4(b) shows the average per-server CPU overhead for $L = 0$ to 6. We do not show error bars, but the maxi-

mum and minimum are within 10.6% of the median value for all results. When $L = 0$ there is no network load and the CPU utilization is close to zero. Figure 4(b) shows that for jumbo packets, the CPU utilization is low despite the overhead associated with passing each packet across the kernel user-space boundary. When all six links are being saturated, CPU utilization is less than 22%. Using 1500-byte packets incurs a higher CPU overhead, over 87% when saturating all links. When we use the packet aggregation optimization this drops to less than 45%. This demonstrates the effectiveness of packet aggregation optimization: it increases throughput and decreases CPU overhead.

4.2.2 Latency

Next, we use a ping service to measure the increase in communication latency introduced by CamCubeOS. The ping service uses the routing service to route packets between two arbitrary servers. The source generates a packet and then forwards it towards the destination server. Each server on path receives the packet, modifies a counter in the payload, and then forwards it. When it reaches the destination, the destination reverses the source and destination identities in the packet and then routes it back towards the source. On-path the runtime and the ping service ensure that the packet is zero-copied. The source sends 10,000 ping packets, sequentially, for 1,500-byte and jumbo packets, and then reports the average round trip time (RTT).

To show the relative performance of the runtime, we also measured the performance of the standard Windows TCP/IP stack performing a ping operation between two servers using UDP and TCP over the switch for both packet sizes. The jumbo frame performance over the switch is poor, presumably because it is a commodity store-and-forward switch. Therefore, we also ran the TCP/IP experiments using a standard cross-over cable directly connecting two servers. In the case of TCP, the source creates a new socket for each ping. This is consistent with a recent analysis of data center network traces [19], which shows that most flows are smaller than 10 KB. If, instead, persistent TCP connections were used, we expect the RTTs to match those obtained with UDP and, hence, we did not run this configuration.

Figure 4(c) shows the average RTT for the different configurations, split by 1,500 and 9,000 byte packets. For CamCubeOS we show the results for a single hop. In all cases, the CamCubeOS performance is comparable to UDP using the cross-over cable. As would be expected, the TCP latency is much higher due to the additional round trips needed to create and close a TCP socket. To support arbitrary routing, multi-hop routing will be required for CamCubeOS. To explore this performance we also configured the ping service to

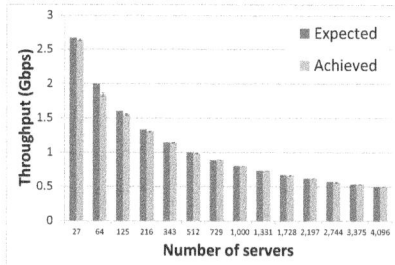

(a) Per-server throughput versus number of servers with an all-to-all traffic pattern.

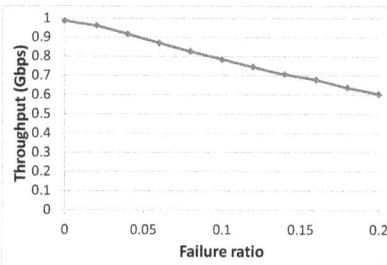

(b) Median throughput per-server versus server failure ratio with an all-to-all traffic pattern (512 servers).

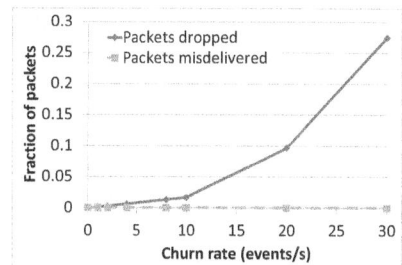

(c) Fraction of packets dropped and misdelivered versus churn rate (512 servers).

Figure 5: Simulation results.

use a 15-hop path. This is the maximum hop count between two servers in a 1,000-server CamCube (i.e., a 10x10x10, with an average path length of 7.5 hops). The average RTT is 2.22 ms for 1,500-byte packets and 5.87 ms for jumbo packets, respectively about 4.2 times and 6.73 times slower than TCP. This is the worst case and demonstrates the latency overhead of routing through servers. In an 8x8x8 CamCube, e.g. 512 servers, the maximum hop count is 6 and the average only 3. The latency would be comparable to using TCP in a traditional 512 switch-based cluster. Further, as many services induce locality often the average hop count is further reduced. As we demonstrate in Section 5, a service built on top of CamCubeOS can significantly outperform the same service running on a traditional switched setup.

4.2.3 Scaling

Next, we explore how our testbed would scale with the number of servers. We do this in simulation with an all-to-all traffic pattern, emulating the shuffle phase in a MapReduce job. Each server sends packets to $N - 1$ servers, and receives packets from $N - 1$ servers. All packets are routed on shortest paths using the multi-hop routing protocol. To keep the experiment simple we do not use a flow control protocol, but instead calculate the expected throughput per server, given N servers, and then have each server generate packets at that rate. In the experiment we measure the achieved throughput per-server, which includes only packets delivered to the server, *not* packets forwarded by the server.

Figure 5(a) shows the expected and achieved throughput per server as we scale the number of servers. The achieved and expected results are close and, as N increases, the expected throughput drops. At 27 servers the throughput is 2.7 Gbps, at 512 servers this has dropped to 1 Gbps and at 4,096 servers this is 500 Mbps. Recall that in a traditional data center this would represent an over-subscription rate of only 1:2 at 4,096 and full bisection bandwidth at 512 (1:1 over-subscription). At core routers over-subscription is normally much higher, 1:20 is not unusual and can be as high as 1:240 [19], and 1:4 at a rack level is considered good.

4.2.4 Server failure sensitivity

So far we have not considered the impact of server and link failures. Figure 5(b) shows the median throughput per server with 512 servers using the same all-to-all traffic pattern used in the previous experiment, when up to 20% of the servers are failed. Failed servers are selected randomly. The results show that the throughput drops linearly with

the number of failures. When 20% of the servers have failed throughput has dropped by 38.77%.

4.2.5 Maintaining keyspace consistency

The final experiment in this benchmarking section evaluates the keyspace consistency. We run an experiment on the simulator using 512 servers, and we induced server churn. The churn rate represents the number of servers that join and fail per second. The inter-failure times are selected randomly from an exponential distribution with a mean of 1/(failure rate), where the failure rate is (churn rate)/2. When a server fails, after a failure duration period, it rejoins the CamCube. The failure duration is set as a function of a target fraction of servers to have failed at any point in time and in these experiments this was set to 10% of the servers failed. The experiment runs for 10 minutes of simulated time. Every active server generates packets destined to a random key at a rate of 1,000 per second. All packet deliveries and drops are recorded. We use an oracle, which has global knowledge, to determine if a packet has been correctly delivered to the server responsible for the key (e.g. the key root server).

Figure 5(c) shows the fraction of packets misdelivered and dropped. Delivering a packet to the wrong server (misdelivered) is an issue with correctness, as the server will handle the packet as though it was responsible for the key. Across all experiments we had no misdelivered packets. Dropped packets impact performance, as the source of the packet will probably need to re-transmit the packet. Even at high churn rates for a data center (two failures per second), the packet drop rate is below 1%. For higher churn rates, the packet drop rate increases up to 27.41% but these correspond to extreme, unrealistic, scenarios in which on average 15 servers would fail every second.

5. KEY-VALUE STORE

To show how to build an application on top of CamCubeOS, we describe and evaluate on our testbed the implementation of a key-value store. Key-value stores such as Amazon Dynamo [15], Google BigTable [9] and Facebook Haystack [6] are widely used and often represent the critical component of a complex system. To achieve high performance, we augmented our persistent key-value store service with a caching service, similar to memcached [26], to cache the results of popular queries.

In this section, we first distill the main design features of the caching and the store service and then we evaluate the performance of the two services combined against a similar setup using a switch-based network.

5.1 Caching Service

Typically, distributed in-memory key-value caches have an API that allows read, write and delete operations on key-value pairs, with the key specified as a string and the value as a byte array. For example in an image store the key could be `image:user3:picture.jpg`, which encodes service, user and image name.

We have implemented a distributed key-value cache that exploits caching techniques from structured overlay applications to improve performance [32, 35]. In particular, the string key is converted into a 160-bit key, *memId*, by taking its SHA1 hash. The key-value pair is stored on the server that is responsible for the key. Hashing ensures that the memIds will be uniformly distributed across the keyspace. On writes the value is simply routed, using key-based routing, to the root server for the memId where the value is stored in memory. On a read the request is routed to the root server, using key-based routing, which looks up the associated value and returns it or produces an error message.

To demonstrate the flexibility of CamCubeOS, we extended the basic cache to handle hot spots, which are not supported in memcached. This is done by dynamically creating replicas of cached values on-demand, as done in many structured overlay applications. We use a function that, given a memId, generates k additional keys that are uniformly distributed in the keyspace. On reads, the lookup source generates the k keys, and then selects the closest in the keyspace from the k keys and memId. The read is routed, using key-based routing, to this key. When a server, C, receives the lookup and it is the destination, it checks if the key-value pair is locally cached. In case of a cache miss, if the server is not the root for memId, the key is routed to memId. When the root for memId receives the read it sends a response to C and records that C has a copy. When the response is received by C, it is cached (so that future requests for the same key can be handled locally) and routed to the original server that performed the lookup request.

When a server is notified by the CamCubeOS API that another server has failed it flushes all cached items for which the failed server would be the root for the memId. If a new value is associated with a key, then the root ensures all other cached copied are flushed, by explicitly contacting servers it knows requested copies of the key to cache.

This is an example of a service inducing locality, to limit load skew caused by hot keys, and to reduce the average lookup hop count. Having the k additional keys uniformly distributed means that average number of hops traversed to perform a lookup is lower.

5.2 Key-value Store Service

Our implementation of a key-value store maintains r replicas of each value inserted. Each value is associated with a 160-bit objId, and a replica is stored on the r servers returned by `GetServersForKey` (see Section 3.2). Therefore, unlike in the key-value cache, the r replicas will be stored on servers that will, under normal operation, be one-hop neighbors in the network. If the server responsible for objId fails, one of the $r - 1$ replicas will become the primary, and the replica selected will be the one responsible for the keyspace in which objId lies after the failure. The store is configurable

to use a disk-based or memory-based store for the key-value pairs. By default we use $r = 3$. It supports versioning of key values, and provides insertion, lookup, delete and a compare and swap operation.

The key-value store is failure tolerant, leveraging the remapping of keys to servers on failure. In the presence of failures, the meta-data is immediately updated to reflect the failure, but re-replication of data is delayed by t seconds, currently $t = 180$, so that servers being rebooted do not generate significant data migration. If a failed server rejoins after t seconds, a recovery protocol updates the stale data on the server in the background. This can involve the transfer of a significant amount of data, and the key-value store is able to continue to service read and write operations concurrently with the recovery protocol.

The key-value store can be used with the key-value cache, and normally, the memId = objId. The cache service is optimized so that, if it is caching items that are stored in the key-value store, it does not locally duplicate the storage.

5.3 Evaluation

In order to evaluate the performance of the key-value store and memory cache, we implemented a simple image store on top of them. Images are stored in a disk-backed key-value store using three-way replication. External clients can insert images into the store, which also causes a small thumbnail image to be automatically generated and inserted into the memory cache. Clients outside the CamCube can lookup the original or thumbnail image. Images and thumbnails are associated with a unique 160-bit key. Similar image stores underpin many social networking-like applications.

In order to generate a workload to drive the experiments we attached ten additional servers to the switch used by CamCube (the *load generators*). Each load generator has a single 1 Gbps link to the switch, therefore supporting an aggregate throughput of 10 Gbps. Each load generator can issue up to 15 concurrent requests, providing an aggregate peak load of 150 concurrent requests. Whenever a request is satisfied a new request is immediately generated, and a request can be an image insertion or lookup. All CamCube servers are front-end servers (*FEs*) that accept incoming TCP connections from the load generators. Load generators randomly select a FE and send a request to it.

We compare against a switch-based configuration, inspired by traditional cluster architectures, in which servers communicate only through the switch, using a standard TCP/IP network stack. In this configuration, each server uses only 1 Gbps link. The reason is that in a multi-tier tree network topology, adding a second network interface to each server increases the bandwidth over-subscription. Maintaining the bandwidth over-subscription requires the uplink capacity from the top of rack switch to be doubled (as well as the capacity of aggregation/core switches). This would be expensive. Without doing this, the increased bandwidth within the rack would only help in-rack communication, not across racks. This would provide no benefit for workloads like MapReduce. We therefore decided, as has prior work, e.g., [3, 21, 22], to keep the currently used network topology, without increasing the number of links per server. To provide a fair comparison, we created a shim that allowed the image store to use TCP for communication. In this way, the same core key-value store code is used in the two configurations and just the communication layer is different.

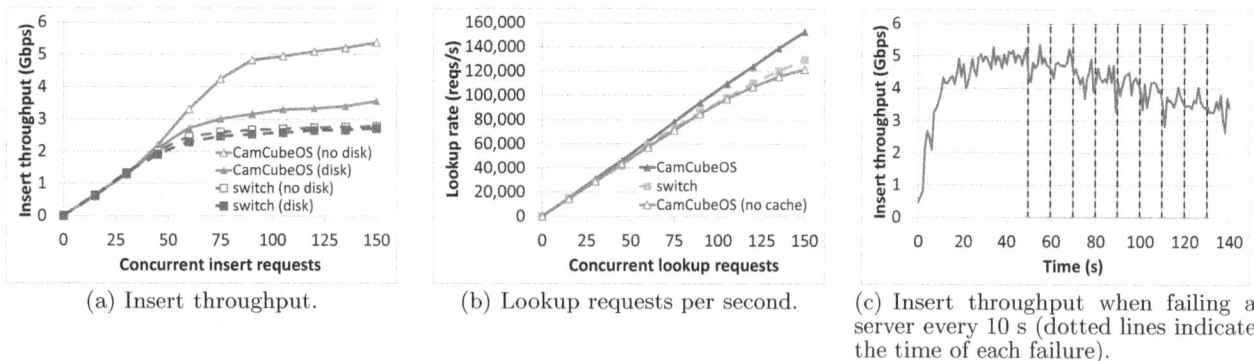

(a) Insert throughput.   (b) Lookup requests per second.   (c) Insert throughput when failing a server every 10 s (dotted lines indicate the time of each failure).

Figure 6: Image store performance for insertion and lookup workloads.

We present results for two simple workloads: an insertion workload where all requests are to insert an image, and a lookup workload. For the insertion workload the load generators have 233 JPEG image files, cached in memory, with an average size of 1.47 MB and the minimum and maximum size of 0.50 MB and 2.63 MB, respectively. A unique key is generated per insertion and an image selected at random. For the lookup workload 23,300 images are inserted, and we then generate requests for thumbnail images, selecting uniformly at random from the set of images inserted.

Figure 6(a) shows the aggregate insertion throughput at the load generators versus the number of concurrent insertion requests, varied from 15 to 150. We show the results for the TCP switch-based version (*switch*) and CamCubeOS. We found that for the CamCubeOS version the bottleneck in performance was the low disk I/O rate and, hence, we show performance with and without the disk write (labeled *disk* and *no disk*, respectively). We use only a single disk per server, and adding further disks would increase the disk bandwidth rates per server to the point where they were not the bottleneck. With and without disk writes enabled, the CamCubeOS implementation outperforms the switch-based version. At 150 concurrent requests, the insert throughput achieved by CamCubeOS is 1.31 times (disk) and 1.93 times (no disk) higher than the switch-based version. The reason is twofold. First, in the switch-based version, the server uplink bandwidth is used for external and internal traffic while for CamCubeOS two distinct networks are used. Second, as explained in Section 3.2, CamCubeOS ensures that, under normal operation, the secondary replicas are one-hop neighbors of the primary replica. This means that the primary replica can use two distinct links to copy the data to the secondary replicas. In contrast, in the switch-based version the traffic to the secondary replicas is sent through the same single uplink that is also handling the external traffic, which significantly reduces the overall throughput.

Figure 6(b) shows the achieved lookup rate in requests per second versus the number of concurrent thumbnail lookup requests. The thumbnails are retrieved from the in-memory cache service, and are on average 3.55 KB in size. To understand the impact of the distributed key-value cache, we run two configurations of the image store on CamCubeOS, one using the key-value store only (*disabled cache*) and one using also the distributed key-value cache. When running without the cache, the CamCubeOS version achieves a slightly lower rate of lookup requests per second than the switch-based version. However, if cache is enabled, the CamCubeOS ver-

sion is able to scale linearly with the number of concurrent requests and sustain the full load of the 10 generators. The reason is that caching exploits locality and reduces latency by decreasing the hop count of each lookup request. At 150 concurrent requests, the median latency for CamCubeOS with distributed cache is 0.83 ms and the 95th percentile is 1.70 ms (respectively 0.97 ms and 2.13 ms with the cache disabled) while the switched based implementation has a median latency of 0.95 ms and a 95th percentile of 2.22 ms.

We also measured the CPU utilization for all CamCube servers. Across all insert workloads, the median CPU utilization among all servers is always lower than 33% and the 95th percentile is always lower than 77% (respectively 16% and 19% for the lookup workloads). This shows that, although all CamCube traffic is being routed hop-by-hop through the servers, the CPU is not the bottleneck.

Last, to evaluate the impact of failures when running on CamCubeOS, we ran an experiment in which we permanently failed 9 randomly selected servers, one every 10 s. We used the insert workload as this is the most critical for our system because it is both computationally and bandwidth intensive. We disabled disk writes and we generated a load of 150 concurrent requests. In Figure 6(c), we plot the insert throughput (one second moving average) versus the experiment time. We let the system run for 50 s to reach a steady state and then we started failing servers. Results show that server failures have small impact on the insert throughput: after 9 servers have been removed from the system, the insert throughput is only 38.85% lower. The reason is that, as explained in Section 3.2, the load of the failed server is evenly distributed across its one-hop neighbors and, hence, the impact of a failure is minimized. Also, the availability of multiple paths partly compensate for the loss of the links attached to the failed servers.

5.4 Source Code Size

CamCubeOS is designed to provide an easy platform on which to design and implement services. It is very difficult to quantify this, but as an indication, we counted the number of lines code for our key-value store (counting semi-colons). The distributed key-value cache service, including its ability to handle hot spots by exploiting physical locality, and the persistent key-value store required only 1,335 lines of C# in total. In contrast memcached version 1.4.5, which does not provide support for replication nor hot spots, is written in 4,671 lines of C. The point-to-point or point-to-key reliable transport service used by the key-value store is 569 lines of C#, respectively. Finally, the image store application is only

151 lines of C#, of which the majority is to implement front end server functionality, as most of the other functionality is achieved using the key-value store and the distributed key-value cache service.

6. BUILDING SERVICES ON CamCubeOS

Many of the applications running in modern data center clusters are key-based and adopt the so-called *partition-aggregate* model [4]. These include key-value stores, e.g., [15, 24, 26], large-scale data analytics platforms such as MapReduce [42] and Dryad/DryadLINQ [23, 40] as well as real time stream processing and web applications, e.g., [7, 43, 48].

These applications represent a great match for CamCubeOS as they can naturally leverage its key-based API and its efficient support for *custom forwarding* and *arbitrary processing* of packets on path rather than relying on inefficient, application-level overlay networks.

In the previous section, we demonstrated the benefits of CamCubeOS in the context of the key-value store application. In this section, we provide further examples of its flexibility. First, as an example of custom forwarding, we report on the design and evaluation of a file distribution service. Next, we illustrate the benefits of in-network processing by briefly discussing the design and implementation of Camdoop. Finally, to show the support for legacy applications, we discuss the TCP/IP service, which enables running existing unmodified TCP/IP applications on top of CamCubeOS.

6.1 File Distribution Service

The file distribution service allows to transmit a file to an arbitrary subset of CamCube servers using a multicast tree. The key-based API offered by CamCubeOS greatly simplifies this task. The tree is built using techniques similar to those used in prior work on building multicast trees on structured overlays [8]. The tree vertexes are represented by keys in the keyspace and parent and children are chosen such that the edges of the trees map onto a single link. Key-based routing is used to route packets from vertex to vertex.

Traditionally, application-level multicast are inefficient due to the mismatch between the physical and the logical topology, which causes link sharing (multiple logical links mapped to the same physical link) and path stretch (a single logical link is mapped to multiple physical links). The CamCubeOS API, instead, exposes the key locality to the developers and makes it easier to ensure that, when there are no failures, there is a one-to-one correlation between the next hop in the keyspace and a link in the physical topology. This allows the full 1 Gbps per server to be achieved.

Building a single distribution tree limits the throughput to the data rate of a single link, i.e., 1 Gbps. In order to increase throughput the service builds six *disjoint* trees, allowing all six links per server to be used. Without failures this enables a file distribution rate of 6 Gbps. In general, if a server is distributing a file to the $N - 1$ other servers in the CamCube then $6(N - 1)$ (unidirectional) links will be utilized, with each link being traversed by a single tree.

This further shows the benefits of knowing the topology and control the routing. However, one of the main benefits of the key-based abstraction supported by CamCubeOS is that it minimizes the effort of maintaining the tree connected in the presence of failures. When a server fails, then the key-based routing will ensure that packets are still delivered to

	Throughput (Gbps)		
Single instance	5.662		
Three concurrent instances	1.852	1.854	1.848

Table 1: Minimum per-member throughput for multicast with a single and three concurrent instances.

the vertex in the keyspace, but the vertex will be mapped to a different server. This means that the packets for that edge will now traverse one or more physical links. If there are multiple paths available, these will be exploited.

6.1.1 Evaluation

To evaluate the performance of this service, we multicast a 750 MB file to a subset of the servers. In the experiments, we measure the achieved throughput by determining the time from when the first packet is sent to when each group member has successfully received the entire file (including any time required for re-transmissions due to packet loss). We then divide 750 MB by the elapsed time to determine the multicast throughput in Gbps. To ensure bandwidth is the bottleneck resource, the file is cached in memory on the source, and the group members store the file in memory.

The link-level queue management provided by CamCubeOS allows the per-link bandwidth to be efficiently shared across competing services. To demonstrate this, we also ran multiple instances of the file distribution service concurrently and we measured the throughput achieved by each.

Table 1 compares the *minimum* throughput per member when running the service in isolation and when running three instances of the file distribution service concurrently, each distributing a 750 MB file to 26 servers. The first observation is that when running in isolation the multicast service achieves a throughput close to the theoretically maximum achievable of 6 Gbps. We also ran with group sizes of 1, 6, and 13 members and obtained similar results, but we omit these for space reasons. In a traditional data center files can be distributed using unicast, IP multicast or application-level multicast. If the servers have 1 Gbps links to the ToR switch, as is normal, this will be the upper throughput bound for any of these approaches.

The results also show that when running three concurrent instances the bandwidth is split evenly between the three instances. Each instance achieves approximately one third (1.9 Gbps) of the throughput achieved by a single instance. This demonstrates that CamCubeOS ensures fair-sharing of the bandwidth across multiple services. It would be trivial to configure weighted-sharing of links.

6.2 Large-scale Data Analytics

For completeness, we briefly report on Camdoop, a CamCube service to run MapReduce jobs. We extensively describe its design and evaluation in [10]. Here, instead, we focus on how it benefited from the CamCubeOS API.

MapReduce-like systems such as Apache Hadoop [42] and Microsoft Dryad [23, 40] are used daily by large-scale companies as well as small and medium businesses to process large amount of data. These systems typically operate in a partition-aggregate fashion. Input data is partitioned across multiple servers and locally processed. These intermediate results are then merged and aggregated together. These systems significantly stress network resources, due to the large amount of data that needs to be shipped across the network during the aggregation phase.

A common property of MapReduce-like jobs is that the output size is often a small fraction of the input size, due to the high degree of aggregation occurring during the process. We leveraged this property in Camdoop by performing partial aggregation of packets on path. This drastically reduces the traffic (and, hence, the job running time) because at each hop, only a fraction of the data received is forwarded. This enables achieving a speed-up of up to two orders of magnitude compared to Hadoop and Dryad/DryadLINQ [10].

CamCubeOS greatly simplified the implementation of Camdoop. Camdoop uses six aggregation *disjoint* trees, built in a way similar to the file distribution service. Due to the ability of CamCubeOS to intercept packets on path, the Camdoop service can easily receive the packets, aggregate their content in a new packet and forward it to the upstream server. Since each vertex is represented by a key, little effort is required to deal with fault tolerance because we leveraged the CamCubeOS key-based routing to keep the tree connected in the presence of link or server failures.

We used the key-based API also to map tasks to servers, using the task ID as the key. In case of failure, tasks are re-assigned using the re-mapping scheme described in Section 3.2. This ensures that tasks get re-scheduled on neighboring servers, thus preserving the tree locality.

6.3 Legacy Applications

Although CamCubeOS has been designed to efficiently run key-based services, it can also support generic workloads, including legacy TCP/IP applications. To support legacy applications we have created a TCP/IP service that enables running unmodified TCP/IP applications on CamCubeOS. To achieve this, we bound the TCP/IP stack to a virtual Ethernet interface. All packets sent to this interface, are intercepted and delivered to the CamCubeOS runtime, which is also able to inject packets into the bottom of the TCP/IP stack. The TCP/IP service encapsulates and tunnels the intercepted IP packets across the CamCube to the destination server, with the exception of ARP requests. These are spoofed, and a MAC address generated that encodes the destination. Applications can use the standard TCP/IP stack and socket API and are unaware that they are running on top of a 3D torus, which is presented as a single layer 2 IP network.

The 3D torus introduces multi-path, and when TCP/IP tunneling this is a challenge. It increases the aggregate throughput between servers, and provides a high resilience to failures, but causes out of order packet delivery. Traditionally, TCP handles out of order packet delivery badly, and it leads to throughput collapse which we also observed. Making multi-path TCP work is a current active area of research [31]. The TCP/IP service uses small buffers at the destination, which allows the TCP/IP service to reorder the packets of each flow.

6.3.1 Evaluation

To understand the performance of running TCP/IP applications on CamCubeOS, we ran an experiment in which every server simultaneously transferred 1 GB of data to each of the other 26 servers using TCP. This creates an all-to-all traffic pattern, similar to the one generated by the MapReduce shuffle phase. We obtained a median aggregate TCP inbound throughput of 1.49 Gbps per server. This is higher than the maximum throughput achievable in a conventional cluster where servers have 1 Gbps uplinks to the switch. However, the maximum throughput achievable is 2.7 Gbps, but out of order packet delivery induced by multi-path limits the throughput achieved.

7. RELATED WORK

Torus-based fabric interconnects have been very popular in the High Performance Computing (HPC) and have recently started being deployed also in data center clusters, using proprietary technologies, e.g., SeaMicro Freedom fabric [47], as well as open industry standards such as Hyper-Transport [44], a consortium including, among others, AMD, Broadcom, Cisco, Dell, HP, NVIDIA, Oracle, and Xilinx.

Compared to existing switched-based networks, these solutions enable reducing capital and operational costs while delivering higher throughput [49]. These systems, however, still rely on traditional networking stacks like TCP/IP or MPI, which completely hide the topology and provide an end-to-end abstraction. This makes it impossible to perform efficient in-network packet processing, which, as we demonstrated in this paper, can significantly improve performance. For instance, the IBM Project Kittyhawk [5] proposes using the BlueGene/P supercomputer in a data center, and then runs unmodified TCP/IP applications, by making the 3D torus topology appear as a flat layer 2 IP network, as does our TCP/IP service. In contrast, CamCubeOS explicitly exposes the topology to allow services to exploit it.

Another key difference between CamCubeOS and mainstream networking stacks is that CamCubeOS natively supports a key-based API. Many of the applications running in clusters are key-based, e.g., [15, 24, 26]. CamCubeOS makes it easier to implement these applications, because it removes the burdens of managing the key space and ensuring consistency in the presence of failures. HPC clusters usually do not handle failures, e.g. BlueGene/L can tolerate three failed links [30], and indeed they use routing protocols that do not necessarily converge with link failure [13,18,39]. Failures are handled by stopping the system and restarting it [17,27]. In contrast, CamCubeOS uses key-based routing to mask failures and simplify failure recovery.

In the networking community there have been several proposals for new networking topologies for the data center, including direct-connect or hybrid ones, e.g., [21, 22, 37]. The goal of these proposals is to increase the bisection bandwidth, often motivated by MapReduce-like workloads, but they still assume that TCP/IP is used on top. CamCubeOS challenges this view and shows that these new topologies provide a great opportunity to rethink established practices in networking in order to achieve high performance and reduce development complexity.

8. CONCLUSIONS

CamCubeOS explores the question: are the current communication abstractions for clusters, derived from networking principles used in enterprise networks and the Internet, the best? Based on the observation that many clusters run key-based applications and the increasing availability of 3D torus fabric interconnects, CamCubeOS is designed from the ground up to support developing and running key-based services. It represents a very different design point from traditional data centers, but the results show that it is feasible and efficient.

Acknowledgements. We thank Thomas Zahn for his contribution to an early version of CamCubeOS, and the anonymous reviewers and our shepherd, Prasenjit Sarkar, for their insightful feedback and advice.

9. REFERENCES

[1] ABU-LIBDEH, H., COSTA, P., ROWSTRON, A., O'SHEA, G., AND DONNELLY, A. Symbiotic Routing in Future Data Centers. In *SIGCOMM* (2010).

[2] ADIGA, N. R., BLUMRICH, M. A., CHEN, D., COTEUS, P., GARA, A., GIAMPAPA, M. E., HEIDELBERGER, P., SINGH, S., STEINMACHER-BUROW, B. D., TAKKEN, T., TSAO, M., AND VRANAS, P. Blue Gene/L torus interconnection network. *IBM Journal of Research and Development 49*, 2 (2005).

[3] AL-FARES, M., LOUKISSAS, A., AND VAHDAT, A. A scalable, commodity data center network architecture. In *SIGCOMM* (2008).

[4] ALIZADEH, M., GREENBERG, A. G., MALTZ, D. A., PADHYE, J., PATEL, P., PRABHAKAR, B., SENGUPTA, S., AND SRIDHARAN, M. Data center TCP (DCTCP). In *SIGCOMM* (2010).

[5] APPAVOO, J., UHLIG, V., AND WATERLAND, A. Project Kittyhawk: building a global-scale computer: Blue Gene/P as a generic computing platform. *OSR 42*, 1 (2008).

[6] BEAVER, D., KUMAR, S., LI, H. C., SOBEL, J., AND VAJGEL, P. Finding a Needle in Haystack: Facebook's Photo Storage. In *Usenix OSDI* (2010).

[7] BORTHAKUR, D., GRAY, J., SARMA, J. S., MUTHUKKARUPPAN, K., SPIEGELBERG, N., KUANG, H., RANGANATHAN, K., MOLKOV, D., MENON, A., RASH, S., SCHMIDT, R., AND AIYER, A. Apache Hadoop Goes Realtime at Facebook. In *SIGMOD* (2011).

[8] CASTRO, M., DRUSCHEL, P., KERMARREC, A.-M., AND ROWSTRON, A. Scribe: A large-scale and decentralized application-level multicast infrastructure. *IEEE JSAC 20*, 8 (2002).

[9] CHANG, F., DEAN, J., GHEMAWAT, S., HSIEH, W. C., WALLACH, D. A., BURROWS, M., CHANDRA, T., FIKES, A., AND GRUBER, R. E. Bigtable: A Distributed Storage System for Structured Data. In *OSDI* (2006).

[10] COSTA, P., DONNELLY, A., ROWSTRON, A., AND O'SHEA, G. Camdoop: Exploiting In-network Aggregation for Big Data Applications. In *NSDI* (2012).

[11] COSTA, P., ZAHN, T., ROWSTRON, A., O'SHEA, G., AND SCHUBERT, S. Why Should We Integrate Services, Servers, and Networking in a Data Center? In *WREN* (2009).

[12] DABEK, F., ZHAO, B., DRUSCHEL, P., KUBIATOWICZ, J., AND STOICA, I. Towards a Common API for Structured Peer-to-Peer Overlays. In *IPTPS* (2003).

[13] DALLY, W. J., AND SEITZ, C. L. Deadlock-free message routing in multiprocessor interconnection networks. *IEEE ToC 36*, 5 (1987).

[14] DEAN, J., AND GHEMAWAT, S. MapReduce: Simplified Data Processing on Large Clusters. In *OSDI* (2004).

[15] DECANDIA, G., HASTORUN, D., JAMPANI, M., KAKULAPATI, G., LAKSHMAN, A., PILCHIN, A., SIVASUBRAMANIAN, S., VOSSHALL, P., AND VOGELS, W. Dynamo: Amazon's Highly Available Key-value Store. In *SOSP* (2007).

[16] DOBRESCU, M., EGI, N., ARGYRAKI, K., CHUN, B.-G., FALL, K., IANNACCONE, G., KNIES, A., MANESH, M., AND RATNASAMY, S. Routebricks: Exploiting parallelism to scale software routers. In *SOSP* (2009).

[17] DUATO, J. A Theory of Fault-Tolerant Routing in Wormhole Networks. *IEEE TPDS 8*, 8 (1997).

[18] GLASS, C. J., AND NI, L. M. The turn model for adaptive routing. *SIGARCH Comput. Archit. News 20*, 2 (1992).

[19] GREENBERG, A., HAMILTON, J. R., JAIN, N., KANDULA, S., KIM, C., LAHIRI, P., MALTZ, D. A., PATEL, P., AND SENGUPTA, S. VL2: A Scalable and Flexible Data Center Network. In *SIGCOMM* (2009).

[20] GUMMADI, K. P., GUMMADI, R., GRIBBLE, S. D., RATNASAMY, S., SHENKER, S., AND STOICA, I. The impact of DHT routing geometry on resilience and proximity. In *SIGCOMM* (2003).

[21] GUO, C., LU, G., LI, D., WU, H., ZHANG, X., SHI, Y., TIAN, C., ZHANG, Y., AND LU, S. BCube: A High Performance, Server-centric Network Architecture for Modular Data Centers. In *SIGCOMM* (2009).

[22] GUO, C., WU, H., TAN, K., SHIY, L., ZHANG, Y., AND LUZ, S. DCell: A Scalable and Fault-Tolerant Network Structure for Data Centers. In *SIGCOMM* (2008).

[23] ISARD, M., BUDIU, M., YU, Y., BIRRELL, A., AND FETTERLY, D. Dryad: distributed data-parallel programs from sequential building blocks. In *EuroSys* (2007).

[24] LAKSHMAN, A., AND MALIK, P. Cassandra: A Decentralized Structured Storage System. *OSR 44*, 2 (2010).

[25] MORRIS, R., KOHLER, E., JANNOTTI, J., AND KAASHOEK, M. F. The Click modular router. In *SOSP* (1999).

[26] NISHTALA, R., FUGAL, H., GRIMM, S., KWIATKOWSKI, M., LEE, H., LI, H. C., MCELROY, R., PALECZNY, M., PEEK, D., SAAB, P., STAFFORD, D., TUNG, T., AND VENKATARAMANI, V. Scaling Memcached at Facebook. In *NSDI* (2013).

[27] NORDBOTTEN, N. A., FLICH, J., SKEIE, T., GOMEZ, M. E., LOPEZ, P., ROBLES, A., DUATO, J., AND LYSNE, O. A routing methodology for achieving fault tolerance in direct networks. *IEEE ToC 55*, 4 (2006).

[28] ORAN, D. OSI IS-IS Intra-domain Routing Protocol. IETF RFC 1142.

[29] PARHAMI, B. *Introduction to Parallel Processing: Algorithms and Architectures.* Kluwer Publishers, 1999.

[30] PUENTE, V., AND GREGORIO, J. A. Immucube: Scalable Fault-Tolerant Routing for k-ary n-cube Networks. *IEEE TPDS 18*, 6 (2007).

[31] RAICIU, C., PAASCH, C., BARRE, S., FORD, A., HONDA, M., DUCHENE, F., BONAVENTURE, O., AND HANDLEY, M. How Hard Can It Be? Designing and implementing a deployable Multipath TCP. In *NSDI* (2012).

[32] RAMASUBRAMANIAN, V., AND SIRER, E. G. Beehive: O(1) lookup performance for power-law query distributions in peer-to-peer overlays. In *NSDI* (2004).

[33] RATNASAMY, S., FRANCIS, P., HANDLEY, M., KARP, R., AND SHENKER, S. A Scalable Content-addressable Network. In *Proceedings of SIGCOMM* (2001).

[34] ROWSTRON, A., AND DRUSCHEL, P. Pastry: Scalable, distributed object location and routing for large-scale peer-to-peer systems. In *Middleware* (2001).

[35] ROWSTRON, A., AND DRUSCHEL, P. Storage management and caching in PAST, a large-scale, persistent peer-to-peer storage utility. In *SOSP* (2001).

[36] SCOTT, S. L., AND THORSON, G. Optimized Routing in the Cray T3D. In *PCRCW* (1994).

[37] SHIN, J.-Y., WONG, B., AND SIRER, E. G. Small-world Datacenters. In *SOCC* (2011).

[38] STOICA, I., MORRIS, R., KARGER, D., KAASHOEK, M., AND BALAKRISHNAN, H. Chord: A scalable peer-to-peer lookup service for internet applications. In *SIGCOMM* (2001).

[39] VALIANT, L. G., AND BREBNER, G. J. Universal schemes for parallel communication. In *STOC* (1981).

[40] YU, Y., ISARD, M., FETTERLY, D., BUDIU, M., ÚLFAR ERLINGSSON, GUNDA, P. K., AND CURREY, J. DryadLINQ: A System for General-Purpose Distributed Data-Parallel Computing Using a High-Level Language. In *OSDI* (2008).

[41] AMD Completes Acquisition of SeaMicro. http://bit.ly/OuOaHm.

[42] Apache Hadoop. http://hadoop.apache.org/.

[43] Google Distribution of Requests . http://bit.ly/hUTaVQ.

[44] HyperTransport Consortium. http://www.hypertransport.org.

[45] Intel acquires Cray Interconnect. http://intel.ly/I8VIAR.

[46] SeaMicro SM10000-XE. http://bit.ly/KlIyAp.

[47] SeaMicro Technology Overview. http://bit.ly/MAwJ4S.

[48] Storm. http://storm-project.net.

[49] Why Torus-Based Clusters? http://bit.ly/MBuGOE.

NUMA-Aware Shared-Memory Collective Communication for MPI

Shigang Li[*]
School of Computer and
Communication Engineering
University of Science and
Technology Beijing
shigangli.cs@gmail.com

Torsten Hoefler
Department of Computer
Science
ETH Zurich
htor@inf.ethz.ch

Marc Snir
Department of Computer
Science
University of Illinois at
Urbana-Champaign
and Argonne National
Laboratory
snir@illinois.edu

ABSTRACT

As the number of cores per node keeps increasing, it becomes increasingly important for MPI to leverage shared memory for intranode communication. This paper investigates the design and optimizations of MPI collectives for clusters of NUMA nodes. We develop performance models for collective communication using shared memory, and we develop several algorithms for various collectives. Experiments are conducted on both Xeon X5650 and Opteron 6100 InfiniBand clusters. The measurements agree with the model and indicate that different algorithms dominate for short vectors and long vectors. We compare our shared-memory allreduce with several traditional MPI implementations – Open MPI, MPICH2, and MVAPICH2 – that utilize system shared memory to facilitate interprocess communication. On a 16-node Xeon cluster and 8-node Opteron cluster, our implementation achieves on average 2.5X and 2.3X speedup over MVAPICH2, respectively. Our techniques enable an efficient implementation of collective operations on future multi- and manycore systems.

Categories and Subject Descriptors

D.1.3 [**Programming Techniques**]: Concurrent Programming—*Parallel Programming*

Keywords

MPI, multithreading, MPI_Allreduce, collective communication, NUMA

---

[*]Shigang Li is currently a visiting graduate student at Department of Computer Science, University of Illinois at Urbana-Champaign.

1. INTRODUCTION

Applications using the Message Passing Interface (MPI) [14] often run multiple MPI processes at each node. As the number of cores per node keeps growing and as nodes exhibit increasingly nonuniform memory, the performance of MPI collectives becomes more and more dependent on the performance of the intranode communication component of such collectives. Currently, implementations of MPI collectives take advantage of shared memory in two ways. In the first way, collectives are built by using point-to-point message passing, which uses shared memory as a transport layer inside a node. Collectives in MPICH2 [28] are implemented in this way. In the second way, Collectives are implemented directly atop shared memory [6, 11, 23]: Data is copied from user space to shared system space so that all the processes in the communicator can share and collectively work on the data. Collectives in Open MPI [6] and some collectives in MVAPICH2 [11] are implemented in this way. The second approach reduces the number of memory transfers [6, 23], but still requires extra data movement. Also, shared memory is usually a limited system resource.

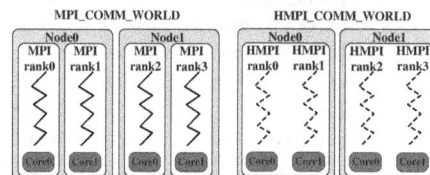

Figure 1: Runtime model of traditional MPI vs. Hybrid MPI (HMPI)

The hybrid MPI library (HMPI) [5] avoids these overheads by replacing the common process-based rank design with a thread-based rank; all MPI ranks (threads) on a node are running within the same address space, as illustrated in Figure 1. HMPI takes advantage of shared memory within a node and utilizes the existing MPI infrastructure for internode communication. A similar technique can be applied to existing MPI implementations by using techniques such as cross-memory attach (XPMEM [24]) to create a globally shared heap for all MPI processes on a node. The detailed techniques for sharing the heap are well understood [20] and thus not a topic of this paper.

Sharing heap data directly can yield significant perfor-

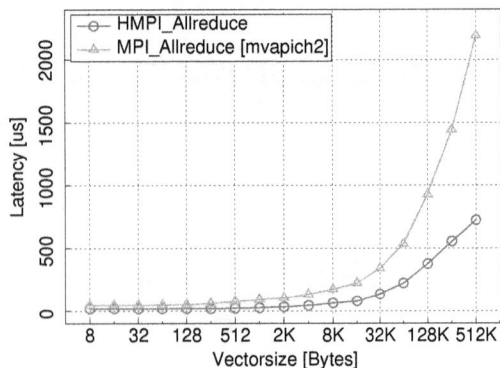

Figure 2: Latency of HMPI_Allreduce vs. traditional MPI_Allreduce on 16 Xeon X5650 nodes

mance gains for the following reasons: (1) communication between MPI ranks within a node requires only one copy, the minimum possible, and (2) synchronization can be accelerated by using shared flags. Applications that run in the process-based model will work with few modifications in the thread-based model: Static variables need to become thread-private. Automatic privatization of global variables [15, 17] can minimize the developer effort. Shared-heap techniques such as XPMEM change the memory allocator to allocate from shared memory, and no further changes are needed.

We demonstrate in this paper the performance advantage of HMPI's thread-based approach, in the context of MPI collectives, in particular, MPI_Allreduce. Figure 2 shows the motivation for our work, namely, that HMPI_Allreduce is significantly faster than traditional MPI_Allreduce. The remainder of this paper discusses a set of algorithmic motifs, such as mixing different tree structures and multidimensional dissemination algorithms; and a set of optimization, such as utilizing shared caches and locality. These enable us to achieve highest performance for collective operations on NUMA machines.

We study three thread-based algorithms for MPI allreduce in detail: *reduce-broadcast*, *dissemination*, and *tiled-reduce-broadcast*. We establish detailed performance models for all algorithms to enable model-based algorithm selection. Experiments are conducted on a 12-core Xeon X5650 cluster and a 32-core Opteron 6100 cluster. On 16 nodes of the Xeon cluster and 8 nodes of the Opteron cluster, HMPI_Allreduce gets on average 2.5X and 2.3X speedup over MVAPICH2 1.6, and gets on average 6.3X and 4.7X speedup over MPICH2 1.4.

The key contributions of this paper are as follows:

1. We design NUMA-aware algorithms for thread-based HMPI_Allreduce on clusters of NUMA nodes.

2. We show a set of motifs and techniques to optimize collective operations on multicore architectures.

3. We establish performance models based on memory access latency and bandwidth to select the best algorithm for different vector sizes.

4. We perform a detailed benchmarking study to assess the benefits of using our algorithms over state-of-the-art approaches.

In the next section, we discuss the models to estimate the cost of intranode data movement, and introduce the implementations and performance models of our NUMA-aware allreduce algorithms, including reduce-broadcast, dissemination, and parallel-reduce followed by a broadcast. Experimental results and analyses are presented in Section 3. Section 3.4 discusses parameter estimation for our model and algorithm selection. A comparison with OpenMP reduction is presented in Section 3.5. Section 3.6 and Section 3.7 present the performance of our thread-based MPI collectives using microbenchmarks and applications on CMP clusters. Section 4 discusses related work, and Section 5 summarizes and concludes.

2. ALLREDUCE ALGORITHMS IN SHARED MEMORY

Several factors, such as thread affinity, memory contention, and cache coherency, must be considered when designing multithreading algorithms. We assume that threads are bound to cores and use the following techniques to address these factors:

1. All the algorithms discussed in the following subsections are NUMA-aware to reduce intersocket memory traffic.

2. To reduce capacity cache misses for large-vector reductions, we use strip mining for large vectors in all algorithms. With this technique, large vectors are divided into chunks so that each chunk can fit into the last-level cache.

3. A high-performance, tree-based barrier is used to synchronize all threads in a communicator. Flag variables used in the synchronization operations are padded to prevent false sharing.

2.1 Performance Model

We use performance models to guide the selection of the best collective algorithms. Since internode communication is not affected by our design, we focus on a performance model for intranode communication. The key operation is a read or write of contiguous data. We assume that the time overhead of consecutive memory access by a thread is approximated as $a + bm$, where m is the vector length (number of cache lines), $a + b$ is the latency for the first cache line access and $1/b$ denotes the bandwidth (relative to cache lines). The average latency for each cache line is less than the latency for the first cache line, because consecutive memory accesses benefit from hardware or software prefetching [9, 1]. The values of a and b depend on whether the data is on the local or the remote socket, the level of memory hierarchy, the cache line state (e.g., modified cache lines need to be written back before they are evicted), and whether one reads or writes the data (e.g., a write miss may cause a load triggered by write-allocate).

The layout of threads is critical when designing the algorithms. For instance, a random mapping of threads in a node may lead to more intersocket communication, which can be several times slower than intrasocket communication [13]. In order to minimize communication overhead, all the following algorithms are designed and implemented hierarchically according to the hierarchy detected by the HWLOC library [4],

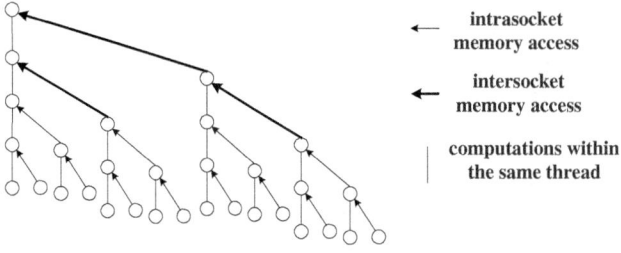

Figure 3: Binary reduction tree, for 1 node with 4 sockets; each socket includes 4 cores.

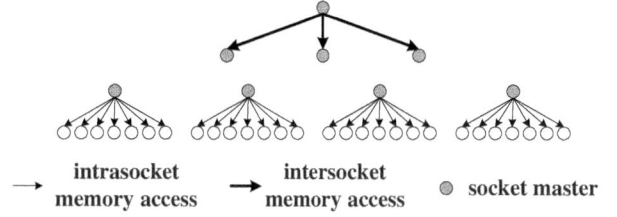

Figure 4: Two-stage broadcast, for 1 node with 4 sockets; each socket includes 4 cores.

namely intramodule (for cores sharing L2 cache), intrasocket (for cores sharing L3 cache), intersocket, and internode. To simplify the problem, when introducing the algorithms implementation, we assume that each core has a private L2 cache and each socket contains a shared L3 cache, such as for the Xeon X5650 and Opteron 6100. The intrasocket memory access time is expressed as $a_\alpha + b_\alpha m$, and the intersocket memory access time is expressed as $a_\beta + b_\beta m$, where $a_\alpha + b_\alpha < a_\beta + b_\beta$ and $1/b_\alpha > 1/b_\beta$. These formulas ignore congestion [13]. To model congestion, we use the formula $a + Bdm$ to represent the delay for d simultaneous accesses where $1/B$ is the total bandwidth of the shared link and $(1/(Bd) \leq 1/b)$. We use $1/B_\alpha$ to represent intrasocked total bandwidth and $1/B_\beta$ to represent intersocket total bandwidth.

We use s for the number of sockets and q for the number of threads running in each socket, for a total of $p = qs$ threads per node.

2.2 Reduce-Broadcast

Our reduce-broadcast algorithm uses a tree reduction, followed by a tree broadcast. For the reduction phase, we use a regular n-ary tree. Each thread performs a reduction after it has synchronized with $n - 1$ children and finished its previous step. If it is the first child of its parent, then it acts as parent in the next round. Otherwise it synchronizes with the parent.

A binary reduction tree is illustrated in Figure 3; vertical lines connect computations within the same thread and arrows show communication across threads. The n-ary tree is mapped onto the node topology so that intersocket communication is used only at the top levels. If h is the height of the intrasocket reduction tree, then $q \leq (n^{h+1} - 1)/(n - 1)$, and $h = \lceil \log_n((n-1)q+1) \rceil - 1$. To simplify this formula, we assume q is much larger than 1, so that $h = \lceil \log_n((n-1)q+1) \rceil - 1 = \lceil \log_n(n-1) + \log_n q \rceil - 1 \approx \lceil 1 + \log_n q \rceil - 1 = \lceil \log_n q \rceil$. Similarly, the height of intersocket n-ary tree can be expressed as $\lceil \log_n s \rceil$. Assuming no congestion, the time for the intrasocket n-ary reduction tree is $(n-1)(a_\alpha + b_\alpha m)\lceil \log_n q \rceil$. However, intrasocket reduction may cause congestion in the lower level of the tree, since simultaneous memory accesses share the last-level cache. However, the number of simultaneous accesses decreases as the tree goes to higher levels. To be more accurate, we use

$$T_{intra-red} = (n-1)\sum_{i=0}^{\lceil \log_n q \rceil} max(a_\alpha + b_\alpha m, \\ a_\alpha + B_\alpha n^i m) \quad (1)$$

to model the time for the intrasocket n-ary reduction tree. For intersocket reduction, no memory accesses share the same link (in modern NUMA processors, sockets are linked with each other by point-to-point links, e.g., Intel QPI and AMD HT). The time for the intersocket n-ary reduction tree is

$$T_{inter-red} = (n-1)(a_\beta + b_\beta m)\lceil \log_n s \rceil \quad (2)$$

The total time for reduction is

$$T_{red} = T_{intra-red} + T_{inter-red} \quad (3)$$

This function is monotonically increasing in n, so that the best algorithm is always obtained for $n = 2$. This is validated by the experiments described in Section 3.2.

When broadcast is done by using shared memory with an n-ary tree, one thread writes the vector, and n threads read the vector simultaneously. Communication will go through the cache, and data is not written back to memory. Caches have a high bandwidth and hence can support a large fan-out. Experiments described in Section 3.2 show that, for the systems under consideration, only two configurations need to be considered: (1) a one-stage broadcast, where all the threads read the vector simultaneously, and (2) a two-stage broadcast, where a "socket master" at each socket reads the vector in the first step, and then all threads within a socket, except the socket master, read the local copy simultaneously, as illustrated in Figure 4. The first approach always gets the best performance on a dual-socket Westmere CMP, and the second approach performs better for the 4-socket Magny-Cours CMP.

In a two-stage broadcast, the time for the intersocket broadcast (no shared intersocket link in this stage) is $(a_\beta + b_\beta m)$, and the time for the intrasocket broadcast is $(a_\alpha + B_\alpha(q-1)m)$, so that the total time overhead is $a_\alpha + B_\alpha(q-1)m + a_\beta + b_\beta m$. In a one-stage broadcast the time is dominated by the intersocket memory accesses and each intersocket link is shared by q memory accesses. Simultaneous remote accesses to the same data benefit from synergistic prefetching [26]: After one thread reads one chunk of data from the remote socket, other threads can read this chunk of data directly from the socket-local shared cache. However, we found that, in practice, it does suffer from congestion to some extent, so that we approximate the time cost of one-stage broadcast as $a_\beta + B_\beta qm$. In general, the broadcast takes time

$$T_{bcst} = min(a_\alpha + B_\alpha(q-1)m + a_\beta + b_\beta m, a_\beta + B_\beta qm) \quad (4)$$

Considering both reduction and broadcast phases for tree-based allreduce, the total time taken by an n-ary reduction tree combined with a one- or two-stage broadcast is

$$T_{red-bcst} = T_{red} + T_{bcst} \quad (5)$$

2.3 Dissemination

The dissemination algorithm [7, 8] achieves complete dissemination of information among p threads in $\lceil \log_2 p \rceil$ synchronized steps. If the number of threads p is a power of 2, it needs $N = \lceil \log_2 p \rceil$ steps to accomplish an allreduce. During step i ($i = 0, 1, ..., N-1$), thread j ($j = 0, 1, ..., p-1$) combines the data from thread $(j - 2^i + p)$ mod p with its own data. This algorithm has fewer steps but more total communication than does the reduce-broadcast algorithm.

The dissemination algorithm can be laid out so that intersocket communication happens only in the last $\lceil \log_2 s \rceil$ steps, as presented in Figure 5. In the last $\lceil \log_2 s \rceil$ steps, all threads within a socket need the same chunk of data from the other sockets. While this approach benefits from synergistic prefetching [26], it does suffer from congestion to some extent in practice.

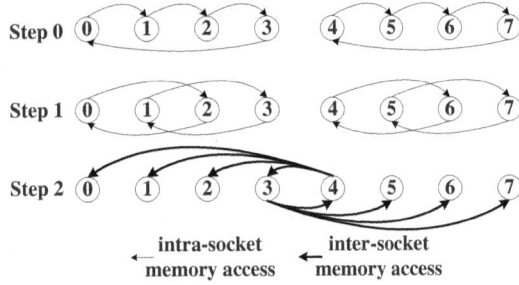

Figure 5: Dissemination, for 1 node with 2 sockets; each socket includes 4 cores.

In each step of dissemination all the threads communicate simultaneously, so we use the total bandwidth $1/B$ to approximate the time overhead. Although p memory accesses share the intersocket link (in the case of 2 sockets), intersocket links always have equal bidirectional bandwidth in modern NUMA processors, so that we can always use q as the number of memory accesses sharing the link. If p is a power of 2, the total time taken by dissemination is

$$T_{dis-pwr2} = (a_\alpha + B_\alpha qm)\lceil \log_2 q \rceil + (a_\beta + B_\beta qm)\lceil \log_2 s \rceil \quad (6)$$

If the number of threads p is not a power of 2, the final results may not be correct using the above algorithm. To solve this problem, we put the excess threads in a different set that is handled separately, so that the number of the remaining threads is the largest possible power of 2. A regular dissemination algorithm can be used for the remaining threads; the excess threads then copy the final result from a thread in the same socket. A dissemination algorithm for $p = 12$ is given in Figure 6.

Let $u = \lfloor log_2 q \rfloor$, $q' = 2^u$ and $r = q - q'$. If p is not a power of 2, then the total time taken by dissemination is

$$T_{dis-non-pwr2} = (a_\alpha + B_\alpha q'm)\lceil \log_2 q' \rceil +$$

$$(a_\beta + B_\beta q'm)\lceil \log_2 s \rceil + 2(a_\alpha + B_\alpha rm) \quad (7)$$

2.4 Tiled Reduce-Broadcast

Since all threads can access all the vectors, a straightforward algorithm is for each thread to compute sequentially one tile of the final result and then broadcast it to all threads. This algorithm works for long vectors and can be expected to have better performance than other algorithms

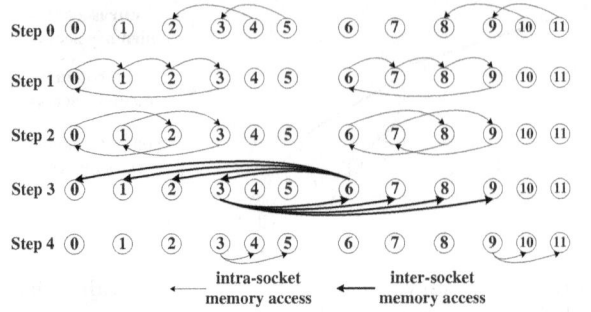

Figure 6: Dissemination, for 1 node with 2 sockets; each socket includes 6 cores.

for large vector sizes, because it can keep all the threads busy and make better use of bandwidth.

We use the tiled approach only within sockets; the limited intersocket bandwidth means that a tree reductions performs better at that stage. Each send buffer of a thread is partitioned into q chunks as evenly as possible, and then each thread simultaneously reduces its corresponding portion into a temporary buffer. In order to prevent false sharing, the temporary buffer is padded with dummy data to the cache line boundary and partitioned at cache line granularity. In Figure 7, $Thread_0$ in $Socket_1$ reduces all the B_0 blocks onto a temporary buffer. Next, we reduce in parallel these q chunks across sockets, using a tree reduction, in $\lceil \log_2 s \rceil$ steps.

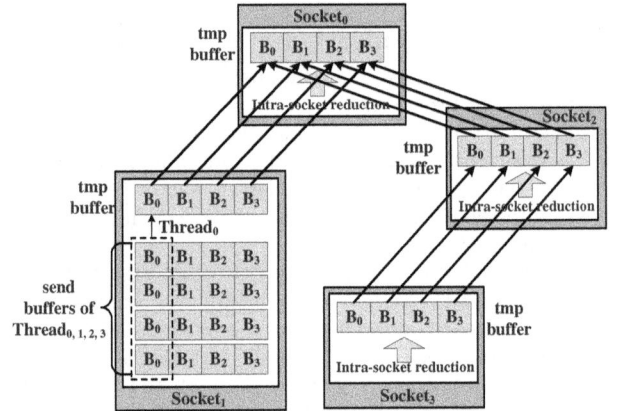

Figure 7: Hierarchical parallel-reduce, for 1 node with 4 sockets; each socket includes 4 cores.

Simultaneous memory accesses happen within each socket, so that we use the total bandwidth $1/B$ to approximate the reduce time. The time spent in the intrasocket reduction is:

$$T_{tiled-intra-red} = (a_\alpha + B_\alpha q(m/q))q = a_\alpha q + B_\alpha qm \quad (8)$$

The time spent in intersocket reduction is

$$\begin{aligned} T_{tiled-inter-red} &= (a_\beta + B_\beta (m/q)q)\lceil \log_2 s \rceil \\ &= (a_\beta + B_\beta m)\lceil \log_2 s \rceil \end{aligned} \quad (9)$$

The total reduction time is

$$T_{tiled-red} = a_\alpha q + B_\alpha mq + (a_\beta + B_\beta m)\lceil \log_2 s \rceil \quad (10)$$

For the broadcast phase, we use one- or two-stage broadcast, as presented in Section 2.2. The total time for tiled-reduce-broadcast is

$$T_{tiled-red-bcst} = a_\alpha q + B_\alpha mq + (a_\beta + B_\beta m)\lceil \log_2 s \rceil$$
$$+ min(a_\alpha + B_\alpha(q-1)m + a_\beta + b_\beta m, a_\beta + B_\beta qm) \quad (11)$$

2.5 Internode Communication

Allreduce can be executed on multiple network nodes by performing a reduce computation within each node, an allreduce across nodes, and a broadcast within each node. The intranode communication is the same as for a reduce-broadcast or a tiled-reduce-broadcast. Therefore, to first approximation, an optimized allreduce is obtained by composing the best intranode allreduce with the best internode allreduce. Internode collectives have been extensively studied [22, 18, 21], so we focus on the intranode part.

Different from reduce-broadcast and tiled-reduce-broadcast, internode dissemination is used after intranode dissemination for the dissemination algorithm across nodes. The internode dissemination is similar to the shared-memory algorithm described in Section 2.3. Assume there are P nodes (P is power of 2). It needs $N = \lceil \log_2 P \rceil$ steps to accomplish internode dissemination. In each step, to reduce communication overhead, only one thread in a node communicates with another node using point-to-point communication. After receiving the data, each thread within the node combines the received data with its own data simultaneously. Again, dissemination may has fewer steps but may have more communication than the other two algorithms. Experiments described in Section 3.6 compare the performance of these three algorithms on distributed memory.

2.6 Other Collective Operations

Our allreduce algorithms can be extended to other collective operations in NUMA shared memory systems. A reduce can be implemented as the reduction phase in allreduce. Different from allreduce, one needs to allocate an extra temporary buffer for each parent thread to store the intermediate results, since only the root thread has an output buffer. Broadcast can be implemented as the broadcast phase of allreduce.

An intranode barrier is implemented as a reduce-broadcast allreduce with zero workload. In the reduction phase, each thread sets a flag variable to indicate its arrival by an n-ary reduction tree. The root thread then informs other threads to continue by a one- or two-stage broadcast tree. For the internode barrier, an existing MPI_Barrier is called by the root thread between the reduction and broadcast phases.

For scatter, a temporary buffer is allocated within each node. The "global" Scatter is called by the "node master" to scatter the send buffer evenly among all the nodes, and the temporary buffer on each node is used as the receive buffer. The temporary buffer on each node then is evenly scattered among all the threads within a node. Similar to the broadcast phase of allreduce, the intranode scatter phase can be implemented as one- or two-stage scatter.

3. EVALUATION

Experiments were conducted on both Intel Xeon X5650 (Westmere) and AMD Opteron 6100 (Magny-Cours) clus-

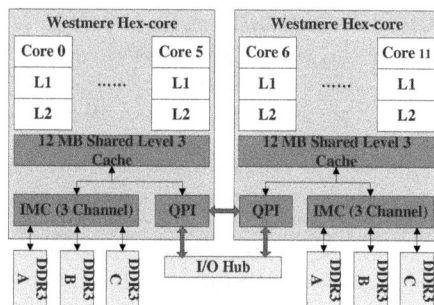

Figure 8: Westmere, 2 sockets, total 12 cores

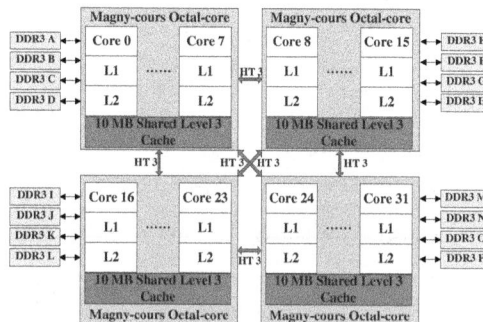

Figure 9: Magny-Cours, 4 sockets, total 32 cores

ters. One Xeon X5650 node has two 2.67 GHz Westmere processor sockets. Each socket has 6 cores and a 12 MB inclusive shared L3 cache. The architecture of the Xeon X5650 is illustrated in Figure 8. One Opteron 6100 node has 2.4 GHz Magny-Cours sockets with 8 cores in each of the sockets. Each socket has a shared 10 MB noninclusive L3 cache; 2 MB out of the 10 MB of L3 cache are used to record the data in L1 and L2 caches. The architecture of the Opteron 6100 is illustrated in Figure 9.

In a Xeon X5650 node, intersocket data transfer goes through the Quick Path Interconnect (QPI), while in an Opteron 6100 node, intersocket data transfer goes through HyperTransport (HT 3) point-to-point links. Both the Xeon X5650 nodes and Opteron 6100 nodes are connected with Voltaire QDR InfiniBand in the cluster. The operating system on the Xeon X5650 cluster is Scientific Linux 6.1; the operating system on Opteron 6100 cluster is CentOS 5.5.

We compare the performance of HMPI's Allreduce with several currently popular MPI implementations, including MPICH2 1.4.1.pl, MVAPICH2 1.6, and Open MPI 1.6 in both shared-memory and distributed-memory environments. All the experiments are run 256 times, and we present the average values in the following figures. To save space, if similar results are obtained from both systems, we present the results only on one architecture.

We define the *speedup* S as $S = \frac{T_{ref}}{T}$. This means that an optimized operation that runs in 50% of the latency (time) of the reference operation is said to have a speedup of 2 (also denoted as 2X).

3.1 Reduce-Broadcast

In this section, we compare the performance of different broadcast and reduction tree structures, in order to select the reduce-broadcast algorithm. Figures 10 and 11 present the performance comparison of different broadcast trees on Westmere and Magny-Cours CMPs respectively. On the 12-core Westmere, a one-stage broadcast where 11 threads read data from the root thread simultaneously always gets the best performance for all vector sizes. The reason is that the inclusive L3 cache of Westmere exhibits affordable contention when all the threads accessing it simultaneously.

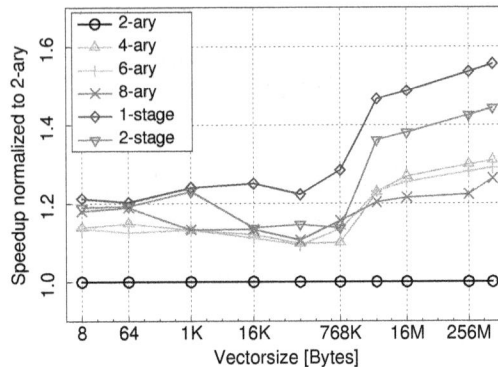

Figure 10: **Performance comparison of different n-ary broadcast trees and 1-stage/2-stage broadcast trees on 12-core Westmere**

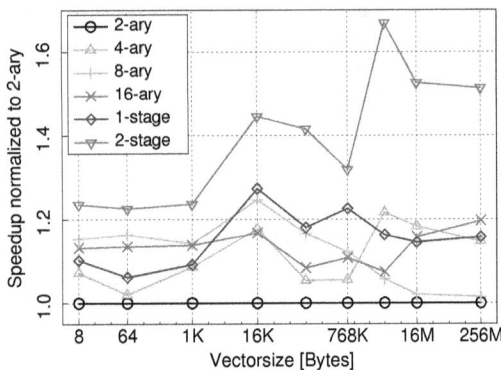

Figure 11: **Performance comparison of different n-ary broadcast trees and 1-stage/2-stage broadcast trees on 32-core Magny-Cours**

Different from Westmere, on the 32-core Magny-Cours, a two-stage broadcast always gets the best performance for all vector sizes. The reason is probably that Magny-Cours has more sockets and cores than does Westmere, so that the benefit of finishing broadcast in one step cannot compensate for the high contention overhead.

In both Figures 10 and 11, flatter broadcast trees become much more advantageous when the vector size is larger than 768 KB. The reason is that the total data set size is larger than the L3 cache and threads need to load the data from main memory (DRAM). The bandwidth to main memory is much lower than the L3 cache, so that reducing the number of passes becomes more important.

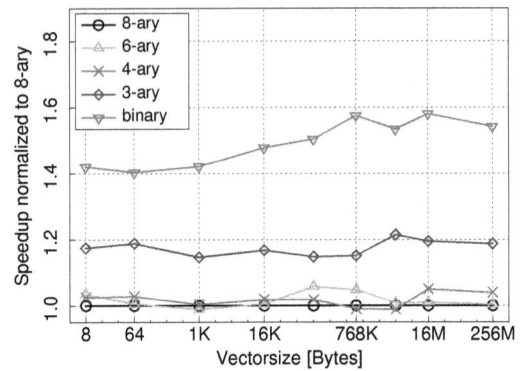

Figure 12: **Performance comparison of different n-ary reduction trees on 32-core Magny-Cours**

Figure 12 presents the performance comparison of different n-ary reduction trees on Magny-Cours. As expected, a binary reduction tree dominates all other n-ary reduction trees. Similar results have been obtained for Westmere. In summary, the best reduce-broadcast algorithm is a binary reduction tree followed by a one-stage or two-stage broadcast tree, which is abbreviated as "tree" algorithm in the remainder of the paper.

3.2 Performance of Tiled-Reduce

We evaluate the performance of the hierarchical tiled-reduce algorithm presented in Section 2.4 with other similar implementations, namely, a naive tiled-reduce and cyclic tiled-reduce [11]. Tiled-reduce does the reduction in parallel but without consideration of the NUMA hierarchy. This leads to high contention for intersocket memory accesses. Mamidalaet al. [11] proposed a cyclic tiled-reduce algorithm where the order of send buffer (input buffer) accesses are interleaved leading to lower contention than tiled-reduce. Figure 13 show the results on Magny-Cours. Cyclic tiled-

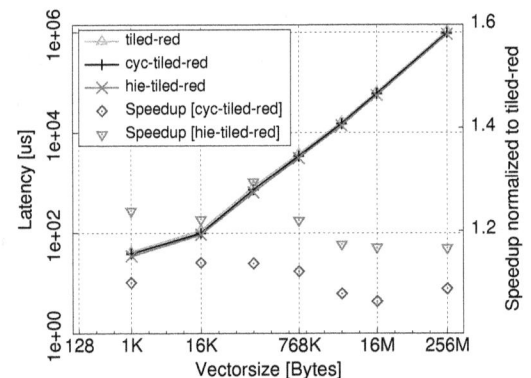

Figure 13: **Tiled-reduce on 32-core Magny-Cours**

reduce performs slightly better than the original tiled-reduce algorithm. The hierarchical algorithm that uses tiled-reduce inside sockets and tree reduction across sockets has significantly better performance. Similar results have been obtained from Westmere.

3.3 HMPI's Allreduce vs. Traditional MPIs

First we compare the best HMPI Allreduce algorithms, including tree, dissemination, and tiled-reduce followed by a broadcast, with the current MPI implementations, including MPICH2, Open MPI 1.6, and MVAPICH2, on shared memory. The number of launched threads in HMPI Allreduce and the number of launched processes in the traditional Allreduce are equal to the number of cores on each architecture. Figure 14 shows the result on Westmere.

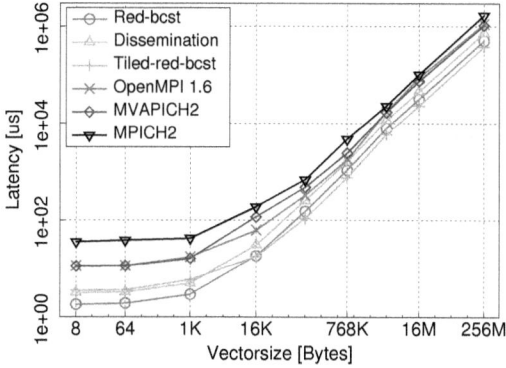

Figure 14: Performance comparison between HMPI's Allreduce algorithms and several MPI implementations on a 12-core Westmere CMP

HMPI's Allreduce always outperforms traditional approaches used in other MPI implementations. This performance is due partially to direct memory access and low overhead of synchronization and partially to the aggressive NUMA optimizations in HMPI. Among all the HMPI Allreduce algorithms, dissemination almost always exhibits the worst performance on both architectures (only better than tiled-reduce-broadcast for small vectors). This probably results from the redundant computation and contention caused by combining reduction and broadcast together, and the extra overhead for nonpower-of-2 thread counts, as reflected in Equation (7).

Among all the MPI implementations, MPICH2 always gets the worst performance. Recall that in MPICH2, collectives are built on the point-to-point message passing using shared memory merely as a transport layer; in Open MPI 1.6 and MVAPICH2, collectives are implemented and optimized independently by eliminating point-to-point message passing as the underlying communication protocol. Implementing collectives on top of point-to-point message passing has the most buffer copies. Our best implementation achieves on average 3.6X lower latency than Open MPI 1.6, 4.3X lower latency than MVAPICH2, and 8.8X lower latency than MPICH2.

Overall, the tree-based algorithm gets the best performance when the vector size is less than 16 KB, while tiled-reduce followed by a broadcast gets the best performance when vector size grows larger than 16 KB. When comparing Equation (5) with Equation (11), the latency of tiled-reduce followed by a broadcast is higher than tree but the bandwidth term is more favorable. When the vectors are small, latency is the limiting factor in the time overhead, so that tree performs better than parallel-reduce followed by a broadcast. When the vector size grows larger and band-

width becomes the bottleneck, tiled-reduce followed by a broadcast performs better than tree. Similar results have been achieved on Magny-Cours.

3.4 Algorithm Selection

In this section we use memory access latency and bandwidth to verify the performance models and then select the best Allreduce algorithms for different vector sizes. Several factors, such as cache coherence protocol, hardware and software prefetch, and page size (TLB), affect the cache line transfer latency and bandwidth. The configurations of these parameters for both Westmere and Magny-Cours are presented below. Page size is set to 4 KB, hardware prefetch and adjacent line prefetcher are turned on, and no software prefetch is used in the original code or in the compiler options. The various cache line states also affect performance. In order to build the performance model accurately, all the data in send buffer and receive buffer are set to the *Modified state*, which models the common scenario of a local write followed by a global communication of the written buffer.

As mentioned, the tree-based algorithm gets the best performance for small vector sizes. The time overhead of a tree-based algorithm is shown in Equation (5), where $n = 2$. We set the vector size to one cache line ($m = 1$) and use experimentally measured cache line transfer latency to verify the model. To determine the latencies, we use BenchIT [13], which provides memory latency benchmarks for multicore and multiprocessor x86-based systems.

Figure 15 shows the results on Xeon X5650. The three curves show the latency of local access, intrasocket access (Core 0 accessing Core 1), and intersocket access (Core 0 accessing Core 6) respectively. By varying the data set size, the performance of the full memory hierarchy is exposed. The latency of reading local L1 cache (Rl) is 1.2 ns, the latency of reading other L1 cache but in the same socket (Rs) is 28.5 ns, and the latency of reading L1 cache on the other socket (Rr) is 105.2 ns.

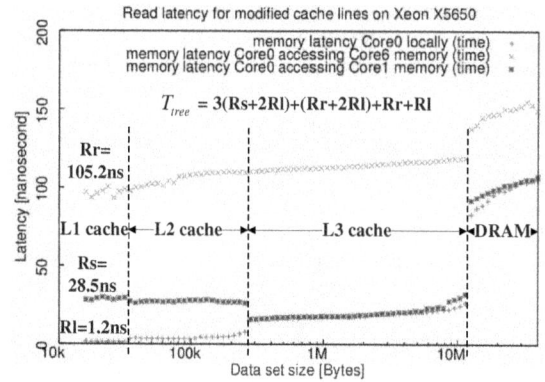

Figure 15: Modified cache line read latency on Westmere. Rl denotes latency of read local L1 cache, Rs denotes latency of read other L1 cache but within the same socket, and Rr denotes latency of read other L1 cache from remote socket.

On the 12-core Westmere, Equation (5) is unfolded as $T_{red-bcst} = (a_\alpha + 2B_\alpha m) + 2(a_\alpha + b_\alpha m) + (a_\beta + b_\beta m) + (a_\beta + B_\beta qm)$, where $m = 1, q = 6$. Figure 16 shows the steps in the tree-based algorithm on Westmere.

(1) In $Step_0$, $Step_1$, and $Step_2$, a thread reads a cache

91

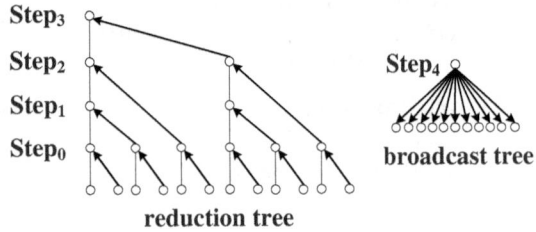

Figure 16: Steps in the tree-based algorithm on Westmere

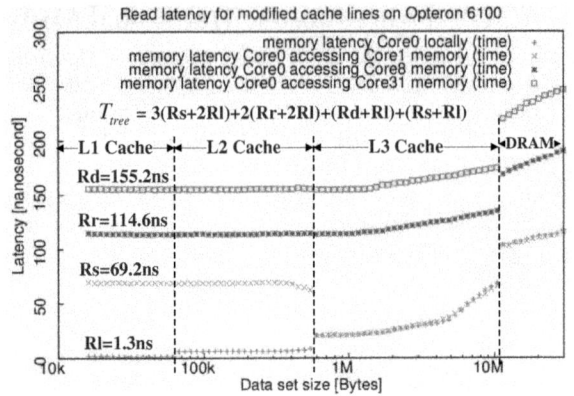

Figure 17: Modified cache line read latency on Magny-Cours. Rr denotes the L1 read latency from a horizontal or vertical remote socket, and Rd denotes the L1 read latency from a diagonal remote socket.

line from its local L1 cache and a cache line from a remote L1 cache but within the same socket and then writes to its local L1 cache. Because writing to the local L1 cache is a write hit, we assume its latency is equal to the read latency. In $Step_0$, there are 3 simultaneous memory accesses within each socket; however, because the data size is very small and the shared L3 cache serves as central unit for intercore communication, the congestion is ignored. Thus, the time overhead of the first three steps is $3(Rs+2Rl)$, corresponding to $(a_\alpha + 2B_\alpha m) + 2(a_\alpha + b_\alpha m)$ in the model.

(2) In $Step_3$, a thread performs the same operations as in the first three steps except that there is an intersocket cache line read. The time overhead of $Step_3$ is $Rr + 2Rl$, corresponding to $(a_\beta + b_\beta m)$ in the model.

(3) In $Step_4$, all other threads read data from the root thread and write to their own receive buffer. Because of the same reason mentioned in $Step_0$, the congestion is ignored. Hence, $Step_4$ can be simplified to one thread reading a cache line from remote socket and writes to local L1 cache. The write is a write hit and we assume it equals to the read latency. So the time overhead in $Step_4$ is $Rr + Rl$, corresponding to $(a_\beta + B_\beta qm)$ in the model.

To sum up, the overall time overhead of tree-based algorithm on Xeon X5650 is $3(Rs+2Rl)+(Rr+2Rl)+(Rr+Rl)=$ 306.7 ns. We use an indirect method to measure the practical runtime, namely, the runtime of one cache line workload minus the runtime of zero workload. The practical runtime is 339.8 ns, which is a little higher than that the model predicted. The deviation is due to complex interactions in the microarchitecture (e.g., pipelining and superscalar units) that have only low-order influence on the runtime and that we thus excluded from the model.

Similar results have been obtained on Magny-Cours. We note that on the four-socket Opteron 6100, the latency of reading an L1 cache line from a diagonal remote socket is higher than that from horizontal or vertical remote socket, as illustrated in Figure 17. The time overhead is $3(Rs + 2Rl) + 2(Rr + 2Rl) + (Rd + Rl) + (Rs + Rl) = 608.4$ ns, in which Rd denotes latency of read other L1 cache from diagonal remote socket. The practical runtime is 647.4 ns, which is also a little higher than that model prediction.

The tiled-reduce followed by a broadcast gets the best performance for large vector sizes. In this section, we utilize the performance models to select the best algorithm for different vector sizes. We measure all the values (latency and bandwidth) in Equation (5) and Equation (11) on Westmere, and we present the predicted runtime obtained from the performance models and the real runtime of parallel reduce followed by a broadcast and tree-based algorithms in

Figure 18. We see that the models can predict latencies accurately and the relative errors are all below 5%.

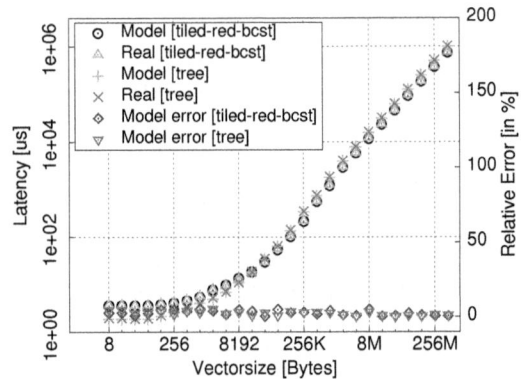

Figure 18: Performance model for tree and tiled-reduce-broadcast on Westmere

Figure 19 shows that the tree-based algorithm gets the best performance for small vector size, while the crosspoint at 16 KB indicates that the best algorithm switches to tiled-reduce followed by a broadcast. Similarly, the crosspoint on Magny-Cours is 14 KB.

3.5 Comparison with OpenMP

We compare our performance with another native shared-memory programming environment, OpenMP. We previously discussed how our techniques can be used in the context of MPI. However, we could not easily quantify the source of the benefits because current MPI implementations do not exploit direct shared-memory communication. Thus, in this section, we implemented HMPI Reduce with the techniques described above and compare it with OpenMP reductions that have been optimized for direct shared-memory accesses.

Figure 20 compares our best Reduce algorithms with an OpenMP REDUCTION clause [16] on Westmere. C based OpenMP does not support reduction on vectors, so we use Fortran based OpenMP reduction for our comparison. We

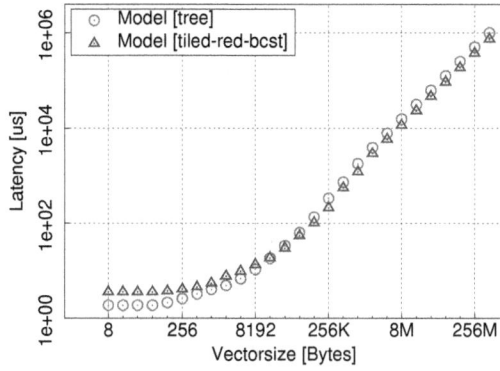

Figure 19: Selecting the best algorithm with the performance model on Westmere

use 12 threads for both HMPI Reduce and OpenMP on Westmere. We see that HMPI Reduce achieves on average 1.5X speedup over OpenMP for all the vector sizes, probably due to the hierarchy-aware HMPI Reduce implementation on NUMA machines.

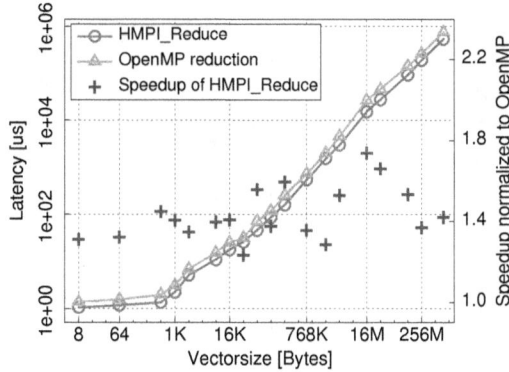

Figure 20: Performance comparison between the best HMPI Reduce algorithm and OpenMP reduction on Westmere

3.6 Performance on Distributed Memory

We now compare the algorithms of thread-based Allreduce on 16-node Xeon cluster combining inter- and intranode communications. As on shared memory, on-node dissemination exhibits the worst performance among our algorithms, as illustrated in Figure 21. For the internode dissemination, each node has to communicate with another node by point-to-point communication, probably causing more communication overhead than the current process-based MPI allreduce implementation [22, 18, 21], which is used for internode allreduce in tree and tiled-reduce-broadcast.

We compare thread-based MPI allreduce, broadcast, and reduce with MPICH2 1.4 and MVAPICH2 1.6. For both MPI and HMPI, the total number of launched ranks is equal to the total number of cores in the cluster. On 16-node Xeon X5650 and 8-node Opteron 6100 clusters, HMPI_Allreduce gets on average 2.5X and 2.3X speedup over MVAPICH2, and gets on average 6.3X and 4.7X speedup over MPICH2. To save space, only the performance comparison between HMPI_Allreduce and MVAPICH2 on 8-node Opteron 6100

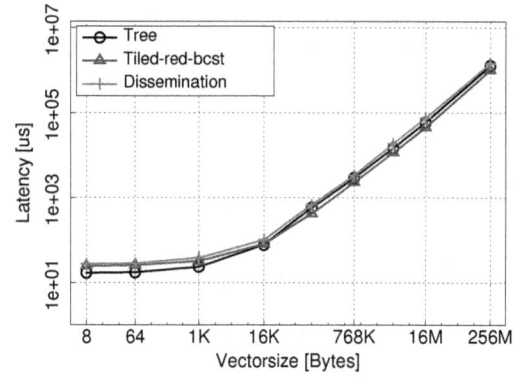

Figure 21: Performance comparison between HMPI_Allreduce algorithms on 16-node Xeon X5650 running on 192 cores

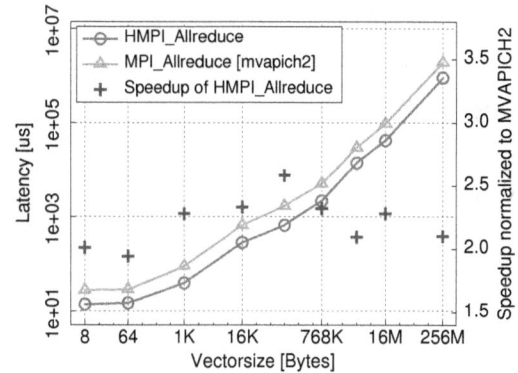

Figure 22: Performance comparison between HMPI's Allreduce and MVAPICH2 on 8-node Opteron 6100 running on 256 cores

cluster is shown in Figure 22. Figures 23 and 24 show the performance of HMPI_Bcast and HMPI_Reduce on the 16-node Xeon X5650 cluster. HMPI_Bcast and HMPI_Reduce get on average 1.8X and 1.4X speedup over MVAPICH2 for all vector sizes respectively. Figure 25 shows that HMPI_Barrier scales better than MVAPICH2. The results indicate that the thread-based MPI collectives design, which is a true zero-copy approach with NUMA-aware topology optimization, has significant advantage over traditional process-based MPI collectives.

3.7 Application Comparison

Two applications, dense matrix vector multiplication and tree-building in Barnes-Hut, are used to evaluate the performance of HMPI mainly stressing our collective optimizations. We compare HMPI implementation with MVAPICH2, which is the best performing MPI implementation in our earlier experiments. The dense matrix vector multiplication is computed for 128 iterations and the matrix size is $49,152 \times 49,152$. The matrix is partitioned columnwise and scattered to all the processes using MPI_Scatter. The vector is broadcast to all the processes using MPI_Bcast. Within each iteration, each process use an MPI_Reduce to sum the corresponding part of the intermediate results. As

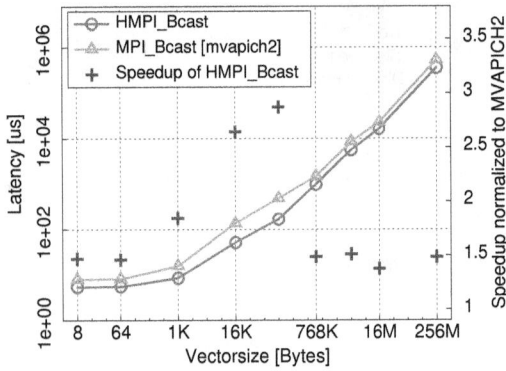

Figure 23: Performance comparison between HMPI's Bcast and MVAPICH2 on 16-node Xeon X5650 running on 192 cores

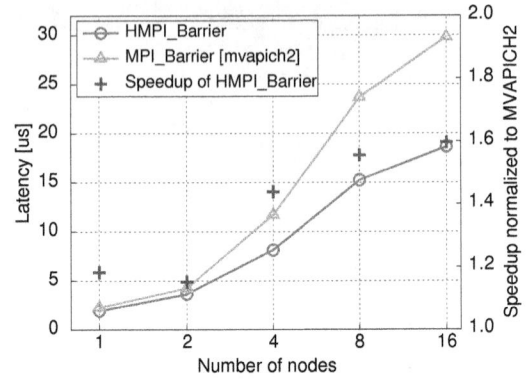

Figure 24: Performance comparison between HMPI_Reduce and MVAPICH2 on 16-node Xeon X5650 running on 192 cores

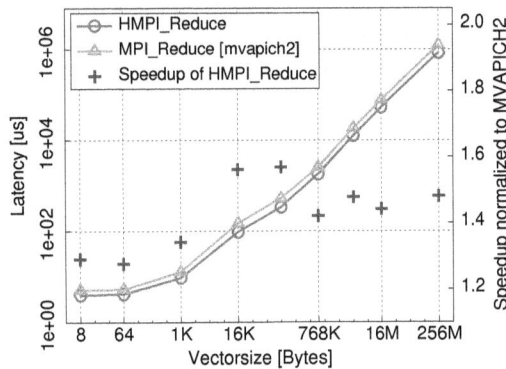

Figure 25: Performance comparison between HMPI_Barrier and MVAPICH2 on Xeon X5650 cluster (12, 24, 48, 96, and 192 cores)

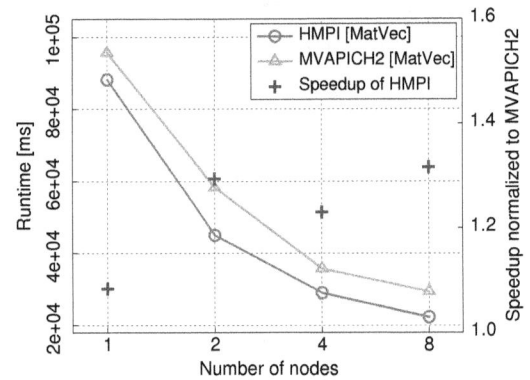

Figure 26: Dense matrix vector multiplication on Xeon X5650 cluster (12, 24, 48, and 96 cores)

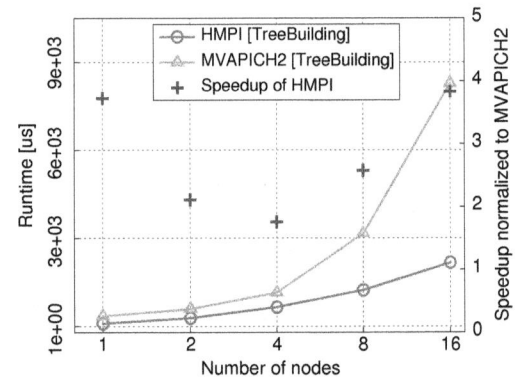

Figure 27: Tree-building in Barnes-hut on Xeon X5650 cluster (12, 24, 48, 96, and 192 cores)

illustrated in Figure 26, HMPI has better scalability and gets on average 1.2X speedup over MVAPICH2.

Allreduce is a key operation in the tree-building algorithm of the Barnes-Hut n-body simulation [27]. Tree building relies on allreduce to achieve high level alignment of space partitions. Processes compute local costs of subspaces and then use an allreduce to sum local costs of subspaces to get the global cost of these subspaces. Because processes split the simulation space recursively, multiple allreduce operations on different vector length are used until there is no fat subspace. We set the number of bodies to 4 million and test the allreduction phase of the tree building algorithm on 1, 2, 4, 8, and 16 Xeon X5650 nodes. HMPI shows on average 2.8X speedup over MVAPICH2. Moreover, as the number of nodes increases, the improvement becomes more apparent, as illustrated in Figure 27. Overall, results on real applications indeed validate the advantage of the thread-based MPI collectives design.

4. RELATED WORK

Several MPI implementations have optimizations for shared memory based on a process per MPI rank model. In MVAPICH2, shared-memory-based collectives have been enabled for MPI applications running over OFA-IB-CH3, OFA-iWARP-CH3, and uDAPL-CH3 stack. Currently, this support is available for the following collective operations: MPI_Allreduce, MPI_Reduce, MPI_Barrier, and MPI_Bcast [11]. Open MPI provides sm BTL (shared-memory Byte Transfer Layer) as a low-latency, high-bandwidth mechanism for transferring data between two processes via shared memory. According to the hardware architecture, Open MPI will choose the best BTL available for each communication. Other MPI implementations, such as LA-MPI [2] and Sun MPI [19], also have support for shared memory.

Graham and Shipman [6] have examined the benefits of creating shared-memory optimized multiprocess collectives for on-node operations. They indicated the importance of taking advantage of shared caches and reducing intersocket memory traffic. Kielmann et al. [10] developed MagPIe, a hierarchy-aware library of collective communication operations for wide area systems. We utilize this hierarchical design method to implement NUMA-aware collectives of HMPI. Tang and Yang [20] presented thread-based MPI system for SMP clusters and showed that multi-threading, which provides a shared-memory model within a process, can yield performance gain for MPI communication because of speeding the synchronization and reducing the buffering and orchestration overhead. Their experimental results indicated that even in a cluster environment for which internode network latency is relatively high, exploiting thread-based MPI execution on each node can deliver substantial performance gains. A hybrid of multiprocess and multithreading runtime system for Partitioned Global Address Space languages is presented in [3].

Tree-based barriers, such as the Combining Tree Barrier [25] and the MCS Barrier [12], are designed to distribute hotspot accesses over a software tree. This rationale is also used in HMPI when designing synchronization operations, such as HMPI_Barrier, and also collective operations, such as tree-based HMPI_Allreduce. Dissemination-based barriers [7, 12] achieve complete dissemination of information among p processes in $log_2 p$ synchronized steps. We utilize this algorithm to implement dissemination-based allreduce which further evolves to 3D dissemination (intrasocket, intersocket and then internode) to reduce communication overhead. Zhang et al. [26] have exploited program-level transformations to lift the parallel programs to be cache-sharing-aware, which motivated us when optimizing the collective algorithms to take advantage of shared cache.

5. CONCLUSIONS AND DISCUSSION

In the era of multicore or manycore, parallel programming languages or libraries need to provide high performance and low power consumption for scientific computing applications on both shared and distributed memory. In this paper, we improve MPI performance, the most popular library interface for high-performance computing, using multithreading for collective communications. Multithreading has several advantages over multiprocessing on shared memory for collectives: direct memory access can reduce buffer copying and system resource overhead; and multithreading features fast synchronization between threads.

For multithreading-based HMPI_Allreduce, we design hierarchy-aware algorithms to reduce intersocket data transfer, utilize shared last-level cache in modern CMPs to reduce data transfer latency, and adopt strip mining to improve the cache efficiency when the dataset size exceeds the capacity of the last-level cache.

We find that tree-based HMPI_Allreduce is best for small vector sizes while tiled-reduce followed by a broadcast is best for large vector sizes. We compare the best allreduce algorithms of HMPI with other MPI implementations. Experimental results show that multithreading yields significant performance improvement for MPI collective communication. On 16-node Xeon cluster and 8-node Opteron cluster,

HMPI_Allreduce gets on average 2.5X and 2.3X speedup over MVAPICH2 1.6, and gets on average 6.3X and 4.7X speedup over MPICH2 1.4. We also establish performance models for all the algorithms of HMPI_Allreduce. The consistency of predicted and measured running time shows the correctness of the performance models, which can be used for algorithm selection on new platforms.

Architecture trends indicate that the number of cores will grow continuously and that deep memory hierarchies will be necessary to reduce power consumption and contention on buses. Thus, we expect that NUMA effects will be even more important on future systems. Our developed techniques, algorithms, and model form a basis for implementing parallel communication algorithms on such future architectures.

6. ACKNOWLEDGMENTS

The work is supported in part by the DOE Office of Science, Advanced Scientific Computing Research, under award number DE-FC02-10ER26011 and DOE Office of Science, Advanced Scientific Computing Research, under award number DE-AC02-06CH11357. Li is supported in part by National Key Basic Research and Development Program of China under No.2013CB329606 and Key Project of the National Twelfth-Five Year Research Program of China under No.2011BAK08B04.

7. REFERENCES

[1] AMD. Software Optimization Guide for AMD Family 15h Processors, January 2012.

[2] R. Aulwes, D. Daniel, N. Desai, R. Graham, L. Risinger, M. Taylor, T. Woodall, and M. Sukalski. Architecture of LA-MPI, a network-fault-tolerant MPI. In *Proceedings of the 18th International Parallel and Distributed Processing Symposium.*, page 15, April 2004.

[3] F. Blagojević, P. Hargrove, C. Iancu, and K. Yelick. Hybrid PGAS runtime support for multicore nodes. In *Proceedings of the Fourth Conference on Partitioned Global Address Space Programming Model*, PGAS '10, pages 3:1–3:10. ACM, 2010.

[4] F. Broquedis, J. Clet-Ortega, S. Moreaud, N. Furmento, B. Goglin, G. Mercier, S. Thibault, and R. Namyst. hwloc: A generic framework for managing hardware affinities in HPC applications. In *Proceedings of the 2010 18th Euromicro Conference on Parallel, Distributed and Network-based Processing*, PDP '10, pages 180–186. IEEE Computer Society, 2010.

[5] A. Friedley, T. Hoefler, G. Bronevetsky, A. Lumsdaine, and C.-C. Ma. Ownership Passing: efficient distributed memory programming on multi-core systems. In *PPoPP'13. Proceedings of the 18th ACM symposium on Principles and Practice of Parallel Programming*, 2013. Accepted at PPoPP'13.

[6] R. L. Graham and G. Shipman. MPI support for multi-core architectures: optimized shared memory collectives. In *Proceedings of the 15th European PVM/MPI Users' Group Meeting on Recent Advances in Parallel Virtual Machine and Message Passing Interface*, pages 130–140, Berlin, Heidelberg, 2008. Springer-Verlag.

[7] D. Hensgen, R. Finkel, and U. Manber. Two

algorithms for barrier synchronization. *Int. J. Parallel Program.*, 17(1):1–17, Feb. 1988.

[8] T. Hoefler, T. Mehlan, F. Mietke, and W. Rehm. Fast barrier synchronization for InfiniBand. In *Parallel and Distributed Processing Symposium, 2006. IPDPS 2006. 20th International*, April 2006.

[9] Intel. Intel 64 and IA-32 Architectures Optimization Reference Manual, April 2012.

[10] T. Kielmann, R. F. H. Hofman, H. E. Bal, A. Plaat, and R. A. F. Bhoedjang. MagPIe: MPI's collective communication operations for clustered wide area systems. In *Proceedings of the seventh ACM SIGPLAN symposium on Principles and practice of parallel programming*, PPoPP '99, pages 131–140, New York, NY, USA, 1999. ACM.

[11] A. Mamidala, R. Kumar, D. De, and D. Panda. MPI collectives on modern multicore clusters: performance optimizations and communication characteristics. In *8th IEEE International Symposium onCluster Computing and the Grid. CCGRID '08.*, pages 130 –137, May 2008.

[12] J. M. Mellor-Crummey and M. L. Scott. Synchronization without contention. *SIGPLAN Not.*, 26(4):269–278, April 1991.

[13] D. Molka, D. Hackenberg, R. Schone, and M. S. Muller. Memory performance and cache coherency effects on an Intel Nehalem multiprocessor system. In *Proceedings of the 2009 18th International Conference on Parallel Architectures and Compilation Techniques*, PACT '09, pages 261–270, Washington, DC, 2009. IEEE Computer Society.

[14] MPI Forum. MPI: A Message-Passing Interface standard. version 2.2, September 2009.

[15] S. Negara, G. Zheng, K.-C. Pan, N. Negara, R. E. Johnson, L. V. Kalé, and P. M. Ricker. Automatic MPI to AMPI program transformation using photran. In *Proceedings of the 2010 Conference on Parallel Processing*, Euro-Par 2010, pages 531–539, Berlin, Heidelberg, 2011. Springer-Verlag.

[16] OpenMP Architecture Review Board. Application Program Interface Version 3.1. July 2011.

[17] M. Pérache, P. Carribault, and H. Jourdren. MPC-MPI: an MPI implementation reducing the overall memory consumption. In *Proceedings of the 16th European PVM/MPI Users' Group Meeting on Recent Advances in Parallel Virtual Machine and Message Passing Interface*, pages 94–103, Berlin, Heidelberg, 2009. Springer-Verlag.

[18] R. Rabenseifner. Optimization of collective reduction operations. *Computational Science-ICCS*, pages 1–9, 2004.

[19] S. Sistare, R. Vaart, and E. Loh. Optimization of MPI collectives on clusters of large-scale SMP's. In *Supercomputing, ACM/IEEE 1999 Conference*, November 1999.

[20] H. Tang and T. Yang. Optimizing threaded MPI execution on SMP clusters. In *Proceedings of the 15th International Conference on Supercomputing*, ICS '01, pages 381–392. ACM, 2001.

[21] R. Thakur and W. Gropp. Improving the performance of collective operations in MPICH. In *Recent Advances in Parallel Virtual Machine and Message Passing Interface. Number 2840 in LNCS, Springer Verlag (2003) 257-267 10th European PVM/MPI User's Group Meeting*, pages 257–267. Springer Verlag, 2003.

[22] R. Thakur, R. Rabenseifner, and W. Gropp. Optimization of collective communication operations in MPICH. *International Journal of High Performance Computing Applications*, 19:49–66, 2005.

[23] V. Tipparaju, J. Nieplocha, and D. Panda. Fast collective operations using shared and remote memory access protocols on clusters. In *Parallel and Distributed Processing Symposium, 2003. Proceedings. International.* IEEE, 2003.

[24] M. Woodacre, D. Robb, D. Roe, and K. Feind. The SGI AltixTM 3000 global shared-memory architecture, 2005.

[25] P.-C. Yew, N.-F. Tzeng, and D. Lawrie. Distributing hot-spot addressing in large-scale multiprocessors. *IEEE Transactions on Computers*, C-36(4):388–395, april 1987.

[26] E. Z. Zhang, Y. Jiang, and X. Shen. Does cache sharing on modern CMP matter to the performance of contemporary multithreaded programs? In *Proceedings of the 15th ACM SIGPLAN Symposium on Principles and Practice of Parallel Programming*, PPoPP '10, pages 203–212. ACM, 2010.

[27] J. Zhang, B. Behzad, and M. Snir. Optimizing the Barnes-Hut algorithm in UPC. In *Proceedings of 2011 International Conference for High Performance Computing, Networking, Storage and Analysis*, SC '11, pages 75:1–75:11. ACM, 2011.

[28] H. Zhu, D. Goodell, W. Gropp, and R. Thakur. Hierarchical collectives in MPICH2. In *Proceedings of the 16th European PVM/MPI Users' Group Meeting on Recent Advances in Parallel Virtual Machine and Message Passing Interface*, pages 325–326, Berlin, Heidelberg, 2009. Springer-Verlag.

Modeling Communication in Cache-Coherent SMP Systems - A Case Study with Xeon Phi[*]

Sabela Ramos
Computer Architecture Group
University of A Coruña
Spain
sramos@udc.es

Torsten Hoefler
Scalable Parallel Computing Lab
ETH Zurich
Switzerland
htor@inf.ethz.ch

ABSTRACT

Most multi-core and some many-core processors implement cache coherency protocols that heavily complicate the design of optimal parallel algorithms. Communication is performed implicitly by cache line transfers between cores, complicating the understanding of performance properties. We developed an intuitive performance model for cache-coherent architectures and demonstrate its use with the currently most scalable cache-coherent many-core architecture, Intel Xeon Phi. Using our model, we develop several optimal and optimized algorithms for complex parallel data exchanges. All algorithms that were developed with the model beat the performance of the highly-tuned vendor-specific Intel OpenMP and MPI libraries by up to a factor of 4.3. The model can be simplified to satisfy the tradeoff between complexity of algorithm design and accuracy. We expect that our model can serve as a vehicle for advanced algorithm design.

Categories and Subject Descriptors

C.4 [**Performance of Systems**]: Modeling techniques

Keywords

Cache coherency; Communication modeling; Shared memory systems; Intel Xeon Phi

1. MOTIVATION

The recent stop of frequency and Dennard scaling while Moore's law still holds, caused processor manufacturers to move into the direction of multi- and many-core architectures. Eight- or sixteen-core CPUs are standard in today's commodity machines, and the number of cores is growing, for example in graphics processing units (GPUs) which are exceedingly used for general purpose computations. However, programming GPUs requires a deviation from traditional latency-optimized programming to stream-optimized computing. Thus, it is considered viable to push the standard architectures, e.g., x86 into the many-core era. Those architectures typically offer automated *cache coherency* to the user, a mechanism where changes in one cache are automatically transferred to other caches. Indeed, coherency protocols are usually the only means of communication between cores. Cache-coherency protocols are often implemented using fully connected crossbars and broadcast protocols for smaller numbers of cores. However, crossbar switches and broadcast protocols do not scale to larger numbers of cores and are commonly replaced by directory-based approaches.

Some ISA's, e.g. x86, do not offer explicit communication functions between cores, thus, communication must be implemented through loads and stores, essentially relying on the underlying cache-coherency protocol. The growing number of cores makes it increasingly important to understand the performance characteristics of such protocols. Analytic performance models, a formalization of such performance characteristics, can be used to design intelligent and scalable multi-core algorithms.

Current broadcast- and directory-based cache coherency protocols are implemented using a rather complex state machine where every cache line (a fixed unit of memory cells) can be in a different state in cache. In this work, we create a complete performance model for communication in cache-coherent systems by assigning a cost to each transition for a cache line in different caches. We then show how to reduce the complexity of the full model to enable its use for algorithm design. We demonstrate how to use this model mechanically for optimizing algorithms as well as the development of optimal algorithms. Our target architecture is the Intel's Xeon Phi accelerator, the currently most scalable cache-coherent single-chip architecture. Our developed algorithms are up to *4.3 times faster* than Intel's hand-tuned implementation in high-performance libraries and compilers (MPI and OpenMP).

In summary, the main contributions of this work are:

- We propose a novel state-based modeling approach for memory communication in cache-coherent systems.

- We demonstrate the applicability of the model to Intel Xeon Phi and show how it can be simplified for algorithm design.

- We demonstrate how our model can be used to design and optimize algorithms far beyond previous hand-optimized versions.

---

[*]This work was performed during a visit of S. Ramos at ETH, financed by HiPEAC

Furthermore, based on those insights, we argue that the addition of explicit communication interfaces for on-chip communication could enhance the performance of parallel algorithms significantly.

2. A PERFORMANCE MODEL FOR COMMUNICATION IN CACHE-COHERENT SYSTEMS

In most multi-core systems, the only way to communicate data from one thread, T_0, to another thread, T_1, is to issue load and store instructions from and to main memory. For example, if T_0 wants to send a word (initially in a register) to T_1, it would store it to a specific memory location which is then read by T_1 (assuming appropriate synchronization).

Early multi-core systems, using the MESI protocol [13], would perform this communication through main memory, i.e., the line would be evicted from T_0's cache to main memory and loaded into T_1's cache from memory. However, the costs to communicate the line to memory and back are significantly more expensive than on-chip transfers. Thus, more recent cache-coherency protocols [10] such as MOESI, MESIF, and extended MESI [1, §2.1.3] protocols allow direct cache-to-cache transfers.

We discuss the MESI protocol as an example and note that it can be extended with additional states to model advanced protocols. Table 1 summarizes the MESI states and their semantics.

Table 1: MESI protocol states

		Who may own it		Is it Modified?
		This core	Other cores	
M	Modified	Yes	No	Yes
E	Exclusive	Yes	No	No
S	Shared	Yes	Yes	No[1]
I	Invalid	No	Yes	-

Since memory is generally arranged in blocks (or lines), we will argue in terms of cache lines in the following. First we assume that the communicated data fits in one line and then we will extend the model to cover multi-line transfers.

The cache coherency protocol state will determine the location of each cache line[2] and the operations needed in order to fetch it, thus the latency of reading or writing will depend on the state of the requested line.

When communicating a cache line, it is always transferred between the caches of two cores running threads T_0 and T_1, respectively. We assume the most general model where the line may be in any state in each cache. Let us assume that T_0 wants to communicate a line that is in state invalid (I) before the communication. Thread T_0 will write the send data and the line would transition from $I \rightarrow M$ in its local cache. The following read by T_1 would transfer the line to $T_1's$ cache and transition it in both caches into the shared state. We assume that each state update and line transfer has a specific cost associated with it.

A program $\mathcal{P}$ now defines a set of transitions for each used cache line in each cache of the parallel computation.

[1]This state can be extended to allow sharing of modified lines as we describe later.

[2]we use "cache line" and "cache line data" synonymously if the meaning can easily be inferred

The possible transitions for each cache line (as mandated by $\mathcal{P}$) can be modeled with a finite automaton with an initial state I (invalid).

We can now model the state changes and costs for all pairs of line states in T_0 and T_1. Figure 1 shows our initial cost model for the transfer of one cache line from T_0 to T_1. Let both threads be running in two different cores using an extended MESI protocol in which a modified line can be shared (other protocols would require slightly different but conceptually identical transition cost graphs). Each vertex represents the state of the line in each of the two cores, while edges represent the transitions. The possible states of a line in one core are M (modified), E (exclusive), S (shared) and I (invalid). Each vertex would be composed by the combination of two of these states to represent the cache line in each of the two cores. Vertices that are not shown represent invalid combinations of protocol states (e.g., the same line cannot be exclusive to two caches!).

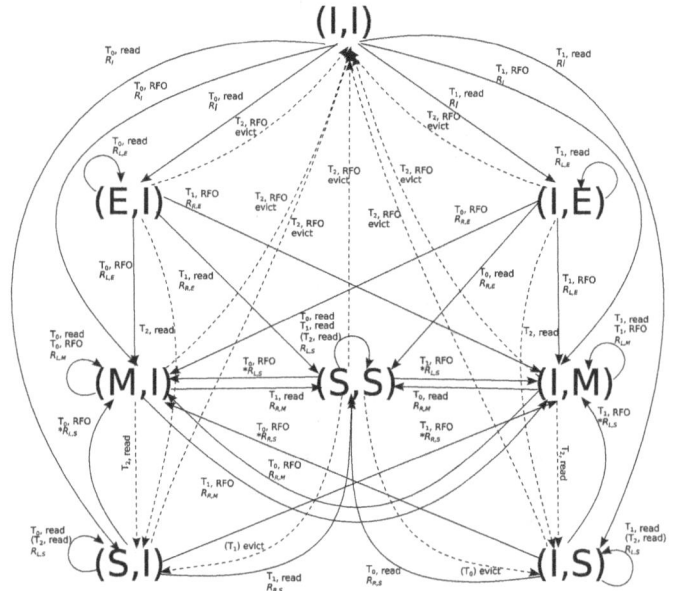

Figure 1: Transition diagram for the MESI protocol for communicating one cache line with two cores. The vertices form combinations of states (see Table 1), and the edges show actions that cause transitions and the associated costs.

Each transition is labeled with the required action (in the form $T_i, action$) and the cost associated. Dotted edges either represent external actions taken by a third thread (T_2) that runs in another core, or local capacity evictions. Thus, those edges do not have any associated cost. The actions can be *read*, *RFO* (request for ownership) and *evict*. When several actions appear at one edge, it indicates that any of them can be taken to transition to the target vertex.

The costs for all line transfers can be modeled in terms of line reads since a cache line is read into the local cache for both, load and store operations. Line writes only happen if lines are evicted to main memory and are thus outside of our cache-to-cache communication model. We denote the costs for reading lines as $R_{\mathcal{L},\mathcal{S}}$, where $\mathcal{L}$ is the location of the line (**L**ocal for the own cache of the thread performing the action, and **R**emote if the line is in other core cache), and $\mathcal{S}$ is the state of the line before the transition (M, E, S, or I). If $\mathcal{S} = I$, the location is not relevant since the line has to be fetched from main memory.

The symbol $*$ preceding some of the costs indicate that there can be an overhead as a consequence of the need to invalidate the line in other caches. This occurs, for example, with an RFO of a shared line: with a modified or exclusive line the target of invalidation is well-defined (the current owner), but with a shared line there can be multiple cores holding the line.

All costs ($R_{\mathcal{L},\mathcal{S}}$) in the model can be benchmarked with a methodology similar to the one proposed by Molka et al. [18]. Due to space limitations, we only discuss the most scalable and thus most interesting architecture, Intel Xeon Phi, in the following. The extended technical report version of this paper [22] contains model parameters for other architectures as well.

2.1 Intel Xeon Phi Architecture

The Intel Xeon Phi coprocessor is a many-core system based on the Intel MIC (Many Integrated Core) architecture. Its cores are arranged on a bidirectional ring bus that provides high scalability. Figure 2 represents the basic architecture of the Xeon Phi including the cores, the bus, the memory controller and the tag directories. The current commercial Xeon Phi (5110P) has 60 simplified Intel CPU cores running at 1056 MHz and supports 4 threads per core with hyperthreading (thus, 240 threads in the die). The cores have a vector unit with 64 byte registers featuring a new vector instruction set known as Intel Initial Many Core Instructions (IMCI). Each core has a 32 kb L1 data cache, 32 kb L1 instruction cache, and a private 512 kb L2 unified cache which is kept coherent by a distributed tag directory system (DTDs). There are 64 tag directories connected to the ring and the address-mapping to the tag directories is based on hash functions over the memory addresses, leading to an even distribution around the ring. The bidirectional ring to which cores and DTDs are connected has three independent rings in each direction [7]: the data block ring (64 bytes wide), the address ring (send/write commands and memory addresses) and the acknowledgment ring (flow control and coherence messages). The memory controllers, also connected to the ring, provide access to the GDDR5 memory (8 GB of global memory). The coprocessor runs a simplified Linux-based OS in one of the cores.

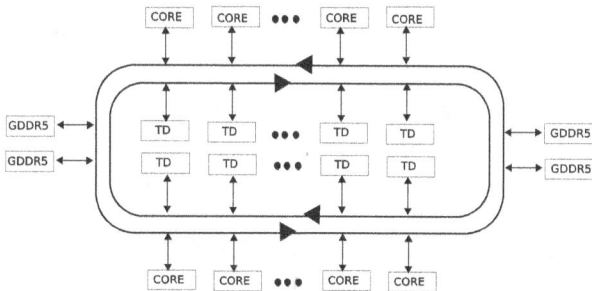

Figure 2: Architecture of the Intel Xeon Phi coprocessor

The main advantage of the Xeon Phi over other accelerators or coprocessors is that it provides the well-known x86 ISA and memory model, hence the programming effort is just focused on how to better exploit performance, but it can be done with known techniques and languages such as OpenMP or MPI. Xeon Phi can be used as a mere coprocessor in which the host offloads code to be accelerated, or as an independent unit that runs a whole application or that communicates in a symmetric manner with the host [1, §6].

2.1.1 Directory-Based Cache Coherency

The cache coherency on Intel Xeon Phi chips is implemented using an extended MESI protocol [1, §2.1.3]. The main difference to standard MESI-based systems is that the shared (S) state was extended with a directory-based cache coherency protocol called GOLS (Globally Owned, Locally Shared) in order to avoid broadcast storms on the address buses. GOLS extends the shared state to allow modified as well as unmodified lines. Each cache needs to consult the GOLS protocol to determine if a line is in modified state or not.

The global coherency is maintained via *Distributed Tag Directories* (DTDs) that hold the GOLS coherency state of each line. Lines are assigned to each DTD using a hash function based on the address of the line. This results in an even load distribution (assuming an even distribution of memory addresses) but does not take advantage of locality in the network. This means that the DTD which is responsible for a line held by a specific core is not local to the core, in fact, on average, it will be at a distance of *15 cores* due to the ring topology. Table 3 describes the different states of the GOLS directory protocol.

Table 3: GOLS protocol states

		Number of owners	Is it Modified?
GOLS	Globally Owned Locally Shared	Several	Yes
GE /GM	Globally Exclusive /Modified	One	Yes or No (the core has M or E)
GS	Globally Shared	Several	No
GI	Globally Invalid	None	-

When a core encounters a cache miss, it requests the line from the according DTD that will answer depending on the GOLS state and will either request the memory or the core owning the line to answer with the line data. If a core owns the line, it will acknowledge the DTD and send the data to the requester cache, which will then acknowledge the DTD that it has received the line, for the DTD to update the line state. In addition, any eviction has to notify the DTD before evicting the line.

A direct consequence of having a distributed directory protocol based on line addresses is that there are high differences in access latencies that are not dependent on the distance among cores but on the DTD that is holding the line. Since we cannot control the address mapping onto DTDs, we will use randomized accesses and work with averages and standard deviations to avoid DTDs bias in the benchmarking results and, thus, in the modeling. In fact, we observed up to a 5x variation in latency when not using randomization.

The protocol states are rather similar to MESI, the only difference lies in the fact that some reads are more expensive due to interaction with the DTDs and the extended shared state. However, the extended MESI model developed in the previous section is sufficient to model all transitions.

	Same core		Adjacent cores		Middle distance		Largest distance	
	avg	stdev	avg	stdev	avg	stdev	avg	stdev
M	8.6	0.2	241.2	21.7	234.7	25.6	240.1	10.4
E	8.6	0.2	227.4	20.6	235.8	25.5	237.4	27.7
S	8.7	0.9	232.0	10.2	233.4	35.0	233.4	22.5
I	277.7	34.0	274.3	25.2	278.8	34.4	284.5	29.6

(a) Results of the BenchIT [18] latency benchmark in nanoseconds

Label	Cost
$R_{L,M}$	8.6
$R_{L,E}$	8.6
$R_{L,S}$	8.7
$R_{R,M}$	234.7
$R_{R,E}$	235.8
$R_{R,S}$	233.4
R_I	277.7

(b) Model parameters (nanoseconds)

Label	Cost
$R_{L,*} = R_L$	8.6
$R_{R,*} = R_R$	235.8
R_I	277.7

(c) Simplified parameters (nanoseconds)

Table 2: Parametrizing and simplifying the model: (a) shows latency results and standard deviations for different distances, (b) extracts the relevant model parameters (cf. Fig. 1), (c) shows the simplified model parameters (cf. Fig. 3).

2.2 Parametrizing the Model for Xeon Phi

We use the BenchIT [18] benchmark to determine the base parameters of our model. The benchmark measures the latency of T_0 reading random lines from a buffer owned by T_1 varying the state of the lines and the placement of T_1. We place T_1 in the same core (distance 0), in an adjacent core (distance 1), in a distant core (distance 15) and in a core located at the opposite side of the ring (distance 30). When T_1 is in the same core as T_0, the reads of M, E, and S lines are performed inside the local cache, but, when T_1 is located in another core, T_0 has to communicate with the DTD in charge of the cache line (the S state is achieved by sharing the line between T_1 and a third thread).

Our measurements in Table 2a show that communication with the DTD makes the distance between the two cores nearly irrelevant. In fact, the distance-invariant performance is a design goal for excellent application scalability on Xeon Phi. Our model parameters can be derived from those measurements (we use the "Middle distance") and are shown in Table 2b. If the line is in I state, that is, it has to be fetched from memory, it does not matter if T_1 is in the local core or in a remote one, and for Table 2b we chose the values for "Same core".

The full model in Table 2b indicates that some of the states in Figure 1 can be collapsed due to nearly identical transition costs. We can form three groups of operations, local reads, remote reads, and reads of invalid lines. Table 2c and Figure 3 summarize the simplified model for Intel Xeon Phi.

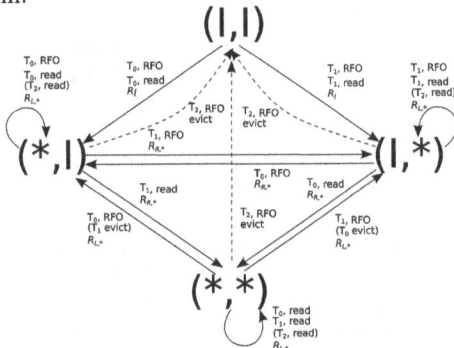

Figure 3: Graph of the simplified MESI transitions of a line within two cores

The simplifications we applied to make the model easier to use for algorithm design are system-specific. We tested the methodology on other systems, such as Sandy Bridge and Nehalem, and found that similar simplifications can be performed. The main difference is that, on those systems, the performance is generally depending on the distance between the caches. We found that this can be included with constant cost-offsets for each distance.

3. COMMUNICATION MODELS

In this section, we utilize the basic cache communication model to develop slightly more complex models for typical communications in parallel programming. The first and simplest model is for a single cache-line ping-pong benchmark where a send-buffer is communicated to a distinct receive buffer. The main difference is that this benchmark involves two memory locations and two lines, instead of one location as in the previous model. Later, we will extend the single-line ping-pong to multiple lines and then investigate the effect of contention while accessing single lines from multiple threads. This will result in a complete model for communications in cache-coherent systems that covers all scenarios that, for example, the LogP model family [9] expresses.

3.1 The Single-line Ping-Pong Model

The single-line ping-pong benchmark resembles the design of traditional ping-pong benchmarks: a send buffer is copied to a buffer at the receiver and, after reception, another buffer is copied back to the sender. This requires two sets of buffers on each process (thread) and a synchronization between sender and receiver. We are using a designated byte, which we call *canary value* in the receive buffer as a synchronization flag such that the receiver waits for the message by repeatedly reading this byte (polling) until the byte changes. Such "canary protocols" are used in practice for small-message synchronizations [12][3]. Figure 4 shows the benchmark schematically.

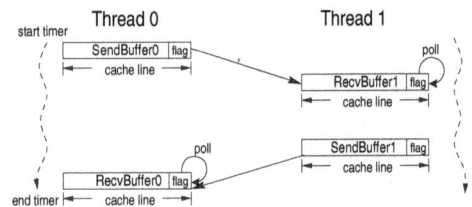

Figure 4: Ping-Pong test between two threads using four buffers.

The desired coherence state for each line is established before each ping-pong exchange. An S state indicates that

---
[3]We remark that such canary protocols are typically limited to a single aligned cache line due to relaxed memory consistency in modern multiprocessors.

the line is shared between the two threads performing the ping-pong. Considering the symmetry of the benchmark, send-buffers from both threads have the same cache coherence state ($\mathcal{S}_s$), and so do the recv-buffers ($\mathcal{S}_r$). The estimation of the latency of a ping-pong can be based upon the latencies of reading each line.

We assume that the protocol is sender-driven, i.e., the sender copies the data to the receiver. To perform the copy, the sender reads its send-buffer, which is in state $\mathcal{S}_s$ in the local cache, in time $R_{L,\mathcal{S}_s}$. This is followed by a read of the correspondent recv-buffer, which is in state $\mathcal{S}_r$ in the remote cache, in time $R_{R,\mathcal{S}_r}$. Then (ignoring the overhead that the write operation could provoke) the receiver reads its recv-buffer, that has been modified by the sender, and thus is in modified state in the sender's cache, in time $R_{R,M}$. This process is repeated with switched roles. Equation (1) shows $\mathcal{T}_1$, the single-line latency and the simplified model. The term O stands for an overhead that might be introduced by the coherency traffic due to having two active communicating threads (ideally, $O = 0$).

$$\mathcal{T}_1 = R_{L,\mathcal{S}_s} + R_{R,\mathcal{S}_r} + R_{R,M} + O = R_L + 2R_R + O \quad (1)$$

We measured 5000 independent iterations (using the high-precision x86 RDTSC counter) with pseudo-random addresses to avoid bias caused by the DTDs. The average and standard deviation form a Gaussian Distribution of the samples. We applied the t-test to each result to assess the statistical significance of our results and modeling. Where the result of the t-test was to reject the null hypothesis of equality of averages between both distributions, the overhead O was estimated as the difference of the distributions. Since the variances are unknown and not equal, we used Welch's t-test [25]. We found that we could reject the equality of averages with more than a 90% confidence in every scenario, confirming that there is an extra overhead imposed by the coherency traffic.

For the two threads T_0 and T_1 on different cores and $\mathcal{S}_s = \mathcal{S}_r = E$, we measured $497.1\mu s$ (standard deviation $\sigma = 77.2\mu s$) while the simplified model predicts $479.1\mu s$ ($\sigma = 36.1\mu s$). For the states $\mathcal{S}_s = I$ and $\mathcal{S}_r = E$, we measured $842.8\mu s$ (standard deviation $\sigma = 102\mu s$) while the simplified model predicts $748.1\mu s$ ($\sigma = 49.6\mu s$)[4].

The state $\mathcal{S}_r = I$ cannot be measured with our method because it cannot be guaranteed that the receive buffer is in invalid state when the sender attempts to fetch it. This is due to the benchmark design: the receiver is polling the recv-buffer and it can fetch it from memory before the sender requests it.

The results show that the overhead $O \simeq 18$ for the in-cache configuration and $O \simeq 95$ if the send-buffer is in memory. However, the overhead is lower than the standard deviation of the measurements, thus, although our t-test shows that it is statistically significant, it could be within the noise of real measurements.

3.2 The Multi-line Ping-Pong Model

We now show how to model multi-line ping-pong transfers, i.e., buffers can contain more than one cache line and, assuming x86 total store order [20], the receiver will only poll for the canary value on the last line of the recv-buffer

while the sender copies the content of the send-buffer. The analysis of different cache states is limited to 8 kb buffers due to the use of four buffers per pair of threads and the L1 cache size (32 kb). From now on, and given that we want to analyze the effect of having threads in different cores, we will assume a one-to-one mapping of threads to cores.

Assuming pipelining, the sender fetches every line in $\frac{2N}{P}R_{\mathcal{L},\mathcal{S}}$ where N is the number of cache lines of each buffer and P is the number of outstanding memory requests per core. After the copy, the receiver reads the last line, that has been modified by the sender, in $R_{R,M}$.

However, this simple model misses several factors that affect performance as the eviction overhead, the hardware prefetcher, the signal buses or the DTD capabilities to serve the outstanding requests. To approach this overhead, we tested a multiplicative factor based on the results, but, although it was asymptotically accurate, the relative error reached the 40-50% for small messages (2-12 lines) when the send-buffer was in I, and around 30% when it was in E. To obtain a more accurate model, we use linear regression with a typical transfer function. Equation (2) shows the model function where o is the asymptotic fetch latency for each cache line (including hardware prefetch, etc.), and p, q model the startup overhead which consists of a fixed part q that is amortized partially by the number of fetched lines with the factor p.

$$\mathcal{T}_N = o \cdot N + q - \frac{p}{N} \quad (2)$$

If we apply this model to a single line broadcast, it will essentially lead to the one-line model discussed before in Section 3.1: $\mathcal{T}_1 = R_L + 2R_R + O = q + o - p$.

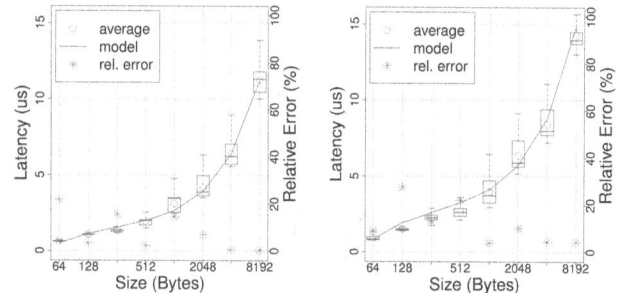

(a) Sender and receiver buffers in Exclusive state. The parameters of the model (in nanoseconds) are $76.0 \cdot N + 1521.0 - \frac{1096.0}{N}$. (b) Sender and receiver buffers in Invalid state. The parameters of the model (in nanoseconds) are $94.9 \cdot N + 2750.0 - \frac{2017.5}{N}$.

Figure 5: Latency and performance model for a multi-line ping-pong

The parametrization of the model has been performed with ping-pong tests using buffers from 64 bytes (one cache line) to 8 kb, varying the initial cache state of the buffers[5].

The results of our ping-pong measurements and the model fits are shown in Figure 5. The measurement for each size were repeated 5000 times and timed separately using x86 RDTSC. The left axis shows boxplots [17] of each value where the horizontal line is the median, the upper and lower parts of the box denote the first and third quartile and the whiskers show the minimum and maximum data values (out-

---

[4]An extensive analysis of every combination of states and locations of the threads has been carried out and are included in the extended version of this article [22].

[5]This test can use the $\mathcal{S}_r = I$ because the receiver is polling only the last line, and when the sender fetches the recv-buffer lines they are all invalidated except for the last one.

liers were removed). We use boxplots to visualize the statistical noise across measurements. The right axis and asterisks show the relative error of the model.

3.3 DTD Contention Model

On Xeon Phi, the DTDs may cause delays when they are contended [7]. Thus, we include an additional contention model to capture this effect. This may not be necessary in broadcast and snooping-based cache-coherency protocols.

Contention is benchmarked using a global send-buffer owned by one thread that every other thread (receivers) copies into a private recv-buffer. When having only two threads, the performance is expected to be $R_{\mathcal{L}_s,\mathcal{S}_s} + R_{\mathcal{L}_r,\mathcal{S}_r}$. For the rest of the section, and given that the sender is an idle thread that only owns the global buffer, we will assume that the number of threads is the number of receivers.

The contention on MIC for cached lines can be estimated with a linear model $\mathcal{T}_C(n_{th}) = c \cdot n_{th} + b$, where n_{th} is the number of threads, and c represents the slope and the overhead imposed when adding a new thread. If $n_{th} = 1$, there is no contention and $\mathcal{T}_C(1) = R_L + R_R = c + b$ (the cost of copying a global send-line into a private recv-line). Equation (4) shows the DTD contention model when buffers are in E state in the owner's cache.

$$\mathcal{T}_C(n_{th}) = R_L + R_R + c \cdot (n_{th} - 1) = b + c \cdot n_{th} \quad (3)$$

However, if the global line is in memory, the performance is limited by the access to memory and the model is similar to the one developed for the multi-line ping-pong in terms of the number of threads accessing the line instead of the message size.

$$\mathcal{T}_C(n_{th}) = c \cdot n_{th} + b - \frac{a}{n_{th}} \quad (4)$$

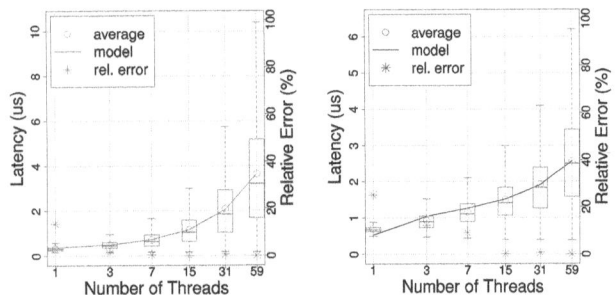

(a) Sender and receiver buffers in Exclusive state. The parameters of the model (in nanoseconds) are $320.5 + 56.2 \cdot n_{th}$.

(b) Sender and receiver buffers in Invalid state. The parameters of the model (in nanoseconds) are $23.4 \cdot n_{th} + 1202.0 - \frac{695.8}{n_{th}}$.

Figure 6: Contention in the access to the same line

Figure 6 shows the results of the benchmark for different number of threads and state of the global and private buffers (E for both in Figure 6a and I in Figure 6b).

3.4 Ring Contention

We have also analyzed how the number of running threads affects the performance of the cache line transfers. For this purpose, we have designed two ping-pong benchmarks. The first one arranges threads into groups of four where the communicating pairs are interleaved (e.g., if a group is formed by T_0, T_1, T_2 and T_3, and T_i is running in core i, the pairs are $T_0 - T_2$, and $T_1 - T_3$). The second benchmark forces pairs

to communicate through the same part of the ring (e.g, with 6 threads, the pairs will be $T2 - T3$, $T1 - T4$, $T0 - T5$) assuming that communications will use the shortest path. Due to the ring structure of the Xeon Phi, from the 16th pair on, communications will go through the other half of the ring.

Regardless of the initial cache state of the buffers, both benchmarks showed that there is no congestion caused by having several pairs of threads communicating simultaneously if they are accessing different memory addresses. The differences that appeared were not related to the number of running threads and the most feasible reason is the assignment of the requested lines to DTDs.

We have shown that the communication model can be parametrized accurately for simple communication tasks such as ping-pong. We now discuss how the model can be used to develop and parametrize suitable algorithms for communications on Xeon Phi.

4. DESIGNING COMMUNICATION ALGORITHMS IN THE MODEL

The communication algorithms tackled are different patterns of data exchange where interference among threads hugely increase variability. E.g., if two threads, T_0 and T_1 have to write to a line that T_2 is polling, waiting for them to write the value, the performance will depend on the order in which the three operations occur, as shown in Figure 7. If T_0 and T_1 write to the line, and then T_2 checks it (Fig. 7a), the cost is $R_I + 2R_R$. But, if T_2 checks it right after the write of T_0 (Fig. 7b), the line makes an extra travel to T_2 before going to T_1, and T_2 has to read it again to get the expected value ($R_I + 3R_R$). And there is still a worse scenario: when T_2 is the first that gets the line (Fig. 7c) and keeps polling, causing the line to travel from T_2's cache to each writer and the other way round, increasing the cost up to $R_I + 4R_R$.

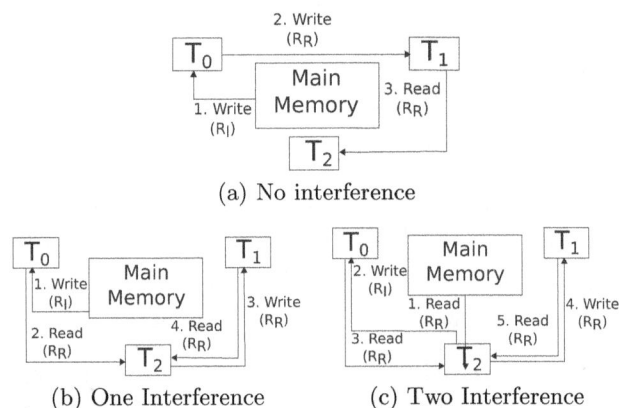

(a) No interference

(b) One Interference

(c) Two Interference

Figure 7: Interference in the access to a cache line by two writers (T_0 and T_1) and a reader that is polling the line waiting for writes.

To capture all the variations, the algorithms are expressed as *Min-Max Models* including the best and the worst case.

In the design of algorithms, it is assumed that data buffers are initially in exclusive state in the owner's cache to simplify the discussion. Similar results were obtained with buffers in invalid state and the models can be adapted by applying the invalid-state equations where the exclusive-state models are used. For the same reason, shared structures are assumed to be in memory (invalid) at the beginning of each algorithm.

4.1 Fast Message Broadcasting

The broadcast operation consists of sending one message from one thread, called *root*, to every other thread. We will talk in terms of trees since they are the more common communication patterns in broadcast algorithms.

In a shared memory scenario, a send-receive pair of operations can be performed in two different ways. In a *sender-driven* approach, the sender copies the data into the recv-buffer, similar to the pingpong benchmark from Section 3.1; the receiver may notify the sender with the canary protocol that the recv-buffer is ready. In a *receiver-driven* approach, the receiver would copy the message after the sender has notified that it is ready (notification forwards). In addition, the receiver has to acknowledge the reception of the message (notification backwards).

For the broadcast operation, where the sender communicates with several receivers, the receiver-driven approach allows simultaneous copies and thus leads to better load balancing for larger numbers of threads despite the additional acknowledgment.

4.1.1 Notification

The notification forwards and backwards uses shared structures in order for them to be accessible to every thread. There, the root can notify that the message is ready to be copied and the rest of threads can confirm that they have received the message, so that the root can free the shared structure. If the algorithm uses a tree, each parent has to communicate with its descendants and every descendant has to notify backwards to is parent, thus, several notification substructures will be needed.

Given that the parent has to provide, along with a notification flag, the data that is going to be copied or the address where it is stored, the notification forwards can be seen as a notification with payload where data and flag can be fetched in a single line. Hence, if data is small enough to fit in the same line, the descendants will poll the notification line and they will copy the data directly from there. If the space in the notification line is not enough, the parent will set the flag and an address (zero-copy protocol) from which descendants will copy the data.

The backwards notification from the descendants to the parent uses cache lines that are independent from the notification forwards structures to avoid interference in the copy of the data. We analyze two variants of this notification: The first one with one cache line in which every thread adds a value after finishing. The parent reads this value and checks if the operation is done. This requires every child thread, to write to the same line, and, since only one thread can write a line at a time, these writes are going to be serialized. In the second variant, each thread avoids serialization by writing its own notification line, but the parent has to read them all to check if the operation is done. We will focus on the use of one line because both the model and the empirical results confirmed that it provides better performance.

The model for the notification backwards assumes that each thread writes an immediate value and thus there is no cost associated with reading an additional cache line.

Since all threads, but the root, write to the same line,

every thread (but the root) has to read and modify the notification line ($R_I + (n_{th} - 2)R_R$). Then, in the best case, the root only reads the line at the end (R_R).

$$\mathcal{T}_{nb,min}(n_{th}) = R_I + (n_{th} - 1) \cdot R_R \quad (5)$$

In the worst case, the root will check the notification line after each time a thread wrote to it. This scenario is modeled by Equation (6).

$$\mathcal{T}_{nb,max}(n_{th}) = R_I + 2(n_{th} - 1) \cdot R_R \quad (6)$$

4.1.2 Small Broadcast

Once the notification has been analyzed, the design of the broadcast algorithm focuses on the stages needed to copy the data from the root into every other descendant. Karp et al. developed an optimal algorithm [14] in the LogP model, but this is very different from our state-based min-max model with separate notification. However, we can use a similar technique to design our optimal tree taking into account that all the descendants of a given node can get the data at the same time.

First of all, we will describe the structure of a generic tree assuming that each level i can use a different number of descendants (k_i) and that the height of the tree is d. In this structure, the number of threads in each level (n_i) of the tree is given by equation 7.

$$n_0 = 1, n_i \le \prod_{j=1}^{i} k_j \quad (7)$$

Hence, the total number of threads can be expressed as:

$$n_{th} \le 1 + \sum_{i=1}^{d} \prod_{j=1}^{i} k_j \quad (8)$$

All of the k_i descendants of one thread from level i are accessing the same line, thus, by increasing the number of descendants, we also increase contention. Hence, every one of these descendants is able to get the data in $\mathcal{T}_C(k_i)$. It is also worth mentioning that different threads accessing different data should not cause any congestion, thus, it is possible to apply the contention model to each group of descendants ignoring other groups of threads. Thus, the latency of copying a message throughout this tree is:

$$\mathcal{T}_{tree} = \sum_{i=1}^{d} \mathcal{T}_C(k_i) = \sum_{i=1}^{d} (c \cdot k_i + b)$$
$$= \sum_{i=1}^{d} (R_R + R_L + c \cdot (k_i - 1)) \quad (9)$$

The optimized tree has to find a tradeoff between the number of threads that get the value at the same time, thus causing congestion ($c \cdot k_i$), and the number of levels of the tree. It is expected that the values of k_i decrease while descending throughout the tree since the lower the value of k_i, the lower the latency of acquiring one message.

Figure 8 presents an example of a 10-threads broadcast tree using (arbitrarily chosen) d=2, $k_1 = 3$, $k_2 = 2$. The backwards arrows indicate from which node the receivers copy the message. Threads from level 1 get the message in $t_1 = c \cdot k_1 + b = 3c + b$ and, then, leaf nodes will copy it in $c \cdot k_2 + b = 2c + b$, thus, the total time will be $t_2 = c \cdot (k_1 + k_2) + 2b = 5c + 2b$.

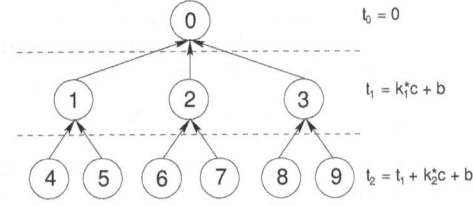

Figure 8: Tree for an 10-threads broadcast assuming $d = 2$, $k_1 = 3$, $k_2 = 2$.

Once the tree structure is defined, we have to take into account the notification. The total time for notification backwards is the time spent from the moment in which the last descendant receive the message until the root is aware that every thread has it. The correspondent equations from Section 4.1.1 must be applied to each level of the tree, providing the cost of notification backwards in the critical path.

Regarding notification forwards (i.e., the parent notifying to its descendants that the buffer is ready to be copied), first, there is a global flag where the root sets the shared structure as occupied by the current operation (R_I). Each descendant has to check the flag and copy the data (that are on the same line), which can be estimated by the contention model (Equation (9)), and then, each parent has to read its own structure (R_I), copy the data into this structure (R_L) and set it as ready (R_L). In the worst case, the descendants can read the flag before it is set and interfere while the parent is copying the data and setting the flag. Moreover, when interference involves several threads, they will cause contention. Although the first reading affected by contention is an invalid line, the contention model for a cached line is used for simplicity purposes. Equation (10) show the best (min) and worst (max) case model for this notification forwards.

$$\mathcal{T}_{fw,min} = R_I + \sum_{i=1}^{d}(R_I + 2R_L) = (d+1)R_I + 2dR_L$$

$$\mathcal{T}_{fw,max} = R_I + \sum_{i=1}^{d}2\left(R_R + \sum_{i=1}^{d}(c \cdot k_i + b)\right)$$

(10)

The optimal tree to perform a one-item broadcast is thus the solution to the minimization problem expressed in equation (11), combining notifications and reception of data.

$$\mathcal{T}_{sbcast} = \min_{d,k_i}\left(\mathcal{T}_{fw} + \sum_{i=1}^{d}(c \cdot k_i + b) + \sum_{i=1}^{d}\mathcal{T}_{nb}(k_i + 1)\right)$$

$$N \leq 1 + \sum_{i=1}^{d}\prod_{j=1}^{i}k_j, \quad \forall i < j, k_i \leq k_j$$

(11)

This equation can be solved with numerical methods to obtain d and all k_i for the optimal broadcast tree.

4.1.3 Large Broadcast

When each thread has to copy N lines using the tree developed for the small broadcast and assuming that the N lines are sent in N_{pack} packets of size N_{cl}, the leafs will not start copying until the first package has arrived.

In order to avoid having idle threads in the first stages, and given that it is possible to divide the N-line message in $N_{pack} = n_{th} - 1$ slices, we can construct an algorithm in

stages in which every thread, but the root, starts copying one different slice of the message. Having every line of the message in the root's cache could cause some contention (the root has to communicate with the DTDs to change the state of each line from E or M to S) and for the next stages, each thread copy one slice of the message from a different thread, having only one thread copying from the same location at the same time. The performance model of this pipelined algorithm is stated in Equation (12).

$$\mathcal{T}_{pipedbcast} = \mathcal{T}_{init} + \mathcal{T}_{1st} + \mathcal{T}_{rest} + \mathcal{T}_{fin}$$
$$\mathcal{T}_{init,min} = R_I + 2R_L$$
$$\mathcal{T}_{1st,min} = 2R_L + \mathcal{T}_C(n_{th} - 1) + \mathcal{T}_{N_{cl}}$$
$$\mathcal{T}_{rest,min} = (n_{th} - 2)(R_R + R_L + \mathcal{T}_{N_{cl}})$$
$$\mathcal{T}_{fin,min} = 2R_R + R_L$$

(12)

This algorithm will use the same notification structure than the small broadcast, but since only one thread accesses this information in each stage, it is possible to have the flag, address and notification in the same line, allowing the receiver to fetch it only once during the stage. Moreover, the owner of the line only checks the notification at the end of the whole algorithm, minimizing interference. The model has been divided in four parts: (1) initialization ($\mathcal{T}_{init}$), in which every thread checks its notification line and sets the local buffer address. (2) First stage ($\mathcal{T}_{1st}$): the root sets its flag to ready (R_L), the rest of threads check it ($\mathcal{T}_C(n_{th} - 1)$ is an upper bound to the real value because the contention model implies the copy of a line and in this scenario threads only read the value) and copy of the first slice of the message ($\mathcal{T}_{N_{cl}}$ using the multi-line model) and sets its own flag to ready (R_L). (3) Rest of stages ($\mathcal{T}_{rest}$), where the rest of packets ($n_{th} - 2$) are copied, including the check for readiness (R_R) and the notification to the owner (R_L). And (4) Finalization ($\mathcal{T}_{fin}$), each thread checks for completion (R_R) and sets the own structure as free (R_L). The extra R_R represents the notification to the root. To avoid interference and serialization in this notification, each thread will notify the first copy in a different stage.

Having only one thread accessing one location at every stage minimizes interference, however, there are still some points in which it can appear. In $\mathcal{T}_{1st}$, as happened in the notification forwards from Equation (10), the polling threads can interfere with the root. Moreover, in $\mathcal{T}_{rest}$, any thread (e.g., T_2) can finish its stage earlier tan others and try to read a flag before it is set, e.g., by T_1. When setting it, T_1 forces the line to be evicted from T_2's cache, that will have to fetch it again later. And finally, it is possible to assume that the last thread writes the notification after the first check for completion, adding some extra costs.

$$\mathcal{T}_{init,max} = R_I + 2(R_R + \mathcal{T}_C(n_{th} - 1)) + R_R$$
$$\mathcal{T}_{1st,max} = 2R_R + \mathcal{T}_C(n_{th} - 1) + \mathcal{T}_{N_{cl}}$$
$$\mathcal{T}_{rest,max} = (n_{th} - 2)(2R_R + \mathcal{T}_{N_{cl}})$$
$$\mathcal{T}_{fin,max} = 2R_R + R_L$$

(13)

Although this algorithm minimizes contention and interference, it can also preclude the benefits of prefetching (Equation (2)) that is only exploited for each packet.

Thus, we analyze a second algorithm, a flat tree, that optimizes for prefetching. In a flat tree, all receivers access the whole message after the root notified them. This algorithm ends when the receivers acknowledge the root that they have copied the message. Since the number of threads colliding is large, the notification system uses two lines, in the same way as the small broadcast. The analysis to be done here is how contention affects the performance of requesting multiple contiguous lines, thus, we have to combine the contention and the multi-line models. For this purpose, we use the slope factor of the multi-line ping-pong model (o) as the time that it takes for one thread to get the message. This operation will be affected by the congestion caused by the rest of threads but the root ($n_{th} - 2$). As intercept or constant factor, we arbitrarily chose the b from the contention model (assuming that the buffers are in exclusive state). In this scenario, the Flat Tree algorithm represents a good tradeoff between the benefits of prefetching and the drawbacks of contention. The rest of the model is equivalent to one stage of the small broadcast tree. Equation (14) reflects the best and worst models for this algorithm.

$$
\begin{aligned}
\mathcal{T}_{ftbcast} &= \mathcal{T}_{notif} + \mathcal{T}_{copy} \\
\mathcal{T}_{copy} &= b + c \cdot (n_{th} - 2) + o \cdot N \\
\mathcal{T}_{notif,min} &= R_I + 3R_L + R_R + T_C(n_{th} - 1) \\
&\quad + (n_{th} - 1)R_R \\
\mathcal{T}_{notif,max} &= R_I + R_L + 3R_R + 2T_C(n_{th} - 1) \\
&\quad + 2(n_{th} - 1)R_R
\end{aligned}
\tag{14}
$$

We expect the second algorithm to perform better for large message sizes.

4.2 Barrier Synchronization

A barrier synchronization involves every thread acknowledging that every other thread has reached the synchronization point. We have modeled it as a dissemination barrier since it has been proven to be the best algorithm for single-port LogP systems, but optimizing the parameters within our min-max models. The dissemination algorithm uses $r = log_m(n_{th})$ rounds in which thread T sends a notification to thread $(T + i(m+1)^r) \mod n_{th}, 0 < i \leq r$ and waits for the notifications from $(T - i(m+1))^r) \mod n_{th}, 0 < i \leq r$. In our shared memory scenario, assuming that every thread owns a notification line, each "send" operation consists of setting a flag and waiting until the receivers acknowledge that they have read this flag; and, "receive" is to notify to the senders the read of the corresponding flags.

In the best case, the owner was the last reader of its line (to check its value in the previous round), having it in cache when setting it to ready (R_L), and, the cost of checking it after every receiver has finished is R_R. Moreover, it has to read m threads' flags and, assuming no interference and that flags are already set, the thread will read and write to them just fetching each line once. Although every thread has to read m lines, they are not contiguous and exposed to be prefetched, thus we will not apply the multi-line model. The contention model does not apply either because, although m threads are accessing each line, they are performing writes that have to be serialized. The total cost is shown in Equation (15). The m value must be chosen to minimize this cost.

$$
\begin{aligned}
\mathcal{T}_{barr,min} &= r(R_L + R_R \cdot m + R_R) \\
r &= \lceil log_m(n_{th}) \rceil
\end{aligned}
\tag{15}
$$

However, in every round, the own line can be in other core's cache, e.g. if other thread is already checking the flag,(R_R) and the notification value can be checked once and

every time that it is modified by a notifier thread ($(2m + 1)R_R$). Finally, if the first read of other thread's flags results in failure (the flag has not been set yet), at least another read of the line has to be performed. Taking into account that other $m - 1$ threads can get the line and modify it in between, this interference could result in $(3m) \cdot R_R + m(m-1)R_R$. Since it is unlikely to happen, the model includes only one interference per line m.

$$
\begin{aligned}
\mathcal{T}_{barr,max} &= r(R_R + 4m \cdot R_R + (2m+1)R_R) \\
r &= \lceil log_m(n_{th}) \rceil
\end{aligned}
\tag{16}
$$

The best m can again be found using numerical methods.

4.3 Small Reduction

A reduction is the application of an operation to data collected from all threads. In this section we will analyze the implementation of the reduction of one item.

The root is receiving from multiple threads, thus, the operation is very different from broadcast. A first approach could be having all those threads writing to a common location. Then, each thread will have to (1) check a flag to see if the buffer is ready (R_R), (2) read the buffer (R_L), (3) apply the reduction operation to the buffer using its private data (R_L), (4) write the result to the data buffer and (5) notify that it has finished (R_R). If several threads are accessing the same buffer, steps 2 to 5 have to be performed in an atomic manner, thus, serializing. To avoid serialization, the root has several buffers in which each descendant writes its data. Then the root reads them all and performs the operation.

This scheme can be structured in a tree similar to the broadcast one. In this tree, each thread from level i has k_i buffers where its k_i children copy their own data. Then, the parent performs the operation with the data from these buffers. In each stage of the tree, the parent has to set a flag (R_I) that their children (k_i) read (causing some contention) before writing to the corresponding buffer ($R_R + R_L$) and notifying that the data is ready (R_R). Once the parent gets the acknowledgment (R_R), it performs the operation (which is modeled using the multi-line model). The tree minimizing Equation 17 forms our solution.

$$
\begin{aligned}
\mathcal{T}_{red,min} &= \sum_{i=1}^{d} [R_I + \mathcal{T}_C(k_i) + (1 + k_i)R_R + R_L + \mathcal{T}_{k_i}] \\
&\quad + R_R
\end{aligned}
\tag{17}
$$

The interference in the notification forwards (some threads read the parent's flag before it is set) and in the notification backwards (the parent checks the notification before it is complete) are reflected in the worst case in Equation (18).

$$
\begin{aligned}
\mathcal{T}_{red,max} &= \sum_{i=1}^{d} [R_I + 2\mathcal{T}_C(k_i) + 2(1 + k_i)R_R + R_L + \mathcal{T}_{k_i}] \\
&\quad + R_R
\end{aligned}
\tag{18}
$$

Here again, we compute the optimal d and k_is using numeric techniques.

5. EVALUATION

The evaluation of the designed algorithms has been performed on an Intel Xeon Phi 5110P with 60 cores at 1052 MHz, the host machine is a Intel Xeon E5-2670 Sandy Bridge with 8 cores at 2.60 Ghz. The Intel MIC software stack is the MPSS Gold update 2.1.4346-16, with the Intel Composer XE 2013.0.079, the Intel Compiler v.13.0 and Intel MPI v.4.1.0.024. The benchmarks used are the EPCC OpenMP Benchmarks 3.0 and the Intel MPI Benchmarks (IMB) 3.2.

The benchmarks used to measure the performance of our algorithms were developed to ensure a given cache state in each of the 1000 iterations. Before each iteration, threads are synchronized with a custom RDTSC-based synchronization and the data lines are placed in the desired cache state.

To guarantee that all threads start at the same time we used the feature that the RDTSC is consistent among cores [1, §2.1.7] in a normal power state of the Xeon Phi. Thus, we generate time intervals for threads to achieve before starting, then assuring that they enter each operation at the same time. A second synchronization before the collective operation is performed. The time is measured for every operation call and the whole distribution of times is used for statistical analysis of the obtained results. The goal is to check whether the model predictions are accurate enough and compare the results with existing solutions.

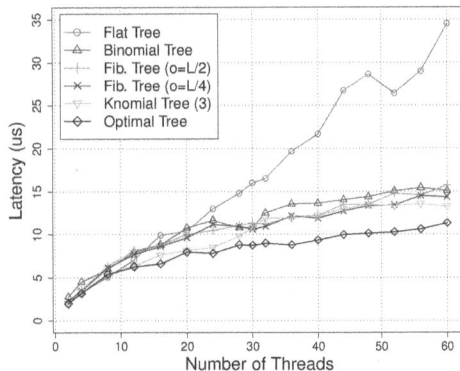

Figure 9: Small Broadcast performance comparing our optimal algorithm with widely used broadcast trees.

Before testing, all the parametrizable algorithms (small broadcast, reduction and synchronization) have been optimized to obtain the best parameters by minimizing the best case models from Section 4. The optimization for the worst case was also taken into account with similar results, hence, only the parameters obtained for the best case model are shown in the graphs. As an example, when having 30 threads, the parameters obtained for a small broadcast were $d = 2$, $k_1 = 5$, $k_2 = 5$; for reduction $d = 3$, $k_1 = 3$, $k_2 = 3$, $k_3 = 2$; and for barrier $m = 6$ ($r = 2$). For 60 threads, the parameters were $d = 3$, $k_1 = 4$, $k_2 = 4$ and $k_3 = 3$ for small broadcast and reduction, and $m = 4$ ($r = 3$) for barrier. Parameters differ for each number of threads and that is the reason of some variations in the models as seen around 28 processes in Figure 12.

All benchmarks launch one thread per core and, when using 60 threads, the variability increases because it is not possible to avoid the core that runs the OS.

Figure 9 shows a comparison between different algorithms for small broadcast: flat tree, binomial tree, k-nomial tree (k=3), Fibonacci tree and our optimal tree, all of them with buffers in E state. For Fibonacci trees [14], given that they are designed for LogP and that in this system it is not exactly applicable, we have chosen $o = L/2$ and $o = L/4$ to construct the tree. As expected, the optimal algorithm developed using the model obtains the lowest latency even though, some of the other algorithms, e.g., Fibonacci Trees, are optimal in other models.

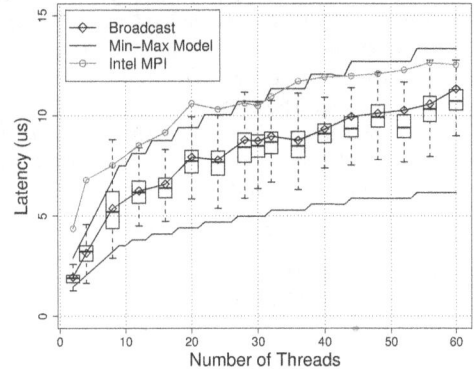

Figure 10: Small Broadcast performance compared to the model and the Intel MPI implementation.

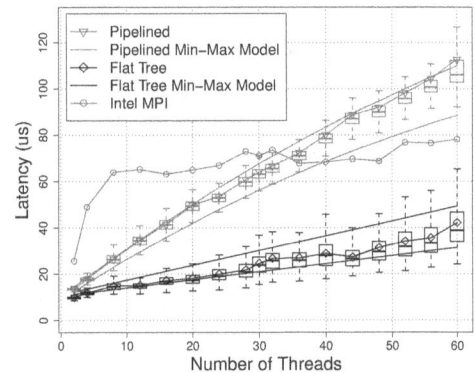

Figure 11: Large Broadcast (8 kb) algorithms compared to the model and the Intel MPI implementation.

Figures 10 to 13 represent the performance obtained with the algorithms modeled in Section 4. Results are presented with the corresponding boxplots and the min-max model. The large broadcast uses 8 kb messages because it is the higher buffer size that was modeled for the multi-line ping-pong, and the operation used in the reduction is a summation. As it can be seen, the min-max model is able to capture the inherent variability of the use of threads and allowed us to obtain the best parameters for the small broadcast, the small reduce and the barrier.

To compare the results with current shared memory communication solutions, the graphs also include the latency obtained with MPI and OpenMP (when applicable). It is worth mentioning that the benchmarks used for OpenMP and MPI measure the average result without synchronizing threads before each iteration and without forcing any cache state, avoiding the eviction of the shared data and taking advantage of temporal locality across iterations. Our benchmark forces the data to be in exclusive state in the buffer owner's cache, thus invalidating it in any other cache.

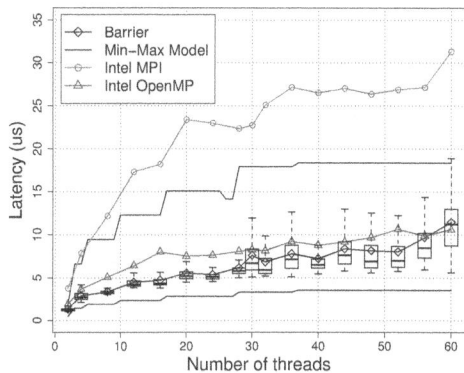

Figure 12: Barrier Synchronization results compared to the model and the Intel OpenMP and MPI implementations.

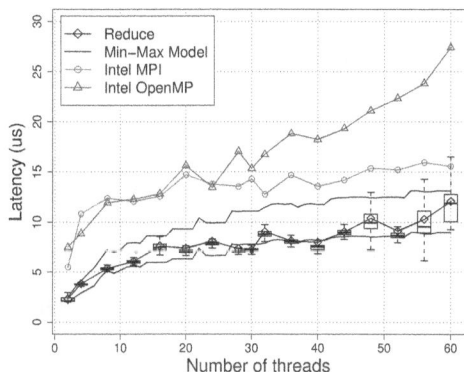

Figure 13: Small Reduction performance compared to the model and the Intel OpenMP and MPI implementations

However, even in that case, our algorithms outperform MPI and OpenMP except for two scenarios. In Figure 12, with 60 threads, the OpenMP barrier obtained a latency that is lower than our algorithm, however, it seems that it is highly optimized for a large number of threads while ours is optimized separately for each number of threads. Moreover, they take advantage of the non-cache-invalidation policy between iterations used in the benchmarks. In the results of the large broadcast (Fig. 11), the "pipelined" algorithm is outperformed by MPI when the number of threads is larger than 32, although it does not happen if the flat tree algorithm is used. As mentioned in Section 4.1.3, the flat tree obtains a good tradeoff between contention and prefetching while the pipelined algorithm is not able to take advantage of prefetching.

6. RELATED WORK

The optimization of parallel computation is based on the study of the architectural features that can influence performance. However, algorithm design requires models that simplify and abstract complex systems, e.g., LogP [9], LogGP [3], LoGPC [19], PlogP [16] or Hockney [11] model the communications in distributed memory systems. On the other hand, models like PRAM [15], that assume that processors can access global memory without cost, study the logical structure of parallel computation removing communication from the analysis. Another approach followed in [5] and [6] is the inclusion of memory concerns in the model to measure the effects that memory buffer copies have

in point-to-point communications. Our work is focused on shared memory architectures were point-to-point communications are translated directly to memory transfers, thus, buffer transformations would be treated as common memory operations.

These models have been successfully used to design optimal algorithms for communication operations. In [14], Karp et al. show that Fibonacci trees are optimal for small broadcasts. The authors of [23] use a simple linear communication model to develop bandwidth-optimal broadcast and reduction algorithms.

With the increase in the number of cores per processor, the modeling of shared memory communications is also crucial to develop efficient algorithms to transfer information through shared memory among the cores of the system. Petrovic et al. [21] discuss communications in the precursor of the Intel Xeon Phi, the Intel SCC. However, this system did not provide cache coherency, which simplifies the interactions among threads greatly.

The cache coherency protocols have been also widely studied, specially in terms of internal memory hierarchy models analyzing the effects of evictions and memory locality. Agarwal et al. [2] presents a comprehensive model for associative caches and other works like [24] or [4] study the behavior of the memory hierarchy on multi-core systems, but focus on the behavior of caches and the optimization of parallel codes avoiding cache misses, and does not discuss the effects of communications among cores.

Early experiences on the Intel Xeon Phi coprocessor [8] showed that this architecture provides scalable performance, which combined with the possibility of obtaining highly parallel applications with standard programming paradigms, makes it really interesting to explore the communications among cores in a shared memory environment.

7. DISCUSSION AND CONCLUSIONS

We found that, especially for small data, the notification system and interference caused by threads in the polling stages, can impact performance more than the actual data transfer. In order to model these effects, we had to resort to min-max models that complicate the algorithm development considerably. Nevertheless, our model allows algorithm designers to abstract away from the architecture and the detailed cache coherency protocols and design algorithms on purely analytic ground. We showed that our models can be combined into a powerful framework for tuning and developing parallel algorithms.

In general, we found that optimizing for cache-coherency protocols is harder than optimizing for systems that offer direct remote memory access. The developed models and techniques are more complex than, for example algorithms in the LogP model. Based on results gathered in [21], we would assume that direct remote cache access (DRCA) would lead to parallel systems with higher performance and better predictability and transparency. Thus, we conjecture that DRCA would greatly simplify the design of parallel algorithms.

However, if such architectures are not an option, our models describe a viable method for designing parallel algorithms on cache-coherent architectures. Indeed, our simplified model can be used rather mechanically to optimize and parametrize well-known algorithms. In addition, we showed how to develop new and optimal algorithms requiring slightly more effort. While all our models do not provide precise predictions rather than a range of possible performance, we demonstrated how they can be used to guide algorithm design and development.

The algorithms we developed with the help of our analytical models show performance improvements over Intel's hand-tuned MPI and OpenMP libraries in nearly all configurations with a maximum improvement of 4.3 times. Our method can also be used for other architectures and algorithms.

Acknowledgments

We thank the Swiss National Supercomputing Center (CSCS), especially Hussein Harake, Thomas Schoenemeyer, and Thomas Schulthess, for providing access to and support with Xeon Phi hardware. S. Ramos thanks the HiPEAC network, the University of A Coruña, the Ministry of Science and Innovation of Spain [Project TIN2010-16735], and the Xunta de Galicia CN2012/211, partially supported by FEDER funds for financial support.

8. REFERENCES

[1] Intel® Xeon Phi™ Coprocessor: Software Developers Guide. https://www-ssl.intel.com/content/www/us/en/processors/xeon/xeon-phi-coprocessor-system-software-developers-guide.html, 2012.

[2] A. Agarwal, J. Hennessy, and M. Horowitz. An Analytical Cache Model. *ACM Trans. Comput. Syst.*, 7(2):184–215, 1989.

[3] A. Alexandrov, M. F. Ionescu, K. E. Schauser, and C. Scheiman. LogGP: Incorporating Long Messages into the LogP Model - One Step Closer towards a Realistic Model for Parallel Computation. In *Proc. 7th Annual ACM Symp. on Parallel Alg. and Arch. (SPAA'95)*, pages 95–105, S. Barbara, CA, USA, 1995.

[4] D. Andrade, B. B. Fraguela, and R. Doallo. Accurate Prediction of the Behavior of Multithreaded Applications in Shared Caches. *Parallel Computing*, 39(1):36 – 57, 2013.

[5] K. W. Cameron, R. Ge, and X. H. Sun. lognP and log3P: Accurate Analytical Models of Point-to-Point Communication in Distributed Systems. *IEEE Trans. Computers*, 53(3):314–327, 2007.

[6] K. W. Cameron and X. H. Sun. Quantifying Locality Effect in Data Access Delay: Memory logP. In *Proc. 17th IEEE Intl. Parallel & Distrib. Processing Symp. (IPDPS'03)*, page (8 pages), Nice, France, 2003.

[7] G. Chrysos. Intel® Xeon Phi™ Coprocessor (Codename Knights Corner). Keynote talk at the 24th Hot Chips: A Symp. on High Perf. Chips, 2012.

[8] T. Cramer, D. Schmidl, M. Klemm, and D. an Mey. OpenMP Programming on Intel Xeon Phi Coprocessors: An Early Performance Comparison. In *Proc. Many-core Applications Research Community (MARC) Symp. at RWTH Aachen University*, pages 38–44, 2012.

[9] D. Culler et al. LogP: towards a Realistic Model of Parallel Computation. *SIGPLAN Not.*, 28(7):1–12, 1993.

[10] D. Hackenberg, D. Molka, and W. E. Nagel. Comparing Cache Architectures and Coherency Protocols on x86-64 Multicore SMP Systems. In *Proc. 42nd Annual IEEE/ACM Intl. Symp. on Microarchitecture (MICRO'42)*, pages 413–422, New York, NY, USA, 2009.

[11] R. W. Hockney. The Communication Challenge for MPP: Intel Paragon and Meiko CS-2. *Parallel Computing*, 20(3):389 – 398, 1994.

[12] T. Hoefler and T. Schneider. Optimization Principles for Collective Neighborhood Communications. In *Proc. 25th ACM/IEEE Intl. Supercomputing Conf. for High Performance Computing, Networking, Storage and Analysis (SC'12)*, Salt Lake City, UT, USA, 2012.

[13] L. Ivanov and R. Nunna. Modeling and Verification of Cache Coherence Protocols. In *Proc. 2001 IEEE Intl. Symp. on Circuits and Systems (ISCAS'01)*, pages 129–132, 2001.

[14] R. M. Karp et al. Optimal Broadcast and Summation in the LogP Model. In *Proc. 5th Annual ACM Symp. on Parallel Alg. and Arch. (SPAA'93)*, pages 142–153, Velen, Germany, 1993.

[15] R. M. Karp and V. Ramachandran. A Survey of Parallel Algorithms for Shared-Memory Machines. Technical report, Berkeley, CA, USA, 1988.

[16] T. Kielmann, H. E. Bal, and K. Verstoep. Fast Measurement of LogP Parameters for Message Passing Platforms. In *Proc. 15th IPDPS 2000 Workshops on Parallel & Distrib. Processing*, pages 1176–1183, 2000.

[17] R. McGill, J. W. Tukey, and W. A. Larsen. Variations of Box Plots. *The American Statistician*, 32(1):12–16, 1978.

[18] D. Molka, D. Hackenberg, R. Schoene, and M. S. Mueller. Memory Performance and Cache Coherency Effects on an Intel Nehalem Multiprocessor System. In *Proc. 18th Intl. Conf. on Parallel Architectures and Compilation Techniques (PACT'09)*, pages 261–270, Raleigh, NC, USA, 2009.

[19] C. A. Moritz and M. I. Frank. LoGPC: Modeling Network Contention in Message-Passing Programs. *IEEE Trans. on Parallel and Distrib. Systems*, 12(4):404–415, 2001.

[20] S. Owens, S. Sarkar, and P. Sewell. A Better x86 Memory Model: x86-TSO. In *Proc. 22nd Intl. Conf. on Theorem Proving in Higher Order Logics (TPHOLs'09)*, pages 391–407, Munich, Germany, 2009.

[21] D. Petrović, O. Shahmirzadi, T. Ropars, and A. Schiper. High-performance RMA-based Broadcast on the Intel SCC. In *Proc. 24th ACM Symp. on Parallelism in Alg. and Arch. (SPAA'12)*, pages 121–130, Pittsburgh, PA, USA, 2012.

[22] S. Ramos and T. Hoefler. Modeling Communications in Cache Coherent Systems . Technical report, University of A Coruña, ETH Zurich, 2013.

[23] P. Sanders, J. Speck, and J. L. Träff. Two-Tree Algorithms for Full Bandwidth Broadcast, Reduction and Scan. *Parallel Comput.*, 35(12):581–594, 2009.

[24] L. G. Valiant. A Bridging Model for Multi-core Computing. *Journal of Computer and System Sciences*, 77(1):154 – 166, 2011.

[25] B. L. Welch. The Generalization of 'Student's' Problem when Several Different Population Variances are Involved. *Biometrika*, (1-2):28–35, 1947.

IBIS: Interposed Big-data I/O Scheduler

Yiqi Xu
Florida International University
11200 S.W. 8th Street
Miami, FL 33199
yxu006@cs.fiu.edu

Adrian Suarez
Florida International University
11200 S.W. 8th Street
Miami, FL 33199
asuar054@fiu.edu

Ming Zhao
Florida International University
11200 S.W. 8th Street
Miami, FL 33199
ming@cs.fiu.edu

ABSTRACT

Existing big-data systems (e.g., Hadoop/MapReduce) do not expose management of shared storage I/O resources. As such, application's performance may degrade in unpredictable ways under I/O contention, even with fair sharing of computing resources. This paper proposes *IBIS*, a new Interposed Big-data I/O Scheduler, to provide performance differentiation for competing applications' I/Os in a shared MapReduce-type big-data system. IBIS is implemented in Hadoop by interposing HDFS I/Os and use an SFQ-based proportional-sharing algorithm. Experiments show that the IBIS provides strong performance isolation for one application against another highly I/O-intensive application. IBIS also enforces good proportional sharing of the global bandwidth among competing parallel applications, by coordinating distributed IBIS schedulers to deal with the uneven distribution of local services in big-data systems.

Categories and Subject Descriptors

C.1.4 [**Parallel Architectures**]: Distributed architectures; D.4.3 [**File System Management**]: Distributed file systems

Keywords

Proportional Sharing, Distributed Storage

1. INTRODUCTION

Big-data applications need to process and analyze massive amounts of data in parallel (e.g., MapReduce [2]) and often have complex I/O phases is highly distributed across many data nodes. Thus, storage systems that can provide high scalability and availability (e.g., Hadoop HDFS [3]) needs to be SLA aware in the shared infrastructure. However, existing big-data systems do not expose management of shared storage I/O resources. As a result, an application's performance may degrade in unpredictable ways when there is I/O contention.

This paper proposes *IBIS*, a new Interposed Big-data I/O Scheduler, to provide performance differentiation for competing applications' I/Os in a shared MapReduce-type big-data system. This scheduler solves the problem of differentiating the I/Os among competing applications *on individual data nodes* and schedule them according to the applications'

bandwidth demands. The proposed IBIS scheduler is able to transparently intercept the I/Os from big-data applications and schedule them on every data node via an I/O interposition layer. IBIS also coordinates I/O scheduling *across distributed data nodes* to allocate the total storage service of the entire big-data system to the parallel tasks of competing applications.

The IBIS prototype is implemented in Hadoop by interposing HDFS I/Os and scheduling them using an SFQ-based proportional-sharing algorithm [4]. Experimental results show that with IBIS, an application's performance can be strongly isolated from the contention by a highly I/O-intensive application (TeraGen) ($< 5\%$ slowdown in total runtime), even with uneven available bandwidth on different nodes.

2. APPROACH

IBIS is designed to *effectively differentiate I/Os from competing applications and allocate the shared storage bandwidth on individual data nodes in a big-data system*. IBIS is based on *virtualization* principles (Figure 1), where an indirection layer exposes the interfaces already in use by the big-data system to access storage, allowing applications to time-share the storage system without modifications, while enforcing performance isolation and differentiation among them. Step 1-5 corresponds to map read, map output, reduce shuffle, reduce merge and reduce write. We chose to introduce virtualization at a DataNode layer of the storage hierarchy to gain more control of I/O executions and utilization while supporting more diverse applications. The DFSClient interface between the tasks and DataNode is modified to allow application-specific information to be carried as part of the request header of each block request issued by the map/reduce task, transparent to the applications.

IBIS also *efficiently coordinates the distributed I/O schedulers across data nodes in order to allocate the global storage bandwidth for the parallel tasks of applications in a big data system*. The total service that an application gets across the whole system is the sum of the services that it obtains from every data node where its tasks run. The amount of local service that it actually obtains from a data node varies across nodes and over time and each local scheduler needs a global view of aggregate I/O throughput to converge to the I/O sharing ratio collectively on all data nodes. To address the challenge of synchronization of global I/O view between data nodes, the IBIS schedulers exchange their local I/O service information and obtain global views of total I/O services by piggybacking upon the existing RPCs between

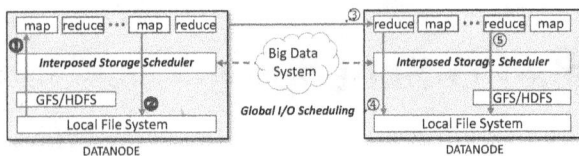

Figure 1: Architecture of IBIS

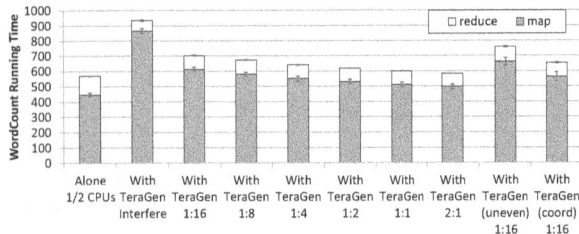

Figure 2: Runtime of WordCount without/with IBIS with varying I/O sharing ratios (WC:TG)

Figure 3: WordCount aggregate I/O throughput under TeraGen contention without and with IBIS (2:1)

TaskTrackers and JobTrackers. The scalability of this global coordination scheme is made possible by the scalability of the JobTrackers (in YARN [1] for large systems). Specifically, local scheduler adjusts the local I/O service ratios among the tasks on its data node in order to achieve global fairness of total I/O service among competing parallel applications, by delaying those that are above their global fair shares and promoting those below their global fair shares.

3. EVALUATION

Hadoop-based IBIS prototype was implemented and evaluated on a testbed consisting of eight nodes each with two six-core 2.4GHz AMD Opteron CPUs, 32GB of RAM, and two 500GB 7.2K RPM SAS disks, interconnected by a Gigabit Ethernet switch. All the nodes run the Debian 4.3.5-4 Linux with the 3.2.20-amd64 kernel and use EXT3 as the local file system. One node runs *JobTracker*, another as *NameNode*, and the other six as *TaskTrackers* and *DataNodes*. HDFS is configured to use one of the two disks on each data node, while the other is used for map intermediate outputs and reduce inputs to reduce self-interference. Each node is assigned 10 map slots and 2 reduce slots, with Hadoop fair scheduler for equal share of slots between two applications so the contention is purely from I/O side.

Figure 2 shows WordCount runtimes when running alone (half CPUs) or against TeraGen (two evenly using all CPUs). TeraGen's I/O contention caused more than 65% runtime increase to WordCount from the 1^{st}(alone) bar to the 2nd bar although native Hadoop fair scheduler assigns the same number of CPUs to both jobs. When applied SFQD scheduler with a depth of 4 from the 3^{rd}(1:16) bar, gradually increasing the share of TeraGen, and achieved within 105% of original alone performance at the ratio of 2:1. The last two bars shows with uneven available bandwidth on one of the data nodes (introduced by another I/O intensive application), uncoordinated (uneven) 1:16 target ratio cannot be reached as when bandwidth is even (3th bar). By adjusting unaffected nodes' bandwidth share, coordinated case on the rightmost bar(coord) can gain performance back.

Figure 3 collects per-second aggregate HDFS system bandwidth allocated to WordCount and TeraGen, without and

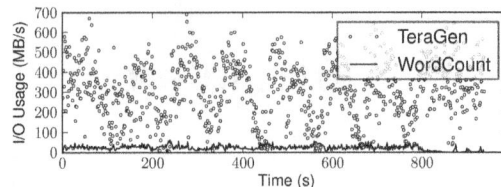

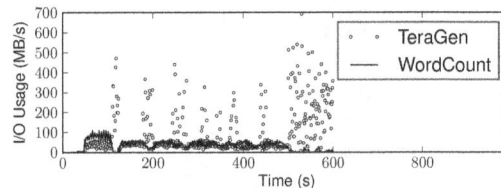

with IBIS(2:1). TeraGen writes suppressing the WordCount I/O without IBIS is on the top figure, while bottom figure shows the effectiveness of IBIS by: *1)* allowing approximately 1/3 of the available bandwidth to TeraGen and 2/3 to WordCount; *2)* allowing TeraGen to consume available bandwidth when WordCount issues less I/O. As a result, WordCount's I/Os are prioritized on all the datanodes and completes faster by 40%.

4. CONCLUSIONS AND FUTURE WORK

This paper proposes IBIS, an Interposed Big-data I/O Scheduler, to provide global I/O performance differentiation to big-data applications. Experimental evaluation shows with IBIS, an application's (WordCount) performance can be strongly isolated from the contention generated by a highly I/O-intensive application (TeraGen) (< 5% slowdown in total runtime). The results also show that IBIS can effectively achieve specified sharing ratio of the global bandwidth between two competing parallel applications by coordination. In the future work, IBIS will support the scheduling of other I/Os used by big-data applications in addition to HDFS I/Os. The I/O scheduling provided by IBIS will then be integrated with the existing CPU scheduling in big-data systems. Both types of resources are essential to the different stages of big-data applications and need to be managed holistically to achieve the application-desired quality of service.

5. REFERENCES

[1] Yet another resource negotiator. hadoop.apache.org/docs/current/hadoop-yarn/.

[2] J. Dean and S. Ghemawat. MapReduce: simplified data processing on large clusters. In *Proceedings of the 6th conference on Symposium on Opearting Systems Design & Implementation - Volume 6*, OSDI'04, page 10, Berkeley, CA, USA, 2004. USENIX Association.

[3] K. Shvachko, H. Kuang, S. Radia, and R. Chansler. The Hadoop Distributed File System. In *2010 IEEE 26th Symposium on Mass Storage Systems and Technologies (MSST)*, pages 1–10. IEEE, May 2010.

[4] Y. Wang and A. Merchant. Proportional-share scheduling for distributed storage systems. In *FAST*, pages 47–60. USENIX, 2007.

ACIC: Automatic Cloud I/O Configurator for Parallel Applications

Mingliang Liu
Tsinghua University
liuml07@gmail.com

Ye Jin
NCSU
yjin6@ncsu.edu

Jidong Zhai
Tsinghua University
zhaijidong@tsinghua.edu.cn

Yan Zhai
UW-Madison
zhaiyan920@gmail.com

Qianqian Shi
Tsinghua University
shiqiezi@gmail.com

Xiaosong Ma
NCSU and ORNL
ma@ncsu.edu

Wenguang Chen
Tsinghua University
cwg@tsinghua.edu.cn

ABSTRACT

To tackle the highlighted I/O bottleneck problem in cloud, we propose ACIC, a system which automatically searches for optimized I/O system configurations from many candidates for each individual application running on a given cloud platform. The top ACIC-recommended configuration improves the applications' performance by a factor of up to 10.5 (3.0 on average), and cost saving of up to 89% (53% on average), compared with a commonly used baseline.

Categories and Subject Descriptors

C.4 [**Performance of Systems**]: Modeling techniques

Keywords

Storage, Modeling, Performance, Cloud Computing

1. INTRODUCTION

More and more HPC users today are running their programs in the cloud [1]. Unfortunately, cloud platforms amplify the growing performance gap between I/O systems and other components [6]. The cloud enables users to setup optimized I/O configurations for **individual** applications upon their execution, instead of configuring I/O system for **all** applications that may run in the system [2]. However, taking advantage of this configurability and deriving optimized per-application I/O configuration are very challenging manually. Moreover, the complexity of both the underlying system and the parallel applications, and the obscureness of I/O system hardware/software details due to virtualization, make white-box modeling and analysis unrealistic.

We propose ACIC (**A**utomatic **C**loud **I**/O **C**onfigurator), which automatically searches for optimized I/O system configurations from many candidates for each individual application running on a given cloud platform. It takes advantage of a black-box machine learning model to train between representative I/O system exploration variables and optimal configuration target (cost and performance). After training the model on the target cloud platform, given the I/O characteristics of a certain application, ACIC evaluates candidate I/O configurations and recommends an optimized configuration for performance or monetary cost. The

originality of our work lies in the cost-saving mechanisms that make such approaches affordable on clouds: *1)* we enable *reusable training* by adopting a generic synthetic I/O benchmark and systematically sample the parameter space; *2)* we propose the potential of building a shared, public I/O performance/cost training database.

2. APPROACH

Figure 1 illustrates the ACIC architecture. The central component of ACIC is a black-box prediction model, which can be bootstrapped with a certain amount of initial training. ACIC takes both the cloud system I/O configuration parameters and application I/O characteristics. ACIC chooses the synthetic benchmark [5] to collect training data because it's generic, highly configurable and open-source. whose parameters are generated from the reduced I/O characteristic space. ACIC collects the performance (cost) metric on the target cloud system configured with the candidate I/O configurations as training data. It trains the black-box prediction model with classification and regression trees (CART) [3], a popular machine learning method. Users provide the I/O characteristics of one individual application as input to the prediction model. The output is the top predicted I/O configurations from many candidates.

Name	Value	Rank
Disk device	{EBS, ephemeral}	10
File system	{NFS, PVFS2}	5
Instance type	{cc1.4xlarge, cc2.8xlarge}	12
I/O server number	{1, 2, 4}	3
Placement	{parttime, dedicated}	7
Stripe size	{64KB, 4MB}	6
Num. of all processes	{32, 64, 128, 256}	14
Num. of I/O processes	{32, 64, 128, 256}	4
I/O interface	{POSIX, MPIIO}	9
I/O iteration count	{1, 10, 100}	13
Data size	{1, 4, 16, 32, 128, 512 (MB)}	1
Request size	{256KB, 4MB, 16MB, 128MB}	8
Read and/or write	{read, write}	2
Collective	{yes, no}	11
File sharing	{share, individual}	15

Table 1: The variables affecting performance and cost.

To summarize, we list the I/O configurations and application I/O characteristics parameters considered in this ACIC prototype in Table 1. To define the range of the values, we studied over 12 HPC applications in several scientific areas with different scale (32 to 256). Concatenated together,

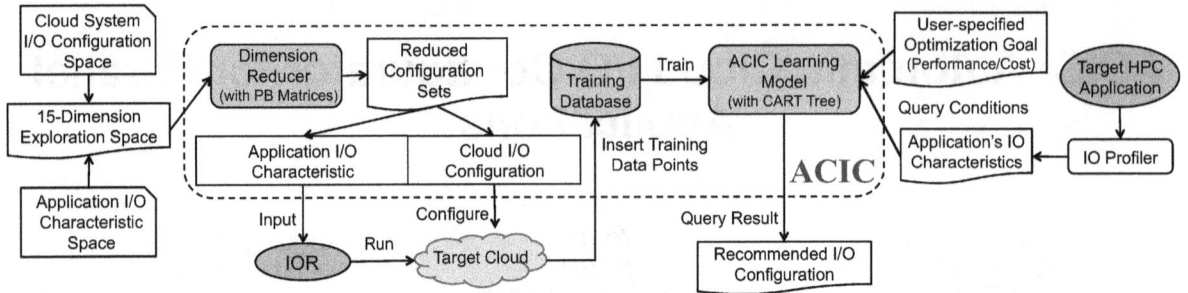

Figure 1: Predicting model architecture

these parameters make a 15-D exploration space as listed in Table 1. The top 6 variables are I/O system options in cloud, while the other ones are workload characteristics. For each parameter, we sample its value range during our bootstrap training. Considering the number of model parameters and their value range, the training space is so huge that tuning both the benchmark input size and I/O system configurations to cover all kinds of HPC applications' behavior is impossible. ACIC employs a dimension reducer using Plackett-Burman (PB) matrices [4] to rank all the I/O parameters and only trains the top 10 of them.

3. EVALUATION

All our experiments are performed on Amazon EC2 Cluster Computing Instances (CCIs) (*cc2.8xlarge*) [1]. We use the Amazon Linux OS 201202, Intel compiler 11.1 and Intel MPI 4.0. The baseline configuration is the popular but simple dedicated NFS server with one EBS disk attached. The performance and cost are calculated as:

$$speed\_up = \frac{time_{baseline/median}}{time_{ACIC}} \quad (1)$$

$$cost\_saving = \frac{cost_{baseline/median} - cost_{ACIC}}{cost_{baseline/median}} \times 100\% \quad (2)$$

We examine the potential difference made by verifying top-k recommendation set from ACIC. This is considering that the parameter filtering done by PB design and the rather sparse parameter sampling we perform may lead to co-champions. Figure 2 shows the execution time and cost improvement achieved by the best configuration among the top 1, 3, and 5 ACIC recommendations and eventually all I/O configurations (the true optimal configuration). The results reveal that the top recommendation (median if ACIC has co-champions) works fairly well, though considering more top candidates does help sometimes (256-process FLASHIO, 32-process mpiBLAST, and 256-process MADbench2). Particularly, we see that in almost all cases, little further gain can be achieved by checking beyond the top 3 ones.

4. CONCLUSION

We propose ACIC, an automatic cloud I/O system configuration tool for HPC applications encompassing several statistical and machine learning techniques to enable application-dependent, incremental model training and black-box performance/cost prediction. We released it to HPC community for free at http://hpc.cs.tsinghua.edu.cn/ACIC

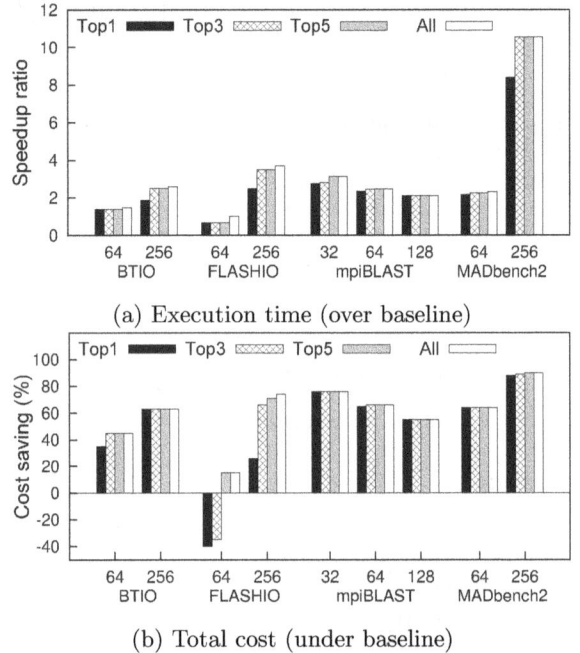

(a) Execution time (over baseline)

(b) Total cost (under baseline)

Figure 2: Effectiveness of top-k ACIC recommendations

5. ACKNOWLEDGEMENTS

Thanks go to our reviewers. This work was supported by the National High Technology Research and Development Program of China (863 Program) No. 2010AA012403.

6. REFERENCES

[1] Amazon. aws.amazon.com/ec2/hpc-applications/, 2011.
[2] M. Liu, J. Zhai, Y. Zhai, X. Ma, and W. Chen. One optimized i/o configuration per hpc application: leveraging the configurability of cloud. In *APSys*, 2011.
[3] L. Olshen and C. Stone. Classification and regression trees. *Wadsworth International Group*, 1984.
[4] R. Plackett and J. Burman. The design of optimum multifactorial experiments. *Biometrika*, 1946.
[5] H. Shan and et. al. Characterizing and Predicting the I/O Performance of HPC Applications Using a Parameterized Synthetic Benchmark. In *SC*, 2008.
[6] Y. Zhai, M. Liu, J. Zhai, X. Ma, and W. Chen. Cloud versus in-house cluster: evaluating amazon cluster compute instances for running mpi applications. In *SC*. ACM, 2011.

Orthrus: a Framework for Implementing High-performance Collective I/O in the Multicore Clusters

Xuechen Zhang
School of Computer Science
Georgia Institute of
Technology
Atlanta, GA, 30332
xczhang@cc.gatech.edu

Jianqiang Ou
ECE Department
Wayne State University
5050 Anthony Wayne Drive
Detroit, MI, 48202, USA
jianqiang.ou@wayne.edu

Kei Davis
CCS Division
Los Alamos National
Laboratory
Los Alamos, NM 87545, USA
kei.davis@lanl.gov

Song Jiang
ECE Department
Wayne State University
5050 Anthony Wayne Drive
Detroit, MI, 48202, USA
sjiang@eng.wayne.edu

ABSTRACT

This paper presents a framework, *Orthrus*, that can accommodate multiple collective-I/O implementations, each optimized for some performance aspects, and dynamically select the best performing one accordingly to current workload and system performance bottleneck. We have implemented *Orthrus* in the ROMIO library. Our experimental results with representative MPI-IO benchmarks show that *Orthrus* can significantly improve the performance of collective I/O under various workloads and system scenarios.

Categories and Subject Descriptors

B.4.3 [**Interconnections(Subsystems)**]: [Parallel I/O]

Keywords

Parallel I/O; parallel file systems; collective I/O.

1. INTRODUCTION

Collective I/O is a technique commonly employed in MPI programs that coordinates and reorganizes the requests from the multiple processes of a program before sending them to data nodes. There are two factors that may compromise its performance. One factor is the potentially high cost for the data exchange operation required in collective I/O. The overhead of data exchange can be significant if a large amount of data needs to be exchanged, especially when these aggregators and the processes communicating with them are on different compute nodes. If there are multiple cores on each node—the common case in today's HPC systems—the ideal scenario in terms of minimizing the cost of data exchange is to have each aggregator only be responsible for accessing data for processes on the same node and so have all data exchange occur within individual nodes. However, such a method for assigning file realms to aggregators may compromise the efficiency of I/O operations on the data nodes—the second factor that compromises collective-I/O's performance goal.

This paper describes a general framework *Orthrus* that allows multiple collective-I/O implementations, each optimized for one (or more) performance aspect(s), such as I/O pattern or relative hardware performance characteristics, to co-exist in a library. Based on a prediction of which would perform best for the current I/O pattern and system load, the framework essentially provides MPI programmers a collective-I/O library that adapts to access pattern changes and other dynamic system characteristics. A major challenge for the framework to achieve effectiveness is in the dynamic prediction of the performance of the various candidate implementations in a given scenario. To solve it, we propose a simple, efficient, accurate, and portable method for selecting the best performer for a collective-I/O operation. It does not take any workload or system information as input and does not involve any complicated modeling or simulation for performance prediction. The key technique is to use performance examination, rather than performance modeling, in the prediction. Each candidate collective-I/O implementation is given opportunities to demonstrate its performance, which is recorded for comparison and selection. By doing so, all of the hard-to-capture information is reflected in the actual performance of a candidate's examination run, which provides an accurate prediction of the performance that would be exhibited should the candidate be selected for executing the collective I/O in the near future.

2. THE DESIGN OF *ORTHRUS*

The crux of the *Orthrus* framework is to know how each candidate implementation would perform if it were used to execute a collective-I/O function call. The strategy of *Orthrus* is to apply each candidate implementation on the real execution of the function call to examine its actual performance. Certainly in the library one application-level call cannot be executed more than once: the overhead would be excessively large and the caching effect would invalidate the performance results from all but the first call. However, with different candidates executing different calls we would need to ensure that their performance results were comparable by invoking these candidates within the same workload, i.e. have the data requested by the calls have the same pattern.

In addition, the performance examination period must constitute only a small fraction of the total collective-I/O time because many candidates might not provide efficient I/O service. To characterize iteration's data access pattern *Orthrus* uses a number of factors, including name of accessed file, number of processes issuing I/O requests, number of requests, and request sizes, and their relative offsets in the file. We refer to these factors collectively as the call's *signature*. Two collective I/O calls are considered to have the same pattern and comparable performance results only when their signatures are the same.

Orthrus carries out its operations as follows. When a collective-I/O call is made, first its signature is compared to the signature of the previous call. If they are not the same, a new candidate examination period is started. If they are the same, then either the system is in a candidate examination period, in which case *Orthrus* keeps testing a candidate implementation, or the system uses the currently selected candidate implementation to execute the call. When a new candidate examination period is started, calls are serviced by the candidates in rotation, each for a fixed number of times (three by default), as long as the signature does not change. The throughput of each candidate is computed as an average to minimize the effect of transient changes in the execution environment. When the examination period ends without a change in signature, the candidate with the highest throughout is selected to execute the calls until the signature changes. During a regular execution period, even if the collective-I/O calls do not change their access pattern, the dynamic system environment, such as communication and I/O request traffic initiated by other programs, could change, and accordingly the best performing candidate for this program might change. To detect such system variations we monitor the throughput of the selected candidate. If the deviation of the throughout exceeds a certain threshold (15% by default) of the average recorded in the candidate examination period the system returns to the examination mode.

To test our idea we implemented two strategies. One, *core-first*, constrains data exchange to be intra-node. In the current implementation of *core-first* there is one aggregator per compute node to represent all the processes running on that node. We choose as the aggregator the process in that node requesting the largest amount of data. The processes' I/O requests are collected by the aggregator, which then sorts them in the ascending order according to the offsets of their requested data. The second strategy, *disk-first*, is designed to optimize for disk efficiency [3]. It sets up the same number of aggregators as the number of data nodes, each collecting and sending requests to one data node. Before that it sorts the requests as *core-first* does. However, *disk-first* ensures that each data node receives requests in one well-ordered sequence in the execution of a collective I/O call, while in *core-first* each data node receives requests from multiple (possibly all) aggregators, and the order of requests from different aggregators is essentially random. We also plug the ROMIO collective [2] implementation into the *Orthrus* framework.

3. PERFORMANCE EVALUATION

We evaluate *Orthrus* when a program using collective I/O runs on a PVFS2 cluster with 11 compute nodes (8-core Xeon) and 6 data nodes. The program (*Matrix*) simulates the I/O pattern exhibited with access of a large matrix file

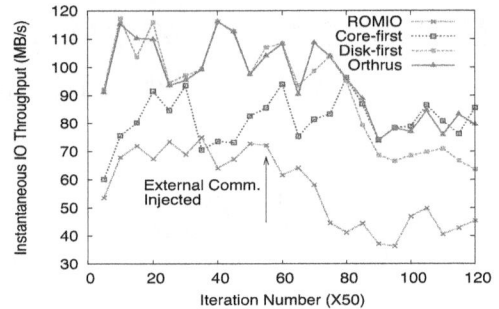

Figure 1: Instantaneous throughput measured for the four schemes after execution of every 250 iterations. The NPB/FT program starts executing at the 60th second.

by multiple processes in a block-by-block fashion. To reveal *Orthrus*'s adaptability to the changes in the run-time environment, from the 60th second of *Matrix*'s execution we ran the NPB/FT program [1] to generate inter-node all-to-all communication. Figure 1 shows the instantaneous I/O throughput of *Matrix*, at each multiple of 250 iterations, using each of the four strategies. Initially *Orthrus* selects *disk-first*. After the injection of the external communication traffic the inter-node bandwidth available to *Matrix* is reduced and its data exchange becomes more expensive. Accordingly the throughputs of *ROMIO* and *disk-first* are reduced by up to 46% and 60%, respectively, and *core-first* shows its performance advantage. As shown in Table 1, during the execution of the benchmark *core-first* generates a much smaller number of IP segments as reported by /proc/net/snmp. When *Orthrus* detects the throughout degradation with *disk-first* it re-evaluates the candidates and responsively switches to *core-first*, significantly reducing inter-node data exchange.

Schemes	*ROMIO*	*core-first*	*disk-first*
# of In Segs.	701,600	337,257	701,056
# of Out Segs.	1,385,008	322,884	1,412,066

Table 1: Average number of incoming and outgoing IP segments transmitted at each compute node

4. CONCLUSION

We have presented the design and implementation of *Orthrus*, a framework that can host multiple collective-I/O implementations and adaptively select the one that provides the highest I/O throughout according to current workload and system dynamics. We have implemented *Orthrus* in the ROMIO library and tested it with multiple sample collective-I/O implementations. Our results show that *Orthrus* can significantly improve the throughput of collective I/O for representative MPI-IO benchmarks.

5. REFERENCES

[1] "FT: Discrete 3D Fast Fourier Transform", *URL: http://www.nas.nasa.gov/publications/npb.html*
[2] R. Thakur, W. Gropp, and E. Lusk, "Data Sieving and Collective I/O in ROMIO", In *Frontiers'99*.
[3] X. Zhang, S. Jiang, and K. Davis, "Making Resonance a Common Case: A High-Performance Implementation of Collective I/O on Parallel File Systems", In *IPDPS'09*.

ElastMan: Autonomic Elasticity Manager for Cloud-Based Key-Value Stores

Ahmad Al-Shishtawy
KTH Royal Institute of Technology
Stockholm, Sweden
ahmadas@kth.se

Vladimir Vlassov
KTH Royal Institute of Technology
Stockholm, Sweden
vladv@kth.se

ABSTRACT

The increasing spread of elastic Cloud services, together with the pay-as-you-go pricing model of Cloud computing, has led to the need of an elasticity controller. The controller automatically resizes an elastic service in response to changes in workload, in order to meet Service Level Objectives (SLOs) at a reduced cost. However, variable performance of Cloud virtual machines and nonlinearities in Cloud services complicates the controller design. We present the design and evaluation of ElastMan, an elasticity controller for Cloud-based elastic key-value stores. ElastMan combines feedforward and feedback control. Feedforward control is used to respond to spikes in the workload by quickly resizing the service to meet SLOs at a minimal cost. Feedback control is used to correct modeling errors and to handle diurnal workload. We have implemented and evaluated ElastMan using the Voldemort key-value store running in a Cloud environment based on OpenStack. Our evaluation shows the feasibility and effectiveness of our approach to automation of Cloud service elasticity.

Categories and Subject Descriptors

C.2.4 [**Computer-Communication Networks**]: Distributed Systems; I.2.8 [**Artificial Intelligence**]: Problem Solving, Control Methods, and Search—*Control theory*

Keywords

Cloud Computing; Elasticity Controller; Key-Value Store

1. INTRODUCTION

Cloud computing [3], with its pay-as-you-go pricing model, provides an attractive environment to provision elastic services as the running cost of such services becomes proportional to the amount of resources needed to handle the current workload.

However, sharing the physical resources among Virtual Machines (VMs) running different applications makes it challenging to model and predict the performance of the VMs [5]. Managing the resources for Web 2.0 applications, in order to guarantee acceptable performance, is challenging because of the highly dynamic workload that is composed of both gradual (diurnal) and sudden (spikes) variations [2].

HPDC'13, June 17–21, 2013, New York, NY, USA.
ACM 978-1-4503-1910-2/13/06.

The pay-as-you-go pricing model, elasticity, and dynamic workload of Web 2.0 applications, call for the need for an elasticity controller that automates the provisioning of Cloud resources. The elasticity controller leverages the horizontal scalability of elastic services by provisioning more resources under high workloads in order to meet required SLOs. The pricing model provides an incentive for the elasticity controller to release extra resources once the workload decreases.

2. ELASTICITY CONTROLLER

The objective of ElastMan is to regulate the performance of key-value stores according to a predefined SLO expressed as the 99th percentile of read operations latency over a fixed period of time (R99p thereafter). To address the challenges of controlling a noisy signal and variable performance of VMs, ElastMan consists of two components, a feedforward controller and a feedback controller. ElastMan relies on the feedforward controller to handle rapid large changes in the workload (e.g., spikes). This enables ElastMan to smooth the noisy 99th percentile signal and use the PI feedback controller to correct errors in the feedforward system model in order to accurately bring the 99th percentile of read operations to the desired SLO value. In other words, the feedforward control is used to quickly bring the performance of the system near the desired value and then the feedback control is used to fine tune the performance.

Due to the nonlinearities in elastic Cloud services, resulting from the diminishing reward of adding a service instance (VM) with increasing the scale, we propose a scale-independent model used to design the feedback controller. This enables the feedback controller to operate at various scales of the service without the need to use techniques such as gain scheduling. To achieve this, our design leverages the near-linear scalability of elastic service.

In the design of the feedback controller, we propose to model the target store using the average throughput per server as the control input. Although we cannot control the total throughput on the system, we can indirectly control the average throughput of a server by adding/removing servers. Adding servers reduces the average throughput per server under the same load, whereas removing servers increases the average throughput per server. Thus, the controller decisions become independent of the number of service instances. The major advantage of our proposed approach to model the store is that the model remains valid as we scale the store, and it does not depend on the number of severs.

For the feedforward controller we use a binary classifier built using logistic regression as proposed in [6]. The model

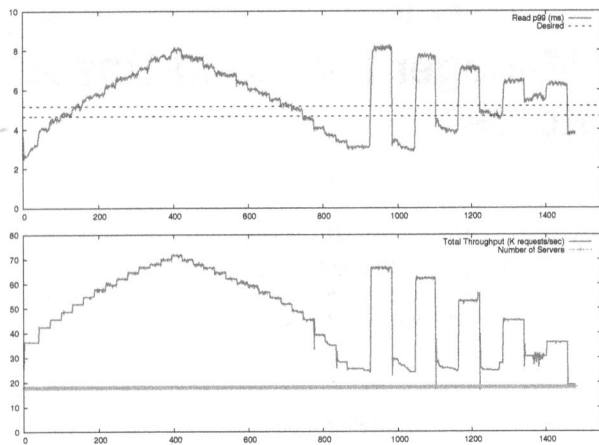

Figure 1: Performance of Voldemont without Elast-Man with fixed number of servers (18 virtual servers) under gradual diurnal workload (0-900 min) and under workload with spikes (900-1500 min)

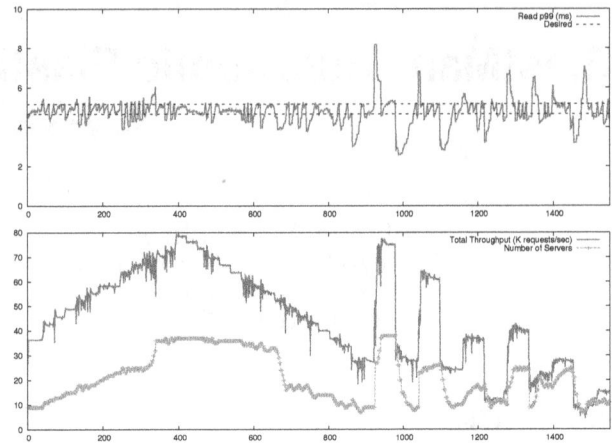

Figure 2: Performance of Voldemort with ElastMan under gradual diurnal workload (0-900 min) and under workload with spikes (900-1500 min)

is trained offline by varying the average intensity and the ratio of read/write operations per server. The final model is a line that splits the plane into two regions. In the region on and below the line, the SLO is met; whereas in the region above the line, SLO is violated. Ideally, the average measured throughput should be on the line, which means that the SLO is met with the minimal number of servers.

3. EVALUATION RESULTS

We have implemented ElastMan in order to evaluate our proposed approach to automation of Cloud service elasticity. In order to evaluate ElastMan, we have chosen the Voldemort (version 0.91) Key-Value Store [4] which is used in production in many applications such as LinkedIn. We run our experiments on a cluster of 11 servers each with two Intel Xeon X5660 processors (24 HW threads), and 44 GB of memory. The cluster runs Ubuntu 11.10. We setup a private Cloud using OpenStack Diablo release [1].

We have tested ElastMan controller with both gradual diurnal workload and sudden changes (spikes) in workload. The goal of ElastMan controller is to keep R99p at a value specified in the service SLO. In our experiments we choose the value to be 5 ms in 1 min period. Fig. 1 depicts the performance of Voldemort without ElastMan, i.e., with a fixed number of servers. Results shows that the store can not meet required SLO most of the time. Fig. 2 depicts the performance of Voldemort with ElastMan. Results show that ElastMan is able to keep the R99p within the desired region most of the time under a gradual workload (0-900 min) as well as under workload with spikes (900-1500 min).

4. CONCLUSIONS

ElastMan combines and leverages the advantages of both feedback and feedforward control. The feedforward control is used to quickly respond to rapid changes in workload. This enables us to smooth the noisy signal of the 99th percentile of read latency and thus use feedback control. The feedback control is used to handle gradual workload and to correct errors in the feedforward control due to the noise that

is caused mainly by the variable performance of Cloud VMs. The feedback controller uses a scale-independent model by indirectly controlling the number of servers (VMs) by controlling the average workload per server. This enables the controller, given the near-linear scalability of key-value stores, to operate at various scales of the store.

5. ACKNOWLEDGMENTS

This research has been funded by the Complex System Engineering project in the ICT-TNG Strategic Research Areas initiative at KTH; the End-to-End Clouds project funded by the Swedish Foundation for Strategic Research; and the FP7 project Clommunity funded by the European Commission.

6. REFERENCES

[1] Openstack: Open source software for building private and public clouds. http://openstack.org/.
[2] M. Arlitt and T. Jin. A workload characterization study of the 1998 world cup web site. *Network, IEEE*, 14(3):30 –37, May/June 2000.
[3] M. Armbrust, A. Fox, R. Griffith, A. D. Joseph, R. Katz, A. Konwinski, G. Lee, D. Patterson, A. Rabkin, I. Stoica, and M. Zaharia. A view of cloud computing. *Commun. ACM*, 53(4):50–58, Apr. 2010.
[4] R. Sumbaly, J. Kreps, L. Gao, A. Feinberg, C. Soman, and S. Shah. Serving large-scale batch computed data with project voldemort. In *The 10th USENIX Conference on File and Storage Technologies (FAST'12)*, February 2012.
[5] O. Tickoo, R. Iyer, R. Illikkal, and D. Newell. Modeling virtual machine performance: challenges and approaches. *SIGMETRICS Perform. Eval. Rev.*, 37(3):55–60, Jan. 2010.
[6] B. Trushkowsky, P. Bodík, A. Fox, M. J. Franklin, M. I. Jordan, and D. A. Patterson. The SCADS director: scaling a distributed storage system under stringent performance requirements. In *Proceedings of the 9th USENIX Conference on File and Storage Technologies*, FAST'11, pages 12–12, USA, 2011.

Supporting Parallel Soft Real-Time Applications in Virtualized Environment

Like Zhou, Song Wu, Huahua Sun, Hai Jin, Xuanhua Shi
Services Computing Technology and System Lab
Cluster and Grid Computing Lab
School of Computer Science and Technology
Huazhong University of Science and Technology, Wuhan, 430074, China
wusong@hust.edu.cn

ABSTRACT

The prevalence of multicore processors and virtualization technology enables parallel soft real-time applications to run in virtualized environment. However, current hypervisors do not provide adequate support for them because of soft real-time constraints and synchronization problems, which result in frequent deadline misses and serious performance degradation. In this paper, we propose a novel parallel soft real-time scheduling algorithm which addresses them well, and implement a parallel soft real-time scheduler, named *Poris*, based on Xen. Our evaluation shows that *Poris* shortens the execution time of PARSEC benchmark by up to 44.12% compared to Credit scheduler.

Categories and Subject Descriptors

D.4.1 [**OPERATING SYSTEMS**]: Process Management— *Scheduling*

Keywords

Virtualization; Soft Real-Time; Parallel; Scheduling

1. INTRODUCTION

With the prevalence of multicore processors in computer systems, many soft real-time applications use parallel programming models to utilize hardware resources better and possibly shorten response time. We call this kind of applications as parallel soft real-time ones, abbreviated as PSRT applications. Examples include cloud-based video streaming, real-time transcoding, computer vision, and gaming, etc. Recent advances in virtualization technology make more and more applications run in virtual machines (VMs). However, when running in virtualized environment, PSRT applications do not behave well and only obtain inadequate performance [3, 4].

On one hand, PSRT applications must respond to requests in a timely fashion due to their soft real-time constraints. A PSRT application can have responses only when the virtual CPU (VCPU) of its hosting VM is scheduled. However, current CPU schedulers in hypervisors do not consider the soft real-time constraints of PSRT applications, which cause frequent deadline misses. On the other hand, PSRT applications have synchronization requirements due to their parallel

feature. In virtualized environment, PSRT applications always run in the VMs with multiple VCPUs. However, the asynchronous CPU scheduling used by hypervisors causes synchronization problems, such as lock-holder preemption [5], which results in a waste of CPU time doing useless work, and then affects the performance of PSRT applications seriously.

In summary, PSRT applications have to face soft real-time constraints and synchronization problems. In this paper, we propose a novel parallel soft real-time scheduling algorithm, which considers them simultaneously.

2. OUR APPROACH

Our approach is based on Xen [1] because it is open-source and widely used. Since the parallel soft real-time scheduling algorithm needs to address soft real-time constraints and synchronization problems simultaneously, the scheduling problem can be divided into two sub-problems: 1) how to schedule VCPUs to ensure soft real-time constraints? 2) how to schedule all the VCPUs of a VM to solve synchronization problems? We present different solutions to address these sub-problems, and the parallel soft real-time scheduling algorithm consists of both solutions.

2.1 How to Handle Soft Real-time Constraints

Soft real-time applications can be divided into event-driven ones and time-driven ones according to their characteristics. Event-driven soft real-time applications are executed when external events arrive. Time-driven soft real-time applications are executed periodically. Some soft real-time applications may have both characteristics.

In order to satisfy the performance of event-driven soft real-time applications, we introduce *real-time* priority, which is higher than *boost* in Xen's Credit scheduler, to achieve timely scheduling for RT-VCPUs. (For simplicity, we call the VM hosting soft real-time applications as RT-VM, and the VCPU of RT-VM as RT-VCPU.) If a RT-VCPU with *under* priority in the run queue receives an external event, the priority of the RT-VCPU is promoted to *real-time*. The RT-VCPU preempts current running VCPU if the priority of RT-VCPU is higher than that of the current running VCPU, and its priority degrades to *under* when the RT-VCPU is descheduled.

Dynamic time-slice mechanism is introduced to guarantee the performance of time-driven soft real-time applications. If there is no RT-VM in the system, long time slice (i.e. 30ms) is used to schedule VCPUs. Otherwise, the time slice

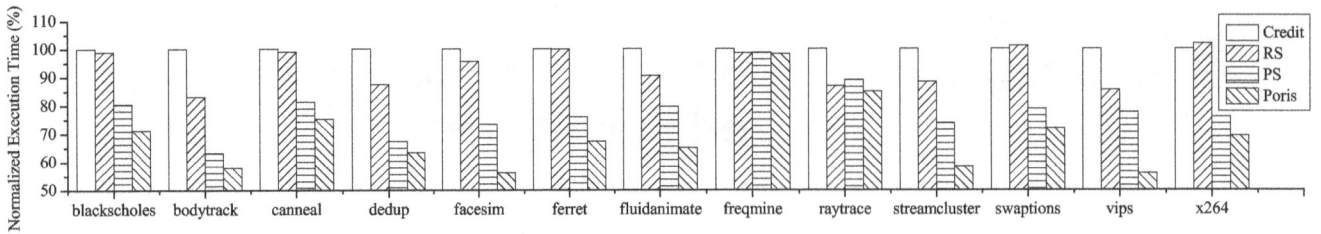

Figure 1: Normalized execution time of PARSEC benchmark under different schedulers

of scheduler is set to the short mode. We first define some variables as follows:

- S: the length of time slice that the scheduler used.
- LTS: long time slice (i.e. 30ms in Credit scheduler).
- N_R: the total number of RT-VCPUs in the system.
- N_V: the number of VCPUs per PCPU, which is the ratio of total number of VCPUs and total number of PCPUs.
- L: the expected latency of soft real-time applications.

S can be calculated by equation (1):

$$S = \begin{cases} LTS & N_R = 0 \\ LTS & N_R > 0 \text{ and } N_V = 1 \\ L/(N_V - 1) & N_R > 0 \text{ and } N_V > 1 \end{cases} \quad (1)$$

2.2 How to Handle Synchronization Problems

We use parallel scheduling to address synchronization problems when PSRT applications run in VMs. It schedules all the VCPUs of a RT-VM at the same time. (As to the non-real-time VMs, the scheduler uses default scheduling strategy, i.e. asynchronous scheduling, to schedule their VCPUs.) Such scheduling strategy can eliminate the synchronization problems of PSRT applications while minimizing the impact on non-real-time applications. The design of parallel scheduling is as follows. First, the scheduler distributes all the VCPUs of a RT-VM across different PCPUs. Second, when a VCPU is scheduled, if it is the first scheduled VCPU of a RT-VM, the priorities of other VCPUs, belonging to the RT-VM, are promoted to *real-time*. The scheduler reinserts the VCPUs into the proper position of corresponding PCPUs' run queue (mostly, it is the head of the run queue), and soft interrupts are sent to corresponding PCPUs to trigger rescheduling.

3. PERFORMANCE EVALUATION

The physical machine has two 2.4GHz Intel Xeon CPUs (two quad-core CPUs), 24GB memory, 1TB SCSI disk and 1Gbps Ethernet card. We use Xen-4.0.1 as the hypervisor and CentOS 5.5 distribution with the Linux-2.6.31.8 kernel as the OS. All the configurations of VMs are as follows: 8VCPUs, 1GB memory and 10GB virtual disk.

We implement a parallel soft real-time scheduler, named *Poris*, based on Xen 4.0.1, and use PARSEC benchmark suite [2] to evaluate the effectiveness of *Poris*. PARSEC benchmark suite contains 13 multithreaded programs from many different areas. All of them are parallel programs, and some of them have soft real-time constraints, such as *vips*, *fluidanimate*, *facesim*, and *streamcluster*. For comparison, we also implement soft real-time scheduler (RS) and parallel scheduler (PS) under Xen-4.0.1 based on the descriptions in Section 2.1 and 2.2 respectively.

In this test, we run PARSEC benchmark in a VM, and set the VM as RT-VM. We specify the thread parameter of PARSEC benchmark as eight threads, and choose *native* data set as the input set. We use three other VMs run CPU-intensive workloads to compete with the RT-VM. The expected latency is set to 15ms. Figure 1 shows the results where the bars are normalized execution time.

As can be seen from the test results, for each individual benchmark, the performance of *Poris* is the best among these schedulers. The performance of *Poris* is up to 44.12% better than Credit, 41.28% better than RS, and 28.02% better than PS.

4. FUTURE WORK

Currently, our approach needs administrators to set the type of a VM manually, and only supports multithreaded soft real-time applications running in a VM. In the future, we will research the adaptive parallel real-time scheduling in which the type of a VM can be identified automatically according to the runtime characteristics of applications, and extend current scheduling algorithm to support multiple VMs running the same PSRT applications.

5. ACKNOWLEDGEMENTS

The research is supported by National Science Foundation of China under grant No.61073024 and 61232008. It is also supported by National 863 Hi-Tech Research and Development Program under grant No.2013AA01A213, Outstanding Youth Foundation of Hubei Province under grant No.2011CDA086S, and MOE-Intel Special Research Fund of Information Technology under grant MOE-INTEL-2012-01.

6. REFERENCES

[1] P. Barham, B. Dragovic, K. Fraser, S. Hand, T. Harris, A. Ho, R. Neugebauer, I. Pratt, and A. Warfield. Xen and the art of virtualization. In *SOSP'03*, pages 164–177, 2003.

[2] Christian Bienia. *Benchmarking Modern Multiprocessors*. PhD thesis, Princeton University, January 2011.

[3] M. Lee, A. S. Krishnakumar, P. Krishnan, N. Singh, and S. Yajnik. Supporting soft real-time tasks in the xen hypervisor. In *VEE'10*, pages 97–108, 2010.

[4] D. Patnaik, A. S. Krishnakumar, P. Krishnan, N. Singh, and S. Yajnik. Performance implications of hosting enterprise telephony applications on virtualized multi-core platforms. In *IPTComm'09*, 2009.

[5] V. Uhlig, J. LeVasseur, E. Skoglund, and U. Dannowski. Towards scalable multiprocessor virtual machines. In *VM'04*, pages 43–56, 2004.

Building and Scaling Virtual Clusters with Residual Resources from Interactive Clouds

R. Benjamin Clay*, Zhiming Shen*, Xiaosong Ma*†
*Dept. of Computer Science, North Carolina State University.
† Computer Science and Mathematics Division, Oak Ridge National Laboratory
{rbclay,zshen5}@ncsu.edu, ma@csc.ncsu.edu

ABSTRACT

The popularity of cloud-based interactive computing services (e.g., virtual desktops) brings new management challenges. Each interactive user leaves abundant but fluctuating residual resources while being intolerant to latency, precluding the use of aggressive VM consolidation. In this paper, we present the Resource Harvester for Interactive Clouds (RHIC), an autonomous management framework that harnesses dynamic residual resources aggressively without slowing the harvested interactive services. RHIC builds ad-hoc clusters for running throughput-oriented "background" workloads using a hybrid of residual and dedicated resources. For a given background job, RHIC intelligently discovers/maintains the ideal cluster size and composition, to meet user-specified goals such as cost/energy minimization or deadlines. RHIC employs black-box workload performance modeling, requiring only system-level metrics and incorporating techniques to improve modeling accuracy under bursty and heterogeneous residual resources. Our results show that RHIC finds near-ideal cluster sizes/compositions across a wide range of workload/goal combinations, significantly outperforms alternative approaches, tolerates high instability in the harvested interactive cloud, works with heterogeneous hardware and imposes minimal overhead.

Categories and Subject Descriptors

C.2.4 [**Computer Systems Organization**]: Computer- Communication Networks—*Distributed systems*

Keywords

Resource Harvesting; Cloud Computing; Volunteer Computing

1. INTRODUCTION

Interactive clouds are becoming more popular, hosting virtual computing laboratories, remote desktop environments and online collaboration tools. For example, North Carolina State University's Virtual Computing Laboratory (VCL) [8] is a production cloud system hosting virtual desktops with a variety of applications for more than 13,000 students at NCSU and other nearby schools. Such systems cater directly to human users, whose behavior yields significant unused *residual* resources due to bursty, unpredictable usage patterns. Traditional techniques such as virtual machine (VM) packing cannot be performed aggressively due to response time requirements (and human impatience), despite low average utilization. Enabling cloud providers to harness these idle resources will yield considerable energy savings, as the *incremental* energy cost of running additional applications using residual CPU is low [5].

Harvesting residual resources in this context requires a well-

Copyright is held by the author/owner(s).
HPDC'13, June 17–21, 2013, New York, NY, USA.
ACM 978-1-4503-1910-2/13/06.

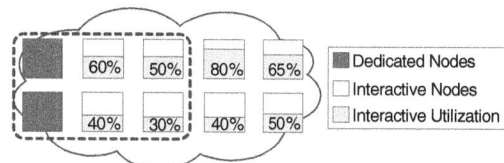

Figure 1: Sample hybrid cloud computing system, with 8 interactive nodes running interactive services. A background job runs on 2 dedicated and 4 volunteer nodes.

designed infrastructure that considers performance, cost-effectiveness and system reliability. In particular, using *interactive nodes* alone will suffer from performance and stability issues. Prior work [6] proposed a hybrid batch cluster design where *volunteer* nodes supplement a core set of stable *dedicated* nodes. As shown in Fig. 1, a set of transient interactive nodes are "padded" with volunteer VMs running a background batch job, which consume residual resources while automatically deferring to the interactive user via hypervisor prioritization. This co-location of interactive and batch workloads is advantageous due to orthogonal temporal characteristics [5]. In preliminary experiments, we demonstrate 20-29% energy and 20-40% cost gains over normal dedicated clusters with only 1% slowdown of interactive workloads.

In this setting, the cloud administrator is faced with the following question: *Given an arbitrary batch job, and limited knowledge about the interactive workloads, what hybrid cluster size and composition will give the best performance for the cost?* This problem can be formulated as a dynamic, virtualized cluster-sizing problem, which brings new challenges not studied in prior work. Unlike in traditional cluster-sizing scenarios, the highly-dynamic nature of this environment introduces substantial complications when modeling and predicting performance, determining an ideal cluster size, and selecting cluster composition.

In this paper, we present the Resource Harvester for Interactive Clouds (RHIC), a generic management framework which autonomically optimizes a hybrid cluster running within residual resources. RHIC provides intelligent cluster sizing for a wide range of throughput-oriented parallel batch workloads. To accomplish this, RHIC combines profiling with black-box performance modeling to make resizing decisions in an iterative, online fashion. We profile the CPU, memory and I/O consumption of each workload and build self-tuning models to translate these system-level metrics into job performance estimates. Finally, we tailor this approach to the hybrid cluster design, by predicting residual resource availability at the volunteers and directly managing I/O saturation at the dedicated nodes. Our multi-faceted approach handles dynamic and unpredictable behavior from a wide range of sources, aggregating unstable resources into a reliable batch platform. The major contributions of this work are:

- To the best of our knowledge, we are the first to propose batch cluster sizing as a tool for resource harvesting in interactive clouds.
- We present an adaptive cluster sizing solution that uses a combination of online profiling and performance modeling to quickly discover and maintain efficient hybrid cluster sizes, relying only on system monitoring data for wide applicability.
- In over 400 experimental runs, our results show that RHIC achieves high accuracy across 28 workload/goal combinations in minimizing cost/energy and enforcing deadlines.

2. RELATED WORK

Our work is related to contributions from several other areas:

Volunteer computing. Volunteer computing (VC), known widely through projects such as Condor [7], has a long history as both a computation paradigm and a method of harvesting wasted cycles. Recently, advancing multitasking technology has made it feasible and attractive to perform *active* volunteer computing [3, 5], where the user and harvester coexist temporally. Active VC poses challenges in maintaining interactive user experience [3] and delivering consistent background performance [1]. The focus of this work is related to the latter challenge: how bursty residual resources can efficiently provide a stable batch execution platform that meets performance and/or cost goals. RHIC's novelty is in modeling the relationship between batch workload progress and resource availability, with techniques to mitigate burstiness, heterogeneity and other artifacts of our hostile environment.

Cluster sizing for parallel batch workloads. Several works have been recently published which perform cluster sizing for parallel batch workloads [2, 4, 9, 10]. RHIC addresses a unique permutation of traditional cluster sizing for parallel batch workloads. We consider several sub-problems which are specific to our harvesting theme, including foreground demand prediction, heuristic node selection, I/O saturation awareness, I/O curve discovery and heterogeneity-tolerant performance modeling. In summary, the differences between RHIC and the aforementioned MapReduce cluster-sizing efforts are as follows: (1) the uniquely unstable environment in which we operate, (2) our support for novel, short-lived jobs, and (3) the general applicability of our modeling approach to a broad class of parallel batch workloads.

Volunteer MapReduce. MOON [6] enhanced Hadoop to operate under passive volunteerism, where a foreground workload and MapReduce are interleaved temporally but not spatially. MOON is a conceptual predecessor to our work, but does not consider active volunteerism or perform cluster sizing.

Workload Consolidation. Co-locating workloads is a well-established technique [11] that is complementary to our approach. RHIC can transparently harvest whatever residual resources are available after consolidation during periods of user "think time".

3. APPROACH

RHIC combines online profiling with periodic job progress and system resource monitoring to adaptively scale the volunteer node set throughout a *background* (batch) job's execution. To handle a dynamic set of interactive nodes, each contributing varying amount of resources, and to achieve online performance modeling independent of the actual workload and batch execution framework, RHIC relies on three key insights derived from our experiments:

- *Insight 1:* Although each foreground interactive workload has unpredictable resource usage bursts, its *average* usage in the near future tends to be more stable.
- *Insight 2:* In our proposed hybrid execution mode, the disk I/O bandwidth afforded by the dedicated nodes can be a major factor limiting the *effective* productivity of a volunteer.

- *Insight 3:* The overall progress of a batch job is determined by the *aggregate* productivity from all selected volunteers, largely independent of the productivity distribution among these nodes.

RHIC's novelty is in leveraging these insights to build problem-tailored models for residual resource avaiability, I/O bottlenecks and batch job runtime in an online fashion. In particular, RHIC collects once-per-second resource and job metrics, periodically updates its models and leverages them to determine the best possible hybrid cluster composition. The new cluster composition is then observed over the following period, when the process repeats. This online reactive approach allows RHIC to handle two sources of uncertainty, novel workloads and unstable interactive users, by predicting near-future behavior while constantly adjusting to past performance. In our preliminary evaluation, RHIC's flexibility on both of these fronts delivers high adaptability and accuracy, as compared to alternative approaches.

4. RESULTS OVERVIEW

We evaluated RHIC with over 400 experiments on a cluster of 6 dedicated and 0-36 volunteer nodes, running four diverse Hadoop workloads and interactive traces taken from NCSU's VCL.

Exhaustive comparison: Compared to an exhaustive search of cluster sizes, RHIC achieves within 5% of the minimum possible cost and 3% of the minimum energy, and adheres closely to deadlines with an average of 2% time to spare.

Alternative algorithm comparison: Compared to two alternative algorithms using fuzzy control and naïve thresholds respectively, RHIC delivers significantly lower error and greater consistency.

Overhead: RHIC's control node consumes less than 2% CPU on average and takes less than $250ms$ to make an exhaustive cluster sizing decision for 36 volunteers.

Impact of Environment Stability: RHIC is very resilient to high instability (2-$8\times$ normal) in interactive cloud sessions.

Other Background Frameworks: RHIC achieves 1% average error for cost and 2% for energy when managing a lightweight compute framework on top of HBase.

Hardware Heterogeneity: RHIC's thin hardware translation layer yields $\leq 2\%$ modeling error for I/O & compute-intensive jobs.

5. ACKNOWLEDGEMENTS

This work has been supported in part by NSF grants 0546301 (CAREER), 0915861, 0937908, and 0958311, in addition to Google Research Awards, IBM Research Awards, a Graduate Merit Award from the College of Engineering at NCSU, as well as a joint faculty appointment between Oak Ridge National Laboratory and NCSU.

6. REFERENCES

[1] A. Chandra and J. Weissman. Nebulas: Using distributed voluntary resources to build clouds. In *HotCloud'09*.

[2] A. D. Ferguson, P. Bodik, S. Kandula, et al. Jockey: Guaranteed job latency in data parallel clusters. In *EuroSys'12*.

[3] A. Gupta, B. Lin, and P. Dinda. Measuring and understanding user comfort with resource borrowing. In *HPDC '04*.

[4] H. Herodotou, F. Dong, and S. Babu. No one (cluster) size fits all: Automatic cluster sizing for data-intensive analytics. In *SOCC '11*.

[5] J. Li, A. Deshpande, J. Srinivasan, et al. Energy and performance impact of aggressive volunteer computing with multi-core computers. In *MASCOTS '09*.

[6] H. Lin, X. Ma, J. Archuleta, et al. Moon: Mapreduce on opportunistic environments. In *HPDC '10*.

[7] M. Litzkow, M. Livny, and M. Mutka. Condor-a hunter of idle workstations. In *DCS '88*.

[8] NCSU. NCSU Virtual Computing Lab. vcl.ncsu.edu/.

[9] J. Polo, C. Castillo, D. Carrera, et al. Resource-aware adaptive scheduling for mapreduce clusters. In *Middleware'11*.

[10] A. Wieder, P. Bhatotia, A. Post, et al. Orchestrating the deployment of computations in the cloud with conductor. In *NSDI '12*.

[11] T. Wood, P. Shenoy, A. Venkataramani, et al. Black-box and gray-box strategies for virtual machine migration. In *NSDI '07*.

SCDA: SLA-aware Cloud Datacenter Architecture for Efficient Content Storage and Retrieval

Debessay Fesehaye
Department of Computer Science
University of Illinois at Urbana-Champaign
dkassa2@illinois.edu

Klara Nahrstedt
Department of Computer Science
University of Illinois at Urbana-Champaign
klara@illinois.edu

ABSTRACT

With the fast growth of (online) content and the need for high quality content services, cloud data centers are increasingly becoming the preferred places to store data and retrieve it from. With a highly variable network traffic and limited resources, efficient server selection and data transfer rate allocation mechanisms become necessary. However, current approaches rely on random server selection schemes and inefficient data transmission rate control mechanisms.

In this paper we present SCDA, an efficient server selection, resource allocation and enforcement mechanism with many salient features. SCDA has prioritized rate allocation mechanism to satisfy different service level agreements (SLA)s on throughput and delays. The allocation scheme can achieve max/min fairness. SCDA has a mechanism to detect and hence mitigate SLA violation in realtime.

We have implemented SCDA in the NS2 simulator. Extensive experimental results confirm some of the design goals of SCDA to obtain a lower content transfer time and a higher throughput. The design of SCDA can achieve a content transfer time which is about 50% lower than the existing schemes and a throughput which is higher than existing approaches by upto than 60%.

Categories and Subject Descriptors

C.2 [**COMPUTER-COMMUNICATION NETWORKS**];
C.2.1 [**Network Architecture and Design**]: Network communications

Keywords

Cloud architecture, max/min fairness, fast transfer, SLA-aware, prioritized rate.

1. INTRODUCTION

Over the past few years there has been an exponential growth of online content and such content generation is expected to grow at 40-35% a year [5]. Users of (multimedia) content have diverse Quality of Service (QoS) requirements. Based on their QoS specifications, content users make service level agreements (SLA) with content and/or network providers. Satisfying QoS requirements with dynamic network and server loads and with limited resource capacities

(link bandwidth, server storage, processing, energy) is challenging. The main problem lies in knowing *where* to *store* contents and *retrieve* them from, by *utilizing* available resources and *detecting SLA* violations.

Addressing this problem involves answering a series of questions. Some of the main questions are the following.

1. *Which* server among a group of servers at different locations is the *least loaded* and power efficient?

2. At what *rate* should content be *written* to server and *retrieved* from it in order to satisfy SLA (lower delay and higher throughput)?

3. How can max/min fairness be ensured where available resource is utilized as long as there is demand for it?

4. How can *SLA violation* be detected in realtime (milliseconds interval) and be mitigated?

5. How can such data transfer rate allocations to different users be enforced without changing routers, switches and the TCP/IP stack?

Existing attempts to solve these problems broadly fall into two categories. The first one is using large content distribution networks (CDNs) such as Akamai. Such CDNs use a large number of edge servers distributed in vast Internet locations. As explained in [7] such schemes select a server for client request based on proximity and latency. Server selection is not based on best content transfer rates and lowest delays. Besides, the scalability of distribution and maintenance of edge-servers scattered in many Internet locations all over the world is costly. The work presented in [7] shows that significant consolidation of Akamai's platform into fewer large data centers is possible without degrading performance.

The second but dominant and emerging content storage and retrieval approach is using cloud data centers. There have been numerous data center architectures [4, 1] to address the above-mentioned challenges. However such architectures do not use an efficient mechanism to select the best servers in the data center. They use random switch (server) selection strategies. They also rely on the transmission control protocol (TCP) to control the rates of the senders. TCP is known to have higher average file completion time (AFCT) than necessary as discussed in [2]. Besides, such approaches are restricted to specific structure of datacenter network interconnect.

In this paper we present the design of SLA-aware Cloud Datacenter Architecture (SCDA) for efficient content storage and retrieval. SCDA among other things addresses the above five questions. The design of SCDA has two main features. The first feature enables SCDA to use multiple name node servers (NNS) using a light weight front-end server (FES) which forwards requests to the name nodes (NNS). This approach solves the weakness of current state-of-the-art cloud-computing architectures (file systems) [6]. In such systems only a single NNS, which can potentially be a bottleneck resource and single point of failure, is used.

The second main feature of SCDA is its ability to avoid congestion and select the less loaded servers using a cross-layer (transport and network layers) concept unlike current well known schemes [1, 4, 6] which rely on TCP and random server selection (RandTCP). SCDA also uses resource monitors (RM) and resource allocators (RA) to do fine grained resource allocation and load balancing. The roles of these SCDA components can be extended to constantly monitor the performance of the cloud against malicious attacks or failures. All the aggregated and monitored traffic metrics can be offloaded to an external server for off-line diagnosis, analysis and data mining of the distributed system.

The data center (cloud) resource *allocation and enforcement* mechanism of SCDA using RMs and RAs is *stateless* and does not need modifications to routers/switches or the TCP/IP stack. The scheme can *detect violation in service level agreements (SLA)* and can help cloud (data center) administrators (admins) to automatically add more resources to resolve detected SLA violations.

The SCDA resource (bandwidth) allocation mechanism is *max-min fair* in that any link bandwidth unused by some flows (bottlenecked elsewhere) can be used by flows which need it. This is a very useful quality any resource allocation mechanism needs to achieve. We also show how SCDA can do more *power aware server selection* as there is heterogeneity in power consumptions by different servers. This heterogeneity can be due to server's location in a rack, due to server age and specifications or due to other compute intensive or background tasks the servers perform. The RM and RA of SCDA are *software components* and can be consolidated into a few powerful servers close to each other to minimize communication overheads and latencies.

An entire description of the SCDA architecture can be found at [3].

2. NUMERICAL RESULTS

We have conducted trace-based packet level detailed simulation experiments by implementing SCDA in the NS2 network simulator. As shown in figures 1 and 2 SCDA outperforms schemes based on random server selction and TCP (RandTCP).

3. REFERENCES

[1] AL-FARES, M., RADHAKRISHNAN, S., RAGHAVAN, B., HUANG, N., AND VAHDAT, A. Hedera: dynamic flow scheduling for data center networks. In *Proceedings of the 7th USENIX NSDI'10* (2010).

[2] DUKKIPATI, N., AND MCKEOWN, N. Why flow-completion time is the right metric for congestion control. *SIGCOMM CCR 36*, 1 (2006), 59–62.

[3] FESEHAYE, D., AND NAHRSTEDT, K. SCDA: SLA-aware Cloud Datacenter Architecture for Efficient Content Storage and Retrieval. Technical report, UIUC, 01 2013.

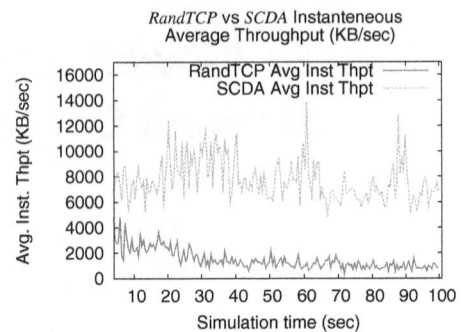

Figure 1: Average Instantaneous Throughput comparison of SCDA and RandTCP based: Using Video Traces without control flows

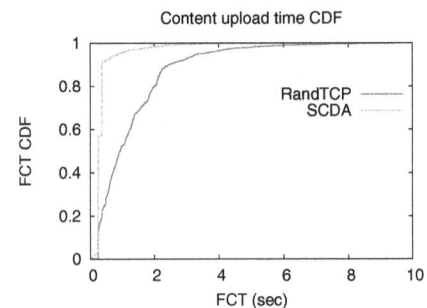

Figure 2: FCT CDF comparison of SCDA and RandTCP based: Using Datacenter Traces with $K = 3$

[4] GREENBERG, A., HAMILTON, J. R., JAIN, N., KANDULA, S., KIM, C., LAHIRI, P., MALTZ, D. A., PATEL, P., AND SENGUPTA, S. Vl2: a scalable and flexible data center network. In *Proceedings of the ACM SIGCOMM '09* (2009), pp. 51–62.

[5] LABOVITZ, C., IEKEL-JOHNSON, S., MCPHERSON, D., OBERHEIDE, J., AND JAHANIAN, F. Internet inter-domain traffic. *SIGCOMM Comput. Commun. Rev. 41*, 4 (Aug. 2010).

[6] SHVACHKO, K., KUANG, H., RADIA, S., AND CHANSLER, R. The hadoop distributed file system. In *Proceedings of the IEEE MSST 2010* (Long Beach, CA, USA, 2010), pp. 1–10.

[7] TRIUKOSE, S., WEN, Z., AND RABINOVICH, M. Measuring a commercial content delivery network. In *Proceedings of the WWW '11* (Hyderabad, India, 2011), pp. 467–476.

Load Balancing in Large-scale Epidemiological Simulations

[Extended Abstract]

Tariq Kamal
NDSSL, VBI, Virginia Tech
Blacksburg VA, USA
tkamal@vbi.vt.edu

Keith R. Bisset
NDSSL, VBI, Virginia Tech
Blacksburg VA, USA
kbisset@vbi.vt.edu

Ali R. Butt
Computer Science, Virginia Tech
Blacksburg VA, USA
butta@cs.vt.edu

Youngyun Chungbaek
NDSSL, VBI, Virginia Tech
Blacksburg VA, USA
ychungba@vbi.vt.edu

Madhav Marathe
NDSSL, VBI, Virginia Tech
Blacksburg VA, USA
mmarathe@vbi.vt.edu

ABSTRACT

Despite the recent advancements in graph partitioning techniques and algorithms, achieving static load balancing in agent-based epidemiological applications is challenging. Input to these simulations is a large agent-location bipartite graph that is highly complex and non-uniform. In this paper, we compare several static load distribution schemes, including our custom strategies, for partitioning a class of bipartite graphs. Computations over such graphs happen between classes of nodes in phases. Our performance evaluations on a 768 core system show that our lower-overhead custom load balancing strategy achieves a 2-fold increase in strong scaling performance compared to the default Round Robin data distribution.

Categories and Subject Descriptors

D.4.8 [**Performance**]: Simulation

Keywords

distributed systems, epidemiological simulations, load balancing

1. INTRODUCTION

Input to agent-based epidemiological applications is a large agent-location bipartite graph that is highly complex and non-uniform. Achieving static load balancing in such applications is challenging. Two main factors impose problems for partitioning algorithms: (i) tasks carry variable computational weights (e.g., non-home locations receive more agents than home locations), which makes Round Robin distribution an ineffective scheme to achieve a balanced load, and, (ii) the computations happen between classes of tasks (agents and locations) in phases. This requires a good partitioning strategy that balances both types of computations across all the compute units while minimizing the edge-cut (i.e., inter-process communication) at the same time.

In this work, we review Metis library for partitioning large bipartite graphs. Metis with the multi-constraint feature gives best-quality partitions at the cost of extremely high memory and runtime overhead. Partitioning overheads are important when simulation running times are very small. To mitigate this, we design a custom partitioning algorithm (Colocation strategy) that is extremely low-overhead and is capable of producing good-quality partitions. We also design a hybrid strategy that reduces the input graph to partition by merging several nodes into fewer super-nodes (based upon the relationship among nodes). The merged graph is partitioned using Metis. The hybrid strategy (MetColoc) has the advantage of producing same as Metis partitions at the cost of much reduced overhead (compared to Metis).

As an example, we review the partitioning strategies for achieving load balancing in EpiSimdemics [1] [2]. EpiSimdemics is one implementation of scalable parallel algorithms that simulate the spread of contagion in large realistic social contact networks using individual-based models. The input to EpiSimdemics is a person-location bipartite graph. There are two types of vetices (or tasks) in the graph: Person tasks and location tasks. The person and location tasks have a producer-consumer relationship. During the two phases of a time-step separated by synchronization, each task is both a producer and consumer, alternatively. Consumers must receive all the events generated by producers before starting to process them. The time used for person computation is estimated by the number of persons and the time used for location computation is estimated by number of incoming edges.

1.1 Contributions

The primary contributions of this work are:
- A simple, semantic aware and low-overhead Colocation algorithm for data distribution
- Reviewing and using Metis library for partitioning bipartite graphs
- Augmenting Metis scheme with knowledge of relationship of entities in simulation to achieve lower-overhead and high-quality partitioning

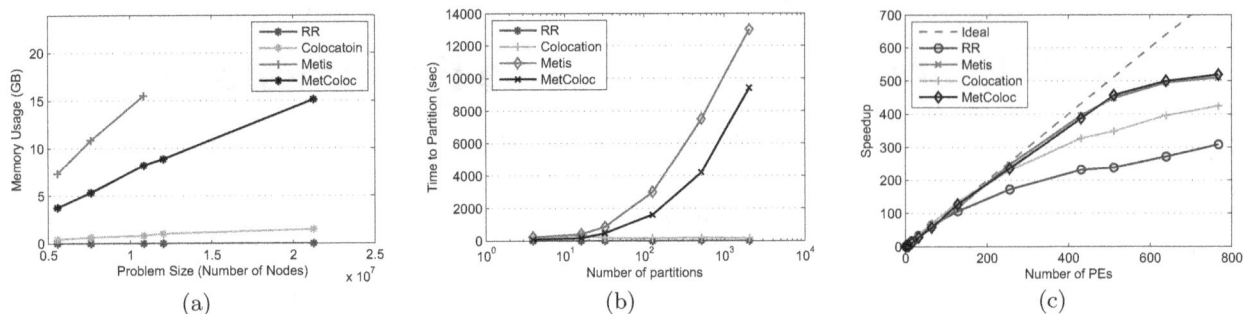

Figure 1: (a) Memory consumption of partitioning strategies when partitioning graphs of various sizes in 768 partitions. Due to large memory requirements, M fails to partition two configurations (of 12 million and 21 million nodes). (b) The execution times of load balancing strategies when creating several partitions of NC graph (10,832,803 nodes). (c) strong scaling speedup for a 120 day simulation of NC. M and MC achieves upto 2x peformance of RR.

2. PARTITIONING SCHEMES

2.1 Round Robin (RR)

RR assigns persons and locations to partitions in a round-robin fashion without regard for their weights. The partitions it creates are usually imbalanced in terms of computations and communication.

2.2 Colocation (C)

C achieves static load balancing with a simple and low overhead greedy approach. It perfectly balances computations by assigning person load in the number of persons and location load in the number of location inedges. On average, 46% of the time, the persons visit their home locations, and to exploit this locality the Colocation algorithm assigns persons and their home-locations to the same partition.

2.3 Metis (M)

We use Metis [3] direct k-way and multi-constraint features to partition our weighted person-location bipartite graph. We prefer Muli-level k-way partitioning over multi-level recursive bisection, as it is faster by a factor of $O(logk)$, and produces better quality partitions in less time [4]. The produced partitions have fewer connected edges between partitions.

2.4 MetColoc (MC)

MC is a custom partitioning strategy that augments Metis with knowledge of person-home-location relationship. The algorithm minimizes the input graph to partition by merging person nodes and their respective home-location node into super-nodes. The merged graph is then partitioned using Metis direct k-way and multi-constraint partitioning.

3. PERFORMANCE EVALUATION

Among the four schemes, M has the highest memory and runtime overhead as shown in Figure 1. M time to partition increases linearly as we increase the number of partitions to create. MC has a smaller graph to process, and takes less time in partitioning compared to M. Figure 1(a),(b) shows that C has smallest partitioning overheads even when creating a large number of partitions.

We also evaluate the strong scaling performance of load distribution strategies on 768 processor cores. Figures 1(c)

shows that M and MC schemes scales best achieving 78% effeciency. The reason is its ability to keep person and location imbalances within specified limits while achieving higher locality (even for a large number of partitions). RR distribution performs quite poorly in exploiting task locality, and even for a small number of partitions (128), more than 99% of communication is remote. C gives well-balanced computational loads and scales up to 640 PEs achieving 62% efficiency compared to 42% of RR.

4. CONCLUSIONS

We have presented four strategies for partitioning bipartite graphs. EpiSimdemics is used as an example; however, the algorithms are equally applicable to a broad class of bipartite network-based dynamical processes. The partitioning algorithms were shown to be more effective than the Round Robin scheme that was originally used. Metis produce better partitions at the cost of more resources used to create partitions.

Acknowledgment

This work has been partially supported by NSF PetaApps Grant OCI-0904844 and DTRA CNIMS Grant HDTRA1-07-C-0113.

5. REFERENCES

[1] C. L. Barrett, K. R. Bisset, S. G. Eubank, X. Feng, and M. V. Marathe. EpiSimdemics: An efficient algorithm for simulating the spread of infectious disease over large realistic social networks. In *SC '08: Proceedings of the 2008 ACM/IEEE conference on Supercomputing*, pages 1–12, Piscataway, NJ, USA, 2008. IEEE Press.

[2] K. Bisset, A. Aji, E. Bohm, L. Kale, T. Kamal, M. Marathe, and J.-S. Yeom. Simulating the spread of infectious disease over large realistic social networks using Charm++. In *Parallel and Distributed Processing Symposium Workshops PhD Forum (IPDPSW), 2012 IEEE 26th International*, pages 507 –518, May 2012.

[3] G. Karypis and V. Kumar. Metis - Unstructured graph partitioning and sparse matrix ordering system, Version 2.0. Technical report, 1995.

[4] G. Karypis and V. Kumar. A fast and high quality multilevel scheme for partitioning irregular graphs. *SIAM Journal on Scientific Computing*, 20(1):359–392, 1998.

Efficient Analytics on Ordered Datasets using MapReduce

Jiangtao Yin
UMass Amherst
jyin@ecs.umass.edu

Yong Liao
Narus Inc.
yliao@narus.com

Mario Baldi
Narus Inc.
mbaldi@narus.com

Lixin Gao
UMass Amherst
lgao@ecs.umass.edu

Antonio Nucci
Narus Inc.
anucci@narus.com

ABSTRACT

Efficiently analyzing data on a large scale can be vital for data owners to gain useful business intelligence. One of the most common datasets used to gain business intelligence is event log files. Oftentimes, records in event log files that are time sorted, need to be grouped by user ID or transaction ID in order to mine user behaviors, such as click through rate, while preserving the time order. This kind of analytical workload is here referred to as RElative Order-pReserving based Grouping (RE-ORG). Using MapReduce/Hadoop, a popular big data analysis tool, in an as-is manner for executing RE-ORG tasks on ordered datasets is not efficient due to its internal sort-merge mechanism. We propose a framework that adopts an efficient group-order-merge mechanism to provide faster execution of RE-ORG tasks and implement it by extending Hadoop. Experimental results show a 2.2x speedup over executing RE-ORG tasks in plain vanilla Hadoop.

Categories and Subject Descriptors

H.3.4 [**Systems and Software**]: Distributed systems

General Terms

Design, Experimentation, Performance

Keywords

MapReduce/Hadoop; distributed framework; ordered dataset

1. PROBLEM STATEMENT

Large corporations produce and collect terabytes of data on a daily basis with the purpose of analyzing them to continually improve their services and operations. Several classes of data used to gain business intelligence have a temporal dimension, such as webpage click streams, network traffic traces, and business transaction records. Furthermore, a lot of analytic tasks over such temporal data require to group data points based on a certain feature and temporally sort them within the group. Many important analytic jobs, including user online activity sessionization, TCP/IP flow construction, and customer statement generation, treat such tasks as a vital part of their execution. The corresponding input datasets can be generally seen as event

log files, in which each record is about an event occurring at a given point in time. Such datasets have the important property that since the records are placed in the dataset as they are generated, they are temporally ordered.

More generally, this kind of dataset can be represented as a list of *records* consisting of a *primary key*, a *secondary key*, and a *value*, sorted by the secondary keys. Several popular and business critical analytics tasks use such a dataset as an input to generate a set of output data points, each one being a function of a *group* of records from the input dataset that satisfy the following conditions: (1) records are grouped based on their primary keys; (2) records in a group are sorted by their secondary keys. We define the *RElative Order-pReserving based Grouping*, or RE-ORG, as the processing that creates groups satisfying the above requirements.

Efficiently executing RE-ORG over large quantity of data in a distributed environment is challenging. MapReduce [3] and its extensions [4, 6–8] have emerged as scalable frameworks for data intensive computation using a large cluster of commodity machines. However, realizing RE-ORG tasks using MapReduce in an as-is manner is not efficient. MapReduce distributes input records to mapper nodes (workers) in the cluster and then groups them by their primary keys on the reducer nodes utilizing an internal *sort-merge* scheme, which cannot take advantage of the fact that the input records are already sorted by secondary key. Sorting records by secondary key in the same group (i.e., having the same primary key) requires to either write custom code or instrument the MapReduce framework (e.g., Hadooop) to do that. Either way, the sorting operation is time consuming.

2. OUR SOLUTION

This work proposes a novel *group-order-merge* (GOM) mechanism to replace the *sort-merge* shuffle scheme of MapReduce, so as to efficiently support the execution of RE-ORG in a distributed environment. The property of the input dataset being sorted by secondary key is used to speed up the execution of RE-ORG. Figure 1 shows how the three phases of the GOM mechanism are distributed between mapper and reducer workers.

Group Phase: A worker (mapper) sequentially extracts the records from its input chunk and groups them by applying a hash function on their primary keys. The output of the group phase is a set of *segments*, each containing a set of *lists*. Each list includes all the records in the processed chunk with the same primary key. Since records are processed sequentially, each list preserves the ordering records have in the input dataset.

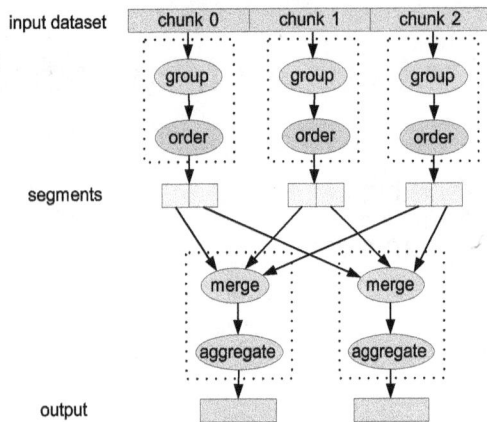

Figure 1: Group-order-merge phases.

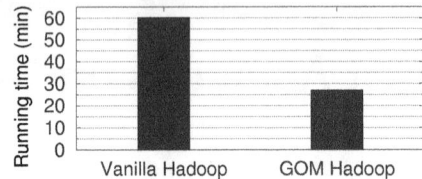

Figure 2: Running time of user sessionization.

sionization task on GOM-enhanced Hadoop was compared to the one of vanilla Hadoop using the stock secondary sort implementation [5]. As it can be seen in Figure 2, the GOM-enhanced Hadoop prototype achieves a 2.2x speedup on the completion time over vanilla Hadoop.

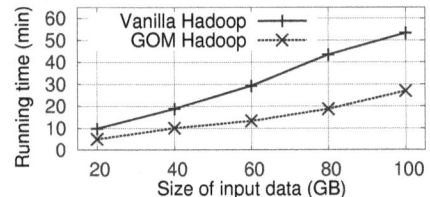

Figure 3: Running times of user sessionization on data with varying size.

Figure 3 shows how the performance of the sessionization task on a 10-node GOM-enhanced Hadoop cluster scales with increasing size of the input dataset compared to the vanilla Hadoop cluster. The 116GB click stream dataset was divided in subsets of different sizes on which the user online activity sessionization task was run. As shown in Figure 3, the running times on the GOM-enhanced framework increase linearly with the size of the input dataset outperforming vanilla Hadoop with any input data size.

Order Phase: Lists in each segment are sorted based on their primary keys. This is an important preparation step to then allow reducer nodes to efficiently merge segments produced by different mapper workers. Note that each list is treated as a whole in the order phase, which is much more efficient than handling each record individually. The sorted segments are then distributed to a set of reducer workers based on the primary key (i.e., one segment to one worker and guaranteeing all lists whose records have the same primary key will be received by the same reducer worker).

Merge Phase: The records contained in segments for the same primary key received from different mappers are merged into one final list. The merging algorithm must ensure that records in the resulting list of each segment preserve their relative ordering as in the input dataset. The fact that lists in the segments received from different mappers are sorted by primary key allows the merging algorithm to have minimum complexity by creating the secondary-key-sorted list corresponding to each primary key value in a single pass.

After the merge phase, data is ready to allow each reducer to perform the aggregation operation on the final secondary-key-sorted list[1].

3. IMPLEMENTATION AND EVALUATION

The group-order-merge (GOM) mechanism was implemented as an alternative shuffle scheme in Hadoop [1] to the default sort-merge one. Hadoop was selected as the basis for the implementation because a RE-ORG task maps very well to the MapReduce programming model and Hadoop is the most popular open-source framework supporting such programming model. The popularity of Hadoop stems from its good performance in handling failures and capability of scaling to a large number of worker nodes. The prototype implementation that provided the results shown below is based on Hadoop version 1.0.3.

A user online activity sessionization task was run on the well known 116GB click stream dataset related to World Cup 1998 [2] using a 10-node cluster. This sessionization task first groups clicks by user and then divides the click stream of each user into browsing sessions based on a time-out threshold (e.g., 5 minutes). The performance of the ses-

---

[1]The aggregation operation is not part of the proposed mechanism, but constitutes the implementation of the actual analytics task.

Acknowledgments

This work is partially supported by NSF grant CNS-1217284.

4. REFERENCES

[1] Apache Hadoop. http://hadoop.apache.org/.
[2] World Cup 1998. http://ita.ee.lbl.gov/html/contrib/WorldCup.html.
[3] J. Dean and S. Ghemawat. MapReduce: Simplified data processing on large clusters. In *OSDI '04*, 2004.
[4] J. Ekanayake, H. Li, B. Zhang, T. Gunarathne, S.-H. Bae, J. Qiu, and G. Fox. Twister: a runtime for iterative MapReduce. In *HPDC '10*, 2010.
[5] T. White. *Hadoop: The Definitive Guide.* O'Reilly Media, Inc., 1st edition, 2009.
[6] J. Yin, Y. Zhang, and L. Gao. Accelerating expectation-maximization algorithms with frequent updates. In *CLUSTER '12*, 2012.
[7] Y. Zhang, Q. Gao, L. Gao, and C. Wang. iMapReduce: A distributed computing framework for iterative computation. In *IPDPSW '11*, 2011.
[8] Y. Zhang, Q. Gao, L. Gao, and C. Wang. PrIter: A distributed framework for prioritized iterative computations. In *SOCC '11*, 2011.

A Framework for Auto-Tuning HDF5 Applications

Babak Behzad
University of Illinois at
Urbana-Champaign

Joseph Huchette
Rice University

Huong Vu Thanh Luu
University of Illinois at
Urbana-Champaign

Ruth Aydt
The HDF Group

Surendra Byna
Lawrence Berkeley National
Laboratory

Yushu Yao
Lawrence Berkeley National
Laboratory

Quincey Koziol
The HDF Group

Prabhat
Lawrence Berkeley National
Laboratory

ABSTRACT

The modern parallel I/O stack consists of several software layers with complex interdependencies and performance characteristics. While each layer exposes tunable parameters, it is often unclear to users how different parameter settings interact with each other and affect overall I/O performance. As a result, users often resort to default system settings, which typically obtain poor I/O bandwidth. In this research, we develop a benchmark guided auto-tuning framework for tuning the HDF5, MPI-IO, and Lustre layers on production supercomputing facilities. Our framework consists of three main components. *H5Tuner* uses a control file to adjust I/O parameters without modifying or recompiling the application. *H5PerfCapture* records performance metrics for HDF5 and MPI-IO. *H5Evolve* uses a genetic algorithm to explore the parameter space to determine well-performing configurations. We demonstrate I/O performance results for three HDF5 application-based benchmarks on a Sun HPC system. All the benchmarks running on 512 MPI processes perform 3X to 5.5X faster with the auto-tuned I/O parameters compared to a configuration with default system parameters.

Categories and Subject Descriptors

H.4 [**Information Systems Applications**]: Miscellaneous; D.2.8 [**Software Engineering**]: Metrics—*complexity measures, performance measures*

General Terms

Performance

Keywords

Parallel I/O, Auto-tuning, Parallel file systems, H5Tuner, H5Evolve, H5PerfCapture, HDF5 Auto-tuning

1. INTRODUCTION

Our goal in this research is developing a benchmark-driven auto-tuning framework for identifying appropriate HDF5, MPI-IO, and Lustre settings on a given platform. Figure 1

shows an overview of our I/O auto-tuning framework with H5Tuner, H5PerfCapture, and H5Evolve. *H5Tuner* provides transparent parameter injection into the parallel I/O calls. It is a shared library which can be preloaded before the HDF5 library, prioritizing it over the native HDF5 functions. *H5PerfCapture*, built on Darshan [1], gathers I/O performance statistics, such as I/O time and number of bytes read/written, and traces HDF5 calls. *H5Evolve* uses a genetic algorithm (GA) to sample the I/O parameter space in order to find high-performing I/O configurations.

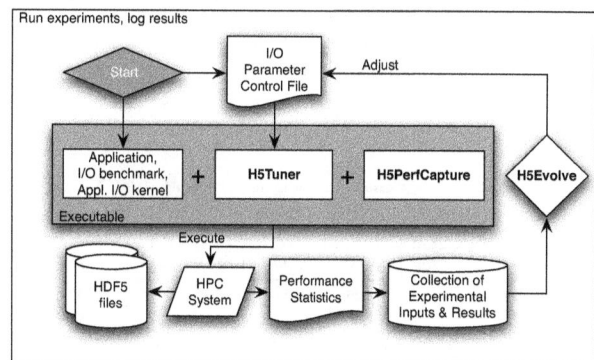

Figure 1: A functional schematic of the the auto-tuning framework

2. RESULTS

We choose three parallel I/O kernels to evaluate our auto-tuning framework: VPIC-IO, VORPAL-IO, and GCRM-IO. These kernels are derived from real scientific applications. We applied the auto-tuning framework for these applications on Texas Advanced Computing Center's Ranger system. We ran the tests on 128 and 512-core concurrency. We hand-selected a number of important parallel I/O parameters from the HDF5 (alignment), MPI-IO (collective buffer size, number of collective buffering nodes) and Lustre (strip count, stripe size) software layers.

Figure 2 shows the GA evolution of overall GCRM-IO kernel runtime using *H5Evolve* on 512 Ranger cores. The x-axis shows the experiment number and the y-axis shows the time taken to complete writing GCRM-IO data. We observed a large variation in I/O time, with spikes corresponding to parameter choices that performed poorly. Over time, the GA adjusts tunable parameters to find good combinations, favoring exploration around well-performing choices. We chose the set of parameters with the smallest I/O time in the last group of experiments (the last GA generation) as the tuned set.

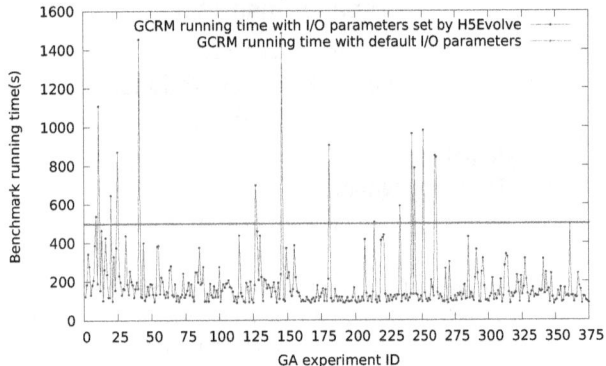

Figure 2: Evolution of GCRM-IO runtime with H5Evolve on Ranger using 512 cores

Tuned Parameters, Runtimes, and Speedup of Tuned over Default						
System	Ranger (128 Cores)			Ranger (512 Cores)		
Application	VPIC-IO	GCRM-IO	VORPAL-IO	VPIC-IO	GCRM-IO	VORPAL-IO
Parameter	Tuned Sets of Parameters Identified by H5Evolve					
Stripe Count	16	32	16	96	96	32
Stripe Size/ CB Buffer Size	16 MB	16 MB	32 MB	128 MB	1 MB	8 MB
CB Nodes	128	96	96	48	64	64
Alignment (thrsh, bndry)	0 KB, 4 KB	0 KB, 64 KB	0 KB, 16 KB	4 KB, 16 KB	0 KB, 64 KB	0 KB, 256 KB
Description	Measured Runtime (seconds) / Bandwidth (MB/s)					
Default Parameters	119.91	135.43	179.97	417.50	498.21	391.72
	258.52	302.73	322.27	308.98	327.17	584.60
Minimum	57.38	44.75	50.76	127.92	84.29	103.99
Maximum	243.88	284.26	357.54	1205.89	1485.36	959.51
Tuned Set	68.11	48.86	53.31	132.64	89.64	108.52
	455.14	839.13	1087.97	972.55	1818.38	2110.21
Speedup	1.76x	2.77x	3.37x	3.14x	5.55x	3.60x

Table 1: Tuned results for Ranger using 128 cores and 512 cores

Table 1 summarizes tuned I/O parameters, runtime, and speedup obtained by the framework for the kernels and platforms for three benchmarks using 128 and 512 cores. We can observe speedups ranging from 1.7x to 3.4x for 128-core scale and those ranging from 3.1x to 5.5x at 512-core scale compared to default I/O settings.

3. RELATED WORK

Auto-tuning has been used extensively in computer science for improving performance of computational kernels [4, 3, 5]. Our study focuses on auto-tuning *I/O subsystem* for writing and reading data to a parallel file system in contrast to tuning a few computational kernels. Yu et al. [7] manually characterize, tune, and optimize parallel I/O performance on Lustre file system of Jaguar. Howison et al. [2] also perform manual tuning of various benchmarks that

select parameters for HDF5, MPI-IO and Lustre parameters on Hopper. You et al. [6] proposed an auto-tuning framework based on queuing theory models for Lustre file system on Cray XT5 systems at ORNL. They search for file system stripe count, stripe size, I/O transfer size, and the number of I/O processes. Developing a mathematical model for different systems can be farther from the real system and may produce inaccurate performance results. In contrast, our framework searches for parameters on real system using search heuristics.

4. CONCLUSIONS

We have presented a general framework for optimizing I/O performance of HDF5 applications. The framework is able to search a configuration space consisting of HDF5, MPI-IO and Lustre parameters to determine good settings. The framework is then able to execute these settings without requiring any effort from the application developer. We have demonstrated the successful application of the framework for three HDF5 benchmarks derived from production simulation codes. We applied the framework on a Sun Constellation cluster, and demonstrate convincing performance improvements over system default settings. We believe that this approach holds much promise in terms of hiding the complexity of the I/O stack and providing performance portability.

5. ACKNOWLEDGMENTS

This work is supported by the Director, Office of Science, Office of Advanced Scientific Computing Research, of the U.S. Department of Energy under Contract No. AC02-05CH11231. This research used resources of the the Texas Advanced Computing Center. The authors would like to acknowledge John Shalf, Mohamad Chaarawi and Marc Snir for their support and guidance.

6. REFERENCES

[1] P. Carns et al. Understanding and improving computational science storage access through continuous characterization. In *27th IEEE Conference on Mass Storage Systems and Technologies*, 2011.

[2] M. Howison et al. Tuning HDF5 for Lustre File Systems. In *Proceedings of 2010 Workshop on Interfaces and Abstractions for Scientific Data Storage (IASDS10)*, 2010.

[3] R. Vuduc, J. Demmel, and K. Yelick. Oski: A library of automatically tuned sparse matrix kernels. In *Proceedings of SciDAC 2005, Journal of Physics: Conference Series*, 2005.

[4] R. C. Whaley, A. Petitet, and J. J. Dongarra. Automated empirical optimization of software and the ATLAS project. *Parallel Computing*, 27(1–2):3–35, 2001.

[5] S. Williams et al. Optimization of sparse matrix-vector multiplication on emerging multicore platforms. In *2007 ACM/IEEE conference on Supercomputing*, SC '07, pages 38:1–38:12, 2007.

[6] H. You, Q. Liu, Z. Li, and S. Moore. The design of an auto-tuning i/o framework on cray xt5 system.

[7] W. Yu et al. Performance characterization and optimization of parallel i/o on the cray xt. In *IPDPS 2008.*, pages 1 –11, april 2008.

Anton: A Special-Purpose Machine that Achieves a Hundred-Fold Speedup in Biomolecular Simulations

David E. Shaw

D. E. Shaw Research and
Center for Computational Biology &
Bioinformatics, Columbia University
New York, NY
David.Shaw@DEShawResearch.com

ABSTRACT

Molecular dynamics (MD) simulation has long been recognized as a potentially transformative tool for understanding the behavior of proteins and other biological macromolecules, and for developing a new generation of precisely targeted drugs. Many biologically important phenomena, however, occur over timescales that have previously fallen far outside the reach of MD technology. We have constructed a specialized, massively parallel machine, called Anton, that is capable of performing atomic-level simulations of proteins at a speed roughly two orders of magnitude beyond that of the previous state of the art. The machine has now simulated the behavior of a number of proteins for periods as long as two milliseconds -- approximately 200 times the length of the longest such simulation previously published -- revealing aspects of protein dynamics that were previously inaccessible to both computational and experimental study. The speed at which Anton performs these simulations is in large part the result of a tightly coupled codesign process in which the machine architecture was developed in concert with novel algorithms, including an asymptotically optimal parallel algorithm (with highly attractive constant factors) for the range-limited N-body problem.

Categories and Subject Descriptors

C.1.4 **[Processor Architectures]**: Parallel Architectures; C.5.1 **[Computer System Implementation]**: Large and Medium ("Mainframe") Computers – *super (very large) computers*; I.6.3 **[Simulation and Modeling]**: Applications; I.6.5 **[Simulation and Modeling]**: Model Development – *modeling methodologies*; I.6.6 **[Simulation and Modeling]**: Simulation Output Analysis; J.2 **[Physical Sciences and Engineering]**: Chemistry; J.2 **[Physical Sciences and Engineering]**: Physics; J.3 **[Life and Medical Sciences]**: Biology and Genetics.

General Terms

Algorithms, Design, Performance.

Keywords

Parallel architectures; Hardware/software co-design; Molecular dynamics simulation; Computational biology; Computational chemistry; Computer-aided drug design.

Biography

David E. Shaw serves as chief scientist of D. E. Shaw Research and as a senior research fellow at the Center for Computational Biology and Bioinformatics at Columbia University. He received his Ph.D. from Stanford University in 1980, served on the faculty of the Computer Science Department at Columbia until 1986, and founded the D. E. Shaw group in 1988. Since 2001, Dr. Shaw has been involved in hands-on research in the field of computational biochemistry. His lab is currently involved in the development of new algorithms and machine architectures for high-speed molecular dynamics simulations of biological macromolecules, and in the application of such simulations to basic scientific research and computer-assisted drug design.

Dr. Shaw was appointed to the President's Council of Advisors on Science and Technology by President Clinton in 1994, and again by President Obama in 2009. He is a member of the National Academy of Engineering, and is a fellow of the American Academy of Arts and Sciences and of the American Association for the Advancement of Science.

HPDC'13, June 17–21, 2013, New York, NY, USA.
ACM 978-1-4503-1910-2/13/06

WuKong: Automatically Detecting and Localizing Bugs that Manifest at Large System Scales

Bowen Zhou, Jonathan Too, Milind Kulkarni, Saurabh Bagchi
Purdue University
West Lafayette, IN
{bzhou, jtoo, milind, sbagchi}@purdue.edu

ABSTRACT

A key challenge in developing large scale applications is finding bugs that are latent at the small scales of testing, but manifest themselves when the application is deployed at a large scale. Here, we ascribe a dual meaning to "large scale"—it could mean a large number of executing processes or applications ingesting large amounts of input data (or both). Traditional statistical techniques fail to detect or diagnose such kinds of bugs because no error-free run is available at the large deployment scales for training purposes. Prior work used *scaling models* to *detect* anomalous behavior at large scales without training on correct behavior at that scale. However, that work *cannot localize* bugs automatically, *i.e.,* cannot pinpoint the region of code responsible for the error. In this paper, we resolve that shortcoming by making the following three contributions: (i) we develop an automatic diagnosis technique, based on *feature reconstruction*; (ii) we design a heuristic to effectively prune the large feature space; and (iii) we demonstrate that our system scales well, in terms of both accuracy and overhead. We validate our design through a large-scale fault-injection study and two case-studies of real-world bugs, finding that our system can effectively localize bugs in 92.5% of the cases, dramatically easing the challenge of finding bugs in large-scale programs.

Categories and Subject Descriptors

D.2.4 [**Software Engineering**]: Software/Program Verification—*Statistical Methods*; D.2.5 [**Software Engineering**]: Testing and Debugging—*Diagnostics*

General Terms

Reliability

Keywords

Scale-dependent Bug, Program Behavior Prediction, Feature Reconstruction

1 Introduction

One of the key challenges in developing large-scale software, i.e., software intended to run on many processors or with very large data sets, is detecting and diagnosing *scale-dependent* bugs. Most bugs manifest at both small and large scales, and as a result, can be identified and caught during the development process, when programmers are typically working with both small-scale systems and small-scale inputs. However, a particularly insidious class of bugs are those that predominantly arise at deployment scales. These bugs appear far less frequently, if at all, at small scales, and hence are often not caught during development, but only when a program is released into the wild and is deployed at large scales. As one example of this class of bugs, there is a performance bug in one version of the popular parallel programming library, MPICH2, that arises when the total amount of data being exchanged between the processes of the parallel application is large [1]. The root cause of the bug is overflow of a 32-bit integer variable.

Interestingly, even if a programmer has access to large-scale inputs and systems, detection and diagnosing scale-dependent bugs can be intractable. As system size and complexity increase, correctly attributing anomalous behavior to a part of a program can be quite challenging. If a bug causes a program to crash at large scale runs, it is obvious that the error lies with the program, and hence debugging efforts can focus on locating (and then fixing) the bug in the program. For bugs that do not have a clear symptom, it may not even be apparent that there *is* a bug in the program. For example, if a bug does not manifest at small scales but arises deterministically at large scales, there is no example of correct behavior at large scales to determine that the observed behavior is anomalous.

Once a bug is detected, the next challenge is to localize[1] the bug. Programs meant to scale up often have large code bases, so simply identifying that there is a bug is not sufficient to fix the bug. Instead, the developer would like to know *where* the bug arose: which module, function, or even line number. Unfortunately, performing this localization manually for large-scale systems is overwhelming. Even if the point where the bug *manifests* can be identified (*e.g.,* by examining a stack dump after a program crashes), this location may be far removed from the source of the bug. Even worse is when the bug does not cause the program to crash, but instead results in incorrect results; in the absence of in-

---
[1]We use the terms "diagnosis" and "localization" interchangeably; both are defined as the action of pinpointing the root cause of the detected error to a region of code.

formation associated with a crash, identifying the source of the error requires examining every possible program location that may be buggy. For example, a hang bug in a popular P2P file-sharing program called Transmission manifests only when the number of peers overflows a fixed-size buffer. However, traditional debugging techniques (*e.g.*, OPROFILE) can at best indicate that a particular method is running for a long time, not that this is a bug. Identifying that the long running time constitutes a bug requires understanding the behavior of the method and *localizing* the bug (even if the method is known to be buggy) requires investigating 252 lines of code. In contrast, a more accurate tool (such as the system we develop) can correctly localize the bug to a specific, 27-line loop.

1.1   Statistical bug diagnosis

A popular approach to detecting and diagnosing bugs is *statistical* debugging. At a high level, a statistical model is built using a set of training runs, which are expected to be *not* affected by the bug. This model captures the expected behavior of a program by modeling the values of selected program *features* (*e.g.*, the number of times a particular branch is taken, or the number of times a particular calling context appears). Then, at deployment time, values of these same features are collected at different points in the execution; if the values of these features fall outside the model parameters, the deployed run represents program behavior different from the training runs and a bug is detected. By examining which program features are deviant, the bug can be localized (to different levels of accuracy; the deviant program feature may just be the one that is most affected by the bug and not be related to the root cause). This approach has been taken by numerous prior bug-detection tools [9, 12, 21].

However, the traditional statistical debugging approach is insufficient to deal with scale-dependent bugs. If the statistical model is trained only on small-scale runs, statistical techniques can result in numerous false positives. Program behavior naturally changes as programs scale up (*e.g.*, the number of times a branch in a loop is taken will depend on the number of loop iterations, which can depend on the scale), leading small scale models to incorrectly label bug-free behaviors at large scales as anomalous. This effect can be particularly insidious in strong-scaling situations, where each process of a program inherently does less work at large scales than at small ones.

While it may seem that incorporating large-scale training runs into the statistical model will fix the aforementioned issue, doing so is not straightforward. If a developer cannot determine whether large-scale behavior is correct, it is impossible to correctly label the data to train the model. Furthermore, many scale-dependent bugs affect *all* the processes and are triggered in *every* execution at large scales. Thus, it would be impossible to get *any* sample of bug-free behavior at large scales for training purposes.

A further complication in building models at large scale is the overhead of modeling. Modeling time is a function of training-data size, and as programs scale up, so, too, will the training data. Moreover, most modeling techniques require global reasoning and centralized computation. Hence, the overheads of performing complex statistical modeling on large-scale training data can rapidly become impractical.

1.2   Detecting scale-dependent bugs

Prior work by us [25] has attempted to address the drawbacks of existing statistical debugging techniques. VRISHA is a tool that exploits *scale-determined* features to detect bugs in large-scale program runs even if the statistical model was only trained on small-scale behavior. At a high level, the intuition behind VRISHA's operation is as follows. Several training runs are collected at different small scales. A statistical model (based on Kernel Canonical Correlation Analysis, or KCCA) is then built from these training runs to infer the relationship between scale and program behavior. In essence, we build a *scaling model* for the program, which can extrapolate the aggregated behavioral trend as the input or system size scales up. Bugs can then be automatically detected by identifying deviations from the trend. Notably, this detection can occur *even if the program is run at a never-before-seen scale.*

Unfortunately, VRISHA suffers from two key drawbacks. First, while KCCA is useful for being able to capture non-linear relationships between scale and behavior, its accuracy decreases as the scales seen in deployment runs become significantly larger than the scales used in training. Hence, VRISHA loses effectiveness when attempting to detect bugs in large-scale systems, primarily reflected in an increase in its false alarms (we show this empirically in Section 5.1).

Second, and more importantly, while the detection of bugs is automatic, VRISHA is only able to identify that the scaling trend has been violated; it cannot determine *which* program feature violated the trend, nor *where* in the program the bug manifested. *Hence, diagnosis in* VRISHA *is a manual process.* The behavior of the program at the various small scales of the training set are inspected to predict expected values for each individual program feature at the problematic large scale, and discrepancies from these manually-extrapolated behaviors can be used to hone in on the bug.

This diagnosis procedure is ineffective under many real-world scenarios. First, if different aspects of program behavior are related to scale through different functions (linear, quadratic, etc.), then each feature must be considered separately when attempting to infer a scaling trend. This inference can be intractable when the feature set is large, as it is for reasonable-sized programs and in situations where many of its features need to be considered to achieve reasonable detection coverage. Second, some scaling trends may be difficult to detect unless a large number of training runs at different scales are considered, again making manual inference of these trends impractical. Finally, some features may not be well-correlated with scale at all, such as the delay in network communication, which will depend on factors external to the particular application being debugged. Without a means to identifying such problematic features, VRISHA will falsely flag them as being erroneous, leading developers on a wild-goose chase.

In follow-on work, ABHRANTA, we tweaked VRISHA's program model to automatically diagnose bugs [24]. However, because ABHRANTA is based on the same KCCA technique as VRISHA, and does not attempt to deal with problematic features, its accuracy precipitously declines as the scale of production runs increases, leading to increasingly inaccurate diagnoses. Consequently, for large-scale runs, it is still necessary to resort to manual inspection to diagnose bugs.

Hence, it is fair to say that neither VRISHA nor ABHRANTA *support automated diagnosis of bugs in large-scale systems.*

1.3 Our approach: WuKong

This paper presents WuKong[2], an *automatic, scalable approach to detecting and diagnosing bugs that manifest at large system scales*. WuKong is designed to model program behavior as a group of *features*, each representing the behavior of a particular part of the program in an execution.

In a typical usage scenario, WuKong is deployed in production runs, after a program has been thoroughly tested at small scales, to detect and diagnose bugs. WuKong works towards diagnosing a bug in three steps. First, during development a series of small-scale bug-free runs are analyzed to derive per-feature behavioral models for the program. Second, during production runs, the behavioral models predict what the correct value for each feature at production scale would be if the large-scale run were bug-free. Finally, the actual value and the predicted value of each feature are compared; if any features behave differently from the prediction, a bug is detected, and the most deviant features are identified as the probable root causes for the bug. Since every feature can be attributed to a particular part of the program, it is straightforward to map suspicious features to locations in the source code of the program.

WuKong is based on the same high level concepts as Vrisha and Abhranta, but provides three key contributions over the previous work:

Automatic bug localization As described above, Vrisha's diagnosis technique requires careful manual inspection of program behaviors both from the training set and from the deployed run. WuKong, in contrast, provides an *automatic* diagnosis technique. WuKong alters Vrisha's modeling technique, using *per-feature regression models*, built across multiple training scales that can accurately *predict* the expected bug-free behavior at large scales.

When presented with a large-scale execution, WuKong uses these models to infer what the value of each feature *would have been* were a run bug-free. If any feature's observed value deviates from the predicted value by a sufficient amount, WuKong detects a bug. With carefully chosen program features that can be linked to particular regions of code (WuKong uses calling contexts rooted at conditional statements, as described in Section 3), ranking features by their prediction error can identify which lines of code result in particularly unexpected behavior. This ranked list therefore provides a roadmap the programmer can use in tracking down the bug.

Feature pruning Not all program behaviors are well-correlated with scale, and hence cannot be predicted by scaling models. Examples of such behaviors include random conditionals (*e.g.*, `if (x < rand())`) or, more commonly, data-dependent behaviors (where the *values* of the input data, rather than the *size* of that data determine behavior). The existence of such hard-to-model features can dramatically reduce the effectiveness of detection and localization: a feature whose behavior seems aberrant may be truly buggy, or may represent a modeling failure. To address this shortcoming, we introduce a novel cross-validation-based *feature pruning* technique. This mechanism can effectively prune features that are hard to model accurately from the training

set, allowing programmers to trade off reduced detectability for improved localization accuracy. We find that our pruning technique can dramatically improve localization with only a minimal impact on detectability.

Scaling A key drawback to many statistical debugging techniques is the scalability of both the initial modeling phase, and the detection phase. As scales increase, the cost of building statistical models of large-scale behavior becomes prohibitive, especially with global modeling techniques. WuKong possesses an intriguing property: because the training models do not need to be built at large scales, WuKong's *modeling cost is independent of system scale*. Hence, WuKong is uniquely suited to diagnosing bugs in very large scale systems. Furthermore, because WuKong's detection strategy is purely local to each execution entity, detection and diagnosis cost scales only linearly with system size, and is constant on a per-process basis.

In this work, we show that our per-feature scaling models can be used to effectively detect and diagnose bugs at large scales (> 1000 processes) even when trained only at small scales (≤ 128 processes). In particular, we show through a fault-injection study that not only can WuKong accurately detect faulty program behaviors in large-scale runs, but that it can correctly locate the buggy program location 92.5% of the time. We show that our modeling errors and overheads are independent of scale, leading to a truly scalable solution.

1.4 Outline

Section 2 presents the data collection of WuKong. Section 3 describes WuKong's new approach to modeling the scaling behavior of programs, including our feature pruning strategy. Section 4 discusses how WuKong uses these models to detect and localize bugs. Section 5 demonstrates, through several case studies, the utility of WuKong for automatically diagnosing bugs, and shows, through a fault-injection study, that WuKong scales effectively to 1024 processes. Section 6 discusses related work, and Section 7 concludes.

2 Data Collection

This section presents the data collection approach used by WuKong to capture program behaviors at different scales. Recall that the goal of WuKong is to diagnose bugs in program runs at large scales, even if it has never observed correct behavior at that large scale. Therefore, WuKong needs to observe program behaviors at a series of training scales to derive the scaling trend.

The fundamental approach of WuKong is to build a statistical model of program behavior that incorporates scale. Essentially, we would like a model that infers the relationship between scale attributes (*e.g.*, number of processes, or input size) and behavior attributes (*e.g.*, trip count of loops, value distribution of variables). We will discuss what information is collected, how WuKong does the data collection, and a few optimizations to reduce the run-time overhead.

2.1 Control and Observational Features

WuKong operates by building a model of behavior for a program. To do so, it must collect data about an application's behavior, and sufficient information about an application's configuration to predict its behavior.

WuKong collects values of two types of features: *control* features and *observational* features. Control features generalize scale: they include all input properties and configu-

---

[2]WuKong, the Monkey King, is the main character in the epic Chinese novel *Journey to the West*, and possesses the ability to recognize evil in any form.

ration parameters to an application that govern its behavior. Example control features include input size, number of processes and, for MPI applications, process rank. Control features can be gathered for a program execution merely by analyzing the inputs and arguments to the program. Observational features capture the observed behavior of the program. Examples include the number of times a syscall is made, or the number of times a libc function is called.

WuKong uses context-sensitive branch profiles as its observational features. Every time a branch instruction is executed, WuKong's instrumentation computes the current calling context, *i.e.,* the call stack, plus the address of the branch instruction, and uses the result as an index to access and update the corresponding tuple of two counters: one recording the number of times this branch is *taken*, and the other recording the number of times this branch is *not taken*. The benefits of choosing such observational features are twofold: (1) by choosing observational features that can be associated with unambiguous program points, WuKong can provide a roadmap to the developer to hone in on the source of the bug; (2) with this selection of observational features, WuKong is geared to observe perturbations in both the *taken* → *not taken* and *not taken* → *taken* directions thereby, in principle, detecting and locating all bugs that perturb control-flow behavior.

Observational and control features are collected separately for each unit of execution we wish to model. For example, when analyzing MPI applications, WuKong collects data and builds a model for each process separately. Currently, the execution unit granularity must be specified by the programmer; automatically selecting the granularity is beyond the scope of this work.

2.2 Optimizing Call Stack Recording

WuKong's run-time overhead comes solely from collecting the observational features, since the control features can be extracted before running the program. This section presents performance optimizations we employ to reduce the run-time overhead for a given set of observational features. Section 3.4 will describe our approach to pruning the observational feature set, whose main goal is to increase the accuracy of detection and diagnosis, but which has the additional benefit of reducing the overhead of data collection.

WuKong's instrumentation operates at the binary code level, where determining the boundary of a function can be difficult, as compilers may apply complex optimizations, *e.g.,* using "jmp" to call a function or return from one, popping out multiple stack frames with a single instruction, issuing "call" to get the current PC, *etc.*. As a result, simply shadowing the "call" and "ret" instructions cannot capture the call stack reliably. Instead, WuKong walks down the call stack from the saved frame pointer in the top stack frame, chasing the chain of frame pointers, and recording the return address of each frame until it reaches the bottom of the call stack. This makes sure that WuKong records an accurate copy of the current call stack irrespective of compiler optimizations.

Based on the principle of locality, we design a caching mechanism to reduce the overhead incurred by stack walking in WuKong. First, whenever WuKong finishes a stack walk, it caches the recorded call stack. Before starting the next stack walk, it compares the value of the frame pointer on top of the cached call stack and the current frame pointer register and uses the cached call stack if there is a match. This optimization takes advantage of the temporal locality that consecutive branches are likely to be a part of the same function and therefore share the same call stack. Note that it is possible in theory to have inaccurate cache hit where consecutive branch instructions with the same frame pointer come from different calling contexts. We expect such a case to be rare in practice, and it did not arise in any of our empirical studies.

3 Modeling Program Behavior

This section describes WuKong's modeling technique. The key component is the construction of per-feature models that capture the relationship between the control features and the value of a particular observational feature. These models can be used to predict the expected observational features for production runs at a scale larger than any seen during training. As a result, the correct behavior (observational feature values) of large scale runs can be reconstructed based on the prediction of the model, and this information can be used for detection and localization.

3.1 Overview

At a high level, WuKong's modeling, detection and localization approach consists of the following components.

(a) Model Building During training, control and observational features are collected at a *series* of small scales. These features are used to construct per-feature regression models that capture non-linear relationships between system scale (the control features) and program behavior (the observational features). Sections 3.2 and 3.3 describe WuKong's modeling strategy in more detail.

(b) Feature Pruning Features whose behavior is inherently unpredictable (*e.g.,* non-deterministic, discontinuous or overly-complex) cannot be accurately modeled by WuKong's regression models. Because model failures can complicate detection and localization (poorly modeled features may deviate significantly from predictions, triggering false positives), WuKong uses a novel, cross-validation-based *feature pruning* strategy to improve the accuracy of detection and localization. Section 3.4 details this approach.

(c) Bug Diagnosis WuKong can detect and diagnose bugs in large-scale production runs by using its models to predict what behavior *should have been* at that large scale. Intuitively, a feature whose predicted value is significantly different from its actual value is more likely to be involved in the bug than a feature whose predicted value is close to its actual value. A test run is flagged as buggy if any one of its features has a significant deviation between its observed and the predicted values. To locate a bug, WuKong simply ranks features by the relative difference between the predicted value and the actual value, and presents the ordered list to the programmer. Section 4 elaborates further.

3.2 Model Building

WuKong models application behavior with a collection of base models, each of which characterizes a single observational feature. The base model is an instance of multiple regression where multiple predictors are considered. Specifically, the base model for each observational feature considers all control features as predictor variables, and the value of the observational feature as the response variable.

Suppose Y is the observational feature in question, and X_i for $i = 1 \ldots N$ are the N control features. We note that a base model of the form:

$$Y = \beta_0 + \sum_{i=1}^{N} \beta_i \cdot X_i \qquad (1)$$

is not sufficient to capture complex relationships between control features and program behavior. It does not account for higher-order relationships between behavior and scale (consider the many algorithms that are $O(n^2)$), and it does not capture interaction between control features (consider a program location inside a doubly-nested loop where the inner loop runs X_i times and the outer loop runs X_j times). To account for this, we apply a logarithmic transform on both the control features and the observational feature, yielding the following base model:

$$\log(Y) = \beta_0 + \sum_{i=1}^{N} \beta_i \log(X_i) \qquad (2)$$

The refined model transforms multiplicative relationships between the variables into additive relationships in the model, allowing us to capture the necessary higher order and interactive effects.

The multiple regression problem is solved by the ordinary least squares method. The solution is given by a vector of coefficients $\beta_0 \ldots \beta_N$:

$$\underset{\beta_0, \ldots, \beta_N}{\arg\min} || \log(Y) - \sum_{i=1}^{N} \beta_i \log(X_i) - \beta_0 ||^2 \qquad (3)$$

The resulting model achieves the best fit for the training data, *i.e.*, it minimizes the mean squared prediction error of Y.

WUKONG limits the regression model to linear terms as our empirical results suggest linear terms are enough to capture the scaling trend of most observational features. Although more complex terms, (*e.g.*, high order polynomials, cross products, etc.) might result in better fit for the training data, they also have a higher risk of overfitting and generalize poorly for the test data.

Since each feature gets its own base model, we do not face the same problem as in Vrisha [25], where a single model must be "reverse-engineered" to find values for individual observational features. Instead, WUKONG can accurately predict each feature in isolation. Moreover, the linear base models leads to more stable extrapolation at large scales, thanks to the lack of over-fitting.

3.3 Base Model Customization

One model does not fit all observational features. Observational features usually scale at differing speeds and the scaling trends of different features may be vastly different. Furthermore, some observational features may depend only on a subset of all control features. Therefore, throwing all control features into the base model for every observational feature may result in over-fitting the data, and lower the prediction accuracy for such features. To handle this problem, we need to customize the base model for each individual observational feature based on the training data. Through the customization process, we want to determine the particular formula used for modeling each individual feature, *i.e.*, which control features should be included as predictor

variables in the model. Essentially, we want the simplest possible model that fits the training data; if making the model more complex only yields a marginal improvement in accuracy, we should prefer the simpler model.

WUKONG's model customization is based on the Akaike Information Criterion (AIC) [4], a measure of relative goodness of fit in a statistical model given by:

$$AIC = -2\ln(L) + 2k \qquad (4)$$

where L is the likelihood of the statistical model, which measures the goodness of fit, and k is the number of parameters in the model, which measures the model complexity. Unlike the more common approach to measuring model accuracy, the coefficient of determination R^2, AIC penalizes more complex models (intuitively, a more complex model must provide a much better fit to be preferred to a simpler model). This avoids over-fitting and ensures that WUKONG produces appropriately simple models for each observational feature.

In a program with N control features, there are 2^N possible models that match the form of Equation 2. If N is small, it is feasible to conduct an exhaustive search through every model configuration to find the appropriate model for each observational feature. However, if N is large, the configuration space might be prohibitively large, making an exhaustive search impractical. In such a scenario, WUKONG uses a greedy, hill-descending algorithm [13]. We begin with a model that includes all control features. At each step, WUKONG considers all models one "move" away from the current model: all models with one fewer control feature than the current model and all models with one more control feature than the current model. Of the candidate models, WUKONG picks the one with the lower AIC and makes it the current model. The process continues until no "move" reduces the AIC compared to the current model. For any single observational feature, the result of model customization is a model that includes a subset of control features that are most relevant to that particular observational feature.

3.4 Feature Selection and Pruning

As described in Section 2, WUKONG uses as its observational features all conditionals in a program, augmented with the dynamic calling context in which that conditional executed. Each time a particular conditional is evaluated, WUKONG increments the value of the appropriate feature.

The logarithmic model in Section 3.2 allows us to readily compute the relative prediction error for a given feature, which we require to identify faulty features (see Section 4). The model built for each observational feature, i, is used to make prediction Y_i' for what the value of that feature *should have been* if the program were not buggy. WUKONG then compares Y_i' to the observed behavior, Y_i and calculates the *relative prediction error* of each observational feature, using the approach of Barnes *et al.* [6]:

$$E_i = |e^{\log(Y_i') - \log(Y_i)} - 1| \qquad (5)$$

Note that a constant prediction of 0 for any feature will result in relative reconstruction error of 1.0; hence, relative errors greater than 1.0 are a clear indication of a poorly-predicted feature.

Unfortunately, not all observational features can be effectively predicted by WUKONG's regression models, leading to errors in both detection and diagnosis. There are two main reasons why an observational feature can be problematic for WuKong. One is that the feature value is non-deterministic: a conditional whose outcome is dependent on a random number, for example. Because such features do not have deterministic values, it is impossible to model them effectively. Recollect that WuKong relies on the assumption that any observational feature is determined by the control features.

A second situation in which a feature cannot be modeled well is if its value is dependent on characteristics not captured by the control features. These could be confounding factors that affect program behavior such as OS-level interference or network congestion. Another confounding factor is *data-dependent* behavior. WuKong uses as its control features scale information about the program, such as number of processes/threads or input data size. If a program's behavior is determined by the *contents* of the input, instead, WuKong does not capture the appropriate information to predict a program's behavior.

WuKong's reconstruction techniques can be thrown off by unpredictable program behavior: the behavioral model will be trained with behavior that is not correlated with the control features, and hence spurious trends will be identified. Note that even a small number of such problematic features can both introduce false positives and seriously affect the accuracy of localization. If WuKong makes a prediction based on spurious trends, even non-buggy behavior may disagree with the (mis)prediction, leading to erroneously detected errors. Second, even if an error is *correctly* detected, because reconstruction will be based on bogus information, it is likely that the reconstruction errors for such problematic features will be fairly high, pushing the true source of errors farther down the list. The developer will be left investigating the sources of these problematic features, which will not be related to any bug.

We note, however, that if we had a means of removing bad features, we could dramatically improve localization performance. Because a bad feature's appearance at the top of WuKong's roadmap occurs far out of proportion to its likelihood of actually being the buggy feature, simply filtering it from the feature set will negatively impact a small number of localization attempts (those where the filtered feature is the source of the bug) while significantly improving all other localization attempts (by removing spurious features from the roadmap). Therefore, WuKong employs a feature filtration strategy to identify hard-to-model features and remove them from the feature list.

To eliminate bad features, WuKong employs cross validation [13]. Cross validation uses a portion of the training data to test models built using the remainder of the training data. The underlying assumption is that the training data does not have any error. More specifically, WuKong employs k-fold cross-validation. It splits the original training data by row (*i.e.* by training run) into k equal folds, treats each one of the k folds in turn as the test data and the remaining $k-1$ folds as the training data, then trains and evaluates a model using each of the k sets of data. For each cross-validation step, we compute the relative reconstruction error of each feature X_i for each of the (current) test runs.

If a particular feature cannot be modeled well during cross validation, WuKong assumes that the feature is unpredictable and will filter it out from the roadmaps generated during the localization phase. WuKong's pruning algorithm operates as follows.

WuKong has a *pruning threshold* parameter, x, that governs how aggressively WuKong will be when deciding that a feature is unpredictable. Given a pruning threshold x, a feature is only kept if it is well-predicted in at least $x\%$ of the training runs during cross-validation. In other words, WuKong will *remove* a feature if more than $(100-x)\%$ of the runs are poorly predicted (*i.e.*, have a relative reconstruction error less than 1.0). For example, if the pruning threshold is 25%, then WuKong prunes any feature for which more than 75% of its (relative) errors are more than than 1.0. The higher x is, the more aggressive the pruning is. If x is 0, then no pruning happens (no runs need be well predicted). If x is 100, then pruning is extremely aggressive (there can be no prediction errors for the feature during cross-validation). Typically, x is set lower than 100, to account for the possibility of outliers in the training data.

Some discontinuous features are hard to eliminate with cross-validation because only a few runs during training have problematic values. Hence, in addition to cross-validation-based feature pruning, WuKong also employs a heuristic to detect potentially-discontinuous observational features based on the following two criteria [15]:

- Discrete value percentage: defined as the number of unique values as a percentage of the number of observations; Rule-of-thumb: $< 20\%$ could indicate a problem.

- Frequency ratio: defined as the frequency of the most common value divided by the frequency of the second most common value; Rule-of-thumb: > 19 could indicate a problem.

If both criteria are violated, the feature has too-few unique values and hence is considered potentially discontinuous. These features are pruned from the feature set, and are not used during detection or diagnosis.

It is important to note that the feature pruning performed by WuKong is a complement to the model customization described in the prior section. Model customization prunes the control features used to model a particular observational feature. In contrast, feature pruning filters the observational features that cannot be effectively modeled by *any* combination of the control features.

4 Debugging Programs at Large Scales

Once the models are built and refined, as described in the previous section, WuKong uses those models to debug programs at large scales. This proceeds in two steps, detection and diagnosis, but the basic operation is the same. When a program is run at large scale, WuKong uses its models to *predict* what each observational feature should be, given the control features of the large-scale run[3]. In other words, WuKong uses its models to predict the *expected* behavior of the program at large scale. These predictions are then used to detect and diagnose bugs, as described below.

---

[3]Note that WuKong makes the crucial assumption that the control features for production runs are correct; this is reasonable since control features tend to be characteristics of program inputs and arguments.

4.1 Bug Detection

WUKONG detects bugs by determining if the behavior of a program execution is inconsistent with the scaling trends captured by the behavioral model. If any feature's observed value differs significantly from its predicted value, WUKONG declares a bug. The question then, is what constitutes "significantly"? WUKONG sets detection thresholds for flagging bugs as follows.

For each observational features, WUKONG tracks the reconstruction errors for that feature across all the runs used in cross validation during training (recall that this cross validation is performed for feature pruning). For each feature, WUKONG determines the maximum relative error (Equation 5) observed during cross validation, and uses this to determine the detection threshold. If M_i is the maximum relative reconstruction error observed for feature i during training, WUKONG computes E_i, the relative reconstruction error *for the test run*, and flags an error if

$$E_i > \eta M_i \qquad (6)$$

where η is a tunable *detection threshold* parameter. Note that η is a global parameter, but the detection threshold for a given feature is based on that feature's maximum observed reconstruction error, and hence each feature has its own detection threshold. What should η be? A lower detection threshold makes flagging errors more likely (in fact, a detection sensitivity less than 1 means that even some known non-buggy training runs would be flagged as buggy), while a higher detection threshold makes flagging errors less likely ($\eta \geq 1$ means that no training run would have been flagged as buggy).

We note that in the context of bug detection, false positives are particularly damaging: each false positive wastes the programmer's time searching for a non-existent bug. In contrast, false negatives, while problematic (a technique that detects no bugs is not particularly helpful!), are less harmful: at worst, the programmer is no worse off than without the technique, not knowing whether a bug exists or not. As a result of this fundamental asymmetry, we bias η towards false negatives to prevent false positives: η should always be set to a greater-than-one constant. We use $\eta = 1.15$ in our experiments; Section 5.1 shows how changing η affects false positive and negative rates.

4.2 Bug Localization

When a bug is detected, to provide a "roadmap" for developers to follow when tracking down the bug, WUKONG ranks all observational features by relative error; the features that deviate most from the predicted behavior will have the highest relative error and will be presented as the most likely sources for the bug. WUKONG produces the entire ranked list of erroneous features, allowing programmers to investigate all possible sources of the bug, prioritized by error. Note that while deviant features are likely to be involved with the bug, the most deviant features may not actually be the source of the bug. Buggy behavior can propagate through the program and lead to other features' going awry, often by much larger amounts than the initial bug (a "butterfly effect"). Nevertheless, as we show in Section 5's fault injection study, the majority of the time the statement that is the root cause of the bug appears at the top of the roadmap.

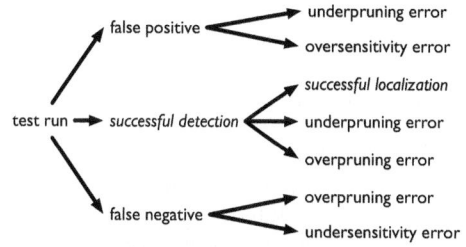

Figure 1: Possible outcomes and errors when using WUKONG to detect and diagnose bugs.

4.3 Sources and types of detection and diagnosis error

WUKONG has two primary configuration parameters that affect the error rates of both its detection scheme and its diagnosis strategy: the feature pruning parameter x, and the detection threshold parameter η. This section describes how these parameters interact intuitively, while the sensitivity studies in Section 5 explore these effects empirically. Figure 1 shows the possible outcomes and error types that can occur when WUKONG is applied to a test run; we discuss these error sources in more detail below.

False positives The most insidious error, from a developer productivity standpoint, is a false positive (an erroneous detection of an error in a bug-free run): if WUKONG throws up a false positive, the developer can spend hours searching for a bug that does not exist. False positives can arise from two sources: *feature underpruning* and *detection oversensitivity*. Feature underpruning occurs when the pruning threshold x is set too low. By keeping too many features, including those that cannot be modeled effectively, WUKONG may detect an error when a poorly-modeled feature leads to a bad prediction, even if the observed feature value is correct. Detection oversensitivity happens when the detection threshold η is too low, which increases the model's sensitivity to slight variations and deviations from the predicted value, increasing the likelihood of a false positive.

If a test run results in a false positive, it is hard to pinpoint the source of the error, as both oversensitivity and underpruning lead to correct features' being mispredicted by WUKONG. Nevertheless, if the erroneous feature was *never* mispredicted during training (*i.e.*, it would not have been pruned even if the pruning threshold were 100%), then oversensitivity is likely at fault.

False negatives False negatives occur when a buggy run is incorrectly determined to be correct by WUKONG, and can occur for two reasons (unsurprisingly, these are the opposite of the issues that result in false positives): *feature overpruning* and *detection undersensitivity*. If *too many* features are pruned, then WUKONG tracks fewer features, and hence observes less program behavior. Because WUKONG can only detect a bug when it observes program behavior changing, tracking fewer features makes it more likely that a bug will be missed. If the detection threshold is raised, then the magnitude of reconstruction error necessary to detect a bug is correspondingly higher, making WUKONG less sensitive to behavior perturbations, and hence less likely to detect a bug.

For false negatives, overpruning is the culprit if the error manifested in a pruned feature, while undersensitivity is the issue if the error manifested in a tracked feature, but WUKONG did not flag the error.

Diagnosis errors Even after WUKONG correctly detects a bug in a program, it may not be able to successfully localize the bug (here, successful localization means that the bug appears within the top k features suggested by WUKONG). The success of localization is primarily driven by x, the feature pruning threshold. Interestingly, there are two types of localization errors, one of which is caused by overpruning, and the other by underpruning. If x is too low, and features are underpruned, then many poorly-modeled features will be included in WUKONG's model. These poorly modeled features can have high reconstruction errors, polluting the ranked list of features, and pushing the true error farther down the list. Conversely, if x is too high and the feature set is overpruned, the erroneous feature may not appear *anywhere* in the list. It may seem weird that the erroneous feature could be pruned from the feature set even while WUKONG detects the bug. This is due to the butterfly effect discussed earlier; even though the buggy feature is not tracked, features that are *affected* by the bug may be tracked, and trigger detection.

For detection errors, it is easy to determine whether overpruning is the source of an error. If the buggy feature is not in the feature set at all, x is too high. Underpruning is harder to detect. It is a potential problem if the buggy feature appears in the feature set but is not highly placed in the ranked list of problematic features. However, the same outcome occurs if the bug cascades to a number of other features, all of which are perturbed significantly as a result, and hence appear high in the list. Due to this error propagation, it is non-trivial to decide whether more aggressive pruning would have improved localization accuracy.

5 Evaluation

This section describes our evaluation of WUKONG. We implemented WUKONG using PIN [20] to perform dynamic binary instrumentation. To collect the features as described in Section 2, we use PIN to instrument every branch in the program to determine which features should be incremented and update the necessary counters. WUKONG's detection and diagnosis analyses are performed offline using the data collected after running a PIN-instrumented program at production scales.

We start by conducting large scale fault injection experiments on AMG2006, a benchmark application from the Sequoia benchmark suite [2]. Through these experiments, we show that (a) our log-transformed linear regression model can accurately predict scale-dependent behavior in the observational features for runs at an unseen large scale; (b) the automatic feature pruning techniques based on cross validation allow us to diagnose injected faults more effectively; (c) as the scale of the test system increases, the modeling time for WUKONG remains fixed without hurting accuracy; and (d) the overhead for instrumentation does not increase with the scales of test systems.

We also present two case studies of real bugs, demonstrating how WUKONG can be used to localize scale-dependent bugs in real-world software systems. These bugs can only be triggered when executed at a large scale. Thus, they are unlikely to manifest in testing, and must be detected at deployed scales. One of the case studies is also used in VR-ISHA [25]. We demonstrate here how WUKONG can be used

to automatically identify which features are involved in the bug and can help pinpoint the source of the fault. The two applications come from different domains, one from high performance computing in an MPI-C program, and the other from distributed peer-to-peer computing in a C program. Since WUKONG works at the binary level for the program features, it is applicable to these starkly different domains.

The fault injection experiments were conducted on a Cray XT5 cluster, as part of the XSEDE computing environment, with 112,896 cores in 9,408 compute nodes. The case studies were conducted on a local cluster with 128 cores in 16 nodes running Linux 2.6.18. The statistical analysis was done on a dual-core computer running Windows 7.

5.1 Fault Injection Study with AMG2006

AMG2006 is a parallel algebraic multigrid solver for linear systems, written in 104K lines of C code. The application is configured to solve the default 3D Laplace type problem with the GMRES algorithm and the low-complexity AMG preconditioner in the following experiments. The research questions we were looking to answer with the AMG2006 synthetic fault injection study are:

- Is WUKONG's model able to extrapolate the correct program behavior at large scales from training runs at small scales?

- Can WUKONG effectively detect and locate bugs by comparing the predicted behavior and the actual behavior at large scales?

- Does feature pruning improve the accuracy and instrumentation overhead of WUKONG?

We began by building a model for each observational feature of AMG2006, using as training runs program executions ranging from 8 to 128 nodes. The control features were the X, Y, Z dimension parameters of the 3D process topology, and the observational features were chosen using the approach described in Section 3.4, resulting in 3 control features and 4604 observational features. When we apply feature pruning with a threshold of 90%, we are left with 4036 observational features for which WUKONG builds scaling models.

Scalability of Behavior Prediction To answer the first research question, we evaluated WUKONG on 31 non-buggy test runs of distinct configurations, *i.e.*, each with a unique control feature vector, using 256, 512 and 1024 nodes to see if WUKONG can recognize these normal large-scale runs as non-buggy in the detection phase. Based on the detection threshold $\eta = 1.15$ and a feature pruning threshold of 90%, WUKONG correctly identified all of the 31 test runs as normal, thus having *zero false positives*. In contrast, the prior state-of-the-art in detection of scale-dependent bugs, VR-ISHA [25], flags six of the 31 runs as buggy, for a 19.4% false positive rate. Recall that false positives are highly undesirable in this context because each false positive leads the developer to chase after a non-existent bug.

Table 1 gives the mean reconstruction error, the time for analysis, and the runtime overhead, due to collecting the observational feature values, at each scale. We see that the average reconstruction error for the features in the test runs is always less than 10% and does not increase with scale *despite using the same model for all scales*. Hence, WUKONG's regression models are effective at predicting the large scale

Scale of Run	Mean Error	Analysis Time (s)	Runtime Overhead
256	6.55%	0.089	5.3%
512	8.33%	0.143	5.4%
1024	7.77%	0.172	3.2%

Table 1: Scalability of WuKong for AMG2006 on test runs with 256, 512 and 1024 nodes.

behavior of the benchmark despite having only seen small scale behavior.

Furthermore, WuKong's run-time overhead does not increase with scale. Indeed, because there is a fixed component to the overhead of Pin-based instrumentation and larger-scale runs take longer, the average run-time overhead of feature collection *decreases* a little as scale increases. On the other hand, the analysis overhead (evaluating the detection and reconstruction models for the test runs) is always less than 1/5th of a second. Hence, with diminishing instrumentation costs and negligible analysis costs, WuKong provides clear scalability advantages over approaches that require more complex analyses at large scales.

Effectiveness in Fault Diagnosis To determine the effectiveness of WuKong's bug detection and localization capabilities, we injected faults into 100 instances of the 1024-node run of AMG2006. Each time a random conditional branch instruction is picked to "flip" throughout the entire execution. The faults are designed to emulate what would happen if a bug changed the control flow behavior at the 1024-node scale but not at the smaller training scales, as manifested in common bug types, such as integer overflow errors, buffer overflows, *etc.*. This kind of injection has been a staple of the dependability community due to its ability to map to realistic software bugs (*e.g.*, see the argument in [22]).

Using the same pruning and detection thresholds as in the scalability study, we evaluated WuKong's ability to (a) detect the faults, and (b) precisely localize the faults. Of the 100 injected runs, 57 resulted in non-crashing bugs, and 93.0% of those were detected by WuKong. For the crashing bugs, the detection method is obvious and therefore, we leave these out of our study. We also tested with alternative values for the detection threshold η as shown by Table 2. This shows, expectedly, that as η increases, *i.e.*, WuKong is less trigger-happy in declaring a run to be erroneous, the false positive rate decreases, until it quickly reaches the desirable value of zero. Promisingly, the false negative rate stays quite steady and low until a high value of η is reached.

We next studied the accuracy of WuKong's localization roadmap. For the runs where WuKong successfully detects a bug, we used the approach of Section 4.2 to produce a rank-ordered list of features to inspect. We found that 71.7% of the time the faulty feature was the *very first feature* identified by WuKong. This compares to a null-hypothesis (randomly selected features) outcome of the correct feature being the top feature a mere 0.35% of the time. With the top 10 most suspicious features given by WuKong, we can further increase the localization rate to 92.5%. Thus, we find that WuKong is effective and precise in locating the majority of the randomly injected faults in AMG2006.

Sensitivity to Feature Pruning We examined the sensitivity of WuKong to the feature pruning threshold. With a detection threshold $\eta = 1.15$, we used three different pruning thresholds: 0%, 90%, and 99%. Table 3 shows how many

η	False Positive	False Negative
1.05	9.7%	5.3%
1.10	6.5%	7.0%
1.15	0%	7.0%
1.20	0%	7.0%
1.25	0%	12.3%

Table 2: The accuracy of detection at various levels of detection threshold with a 90% pruning threshold.

features were filtered during pruning, the false positive rate of detection, the false negative rate of detection, the percentage of detected faulty runs where the faulty feature appears among the top 1, top 5 and top 10 of ranked features. Note that if the buggy feature is pruned for a faulty run, localization will always fail.

We see that performing a small amount of feature pruning can dramatically improve the quality of WuKong's detection and localization accuracy: at a threshold of 90%, false positives are completely eliminated from the detection result, compared with a 6.5% false positive rate when no feature pruning is done; in the meantime, over 92.5% of the faulty features appear in the top 10 features suggested by WuKong, a jump from 85.2% in the case of no pruning. We note that being too aggressive with pruning can harm localization: with a threshold of 99% (where all but the most accurately modeled features are pruned), only 78.0% of the cases are successfully located, as too many features are filtered out, resulting in many situations where a bug arises in a feature that is not modeled by WuKong.

Effect of Fault Propagation Occasionally WuKong may detect an error that it cannot localize because the buggy feature has been pruned from the feature set. Because faults can propagate through the program, affecting many other features, WuKong may still detect the error in one of these dependent features despite not tracking the buggy feature. In 4% of the buggy runs in our fault injection study, with a 90% pruning threshold, the bug is detected but cannot be localized because the faulty feature is pruned (see Section 4.3 for a discussion of this seeming contradiction).

In such scenarios, we further investigate whether WuKong's diagnosis could still help developers zoom in to the root cause of a bug. In our study, there were two faults detected by WuKong with root causes in features that were pruned. The two faults targeted the same branch instruction, though with different contexts. In these cases, the top-most feature located by WuKong resides in the same case-block of a `switch` statement as the fault. Moreover, the closest feature to the fault in the top-10 roadmap is a mere 19 lines from the true fault. Given the sheer amount of code in AMG2006, it is clear that WuKong can still help the developer hone in on the relevant code area for bug hunting, even if the precise feature cannot be identified.

5.2 Case Study 1: Performance Degradation in MPICH2

To evaluate the use of WuKong in localizing bugs in real-world scenarios, we consider a case study from Vrisha [25], based on a bug in MPICH2's implementation of ALLGATHER.

ALLGATHER is a collective communication operation defined by the MPI standard, where each node exchanges data with every other node. The implementation of ALL-

Threshold	Features Pruned	Detection		Localization		
		False Positive	False Negative	Located Top 1	Located Top 5	Located Top 10
0%	0%	6.5%	5.3%	64.8%	68.5%	85.2%
90%	12.3%	0%	7.0%	71.7%	77.4%	92.5%
99%	22.5%	0%	12.3%	56.0%	62.0%	78.0%

Table 3: The accuracy and precision of detection and localization at various levels of feature pruning with detection threshold parameter $\eta = 1.15$.

```
if ((recvcount*comm_size*type_size < MPIR_ALLGATHER_LONG_MSG)
    && (comm_size_is_pof2 == 1)) {
/*** BUG IN ABOVE CONDITION CHECK DUE TO OVERFLOW ***/
/* ALGORITHM 1 */
...
} else if (...) {
/* ALGORITHM 2 */
...
} else {
/* ALGORITHM 3 */
...
}
```

Figure 2: MPICH2 bug that manifests at large scale as performance degradation.

GATHER in MPICH2 (before v1.2) contains an integer overflow bug [1], which is triggered when the total amount of data communicated goes beyond 2GB and causes a 32-bit `int` variable to overflow (and hence is triggered when input sizes are large or there are many participating nodes). The bug results in a sub-optimal communication algorithm being used for ALLGATHER, severely degrading performance.

We built a test application to expose the ALLGATHER bug when more than 64 processes are employed. The control features were the number of processes in the execution, and the rank of each process, while the observational features were 4126 unique calling contexts chosen as described in Section 3.4. After feature pruning with our default pruning threshold of 90%, WUKONG is left with 3902 features. The model is trained on runs with 4–16 processes (all non-buggy), while we attempted to predict the normal behavior for 64-process runs. When the buggy 64-process version was run, WUKONG was able to successfully detect the bug. The next question was whether WUKONG could aid in the localization of the bug.

First, we used WUKONG to reconstruct the expected behavior of the 64-process run and compared it with the observed buggy run. We find that while most features' observed values closely match the predictions, some features are substantially different from the predicted values. As displayed in Figure 3, even though the bug involves a single conditional, numerous features are impacted by the fault. However, when we examined the top features suggested by WUKONG, we found that all features shared a common call stack prefix which was located inside the branch that would have been taken had the bug not been triggered. Thus, by following the roadmap laid out by WUKONG, we could clearly pinpoint the ill-formed "if" statement, the root cause of the bug as shown in Figure 2. Here we indirectly located the bug based on the most suspicious features provided by WUKONG because the bug did not happen right on one of the observational features we were tracking. We plan to explore direct methods to locate bugs beyond the set of observational features, such as program slicing, in future work.

Because WUKONG's regression models were built using training data collected with a buggy program, an obvious

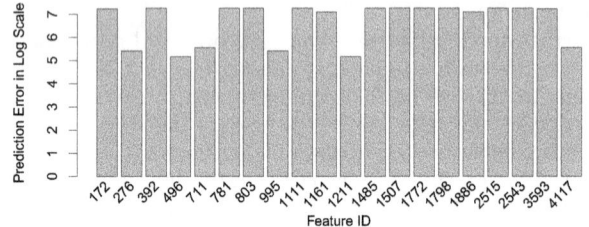

Figure 3: The top suspicious features for the buggy run of MPICH2 ALLGATHER given by WUKONG.

```
while (1) {
    l = strtol((char*)buf + i, &q, 10);
    if(q && *q == ':' && l > 0) {
        if(j + l > MAX_VALUES_SIZE)
            continue;
        /*** BUG: i INCREMENT IS SKIPPED ***/
        i = q + 1 + l - (char*)buf;
        ...
    } else {
        break;
    }
}
```

Figure 4: The deadlock bug appears in Transmission, and manifests when a large number of peers are contained in a single DHT message.

question to ask is whether WUKONG is actually predicting what the correct, non-buggy behavior should be, or whether it is merely getting lucky. To test this, we applied a patch fixing the ALLGATHER bug and performed a test run on 64 processes using the now-non-buggy application. We then compared the observed (non-buggy) behavior to the behavior predicted by WUKONG's model. We find that the average prediction error is 7.75% across all features. In other words, WUKONG is able to predict the *corrected* large-scale behavior; WUKONG correctly predicted how the program would behave if the bug were fixed!

5.3 Case Study 2: Deadlock in Transmission

Transmission is a popular P2P file sharing application on Linux platforms. As illustrated in Figure 4, the bug [3] exists in its implementation of the DHT protocol. Transmission leverages the DHT protocol to find peers sharing a specific file and to form a P2P network with found peers. When Transmission is started, the application sends messages to each bootstrapping peer to ask for new peers. Each peer responds to these requests with a list of its known peers. Upon receiving a response, the joining node processes the message to extract the peer list. Due to a bug in the DHT processing code, if the message contains more than 341 peers, longer than the fixed 2048-byte message buffer, it will enter an infinite loop and cause the program to hang. Hence, this bug would more likely manifest when the program is joining a large P2P network where the number of peers contained in a single DHT message can overflow the message buffer.

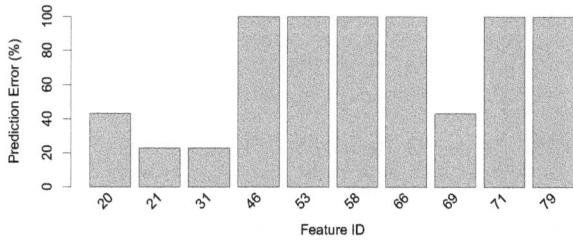

Figure 5: The top suspicious features for the buggy run of Transmission given by WuKong.

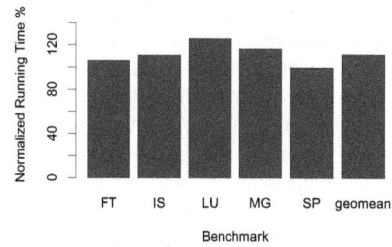

Figure 6: Runtime overhead of WuKong on NPB benchmarks.

This bug could be easily detected using full-system profiling tools such as OPROFILE that could show that the message processing function is consuming many cycles. However, this information is insufficient to tell whether there is a bug in the function or whether the function is behaving normally but is just slow. WuKong is able to definitively indicate that a bug exists in the program.

For this specific bug, given the information provided by OPROFILE, we can focus on the message processing function which is seen most frequently in the program's execution. We treat each invocation of the message processing function as a single execution instance in our model and use the function arguments and the size of the input message as the control features. For the observational features, we use the same branch profile as in the previous experiments, and the associated contexts, to any shared libraries. This gives 83 features and no feature is pruned with our default 90% pruning threshold.

To train WuKong, we use 16 normal runs of the message processing function, and apply the trained model to 1 buggy instance. WuKong correctly determines that the buggy instance is truly abnormal behavior, and not just an especially long-running function. Having established that the long message processing is buggy, WuKong reconstructs the expected behavior and compares it to the observed behavior to locate the bug, as in Figure 5. The rank ordering of deviant features highlights Features 53 and 66, which correspond to the line `if (q && *q == ':' && l > 0)` at the beginning of Figure 4, exhibiting an excessive number of occurrences as a direct consequence of the bug. This feature is a mere 3 lines above the source of the bug.

5.4 Overhead

To further evaluate the overhead of WuKong, we used 5 programs from the NAS Parallel Benchmarks, namely CG, FT, IS, LU, MG and SP[4]. All benchmarks are compiled in a 64-process configuration and each is repeated 10 times to get an average running time. Figure 6 shows the average run-time overheads caused by WuKong for each of these benchmarks. The geometric mean of WuKong's overhead is 11.4%. We note that the overhead with the larger application, AMG2006, is smaller (Table 1).

It is possible to reduce the cost of call stack walking—the dominant component of our run-time overhead—by using a recently demonstrated technique called Breadcrumbs [7] and its predecessor called Probabilistic Calling Context (PCC) [8], both of which allow for efficient recording of dy-

namic calling contexts. Breadcrumbs builds on PCC, which computes a compact (one word) encoding of each calling context that client analysis can use in place of the exact calling context. Breadcrumbs allows one to reconstruct a calling context from its encoding using only a static call graph and a small amount of dynamic information collected at cold (infrequently executed) callsites. We defer to future work the implementation of these techniques in WuKong to capture calling contexts at even lower overheads.

6 Related work

There is a substantial amount of work concerning statistical debugging [5, 9–11, 14, 16–19, 21, 23, 25]. Some of these approaches focus primarily on detection, with diagnosis as a secondary, often ad hoc capability [9, 16, 21, 25], while others focus primarily on assisting bug diagnosis [5, 10, 11, 14, 17–19, 23].

The typical approach taken for detection by statistical approaches [9, 16, 21, 25] is to characterize a program's behavior as an aggregate of a set of features. A model is built based on the behavior of a number of training runs that are known to be buggy or non-buggy. To determine if a particular program execution exhibits a bug, the aggregate characteristics of the test program are checked against the modeled characteristics; deviation is indicative of a bug. The chief drawback to many of these approaches that they do not account for scale. If the system or input size of the training runs differs from the scale of the deployed runs, the aggregate behavior of even non-buggy runs is likely to deviate from the training set, resulting in false positives. Some approaches mitigate this by also detecting bugs in parallel executions if some processes behave differently from others [21]; this approach does not suffice for bugs which arise equally in all processes (such as our MPICH2 case study).

Other statistical techniques eschew detection, in favor of attempting to debug programs that are known to have faults [5, 10, 11, 14, 17–19, 23]. These techniques all share a common approach: a large number of executions are collected, each with aggregate behavior profiled and labeled as "buggy" or "non-buggy." Then, a classifier is constructed that attempts to separate buggy runs from non-buggy runs. Those features that serve to distinguish buggy from non-buggy runs are flagged as involved with the bug, so that debugging attention can be focused appropriately. The key issue with all of these techniques is that (a) they rely on *labeled* data—whether or not a program is buggy must be known; and (b) they require a large number of *buggy* runs to train the classifier. In the usage scenario envisioned for WuKong, the training runs are all known to be bug-free, but bug detection must be performed *given a single buggy run*. We are not attempting to debug widely distributed

---
[4]The overhead numbers for our two case studies are not meaningful—for MPICH2, we created a synthetic test harness; and for Transmission, we relied on a prior use of profiling to identify a single function to instrument.

faulty programs that can generate a large number of sample points, but instead are attempting to localize bugs given a single instance of the bug. Hence, classification-based techniques are not appropriate for our setting.

The closest prior work is our own—ABHRANTA [24], which shares part of the goal of this paper, namely, to localize bugs that appear at large scales. However, it uses the same modeling strategy as VRISHA, Kernel Canonical Correlation Analysis (KCCA), simplifying some portions of the model to ease the task of localization. To be specific, it uses only linear functions for the canonical correlation analysis for the mapping of the observational features. Since it uses KCCA (or CCA in parts), it suffers from the same issue—that its model becomes increasingly inaccurate as the difference increases between the scales of the training runs and those of the production runs. Further, since WUKONG uses the simpler regression model, it runs less risk of overfitting and is conceptually simpler to deal with. Finally, ABHRANTA did not consider the fact that some features are not dependent on scale or otherwise unable to be modeled and should therefore be pruned prior to the analysis. Thus, it is fair to say that ABHRANTA realized only part of the goal of the current paper and can perform reasonably well only in relatively small scale systems without overly-complex behaviors.

7 Conclusions

With the increasing scale at which programs are being deployed, both in terms of input size and system size, techniques to automatically detect and diagnose bugs in large-scale programs are becoming increasingly important. This is especially true for bugs that are scale-dependent, and only manifest at (large) deployment scales, but not at (small) development scales. Traditional statistical techniques cannot tackle these bugs, either because they rely on data collected at the same scale as the buggy process or because they require manual intervention to diagnose bugs.

To address these problems, we developed WUKONG, which leverages novel statistical modeling and feature selection techniques to automatically diagnose bugs in large scale systems, even when trained only on data from small-scale runs. This approach is well-suited to modern development practices, where developers may only have access to small scales, and bugs may manifest only rarely at large scales. With a large-scale fault injection study and two case studies of real scale-dependent bugs, we showed that WUKONG is able to automatically, scalably, and effectively diagnose bugs.

Acknowledgments

We would like to acknowledge the Extreme Science and Engineering Discovery Environment (XSEDE), supported by National Science Foundation grant number OCI-1053575, for use of the clusters for experiments. We would like to acknowledge GrammaTech for providing us an academic license for CodeSurfer, a static analysis tool for C/C++.

References

[1] https://trac.mcs.anl.gov/projects/mpich2/changeset/5262.

[2] https://asc.llnl.gov/sequoia/benchmarks/.

[3] https://trac.transmissionbt.com/changeset/11666.

[4] H. Akaike. A new look at the statistical model identification. *Automatic Control, IEEE Transactions on*, 19(6):716 – 723, dec 1974.

[5] D. Andrzejewski, A. Mulhern, B. Liblit, and X. Zhu. Statistical debugging using latent topic models. In *ECML '07*.

[6] B. J. Barnes, B. Rountree, D. K. Lowenthal, J. Reeves, B. de Supinski, and M. Schulz. A regression-based approach to scalability prediction. In *ICS '08*.

[7] M. Bond, G. Baker, and S. Guyer. Breadcrumbs: efficient context sensitivity for dynamic bug detection analyses. In *PLDI '10*.

[8] M. Bond and K. McKinley. Probabilistic calling context. In *OOPSLA '07*.

[9] G. Bronevetsky, I. Laguna, S. Bagchi, B. R. de Supinski, D. H. Ahn, , and M. Schulz. AutomaDeD: Automata-Based Debugging for Dissimilar Parallel Tasks. In *DSN '10*.

[10] T. M. Chilimbi, B. Liblit, K. Mehra, A. V. Nori, and K. Vaswani. Holmes: Effective statistical debugging via efficient path profiling. In *ICSE '09*.

[11] L. Dietz, V. Dallmeier, A. Zeller, and T. Scheffer. Localizing bugs in program executions with graphical models. In *NIPS '09*.

[12] Q. Gao, F. Qin, and D. Panda. DMTracker: Finding Bugs in Large-Scale Parallel Programs by Detecting Anomaly in Data Movements. In *SC '07*.

[13] T. Hastie, R. Tibshirani, and J. Friedman. *The Elements of Statistical Learning (2nd edition)*. Springer-Verlag, 2008.

[14] J. A. Jones and M. J. Harrold. Empirical evaluation of the tarantula automatic fault-localization technique. In *ASE '05*.

[15] M. Kuhn and K. Johnson. An Introduction to Multivariate Modeling Techniques. http://zoo.cs.yale.edu/classes/cs445/slides/Pfizer_Yale_Version.ppt.

[16] G. L. Lee, D. H. Ahn, D. C. Arnold, B. R. de Supinski, M. Legendre, B. P. Miller, M. Schulz, and B. Liblit. Lessons Learned at 208K: Towards Debugging Millions of Cores. In *SC '08*.

[17] B. Liblit, A. Aiken, A. X. Zheng, and M. I. Jordan. Bug isolation via remote program sampling. In *PLDI '03*.

[18] B. Liblit, M. Naik, A. X. Zheng, A. Aiken, and M. I. Jordan. Scalable statistical bug isolation. In *PLDI '05*.

[19] C. Liu, L. Fei, X. Yan, J. Han, and S. P. Midkiff. Statistical debugging: A hypothesis testing-based approach. *IEEE Trans. Softw. Eng.*, 32:831–848, October 2006.

[20] C.-K. Luk, R. Cohn, R. Muth, H. Patil, A. Klauser, G. Lowney, S. Wallace, V. J. Reddi, and K. Hazelwood. Pin: building customized program analysis tools with dynamic instrumentation. In *PLDI '05*.

[21] A. V. Mirgorodskiy, N. Maruyama, and B. P. Miller. Problem diagnosis in large-scale computing environments. In *SC '06*.

[22] K. Tseng, D. Chen, Z. Kalbarczyk, and R. Iyer. Characterization of the error resiliency of power grid substation devices. In *DSN '12*.

[23] A. X. Zheng, M. I. Jordan, B. Liblit, M. Naik, and A. Aiken. Statistical debugging: simultaneous identification of multiple bugs. In *ICML '06*.

[24] B. Zhou, M. Kulkarni, and S. Bagchi. Abhranta: Locating bugs that manifest at large system scales. In *HotDep '12*.

[25] B. Zhou, M. Kulkarni, and S. Bagchi. Vrisha: using scaling properties of parallel programs for bug detection and localization. In *HPDC '11*.

A 1 PB/s File System to Checkpoint Three Million MPI Tasks[*]

Raghunath
Rajachandrasekar
The Ohio State University
rajachan@cse.ohio-
state.edu

Adam Moody
Lawrence Livermore
National Laboratory
moody20@llnl.gov

Kathryn Mohror
Lawrence Livermore
National Laboratory
kathryn@llnl.gov

Dhabaleswar K.
(DK) Panda
The Ohio State University
panda@cse.ohio-
state.edu

ABSTRACT

With the massive scale of high-performance computing systems, long-running scientific parallel applications periodically save the state of their execution to files called checkpoints to recover from system failures. Checkpoints are stored on external parallel file systems, but limited bandwidth makes this a time-consuming operation. Multilevel checkpointing systems, like the Scalable Checkpoint/Restart (SCR) library, alleviate this bottleneck by caching checkpoints in storage located close to the compute nodes. However, most large scale systems do not provide file storage on compute nodes, preventing the use of SCR.

We have implemented a novel user-space file system that stores data in main memory and transparently spills over to other storage, like local flash memory or the parallel file system, as needed. This technique extends the reach of libraries like SCR to systems where they otherwise could not be used. Furthermore, we expose file contents for Remote Direct Memory Access, allowing external tools to copy checkpoints to the parallel file system in the background with reduced CPU interruption. Our file system scales linearly with node count and delivers a 1 PB/s throughput at three million MPI processes, which is 20x faster than the system RAM disk and 1000x faster than the parallel file system.

Categories and Subject Descriptors

C.4 [**PERFORMANCE OF SYSTEMS**]: Fault tolerance; D.4.3 [**File Systems Management**]: Distributed file systems; D.4.5 [**Reliability**]: Checkpoint/restart

Keywords

HPC, Multilevel Checkpointing, File Systems, Persistent-Memory, SSD, RDMA, Fault-Tolerance

[*]This article has been authored by Lawrence Livermore National Security, LLC under Contract #DE-AC52-07NA27344 with the U.S. Department of Energy.

1. INTRODUCTION

In high-performance computing (HPC), tightly-coupled, parallel applications run in lock-step over thousands to millions of processor cores. These applications simulate physical phenomena such as hurricanes or the effect of aging on the nuclear weapons stockpile. The results of these simulations are important and time-critical, e.g., we want to know the path of the hurricane before it makes landfall. Thus, these applications are run on the fastest supercomputers in the world at the largest scales possible. However, due to the increased component count, large-scale executions are more prone to experience faults, with Mean Times Between Failures (MTBF) on the order of hours or days due to hardware breakdowns and soft errors [12, 17, 24, 25, 28].

HPC applications survive failures by saving their state in files called checkpoints on stable storage, usually a globally-accessible parallel file system. When a fault occurs, the application rolls back to a previously saved checkpoint and restarts its execution. Although parallel file systems are optimized for concurrent access by large scale applications, checkpointing overhead can still dominate application run times, where a single checkpoint can take on the order of tens of minutes [14, 22]. A 2005 study by Los Alamos National Laboratory shows that about 60% of an HPC application's wall-clock time was spent in checkpoint/restart alone [21]. Similarly, a study from Sandia National Laboratories predicts that a 168-hour job on 100,000 nodes with a node MTBF of 5 years will spend only 35% of its time in compute work and the rest of its time in checkpointing activities [11]. On current HPC systems, checkpointing utilizes 75-80% of the I/O traffic [1, 20]. On future systems, checkpointing activities are predicted to dominate compute time and overwhelm file system resources [10, 18].

Multilevel checkpointing systems are a recent optimization to this problem and reduce I/O times significantly [7, 18]. They utilize node-local storage for low-overhead, frequent checkpointing, and only write a select few checkpoints to the parallel file system. Node-local storage is appealing because it scales with the size of the application; as more compute nodes are used, more storage is available. Unfortunately, node-local storage is a scarce resource. While a handful of HPC systems have storage devices such as SSDs on all compute nodes, most systems only have main memory, and some of those do not provide any file system interface to this memory, e.g., RAM disk. Additionally, to use an in-memory file system, an application must dedicate sufficient memory to store checkpoints, which may not always be feasible or desirable.

We address these problems with a new in-memory file system called CRUISE: Checkpoint Restart in User SpacE. CRUISE is optimized for use with multilevel checkpointing libraries to provide low-overhead, scalable file storage on systems that provide some form of memory that persists beyond the life of a process, such as System V IPC shared memory. CRUISE supports a minimal set of POSIX semantics such that its use is transparent when checkpointing HPC applications. An application specifies a bound on memory usage, and if its checkpoint files are too large to fit within this limit, CRUISE stores what it can in memory and then *spills-over* the remaining bytes in slower but larger storage, such as an SSD or the parallel file system. Finally, CRUISE supports Remote Direct Memory Access (RDMA) semantics that allow a remote server process to directly read files from a compute node's memory.

In this paper, we make the following contributions:

- Thorough discussion and evaluation of design alternatives for our in-memory file system
- Detailed description of the design and architecture of CRUISE
- A new mechanism for honoring memory usage bounds, namely, spill-over
- Interfaces to allow external asynchronous data-transfer libraries to interact with CRUISE
- Large-scale performance and scalability evaluation of CRUISE

2. DESIGN GOALS AND BACKGROUND

In this section, we list our design goals and present background on the checkpointing library and the I/O workload characteristics for which we designed CRUISE.

2.1 Design Goals for CRUISE

We were guided by several goals when architecting CRUISE. First, we wanted to provide a file system on machines that have no local storage other than memory. Second, we wanted a framework to support spill-over for checkpoints that are too large to fit in the available local storage. Third, we wanted to enable remote access to checkpoint data using RDMA. Remote access to data stored in compute node memory enables it to be copied to slower, more resilient storage in the background. Fourth, we wanted to develop a file system that could perform near memory speeds to allow for low checkpointing overhead. Finally, we wanted to implement these capabilities with methods that are portable across a range of HPC platforms. In particular our initial target systems are Linux clusters and IBM Blue Gene/Q systems.

2.2 The SCR Library

We developed CRUISE to extend the capabilities of the Scalable Checkpoint/Restart (SCR) library [26].[1] SCR is a multilevel checkpointing system that enables MPI applications to attain high bandwidth for checkpoint and restart I/O [18]. SCR achieves this by saving checkpoints to node-local storage instead of the parallel file system. It can use any available file storage, e.g., RAM disks, magnetic hard-drives, or SSDs. SCR caches recent checkpoints, and discards an older checkpoint with each newly saved one. SCR applies redundancy schemes to the cache, so it can recover

---

[1]Although we developed CRUISE to support SCR, it is generally applicable to any multilevel checkpointing library.

checkpoint files even if a failure disables a small portion of the system. It periodically flushes a cached checkpoint to the parallel file system in order to withstand catastrophic failures.

SCR's design is based on two key properties. First, a job only needs its most recent checkpoint—as soon as the job writes the next checkpoint, a previous checkpoint can be deleted. Second, the majority of failures only disable a small portion of the system, leaving most of the system intact. For example, the results obtained in [18] showed that 85% of failures disabled less than 1% of the compute nodes on the clusters in question.

2.3 Checkpoint/Restart I/O Characteristics

Checkpoint/restart I/O workloads have certain characteristics that allow us to optimize our design and implementation of CRUISE. In this work, we only consider *application-level checkpointing*, where the application explicitly writes its data to files. This differs from *system-level checkpointing* in which the entirety of the application's memory is saved by an external agent. Application-level checkpointing is typically more efficient, because only the data that is needed for restart is saved, instead of the entire memory. Here, we detail the characteristics of typical application-level checkpoint I/O workloads.

A single file per process. Many applications save state in a unique file per process. This checkpointing style is a natural fit for multilevel checkpointing libraries. In fact, SCR imposes the additional constraint that a process may not read files written by another process. As such, there is no need to share files between processes, so storage can be private to each process, which eliminates inter-process consistency and reduces the need for locking.

Dense files. In general, POSIX allows for sparse files in which small amounts of data are scattered at distant offsets within the file. For example, a process could create a file, write a byte, and then seek to an offset later in the file to write more data, leaving a hole. File systems may then optimize for this case by tracking the locations and sizes of holes to avoid consuming space on the storage device. However, checkpoints typically consist of a large volume of data that is written sequentially to a file. Thus, it will suffice to support non-sequential writes in CRUISE without incurring the overhead of tracking these holes to optimize data placement.

Write-once-read-rarely files. A checkpoint file is not modified once written, and it is only read during a restart after a failure, which is assumed to be a rare event relative to the number of checkpoints taken. This property makes it feasible to access file data by external methods such as RDMA without concern for file consistency. Once written, the file contents do not change.

Temporal nature of checkpoint data. Since an application restarts from its most recent checkpoint, older checkpoints can be discarded as newer checkpoints are written. SCR records its own metadata to track checkpoint times, so we need not track POSIX file timestamps in CRUISE. Also, SCR only stores a few checkpoints at a time, so CRUISEuses small fixed-sized arrays to record file metadata.

Globally coordinated operation. Typically, parallel application processes coordinate with each other to ensure that all message passing activity has completed before saving a checkpoint. This coordination means that all processes block until the checkpointing operation is complete, and when a failure occurs, all processes are restarted at the same time. This means that CRUISE can clear all locks when the file system is remounted.

Although, we designed CRUISE to take advantage of the above characteristics, it can be extended to handle other variants. In particular, with slight modification, it is also applicable to uncoordinated checkpointing.

3. DESIGN ALTERNATIVES

Logically, CRUISE requires two layers of software: the first layer intercepts POSIX calls made by the application or checkpoint library, and the second layer interacts with the storage media to manage file data. We considered several design alternatives for each layer that differ in imposed overheads, performance, portability, and capability to support our design goals.

3.1 Intercepting Application I/O

With CRUISE, our objective is to transparently intercept existing application I/O routines such as read(), write(), fread(), and fwrite(), and metadata operations such as open(), close(), and lseek(). We considered two options for implementing the interception layer: FUSE and I/O wrappers.

3.1.1 FUSE-based File System

A natural choice for intercepting application I/O in user-space is to use the Filesystem in User Space (FUSE) module [3]. A file system implementation that uses FUSE can act as an intermediary between the application and the actual underlying file system, e.g., a parallel file system.

The FUSE module is available with all mainstream Linux kernels starting from version 2.4.x. The kernel module works with a user-space library to provide an intuitive interface for implementing a file system with minimal effort and coding. Given that a FUSE file system can be mounted just as any other, it is straight-forward to intercept application I/O operations transparently. However, a significant drawback is that FUSE is not available on all HPC systems. Some HPC systems do not run Linux, and some do not load the necessary kernel module.

Another problem is relatively poor performance for checkpointing workloads. First, because I/O data traverses between user-space and kernel-space multiple times, FUSE can introduce a significant amount of overhead on top of any overhead added by the file system implementation. Second, the use of FUSE implies a large number of small I/O requests for writing checkpoints. By default, FUSE limits writes to 4 KB units. Although the unit size can be optionally increased to 128 KB, that is relatively small for checkpoint workloads that can have file sizes on the order of hundreds of megabytes per process. When FUSE is used in such workloads, many I/O requests are generated at the Virtual File System (VFS) layer leading to several context switches between the application and the kernel.

We quantified the overhead incurred by FUSE using a dummy file system that simply intercepts I/O operations from an application and passes the data to the underlying file system, a kernel-provided RAM disk in this experiment. Direct I/O was used to isolate the effects of the VFS cache. For these runs, we measured the write() throughput of a single process that wrote a 50 MB file to both native RAM disk, and to the dummy FUSE mounted atop the RAM disk. We

Location	Throughput (MB/s)
NFS	84.50
HDD	97.43
Parallel FS	764.18
SSD	1026.39
RAM disk	8555.26
Memory	15097.85

Table 1: I/O throughput for the storage hierarchy on the OSU-RI system described in Section 7.1

found that the bandwidth achieved by FUSE was 80 MB/s, while the bandwidth of RAM disk was 1,610 MB/s. Due to the large overheads of using FUSE, the FUSE file system only gets approximately 5% of the performance of writing to RAM disk directly.

3.1.2 Linker-Assisted I/O Call Wrappers

The other alternative we considered for intercepting application I/O was to use a set of wrapper functions around the native POSIX I/O operations. The GNU Linker (ld) supports intercepting standard I/O library calls with user-space wrappers. This can be done statically during linktime, or dynamically at run time using LD_PRELOAD. This method works without significant overhead because all control remains completely in user-space without data movement to and from the kernel. The difficulty is that a significant amount of work is involved to write wrappers for all of the POSIX I/O routines that an application might use.

Two goals for CRUISE are portability and low overhead for checkpoint workloads, so in spite of the additional work required to write linker-assisted wrapper functions, we opted for this method due to its better performance and portability.

3.2 In-Memory File Storage

Table 1 illustrates the I/O throughput of different levels in the storage hierarchy. We show the performance for several stable storage options: the Network File System (NFS), spinning magnetic hard-disk (HDD), parallel file system, and solid-state disk (SSD). We also show the performance of two memory storage options, RAM disk and shared memory via a memory-to-memory copy operation (Memory). Of course, the memory-based storage options far out-perform stable storage. A key design goal of CRUISE is to store application checkpoint files in memory to improve performance and, more importantly, to serve as a local file system on HPC systems that provide no other form of local storage. Here, we discuss three options that we considered for in-memory storage, RAM disk, a RAM disk-backed memory map, and a persistent memory segment.

3.2.1 Kernel-Provided RAM disk

RAM disk is a kernel-provided virtual file system backed by the volatile physical memory on a node. RAM disk can be mounted like any other file system, and the data stored in it persists for the lifetime of the mount. The kernel manages the memory allocated to RAM disk, enabling persistence beyond the lifetime of user-space processes but not across node reboots or crashes. RAM disk also provides standard file system interfaces and is fully POSIX-compliant, making it a natural choice for in-memory data storage.

However, by comparing the RAM disk to the memory copy performance in Table 1, it is evident that RAM disk does not fully utilize the throughput offered by the physical memory subsystem. Another drawback with RAM disk is that one can not directly access file contents with RDMA.

3.2.2 A RAM disk-Backed Memory-Map

The drawbacks regarding performance and RDMA capability could be addressed by memory mapping a file residing in RAM disk. This approach could fully utilize the bandwidth offered by the physical memory subsystem simply by copying checkpoint data from application buffers to the memory-mapped region using memcpy(). Once the checkpoint is written to the memory-map, it can be synchronized with the backing RAM disk file using msync(). Then one can simply read the normal RAM disk file during recovery.

However, given that the file backing the memory-map resides in the memory reserved for RAM disk, the checkpoint data occupies twice the amount of space. Moreover, there are difficulties involved with tracking consistency between the memory-mapped region and the backing RAM disk file.

3.2.3 Byte-Addressable Persistent Memory Segment

The third approach we considered was to directly store the checkpoint data in physical memory. Our target systems all provide a mechanism to acquire a fixed-size segment of byte-addressable memory which can persist beyond the lifetime of the process that creates it. This includes systems such as the recent IBM Blue Gene/Q that provides so-called *persistent memory*, and all Linux clusters that provide System V IPC shared memory segments.

The downside of this method is that it requires implementation of memory allocation and management, data placement, garbage collection, and other such file system activities. In short, the difficulty lies in implementing the numerous functions and semantics of a POSIX-like file system.

The advantages are the fine-grained management of the data and access to the entire bandwidth of the memory device. Additionally, we expect this approach to work with future byte-addressable Non-Volatile Memory (NVM) or Storage Class Memory (SCM) architectures.

Although the use of a byte-addressable memory segment requires significant implementation effort to perform the activities of a file system, we chose this method for CRUISE for its portability and performance.

3.3 Limitations of the Kernel Buffer Cache

One could argue that the buffer cache maintained in the kernel is a viable alternative that satisfies most of the design goals for CRUISE. The benefits of using the buffer cache include fast writes, asynchronous flush of data to a local or remote file system, and dynamic management of application and file system memory.

However, the potential pitfalls of using the buffer cache in a multilevel checkpointing system outweigh these benefits. One, with multilevel checkpointing, there are situations wherein a cached checkpoint need not be persisted to stable storage. The kernel, however, cannot make this distinction and may unnecessarily flush all data in the buffer cache to the underlying storage system. Two, using the buffer cache involves copies between user and kernel space, reducing write throughput. Three, using the buffer cache does not permit direct access to data for the RDMA capability, which is desirable for asynchronous checkpoint staging. And four, we lose control over when data is moved from the compute node

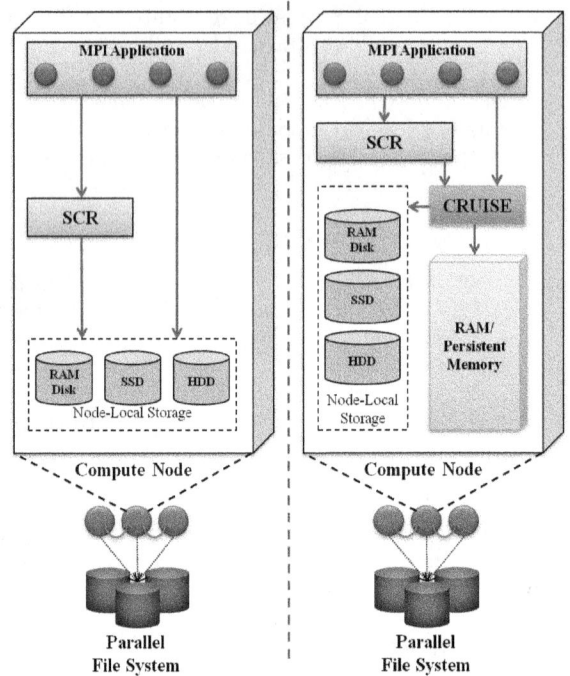

Figure 1: Architecture of CRUISE

to the remote file system. With an in-memory file system like CRUISE, we can orchestrate data movement such that it does not impact the performance of large-scale HPC applications with file system noise. CRUISE is an initial proof-of-concept system intended to work with byte-addressable NVM architectures that cannot be serviced by the buffer cache.

4. ARCHITECTURE AND DESIGN

In this section, we present our design of CRUISE. We begin with a high-level overview. We follow with details on simplifications we made to support checkpoint files, and our approaches for lock management, spill-over, and RDMA support.

4.1 The Role of CRUISE

In Figure 1, we show a high-level view of the interactions between components in SCR and CRUISE. On the left, we show the current state-of-the-art with SCR, and on the right, we show SCR with CRUISE. In both cases, all compute nodes can access a parallel file system. Additionally, each compute node has some type of node-local storage media such as a spinning disk, a flash memory device, or a RAM disk.

In the SCR-only case, the MPI application writes its checkpoints directly to node-local storage, and it invokes the SCR library to apply cross-node redundancy schemes to tolerate lost checkpoints due to node failures. For the highest level of resiliency, SCR writes a selected subset of the checkpoints to the parallel file system. By using SCR, the application incurs a lower overhead for checkpointing but maintains high resiliency. However, SCR cannot be employed on clusters with insufficient node-local storage.

In the SCR-CRUISE case, checkpoints are directed to CRUISE. All application I/O operations are intercepted by the CRUISE library. File names prefixed with a special mount name are

146

processed by CRUISE, while operations for other file names are passed to the standard POSIX routines. CRUISE manages file data in a pre-allocated persistent memory region. Upon exhausting this resource, CRUISE transparently spills remaining file data to node-local storage or the parallel file system. This configuration enables applications to use SCR on systems where there is only memory or where node-local storage is otherwise limited.

As an additional optimization, CRUISE can expose the file contents stored in memory to remote direct memory access. When SCR determines that a checkpoint set should be written to the parallel file system, an asynchronous file-transfer agent running on a dedicated I/O node can extract this data via RDMA using an CRUISE API that lists the memory addresses of the blocks of the files.

4.2 Data Structures

The CRUISE file system is maintained in a large block of persistent memory. The size of this block can be specified at compile time or run time. So long as the node does not crash, this memory persists beyond the life of the process that creates it so that a subsequent process may access the checkpoints after the original process has failed. When a subsequent process mounts CRUISE, the base virtual address of the block may be different. Thus, internally all data structures are referenced using byte offsets from the start of the block. The memory block does not persist data through node failure or reboot. In those cases, a new persistent memory block is allocated, and SCR restores any lost files by way of its redundancy schemes.

Figure 2 illustrates the format of the memory block. The block is divided into two main regions: a metadata region that tracks what files are stored in the file system, and the data region that contains the actual file contents. The data region is further divided into fixed-size blocks, called *data-chunks*. Although not drawn to scale in Figure 2, the memory consumed by the metadata region only accounts for a small fraction of the total size of the block.

We assume that a CRUISE file system only contains a few checkpoints at a time, which simplifies the design of the required data structures. As discussed in Section 2.2, SCR deletes older node-local checkpoints once a new checkpoint has been written, freeing up space for newer checkpoints to be stored. Thus, we are safe to assume a small number of files exist at any time.

Because CRUISE handles a limited number of files for each process, we design our metadata structures to use small, fixed-size arrays. Each file is then assigned an internal *FileID* value, which is used as an index into these arrays. CRUISE manages the allocation and deallocation of FileIDs using the free_fid_stack. When a new file is created, CRUISE pops the next available FileID from the stack. When a file is deleted, its associated FileID is pushed back onto the stack. For each file, we record the file name in the *File List* array, and we record the file size and the list of data-chunks associated with the file in an array of *File Metadata* structures. The FileID is the index for both arrays.

CRUISE adds the name of a newly created file to the File List in its appropriate position, and sets a flag to indicate that this position is in use. For metadata operations that only provide the file name, such as open(), rename(), and unlink(), CRUISE scans the File List for a matching name to discover the FileID, which can then be used to index into

the array of File Metadata structures. For calls which return a POSIX file descriptor, like open(), we associate a mapping from the file descriptor to the FileID so that subsequent calls involving the file descriptor can index directly to the associated element in the File List and File Metadata structure arrays.

The File Metadata structure is logically similar to an *inode* in traditional POSIX file systems, but it does not keep all of the metadata kept in inodes. The File Metadata structure simply holds information pertaining to the size of the file, the number of data-chunks allocated to the file, and the list of data-chunks that constitute the file.

Finally, the free_chunk_stack manages the allocation and deallocation of data-chunks. The size and number of data-chunks are fixed when the file system is created. Each data-chunk is assigned a *ChunkID* value. The free_chunk_stack tracks ChunkIDs that are available to be assigned to a file. When a file requires a new data-chunk, CRUISE pops a value from the stack and records the ChunkID in the File Metadata structure. When a chunk is freed, e.g., after an unlink() operation, CRUISE pushes the corresponding ChunkID back on the stack.

4.3 Spill Over Capability

Some HPC applications use most of the memory available on each compute node, and some also save a significant fraction of that memory during a checkpoint. In such cases, the memory block allocated to CRUISE may be too small to store the checkpoints from the processes running on the node. For this reason, we designed CRUISE to transparently spill over to secondary storage, such as a local SSD or the parallel file system.

During initialization, a fixed-amount of space on the spill-over device is reserved in the form of a file. As with the memory block, the user specifies the location and size of this file. The file is logically fragmented into a pool of data-chunks, and the allocation of these chunks is managed by the free_spillover_stack, which is kept in the persistent memory block. For each chunk allocated to a file, the File Metadata structure also records a field to indicate whether the chunk is in the memory or the spill-over device. When allocating a new chunk for a file, CRUISE allocates a chunk from the spill-over storage only when there are no remaining free chunks in memory.

4.4 Simplifications

We made simplifications over POSIX semantics in CRUISE for directories, permissions, and time stamps.

CRUISE does not support directories. However, CRUISE maintains the illusion of a directory structure by using the entire path as the file name. This support is sufficient for SCR and simplifies the implementation of the file system. When files are transferred from CRUISE to the parallel file system, the directory structure can be recreated since the full paths are stored.

CRUISE does not support file permissions. Since compute nodes on HPC systems are not shared by multiple users at the same time, there is no need for administering file permissions or access rights. All files stored within CRUISE can only be accessed by the user who initiated the parallel application. SCR restores normal file permissions when files are transferred from CRUISE to the parallel file system.

CRUISE does not track time stamps. SCR manages infor-

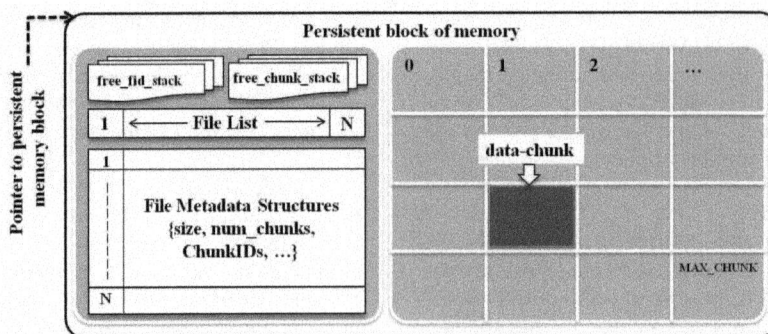

Figure 2: Data Layout of CRUISE on the Persistent Memory Block

mation about which checkpoints are most recent and which can be deleted to make room for new checkpoint files, so time stamps are not required. Typically, versioning mechanisms tend to be a mere sequential numbering of checkpoints, in the order in which they were saved. Updating time stamps on file creation, modification, or access incurs unnecessary overhead, so we remove this feature from CRUISE.

4.5 Lock Management

For some flexibility between performance and portability, the persistent memory block may either be shared by all processes running on a compute node, or there may be a private block for each process. The patterns of checkpoint I/O supported by SCR do not require shared-file access between MPI processes; in fact, SCR prohibits it. Given this, we can assume that no two processes will access the same data-chunk, nor will they update the same File Metadata structure. However when using a single shared block, multiple processes interact with the stacks that manage the free FileIDs and data-chunks. When operating in this mode, the push and pop operations must be guarded by exclusive locks.

Since stack operations are on the critical path, we need a light-weight locking mechanism. We considered two potential mechanisms for locking common data structures. One option is to use System V IPC semaphores and the other is to use Pthread spin-locks. Semaphores provide a locking scheme with a high-degree of fairness, and processes sleep while waiting to acquire the lock, freeing up compute resources. However, the locking and unlocking routines are heavy-weight in terms of the latency incurred. Spin-locks, on the other hand, provide a low-latency locking solution, but they may lack fairness and can lead to wasteful busy-waiting.

When using SCR, all processes in the parallel job synchronize for the checkpoint operation to complete before starting additional computation. This synchronization ensures some degree of fairness between processes across checkpoints. Furthermore, in the case of HPC applications, busy-waiting on a lock does not reduce performance since users do not oversubscribe the compute resources. Thus, we elected to use spin-locks in CRUISE to protect the stack operations.

4.6 Remote Direct Memory Access

RDMA allows a process on a remote node to access the memory of another node, without involving a process on the target node. The main advantage of RDMA is the *zero-copy communication* capability provided by high-performance interconnects such as InfiniBand. This allows the transfer of

data directly to and from a remote process' memory, bypassing kernel buffers. This minimizes the overheads caused by context switching and CPU involvement.

Several researchers have studied the benefits of RDMA-based asynchronous data movement mechanisms [4, 5, 23]. An I/O server process can pull checkpoint data from a compute node's memory without requiring involvement from the application processes, and then write the data to slower storage in the background. This reduces the time for which an application is blocked while writing data to stable storage.

A vast majority of the asynchronous RDMA-based data movement libraries have two sets of components: one or more local RDMA agents that reside on each compute node, and smaller pool of remote RDMA agents hosted on storage nodes or dedicated data-staging nodes. Typically, each data-staging RDMA agent provides data movement services for a small group of compute nodes rather than serving all of them, making this a scalable solution. On receiving a request to move a particular file to the parallel file system, the compute-node RDMA agent reads a portion of the file from disk to its memory space, prepares it for RDMA, and then signals the RDMA agent on the data-staging node. However, the additional memory copy to read the file data into memory for RDMA incurs a significant overhead.

Given that the data managed in CRUISE is already in memory, this additional memory copy operation can be avoided by issuing in-place RDMA operations. To achieve this, we expose an interface for discovering the memory locations of files for efficient RDMA access in CRUISE. The local agent can then communicate the memory locations to the remote agent. This method eliminates the additional memory copies and enables the remote agent to access the files without further interaction with the local agent.

Figure 3 illustrates the protocol for the interface, which works by the following description: (**1**) On initialization, the local and remote RDMA agents establish a network connection for RDMA transfers. (**2**) The local RDMA agent uses the function get_data_region() exposed by CRUISE to get the starting address of the memory region in which CRUISE stores its data chunks, and the size of this memory region. The local RDMA agent then registers the memory region for RDMA operations. (**3**) Following this, the local RDMA agent sleeps until it receives a request from SCR to flush a checkpoint file to the parallel file system.

(**4**) On receiving a request from SCR, the local agent invokes get_chunk_meta_list() exposed by CRUISE, which returns a list of metadata information about each data chunk in the file. This includes the logical ChunkID, the memory

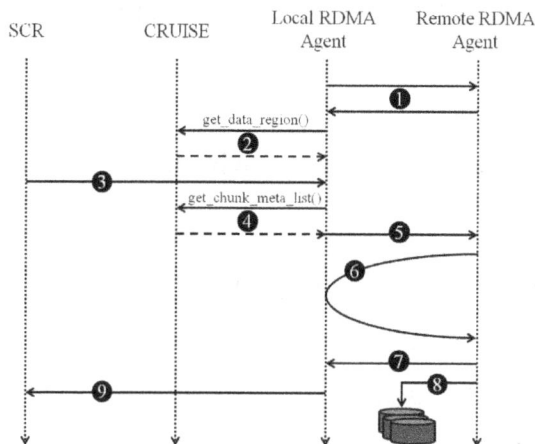

Figure 3: Protocol to RDMA files out of CRUISE

address of the chunk if it is in memory, the offset of the chunk if it is in a spill-over file, and a flag to indicate if the chunk is located inside the memory region or the spill-over file. If a chunk has been spilled-over to an SSD, the local agent issues a `read()` to copy that particular chunk to its address space before initiating an RDMA transfer. **(5)** Then, the local agent sends a control message to the remote agent with the information about the memory addresses to transfer. **(6)** The remote process reads the data chunks directly from the data region managed by CRUISE, without involving the local RDMA agent or the application processes.

(7) After the data has been read from the list of addresses, the remote agent sends a control message to the local agent informing it that it is safe for these buffers to be replaced for subsequent transfers. **(8)** The remote agent writes the data it receives into the parallel file system. Note that it is the duty of the remote agent to pipeline the loop of steps (5)-(8) to make optimum use of the network bandwidth and to overlap the communication and I/O phases. **(9)** When the file transfer is complete, the local agent informs SCR to complete the transfer protocol.

5. IMPLEMENTATION OF CRUISE

Here, we illustrate the implementation of the CRUISE file system by detailing initialization and two representative operations: the `open()` metadata operation and the `write()` data operation.

5.1 Initializing the File System

To initialize CRUISE, a process must mount CRUISE with a particular prefix by calling a user-space API routine. At mount time, CRUISE creates and attaches to the persistent memory block. It initializes pointers to the different data structures within this block, and it clears any locks which may have been held by previous processes. If the block was newly created, it initializes the various resource stacks. Once CRUISE has been mounted at some prefix, e.g., `/tmp/ckpt`, it intercepts all I/O operations for files at that prefix. For all other files, it forwards the call to the original I/O routine.

5.2 open() Operation

Figure 4 lists pseudo-code for the `open()` function. When CRUISE intercepts any file system call, it first checks to see if the operation should be served by CRUISE or if it should

```
1:  open(const char *path, int flags, ...)
2:  if path matches CRUISE mount prefix then
3:        lookup corresponding FileID
4:        if path not in File List then
5:              pop new FileID from free_fid_stack
6:              if out of FileIDs then
7:                    return EMFILE
8:              end if
9:              insert path in File List at FileID
10:             initialize File Metadata for FileID
11:       end if
12:       return FileID + RLIMIT_NOFILE
13: else
14:       return __real_open(path, flags, ...)
15: end if
```

Figure 4: Pseudo-code for `open()` function wrapper

```
1:  write(int fd, const void *buf, size_t count)
2:  if fd more than RLIMIT_NOFILE then
3:        FileID = fd - RLIMIT_NOFILE
4:        get File Metadata for FileID
5:        compute number of additional data-chunks
              required to accommodate the write
6:        if additional data-chunks needed then
7:              pop data-chunks from free_chunk_stack
8:              if out of memory data-chunks then
9:                    pop data-chunks from
                          the free_spillover_stack
10:             end if
11:             store new ChunkIDs in File Metadata
12:       end if
13:       copy data to chunks
14:       update file size in File Metadata
15:       return number bytes written
16: else
17:       return __real_write(fd, buf, count)
18: end if
```

Figure 5: Pseudo-code for `write()` function wrapper

be passed to the underlying file system. In `open()`, CRUISE compares the *path* argument to the prefix at which it was mounted. CRUISE intercepts the call if the file prefix matches the mount point; otherwise it invokes the real `open()`.

When CRUISE intercepts `open()`, it scans the File List to lookup the FileID for a file name matching the *path* argument. If it is not found, CRUISE allocates a new FileID from the `free_fid_stack`, adds the file to the File List, and initializes its corresponding File Metadata structure. As a file descriptor, CRUISE returns the internal FileID plus a constant `RLIMIT_NOFILE`. RLIMITs are system specific limits imposed on different types of resources, including the maximum number of open file descriptors for a process. The CRUISE variable `RLIMIT_NOFILE` specifies a value one greater than the maximum file descriptor the system would ever return. CRUISE differentiates its own file descriptors from system file descriptors by comparing them to this value.

5.3 write() Operation

Figure 5 shows the pseudo-code for the `write()` function. CRUISE first compares the value of *fd* to `RLIMIT_NOFILE` to determine whether *fd* is a CRUISE or system file descriptor. If it is a CRUISE file descriptor, CRUISE converts *fd* to

149

a FileID by subtracting `RLIMIT_NOFILE`. Using the FileID, `CRUISE` looks up the corresponding File Metadata structure to obtain the current file size and list of data-chunks allocated to the file. From the current file pointer position and the length of the write operation, `CRUISE` determines whether additional data-chunks must be allocated. If necessary, it acquires new data-chunks from `free_chunk_stack`. If the persistent memory block is out of data-chunks, `CRUISE` allocates chunks from the secondary spill-over pool. It appends the ChunkIDs to the list of chunks in the File Metadata structure, and then it copies the contents of *buf* to the data-chunks. `CRUISE` also updates any relevant metadata such as the file size.

6. FAILURE MODEL WITH SCR

`CRUISE` is designed with the semantics of multilevel checkpointing systems in mind. The core principle of multilevel checkpointing is to use light-weight checkpoints, such as those written to `CRUISE`, to handle the most common failures. Less frequent but more severe failures restart the application from a checkpoint on the parallel file system. In this section, we detail the integration of `CRUISE` with SCR.

SCR supports HPC applications that use the Message Passing Interface (MPI). SCR directs the application to write its files to `CRUISE`, and after the application completes its checkpoint, SCR applies a redundancy scheme that protects the data against common failure modes. The redundancy data and SCR metadata are stored in additional files written to `CRUISE`. On any process failure, SCR relies on the MPI runtime to detect the failure and kill all remaining processes in the parallel job. Note that processes can fail or be killed at any point during their execution, so they may be interrupted while writing a file, and they may hold locks internal to `CRUISE`.

If a failure terminates a job, SCR logic in the batch script restarts the job using spare nodes to fill in for any failed nodes. During the initialization of the SCR library by the new job, each process first mounts `CRUISE` and then invokes a global barrier. During the mount call, `CRUISE` clears all locks. The subsequent barrier ensures that locks are not allocated again until all processes return from the mount call. After the barrier, each process attempts to read an SCR metadata file from `CRUISE`. SCR tracks the list of checkpoint files stored in `CRUISE`, and it records which files are complete. It deletes any incomplete files, and it attempts to rebuild any missing files by way of its redundancy encoding. If SCR fails to rebuild a checkpoint, it restores the job using a checkpoint from the parallel file system.

Note that because `CRUISE` stores data in persistent memory, like System V shared memory, data is not lost due to simple process failure. All processes in the first job can be killed, and processes in the next job can reattach to the memory and read the data. However, data is lost if the node is killed or rebooted. In this case, `CRUISE` creates a new, empty block of persistent memory, and SCR is responsible for restoring missing files using its redundancy schemes.

`CRUISE` also relies on external mechanisms to ensure data integrity. `CRUISE` relies on ECC hardware to protect file data chunks stored in memory, and it relies on the integrity provided by the underlying file system for data chunks stored in spill over devices. For this latter case, we only need to ensure that `CRUISE` synchronizes data to the spill over device when the application issues a `sync()` call or closes a file.

7. EXPERIMENTAL EVALUATION

Here we detail our experimental evaluation of `CRUISE`. We performed both single- and multi-node experiments to investigate the throughput and scalability of the file system.

7.1 Experimentation Environment

We used several HPC systems for our evaluation.

OSU-RI is a 178-node Linux cluster running RHEL 6 at The Ohio State University. Each node has dual Intel Xeon processors with 4 CPUs and 12 GB of memory. *OSU-RI* also has 16 dedicated storage nodes, each with 24 GB of memory and a 300GB OCZ VeloDrive PCIe SSD. We used the GCC compilers for our experiments, version 4.6.3.

Sierra and *Zin* are Linux clusters at Lawrence Livermore National Laboratory that run the TOSS 2.0 operating system, a variant of RHEL 6.2. Both of these are equipped with Intel Xeon processors. On Sierra, each node has dual 6-core processors and 24 GB of memory; and on Zin, each node has dual 8-core processors and 32 GB of memory. Both clusters use the InfiniBand QDR interconnect. The total node counts on the clusters are 1,944 and 2,916 respectively. We used the Intel compiler, version 11.1.

Sequoia is an IBM Blue Gene/Q system with 98,304 compute nodes. Each node has 16 compute cores and 16 GB of memory. The compute nodes run IBM's Compute Node Kernel and are connected with the IBM Blue Gene torus network. We used the native IBM compiler, version 12.1.

7.2 Microbenchmark Evaluation

In this section, we give results from several experiments to evaluate the performance of `CRUISE`. First, we explore the impact of NUMA effects on intra-node scalability. Next, we evaluate the effect of data-chunk sizes on performance. Finally, we evaluate the spill-over capability of `CRUISE`. All results presented are an average of five iterations.

7.2.1 Non-Uniform Memory Access

With the increase in the number of CPU cores and chip density, the distance between system memory banks and processors also increases. If the data required by a core does not reside in its own memory bank, there is a penalty incurred in access latency to fetch data from a remote memory bank. In order to evaluate this cost, we altered `CRUISE` so that memory pages constituting the data-chunks are allocated in a particular NUMA bank. Table 2 lists the outcome of our evaluation on a single node of OSU-RI.

OSU-RI nodes have 8 processing cores; 4 cores share a memory bank. The table shows the `CRUISE` bandwidth obtained by allocating a shared memory block for 4 process running on the first four CPU cores, either on the local bank, on the remote bank, or by interleaving pages across the two banks. The "local bank" case always delivers the best bandwidth, the "remote bank" case always performs the worst, and the "interleaved" case strikes a balance between the two. The difference is most exaggerated with 4 processes, for which local bandwidth is 8.3 GB/s compared to only 5.7 GB/s for remote. Thus, `CRUISE` bandwidth drops by more than 30% if we are not careful to allocate data-chunk memory appropriately. To this end, we determine on which core a process is running when it mounts `CRUISE`. We use this information to determine from which NUMA bank to allocate data chunks for this process. HPC applications

# Procs (N)	Single Memory Block			N-Memory Blocks		
	Local Bank	Remote Bank	Mixed	Local Bank	Remote Bank	Mixed
1	3.74	2.63	3.09	3.74	2.63	3.09
2	6.54	4.51	5.16	6.58	4.50	5.33
3	7.84	5.28	6.33	7.84	5.29	6.33
4	8.29	5.70	6.81	8.28	5.69	6.80

Table 2: Impact of Non-Uniform Memory Access on Bandwidth (GB/s)

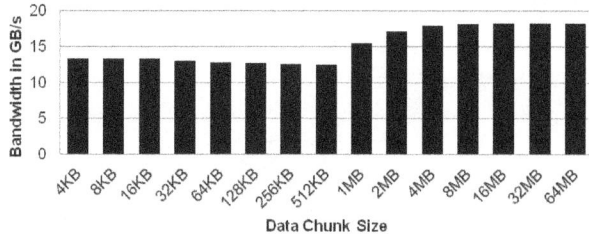

Figure 6: Impact of Chunk Sizes

typically pin processes to cores, so processes do not migrate from one NUMA bank to another during the run.

7.2.2 Impact of Chunk Sizes

One important parameter that affects the performance of CRUISE is the size of the data-chunk used to store file data. The chunk size determines the unit of data with which a write() or read() operation works. To study the impact of chunk sizes, we used the same benchmark from before in which 12 processes each write 64 MB of data to a file in CRUISE on a single node of Sierra. We then vary the chunk size from 4 KB up to 64 MB. In Figure 6, the x-axis shows the chunk size and the y-axis indicates the aggregate bandwidth obtained. As the graph indicates, we see performance benefits with larger chunk sizes. These benefits can be attributed to the fact that a file of a given size requires fewer chunks with increasing chunk sizes, which in turn leads to fewer bookkeeping operations and fewer calls to memcpy(). However, the aggregate bandwidth obtained here saturates that of the memory bank at 18.2 GB/s when chunks larger than 16 MB are used. Although this trend might remain the same across different system architectures, the actual thresholds could vary. To facilitate portability, we leave the chunk size as a tunable parameter.

In addition to having relatively larger chunks for performance reasons, it is also beneficial when draining checkpoints using RDMA as discussed in Section 4.6. One-sided RDMA put and get operations are known to provide higher throughput on high-performance interconnects such as InfiniBand when transferring large data sizes.

7.2.3 Spill-over to SSD

With the next set of experiments, we use a system with local SSD to evaluate the data spill-over capability in CRUISE. As discussed in Section 4.3, if the file data is too large to fit entirely in memory, CRUISE spills the extra data to secondary storage. In such scenarios, we can theoretically estimate the file system throughput using the following formula:

$$T_{spillover} = \frac{size_{tot}}{\frac{size_{MEM}}{T_{MEM}} + \frac{size_{SSD}}{T_{SSD}}}$$

Where, $T_{spillover}$ is the throughput with spill-over enabled; $size_{tot}$ is the total size of the checkpoint; $size_{MEM}$ is the size of the checkpoint stored in memory; $size_{SSD}$ is the size stored to the SSD; and T_{MEM} and T_{SSD} are the native throughput of memory and the SSD device.

We developed tests to study the performance penalties involved with saving parts of a checkpoint in memory and the rest to an SSD. Table 3 lists seven different test scenarios for a 512 MB-per-process checkpoint. Test #1 is the ideal scenario where 100% of the file is stored in memory, and Test #7 is the worst-case scenario where CRUISE must store the entire checkpoint to disk. With Tests #2-6, the size of the file that spills to the SSD increases by a factor of two.

All of these tests were run on a single storage node of OSU-RI that has a high-speed SSD installed. We first ran Tests #1 and #7 to measure the native throughput of memory and the SSD on the system, and we substituted these values into the above formula to compute the expected performance of the other cases. We then limited the memory available to CRUISE according to the test case, and conducted the other tests to measure the actual throughput. The theoretical and actual results are tabulated in Table 3.

Test #	% in SSD	Spill Size (MB)	Theoretical Throughput	Actual Throughput
1	0	0	15074.17	15074.17
2	3.125	16	10349.12	10586.61
3	6.25	32	7879.33	8134.46
4	12.5	64	5333.61	5312.26
5	25	128	3240.00	3110.58
6	50	256	1815.06	2163.93
7	100	512	965.67	965.67

Table 3: CRUISE throughput (MB/s) with Spill-over

The experiment clearly shows that with an increase in the percentage of a checkpoint that has to be spilled to the SSD or any such secondary device, the total throughput of the checkpointing operation reduces. For instance, in case of Test#6, with exactly half the checkpoint spilling to the SSD, the total throughput is reduced by almost 86%. Also, the actual results closely match the theoretical estimates, which validates our basic formula.

7.3 Intra-Node Scalability

In Figure 7, we show the intra-node scalability of CRUISE compared with RAM disk and a memcpy() operation on a single node of Sierra and Sequoia. The x-axis indicates the number of processes on the node, and the y-axis gives the aggregate bandwidth of the I/O operation in GB/s summed across all processes. Each process is bound to a single CPU-core of the compute node and writes and deletes a file five times, reporting its average bandwidth. On Sierra, the file size was 100 MB; on Sequoia, the file size was 50 MB.

The performance of the memory-to-memory copies repre-

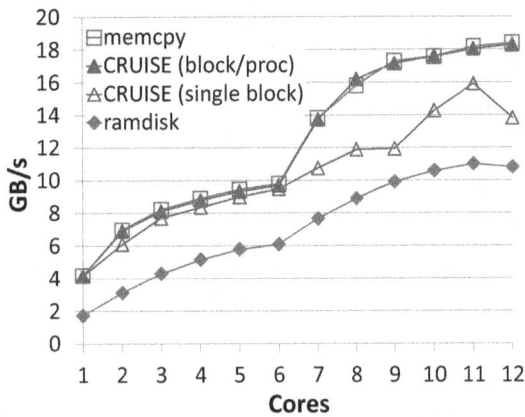

(a) Sierra node   (b) Sequoia node

Figure 7: Intra-Node Aggregate Bandwidth Scalability

sents an upper bound on the performance achievable with our in-memory file system. To measure this bound, our benchmark simply copies data from one user-level buffer to another using standard `memcpy()` calls (red lines in Figure 7). The maximum aggregate bandwidth tops out around 18 GB/s on Sierra and roughly 13 GB/s on Sequoia.

One notable trend in the plot for Sierra is the double-saturation curve. Sierra is a dual-socket NUMA machine with 6 cores per NUMA bank. As the process count increases from 1 to 6, all processes are bound to the first socket and the performance of the local NUMA bank begins to saturate. Then, as the process count increases to 7, the seventh process runs on the second socket and uses the other NUMA bank leading to a jump in aggregate performance. Finally, this second NUMA bank begins to saturate as the process count is increased further from 7 to 12.

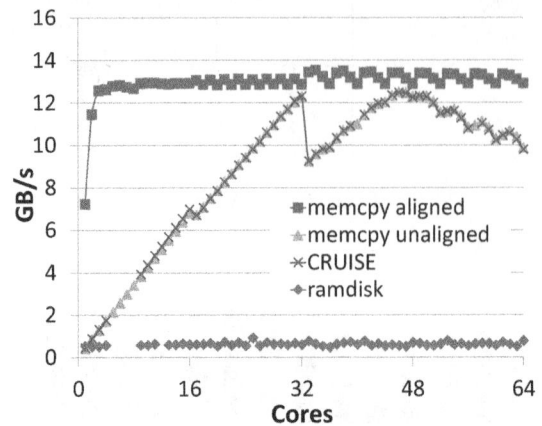

On Sequoia, each node has 16 compute cores, each of which supports 4-way simultaneous multi-threading. Therefore, we can evaluate the aggregate throughput for up to 64 processes on a node. On this system, we found a significant difference in `memcpy` performance depending on how buffers are aligned. If source and destination buffers are aligned at 64-byte boundaries, a fast `memcpy` routine is invoked that utilizes Quad Processing eXtension (QPX) instructions. Otherwise, the system falls back to a more general, but slower `memcpy` implementation. We plot results for both versions. The aligned memory copies (red line) saturate the physical memory bandwidth with a small number of parallel threads. It delivers a peak bandwidth of 13.5 GB/s with 32 processes. The unaligned variant (green line) scales linearly up to 32 processes where it reaches its peak performance of 12 GB/s.

We do not see the double-saturation curves as in the case of Sierra, because the compute nodes on Blue Gene/Q systems have a crossbar switch that connects all cores to all of memory, so there are no NUMA effects. However, there are some interesting points where trends change significantly. The Blue Gene/Q architecture configures hardware as though the total number of tasks is rounded up to the next power of two in certain cases. These switch points apparently impact the memory bandwidth available to the tasks, particularly when going from 16 to 17 processes per node and again from 32 to 33. Beyond 32 processes per node, memory bandwidth

initially drops but increases to another saturation point with about 45 processes. For process counts from 45 to 64, memory bandwidth steadily decreases again. We are still investigating the reason why memory bandwidth is affected this way. Having said that, applications are unlikely to run with process counts other than powers of two on a node.

We now examine the RAM disk performance (blue lines). With each iteration, each process in our benchmark writes and deletes a file in RAM disk. On Sierra, the aggregate bandwidth for RAM disk is nearly half of that for `memcpy`. On Sequoia, the performance is even worse. The memory copy performance increases with increasing cores, but the RAM disk performance is flat at ~ 0.6 GB/s.

On Sierra, we evaluated the performance of CRUISE with a private block per process (purple, filled triangle) and with all processes on the node sharing a single block (purple, hollow triangle). There is a clear difference in performance between these modes. When using private blocks, the performance of CRUISE is close to that of `memcpy`, achieving nearly the full memory bandwidth. With a single shared block, CRUISE closely tracks the `memcpy` performance up to 6 processes, but then it falls off that trend with higher process counts.

A portion of the difference is due to locking overheads. However, experimental results showed these effects to be small for the 64 MB data-chunk size used in these tests. Instead, the majority of the difference appears to be due to the costs of accessing non-local memory. To resolve this problem, we intend to modify CRUISE to manage a set of free chunks for each NUMA bank and then select chunks from the appropriate bank depending on the location of the process making the request.

On Sequoia, we currently do not make an effort to align buffers in CRUISE. CRUISE has control over the alignment of the data-chunks, but it has no control over the offset of the buffers passed by the application. Thus, the performance of CRUISE (purple line) closely follows that of the unaligned `memcpy` (green line). We could modify CRUISE to fragment data-chunks and use aligned buffers more often. This would boost performance at the cost of using more storage space, but it could be a worthwhile optimization for large writes.

152

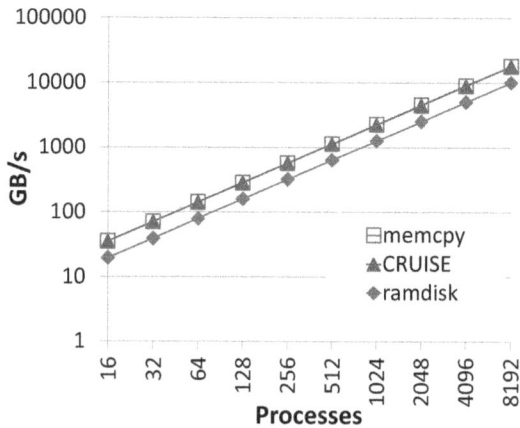

(a) Zin Cluster (Linux)　　　　　　(b) Sequoia Cluster (IBM Blue Gene/Q)

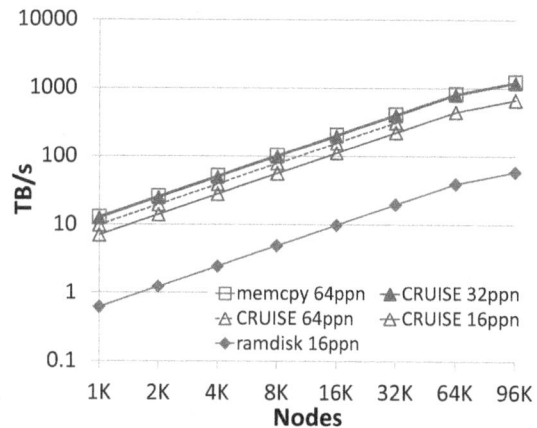

Figure 8: Aggregate Bandwidth Scalability of CRUISE

7.4 Large-Scale Evaluation

CRUISE is designed to be used with large-scale clusters that span thousands of compute nodes. We evaluated the scaling capacity of this framework, and we show the results in Figure 8. We conducted these evaluations on Zin and Sequoia. For each of these clusters, we measured the throughput of CRUISE with increasing number of processes. In these experiments, we configured CRUISE to allocate a persistent memory block per process. On Zin, each process writes a 128MB file; on Sequoia, each writes a 50MB file. We compare CRUISE to RAM disk and a memory-to-memory copy of data within a process' address space using memcpy(). Since CRUISE requires at least one memory copy to move data from the application buffer to its in-memory file storage, the memcpy performance represents an upper-bound on throughput.

On Zin (Figure 8(a)), the number of processes writing to CRUISE was increased by a factor of two up to 8,192 processes along the x-axis. The y-axis shows the bandwidth(GB/s) in log-scale. As the graphs indicate, a perfect-linear scaling can be observed on this cluster. Furthermore, CRUISE takes complete advantage of the memory system's bandwidth (the CRUISE plot overlaps the memcpy plot). The throughput of CRUISE at 8,192 processes is 17.6 TB/s, which is only slightly below the memcpy throughput of 17.7 TB/s. The throughput of RAM disk is nearly half that of CRUISE at 9.87 TB/s. These runs used 17.5% of the available compute nodes. Extrapolation of this linear scaling to the full 46,656 processes would lead to a throughput for CRUISE of over 100 TB/s.

Figure 8(b) shows the scaling trends on Sequoia. Because Sequoia is capable of 4-way simultaneous multi-threading, a total of 6,291,456 parallel tasks can be executed. The x-axis provides the node-count for each data point, and the y-axis shows the bandwidth(TB/s) in log-scale. For clarity, we only show the configurations that deliver the best results for aligned memcpy and RAM Disk. We show the results when using 16, 32, and 64 processes per node for CRUISE. At the full-system scale of 6 million processes (64 processes/node), the aggregate aligned memcpy bandwidth reaches 1.21 PB/s. As observed in Figure 7(b), CRUISE nearly saturates this bandwidth to deliver a throughput of 1.16 PB/s when running with 32 processes per node. This is 20x faster than the

system RAM disk, which provides a maximum throughput of 58.9 TB/s, and it is 1000x faster than the 1 TB/s parallel file system provided for the system.

8. RELATED WORK

Linker support to intercept library calls has been around for a while. *Darshan* [8] intercepts an HPC application's calls to the file system using linker support to profile and characterize the application's I/O behavior. Similarly, *fakechroot* [2] intercepts chroot() and open() calls to emulate their functionality without privileged access to the system.

Other researchers have investigated saving files in memory for performance. The MemFS project from Hewlett Packard [19] dynamically allocates memory to hold files. However, there is no persistence of the files after a process dies and MemFS requires kernel support. McKusick et al. present an in-memory file system [16]. This effort also requires kernel support, and it requires copies from kernel buffers to application buffers which would cause high overhead.

MEMFS is a general purpose, distributed file system implemented across compute nodes on HPC systems [27]. Unlike our approach, they do not optimize for the predominant form of I/O on these systems, checkpointing. Another general purpose file system for HPC is based on a concept called containers which reside in memory [15]. While this work does consider optimizations for checkpointing, its focus is on asynchronous movement of data from compute nodes to other storage devices in the storage hierarchy of HPC systems. Our work primarily differs from these in that CRUISE is a file system optimized for fast node-local checkpointing.

Several efforts investigated checkpointing to memory in a manner similar to that of SCR [7, 9, 13, 23, 29, 30]. They use redundancy schemes with erasure encoding for higher resilience. These works differ from ours in that they use system-provided in-memory or node-local file systems, such as RAM disk, to store checkpoints. Rebound checkpoints to volatile memory but focuses on single many-core nodes and optimizes for highly-threaded applications [6].

153

9. SUMMARY AND FUTURE WORK

In this work, we have developed a new file system called CRUISE to extend the capabilities of multilevel checkpointing libraries used by today's large scale HPC applications. CRUISE runs in user-space for improved performance and portability. It performs over twenty times faster than kernel-based RAM disk, and it can run on systems where RAM disk is not available. CRUISE stores file data in main memory and its performance scales linearly with the number of processors used by the application. To date, we have benchmarked its performance at 1 PB/s, at a scale of 96K nodes with three million MPI processes writing to it.

CRUISE implements a spill-over capability that stores data in secondary storage, such as a local SSD, to support applications whose checkpoints are too large to fit in memory. CRUISE also allows for Remote Direct Memory Access to file data stored in memory, so that multilevel checkpointing libraries can use processes on remote nodes to copy checkpoint data to slower, more resilient storage in the background of the running application.

As a next step, we would like to study the impact of in-memory checkpoint compression to conserve storage space. Furthermore, it is of our interest to investigate various caching policies, when using compression and spill-over capabilities, to improve I/O of frequently accessed file data.

Acknowledgments

The authors would like to thank the anonymous reviewers for their comments and suggestions that helped us improve the paper. This project is supported in part by NSF grants CCF-0937842 and OCI-1148371. (LLNL-CONF-592884)

References

[1] The ASC Sequoia Draft Statement of Work. https://asc.llnl.gov/sequoia/rfp/02_SequoiaSOW_V06.doc, 2008.

[2] fakechroot. https://github.com/fakechroot/fakechroot/wiki.

[3] Filesystem in Userspace. http://fuse.sourceforge.net.

[4] H. Abbasi, J. Lofstead, F. Zheng, S. Klasky, K. Schwan, and M. Wolf. Extending I/O through high performance data services. In *IEEE Cluster*, 2007.

[5] H. Abbasi, M. Wolf, G. Eisenhauer, S. Klasky, K. Schwan, and F. Zheng. DataStager: Scalable Data Staging Services for Petascale Applications. In *HPDC*, 2009.

[6] R. Agarwal, P. Garg, and J. Torrellas. Rebound: Scalable Checkpointing for Coherent Shared Memory. *SIGARCH Comput. Archit. News*, 2011.

[7] L. Bautista-Gomez, D. Komatitsch, N. Maruyama, S. Tsuboi, F. Cappello, and S. Matsuoka. FTI: High Performance Fault Tolerance Interface for Hybrid Systems. In *SC*, 2011.

[8] P. Carns, K. Harms, W. Allcock, C. Bacon, S. Lang, R. Latham, and R. Ross. Understanding and Improving Computational Science Storage Access through Continuous Characterization. 2011.

[9] B. Eckart, X. He, C. Wu, F. Aderholdt, F. Han, and S. Scott. Distributed Virtual Diskless Checkpointing: A Highly Fault Tolerant Scheme for Virtualized Clusters. *IEEE International Parallel and Distributed Processing Symposium Workshops*, 2012.

[10] E. N. Elnozahy and J. S. Plank. Checkpointing for Peta-Scale Systems: A Look into the Future of Practical Rollback-Recovery. *IEEE Transactions on Dependable and Secure Computing*, 2004.

[11] K. Ferreira, R. Riesen, R. Oldfield, J. Stearley, J. Laros, K. Pedretti, T. Kordenbrock, and R. Brightwell. Increasing Fault Resiliency in a Message-Passing Environment. *Sandia National Laboratories, Tech. Rep. SAND2009-6753*, 2009.

[12] J. N. Glosli, K. J. Caspersen, J. A. Gunnels, D. F. Richards, R. E. Rudd, and F. H. Streitz. Extending Stability Beyond CPU Millennium: A Micron-Scale Atomistic Simulation of Kelvin-Helmholtz Instability. In *SC*, 2007.

[13] F. Isaila, J. Garcia Blas, J. Carretero, R. Latham, and R. Ross. Design and Evaluation of Multiple-Level Data Staging for Blue Gene Systems. *TPDS*, 2011.

[14] K. Iskra, J. W. Romein, K. Yoshii, and P. Beckman. ZOID: I/O-Forwarding Infrastructure for Petascale Architectures. In *PPoPP*, 2008.

[15] D. Kimpe, K. Mohror, A. Moody, B. V. Essen, M. Gokhale, K. Iskra, R. Ross, and B. R. de Supinski. Integrated In-System Storage Architecture for High Performance Computing. In *Workshop on Runtime and Operating Systems for Supercomputers*, 2012.

[16] M. McKusick, M. Karels, and K. Bostic. A Pageable Memory-Based Filesystem. In *Proceedings of the United Kingdom UNIX Users Group Meeting*, 1990.

[17] S. E. Michalak, K. W. Harris, N. W. Hengartner, B. E. Takala, and S. A. Wender. Predicting the Number of Fatal Soft Errors in Los Alamos National Laboratory's ASC Q Supercomputer. *IEEE Transactions on Device and Materials Reliability*, 2005.

[18] A. Moody, G. Bronevetsky, K. Mohror, and B. R. d. Supinski. Design, Modeling, and Evaluation of a Scalable Multi-level Checkpointing System. In *SC*, 2010.

[19] H. Packard. MemFSv2 - A Memory-based File System on HP-UX 11i v2 . In *Technical Whitepaper*, 1990.

[20] F. Petrini. Scaling to Thousands of Processors with Buffer Coscheduling. In *Scaling to New Height Workshop*, Pittsburgh, PA, 2002.

[21] I. R. Philp. Software Failures and the Road to a Petaflop Machine. In *1st Workshop on High Performance Computing Reliability Issues (HPCRI)*, 2005.

[22] R. Ross, J. Moreira, K. Cupps, and W. Pfeiffer. Parallel I/O on the IBM Blue Gene/L System. Technical report, Blue Gene/L Consortium Quarterly Newsletter.

[23] K. Sato, A. Moody, K. Mohror, T. Gamblin, B. R. de Supinksi, N. Maruyama, and S. Matsuoka. Design and Modeling of a Non-blocking Checkpointing System. In *SC*, 2012.

[24] B. Schroeder and G. Gibson. Understanding Failure in Petascale Computers. *Journal of Physics Conference Series: SciDAC*, June 2007.

[25] B. Schroeder and G. A. Gibson. A Large-Scale Study of Failures in High-Performance Computing Systems. In *DSN*, June 2006.

[26] SCR. Scalable Checkpoint/Restart Library. http://sourceforge.net/projects/scalablecr/.

[27] J. Seidel, R. Berrendorf, M. Birkner, and M.-A. Hermanns. High-Bandwidth Remote Parallel I/O with the Distributed Memory Filesystem MEMFS. In *EuroPVM/MPI*. 2006.

[28] E. Vivek Sarkar, editor. *ExaScale Software Study: Software Challenges in Exascale Systems*. 2009.

[29] G. Wang, X. Liu, A. Li, and F. Zhang. In-Memory Checkpointing for MPI Programs by XOR-Based Double-Erasure Codes. In *EuroPVM/MPI*, 2009.

[30] G. Zheng, L. Shi, and L. V. Kalé. FTC-Charm++: An In-Memory Checkpoint-Based Fault Tolerant Runtime for Charm++ and MPI. In *IEEE Cluster*, 2004.

AI-Ckpt: Leveraging Memory Access Patterns for Adaptive Asynchronous Incremental Checkpointing

Bogdan Nicolae
IBM Research
Dublin, Ireland
bogdan.nicolae@ie.ibm.com

Franck Cappello
Joint Laboratory for Petascale Computing
INRIA, France
University of Illinois at Urbana-Champaign, USA
fci@lri.fr

ABSTRACT

With increasing scale and complexity of supercomputing and cloud computing architectures, faults are becoming a frequent occurrence, which makes reliability a difficult challenge. Although for some applications it is enough to restart failed tasks, there is a large class of applications where tasks run for a long time or are tightly coupled, thus making a restart from scratch unfeasible. Checkpoint-Restart (CR), the main method to survive failures for such applications faces additional challenges in this context: not only does it need to minimize the performance overhead on the application due to checkpointing, but it also needs to operate with scarce resources. Given the iterative nature of the targeted applications, we launch the assumption that first-time writes to memory during asynchronous checkpointing generate the same kind of interference as they did in past iterations. Based on this assumption, we propose novel asynchronous checkpointing approach that leverages both current and past access pattern trends in order to optimize the order in which memory pages are flushed to stable storage. Large scale experiments show up to 60% improvement when compared to state-of-art checkpointing approaches, all this achievable with an extra memory requirement of less than 5% of the total application memory.

Categories and Subject Descriptors

D.4.5 [**Operating Systems**]: Reliability

General Terms

Design, Performance, Experimentation

Keywords

scientific computing, high performance computing, cloud computing, fault tolerance, checkpoint restart, asynchronous checkpointing, adaptation to access pattern

1. INTRODUCTION

Scientific and data-intensive computing have matured over the last years in all fields of science and industry. They provide an indispensable tool for new insight and solutions to complex problems through modeling, simulation and data analysis. From private-owned data-centers to leadership-class supercomputing facilities, the drive for more computational capabilities has made petascale architectures a reality [2], with predictions of reaching exascale by the end of this decade [22].

Such an explosion of scale introduces many challenges, among which a crucial challenge is *fault tolerance*. With failure rates predicted in the order of tens of minutes [22] and applications running for extended periods of time over a large number of nodes, an assumption about complete reliability is highly unrealistic. Thus, one must consider failures as rather the norm than the exception. Furthermore, since application processes are tightly coupled and depend on each other to make progress with the computation, the failure of one process eventually leads to the failure of all processes. Thus, for the class of problems that we consider, fault tolerance becomes particularly difficult.

Checkpoint-Restart (CR) [14] is a popular approach to provide fault-tolerance for scientific applications. Fault tolerance is achieved by saving recovery information periodically during failure-free execution and restarting from that information in case of failures, in order to minimize the wasted computational time and resources. Although alternatives to CR based on redundancy [7, 30]) have been considered before, such approaches have rarely been adopted in practice for scientific applications due to high performance and resource overhead.

Faced with increasing scale, achieving efficient CR becomes a challenging task. Simple approaches such as synchronous checkpointing become unfeasible: due to high checkpointing frequency, the application would spend the majority of time taking checkpoints rather that running useful computations, with dump times predicted by Jones et al. [21] in the order of several hours. Thus, it becomes increasingly important to devote attention to asynchronous mechanisms that parallelize the checkpointing and computations in order to hide the checkpointing latency. This however is a nontrivial task: it implies capturing and storing the the state of a computation while allowing the computation to progress at the same time. Since this state is mostly composed of allocated memory (used henceforth to refer to the state itself), the checkpointing process and the computation will compete for this memory, which implies the need to minimize potential conflicts.

An important factor that augments this issue is *the need to operate with scarce resources*. Although large-scale datacenters have a lot of memory, this is a precious resource that is expensive to leverage for potential memory copies that help diminish the conflicts between the computation and checkpointing. This happens for several reasons. First, problem sizes attacked by modern applications have been growing fast, causing a declining memory bytes-to-FLOP ratio: from 0.85 for the No. 1 machine on Top500 in 1997 to 0.01 for projected exa-flop machines [3]. Thus, more and more memory is needed for the computation itself, leaving little extra memory for other operations. Second, extra memory generates operational costs either in terms of energy consumption or direct extra charges to users. The latter aspect is of particular interest in the context of HPC cloud platforms, which are increasingly considered as a cost-effective alternative for running HPC applications. Under such circumstances, virtual machine (VM) instances are more expensive the more memory they provide, prompting the need to provide a configuration where the application uses as little extra memory as possible besides what is absolutely need.

In this paper we propose *Adaptive Incremental Checkpointing* (AI-Ckpt), an asynchronous checkpointing runtime specifically designed to operate with scarce extra memory/local storage. Unlike conventional approaches, we introduce a novel checkpointing strategy that is highly versatile: it dynamically adapts to the access pattern of the application and predicts future memory accesses in order to minimize the interference of the background checkpointing process on the application.

We summarize our contributions below:

- We present a series of design principles that facilitate efficient asynchronous checkpointing. In particular, we leverage the assumption that for the iterative application class we consider, first-time writes to memory regions that need to be checkpointed asynchronously generate the same kind of interference as for the previous iterations and thus it is possible to commit the checkpointing data to stable storage in an optimized order that avoids memory access contention between the application execution and the checkpointing process.

- We show how to materialize these design principles in practice through a series of algorithmic descriptions, that are then applied to implement a checkpointing runtime library capable of tracking both user-defined memory contents explicitly or dynamic memory allocations implicitly (Sections 3.3 and 3.4).

- We evaluate our approach in a series of experiments, using both synthetic benchmarks and two real-life scientific applications. These experiments demonstrate significant improvement in overall checkpointing time, while reducing at the same time the negative impact of checkpointing overhead on the performance of the application (Section 4).

2. RELATED WORK

The simplest way to deal with CR is to leave the this issue to the application developer, which is known as *application-*

level checkpointing. In this case, checkpointing can be hand-optimized by leveraging application-specific properties, however at the cost of added complexity that can become prohibitively expensive [24]. At the other extreme is *system-level checkpointing*. In this case, checkpointing is completely transparent with respect to the application, however it is inherently difficult to make feasible because of much larger state size [28] that needs to be saved and the need to employ a checkpointing protocol [14] to guarantee consistency. To fill the gap between the two, an alternative is to provide checkpointing through a run-time library: the checkpoint contents and the places where checkpoints should be taken are application defined, but the how to save the checkpointing data is the responsibility of the system. This is called *user-defined* checkpointing and is employed in several approaches [6, 25].

Regardless of the employed approach, the checkpointing data needs to be saved in a persistent fashion to stable storage that can survive failures. Given the huge amount of checkpointing data that needs to be saved and the widening gap between computational capabilities and I/O bandwidth, this can quickly lead to unacceptable overheads and poor scalability.

One direction that can be explored in order to alleviate this issue is how to reduce the checkpoint sizes. In this context, *incremental checkpointing* was proposed: it is based on the idea that checkpointing data does not fully change from one checkpoint to another, thus storing only incremental differences is enough to restart. Incremental approaches can be broadly classified into two categories: *page-based* and *deduplication-based*. Page-based approaches [31, 17] trap writes to memory in order track all changes and build a set of dirty pages that need to be saved. De-duplication based approaches [4] on the other hand identify differences by means of computation (most often hashing). It is also possible to combine these approaches into hybrid schemes, e.g. hybrid page-based/deduplication-based schemes [16] or hybrid incremental/full checkpointing schemes [32]. Furthermore, de-duplication can be extended beyond the scope of a single process by identifying memory pages with identical content across groups of processes [27]. In either case, incremental checkpointing can complemented with compression techniques [26] to further reduce the checkpoint sizes.

Another direction that helps alleviate the overhead of checkpointing is to depart from synchronous checkpointing. One idea in this context is to design quasi-synchronous checkpointing algorithms that prevent contention to stable storage [23]. Another idea is to use multi-level checkpointing [6, 25, 12], i.e. dump the checkpointing data on fast local storage and then asynchronously flush this data to global storage. Dorier et al. [13] have shown significant benefits of this idea for multi-core architectures, however at the expense of using a large shared memory buffer where the checkpointing data from all cores is aggregated. To limit the memory usage and overhead of copies, a third possible idea is to avoid blocking the application during checkpointing altogether, by using asynchronous techniques such as *copy-on-write*.

Extensive related work has also been undertaken in the area of *live migration*, in particular *pre-copy* [10] and its derivatives. Like asynchronous checkpointing, precopy aims to transfer the memory contents from a source to a destination while the source continues execution and potentially changes the contents. However, the goal here is to converge to a state where both source and destination have identical memory contents in order to be able to transfer control to the destination and continue execution from there. The convergence does not imply any ordering constraints and in fact it is beneficial to delay transferring frequently changed contents [10, 20, 29]. On the other hand, in the case of asynchronous checkpointing, the memory contents cannot be overwritten before it was transferred to the checkpoint, which introduces additional ordering constraints and thus makes the problem more difficult.

Our own work focuses on efficient asynchronous checkpointing in spite of limited extra available memory. We believe the key to do so is to adapt to the access pattern of the application in order to leverage the little spare extra memory as efficiently as possible for copy-on-write. Although there are several established ways to reason about memory access patterns, notably the working set model [11] and by extension to our context the writable working set [10], the synchronization issues raised by asynchronous checkpointing shift the focus to ordering rather than frequency of use (in particular, only first time writes between checkpoint requests need to be considered - see Section 3.1). To our best knowledge, we are the first to formulate the assumptions and explore the benefits of adapting to such specific access pattern requirements and ordering constraints.

3. OUR APPROACH

This section presents the general design principles with an algorithmic description and shows how to implement and integrate them in a typical large scale distributed architecture.

3.1 Design principles

Define and manage protected memory regions. AI-Ckpt enables both user-defined checkpointing and transparent checkpointing. In case of the former, it is the responsibility of the user to define what memory regions are important and needed on restart, which is achieved by using specific memory allocation primitives. In case of the latter, AI-Ckpt automatically captures all memory allocations and considers the requested regions important for restart. Regardless of how such memory regions were defined, they are directly managed by AI-Ckpt, as detailed below. Henceforth we call such memory regions "protected".

Leverage dirty-page tracking to capture write access pattern and checkpoint increments asynchronously. We leverage dirty page tracking in order to simultaneously enable both incremental and asynchronous checkpointing. This works as follows: whenever a checkpointing request is received, all memory regions managed by AI-Ckpt are marked as read-only. At the same time, in background, all pages that were modified so far (i.e. marked as "dirty") are flushed to stable storage. Initially, any new protected memory region is marked as read-only. The application does not block during the checkpoint request. Instead, any write to protected memory regions is trapped and handled in a special fashion. First of all, the corresponding page is marked as "dirty" for the next checkpoint request. When this next checkpoint request eventually arrives, it is trivial to establish what pages were modified since the last checkpoint by simply checking their dirty status. Second, it can happen that

the background checkpointing has not managed to flush the page yet. In this case, it is not possible to simply continue with the write, as doing so will corrupt the content that is expected to be flushed. To deal with this issue, there are two options: either wait until the page was successfully flushed or employ copy-on-write. Finally, once the page has been properly handled, the write protection is lifted and the write to the page (and any other subsequent writes) can continue normally.

Note that asynchronous checkpointing is susceptible to jitter, which for HPC applications is particularly problematic [19] due to the tightly-coupled nature that leads to accumulation of delays. In our context, it is not enough to hide the latency of transfers between memory and persistent storage using traditional approaches such as dedicated I/O cores, because an important source of jitter is the delays caused by waiting. Thus, for the rest of this section we concentrate on this aspect.

Use bounded copy-on-write to avoid wait delays. A popular technique to avoid waiting is to simply create a private copy of the page and apply the write there, which is known as *copy-on-write*. In our case, is not possible to employ copy-on-write in the traditional sense, because this would disrupt the address space expected by the application. Thus, the only possibility left is to create a private copy for the background checkpointing process and perform the actual write on the original page. This works only if the original page is not already in the process of being flushed, otherwise a wait is necessary. Furthermore, this approach cannot be abused indefinitely to avoid waiting: besides the obvious limitation of spare memory available other than for application needs, too much copy-on-write could potentially have a high negative impact on performance that offsets the benefits of avoiding a wait. Thus, we limit the amount of memory available for copy-on-writes to a fixed value that can be configured by the user before launching the application.

Adapt dirty page flushing to access pattern. In its simplest form, the strategy used to flush dirty pages follows a predefined order that is independent of the access pattern. Although quite popular and easy to implement, such an approach is not feasible if operating under a limited amount of memory reserved for copy-on-write. This results from the fact that once the copy-on-write memory buffer is full, the application has to wait until either the page it is trying to write has been flushed or enough free space was released back to the copy-on-write buffer (which enables it to perform a new copy-on-write and thus avoid waiting).

Obviously, a strategy that does not care about the access pattern can hit on the worst case scenario where it flushes all other pages except the page that is waited for or any of the pages that triggered a copy-on-write. To eliminate this effect, we propose a strategy that adapts to the access pattern. More specifically, if the application is waiting for a page, we reschedule that page such that it is flushed as soon as possible. Even if the application is not waiting for any page, we still prefer pages that triggered copy-on-write, as this keeps the buffer free for "dark times" when frequent copy-on-writes might quickly fill it up.

Leverage access pattern history to optimize flushing. Scientific high performance computing applications are typ-

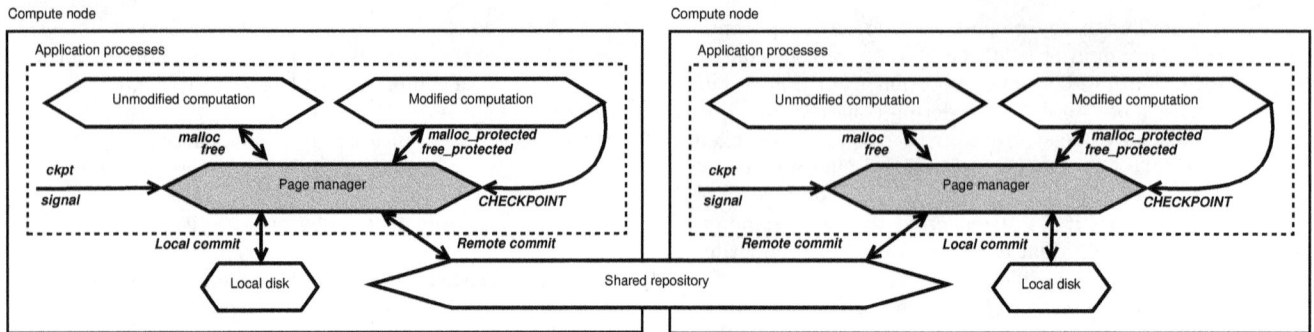

Figure 1: Distributed architecture that integrates our approach via the page manager (dark background).

ically iterative: each process first synchronizes with other processes (typically by message passing), then performs a complex computation on some in-memory data (which involves an alteration of a significant part of it). Most commonly, after a predefined amount of iterations was completed, all processes are checkpointed.

Given this repetitive nature, processes tends to generate highly similar access patterns between checkpoints. Thus, we propose to leverage this fact to further enhance the ability to adapt to the access pattern. Since only first-time writes to memory pages can introduce delays between consecutive checkpoint requests, we propose to record for all such first time writes *when* they happened and under *what circumstances*.

Although we could record the exact timestamp, for simplification reasons we consider that the access order is enough to estimate the "when". With respect to the circumstances, we are interested in the type of interference that this access caused to the asynchronous checkpointing process. This translates to several possible scenarios: (1) a copy-on-write was performed for the page; (2) the application had to wait for the page to be flushed first (because no more copy-on-write slots were available or because the page was in the process of being written to storage); (3) the page was accessed while the checkpointing was still in progress but it didn't trigger any copy-on-write or wait because it was flushed before; and finally (4) the page was accessed after the checkpointing has completed.

We maintain this information for the whole duration between two consecutive checkpoint requests, which we will herein refer to as *epoch*. Armed with this knowledge, we aim to minimize the interference that the application and the background checkpointing process experience. Based on the assumption that page accesses exhibit a similar behavior to that recorded in the previous epoch, we first commit to storage preferentially those pages that have history of "bad behavior" (i.e. caused waits or copy-on-writes) and only then proceed to commit those pages that had a "good behavior". Furthermore, when multiple pages exhibit a similar behavior, we prefer the page that was accessed the earliest.

A detailed algorithmic description of how this works is presented in Section 3.3. Note that for simplification reasons, we describe here only the case when the epoch matches the iterative behavior of the application (i.e. checkpoints requested every N iterations). In order to deal with "unaligned" epochs, one potential solution is to maintain enough past first-time writes to cover a full iteration, then use this

information to "align" the epoch to the iterative behavior (e.g. based on its first few writes). However, providing such a solution is outside the scope of this work.

3.2 Architecture

A simplified distributed architecture that integrates our approach is depicted in Figure 1.

Each compute node runs the *application processes*, which include either a *modified* or *unmodified* computation. In the first case, the application directly controls what memory regions are protected (using malloc_protected and free_protected). In the second case, memory management is handled transparently by capturing all malloc/calloc/realloc as well as free calls.

All memory pages that correspond to the protected memory regions are monitored by the *page manager*, which is the central actor of our approach and is responsible to implement our adaptive asynchronous checkpointing approach. The moment when to initiate the checkpointing is determined either explicitly by the application (which can directly call the CHECKPOINT primitive) or by any other external process (by sending a signal to the page manager, which will then internally call the CHECKPOINT primitive).

The page manager is designed in a modular fashion such that it is easy to plug in different storage backends where the dirty pages can be committed. These can range from POSIX-enabled filesystems (local file systems or parallel file systems deployed remotely, e.g. *PVFS* [9]) to specialized high-availability cloud repositories (such as *Amazon S3* [5]). Furthermore, it can easily complement dedicated checkpointing repositories designed for specific roles (such as virtual disk snapshotting [28]).

Also note that although local storage is particularly attractive as a place to store checkpoints (because it is much faster and more scalable compared to parallel file systems or other conventional remote storage options), it is prone to failures and thus unreliable. However, there are several options to overcome this issue, with data replication on different nodes being the most straight-forward. More cost-effective solutions based on erasure codes are also possible in order to reduce both performance overhead and storage space requirements, as demonstrated by our previous work [18].

3.3 Zoom on the page manager

The *page manager* consists of two independent modules that run concurrently and compete for access to the monitored memory pages: (1) a module that asynchronously commits all dirty pages accumulated at the moment when a checkpoint is requested (ASYNC_COMMIT); and (2) a module that traps all first writes during application runtime after the checkpoint was requested (PROTECTED_PAGE_HANDLER).

The application can initiate a new checkpoint by calling the CHECKPOINT primitive (Algorithm 1). Upon receipt of this request, the page manager first checks if the previous checkpoint is still in progress ($CheckpointInProgress =$ **true**), waiting for it to complete if this is the case. Once the previous checkpoint was successfully committed to storage, it initializes three data structures used by the two modules to synchronize: $Dirty$, which represents the set of all dirty pages, accessed after the CHECKPOINT call, $AT[p]$ which represents the type of access that was triggered by a page p in $Dirty$ and finally $Index[p]$ which represents the order of p in $Dirty$.

Algorithm 1 Initiate a new checkpoint

1: **procedure** CHECKPOINT
2:     **if** $CheckpointInProgress$ **then**
3:         **wait until** $CheckpointInProgress =$ **false**
4:     **end if**
5:     $LastDirty \leftarrow Dirty$
6:     $LastAT \leftarrow AT$
7:     $LastIndex \leftarrow Index$
8:     $Dirty \leftarrow \emptyset$
9:     $AccessOrder \leftarrow 0$
10:     **for all** $p \in Pages$ **do**
11:         write protect p
12:         $AT[p] \leftarrow UNTOUCHED$
13:         $Index[p] \leftarrow 0$
14:     **end for**
15:     **for all** $p \in LastDirty$ **do**
16:         $State[p] \leftarrow PAGE\_SCHEDULED$
17:     **end for**
18:     $CheckpointInProgress \leftarrow$ **true**
19:     notify ASYNC_COMMIT
20: **end procedure**

The type of access triggered by a page p can take one of the following values: $UNTOUCHED$, which is the initial value and means the page was not yet accessed; COW, which means p has triggered a copy-on-write; $WAIT$, which means PROTECTED_PAGE_HANDLER had to wait until p was committed; $AVOIDED$, which means p was accessed after it was committed, but before the checkpointing process has finished; and finally $AFTER$, which means p was accessed after the checkpointing process has successfully completed.

Each of $Dirty$, AT and $Index$ has a corresponding data structure prefixed by $Last$, which has the same semantics as the original except for the fact that it represents the statistics of previous epoch rather than the current one. Finally, a fourth data structure $State[p]$ describes the state of p, which can be one of the following values: $PAGE\_PROCESSED$, which is the initial value and means p was already processed by the checkpointing process (either already committed or untouched); $PAGE\_SCHEDULED$, which means p is dirty and needs to be committed (but this was not already done); and finally $PAGE\_INPROGRESS$, which means p was locked and is in the process of being committed.

Obviously, CHECKPOINT needs to reset the access type of all pages to $UNTOUHCED$ and then write protect them

in order to trap all future modifications. After resetting $Dirty$, all pages that were modified since the last checkpoint (now in $LastDirty$) will be marked as $PAGE\_SCHEDULED$. Once this step is complete, ASYNC_COMMIT can proceed to commit the dirty pages.

Algorithm 2 Handle a write to a protected page

1: **procedure** PROTECTED_PAGE_HANDLER(p)
2:     **if** $State[p] = PAGE\_SCHEDULED \wedge |CowPage| < Threshold$ **then**
3:         $CowPage[p] \leftarrow$ copy of p
4:         $AT[p] \leftarrow COW$
5:     **else if** $State[p] = PAGE\_PROCESSED$ **then**
6:         **if** $CheckpointInProgress$ **then**
7:             $AT[p] \leftarrow AVOIDED$
8:         **else**
9:             $AT[p] \leftarrow AFTER$
10:         **end if**
11:     **else**
12:         $WaitedPage \leftarrow p$
13:         **while** $State[p] \neq PAGE\_PROCESSED$ **do**
14:             wait for notification from ASYNC_COMMIT
15:         **end while**
16:         $WaitedPage \leftarrow$ **nil**
17:         $AT[p] \leftarrow WAIT$
18:     **end if**
19:     $Dirty \leftarrow Dirty \cup \{p\}$
20:     $AccessOrder \leftarrow AccessOrder + 1$
21:     $Index[p] \leftarrow AccessOrder$
22:     remove write protection from p
23: **end procedure**

In the mean time, any modification to a write protected page p will be trapped by PROTECTED_PAGE_HANDLER. This process is detailed in Algorithm 2. More specifically, if p was scheduled but not yet committed and there are enough copy-on-write slots available ($|CowPage| < Threshold$), then a new copy-on-write slot can be used. Otherwise, if p was already committed, nothing needs to be done except setting its access type to $AVOIDED$ or $AFTER$. Finally, the only possibility left is that p is in progress or there are not enough copy-on-write slots left. In this case, we need to wait until p was committed. In order to avoid waiting as much as possible, a hint is created for ASYNC_COMMIT, by assigning a special marker $WaitedPage$ to p. This marker will be used by ASYNC_COMMIT to maximize the priority of p (i.e. commit it as soon as possible). Once p has been successfully handled, it is added to the $Dirty$ set, after which its access order index is set and finally its write protection is removed.

The dirty pages are committed in an iterative fashion, as detailed in Algorithm 3. As long as there are still dirty pages left in $LastDirty$, ASYNC_COMMIT selects one such page p (using SELECT_NEXT_PAGE). If p resulted in a copy-on-write, its copy is committed and the corresponding slot released. Otherwise, p is locked (i.e. $PAGE\_INPROGRESS$), directly written to storage and then unlocked (i.e. marked as $PAGE\_PROCESSED$). In either case, p is removed from $LastDirty$ and the next iteration is started.

The central aspect of this iterative process is how to select the next page to be committed, which is detailed in Algorithm 4. Obviously, if $WaitedPage \neq$ **nil**, then $WaitedPage$ must be committed as soon as possible, in order to be able to unblock PROTECTED_PAGE_HANDLER and thus enable the

Algorithm 3 Commit modified pages asynchronously to storage

```
1:  procedure ASYNC_COMMIT
2:      while true do
3:          wait for notification from CHECKPOINT
4:          while LastDirty ≠ ∅ do
5:              p ← SELECT_NEXT_PAGE
6:              if AT[p] = COW then
7:                  commit CowPage[p] to storage
8:                  release slot of p in CowPage
9:              else
10:                 State[p] ← PAGE_INPROGRESS
11:                 commit p to storage
12:                 State[p] ← PAGE_PROCESSED
13:                 notify PROTECTED_PAGE_HANDLER
14:             end if
15:             LastDirty ← LastDirty \ {p}
16:         end while
17:         CheckpointInProgress ← false
18:     end while
19: end procedure
```

application to continue. Furthermore, if there are pages that triggered copy-on-write, they will be preferentially committed in order to release copy-on-write slots as soon as possible. If neither of these two cases applies, then a page is selected based on the access pattern exhibited by the application before the checkpoint request, under the assumption that it will reflect the future access pattern. More specifically, preference is given to the pages that were marked *WAIT*, then those pages that were marked *COW* and finally those pages that were marked *AVOIDED*. This way, the pages that could have the potentially worst interference are committed first, thus minimizing the chance of future interference. Pages that are marked *AFTER* are given the least priority, as they are likely to keep this status until the next checkpoint request and thus are not likely to generate interference. In either case, if more than one page has the same access type, preference is given to the page that was accessed the earliest before the checkpoint request (i.e. smallest *LastIndex*).

Algorithm 4 Select next page to commit to storage

```
1:  function SELECT_NEXT_PAGE
2:      if WaitedPage ∈ LastDirty then
3:          return WaitedPage
4:      end if
5:      if ∃p ∈ LastDirty | AT[p] = COW then
6:          return p
7:      end if
8:      if ∃p ∈ LastDirty | LastAT[p] = WAIT then
9:          return p | LastIndex[p] is minimal
10:     end if
11:     if ∃p ∈ LastDirty | LastAT[p] = COW then
12:         return p | LastIndex[p] is minimal
13:     end if
14:     if ∃p ∈ LastDirty | LastAT[p] = AVOIDED then
15:         return p | LastIndex[p] is minimal
16:     end if
17:     return any remaining p ∈ LastDirty
18: end function
```

3.4 Implementation

We implemented *AI-Ckpt* in form of two libraries. The first library implements the *page manager*, while exposing the CHECKPOINT primitive to the application. It also exposes two specific memory allocation/deallocation routines: malloc_protected and free_protected. These routines can be used to control directly at application-level what memory contents needs to be checkpointed.

For the case when transparency is desired, we implemented a second library that traps all dynamic memory allocations performed by the application and automatically reports all involved pages to the page manager. To this end, we built our own custom memory allocator on top of *jemalloc* [15], a scalable high performance malloc implementation designed to efficiently support concurrent allocations. The application itself needs not necessarily be linked against this second library, as it is enough to preload the library in order to replace the standard system malloc implementation. This is particularly useful when the application

The page manager was implemented from scratch using the *Boost* C++ collection of libraries, which introduces several optimized implementations of hash tables and balanced trees that we used to adopt the algorithms presented in Section 3.3 with minimal overhead.

In order to trap writes to memory, we rely on the mprotect system call to mark specific pages as read only. If the application attempts to write to such pages, the kernel will trigger a SIGSEGV signal, which we trap using a custom signal handler that implements PROTECTED_PAGE_HANDLER (Algorithm 2). This mechanism involves certain non-trivial aspects that require closer consideration. In particular, if the application passes read-only memory regions to certain system calls that are supposed to write to the memory (for example read), these system calls will not trigger a SIGSEGV but rather fail. To circumvent this issue, we trap such system calls and artificially trigger the necessary SIGSEGVs before launching the system call itself.

4. EVALUATION

After briefly describing the experimental setup and methodology, we evaluate in this section our approach both in synthetic and real life settings.

4.1 Experimental setup

The experiments were performed on *Grid'5000*, an experimental testbed for distributed computing that federates nine sites in France, as well as *Shamrock*, an experimental platform of the Exascale Systems group of IBM Research in Dublin, Ireland.

For the Grid'5000 experiments, we used 42 nodes of the Rennes site, each of which is equipped with a quadcore Intel Xeon X5570 x86_64 CPU, local disk storage of 500 GB (access speed ≃55 MB/s using SATA II ahci driver) and 24 GB of RAM. The nodes are interconnected with Gigabit Ethernet (measured 117.5 MB/s for TCP sockets with MTU = 1500 B with a latency of ≃0.1 ms). Each node is powered by recently updated Debian Sid distribution where OpenMPI 1.4.3 was installed and set up. In this setting, we store the checkpoints in a "conventional" fashion by using a parallel file system. To this end, we reserve 10 nodes to act at storage elements and deploy the *PVFSv2* [9] parallel file system on them. The rest of 32 nodes are used to run our MPI applications and have access to the PVFS deployment through the POSIX interface made available through the PVFS FUSE module.

The Shamrock testbed consists of 160 nodes interconnected with Gigabit Ethernet, each of which features an Intel Xeon X5670 CPU (6 cores, 12 hardware threads), HDD local storage of 1 TB and 128 GB of RAM. For the purpose of this work, we used a reservation of 28 nodes. Each node runs the Red Hat 6.2 Enterprise Linux distribution, while the MPI library installed is MPICH2 1.4.1. In this case, all nodes are reserved for running the applications, while the checkpoints are written to local storage. This setting has a potential for higher I/O scalability (as discussed in Section 3.2) and thus pushes our approach to the limits, as there are fewer opportunities to take of long I/O delays.

For the rest of this paper, we will refer to the two experimental setups simply as Grid'5000 and, respectively, Shamrock. In both setups, the memory page size used throughout our experiments is fixed at 4 KB, the default of the operating system.

4.2 Methodology

We compare three approaches throughout our evaluation:

Asynchronous incremental checkpointing using our approach.

In this setting we use AI-Ckpt to capture all dynamic memory allocations performed by the application and treat all CHECKPOINT requests according to the strategy presented in Section 3.3. We denote this setting our−approach for the rest of the paper.

Asynchronous incremental checkpointing without adaptation to access pattern.

We compare our approach with the case when the access pattern generated before the CHECKPOINT request is not taken into consideration while dumping the checkpointing data to storage. More specifically, this setting is similar to the previous one (i.e. all memory write accesses are trapped for the purpose of building the set of dirty pages that needs to be dumped to storage), except for the fact that the dirty pages are simply dumped in ascending order of their address. For the rest of this paper, we refer to this setting as async−no−pattern.

Synchronous incremental checkpointing.

The third setting we compare our approach with is a synchronous checkpointing approach that blocks inside the CHECKPOINT primitive until all checkpointing data has been successfully dumped to storage. In this setting, dirty page tracking is still used for the purpose of identifying the incremental changes since the last checkpoint, however this mechanism is greatly simplified due to the fact that the application and the checkpointing process do not compete for the dirty pages. For the rest of this paper, we refer to this setting as sync.

These approaches are compared based on the following metrics:

- *Impact on application performance*: is the performance degradation perceived by the application during checkpointing, compared to the case when no checkpointing is performed. For the purpose of this work, we are in-

terested in the impact on the total runtime of various memory-intensive benchmarking scenarios and a real HPC scientific application.

- *Checkpointing time*: is the time elapsed between the moment when the CHECKPOINT primitive has been called and all dirty pages have been successfully committed to storage. For sync, this corresponds to the duration of time during which the application blocked in the CHECKPOINT call. For the other two approaches, the duration is directly reported by *AI-Ckpt*.

- *Access type statistics*: we are interested in statistics about the types of accesses that were triggered by the page faults, as these can explain the various observable differences in checkpointing time and performance overhead. In particular, it is desirable to have as few as possible WAITs, as they are the main source of delays for the other two metrics.

4.3 Checkpointing performance of memory-intensive benchmarks

Our first series of experiments aims to gather insight into how the memory access pattern can influence asynchronous checkpointing. To this end, we have developed a memory-intensive benchmark that allocates a large memory region and then runs a number of iterations, each of which touches the full memory content byte-by-byte in a specified order. Each time a fixed number of iterations has been completed, the CHECKPOINT primitive is called. For the purpose of this work, we fixed the number of iterations to 39, with a checkpoint request issued every 10 iterations (for a total of 3 checkpoints, each of which is overlapping with the benchmark and competes for memory accesses).

In order to understand how the order of memory writes impacts the checkpointing performance, we implemented three access patterns: *Ascending* (i.e. the memory region is accessed page-by-page from the beginning towards the end), *Random* (i.e. a random permutation of the indexes of all pages is generated and used as a fixed access order for all iterations) and finally *Descending* (i.e. the memory region is accessed page-by-page from the end towards the beginning). For each page, a simple transformation is performed: all bytes are incremented by one.

Each experiment consists in running our benchmark on one of the Grid'5000 nodes, while recording the completion time and statistics about the access types triggered by the pages. The size of the memory region is fixed at 256 MB, while the size of the copy-on-write buffer is fixed at 16 MB.

The increase in execution time for the benchmark, compared to the baseline (i.e when no checkpointing is performed), is illustrated in Figure 2(a). As expected, sync has the highest overhead of all three approaches, which is maintained at constant level regardless of access pattern. Comparing our approach to async−no−pattern reveals only small differences for the *Ascending* access pattern, which is understandable considering the fact that the actual order in which the pages are accessed matches the static order in which the pages are selected by async−no−pattern. However, when this is not the case any longer (i.e. for *Random* and *Descending*), significant differences start to appear, reaching as high as 33% and respectively 50% lower overhead in favor of our approach. Compared to sync, our approach exhibits up to 72% lower overhead.

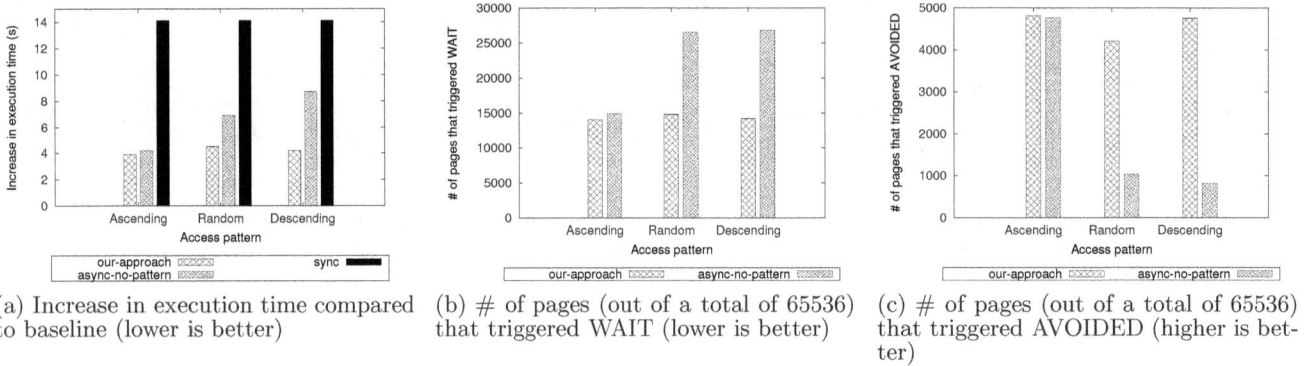

(a) Increase in execution time compared to baseline (lower is better)

(b) # of pages (out of a total of 65536) that triggered WAIT (lower is better)

(c) # of pages (out of a total of 65536) that triggered AVOIDED (higher is better)

Figure 2: Performance results and statistics about access types triggered by pages for a memory-intensive benchmark

In order to understand these findings better, we illustrate statistics about the types of accesses triggered by the pages during the runtime of the benchmark. All statistics are measured between two consecutive checkpoints and the average for the three checkpoints is reported. Since the whole memory region is changed between two consecutive checkpoints, the total number of pages that is flushed to storage remains constant at 65536 for all three checkpoints. As can be noticed, the strategy used by our approach to adapt to the access pattern brings clear advantages over async−no−pattern, especially for *Random* and *Descending*. For these last two access patterns, our approach waits on almost 50% less pages (Figure 2(b)), while managing to avoid both waits and copy-on-writes in a proportion of more than 4x the level of async−no−pattern (Figure 2(c)).

4.4 Case study: Checkpointing performance of CM1

Our next series of experiments illustrates the behavior of our proposal in real life. For this purpose we have chosen *CM1*, a three-dimensional, non-hydrostatic, non-linear, time-dependent numerical model suitable for idealized studies of atmospheric phenomena. This application is used to study small-scale processes that occur in the atmosphere of the Earth, such as hurricanes.

CM1 is representative of a large class of HPC stencil applications that model a phenomenon in time which can be described by a spatial domain that holds a fixed set of parameters in each point. The problem is solved iteratively in a distributed fashion by splitting the spatial domain into subdomains, each of which is managed by a dedicated MPI process. At each iteration, the MPI processes calculate the values for all points of their subdomain, then exchange the values at the border of their subdomains with each other. After a certain number of iterations have been successfully completed, each MPI process triggers a checkpoint, then followed by a barrier to synchronize with all other MPI processes and finally it resumes execution.

Since CM1 is written in Fortran, it was not possible to directly use malloc_protected and free_protected. However, thanks to our custom memory allocator we were able to intercept all dynamic memory allocations triggered by the allocatable data structures, which cover all checkpointing data that needs to

be saved. In order to expose the CHECKPOINT call, we implemented a minimalist wrapper library for Fortran. Using this library, we replaced the hand-optimized synchronous checkpointing implemented in CM1 with a simple call to CHECKPOINT.

For the purpose of this work, we have chosen as input data a 3D hurricane that is a version of the Bryan and Rotunno simulations [8]. We run the simulation of this 3D hurricane on Grid'5000, with each MPI process deployed on a dedicated compute node. The checkpointing frequency is set at 50 seconds of simulated time, which for this configuration results in approx. 400 MB worth of memory content that is changed, out of a total of 728 MB. We fix the total simulation time to 180s, which is enough to trigger three checkpoints.

We aim to study two aspects: (1) how well our approach scales compared to the other two approaches and (2) how the size of the copy-on-write buffer impacts the performance of our approach compared to the other two approaches. These aspects are detailed below.

4.4.1 Weak scalability

Our first experiment studies the weak scalability of our approach by solving the same problem using a different precision, in such way that the size of the subdomain solved by each process remains constant at 200x200. The experiment consists in deploying an increasing number of processes, starting from one and going up to 32. We let the application run until completion and record the increase in execution time (compared to the baseline, i.e. an execution with checkpointing deactivated) as well as the average checkpointing time for the second and third checkpoint (we omit the first checkpoint as it is a full checkpoint). The copy-on-write buffer size is fixed at 16 MB.

Results are shown in Figure 3. With respect to checkpointing time (Figure 3(a)), a sharp increase can be observed in the case of sync. This effect is caused by two factors: (1) an increasing I/O pressure is generated on the storage nodes that host PVFS as the number MPI processes increases; and (2) the small system page size causes multiple concurrent small writes to PVFS, which increases the number of multiple connections that the storage servers have to handle in parallel, thus the high overhead. On the other hand, our approach and async−no−pattern are much more scalable

162

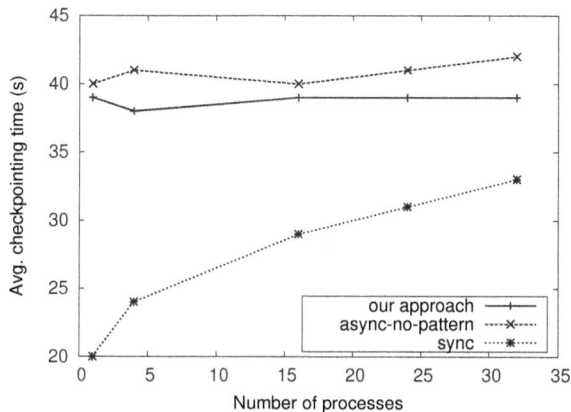

(a) Avg. checkpointing time (lower is better) (b) Increase in execution time compared to baseline (lower is better)

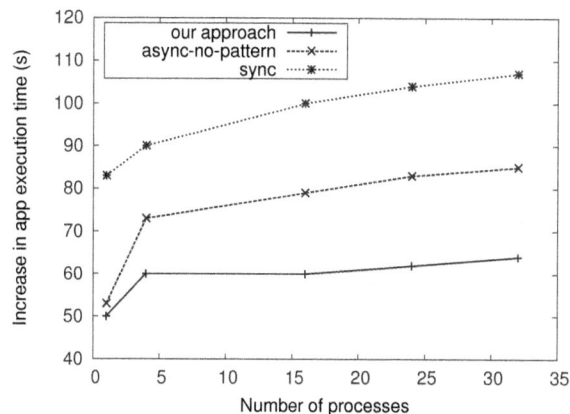

Figure 3: Weak scalability of CM1: 400 MB/728 MB worth of incremental memory changes/process, 1 process/node

with respect to checkpointing time. Although in absolute terms the checkpointing time is higher, this is not surprising considering that the checkpointing runs in parallel with the application, and thus has to compete with it for network bandwidth. Furthermore, this also explains the much better scalability: instead of concentrated bursts of I/O as generated by sync, both asynchronous approaches distribute the I/O more evenly between checkpoints, thus reducing the I/O pressure on the storage nodes. Finally we observe that our approach marginally reduces the checkpointing time compared to async−no−pattern, which is a consequence of the interference between the network traffic generated by the application and the network traffic generated by the checkpointing.

The benefit of access pattern adaptation becomes clearly visible in the increase of execution time compared to the baseline (Figure 3(a)). In this case, our approach avoids waiting for around 6000 less pages/checkpoint when compared to async−no−pattern. This directly reflects on the increase in execution time: compared to our approach, async−no−pattern is almost 33% slower when considering the extreme of 32 processes. Since sync has to wait for all pages to be committed, it is not surprising that it exhibits the worst performance: compared to our approach, it is almost 67% slower.

4.4.2 Impact of copy-on-write buffer size on checkpointing performance

Our next experiment studies the impact of copy-on-write buffer size on the performance of checkpointing. Like in the previous setting, the size of the subdomain solved by each process remains constant at 200x200, however, this time we fix the size of the problem at the maximum of 32 processes and range the buffer size from 0 MB to 256 MB. For each buffer size, we let the application run until completion and record the execution time and statistics about the number of pages that were waited for.

Results are shown in Figure 4(a). We illustrate the percentile increase in checkpointing overhead for both our approach and async−no−pattern when compared to sync (that is, the

difference in completion time between the asynchronous approach and baseline is divided by the difference in completion time between sync and baseline, after which it is subtracted from one and multiplied by one hundred).

As can be observed, when the copy-on-write buffer size is 0 (i.e. copy-on-write is deactivated), both asynchronous approaches perform very closely and exhibit a rather small benefit over synchronous checkpointing, barely reaching 5%. We traced back this result to the fact that of all pages that were committed, most of them had to be waited for. Thus, it seems the lack of a copy-on-write buffer limits the ability of our approach to keep up in sync with the rate of memory changes and/or survive deviations from the access pattern of the previous epoch. However, when gradually increasing the copy-on-write buffer size, a higher reduction in checkpointing overhead is noticeable for both asynchronous approaches. This reduction is especially dramatic for our approach, more than doubling at each step and keeping way ahead over async−no−pattern, which starts to see a significant reduction only beginning with 16 MB. As the copy-on-write buffer gets larger, the difference between our−approach and async−no−pattern gradually gets smaller, eventually evening out at 256 MB when the number of copy-on-write slots is high enough to avoid all page waits. According to these observations, we conclude that adaptation to access pattern has an advantage over no adaptation in all cases, with the most dramatic differences occurring for small copy-on-write buffer sizes, which gives our approach the upper edge.

4.5 Case study: Checkpointing performance of MILC

Our second case study focuses on another high performance computing application: *MIMD Lattice Computation (MILC)*. This application is particularly useful in the field of quantum chromodynamics (QCD), which describes the interactions of the quarks and gluons that form particles such as protons, neutrons and mesons.

MILC treats continuum space-time as a four-dimensional

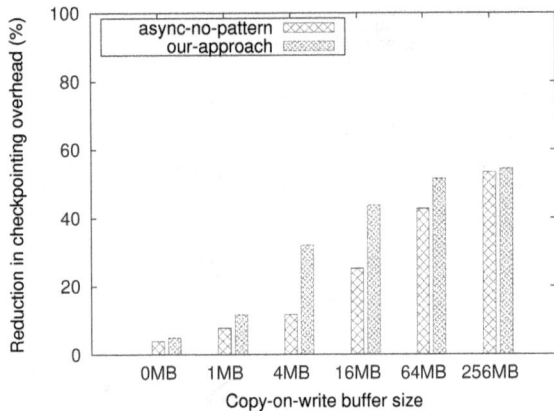

(a) CM1: 32 processes (higher is better)

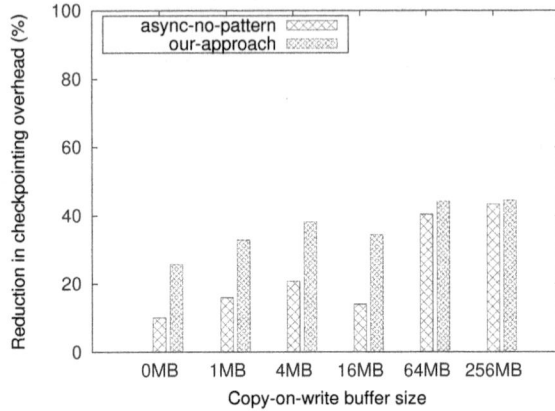

(b) MILC: 280 processes (higher is better)

Figure 4: Impact of copy-on-write buffer size on the performance of checkpointing: reduction in overhead compared to sync

hypercube lattice that is called lattice QCD. In this discretization, lattice sites carry fields representing quarks and the links between lattice sites carry gluon fields. Each link between nearest neighbors in this lattice is associated with a 3-dimensional SU(3) complex matrix for a given field. The fields evolve using an iterative procedure (configuration generation phase), and after a sufficient number of steps the system has changed enough that the new configuration is archived for further analysis. Many different physics projects can use this configuration. To speed-up this process, the lattice is split into subdomains and distributed among MPI processes.

For the purpose of this work, we adapted the NERSC-6 procurement version of the MILC benchmark [1] in order to use AI-Ckpt. To minimize modifications to the benchmark, we use our custom memory allocator to transparently intercept all memory allocations. Our only modification was to add a call to the CHECKPOINT primitive at the end of the computation of each trajectory. We run the benchmark on Shamrock, with each node running 10 MPI processes (leaving two spare I/O cores). We fix the number of trajectories to 3, which corresponds to three evenly spaced checkpoints throughout the runtime. In this scenario, each process touches approx. 830 MB out of a total allocated memory of 868 MB.

As with CM1, we are interested in both the scalability of our approach compared to the other two approaches and the impact of the copy-on-write buffer size.

4.5.1 Weak scalability

This studies the weak scalability of our approach by solving an increasingly larger size of the problem in such way that each process solves a fixed subdomain of the lattice that is 20x32x32x18 large. We deploy an increasing number of processes starting from 10 (1 node) up to 280 (28 nodes). We record the average checkpointing time and the increase in execution time (compared to the baseline, i.e. an execution with checkpointing deactivated). The copy-on-write buffer is deactivated for this scenario.

Unlike the case of CM1, we used local storage in order

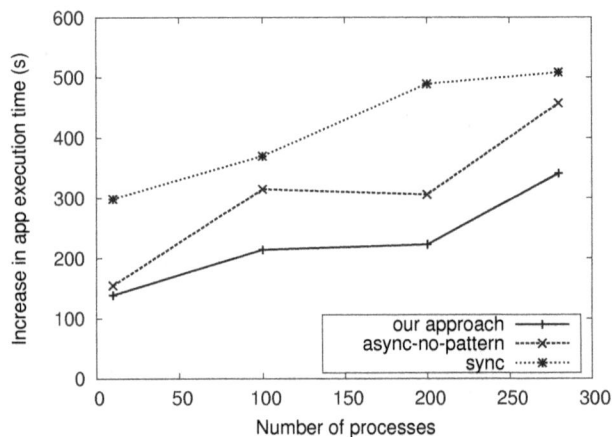

Figure 5: Weak scalability of MILC with 830 MB/866 MB worth of incremental memory changes/process, 10 processes/node: increase in execution time compared to baseline (lower is better)

to persist the modified memory pages of the checkpoints. This enables better overall I/O scalability considering the much larger scale of the problem (i.e. 20 times more checkpointing data compared to CM1) and better reflects more recent trends. On the other hand, it pushes our approach to the limits due to less I/O contention and more homogeneous I/O delays that give sync better scalability and thus better overall chances to compare more favourably to the two asynchronous approaches.

Under these circumstances, for all three approaches the average checkpointing time remains almost constant and fluctuates around $210s \pm 10s$, with a slight advantage for sync due to the fact that no overlapping occurs with the application runtime. This shows that the impact of I/O distribution and contention is of less importance as in the case of CM1.

To understand how the access pattern adaptation manages to reduce the checkpointing overhead and improve the time-to-completion for the application, we depict the increase of execution time compared to the baseline in Figure 5. As can be observed, our approach outperforms sync by more than 25%, which is more than double the improvement experienced by async−no−pattern (11%). This result is highly significant considering the use of local storage: it shows that even when I/O delays are short and do not increase with larger scale, access pattern adaptation maintains its benefits compared to sync and is more scalable than async−no−pattern, whose advantage over sync experiences an overall decreasing trend.

4.5.2 Impact of copy-on-write buffer size on check-pointing performance

Similar to the case of CM1, we study the impact of copy-on-write buffer size on the performance of checkpointing for MILC: we fix the problem size to its maximal extent (280 processes) but vary the copy-on-write buffer size.

Results are shown in Figure 4(b). Again, we illustrate the percentile increase in checkpointing overhead for both our−approach and async−no−pattern when compared to sync. Unlike the case of CM1, when the copy-on-write buffer size is 0 (i.e. copy-on-write is deactivated), a large benefit of our−approach over async−no−pattern is already visible. Thus, in this case the rate at which memory is changed and/or deviations from the access pattern of the previous epoch are much smaller. When gradually increasing the copy-on-write buffer size, both approaches experience a higher reduction in checkpointing overhead. As can be observed, our−approach constantly outperforms async−no−pattern by more than 100% up to 64 MB, when the difference between the two approaches gradually gets smaller and evens out at 256 MB. As in the case of CM1, adaptation to access pattern always outperforms no adaptation, with the largest differences observable for for small copy-on-write buffer sizes.

5. CONCLUSIONS AND FUTURE WORK

Checkpoint-Restart (CR) is a key method to provide fault tolerance for large-scale scientific applications. With increasing scale, CR faces an additional challenge: besides the implicit goal of minimizing the performance overhead during fault-free execution, it has to operate with limited extra available memory besides the one allocated by the application for computational needs.

In this paper, we have proposed *AI-Ckpt*, a runtime environment that enables asynchronous incremental checkpointing. Unlike other state-of-art CR approaches, our proposal is specifically optimized to both adapt to the current memory access pattern and learn from the previous access pattern in order to flush dirty pages during background checkpointing with minimal impact on the running application.

We demonstrated the benefits of our approach through experiments that involve dozens of nodes and hundreds of processes, using both benchmarks and real applications. Compared to naive asynchronous incremental checkpointing, we show up to 30% less checkpointing performance overhead in the real world, which grows up to 60% when compared to synchronous checkpointing. All these benefits are achievable for small copy-on-write buffers that represent less than 5% of the total application memory.

Overall, we conclude that leveraging the current and past memory access patterns during asynchronous checkpointing can significantly lower the overhead on application performance, especially for those that exhibit an iterative nature and generate repetitive memory access patterns. This idea can be further enhanced with small copy-on-write buffers to better handle unexpected deviations from the access pattern between consecutive checkpoints and thus further reduce the overhead of asynchronous checkpointing. Although this effect is naturally present even when there is no awareness of access pattern, much larger overhead reductions are possible at much smaller copy-on-write buffer sizes when leveraging the access pattern. This is a double-win scenario: the application both finishes faster and consumes less memory.

Based on these results, we plan to further explore how to leverage adaptation to the access pattern in the context of CR. In particular, for simplification reasons we scheduled the flushing of dirty pages based on access order, without taking into account the temporal aspect. Thus, one interesting direction to explore is whether introducing timestamps makes room for further optimizations.

Acknowledgments

This work was supported in part by the Joint Laboratory for Petascale Computing, an initiative of INRIA, UIUC, NCSA and Argonne National Laboratory. The experiments presented in this paper were carried out using the Shamrock cluster of IBM Research, Ireland and the Grid'5000/ ALADDIN-G5K experimental testbed, an initiative of the French Ministry of Research through the ACI GRID incentive action, INRIA, CNRS and RENATER and other contributing partners (see http://www.grid5000.fr/).

6. REFERENCES

[1] Nersc 6 procurement benchmark. http://www.nersc.org.

[2] Top 500 supercomputing sites. http://top500.org.

[3] DOE Exascale Initiative Technical Roadmap. Technical report, US Department of Energy, 2009.

[4] S. Agarwal, R. Garg, M. S. Gupta, and J. E. Moreira. Adaptive incremental checkpointing for massively parallel systems. In *ICS '04: Proceedings of the 18th Annual International Conference on Supercomputing*, pages 277–286, St. Malo, France, 2004. ACM.

[5] Amazon Simple Storage Service (S3). http://aws.amazon.com/s3/.

[6] L. Bautista-Gomez, S. Tsuboi, D. Komatitsch, F. Cappello, N. Maruyama, and S. Matsuoka. FTI: High Performance Fault Tolerance Interface for Hybrid Systems. In *SC '11: Proceedings of 24th International Conference for High Performance Computing, Networking, Storage and Analysis*, pages 32:1–32:32, Seattle, USA, 2011. ACM.

[7] R. Brightwell, K. Ferreira, and R. Riesen. Transparent redundant computing with mpi. In *EuroMPI'10: Proceedings of the 17th European MPI user's group meeting conference on recent advances in the message passing interface*, pages 208–218, Stuttgart, Germany, 2010.

[8] G. H. Bryan and R. Rotunno. The maximum intensity of tropical cyclones in axisymmetric numerical model simulations. *Journal of the American Meteorological Society*, 137:1770–1789, 2009.

[9] P. H. Carns, W. B. Ligon, R. B. Ross, and R. Thakur. PVFS: A parallel file system for Linux clusters. In *Proceedings of the 4th Annual Linux Showcase and Conference*, pages 317–327, Atlanta, USA, 2000.

[10] C. Clark, K. Fraser, S. Hand, J. G. Hansen, E. Jul, C. Limpach, I. Pratt, and A. Warfield. Live migration of virtual machines. In *NSDI'05: Proceedings of the 2nd Symposium on Networked Systems Design & Implementation*, pages 273–286, Boston, USA, 2005.

[11] P. J. Denning. Working sets past and present. *IEEE Trans. Softw. Eng.*, 6(1):64–84, Jan. 1980.

[12] X. Dong, Y. Xie, N. Muralimanohar, and N. P. Jouppi. Hybrid checkpointing using emerging nonvolatile memories for future exascale systems. *ACM Trans. Archit. Code Optim.*, 8(2):6:1–6:29, June 2011.

[13] M. Dorier, G. Antoniu, F. Cappello, M. Snir, and L. Orf. Damaris: How to Efficiently Leverage Multicore Parallelism to Achieve Scalable, Jitter-free I/O. In *CLUSTER '12 - Proceedings of the 2012 IEEE International Conference on Cluster Computing*, Beijing, China, 2012.

[14] E. N. M. Elnozahy, L. Alvisi, Y.-M. Wang, and D. B. Johnson. A survey of rollback-recovery protocols in message-passing systems. *ACM Comput. Surv.*, 34:375–408, September 2002.

[15] J. Evans. A scalable concurrent malloc(3) implementation for FreeBSD. In *Proceedings of BSDCan 2006*, Ottawa, Canada, 2006.

[16] K. B. Ferreira, R. Riesen, R. Brighwell, P. Bridges, and D. Arnold. libhashckpt: hash-based incremental checkpointing using gpu's. In *EuroMPI'11: Proceedings of the 18th European MPI Users' Group Conference on Recent Advances in the Message Passing Interface*, pages 272–281, Santorini, Greece, 2011. Springer-Verlag.

[17] R. Gioiosa, J. C. Sancho, S. Jiang, F. Petrini, and K. Davis. Transparent, incremental checkpointing at kernel level: a foundation for fault tolerance for parallel computers. In *SC '05: Proc of 18th International Conference for High Performance Computing, Networking, Storage and Analysis*, pages 9:1–9:14, Seattle, USA, 2005.

[18] L. B. Gomez, B. Nicolae, N. Maruyama, F. Cappello, and S. Matsuoka. Scalable Reed-Solomon-based Reliable Local Storage for HPC Applications on IaaS Clouds. In *Euro-Par '12: 18th International Euro-Par Conference on Parallel Processing*, pages 313–324, Rhodes, Greece, 2012.

[19] T. Hoefler, T. Schneider, and A. Lumsdaine. Characterizing the influence of system noise on large-scale applications by simulation. In *SC '10: Proceedings of the 23rd ACM/IEEE International Conference for High Performance Computing, Networking, Storage and Analysis*, pages 1–11, New Orleans, USA, 2010.

[20] K. Z. Ibrahim, S. Hofmeyr, C. Iancu, and E. Roman. Optimized pre-copy live migration for memory intensive applications. In *SC '11: 24th International Conference for High Performance Computing, Networking, Storage and Analysis*, pages 40:1–40:11, Seattle, USA, 2011.

[21] W. M. Jones, J. T. Daly, and N. DeBardeleben. Application Monitoring and Checkpointing in HPC : Looking Towards Exascale Systems. In *ACM-SE '12: Proceedings of the 50th Annual Southeast Regional Conference*, pages 262–267, Tuscaloosa, USA, 2012.

[22] P. Kogge, K. Bergman, S. Borkar, D. Campbell, W. Carlson, W. Dally, M. Denneau, P. Franzon, W. Harrod, K. Hill, J. Hiller, S. Karp, S. Keckler, D. Klein, R. Lucas, M. Richards, A. Scarpelli, S. Scott, A. Snavely, T. Sterling, W. Stanley, and K. Yelick. ExaScale Computing Study: Technology Challenges in Achieving Exascale Systems. Technical report, DARPA, 2008.

[23] D. Manivannan, Q. Jiang, J. Yang, and M. Singhal. A quasi-synchronous checkpointing algorithm that prevents contention for stable storage. *Inf. Sci.*, 178(15):3109–3116, Aug. 2008.

[24] P. McGrath and B. Tangney. Scrabble: A distributed application with an emphasis on continuity. *Softw. Eng. J.*, 5(3):160–164, July 1990.

[25] A. Moody, G. Bronevetsky, K. Mohror, and B. R. d. Supinski. Design, modeling, and evaluation of a scalable multi-level checkpointing system. In *SC '10: Proceedings of the 23rd International Conference for High Performance Computing, Networking, Storage and Analysis*, pages 1–11, New Orleans, USA, 2010.

[26] B. Nicolae. On the Benefits of Transparent Compression for Cost-Effective Cloud Data Storage. *Transactions on Large-Scale Data- and Knowledge-Centered Systems*, 3:167–184, 2011.

[27] B. Nicolae. Towards Scalable Checkpoint Restart: A Collective Inline Memory Contents Deduplication Proposal. In *IPDPS '13: The 27th IEEE International Parallel and Distributed Processing Symposium*, pages 1–10, Boston, USA, 2013.

[28] B. Nicolae and F. Cappello. BlobCR: Efficient Checkpoint-Restart for HPC Applications on IaaS Clouds using Virtual Disk Image Snapshots. In *SC '11: 24th International Conference for High Performance Computing, Networking, Storage and Analysis*, pages 34:1–34:12, Seattle, USA, 2011.

[29] B. Nicolae and F. Cappello. A Hybrid Local Storage Transfer Scheme for Live Migration of I/O Intensive Workloads. In *HPDC '12: 21th International ACM Symposium on High-Performance Parallel and Distributed Computing*, pages 85–96, Delft, The Netherlands, 2012.

[30] S. Rajagopalan, B. Cully, R. O'Connor, and A. Warfield. SecondSite: Disaster Tolerance as a Service. In *VEE '12: Proceedings of the 8th ACM SIGPLAN/SIGOPS conference on Virtual Execution Environments*, pages 97–108, London, UK, 2012. ACM.

[31] M. Vasavada, F. Mueller, P. H. Hargrove, and E. Roman. Comparing different approaches for incremental checkpointing: The showdown. In *Linux'11: The 13th Annual Linux Symposium*, pages 69–79, 2011.

[32] C. Wang, F. Mueller, C. Engelmann, and S. L. Scott. Hybrid Checkpointing for MPI Jobs in HPC Environments. In *ICPADS '10: Proc. of the 16th International Conference on Parallel and Distributed Systems*, pages 524–533, Shanghai, China, 2010.

Correcting Soft Errors Online in LU Factorization

Teresa Davies
Colorado School of Mines
Golden, CO, USA
tdavies@mines.edu

Zizhong Chen
University of California, Riverside
Riverside, CA, USA
chen@cs.ucr.edu

ABSTRACT

In high-performance systems, the probability of failure is higher with more processors. Errors in calculations may occur that cannot be detected by outside means. To address this problem, we create a checksum-based approach that detects and recovers from calculation errors. We apply this approach to the LU factorization algorithm used by High Performance Linpack. Our approach has low overhead; in contrast to an existing approach that requires repeated calculation, it repeats only a fraction of the calculation during recovery. Because of error propagation, the existing approach has to repeat calculations when soft errors occur. Our approach detects and corrects errors during the calculation before they are propagated. The frequency of checking can be adjusted for the error rate, resulting in a flexible method of fault tolerance.

Categories and Subject Descriptors

C.4 [**Performance of Systems**]: Fault tolerance

General Terms

Reliability

Keywords

High Performance Linpack benchmark; LU factorization; fault tolerance; algorithm-based recovery; soft errors

1. INTRODUCTION

Modern computer systems are becoming more vulnerable to soft errors because they contain larger numbers of smaller, denser components. The more components there are, the more likely a failure. Dealing with soft errors is becoming more of a concern [4, 5, 13, 22, 23], with both hardware and software solutions proposed. Although methods exist to detect errors in stored values, the more calculations there are, the more likely it is that an error will go undetected. If a soft error changes the data only, it is possible that the error will be completely undetected until the calculation returns the wrong answer at the end, because no other way of detecting soft errors exists [10, 17]. For a large matrix operation, one error could be propagated to a large fraction of the matrix. Therefore, it is useful to be able to detect soft errors online after they occur, and to recover the correct value in order to continue. A method that is designed for a specific matrix operation will have lower overhead than a more general technique.

An existing technique is algorithm-based fault tolerance (ABFT) [3, 11, 18, 24], which puts a checksum onto a matrix, and the sum will stay correct through an operation on the matrix. If the sum is incorrect at the end of the calculation, it indicates that an error occurred. Depending on the approach and the type of error, the sum may be used to determine the correct values, or the calculation may be repeated. Using a sum to correct an error at the end of the calculation is limited in the number of errors it can handle, so it is likely that, when ABFT is used, an error will cause the entire calculation to be repeated. With the LU factorization, error propagation happens frequently enough to make it impossible to recover from the checksums at the end of the calculation. Instead, we will recover as soon as errors occur.

In the LU factorization, a single error can be propagated to large sections of the matrix [12]. This can include affecting the checksums as well. Soft errors are not easily detected, so it is necessary to check the matrix for correctness often enough that the errors will not be propagated to the extent that they can no longer be recovered. We have found that different sections of the matrix have different sensitivity to errors, so that some sections do not have to be verified as frequently.

Previously, a global checksum of a matrix has been used to make the LU factorization able to recover from fail-stop failures [9]. This approach used a single checksum, and relied on getting the information about a failure from some other source. When a process dies, it is apparent that there has been a failure, and it should also be possible to obtain the information about which process has failed. In contrast, soft errors often do not result in any noticeable sign that an error has occurred. The only indication of a soft error might be that the result of a calculation is wrong. Therefore, in our approach it is necessary to have two separate checksums of each matrix element - one that indicates that an error occurred, and one that can be used to recover. The matrix elements must be periodically verified using one set of checksums. If the check shows that an error has occurred, the first checksums are not enough to recover from it; the checksum does not match, indicating an error occurred, but it does not contain enough information to also repair the error. A second set of checksums is needed to allow recovery to take place.

We have taken the idea of a checksum on a matrix and extended it, finding the way to set up a checksum on a matrix so that it is correct throughout the calculation. For the LU factorization, we are able to provide fault tolerance using a row checksum, where the sums are of elements in the same row. The global checksum alone can be used to recover from the loss of a process, assuming that the system can tell the program when a failure occurs. With multiple checksums we can both detect and recover errors - with soft errors, there is no other way to detect them, so at least two checksums are needed.

This approach has low overhead. With ABFT the entire calculation has to be repeated when there are more errors than the number of checksums can recover. In our method, a single iteration - a small fraction - of the calculation is repeated when an error occurs. Therefore the expected amount of recalculation due to errors is much smaller than with ABFT. The overhead when no error occurs is $O(\frac{1}{N})$, where the matrix is $N \times N$, and can be adjusted to the error rate.

In this paper, we

- show that certain sections of the matrix do not have to be verified as frequently, making the overhead of verification lower

- prove that a large section of the sums that need to be verified for soft error detection are zeros after a certain point in the calculation, making the verification have lower overhead

- demonstrate that the checksum is not automatically maintained during the LU factorization

- set up global and local checksums in such a way that they are maintained after each iteration of the HPL algorithm

- demonstrate that a soft error can be detected, located, and corrected in the middle of the computation with lower overhead than ABFT

In section 2 other approaches are discussed. In section 3 the type of failure is discussed. In section 4 the algorithm HPL is described. In section 5 the details of our method are described, including how the checksum is used and how errors are detected and recovered. In section 6 the theoretical performance of the method is given. In section 7 the experimental performance is given.

2. RELATED WORK

To both detect and correct soft errors, multiple checksums are needed. One approach is to use differently weighted checksums of the same elements in the matrix [6,8,14]. This approach requires finding optimal weights for numerical stability, which is a difficult problem. Our approach uses only single checksums of different sets of elements to achieve the same effect as multiple checksums. One checksum is kept of the local matrix on each process, and another checksum is

kept of the global matrix. The local checksum can be used to detect errors, and the global checksum to correct them. Any approach that uses a single checksum could be extended to use multiple weighted checksums to provide tolerance of more errors.

Algorithm-based fault tolerance [1–3, 15, 18, 19, 21] is a technique that has been used to detect miscalculations in matrix operations. This technique consists of adding a checksum row or column to the matrices being operated on. For many matrix operations, some sort of checksum can be shown to be correct at the end of the calculation, and can be used to find errors after the calculation is done. It can be used for the LU factorization with a single additional row and column added onto the matrix, which has the sum of all elements in its row or column.

The original algorithm-based fault tolerance uses a checksum to determine at the end whether the calculation had been successful or not. If the sums are not consistent with the final result, the calculation is repeated. If the probability of a failure is p, the expected number of runs is $\frac{1}{1-p}$. If p is small, then the overhead of using this method on average is low, but the cost of repeating is larger the higher the probability of failure. The probability of failure increases linearly with the number of processors.

3. FAILURE MODEL

3.1 Types of errors

One of the main types of errors that can occur is a process failure, also called a fail-stop failure. This work does not explicitly deal with fail-stop failures; however, this technique can be used to recover the data lost when a process fails [9]. The recovery procedure is the same whether an entire process is lost or the local matrix on a process is corrupted. Either way, the global checksum and the surviving processes can be used to recover from the error.

The type of failure that we handle with this technique is a fail-continue failure, also called a soft error, where the failure is not evident except by the fact that the application has the wrong data.

3.2 Soft error

We use a set of checksums to both detect and correct soft errors. Errors can be corrected by this technique when we assume that they can occur in any part of the matrix. Once a section of the matrix is factored, it is not modified again. Errors that occur in the factored parts of the matrix are not critical to correct, so they do not have to be detected immediately. In fact, errors in this part of the matrix can be left until the end of the factorization to correct, unless a certain pattern of multiple errors is expected. Therefore, this technique usually focuses on detecting and correcting errors in the part of the matrix that has not been completed.

We assume that the failure is not detectable from outside the application. This is different from a larger hardware failure where it is obvious from other signs where the problem is located. Because it is most likely not possible to know if or where a soft error has occurred, an important part of our technique is verifying the results of the calculation periodically. An error is detected by a failure in verification, which indicates that recovery is necessary.

In HPL, error propagation can cause a single error to affect nearly the entire matrix. Therefore, the verification must be done often enough to catch errors before they can affect enough of the matrix to make recovery impossible. The results of a part of the calculation can be verified before they are broadcast to other processes, which is when propagation occurs. When an error is detected before it affects multiple processes in a row of the process grid, it is still possible to recover.

4. ERROR PROPAGATION IN HIGH PERFORMANCE LINPACK

HPL performs a dense LU decomposition using a right-looking algorithm. The matrix is stored in a two-dimensional block-cyclic data distribution [9]. Matrices are often stored in 2D block cyclic fashion [7, 16, 20]. These are the most important features of HPL to this technique.

Generally matrix operations are done in parallel because the matrix involved is very large. The matrix will most likely not fit in the memory of one processor, and so it will be distributed so that each process has one part of the matrix. Therefore an important part of recovering from errors is the fact that the affected part of the matrix is not duplicated anywhere else, and has to be recovered.

4.1 Right-looking LU factorization

The right-looking algorithm is the version of LU factorization that updates the trailing matrix, unlike other versions. In other versions, it is possible to put off the update of a particular section of the matrix until just before that section is going to be factored. However, this approach means that large sections of the matrix are unchanged after each iteration. Only the processes holding a small section of the matrix are working at any particular time, making the efficiency of these versions lower. Our technique requires the matrix to be updated each step, which is what is done in the right-looking version.

The factorization in HPL is done by iterating over panels, which are sections of columns the width of the block size. An example panel is shown being factored in figure 1. Each iteration takes its panel from the trailing matrix of the previous iteration (section A_{22} in figure 1), so the height of the panel decreases by one block size each iteration.

Algorithm 1 An iteration has three main steps that are of interest for our technique.

---

    for i = 0 to N/nb **do**
        factor the panel at (i*nb, i*nb)
        broadcast the panel to the rest of the matrix
        update the matrix using the factored panel
    end for

Each step - the panel factorization, the row panel update, and the trailing matrix update - changes only its particular section of the matrix. After the first two steps, matrix elements are broadcast to be used in the updates. The broadcast is where errors can be propagated outside of processes, which is when an error could potentially become unrecoverable. Since we use row checksums only, we are only concerned about error propagation along rows. It turns out that propagation along rows can only happen during the broadcast after the panel factorization. Therefore, it is sufficient to verify the checksums only after the panel factorization of each iteration in order to guarantee that all errors will be

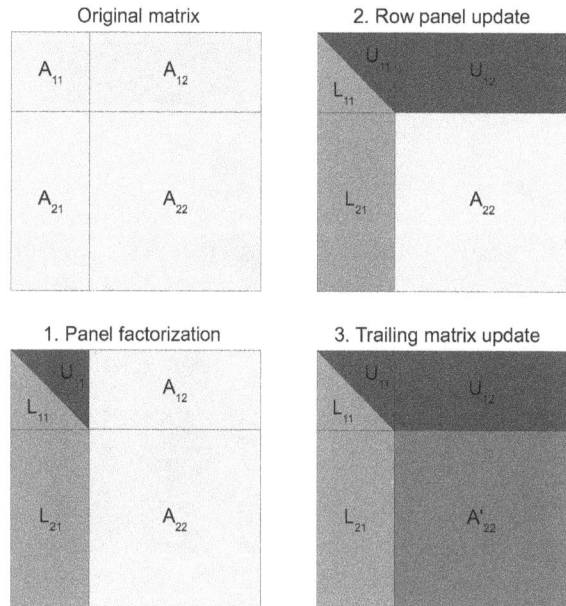

Figure 1: Relevant sections of a matrix in the factorization of one panel.

detected while it is still possible to recover successfully, as long as only one error occurs. It is necessary to verify the trailing matrix with a frequency depending on the failure rate.

Algorithm 2 Error checking is added to the main factorization loop as shown

---

    for i = 0 to N/nb **do**
        factor the panel at (i*nb, i*nb)
        verify the panel
        if the panel contains an error **then**
            perform recovery
            return to the beginning of this loop iteration
        end if
        broadcast the panel to the rest of the matrix
        update the matrix using the factored panel
        if it is time to verify the entire matrix **then**
            verify the matrix
            if the matrix contains an error **then**
                perform recovery
            end if
        end if
    end for

In algorithm 2, the step "verify the panel" must be done to ensure that the values that are being broadcast are correct. It uses the local checksums to verify the result of the panel factorization. The step "verify the matrix" means checking the trailing matrix for correctness. This step takes longer than verifying just the panel, and it is less critical. An error outside of the current panel will only make recovery impossible if it is a second error that occurs before the first error can be corrected. Therefore, the frequency of verifying the trailing matrix depends on the expected error rate.

If a recovery is needed, it is done using the global checksums. A recovery just after the panel factorization will ac-

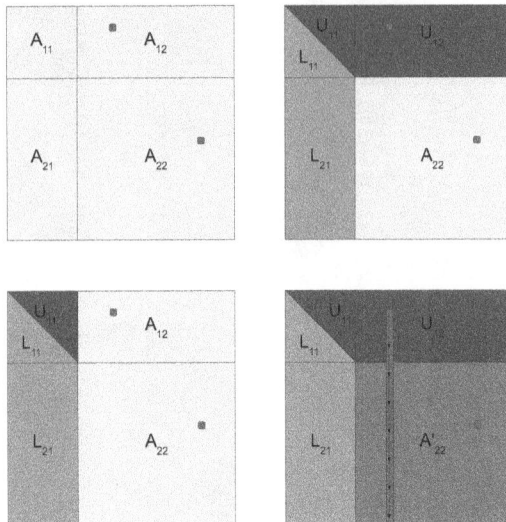

Figure 2: An error in the row panel is propagated down the column. If there is a second error in the matrix, it creates a situation where there are two errors in the same row, making recovery impossible.

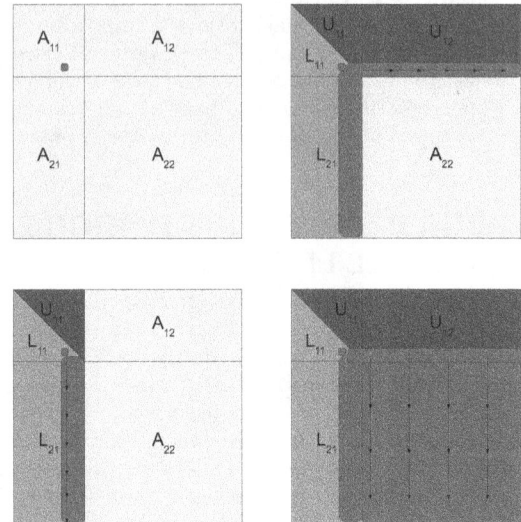

Figure 3: A single error can be propagated to a very large section of the matrix when it occurs in the panel.

tually undo the result of the factorization: at this point in the loop iteration, only the panel has been factored, and the panel has just been shown to contain an error. Therefore, the entire panel must be replaced with the recovered version. The recovery is done using elements that are still in the state from the previous iteration, so the result will be to recover the panel from before it was factored.

However, in the case an error is found during the trailing matrix verification, this is the last step in the loop: the entire matrix has now been updated to the next step in the factorization. Therefore, the entire matrix is consistent with the end of an iteration, and the recovery of any part of the matrix will not require any work to be repeated.

The recovery depends on there not being uncorrected errors outside of the panel. This error check must be done periodically, with a frequency determined by the error rate. If the entire matrix is verified occasionally, then when an error is found in the panel we can assume that the other elements involved in the recovery will be correct. There is still a chance of an error occurring between the last full verification and the recovery, but it is very unlikely.

4.2 Error Propagation

Errors that occur in different sections of the matrix have different levels of risk to the correctness of the calculation. Step 1 of figure 1, the column panel factorization, is the most important to verify. Errors that occur here will be propagated across the rows. This panel is used to update the rest of the matrix. An error will affect the elements in the same row to the right of the affected element. Because the global checksum is across rows, when more than one process in a row is affected, recovery becomes impossible. This panel is factored separately, then it is broadcast to the rest of the matrix. The verification must be done before the broadcast to prevent errors from being propagated. Because of the way the local checksum is set up, the stored sums for

most of this panel will be zeros as long as no error occurred. This check is the shortest, because only one block of sums need to be recalculated.

Step 2 is the row panel update, and is also sensitive to errors. An error in this section is not immediately damaging. It is propagated down the column it occurs in, which does not make recovery impossible. However, since the entire column is affected, a second error in a different location would make recovery impossible unless it happened to occur in the same process column. Therefore it is important to check this section for correctness as well, although it is possible to lengthen the period between verifications depending on the error rate. The sums in this panel all need to be recalculated for the verification, so it takes longer than the column panel verification. Figure 2 shows a situation where an error in the row panel that is not corrected can be propagated in such a way that a second error will make recovery impossible.

Step 3 is the trailing matrix update, and is least sensitive to errors. An error in this section is not propagated until it becomes part of a panel in a later iteration, at which point it can be handled by the panel verification. There is still a possibility that a second error could make recovery impossible, but the probability that an error would do so is lower than for the row panel. It can be necessary to verify this section of the matrix as well, again depending on the error rate, and less frequently than the row panel verification. Again this verification takes longer than the row panel verification, because every sum in the trailing matrix must be recalculated.

Figure 3 shows how much an error is propagated when it occurs in the U section of the panel. The error is propagated down the entire column that it occurs in during the panel factorization. This is the point when it would be detected by our method, before it can become impossible to recover. The corrupted elements are in one process column, so recovery is possible. If it were not recovered at this point, the error

Figure 4: An example matrix, shown first in the original global view, then as it would be distributed on a 3×2 grid with a block size of 2.

19	3	1	12	1	16	1	3	11	0
-19	3	1	12	1	16	1	3	11	0
-19	-3	1	12	1	16	1	3	11	1
-19	-3	-1	12	1	16	1	3	11	0
-19	-3	-1	-12	1	16	1	3	11	0
-19	-3	-1	-12	-1	16	1	3	11	0
-19	-3	-1	-12	-1	-16	1	3	11	0
-19	-3	-1	-12	-1	-16	-1	3	11	0
-19	-3	-1	-12	-1	-16	-1	-3	11	0

19	3	1	3	1	12	11	0	1	16
-19	3	1	3	1	12	11	0	1	16
-19	-3	1	3	-1	-12	11	0	1	16
-19	-3	1	3	1	-12	11	0	-1	16
-19	-3	-1	-3	-1	-12	11	0	-1	-16
-19	-3	1	3	1	12	11	1	1	16
-19	-3	1	3	1	12	11	0	1	16
-19	-3	1	3	-1	-12	11	0	-1	-16
-19	-3	-1	3	-1	-12	11	0	-1	-16

Figure 5: The matrix after local sums are appended to the matrices in each process, and how this addition affects the global matrix.

19	3	22	1	3	4	1	12	13	11	0	11	1	16	17	0	0	0
-19	3	-16	1	3	4	1	12	13	11	0	11	1	16	17	0	0	0
-19	-3	-22	1	3	4	-1	-12	-13	11	0	11	1	16	17	0	0	0
-19	-3	-22	1	3	4	-1	-12	-13	11	0	11	-1	16	15	0	0	0
-19	-3	-22	-1	-3	-4	-1	-12	-13	11	0	11	-1	-16	-17	0	0	0
-19	-3	-22	1	3	4	1	12	13	11	1	12	1	16	17	0	0	0
-19	-3	-22	1	3	4	1	12	11	11	0	11	1	16	17	0	0	0
-19	-3	-22	1	3	4	-1	-12	-13	11	0	11	-1	-16	-17	0	0	0
-19	-3	-22	-1	3	2	-1	-12	-13	11	0	11	-1	-16	-17	0	0	0

19	3	22	1	12	13	1	16	17	1	3	4	11	0	11	0	0	0
-19	3	-16	1	12	13	1	16	17	1	3	4	11	0	11	0	0	0
-19	-3	-22	1	12	13	1	16	17	1	3	4	11	1	12	0	0	0
-19	-3	-22	1	12	11	1	16	17	1	3	4	11	0	11	0	0	0
-19	-3	-22	-1	-12	-13	1	16	17	1	3	4	11	0	11	0	0	0
-19	-3	-22	-1	-12	-13	-1	16	15	1	3	4	11	0	11	0	0	0
-19	-3	-22	-1	-12	-13	-1	-16	-17	1	3	4	11	0	11	0	0	0
-19	-3	-22	-1	-12	-13	-1	-16	-17	-1	3	2	11	0	11	0	0	0
-19	-3	-22	-1	-12	-13	-1	-16	-17	-1	-3	-4	11	0	11	0	0	0

would be propagated to every row in the row panel that had an error in the column panel. Finally, the error is spread to the entire trailing matrix.

5. SOFT ERROR DETECTION, LOCATION, AND CORRECTION

5.1 Checksum Setup

We use two types of checksums, global and local. The local checksum is a sum of elements in the local matrix on each process, and is stored in the same local matrix. The global checksum is a sum of local matrices, and it is stored in additional processes. The local checksum is verified periodically; if the sum is not correct, then the global sum is used for recovery. No extra communication is needed unless an error occurs.

Any checksum of elements in the same row can be maintained at the end of an iteration. However, in this technique we verify the checksums after the panel factorization, where the panel is factored but the rest of the matrix is not updated. Therefore we use local checksums by blocks - the elements in the block are added up across the row and stored just after the block, and the block size is increased by one. After the panel factorization, the checksums within the panel are correct because they involve only elements of the panel.

If an error is detected by the check after the panel factorization, the recovery will take the matrix state back to the beginning of the iteration and the panel factorization will have to be repeated. At the point just after the panel factorization, the panel only is updated (section 1 in figure 1). The global sums, which are used for recovery, have not yet been changed from their state in the previous iteration. When an error is detected in the panel, it is necessary to replace the entire panel with a recovered version due to error propagation. The recovered panel is constructed using elements that are still in the state of the previous iteration; therefore, the panel recovered will be the one from the previous iteration, and the panel factorization will have to be repeated. With this method there is no other way to recover:

any error detected in the panel factorization will require a recovery back to just before the factorization. With only one local sum, even an incorrect sum will cause a recovery, since with a single sum it is impossible to tell which element of the sum is incorrect.

Figure 4 shows an example matrix that will have a checksum added. The matrix is distributed on the process grid according to the 2D block cyclic distribution. Figure 5 shows the same matrix with row sums added to each local matrix. The elements in one block of a row of a local matrix are summed, and the result is stored just after the block that it is the sum of. The block size is increased by one so that the sums are always included with their elements in operations. Maintaining checksums at a fine-grained level requires operating on both a sum and the elements that go into it at the same time. Figure 6 shows the matrix after global sums in additional processes are added. These sums are the sum of the local matrices, stored in extra processes. In the global view of the matrix, these checksums appear to be spread out periodically through the matrix. However, where the sums are located in the global matrix does not impact their correctness.

5.2 Proof of Correctness for Checksum

Each iteration of the LU factorization operates on the trailing matrix from the previous step. Once factored, the sections of L and U are not changed again. Beginning with a matrix with row checksums, one factorization step results in panels of L and U, and a trailing matrix with correct row checksums. Since one step maintains the checksum, it is maintained through the entire calculation.

The panel factorization on a matrix indexed starting from 1, with a block size of nb, is

```
for i = 1 to nb
    A(i+1:n,i) = A(i+1:n,i)/A(i,i)
    A(i+1:n,i+1:nb) -= A(i+1:n,i)*A(i,i+1:nb)
```

Checksums are included in this calculation at the end of each block, so sections of the matrix where the index goes to nb will have checksums appended.

The first step in this loop creates elements of L, which are not maintained with checksums in our approach. The second step uses the modified elements from the first step. Therefore, the elements at the end of the step in terms of the elements from the beginning of the step are

```
A(i+1:n,i+1:nb) - A(i+1:n,i)*A(i,i+1:nb)/A(i,i)
```

THEOREM 5.1. *After one iteration of the main loop in the HPL algorithm, if the matrix started with correct global and local checksums, then the resulting matrix sections of U and the trailing matrix will each have correct global and local checksums.*

Each iteration operates on the trailing matrix from the previous iteration. As we will show below, the trailing matrix begins the iteration with all checksums within the trailing matrix consisting only of elements from the trailing matrix. Therefore it can be treated as an entire matrix, independent of the sections that are already completely factored. Before the panel factorization, the panel is set up with a checksum:

$$\left[A_{1:n,1:nb} \sum_{j=1}^{nb} A_{1:n,j} \right]$$

At each iteration for i from 1 to nb, only the matrix $A_{i:n,i:nb}$ is involved. So if the previous iteration resulted in correct checksum relationships, then row i in iteration i will have a correct checksum and will not be changed again in the panel factorization. Iteration i results in

$$\left[A_{i+1:n,i+1:nb} \sum_{j=i}^{nb} A_{i+1:n,j} \right]$$

$$- A_{i+1:n,i} \left[A_{i,i+1:nb} \sum_{j=i}^{nb} A_{i,j} \right] / A_{i,i}$$

$$= \left[A_{i+1:n,i+1:nb} - A_{i+1:n,i} \cdot A_{i,i+1:nb}/A_{i,i} \right.$$
$$\left. \sum_{j=i}^{nb} A_{i+1:n,j} - A_{i+1:n,i} \sum_{j=i}^{nb} A_{i,j}/A_{i,i} \right]$$

$$= \left[A_{i+1:n,i+1:nb} - A_{i+1:n,i} \cdot A_{i,i+1:nb}/A_{i,i} \right.$$
$$\left. \sum_{j=i}^{nb} A_{i+1:n,j} - A_{i+1:n,i} \cdot A_{i,j}/A_{i,i} \right]$$

$$= \left[A_{i+1:n,i+1:nb} - A_{i+1:n,i} \cdot A_{i,i+1:nb}/A_{i,i} \right.$$
$$A_{i+1:n,i} - A_{i+1:n,i} \cdot A_{i,i}/A_{i,i}$$
$$\left. + \sum_{j=i+1}^{nb} A_{i+1:n,j} - A_{i+1:n,i} \cdot A_{i,j}/A_{i,i} \right]$$

$$= \left[A_{i+1:n,i+1:nb} - A_{i+1:n,i} \cdot A_{i,i+1:nb}/A_{i,i} \right.$$
$$\left. \sum_{j=i+1}^{nb} A_{i+1:n,j} - A_{i+1:n,i} \cdot A_{i,j}/A_{i,i} \right]$$

At the end of iteration i, the sum to the panel is the sum from $i+1$ to nb. So iteration $i+1$ will operate on a panel and a checksum that includes only elements that are involved in the iteration.

Adding a checksum to a matrix can be represented as multiplying the matrix by another matrix H_r, which is set up to produce the appropriate checksum, and is assumed below to have the correct dimensions for the matrix in question. For example, the H_r that adds a row checksum to a 3×3 matrix is

$$\begin{pmatrix} 1 & 0 & 0 & 1 \\ 0 & 1 & 0 & 1 \\ 0 & 0 & 1 & 1 \end{pmatrix}$$

After the panel factorization, the row panel is updated according to the equation $A = LU$, where $A = A_{1:nb,nb+1:n}$, L is the lower triangle of $A_{1:nb,1:nb}$ with the diagonal replaced with ones, and U is the new value of $A_{1:nb,nb+1:n}$. This step maintains the checksum because of the original ABFT idea: since A with a checksum can be represented as $A \cdot H_r$, $A \cdot H_r = (LU) \cdot H_r = L(U \cdot H_r)$, so that U has a checksum as well. The checksum is actually the sum across the entire row, while the part of the matrix being updated is the entire row except for the first nb columns. Therefore, the sums are correct for the entire block of the first nb rows of U. The first nb columns have already been calculated, so they are not included. Nevertheless, the sums will be correct.

Referring to the parts of the matrix shown in figure 1, the relationship is $[A_{11} A_{12}] = L_{11}[U_{11}U_{12}]$, so $A_{12} = L_{11}U_{12}$. With a checksum,

$$[A_{11} A_{12}]H_r = L_{11}[U_{11}U_{12}]H_r = L_{11}\left([U_{11}U_{12}]H_r\right)$$

The checksum on the right hand side is a checksum of U only.

5.3 Local Checksum after Panel Factorization

The checksum verification in general requires recalculating the sums and comparing to the stored values. The overhead involved could be significant because of the memory access required. However, for the most frequent verification, the operation is faster.

All checksums are of either the original matrix or of U. Once elements that went into a checksum have been replaced by elements of L, the checksum reflects the fact that the equivalent position in U has a zero. When the panel is factored, the first $nb \times nb$ block contains a part of U, but the rest is L. In this section, the checksums will all be zeros. Therefore, no computation is required, and the memory access is less, for the main part of the panel verification. Since this verification must be done every iteration, a lower overhead for it is useful.

THEOREM 5.2. *The sums of L in the panel will be zeros immediately after the factorization of that panel if and only if no errors occurred at any point earlier in the calculation either in the panel or in the columns the panel belongs to.*

If there are no errors, then the L sums are zero. As shown in the proof of the correctness of the checksum, the sums are correct only for U. This is achieved by the algorithm when the sum elements that are below the diagonal go to zero. These elements are not stored as part of U because they are zeros. Therefore, when the elements that formerly went into the sum are all storing part of L, the sum will be zero. The panel factorization is done in a loop from 1 to nb. After iteration $nb - 1$, the sum is from nb to nb, or just the last element. After iteration nb, no elements go into the sum, so it is zero.

Figure 6: The matrix after global sums are also added, with the global view of the matrix with all checksums.

```
 19   3  22 |  1   3   4 |  1  12  13 | 11   0  11 |  1  16  17 |  0   0   0 | 21  31  52 | 12   3  15
-19   3 -16 |  1   3   4 |  1  12  13 | 11   0  11 |  1  16  17 |  0   0   0 |-17  31  14 | 12   3  15
-19  -3 -22 |  1   3   4 | -1 -12 -13 | 11   0  11 |  1  16  17 |  0   0   0 |-19   1 -18 | 12   3  15
-19  -3 -22 |  1   3   4 | -1 -12 -13 | 11   0  11 | -1  16  15 |  0   0   0 |-21   1 -20 | 12   3  15
-19  -3 -22 | -1  -3  -4 | -1 -12 -13 | 11   0  11 | -1 -16 -17 |  0   0   0 |-21 -31 -52 | 10  -3   7
-19  -3 -22 |  1   3   4 |  1  12  13 | 11   1  12 |  1  16  17 |  0   0   0 |-17  25   8 | 12   4  16
-19  -3 -22 |  1   3   4 | -1  12  11 | 11   0  11 |  1  16  17 |  0   0   0 |-19  25   6 | 12   3  15
-19  -3 -22 |  1   3   4 | -1 -12 -13 | 11   0  11 | -1 -16 -17 |  0   0   0 |-21 -31 -52 | 12   3  15
-19  -3 -22 | -1   3   2 | -1 -12 -13 | 11   0  11 | -1 -16 -17 |  0   0   0 |-21 -31 -52 | 10   3  13
```

```
 19   3  22 |  1  12  13 |  1  16  17 | 21  31  52 |  1   3   4 | 11   0  11 |  0   0   0 | 12   3  15
-19   3 -16 |  1  12  13 |  1  16  17 |-17  31  14 |  1   3   4 | 11   0  11 |  0   0   0 | 12   3  15
-19  -3 -22 |  1  12  13 |  1  16  17 |-17  25   8 |  1   3   4 | 11   1  12 |  0   0   0 | 12   4  16
-19  -3 -22 | -1  12  11 |  1  16  17 |-19  25   6 |  1   3   4 | 11   0  11 |  0   0   0 | 12   3  15
-19  -3 -22 | -1 -12 -13 |  1  16  17 |-19   1 -18 |  1   3   4 | 11   0  11 |  0   0   0 | 12   3  15
-19  -3 -22 | -1 -12 -13 | -1  16  15 |-21   1 -20 |  1   3   4 | 11   0  11 |  0   0   0 | 12   3  15
-19  -3 -22 | -1 -12 -13 | -1 -16 -17 |-21 -31 -52 |  1   3   4 | 11   0  11 |  0   0   0 | 12   3  15
-19  -3 -22 | -1 -12 -13 | -1 -16 -17 |-21 -31 -52 | -1   3   2 | 11   0  11 |  0   0   0 | 10   3  13
-19  -3 -22 | -1 -12 -13 | -1 -16 -17 |-21 -31 -52 | -1  -3  -4 | 11   0  11 |  0   0   0 | 10  -3   7
```

If there are errors, then the L sums are not zero (which is the same as saying if the L sums are zero, then there are no errors). As stated above, the elements of the panel are updated in a loop:

```
for i = 1 to nb
    A(i+1:n,i) = A(i+1:n,i)/A(i,i)
    A(i+1:n,i+1:nb) -= A(i+1:n,i)*A(i,i+1:nb)
```

When an element in $A_{i+1:n,i}$ has an error during the first line of the loop, it will affect the second line as well. In the second line the checksums are updated. If an element of $A_{i+1:n,i}$ is incorrect, then the value subtracted from $A_{i+1:n,i+1:nb}$ will be incorrect. In the case of the checksums, they will be nonzero.

Figure 7 shows the different sections where errors could occur. The matrix shown is the trailing matrix from the previous iteration, which is the only area of the matrix where values are changed, and therefore is the only area where errors can occur with our assumption of errors only occurring from calculations. The error shown in case 1 is when an error occurs in L. In this case, since L is not included in the checksums, the error will remain, and no recovery will be done. In case 2, the error will be detected by the checksum in the same block, and a recovery of the entire panel will be required. Case 3 is detected by the sums being nonzero. Errors shown in case 4 and case 5 can be detected with one verification, and recovered at the same time, even if both occur. This is possible because errors in different rows do not interact; multiple errors can always be recovered as long as they occur in different rows.

5.4 Error Detection and Location

In order to detect a single error, it is sufficient to verify the sums of the panel after each panel factorization. The reason is the way that errors are propagated. There are three phases of each iteration: panel factorization, broadcast and row panel update, and trailing matrix update. During the updates of the upper row panel and the trailing matrix, rows are combined. Any error in these sections will be spread down its column. Because global checksums are kept across rows, an error of this sort can be recovered. When it is propagated down a column, it amounts to one erroneous

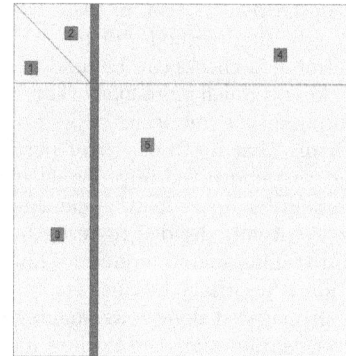

Figure 7: The small boxes indicate the sections of the matrix where errors could occur at different points in an iteration.

local matrix per row. As long as the error is kept to one process column, it can be recovered.

The panel factorization is the part of the iteration where there is a possibility of an unrecoverable error occurring. After the panel is factored, it is broadcast to the rest of the matrix, which is multiplied by the panel. In this case an error would affect entire rows, making recovery impossible. When multiple local matrices in a row are affected, the error cannot be recovered. Therefore, to guarantee recovery, the results of the panel factorization must be verified with local sums before there is any communication, so that a potential error is contained to the column containing the current panel.

Verifying the panel factorization consists of recalculating the sums for the U section of the panel, and of checking that the rest of the sums are zeros. If any sum is found to be incorrect, the entire panel must be recovered and the factorization repeated. The calculation has to be repeated because the global checksums, which the recovery is done from, have not been updated at the time of the panel factorization, so the recovered local matrices will be from the beginning of the iteration before the factorization. Although an error in the panel factorization could be propagated to the entire panel or not, the recovery can only restore the original unfactored panel, so the entire panel must be recovered in any case.

It is possible to detect all errors with only the check after the panel factorization. With this approach, the verification process requires only the calculation of sums in $nb \times nb$ blocks, as well as checking if the sums in the rest of the panel are zeros. Therefore, it has extremely low overhead, significantly less than if even the trailing matrix is also verified. However, this method is vulnerable to multiple errors. The approach of only verifying the panel means that an error could potentially occur a long time before it can be detected. Any error is guaranteed not to leave its column until it becomes part of the panel to be factored, at which point it will be detected and corrected. However, this delay leaves the method vulnerable to a second error. If another error occurs before the first error is detected, recovery is impossible and the calculation must be repeated. What this means for the recovery process is that all of the local matrices must be verified with their sums before using them to recover the corrupted panel. Also, in cases where the error rate is high enough, this method will not be effective. In that case, more frequent checks can be used to detect errors immediately, making it much more likely that each error will be handled before another can occur.

In order to ensure that up to one error per iteration can be handled, and to remove the improbable but fatal possibility of two errors far apart in time causing an impossible recovery, we eventually decided to verify both the panel factorization and trailing matrix update. The panel factorization verification is necessary because errors that occur in this step will be propagated along rows, making recovery impossible. The verification after the trailing matrix update, which is at a time when the checksums in the entire matrix are consistent, ensures that the matrix will be entirely correct going into the next iteration, and that no error will go undetected for a long period of time.

5.5 Soft Error Correction

An error on the diagonal within the panel will be propagated down the column and along all of the rows that are affected by the first propagation. This type of error would corrupt the entire trailing matrix if it were not caught immediately after the factorization, at which point it is still contained within one column of the process grid. An error above the diagonal will propagate down its column, which is harmless in this method. An error below the diagonal will propagate across its row, which is another type that must be caught before it can leave the panel.

An error that occurs in the row panel section of the matrix will be propagated down the column. It cannot cause an impossible recovery until part of the affected area is in the current panel. At this point, an entire column with erroneous values will exist in the panel, but the errors cannot propagate outside the column if the error is detected immediately after the panel factorization.

An error that occurs in the trailing matrix will not be propagated during the update. The error will have no effect until it is part of either the column or row panel, at which point it has the same effect as an error that occurred in one of those areas.

When an error is detected in the panel, it is necessary to recover, not just the entire panel, but the entire column it belongs to. This is because of the situation where an error occurs in place where it is propagated down a column but not immediately detected. This type of error will affect part of the matrix that has already been factored, and this part of the matrix will have to be recovered as well. The recovery is possible even though the error occurred earlier and is in an entire column. Errors cannot spread outside of a single column unless they are part of the panel, and up to one corrupted process per row can be recovered.

Figure 8 shows the idea of the detection and recovery technique with a simple example. With a real block size, more elements go into each local sum - perhaps 32 or 64. Even if multiple elements in the same row are affected, the checksum will indicate an error as long as the elements do not change in such a way that their sum remains the same - for instance, if two values are changed in a way that cancel each other out. The error propagation that can still happen even with the checking that we do is only down columns. Therefore, for more than one error to occur among the elements that go into one local checksum, two soft errors would have to occur within a short time.

The situation where a single error has propagated down a column before being detected is easily handled by our method, although many elements might be affected. We are unable to locate the specific element within the local matrix without communication. Doing this would require a second local checksum. Instead, we recover the entire affected local matrix using the global checksum. Locating the error before recovering only the elements with errors can require as much communication as just recovering the entire local matrix, when an error is propagated down an entire column.

It is possible, as an example, to see how the exact location of the error can be found. In the example in figure 8, the sums need to be checked to find the failure. The elements in equivalent locations in the equivalent blocks of the local matrices are compared. This is done by doing the matrix addition and comparing the elements, but for this example we look at one element at a time to demonstrate. All of the sums need to be verified at the appropriate times, but looking just at the row where the error is, $-19 + (-1) + (-1) = -21$, but $-3 + 10 + 16 = 23$, while the stored sum is 1. The last sum $-22 + (-13) + 15 = -20$ also checks as correct. The global sum shows that the second element in the block is incorrect, so it is replaced with a variable in the local sum and solved for: $-1 + x = -13$, so $x = -12$.

6. PERFORMANCE ANALYSIS

6.1 Overhead of checksum setup and error detection

Calculating the checksum at the beginning of the calculation requires calculating the local checksum, followed by a reduce for the global checksum.

The overhead when no failure has occurred consists of the time to verify the local checksums in each iteration. The sums are verified twice per iteration, once for just the panel and once for the entire trailing matrix. The verification of the panel requires that nb numbers are summed, then the result is compared to the stored value. The verification of the trailing matrix requires each block in the local matrix to be summed and verified. If the maximum number of

19	3	22	1	3	4	1	12	13	11	0	11	1	16	17	0	0	0	21	31	52	12	3	15
-19	3	-16	1	3	4	1	12	13	11	0	11	1	16	17	0	0	0	-17	31	14	12	3	15
-19	-3	-22	1	3	4	-1	-12	-13	11	0	11	1	16	17	0	0	0	-19	1	-18	12	3	15
-19	-3	-22	1	3		-1	10	-13	11	0	11	-1	16	15	0	0	0	-21	1	-20	12	3	15
-19	-3	-22	-1	-3	-4	-1	-12	-13	11	0	11	-1	-16	-17	0	0	0	-21	-31	-52	10	-3	7
-19	-3	-22	1	3	4	1	12	13	11	1	12	1	16	17	0	0	0	-17	25	8	12	4	16
-19	-3	-22	1	3	4	-1	12	11	11	0	11	1	16	17	0	0	0	-19	25	6	12	3	15
-19	-3	-22	1	3	4	-1	-12	-13	11	0	11	-1	-16	-17	0	0	0	-21	-31	-52	12	3	15
-19	-3	-22	-1	3	2	-1	-12	-13	11	0	11	-1	-16	-17	0	0	0	-21	-31	-52	10	3	13

Figure 8: The element -12 is replaced by 10. The sum verification shows that an error exists: $-1 + 10 \neq -13$. This is not enough to tell which element is incorrect. The reduce is done on the whole panel, and the result for this element is $1 - 16 - (-3) = 12$, restoring the correct element.

blocks in a local matrix is B, and the average time to sum nb numbers and do one comparison is t_{nb}, then the total time for both comparisons in one row is

$$t_{nb}(B + 1)$$

To repeat it for every row in a local matrix, if the matrix and grid are both square, is $t_{nb}(B+1)Bnb$. This operation occurs every iteration. If the total matrix size is n, the number of iterations is $\frac{n}{nb}$. Therefore the total overhead for the calculation is

$$nt_{nb}(B + 1)B$$

The value of t_{nb} depends on the time it takes to access the memory.

The panel verification, which takes $nt_{nb}B$, must be done every iteration. However, the trailing matrix verification, which takes $nt_{nb}B^2$, can be done less often. The frequency of checking the entire matrix depends on the error rate. If two errors occur between trailing matrix verifications, it is likely to be impossible to recover. Therefore the interval for checking the trailing matrix can be adjusted so that the probability of two errors occurring in that time is acceptably low. If the interval is T_i, with a time between errors of T_f, the probability of an error in that interval is $\frac{T_i}{T_f}$, so the probability that two errors occur is $\left(\frac{T_i}{T_f}\right)^2$ Since the overhead of the entire matrix check is B times that of the panel verification, doing the check less often is worthwhile.

6.2 Overhead of checking for errors in stored values

This technique mainly focuses on errors in the unfactored parts of the matrix, because these are the errors that can be propagated and make large parts of the matrix incorrect. However, errors could occur in the factored section of the matrix. Since these errors will not be propagated, multiple errors can be corrected in some cases. Only multiple errors in the same row can make it impossible to recover. Even if multiple errors occur in one row within one process, this will still be recoverable because the entire local matrix can be recovered from the other processes in the same row. So unless it is likely that errors will appear in multiple processes that are all in the same row in the process grid, errors can be corrected in the stored values with a high probability of success by doing a verification (and recovery if necessary) on the matrix after the factorization is complete. This verification would actually only apply to the U matrix. During the entire calculation, L is not maintained because it is not

necessary to the solution to the problem at the end, so the same applies here.

The time to check the entire factored matrix for errors is similar to the time to verify the trailing matrix, $nt_{nb}B^2$, because it involves verifying up to the entire local matrix in some processes. No communication is required just for the verification, so the time to finish the verification is the time for the slowest process to finish.

6.3 Overhead of computation

The time for one iteration aside from the verification overhead is made of the panel factorization, the broadcast, and the trailing matrix update. For the panel factorization: repeated nb times, do B divisions followed by a matrix multiplication and subtraction. Some communication is also required to determine the pivots. After the factorization the panel is broadcast to the processes containing the trailing matrix. The trailing matrix update requires more communication. The row and column panels are multiplied, and the result is subtracted from the trailing matrix.

The block size is increased by one, and the entire matrix is increased by the size of the local matrices in one column of the process grid. The number of iterations is not increased because the global checksum elements can be skipped in the factorization. When a panel made of global checksum elements is reached, the sums in it are already zeros because the elements going into them are in the lower diagonal, which is zeros in the U matrix.

The only parts of an iteration that are affected by there being more processors are the parts with communication. There are broadcasts in both rows and columns, but only broadcasting in rows is affected because there are no column checksums. If the original matrix dimension is P, then with a checksum added it is $P + 1$. So the overhead of each iteration is the difference between a broadcast among $P + 1$ processors and a broadcast among P processors. Depending on the implementation, the value varies. With a binomial tree, the overhead would be $\log(P+1) - \log P$. Using pipelining, where the time for the broadcast is nearly proportional to the size of the message, the overhead is even smaller.

The number of iterations is the same, and the length of each iteration is close to the same as when no fault tolerance is used. Any difference in the computation time comes from the increase in the block size. With typical block sizes, this increase might be between 0.5% and 2%.

6.4 Overhead of recovery

The overhead of correcting an error is the time for a reduce, along with the calculation of the panel factorization

Table 1: Ra: $N \times N$ matrix on $P \times P$ process grid, T_p is the panel verification time, and T_t is the trailing matrix verification time, block size 256, time in seconds, performance in Gflops

N	P	Total time	T_p (% overhead)	T_t (% overhead)	Performance
48000	12	128.10	3.40 (2.65)	31.66 (24.71)	575.6
64000	16	170.77	4.78 (2.79)	41.29 (24.17)	1023
80000	20	234.84	6.14 (2.61)	53.13 (22.62)	1454
96000	24	331.42	7.49 (2.25)	62.87 (18.96)	1780
112000	28	404.23	8.89 (2.19)	75.42 (18.65)	2317
128000	32	448.77	10.09 (2.24)	85.45 (19.04)	3115

Table 2: Kraken: $N \times N$ matrix on $P \times P$ process grid, T_p is the panel verification time, T_t is the trailing matrix verification time, block size 256, time in seconds, performance in Gflops

N	P	Total time	T_p (% overhead)	T_t (% overhead)	Performance
144000	72	242.38	5.63 (2.32)	16.85 (6.95)	8213
168000	84	368.16	6.57 (1.78)	19.68 (5.34)	8586
192000	96	307.70	7.51 (2.44)	22.50 (7.31)	15340
216000	108	405.24	8.46 (2.08)	25.32 (6.24)	16580
240000	120	459.27	9.39 (2.04)	28.13 (6.12)	20070
264000	132	553.96	10.32 (1.86)	30.96 (5.58)	22140
288000	144	606.51	11.28 (1.85)	33.75 (5.56)	26260
312000	156	725.67	12.23 (1.68)	36.57 (5.03)	27900

that has to be repeated if the error is found in the panel check. The time to do a reduce is comparable but less than the time of a broadcast. Therefore the total cost of recovery is similar to the time one iteration takes, without the trailing matrix update. The overhead of one recovery as a fraction of the total time is approximately $\frac{nb}{n}$. Since the block size is much smaller than the total matrix size, the overhead fraction is small. Our technique should have low overhead because it does not use communication during an error-free run. However, it does access large parts of the matrix during some checks. We have tested the technique experimentally to see how much the memory access affects the overhead.

6.5 Comparison to alternatives

Generally, the alternative method to our technique is ABFT, using a checksum to verify the result at the end and repeating the entire calculation if there was an error. With multiple weighted checksums, it is possible to recover a certain number of errors - another checksum is needed for each expected error. Another option that is available with HPL is residual checking. The solution x to the system $Ax = b$ is multiplied by A and compared to b, which shows whether the solution is correct. The calculation can be repeated if the solution is incorrect. This approach is essentially the same as ABFT - only one row and column are added for ABFT, and the difference between factoring a $N \times N$ matrix and a $N + 1 \times N + 1$ matrix is small, especially when N is large.

As long as the expected time between failures is greater than the running time of the calculation, the number of times the calculation has to be run is a geometric random variable. If the expected time to failure is T_f and the running time of the calculation is T, the probability of an error occurring is $\frac{T}{T_f}$. The probability of an error-free run is $1 - \frac{T}{T_f} - \frac{T^2}{T_f^2} - \cdots \approx 1 - \frac{T}{T_f}$. So the expected time that it will take to complete an error-free run is

$$\frac{1}{1 - \frac{T}{T_f}} = \frac{T_f}{T_f - T}$$

When the expected time to a failure is less than the run time, as the error rate increases it becomes increasingly unlikely that the calculation will ever finish using ABFT.

7. EXPERIMENTAL RESULTS

7.1 Platforms

We evaluate the proposed fault tolerance scheme on the following platforms:

Kraken at the University of Tennessee: 99,072 cores in 8,256 nodes. Each node has two Opteron 2435 "Istanbul" processors linked with dual HyperTransport connections. Each processor has six cores with a clock rate of 2600 MHz supporting 4 floating-point operations per clock period per core. Each node is a dual-socket, twelve-core node with 16 gigabytes of shared memory. Each processor has directly attached 8 gigabytes of DDR2-800 memory. Each node has a peak processing performance of 124.8 gigaflops. Each core has a peak processing performance of 10.4 gigaflops. The network is a 3D torus interconnection network. We used Cray MPI implementation MPT 3.1.02.

Table 3: With a $N \times N$ matrix, the ratio of trailing matrix verification to panel verification on Ra and Kraken

Ra N	Ra ratio	Kraken N	Kraken ratio
48000	9.32	144000	2.99
64000	8.66	168000	3.00
80000	8.67	192000	2.99
96000	8.43	216000	3.00
112000	8.52	240000	3.00
128000	8.50	264000	3.00
		288000	3.01
		312000	2.99

Ra at Colorado School of Mines: 2,144 cores in 268 nodes. Each node has two 512 Clovertown E5355 quad-core processor at a clock rate of 2670 MHz supporting 4 floating-point operations per clock period per core. Each node has 16 GB memory. Each node has a peak processing performance of 85.44 gigaflops. The network uses a Cisco SFS 7024 IB Server Switch. We used OpenMPI 1.4.

7.2 Overhead without failure

The overheads of this technique when no failure occurs are constructing the checksum at the beginning and verifying the results periodically during the computation. There are two types of verification, the panel and the trailing matrix. The panel verification must be done every iteration, so its overhead is the minimum possible. The trailing matrix verification takes longer, but can be done at a variable rate. The measured overhead is for the trailing matrix update done every iteration.

The overhead of verifying the checksums in each iteration is given in tables 1 and 2. The percentage overhead of the trailing matrix verification is close to $\frac{1}{N}$. The overhead of verifying the panel only is lower, but does not decrease as quickly with decreasing matrix size.

If only the elements involved in the verification are retrieved from memory, the ratio of the trailing matrix check to the panel check should be approximately the number of column blocks in a local matrix, or $\frac{N}{P\hat{n}b}$. For the experiments on Ra this value is 15.6, and for the experiments on Kraken it is 7.8. However, the ratios do not match these values, as shown in table 3. The panel verification times from both sets of experiments appear to be about a factor of two larger than the predicted values. The reason for this is most likely that the part of the matrix put in the cache during the operation includes elements that are not part of the panel. The trailing matrix verification needs the entire local matrix, so it ends up making a better use of the cache than the panel verification. If just the elements in the panel could be retrieved from memory, then the panel verification should take about half as long.

7.3 Overhead with Failure: Our approach compared to ABFT

In figure 9, the expected runtime using ABFT is shown assuming an average time between soft errors of both 40 and 80 minutes for the entire system. These values are chosen to

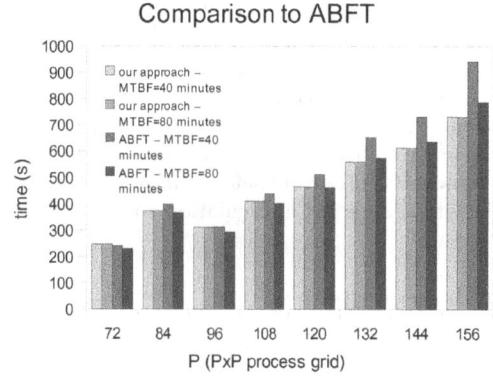

Comparison to ABFT

Figure 9: The expected run time is shown for our method and ABFT, with a mean time between failures of 40 and 80 minutes for each one.

illustrate a situation where our technique would be useful - it is not necessary to take these measures to survive failures unless the failure rate is close to the runtime of the program. When the runtime of the program is orders of magnitude less than the expected time between failures, the probability that a failure will actually occur during a run is low enough to make ABFT the best approach. On a very large system, the error rate would increase and the running time of some applications would also increase, bringing it into the range where our technique is useful.

With a time between failures that is between one and two orders of magnitude longer than the runtime, our technique shows its advantage over ABFT. As the time between failures gets shorter relative to the runtime, our technique gains even more advantage over ABFT.

All times shown include the runtime from an experiment without any fault tolerance and the expected overhead of the specified technique. For our technique, this is the time to verify the checksums and correct errors. For ABFT, this is the expected runtime given that a certain number of repetitions will be required due to propagated errors that make recovery from the checksums impossible.

As the number of processors increases, the expected time for ABFT increases at a faster rate than the time with our checksums. The difference that the error rate makes in the runtime for our method is much less than for ABFT. The expected time for ABFT increases as the error rate increases, and as the number of processors increases. The increase in expected time with an increase in error rate for ABFT is large, while the increase in expected time for our approach is much less. For the numbers of processes shown, ABFT starts with an advantage for the less frequent error rate. However, its expected time increases much more quickly with an increase in the number of processes. To run very large calculations, ABFT becomes impractical. Even for the largest sizes shown here, the overhead of using ABFT is significant.

8. CONCLUSION

We have created a fault tolerance method that handles soft errors in the LU factorization. Our technique uses global and local checksums to both detect and correct soft errors when they occur, preventing repeated calculation. The frequency of checking can be adjusted to the error rate. This technique is intended for situations where the error rate is high. Any technique that corrects the errors at the end of the calculation can only correct a limited number of errors. By correcting errors online, our technique makes it possible to survive any number of subsequent errors. Our technique corrects almost all soft errors before they can be propagated and makes it possible for a calculation to run in spite of a high error rate.

Acknowledgments

The authors would like to thank the reviewers for their insightful comments and valuable suggestions. This research is partly supported by US National Science Foundation, under grants #CNS-1304969, #CCF-1305622, and #OCI-1305624.

We would like thank the following institutions for the use of their computing resources:

- The National Institute for Computational Sciences: Kraken

- The Golden Energy Computing Organization: Ra

9. REFERENCES

[1] C. J. Anfinson and F. T. Luk. A linear algebraic model of algorithm-based fault tolerance. *IEEE Transactions on Computers*, 37(12), December 1988.

[2] P. Banerjee and J. Abraham. Bounds on algorithm-based fault tolerance in multiple processor systems. *IEEE Transactions on Computers*, 2006.

[3] P. Banerjee, J. T. Rahmeh, C. B. Stunkel, V. S. S. Nair, K. Roy, V. Balasubramanian, and J. A. Abraham. Algorithm-based fault tolerance on a hypercube multiprocessor. *IEEE Transactions on Computers*, C-39:1132–1145, 1990.

[4] G. Bronevetsky and B. de Supinski. Soft error vulnerability of iterative linear algebra methods. In *International Conference on Supercomputing*, 2008.

[5] G. Bronevetsky, B. R. de Supinski, and M. Schulz. A foundation for the accurate prediction of the soft error vulnerability of scientic applications. In *IEEE Workshop on Silicon Errors in Logic - System Effects*, 2009.

[6] Z. Chen. Optimal real number codes for fault tolerant matrix operations. In *Proceedings of the ACM/IEEE SC2009 Conference on High Performance Networking, Computing, Storage, and Analysis*, Portland, OR, USA, November 2009.

[7] Z. Chen and J. Dongarra. Algorithm-based fault tolerance for fail-stop failures. *IEEE Transactions on Parallel and Distributed Systems*, 19(12), 2008.

[8] Z. Chen and J. J. Dongarra. Condition numbers of gaussian random matrices. *SIAM J. Matrix Anal. Appl.*, 27:603–620, July 2005.

[9] T. Davies, C. Karlsson, H. Liu, C. Ding, and Z. Chen. High performance linpack benchmark: A fault tolerant implementation without checkpointing. In *Proceedings of the 25th ACM International Conference on Supercomputing*. ACM Press, 2011.

[10] C. Ding, C. Karlsson, H. Liu, T. Davies, and Z. Chen. Matrix multiplication on gpus with on-line fault tolerance. In *Proceedings of the 9th IEEE International Symposium on Parallel and Distributed Processing with Applications*. IEEE Computer Society Press, 2011.

[11] P. Du, A. Bouteiller, G. Bosilca, T. Herault, and J. Dongarra. Algorithm-based fault tolerance for dense matrix factorizations. In *17th ACM SIGPLAN Symposium on Principles and Practice of Parallel Programming (PPoPP' 12)*, 2012.

[12] P. Du, P. Luszczek, S. Tomov, and J. Dongarra. High performance dense linear system solver with soft error resilience. In *IEEE Cluster*, 2011.

[13] S. Feng, S. Gupta, A. Ansari, and S. Mahlke. Shoestring: probabilistic soft error reliability on the cheap. In *Proceedings of the fifteenth edition of ASPLOS on Architectural support for programming languages and operating systems*, ASPLOS '10, pages 385–396, New York, NY, USA, 2010. ACM.

[14] A. Garrett, Z. Chen, and D. E. Smith. Constructing numerically stable real number codes using evolutionary computation. In *Proceedings of the 12th annual conference on Genetic and evolutionary computation*, GECCO '10, pages 1163–1170, New York, NY, USA, 2010. ACM.

[15] J. A. Gunnels, R. A. van de Geijn, D. S. Katz, and E. S. Quintana-Orti. Fault-tolerant high-performance matrix multiplication: Theory and practice. In *The International Conference on Dependable Systems and Networks*, 2001.

[16] D. Hakkarinen and Z. Chen. Algorithmic Cholesky factorization fault recovery. In *Proceedings of the 24th IEEE International Parallel and Distributed Processing Symposium*, Atlanta, GA, USA, April 2010.

[17] I. S. Haque and V. S. Pande. Hard data on soft errors: A large-scale assessment of real-world error rates in gpgpu. *CoRR*, abs/0910.0505, 2009.

[18] K.-H. Huang and J. A. Abraham. Algorithm-based fault tolerance for matrix operations. *IEEE Transactions on Computers*, C-33:518–528, 1984.

[19] J. Jou and J. Abraham. Fault-tolerant matrix arithmetic and signal processing on highly concurrent computing structures. In *Proceedings of the IEEE*, volume 74, May 1986.

[20] Y. Kim. *Fault Tolerant Matrix Operations for Parallel and Distributed Systems*. PhD thesis, University of Tennessee, Knoxville, June 1996.

[21] F. T. Luk and H. Park. An analysis of algorithm-based fault tolerance techniques. *Journal of Parallel and Distributed Computing*, 5(2):172–184, 1988.

[22] K. Malkowski, P. Raghavan, and M. Kandemir. Analyzing the soft-error resilience of linear solvers on multicore multiprocessors. In *24th IEEE International Parallel and Distributed Processing Symposium*, 2010.

[23] M. Nicolaidis. Time redundancy based soft-error tolerance to rescue nanometer technologies. In *VLSI Test Symposium, 1999. Proceedings. 17th IEEE*, pages 86 –94, 1999.

[24] J. Silva, P. Prata, M. Rela, and H. Madeira. Practical issues in the use of ABFT and a new failure model. In *Fault-Tolerant Computing, 1998. Digest of Papers. Twenty-Eighth Annual International Symposium on*, pages 26 –35, June 1998.

A Preemption-based Runtime to Efficiently Schedule Multi-process Applications on Heterogeneous Clusters with GPUs

Kittisak Sajjapongse, Xiang Wang, Michela Becchi

Dept. of Electrical and Computer Engineering
University of Missouri - Columbia

ks5z9@mail.missouri.edu, xw7b4@mail.missouri.edu, becchim@missouri.edu

ABSTRACT

In the last few years, thanks to their computational power, their progressively increasing programmability and their wide adoption in both the research community and in industry, GPUs have become part of HPC clusters (for example, the US Titan and Stampede and the Chinese Tianhe-1A supercomputers). As a result, widely used open-source cluster resource managers (e.g. SLURM and TORQUE) have recently been extended with GPU support capabilities. These systems, however, provide simple scheduling mechanisms that often result in resource underutilization and, thereby, in suboptimal performance.

In this paper, we propose a runtime system that can be integrated with existing cluster resource managers to enable a more efficient use of heterogeneous clusters with GPUs. Differently from previous work, we focus on multi-process GPU applications including synchronization (for example, hybrid MPI-CUDA applications). We discuss the limitations and inefficiencies of existing scheduling and resource sharing schemes in the presence of synchronization. We show that preemption is an effective mechanism to allow efficient scheduling of hybrid MPI-CUDA applications. We validate our runtime on a variety of benchmark programs with different computation and communication patterns.

Categories and Subject Descriptors

C.1.4.1 [**Computer Systems Organization**]: Processor Architectures - Parallel Architectures, Distributed Architectures.

Keywords

Distributed computing, runtime systems, virtualization, GPU, CUDA, Message Passing Interface.

1. INTRODUCTION

In the last decade many-core GPUs have been successfully used to accelerate a wide variety of applications belonging to different domains: linear algebra, computational finance, physics, bioinformatics, and weather prediction, among others. In the last five years, thanks to their computational power, their progressively increased programmability and their wide adoption in both the research community and in industry, GPUs have started to become part of HPC clusters. As of November 2012, three of the fastest supercomputers[1] in the world include many-core GPUs. Specifically, Titan uses 18,688 CPUs paired with an equal number of Nvidia Kepler GPUs; Tianhe-1A is equipped

with 7,168 Nvidia Fermi GPUs and 14,336 CPUs; Stampede, which consists of 6,400 nodes, is planned to include almost one Intel Xeon Phi coprocessor per node and 128 Nvidia Kepler GPUs. In addition, in 2011 several vendors, such as Amazon, Nimbix and Hoopoe, have started offering GPU instances as part of their cloud services.

The adoption of GPUs in cluster and cloud environments has led to the need for cluster resource managers that handle nodes that include CPUs coupled with coprocessor devices. Widely used open-source cluster resource managers, such as SLURM[2] and TORQUE[3], have recently been extended with GPU support capabilities. These systems, however, provide simple scheduling mechanisms that often result in resource underutilization and, thereby, in suboptimal performance. In particular, TORQUE and SLURM do not allow GPU sharing across applications, and allocate to each application as many GPUs as requested by the user. This design choice is due to the fact that these resource managers rely on the CUDA runtime, which does not offer adequate support to concurrency (particularly in the presence of applications with conflicting memory requirements) [1].

Recent projects – GViM [2], vCUDA [3], rCUDA [4] and gVirtuS [5] – have proposed virtualization frameworks to enable GPUs in cluster and cloud environments. These solutions either rely directly on the scheduling mechanisms provided by the CUDA runtime, or include queuing schemes that enable load balancing and serialize the execution of applications on the same GPU. In the former case, the mapping of applications to GPUs is explicitly guided by the user, leading to load imbalances and errors in the presence of applications with conflicting memory requirements (that is, whose aggregate memory requirements exceed the GPU capacity). In the latter, serialization can cause CPU and GPU underutilization and, thereby, suboptimal performance.

More advanced and effective GPU allocation schemes have been proposed in [6] and [1]. In particular, Ravi et al. [6] have designed a runtime component allowing concurrent execution on GPU of kernel functions invoked by different applications. This functionality, however, is restricted to applications with no conflicting memory requirements, and is going to be supported by Nvidia in the Kepler architecture (through the Hyper-Q technology[4] and CUDA 5). In our previous work [1] we have designed a virtual memory-based runtime system that enables GPU time-sharing even in the presence of applications with conflicting memory requirements. This mechanism is particularly beneficial for jobs that alternate between CPU and GPU execution phases. In addition, our runtime component automatically and transparently migrates applications from less powerful to more powerful GPUs when the latter become idle.

---

[1] http://www.top500.org

---

[2] https://computing.llnl.gov/linux/slurm

[3] http://www.adaptivecomputing.com/products/open-source/torque

[4] http://www.nvidia.com/content/PDF/kepler/NVIDIA-Kepler-GK110-Architecture-Whitepaper.pdf

These proposals, however, have an important limitation. The underlying scheduling schemes focus on single-process single-threaded applications, and may lead to inefficiencies in case of multi-threaded or multi-process applications, especially in the presence of synchronization. Some scientific applications, such as Gromacs[5], have parallel implementations based on either MPI, or on CUDA. Today's heterogeneous clusters include different forms of parallelism: (i) a cluster consists of many compute nodes; a node may contain (ii) several CPU cores and (iii) several GPUs; each GPU contains (iv) hundreds of cores. To take advantage of this heterogeneous parallelism, it is conceivable that, in the near future, more and more applications will combine multiprocessing through MPI, CPU-multithreading through POSIX threads and OpenMP, and GPU-multithreading through CUDA and OpenCL (and other multiprocessing or multithreading programming models and libraries).

In this work, we study the efficient scheduling of concurrent multi-process or multi-threaded applications that use GPUs and include synchronization points. In particular, we focus on technologies required at the node-level in order to allow efficient scheduling on heterogeneous clusters. We implement such technologies within our previously proposed runtime system [1]. As explained in Section 3, such node-level component can be integrated with cluster-level resource managers (such as TORQUE and SLURM) to allow efficient scheduling on CPU-GPU clusters. In addition, by performing CUDA call interception, our runtime operates transparently on unmodified CUDA applications (and can be extended to support OpenCL).

Our contributions can be summarized as follows:

- Through different use-cases, we explain the limitations of existing scheduling mechanisms and GPU sharing schemes in the presence of multi-threaded and multi-process applications that include synchronization.
- We propose *GPU preemption* as a mechanism to overcome such limitations and efficiently schedule multi-process applications on CPU-GPU nodes and clusters. We implement GPU preemption in our runtime system [1].
- We propose a workload generator to automatically create MPI-CUDA applications with different characteristics (number and duration of CPU and GPU phases, type of synchronization and communication patterns, among others).
- We compare our preemption-based scheduling with traditional batch-scheduling and a recently proposed GPU sharing scheme [1] on workloads with various computation and communication patterns.

To the best of our knowledge, this is the first investigation which uses GPU preemption in order to improve the GPU utilization and increase the performance of multi-process applications deployed on heterogeneous nodes and clusters.

2. BACKGROUND & MOTIVATIONS

In this section, we provide some additional background and better motivate our proposal. In Section 2.1, we discuss the applications that we target. In Section 2.2, we explain the operation of two existing mapping and scheduling mechanisms (batch scheduling and controlled *n*-way GPU sharing) and of our proposed preemption-based GPU sharing. In Section 2.3, we discuss several scenarios that make our scheme preferable to existing ones.

---
[5] http://www.gromacs.org

2.1 Target applications

In this work, we focus on multi-process applications that include synchronization and employ GPUs. The examples in this paper are MPI applications that invoke GPU-related tasks (e.g., CUDA kernels). However, our study also covers multi-threaded applications (written using POSIX threads, OpenMP or other CPU multi-threading libraries) and consisting of CPU-threads that perform GPU-related calls.

Processes belonging to MPI applications are expected to periodically synchronize and communicate. For examples, MPI applications typically include group communication primitives (e.g, `MPI_Bcast`, `MPI_Gather`, `MPI_Scatter`, `MPI_Alltoall`), pair-wise communication primitives (e.g., `MPI_Send`, `MPI_Recv`), and barrier synchronizations (`MPI_Barrier`). Between synchronization points some computation work is performed; in some cases, such work can be offloaded to GPU. Many MPI applications are iterative: every iteration includes some computation and some communication.

The processes of an MPI application may experience performance differences due to intrinsic load-imbalance or to the presence of compute nodes and GPUs with different compute capabilities. In the presence of synchronization and communication primitives, processes that complete earlier need to wait for processes that finish later. These imbalances may cause resource underutilization, and should be taken into account by the job scheduler.

2.2 Scheduling mechanisms

2.2.1 Batch-scheduling

Most of the cluster schedulers in use today, such as the open-source TORQUE and SLURM, perform batch scheduling. Specifically, they allocate to each application as many GPUs as requested, and do so for the whole application lifetime. Further, by directly relying on the CUDA runtime, they do not provide GPU sharing mechanisms.

This form of batch scheduling has two major limitations. First, when the number of processes requesting GPUs is larger than the number of available GPU devices, batch schedulers fail to allocate the requested resources and to execute the application. Not only does this represent a lack of scheduling flexibility, but it also exposes to the user the configuration of the underlying architecture. Second, this scheme leads to resource underutilization in the presence of long CPU execution phases and load-imbalance, thus reducing the throughput of the whole cluster. This situation is illustrated in Figure 1(a), which depicts the batch scheduling of three applications (A, B, and C) on four GPUs. Application A consists of four processes, each going through two GPU phases; applications B and C consist of two processes, each including a single GPU phase. All applications present a global synchronization at the end of each GPU phase. In the figure, A_{jk} represents the kth GPU phase of process j belonging to application A; black blocks represent idle GPU times. As can be seen, processes A_1, A_2 and A_4 must wait for process A_3 to complete the first phase before proceeding to the next one. As a result, GPU_0, GPU_1 and GPU_3 remain idle for part of the execution. Similar considerations apply in the next execution phases. Such problem is common to batch schedulers that do not allow applications to time-share GPUs.

2.2.2 Controlled n-way GPU Sharing

In our previous work [1] we have proposed a runtime system to allow multiple processes to time-share GPUs even in the presence

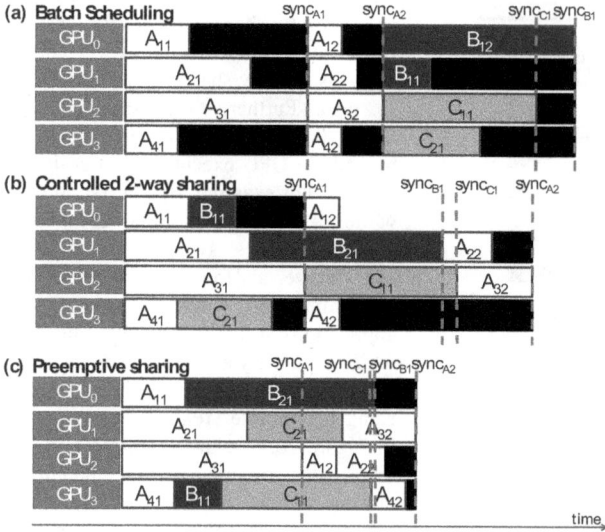

Figure 1: Operation of different scheduling mechanisms in the presence of multi-process applications with synchronizations and *intra-application imbalance*. Application *A* consists of 4 processes and includes 2 GPU execution phases, with a global synchronization at the end of each. Applications *B* and *C* consist of two processes and a single GPU execution phase, also ending with a global synchronization. Synchronizations are represented through (red) dashed vertical lines. A_{jk} represents the kth GPU phase of process j belonging to application *A*. Idle GPU times are represented in black.

of conflicting memory requirements. Controlled GPU sharing among *n* processes (*n-way GPU sharing*) is enabled by associating to each physical GPU a predefined number *n* of virtual GPUs (*vGPUs*). Processes are mapped to virtual GPUs, and vGPUs time-share the underlying physical GPU. Thus, processes mapped onto vGPUs associated to the same physical GPU will time-share the GPU device and execute concurrently. Processes are mapped to vGPUs in a round-robin fashion, prioritizing idle GPU devices. We have shown that this mechanism is particularly beneficial in case of single-process applications that alternate between CPU and GPU execution phases. Specifically, GPU time-sharing allows hiding CPU execution phases behind GPU execution phases of co-scheduled applications.

The proposed mechanism has an important limitation: the associated scheduling scheme focuses on single-process applications and does not consider synchronization issues related to multi-process applications. In the runtime system described in [1], once scheduled for execution, a process is mapped to a vGPU for its whole life-time, unless a more powerful GPU becomes available or a memory swap request occurs. As a consequence, in order for a multi-process application to proceed with its execution, its processes must all be scheduled onto vGPUs at the same time. This may cause performance problems in highly utilized systems. Although the framework is capable of migrating processes to different GPUs, such migration occurs only in the presence of conflicting memory requirements or when some GPUs become idle, but does not take into account performance considerations related to multi-process applications.

In Figure 1(b) we show how the runtime system proposed in [1] would schedule the applications *A*, *B* and *C* described above, assuming two-way sharing (that is, two vGPUs per physical GPU). Note that the processes are mapped to vGPUs in a round-

robin fashion and prioritizing idle GPUs. Assuming that the processes are initially queued as $[A_1, A_2, A_3, A_4, B_1, B_2, C_1, C_2]$, processes A_1 and B_1 will share GPU_0, processes A_2 and B_2 will share GPU_1, processes A_3 and C_1 will share GPU_2 and processes A_4 and C_2 will share GPU_3. As can be seen, sharing allows hiding idle time of one process behind the GPU phase of a co-scheduled process. For example, B_1, B_2 and C_2 can in this case start executing while A_1, A_2 and A_4 wait for A_3 to reach the first synchronization point $sync_{A1}$. However, some GPU underutilization still takes place, especially when processes belonging to the same application exhibit significant imbalance in their execution time. The interested reader can verify that a better schedule would have resulted from co-locating processes A_2 and C_1, processes A_3 and C_2 and processes A_4 and B_2. However, the proposed runtime does not have the capability of automatically making such scheduling decision.

We conclude with two observations. First, despite its limitations, controlled GPU sharing has allowed a better schedule than batch scheduling. Second, one could think of increasing the scheduling flexibility by allowing more processes to share the same GPU (by increasing the number of vGPUs). However, as described in [1], this is not always the optimal choice, since increasing the number of processed mapped to the same physical GPU increases the probability of memory conflicts (thus causing swapping overheads). In addition, scheduling inefficiencies would anyway arise when increasing the number of processes per application.

2.2.3 Preemptive GPU Sharing

In this work we introduce the concept of *preemptive GPU sharing* as a mechanism to further improve the performance by reducing the idle time of the GPU devices. The basic idea is the following: processes that underutilize the GPU should be *preempted* from using it, so to allow other processes to execute. Processes waiting at a synchronization point are good candidates from preemption. Once the synchronization has been performed, preempted processes can be rescheduled for execution on the same or on a different GPU.

In Figure 1(c) we show how preemptive GPU sharing would schedule the applications *A*, *B* and *C* discussed above on four GPUs. This time, we assume that no *n*-way GPU sharing takes place. Pending processes are scheduled for execution as soon as a GPU becomes idle. As can be seen, in this case the scheduler preempts processes A_1, A_2 and A_4 while waiting for A_3 to reach the synchronization point $sync_{A1}$, and lets B_2, C_2 and B_1 execute on GPU_0, GPU_1 and GPU_3, respectively. When the short-running B_1 completes the execution of its GPU phase B_{11}, it is also preempted and GPU_3 is assigned to C_1. The idle times of all GPUs are minimized. From this example, we can see that preemption allows effectively hiding the idle time of one application behind the execution time of other applications. This scheme provides performance benefits not only over batch scheduling, but also over controlled *n*-way GPU sharing.

2.3 Use cases for preemption

There are at least three scenarios that make preemptive GPU sharing preferable to both batch scheduling and controlled *n*-way sharing (from now on, we will omit "controlled" for simplicity).

All these use cases involve multi-processes (or multi-threaded) applications with synchronization.

SCENARIO 1: When processes belonging to the same application

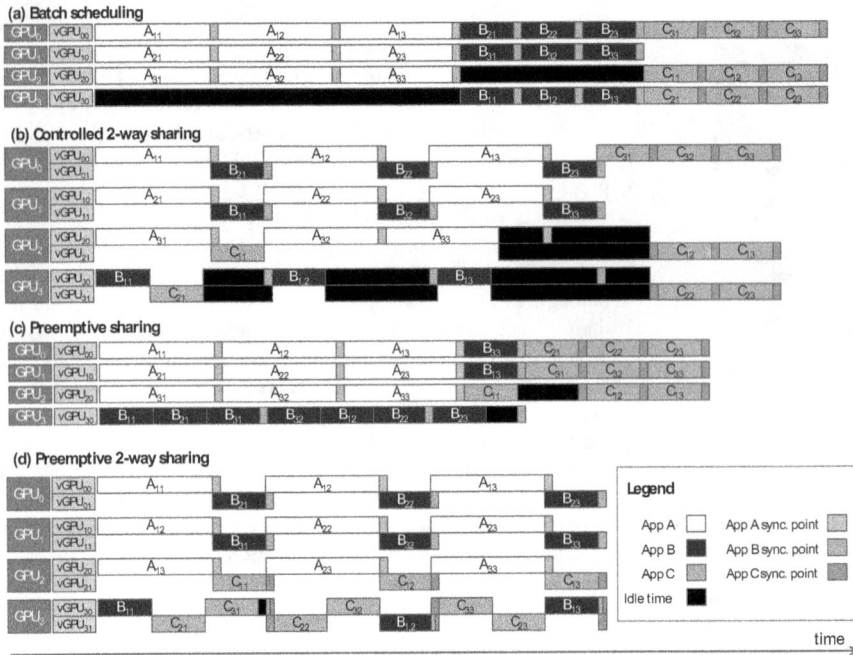

Figure 2: Operation of different scheduling mechanisms in the presence of multi-process applications with synchronizations and *inter-application imbalance*. Applications *A*, *B* and *C* consist of 3 processes and include 3 GPU execution phases, with a global synchronization at the end of each. A_{jk} represents the kth GPU execution phase of process *j* belonging to application *A*. Idle GPU times are represented in black.

exhibit significant imbalance in their execution time and GPU utilization. This is a form of *intra-application imbalance*.

SCENARIO 2: When the workload composition is such to prevent all processes belonging to the same application to be scheduled on the available GPUs at the same time. This is a form of *inter-application imbalance*.

SCENARIO 3: When an application has more processes than physical GPUs (in case of batch scheduling) or than virtual GPUs (in case of *n*-way sharing).

Scenario 1 (intra-application imbalance) is exemplified in Figure 1 and has been already described above.

Scenario 2 (inter-application imbalance) is represented in Figure 2. In this example, we assume again to have three applications *A*, *B* and *C* and four GPUs (*GPU₀-GPU₃*). The applications consist of three processes, each executing three GPU phases; again, there is a global synchronization at the end of each GPU phase. This time, however, each application is internally balanced: processes belonging to the same application have the same execution time in each execution phase. We assume that, at each synchronization point, some CPU code executes. The inter-application imbalance is due to the fact that each application has three processes but the system has four GPUs.

As can be seen in Figure 2(a), inter-application imbalance causes GPU underutilization when batch scheduling is performed. In fact, while *A* runs on *GPU₀-GPU₂*, *GPU₃* stays idle. This is because both *B* and *C* require three GPUs, and are therefore queued until such GPU resources become available. This situation occurs again later when scheduling application *C* (*GPU₂* stays idle until *B* completes execution and frees two more GPUs).

A better schedule is achieved by 2-way sharing, as shown in Figure 2(b). For illustration, we also show the virtual GPUs associated to each physical device. In this case, some waiting

times are hidden by allowing two processes to share a GPU (for example, *GPU₀* is initially shared by *A₁* and *B₂*, *GPU₁* is initially shared by *A₂* and *B₃*, and so on.). Further, GPU sharing allows hiding the CPU execution of one process behind the GPU execution of a co-located process. For example, *B₂* can run on *GPU₀* while *A₁* performs CPU computation (which includes synchronization code), and vice-versa. However, the presence of synchronization within the three applications still leads to GPU idle times, which ultimately affect the performance.

An even better schedule is achieved by using preemptive GPU sharing, as shown in Figure 2(c). In this case, the GPU idle time is minimized by preempting processes that are inactive waiting at synchronization points, and by remapping them to GPUs after the synchronization has been performed. Further, an optimal schedule is achieved by combining 2-way sharing and preemption, as shown in Figure 2(d). This solution benefits from the advantages of both schemes: on one hand, CPU execution phases of one process (including data communication and synchronization) are hidden behind the GPU execution phases of a co-located process; on the other hand, the use of preemption allows minimizing the GPU idle times. We observe that further increasing the level of GPU sharing (by associating to each physical device a larger number of vGPUs) would not bring additional benefits. In fact, the increased probability of conflicting memory requirements among co-located processes and the added overhead would have detrimental effects on the performance.

Scenario 3 can be explained as follows. As detailed above, batch scheduling allocates to each application as many GPUs as requested by its processes, and does not allow GPU sharing. Thus, if one application consists of more processes than the physical GPUs available in the system, such application will not be serviced. Controlled *n*-way sharing reduces this problem by allowing multiple processes to share a physical GPU, and by reassigning a GPU as soon as it becomes idle. However, once scheduled, a process will be mapped onto a GPU for its whole execution time. This works well in the absence of synchronization within the applications. However, let us assume to perform *n*-way sharing of *k* GPU devices, and to have an application that presents global synchronizations and *p* processes, with $p > nk$. In this case, the execution will reach a deadlock situation such that processes *1* to *nk* will be idle waiting on the global synchronization, while processes *nk+1* to *p* will be waiting for a free GPU. GPU preemption allows avoiding this problem.

3. SYSTEM DESIGN

In our previous work [1] we have proposed a node-level runtime component that can be used in combination with cluster-level schedulers (such as TORQUE and SLURM) to provide an integrated resource management framework for heterogeneous clusters that include GPUs. In particular, the integration of our node-level runtime with TORQUE and SLURM allows GPU sharing even in the presence of conflicting memory requirements among processes mapped to the same GPU. In this work, we implement preemptive GPU sharing within such runtime component. This enables the efficient scheduling of multi-process GPU applications with synchronization, which we have not targeted in our previous work. In Section 3.1, we summarize the design of our node-level runtime system (the interested reader can refer to [1] for more details). In Section 3.2, we describe the implementation of preemptive GPU sharing within such runtime component, and discuss the challenges faced in the design and the implementation alternatives that we have considered.

3.1 Design of our node-level runtime

Our node-level runtime can be considered a light-weight operating system for GPUs: it provides *resource allocation*, *process management* and *virtual memory* functionalities to so-called *contexts*, which are basically processes requesting the use of GPU resources. To cooperate with a cluster-level scheduler, our runtime component must be installed on all the nodes of a cluster. The integration between the cluster-level resource manager and our node-level runtime is implemented through library call interception. Our component consists of a front-end library and a back-end demon. The former redefines all CUDA runtime library calls. The cluster-level scheduler maps processes onto compute nodes. During execution, the CUDA library calls issued by the processes are intercepted by our front-end library and redirected to the back-end demon on the node where the process has been scheduled. The back-end demon is the core of our runtime system.

The design of our node-level runtime is represented in Figure 3. Its main components are: *connection manager, context queues, dispatcher, virtual GPUs, memory manager,* and *queue monitor*. The queue monitor and the waiting context queue were not part of the original design [1], and have been introduced to support preemption more efficiently. The main functionalities of these components are summarized below.

Connection manager – The connection manager is the entry point to the back-end demon. It receives CUDA calls from the front-end library, generates a back-end *context* for each process requesting GPU resources, associates each CUDA call to the appropriate context, and places new contexts into an appropriate context queue. These contexts will then be fetched by the dispatcher for scheduling on available GPU resources.

Context queues – The runtime system uses four context queues. (i) The *assigned context queue* contains a list of contexts that have been already scheduled on a GPU resource. (ii) The *ready context queue* stores contexts that have pending CUDA calls and are ready to be scheduled on a GPU resource. (iii) The *waiting context queue* stores contexts that have been preempted and unassigned from a GPU resource. (iv) The *failed context queue* contains contexts which have reported some CUDA error, and need recovery actions.

Dispatcher – The dispatcher performs scheduling functionalities by mapping ready contexts onto free virtual GPUs. Further, it cooperates with the memory manager to ensure correct operation in the presence of co-scheduled processes with conflicting GPU memory requirements.

Virtual GPUs (vGPUs) – Virtual GPUs represent the interface of our back-end demon to the CUDA runtime: each vGPU has an associated context and its main role is to issue CUDA calls belonging to such context to the CUDA runtime. Virtual GPUs allow multiple contexts to time-share a physical GPU. In our system, each GPU device is associated a number of vGPUs: contexts mapped by the dispatcher to virtual GPUs associated to

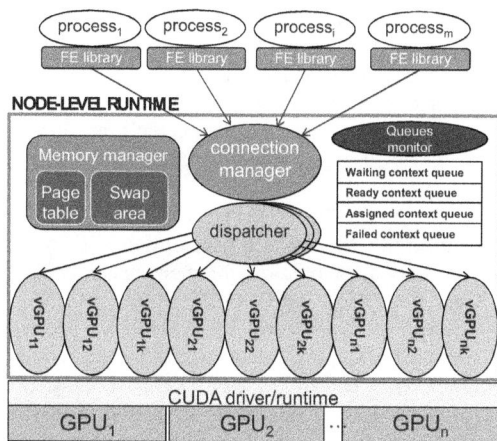

Figure 3: Design of our node-level runtime component.

the same physical GPU will time-share the device. In [1] we have shown that limiting the number of vGPUs per physical GPU prevents the back-end from overloading the CUDA runtime and helps reducing GPU memory conflicts. In our implementation, vGPUs have also the ability to preempt the associated context and move it from the assigned to the waiting context queue.

Memory manager – The memory manager implements a virtual memory abstraction for GPU, which allows handling concurrent applications with conflicting memory requirements. To serve its purpose, this component uses a *swap area* and a *page table*. The former preserves a copy of the data associated to each context; the latter contains directory information to the swap area, and is used to trigger automatic data transfers. The runtime system has the ability to defer data transfers between host and device, and to trigger automatic data transfers that have not been explicitly required by the application. This capability allows contexts to be dynamically mapped to GPUs and unmapped from them, and is therefore an essential mechanism to support preemption.

Queue monitor – This component actively monitors all contexts in the waiting queue, and, whenever appropriate (for example, after an MPI synchronization has been performed), moves them to the ready queue. It is implemented as a backend thread.

3.2 Supporting preemptive GPU sharing

3.2.1 Defining the preemption policy

We want to introduce a preemption mechanism that allows efficient GPU sharing for multi-process applications. To this end, we must define a preemption policy to be used: we must determine *when* preemption must be triggered. Since we are designing a light-weight operating system, we start by considering common OS preemption mechanisms. In operating systems, preemption is commonly implemented using the concept of time-quantum. Each process executes for a period of time, usually in the order of hundreds of micro-seconds. When the time-quantum expires, the process which currently occupies the processor is switched off from the processor and its state and registers are saved in its process-control-block.

However, this approach would be inefficient for our application. The motivations can be summarized as follows. First, GPU preemption can incur substantial overhead: a context-switch for GPU involves data transfers between host and device and the replay of all initializations routines (e.g., _cudaRegisterFatBinary, _cudaRegisterFunction, etc.) to the CUDA runtime. Thus, to avoid inefficiencies, the preemption rate should be kept low. Second, GPU preemption should be performed between kernel calls, and not in the middle of a kernel's execution. Since different kernels may have different execution times, using a time quantum approach may be problematic.

Instead, we consider the following two preemption policies.

1. Maximum idle time-driven preemption – In this approach, assigned contexts are monitored for their inactivity period. If a context does not utilize the GPU for a predefined period (the *maximum idle time*), then it will be preempted. The idea behind this policy is that processes waiting at synchronization points will stop issuing CUDA calls and therefore their associated contexts will become idle. During this inactivity period the GPU can be yielded to other ready contexts. The main advantage of this policy is its relatively simple implementation; the disadvantages are the need for mechanisms to measure the inactivity period and to tune the maximum idle time parameter.

2. Synchronization call-driven preemption – In this approach, contexts are preempted when they invoke synchronization routines, such as MPI collective calls. The main advantage of this approach is that GPU is yielded immediately upon reaching a synchronization point, and not after an idle time. The main disadvantages of this policy are two. First, it requires our runtime to intercept and handle not just CUDA calls, but also MPI calls (and possibly other multi-threading synchronization routines). Second, unless complex bookkeeping of the communicating processes is performed, this policy may lead to unnecessary preemptions (for example, preemption may occur also when the last process involved in the synchronization reaches the synchronization point).

We implemented both approaches, but achieved better results with the first one. In fact, the second approach was penalized by the overhead due to unnecessary preemptions. In the remainder of the paper, we will only present results obtained with the first approach.

3.2.2 Implementation

When a user submits a multi-process application to the system, the runtime receives a connection from each process and creates a context for each of them. The contexts are initially put into the ready queue by the connection manager, where they wait for the dispatcher to perform scheduling operations. When a context from a multi-process application scheduled onto a vGPU reaches a global synchronization point, it may exhibit inactivity periods in two situations. First, it may need to wait for other slower contexts to also reach the synchronization point even if they are all concurrently scheduled onto vGPUs. Second, some of the other contexts in the same application may still be unassigned. In the latter case, there are not enough vGPUs to accommodate all the contexts. We describe the changes made to the system to support preemption and address these situations.

We implemented in our runtime system the preemption cycle represented in Figure 4. In particular, virtual GPUs are extended to actively monitor the inactivity period of their assigned context. To reduce the overhead, we activate this monitoring routine only when the ready context queue is not empty. In other words, preemption is inactivated when there are no pending contexts waiting for a GPU resource. If monitoring is enabled and a context's inactivity period exceeds the maximum idle time, then the corresponding vGPU will preempt such context.

Upon preemption, the following actions are performed. First,

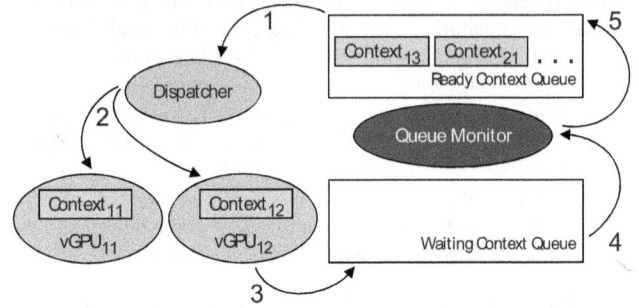

Figure 4: Preemption cycle.

the vGPU stops executing the context (that is, it stops issuing its calls to the CUDA runtime). Second, the vGPU saves the state of the context, by transferring all data residing on the GPU back to the virtual memory space of the context on CPU. Third, the vGPU moves the context to the waiting queue. The context will now be periodically monitored by the queue monitor to check whether it has completed synchronization and is ready to be moved back to the ready queue. The queue monitor accomplished this by observing whether the context has more CUDA tasks issued through the frontend library. If the waiting queue contains several contexts, the queue monitor observes them in a round-robin fashion and moves the context with more CUDA tasks back to the ready queue. The dispatchers can then re-schedule the context to the same or to a different vGPU.

We further clarify this mechanism with an example, as illustrated in Figure 4. Suppose that we have a multi-process and a single-process application. The multi-process application consists of three contexts: $Context_{11}$, $Context_{12}$ and $Context_{13}$. The single-process application consists of a single context: $Context_{21}$. Initially, the dispatcher fetches $Context_{11}$ and $Context_{12}$ from the ready queue (step 1), and then schedules the two contexts to the vGPUs (step 2). These two contexts execute until they reach a global synchronization point. At this point, $Context_{11}$ and $Context_{12}$ become idle waiting for $Context_{13}$, which is in turn waiting in the ready queue. After the maximum idle time period elapses, the vGPUs determine that preemption is necessary because the ready queue is not empty (it contains $Context_{13}$ and $Context_{21}$). The vGPUs, therefore, preempt $Context_{11}$ and $Context_{12}$ and move them to the waiting queue (step 3). At this point, the dispatcher can schedule $Context_{13}$ and $Context_{21}$ onto the two vGPUs. As $Context_{13}$ and $Context_{21}$ progress, $Context_{11}$ and $Context_{12}$ are monitored for readiness by the queue monitor (step 4). After all contexts belonging to the multi-process application synchronize, their processes will start issuing CUDA calls. Eventually, $Context_{11}$ and $Context_{12}$ are moved by the queue monitor back to the ready queue (step 5). The preemption cycle repeats until the pending queue becomes empty, or until the multi-process application terminates.

4. EXPERIMENTAL EVALUATION

The goal of our experiments is to evaluate our proposed preemptive GPU sharing scheme and compare it with batch scheduling and with controlled *n*-way GPU sharing using a collection of benchmark programs with various characteristics. In particular, we want to evaluate how the number of processes per application, the duration of the CPU and GPU computation within the application, the communication pattern, and the degree of intra- and inter-application imbalance affect the performance of the considered scheduling and sharing schemes.

4.1 Benchmark description

Since there is no established benchmark suite for applications that combine MPI and CUDA library calls, we decided to write a benchmark generator for such programs. Our benchmark generator is a C++ tool that automatically generates MPI-CUDA applications according to user-specified parameters.

To define the basic structure of the applications to be generated, we analyzed the structure of the NAS Parallel Benchmarks[6], which include a variety of MPI applications. We observed that several such applications are iterative. Every iteration consists of one or more execution phases; in turn, each execution phase contains some communication and some computation code. We decided to generalize this computation pattern by allowing offloading some computation to the GPU. Specifically, in our model every execution phase consists of some communication, some CPU and some GPU computation (which, in turns, includes data transfers between host and device and some GPU kernel invocations).

The parameters that drive the generation of the benchmark applications are listed in Table 1. In the table, all parameters (but the first) refer to a single MPI process. As can be seen, the generated applications mainly differ in their communication patterns, their CPU and GPU computation intensity, their interleaving of computation between CPU and GPU, and their duration. CPU and GPU computation are currently implemented using a number of vector additions of various sizes. To realize the specified CPU and GPU durations, we dynamically modify the number of vector additions executed (we have profiled the CPU and GPU execution time of vector additions of predefined sizes).

Table 1 also specifies the parameter settings used in the experiments presented in this work. The duration of the execution phases and the size of the MPI data transfers were chosen according to profile information collected in the analysis of the NAS Parallel Benchmarks. We assumed that, in each execution phase, the computation can take place either completely on GPU, or partially on CPU (to this purpose, we varied the CPU phase duration as shown in the table). In our preliminary experiments, we used the all-to-all communication pattern. However, in most of our experiments we focused on three communication patterns: broadcast and scatter-gather communication, and barrier synchronization, which are characteristics of applications such as distributed matrix multiplication and N-body simulation.

4.2 Experimental setup & evaluation metric

Hardware setup – The experiments described in Section 4.3 and 4.4 were performed on a single node; the ones presented in Section 4.5 were performed on a two-node cluster. The hardware setup of our cluster is summarized in Table 2. Single-node experiments were conducted on $Node_1$.

[6] http://www.nas.nasa.gov/publications/npb.html

Table 1: Description and setting of the parameters of our benchmark generator.

Parameters	Description	Settings in the experiments		
		Preliminary	*Node-level*	*Cluster-level*
Number of processes	Number of MPI processes	4	4	4, 6, 8
Communication type	MPI communication type	All-to-all	Broadcast, Scatter-Gather, Barrier synchron.	Scatter-Gather
Number of iterations	Number of iterations executed by each MPI process	200	200 (0.3 sec/kernel), 20 (3.0 sec/kernel)	200
Number of execution phases	Number of phases per iteration	1	1	1
GPU phase duration	Duration of per-phase GPU computation	0.5 sec	0.3 sec - 3.0 sec	0.3 sec
CPU phase duration	Duration of per-phase CPU computation	0	0%, 50%, 100% the GPU phase duration	0
Size of GPU transfers	Size of memory transfers between CPU and GPU	100KB	100KB	100KB
Size of MPI transfers	Size of data transferred by each communication primitive	400KB	400KB (broadcast, gather-scatter) 0KB otherwise	100KB * # of processes

Software setup – All experiments described in this Section were performed using the runtime system described in Section 3. Batch scheduling is implemented by setting the number of virtual GPUs per physical GPU to 1. As far as the implementation of MPI is concerned, we use MPICH2 (http://www.mpich.org).

Maximum Idle Time Setting – Our proposed preemptive GPU sharing scheme requires setting the *maximum idle time* parameter, which indicates how long a GPU should remain idle before the runtime system performs a preemption operation. Setting this parameter involves evaluating a trade-off between runtime overhead and GPU underutilization. If the maximum idle time is set to a large value, preemption will be rarely invoked, leading to minimal runtime overhead but possibly to GPU underutilization. Conversely, if this parameter's value is too low, preemption operations may be triggered too frequently, causing the runtime overhead to outweigh the benefits from an increased GPU utilization. To set this parameter, we have measured the runtime overhead due to preemption and involved with binding a process to a virtual GPU. We have found that setting the maximum idle time to 0.01 seconds allows a good trade-off between runtime overhead and GPU underutilization, and we have used this setting in all experiments presented in this section.

Evaluation Metric – In all our experiments, we have measured the *overall execution time* for running a variable number of MPI jobs on a single node or on a two-node cluster. In the charts presented in Section 4.4, we show the *speedup* (in terms of overall execution time) reported by *n*-way and preemptive GPU sharing over simple batch scheduling.

4.3 Preliminary experiments

Before exploring different computation and communication patterns, we compared the considered scheduling and GPU sharing schemes using a 4-job workload that employs the `MPI_Alltoall` communication primitive (see column 3 in Table 1). We recall that this set of experiments was performed on the 4-GPU $Node_1$ machine. We considered the first two situations described in Section 2.3: intra- and inter-application imbalance. In both cases, we compared batch scheduling, 2- and 4-way sharing, preemptive sharing, and the combination of preemption and 2-way sharing (preemptive 2-way sharing). The results are shown in Figure 5.

Figure 5-a covers the *intra-application imbalance* case. In this

Table 2: Characteristics of the nodes

Node	Attributes	Values
Node₁	# CPU cores	8
	CPU cores	Intel Xeon® E5620, 2.4 GHz 12 MB cache
	Main memory	48 GB
	Operating System	CentOS 5
	CUDA version	3.2
	# GPUs	4
	GPUs	Nvidia GeForce GTX 480 15 SM x 32 cores 1 GB Global memory
Node₂	# CPU cores	12
	CPU cores	Intel Xeon ® E5-2620, 2.00GHz 15 MB cache
	Main memory	64 GB
	Operating System	CentOS 6
	CUDA version	3.2
	# GPUs	3
	GPUs	Nvidia Tesla C2070 14 SM x 32 cores ~6 GB Global memory
		Nvidia Tesla C2075 14 SM x 32 cores ~6 GB Global memory
		Nvidia Tesla C2050 14 SM x 32 cores ~3 GB Global memory

set of experiments, every job consists of 4 processes. Intra-application imbalance is due to the fact that one process is slower than the other three. Specifically, its *GPU phase duration* parameter (0.5 sec) is set to be higher than that of the other three processes by a factor *percentage imbalance*. This factor is varied along the x-axis of Figure 5-a from 10% to 50%, thus leading to an increasing amount of intra-application imbalance.

Figure 5-b covers the *inter-application imbalance* situation. In this case, all the processes within each job have the same CPU and GPU execution time. However, the workload composition is now heterogeneous: the number of processes is not uniform across the jobs. In particular, workload composition $j_1 \times [p_1] + j_2 \times [p_2]$ indicates that j_1 jobs consist of p_1 processes and j_2 jobs consists of p_2 processes. Note that all configurations contain jobs consisting

of 3 processes. Since the node has 4 GPUs, these jobs cause imbalance. In particular, the number of jobs with 3 processes is varied along the x-axis, leading to an increasing amount of inter-application imbalance.

From these preliminary experiments, we can make the following observations. First, batch scheduling fails to capture both intra- and inter-application imbalance, and to correct their negative effects on the performance. In fact, when using batch scheduling, the overall execution time stays constant across all the experiments, and depends on the slowest job. Second, in case of intra-application imbalance, n-way sharing leads to performance improvements over batch scheduling, and this gain increases with the imbalance. In fact, GPU sharing allows the idle time of one process to be hidden behind the GPU execution of co-located processes. In case of inter-application imbalances, n-way sharing is beneficial only when the workload is highly imbalanced and when 4 processes are allowed to share the same GPU device. Third, by increasing the GPU utilization, preemptive GPU sharing greatly outperforms the other schemes in both the intra- and the inter-application imbalance scenarios. Again, the performance gain increases with the degree of imbalance. Finally, best performance can be achieved by combining 2-way sharing and preemption (preemptive 2-way sharing case). This trend has been observed in all experiments performed. For readability, in the remainder of this section we will consider only batch scheduling, 4-way sharing and preemptive 2-way sharing, and report the speedup of these two sharing schemes over batch scheduling.

4.4 Node-level experiments

In this section, we show a set of node-level experiments meant to evaluate the proposed scheduling and sharing schemes on workloads characterized by a variety of computation and communication patterns. The parameter settings of the workload generator used for this group of experiments are shown in the 4th column of Table 1. As can be seen, the exploration space can be described as follows. First, we consider three collecting communication patterns: broadcast, scatter-gather and barrier synchronization. Second, we use shorter and longer GPU phases (namely, 0.3 and 3 sec, respectively). Third, we add an increasing amount of CPU computation to each execution phase: specifically, we consider three settings: one with no CPU computation, one where the CPU computation is half as long as the GPU computation, and one where the two have the same duration (CPU phase duration parameter set to 0%, 50% and

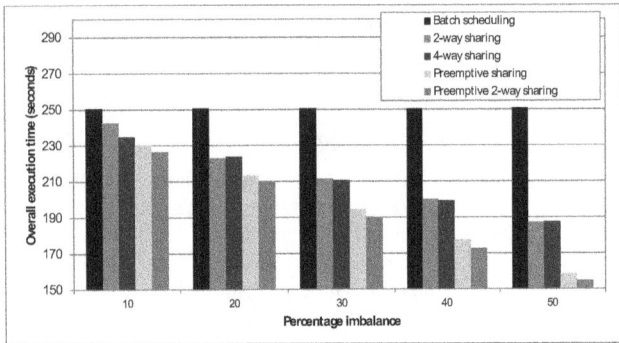

(5-a) – Intra-application imbalance

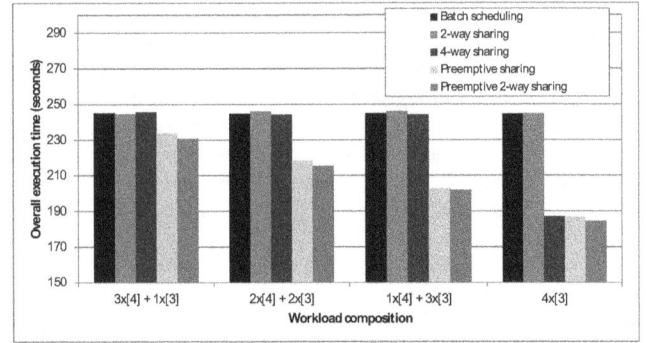

(5-b) – Inter-application imbalance

Figure 5: Preliminary experiments: comparison among 5 scheduling and sharing schemes for a 4-job workload including *all-to-all* communication primitives. In (5-a), each job consists of 4 processes, and the *GPU phase duration* parameter of one of these processes is higher than that of the other three by a factor *percentage imbalance*. In (5-b), workload composition $j_1 \times [p_1] + j_2 \times [p_2]$ indicates that j_1 jobs consist of p_1 processes and j_2 jobs consists of p_2 processes.

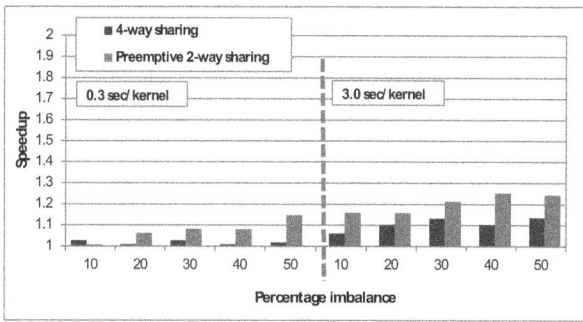
(6-a)   Worst case

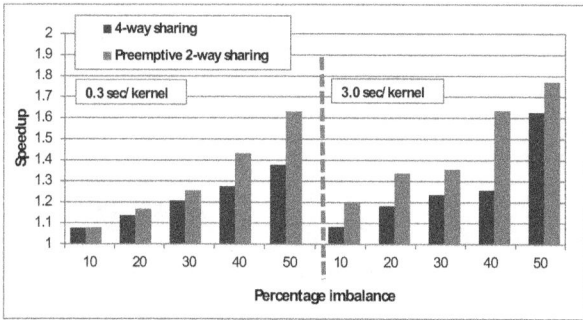
(6-b)   Best case

Figure 6: Intra-application imbalance - speedup for broadcast communication pattern.

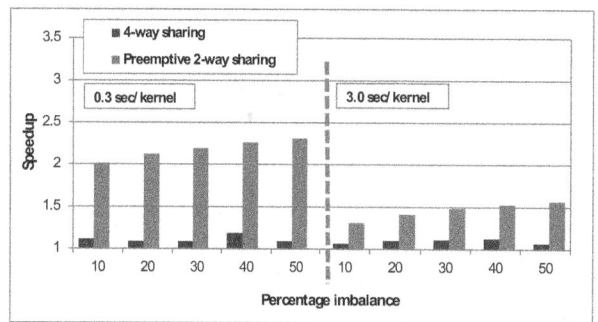
(7-a)   Worst case

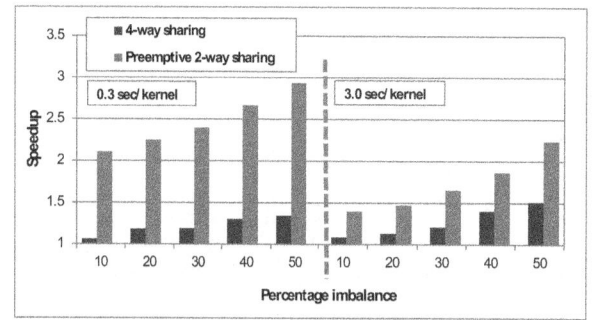
(7-b)   Best case

Figure 7: Intra-application imbalance - speedup for scatter-gather communication pattern.

100%, respectively). We want every process to use the GPU for approximately 60 seconds in all experiments. To this end, we vary the number of iterations (20 or 200) depending on the GPU phase duration used. Note that this will affect the synchronization rate (since each iteration contains a communication/synchronization primitive). As in our preliminary experiments, we want to evaluate the speedup of the sharing schemes over batch scheduling in two situations: intra- and inter-application imbalance. In all cases, we use a workload consisting of 4 jobs.

Intra-application imbalance - In this first set of experiments, all jobs consist of 4 processes with no CPU computation (except for inter-process communication). The default kernel time is set either to 0.3 or to 3 seconds to allow two synchronization rates. To introduce intra-application imbalance, we decrease the GPU phase duration of some processes in each job by 10 to 50 percent of the default kernel time. We consider two workload configurations, that we call *best case* and *worst case*. In the former, three out of four processes per application are made faster. In the latter, only one process per application is faster than the other three.

The results reported on workloads using the broadcast, the gather-scatter and the barrier communication patterns are shown in Figure 6, 7 and 8, respectively. As can be seen, preemption achieves better performance in almost every case. In a few cases (e.g., broadcast communication pattern & low imbalance percentage), the preemption overhead can have a dominant effect and deteriorate the performance. A speedup of 1.7X, 2.9X and 2.9X over the batch scheduling can be observed in the broadcast, scatter-gather and barrier communication cases, respectively. Batch scheduling and 4-way sharing fail to capture the effect of heterogeneity, especially in *worst case* configurations. We also note that the speedup observed with broadcast communication is relatively small compared to that achieved with the other communication patterns. Processes that perform broadcast

communication exhibit fewer inactivity periods than processes using other patterns. This is because the broadcast operation does not require every process to enter the communication routine at the same time in order to proceed. Different processes can progress independently even under the imbalance. The overhead of the communication can, therefore, be adequately hidden even by the 4-way sharing mechanism.

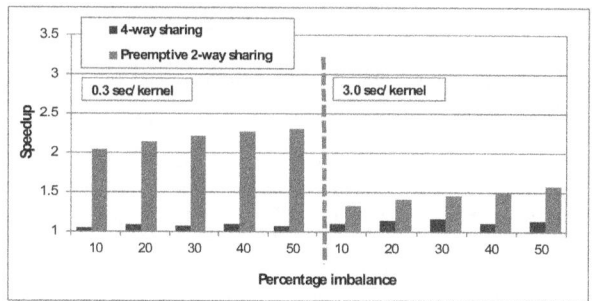
(8-a)   Worst case

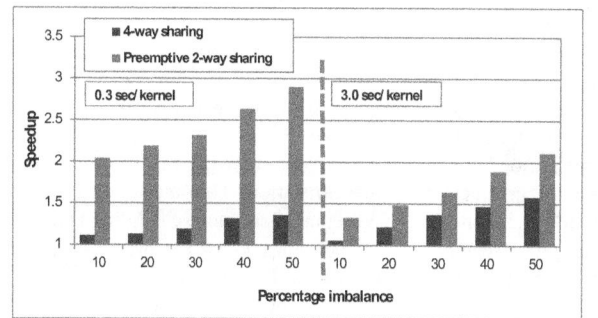
(8-b)   Best case

Figure 8: Intra-application imbalance - speedup for barrier synchronization pattern.

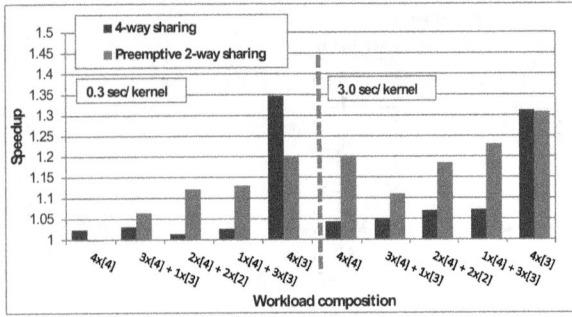

(9-a)   0% CPU phase

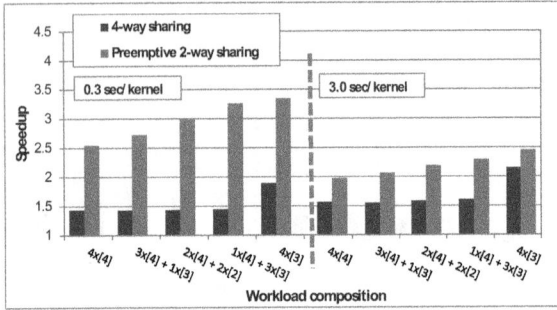

(9-b)   50% CPU phase

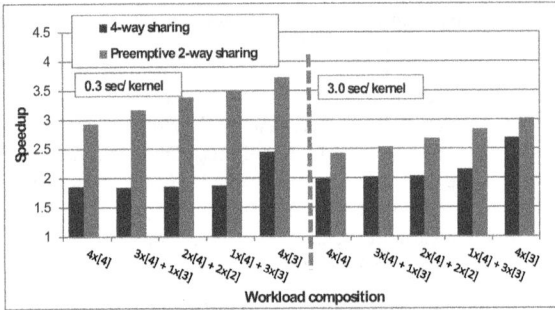

(9-c)   100% CPU phase

Figure 9: Inter-application imbalance - speedup for broadcast pattern.

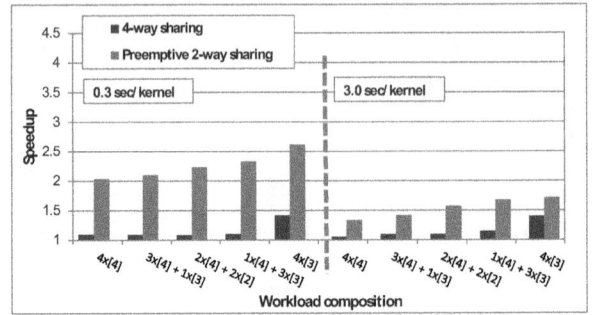

(10-a)   0% CPU phase

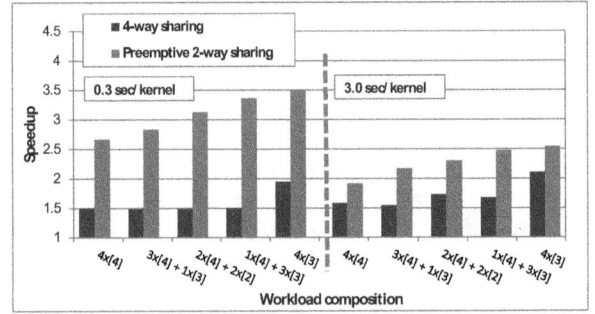

(10-b)   50% CPU phase

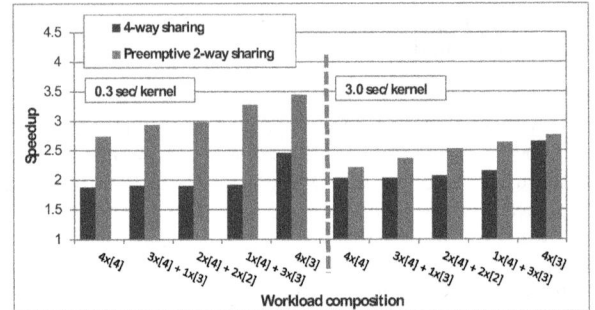

(10-c)   100% CPU phase

Figure 10: Inter-application imbalance - speedup for scatter-gather pattern.

Inter-application imbalance – In this second set of experiments, there is no execution imbalance within each job. However, inter-application imbalance is introduced by allowing different jobs in the workload to include a different number of processes. As in our preliminary experiments, we use mixes of jobs with four and three processes each, and vary the number of jobs consisting of three processes.

The results reported on workloads that use the broadcast, the gather-scatter and the barrier communication patterns are shown in Figure 9, 10 and 11, respectively. The workload composition along the *x*-axis of these charts can be read as in the preliminary experiments. We make the following observations. First, preemption can again effectively improve the performance by minimizing the GPU underutilization. This mechanism achieves up to a 3.5X and a 2.1X speedup over batch scheduling and 4-way sharing, respectively. Second, when using the broadcast pattern, performance improvements can be observed in most of the configurations. As we have learned from the previous experiments, the broadcast pattern rarely blocks processes when performing communication. Therefore, 4-way sharing is sufficient to hide the communication latency. In addition, the preemption overhead can be unjustified in case of balanced workload

compositions (e.g. *4x[4]*). We further observe that, as we increase the percentage of the CPU phase, the speedup of preemption over 4-way sharing decreases slightly. In fact, 4-way sharing can overlap the GPU and CPU phases of different applications without incurring preemption overhead.

4.5 Cluster-level experiments

In this section, we show the results of experiments conducted on the two-node heterogeneous cluster of Table 2. The jobs, whose characteristics are summarized in the 5th column of Table 1, use the scatter-gather communication pattern, do not include CPU computation (except for MPI communication), and do not present intra-application imbalance. We conduct 3 sets of experiments using 4, 6 and 8 processes per job, respectively. In all experiments, the workload consists of 8 jobs.

Figure 12 reports the execution time using batch scheduling, 4-way sharing, and preemptive 2-way sharing. The dataset in case of batch scheduling and 8 processes per job is missing because our cluster has a total of 7 GPUs, and, as explained in Section 2.3 (scenario 3), batch scheduling cannot support applications requesting more GPUs than physically available in the system. As can be seen, 4-way sharing and preemptive GPU sharing lead to a

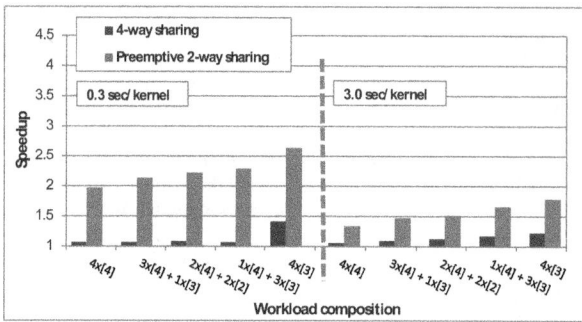

(11-a)   0% CPU phase

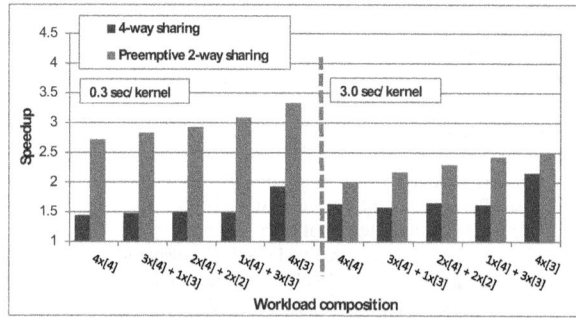

(11-b)   50% CPU phase

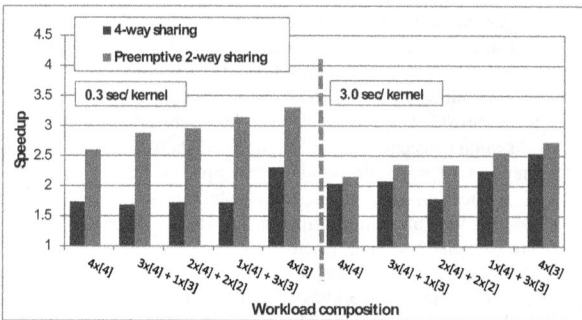

(11-c)   100% CPU phase

Figure 11: Inter-application imbalance - speedup for barrier pattern.

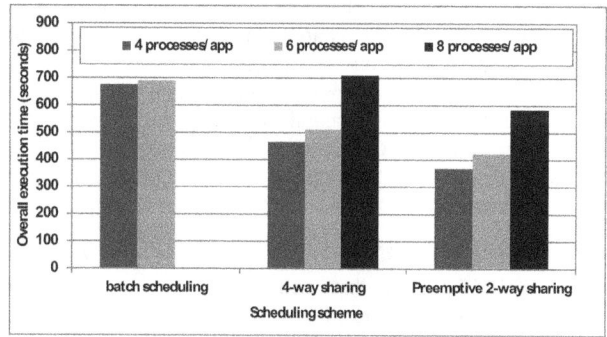

Figure 12: Overall execution time in cluster settings.

25-30% and a 40-45% performance improvement over batch scheduling, respectively. In addition, both sharing mechanisms allow the execution of jobs with more processes than available GPUs. As explained in Section 2.3, 4-way sharing would not be able to support jobs with more than 7*4=28 processes. Preemption-based scheduling is the only mechanism able to support applications with any number of processes even in the presence of synchronization.

5. RELATED WORK

Resource sharing among applications in non-dedicated environments has been extensive studied. Many scheduling algorithms targeting homogeneous nodes and clusters have been proposed, with the goal of maximizing both the performance of individual applications and the resource utilization [7-13]. In particular, Mars et al. [7, 8] proposed co-location mechanisms to allow applications to efficiently share CPU resources while minimizing the performance degradation due to contention.

Gang-scheduling is a scheduling scheme that aims to minimize the cost of communication among parallel applications. Similarly to batch scheduling, gang scheduling schedules processes belonging to the same application on different resources at the same time. Gang scheduling, however, allows some degree of resource sharing. Feitelson et al. [14] presented a performance evaluation of gang-scheduling in shared-memory systems. Hori et al. [15] proposed an implementation of gang-scheduling for multi-node systems. Because gang-scheduling makes scheduling decisions across all involved nodes, it may incur high synchronization overhead and has limited scalability.

More recent work proposed co-scheduling schemes for parallel applications in CPU cluster environments [16-20]. In particular, Arpaci-Dusseau et al. [18] proposed communication-based co-scheduling. In their scheme, information such as the response time and the type of communication among the processes in a parallel application is used to guide scheduling and sharing decisions. Choi et al. [16] proposed a co-scheduling scheme that blocks processes involved in point-to-point communication and tries to co-schedule processes that perform collective communication. Our preemptive scheduling is in spirit similar to the spin-block communication described in [17, 18], in which communicating processes spin for a predefined period, and then block if the communication is not completed within such period. It must be observed that all the studies mentioned above target only on multi-core CPUs and homogenous CPU clusters and do not address performance heterogeneity. Further, no effort has been made to extend these proposals to nodes and clusters that include accelerators and many-core devices, such as GPUs.

With the increased popularity of GPUs, a number of studies on scheduling algorithms for GPU nodes and clusters have been performed. Many of them propose frameworks to schedule jobs in heterogeneous CPU-GPU clusters so as to maximize the overall system throughput. Recently, Ravi et al. [21] have proposed scheduling schemes to efficiently map applications onto different types of resources (CPU/GPU). Scheduling decisions are based on profiling information and user-input. Scheduling and sharing schemes aimed to maximize the users' satisfaction and the provider's profit have been presented in [22] for homogeneous CPU clusters and in [23] for heterogeneous CPU-GPU clusters. All these proposals present cluster-level scheduling schemes, and assume the availability of profiling information. Node-level GPU sharing has been studied in [6], which presents a kernel consolidation framework for GPUs. Although scheduling and sharing on GPUs have been covered by various proposals [1, 6, 21, 23, 24], the effects of synchronization within multi-process applications on sharing are not well understood. To the best of our knowledge, we are the first to evaluate this problem, and to point out how the presence of load imbalance and performance heterogeneity can lead to GPU underutilization and suboptimal performance.

Calhoun et al. [25] presented a study of GPU kernel preemption based on time-quanta. Their preemption mechanism needs compiler's assistance in order to augment the GPU kernel with preemption routines. In our experience, most GPU kernels are relatively short running, and preemption at such a fine granularity is not justified when considering the overhead due to unbinding a context from a virtual GPU and mapping a new context to it. Because of this overhead, we take a different approach and allow only inter-kernel preemption.

6. CONCLUSION

In this work we have discussed the limitations of existing scheduling mechanisms and GPU sharing schemes in the presence of multi-threaded and multi-process applications that include synchronization. In particular, we have shown that that these mechanisms lead to inefficiencies in the presence of intra- and inter-application imbalances. We have then proposed GPU preemption as a mechanism to overcome such limitations and to efficiently schedule multi-process applications on CPU-GPU nodes and clusters, and have implemented GPU preemption in our node-level runtime system. We have proposed a workload generator to automatically create MPI-CUDA applications with different characteristics (CPU and GPU intensity, type of synchronization and communication patterns, and others). Finally, we have used the proposed workload generator to compare batch scheduling, controlled *n*-way GPU sharing, and our preemptive GPU sharing on different job mixes. Our results confirm that, despite its runtime overhead, preemptive GPU sharing is an effective mechanism to improve the performance of MPI-CUDA applications, especially in the presence of load imbalances. The performance improvements are achieved by minimizing the GPU underutilization.

7. ACKNOWLEDGMENTS

This work has been supported by NSF award CNS-1216756 and by a gift from NEC Laboratories America and equipment donations from Nvidia Corporation.

8. REFERENCES

[1] M. Becchi, K. Sajjapongse *et al.*, "A virtual memory based runtime to support multi-tenancy in clusters with GPUs," in Proc. of the 21st Int'l Symp. on High-Performance Parallel and Distributed Computing, 2012, pp. 97-108.

[2] V. Gupta, A. Gavrilovska *et al.*, "GViM: GPU-accelerated virtual machines," in Proc. of the 3rd ACM Workshop on System-level Virtualization for High Performance Computing, 2009, pp. 17-24.

[3] L. Shi, H. Chen, and J. Sun, "vCUDA: GPU accelerated high performance computing in virtual machines," in Proc. of the IEEE Int'l Symposium on Parallel&Distributed Processing, 2009, pp. 1-11.

[4] J. Duato, A. J. Pena *et al.*, "Enabling CUDA acceleration within virtual machines using rCUDA," in Proc. of the 18th Int'l Conference on High Performance Computing, 2011, pp. 1-10.

[5] G. Giunta, R. Montella *et al.*, "A GPGPU transparent virtualization component for high performance computing clouds," in Proc. of the 16th Int'l Euro-Par conference on Parallel processing: Part I, 2010, pp. 379-391.

[6] V. T. Ravi, M. Becchi *et al.*, "Supporting GPU sharing in cloud environments with a transparent runtime consolidation framework," in Proc. of the 20th Int'l Symp. on High performance distributed computing, 2011, pp. 217-228.

[7] J. Mars, N. Vachharajani *et al.*, "Contention aware execution: online contention detection and response," in Proc. of the 8th annual IEEE/ACM Int'l Symp. on Code generation and optimization, Toronto, 2010, pp. 257-265.

[8] J. Mars, L. Tang *et al.*, "Bubble-Up: increasing utilization in modern warehouse scale computers via sensible co-locations," in Proc. of the 44th Annual IEEE/ACM Int'l Symp. on Microarchitecture, 2011, pp. 248-259.

[9] M. Kambadur, T. Moseley *et al.*, "Measuring interference between live datacenter applications," in Proc. of the Int'l Conf. on High Performance Computing, Networking, Storage and Analysis, 2012, pp. 1-12.

[10] C. Anglano, "A Performance Comparison of Coscheduling Strategies for Workstation Clusters," *Cluster Computing*, vol. 4, no. 2, pp. 121-131, 2001.

[11] G. S. Choi, S. Agarwal *et al.*, "Performance Comparison of Coscheduling Algorithms for Non-Dedicated Clusters Through a Generic Framework," *Int. J. High Perform. Comput. Appl.*, vol. 21, no. 1, pp. 91-105, 2007.

[12] D. G. Feitelson, and L. Rudolph, "Coscheduling Based on Run-Time Identification of Activity Working Sets," *International Journal of Parallel Programming*, vol. 23, pp. 135--160.

[13] A. Yoo, and M. A. Jette, "An Efficient and Scalable Coscheduling Technique for Large Symmetric Multiprocessor Clusters," in Revised Papers from the 7th International Workshop on Job Scheduling Strategies for Parallel Processing, 2001, pp. 21-40.

[14] D. G. Feitelson, L. Rudolph, and U. Schwiegelshohn, "Parallel job scheduling: a status report," in Proc. of the 10th Int'l Conf. on Job Scheduling Strategies for Parallel Processing, 2005, pp. 1-16.

[15] A. Hori, H. Tezuka, and Y. Ishikawa, "Highly efficient gang scheduling implementation," in Proc. of the 1998 ACM/IEEE Conf. on Supercomputing (CDROM), 1998, pp. 1-14.

[16] G. S. Choi, J.-H. Kim *et al.*, "Coscheduling in Clusters: Is It a Viable Alternative?," in Proc. of the 2004 ACM/IEEE Conf. on Supercomputing, 2004, pp. 16.

[17] P. Sobalvarro, S. Pakin *et al.*, "Dynamic Coscheduling on Workstation Clusters," in Proc. of the Workshop on Job Scheduling Strategies for Parallel Processing, 1998, pp. 231-256.

[18] A. C. Arpaci-Dusseau, "Implicit coscheduling: coordinated scheduling with implicit information in distributed systems," *ACM Trans. Comput. Syst.*, vol. 19, no. 3, pp. 283-331, 2001.

[19] A. C. Dusseau, R. H. Arpaci, and D. E. Culler, "Effective distributed scheduling of parallel workloads," in Proce. of the 1996 ACM SIGMETRICS Int'l Conf. on Measurement and modeling of computer systems, 1996, pp. 25-36.

[20] S. Agarwal, A. B. Yoo *et al.*, "Co-ordinated coscheduling in time-sharing clusters through a generic framework," in Proc. of the IEEE Int'l Conf. on Cluster Computing, 2003, pp. 84-91.

[21] V. T. Ravi, M. Becchi *et al.*, "Scheduling Concurrent Applications on a Cluster of CPU-GPU Nodes," in Proc. of the 2012 12th IEEE/ACM Int'l Symp. on Cluster, Cloud and Grid Computing, 2012, pp. 140-147.

[22] D. E. Irwin, L. E. Grit, and J. S. Chase, "Balancing Risk and Reward in a Market-Based Task Service," in Proc. of the 13th IEEE Int'l Symp. on High Performance Distributed Computing, 2004, pp. 160-169.

[23] V. T. Ravi, M. Becchi *et al.*, "ValuePack: value-based scheduling framework for CPU-GPU clusters," in Proc. of the Int'l Conf. on High Performance Computing, Networking, Storage and Analysis, 2012, pp. 1-12.

[24] R. Phull, C.-H. Li *et al.*, "Interference-driven resource management for GPU-based heterogeneous clusters," in Proc. of the 21st Int'l Symp. on High-Performance Parallel and Distributed Computing, 2012, pp. 109-120.

[25] J. Calhoun, and J. Hai, "Preemption of a CUDA Kernel Function," in Software Engineering, Artificial Intelligence, in Proc. of the Int'l Conf. in Networking and Parallel & Distributed Computing, 2012, pp. 247-252.

On the Efficacy of GPU-Integrated MPI for Scientific Applications

Ashwin M. Aji[*], Lokendra S. Panwar[*], Feng Ji[†], Milind Chabbi[‡], Karthik Murthy[‡],
Pavan Balaji[§], Keith R. Bisset[¶], James Dinan[§], Wu-chun Feng[*],
John Mellor-Crummey[‡], Xiaosong Ma[†], Rajeev Thakur[§]

[*]Dept. of Comp. Sci., Virginia Tech, {aaji,lokendra,feng}@cs.vt.edu
[†]Dept. of Comp. Sci., North Carolina State Univ., fji@ncsu.edu, ma@csc.ncsu.edu
[‡]Dept. of Comp. Sci., Rice University, {mc29,ksm2,johnmc}@rice.edu
[§]Math. and Comp. Sci. Div., Argonne National Lab., {balaji,dinan,thakur}@mcs.anl.gov
[¶]Virginia Bioinformatics Inst., Virginia Tech, kbisset@vbi.vt.edu

ABSTRACT

Scientific computing applications are quickly adapting to leverage the massive parallelism of GPUs in large-scale clusters. However, the current hybrid programming models require application developers to explicitly manage the disjointed host and GPU memories, thus reducing both efficiency and productivity. Consequently, GPU-integrated MPI solutions, such as MPI-ACC and MVAPICH2-GPU, have been developed that provide unified programming interfaces and optimized implementations for end-to-end data communication among CPUs and GPUs. To date, however, there lacks an in-depth performance characterization of the new optimization spaces or the productivity impact of such GPU-integrated communication systems for scientific applications.

In this paper, we study the efficacy of GPU-integrated MPI on scientific applications from domains such as epidemiology simulation and seismology modeling, and we discuss the lessons learned. We use MPI-ACC as an example implementation and demonstrate how the programmer can seamlessly choose between either the CPU or the GPU as the logical communication end point, depending on the application's computational requirements. MPI-ACC also encourages programmers to explore novel application-specific optimizations, such as internode CPU-GPU communication with concurrent CPU-GPU computations, which can improve the overall cluster utilization. Furthermore, MPI-ACC internally implements scalable memory management techniques, thereby decoupling the low-level memory optimizations from the applications and making them scalable and portable across several architectures. Experimental results from a state-of-the-art cluster with hundreds of GPUs show that the MPI-ACC–driven new application-specific optimizations can improve the performance of an epidemiology simulation by up to 61.6% and the performance of a seismology modeling application by up to 44%, when compared with traditional hybrid MPI+GPU implementations. We conclude that GPU-integrated MPI significantly enhances programmer produc-

tivity and has the potential to improve the performance and portability of scientific applications, thus making a significant step toward GPUs being "first-class citizens" of hybrid CPU-GPU clusters.

Categories and Subject Descriptors: C.1.3 [*Processor Architectures*]: Other Architecture Styles – Heterogeneous (hybrid) systems; D.1.3 [*Programming Techniques*]: Concurrent Programming – Parallel programming

Keywords: MPI; GPGPU; MPI-ACC; Computational Epidemiology; Seismology

1. INTRODUCTION

Graphics processing units (GPUs) have gained widespread use as general-purpose computational accelerators and have been studied extensively across a broad range of scientific applications [13, 20, 25, 30]. The presence of GPUs in high-performance computing (HPC) clusters has also increased rapidly because of their unprecedented performance-per-power and performance-per-price ratios. In fact, 62 of today's top 500 fastest supercomputers (as of November 2012) employ general-purpose accelerators, 53 of which are GPUs [4].

While GPU-based clusters possess tremendous theoretical peak performance because of their inherent massive parallelism, the scientific codes that are hand-tuned and optimized for such architectures often achieve poor parallel efficiency [4, 9]. The reason is partially that data must be explicitly transferred between the disjoint memory spaces of the CPU and GPU, a process that in turn fragments the data communication model and restricts the degree of communication overlap with computations on the CPU *and* the GPU, thus effectively underutilizing the entire cluster. Also, significant programmer effort would be required to recover this performance through vendor- and system-specific optimizations, including GPU-Direct [3] and node and I/O topology awareness. Consequently, GPU-aware extensions to parallel programming models, such as the Message Passing Interface (MPI), have recently been developed, for example, MPI-ACC [6, 19] and MVAPICH2-GPU [28]. While such libraries provide a unified and highly efficient data communication mechanism for point-to-point, one-sided, and collective communications among CPUs and GPUs, an in-depth characterization of their impact on the execution profiles of scientific applications is yet to be performed. In this paper, we study the efficacy of GPU-integrated MPI libraries for GPU-accelerated scientific applications, and we discuss the lessons learned. Our specific contributions are the following:

- We perform an in-depth analysis of hybrid MPI+GPU codes from two scientific application domains, namely, computational epidemiology [7, 9] and seismology modeling [23], and we identify the inherent inefficiencies in their fragmented data movement and execution profiles.

- We use MPI-ACC as an example GPU-integrated MPI solution and explore new design spaces for creating novel application specific optimizations.

- We evaluate our findings on *HokieSpeed*, a state-of-the-art hybrid CPU-GPU cluster housed at Virginia Tech. We use HPCToolkit [5], a performance analysis and visualization tool for parallel programs, to understand the performance and productivity tradeoffs of the different optimizations that were made possible by MPI-ACC.

We demonstrate how MPI-ACC can be used to easily explore and evaluate new optimization strategies. In particular, we overlap MPI-ACC CPU-GPU communication calls with computation on the CPU *as well as* the GPU, thus resulting in better overall cluster utilization. Moreover, we demonstrate how MPI-ACC provides the flexibility to the programmer to seamlessly choose between CPU or GPU to execute the next task at hand, thus enhancing programmer productivity. For example, in the default MPI+GPU programming model, the CPU is traditionally used for prerequisite tasks, such as data marshaling or data partitioning, before the GPU computation. In contrast, MPI-ACC provides a logical integrated view of CPUs and GPUs so that the programmer can choose to move the raw data to the remote GPU itself, then execute the prerequisite tasks and the actual computation as consecutive GPU kernels. In addition, MPI-ACC internally implements scalable memory management techniques, thereby decoupling the low-level memory optimizations from the applications and making them scalable and portable across several architecture generations. In summary, we show that with MPI-ACC, the programmer can easily evaluate and quantify the tradeoffs of many communication-computation patterns and choose the ideal strategy for the given application and machine configuration. Our experimental results on HokieSpeed indicate that MPI-ACC–driven optimizations and the newly created communication-computation patterns can help improve the performance of the epidemiology simulation by 14.6% to up to 61.6% and the seismology modeling application by up to 44% over the traditional hybrid MPI+GPU models.

The rest of the paper is organized as follows. Section 2 introduces the current MPI and GPU programming models and describes the current hybrid application programming approaches for CPU-GPU clusters. Sections 3 and 4 explain the execution profiles of the epidemiology and seismology modeling applications, their inefficient default MPI+GPU designs, and the way GPU-integrated MPI can be used to optimize their performances while improving productivity. Section 5 discusses related work, and Section 6 summarizes our conclusions.

2. APPLICATION DESIGN FOR HYBRID CPU-GPU SYSTEMS

2.1 Default MPI+GPU Design

Graphics processing units have become more amenable to general-purpose computations over the past few years, largely as a result of

```
1  computation_on_GPU(gpu_buf);
2  cudaMemcpy(host_buf, gpu_buf, size, D2H ...);
3  MPI_Send(host_buf, size, ...);
```

(a) Basic hybrid MPI+GPU with synchronous execution – high productivity and low performance.

```
1   int processed[chunks] = {0};
2   for(j=0;j<chunks;j++) {
3     computation_on_GPU(gpu_buf+offset, streams[j]);
4     cudaMemcpyAsync(host_buf+offset, gpu_buf+offset,
5                     D2H, streams[j], ...);
6   }
7   numProcessed = 0; j = 0; flag = 1;
8   while (numProcessed < chunks) {
9     if(cudaStreamQuery(streams[j] == cudaSuccess) {
10      MPI_Isend(host_buf+offset,...); /* start MPI */
11      numProcessed++;
12      processed[j] = 1;
13    }
14    MPI_Testany(...); /* check progress */
15    if(numProcessed < chunks) /* find next chunk */
16      while(flag) {
17        j=(j+1)%chunks; flag=processed[j];
18      }
19  }
20  MPI_Waitall();
```

(b) Advanced hybrid MPI+GPU with pipelined execution – low productivity and high performance.

```
1  for(j=0;j<chunks;j++) {
2    computation_on_GPU(gpu_buf+offset, streams[j]);
3    MPI_Isend(gpu_buf+offset, ...);
4  }
5  MPI_Waitall();
```

(c) GPU-integrated MPI with pipelined execution – high productivity and high performance.

Figure 1: Designing hybrid CPU-GPU applications. For the manual MPI+GPU model with OpenCL, clEnqueueReadBuffer and clEnqueueWriteBuffer would be used in place of cudaMemcpy. For GPU-integrated MPI models such as MPI-ACC, the code remains the same for *all* platforms (CUDA or OpenCL) and supported devices.

the more programmable GPU hardware and increasingly mature GPU programming models, such as CUDA [2] and OpenCL [15]. Today's discrete GPUs reside on PCIe and are equipped with very high-throughput GDDR5 *device* memory on the GPU cards. To fully utilize the benefits of the ultra-fast memory subsystem, however, current GPU programmers must explicitly transfer data between the main memory and the device memory across PCIe, by issuing direct memory access (DMA) calls such as cudaMemcpy or clEnqueueWriteBuffer.

The Message Passing Interface (MPI) is one of the most widely adopted parallel programming models for developing scalable, distributed memory applications. MPI-based applications are typically designed by identifying parallel tasks and assigning them to multiple processes. In the default hybrid MPI+GPU programming model, the compute-intensive portions of each process are offloaded to the local GPU for further acceleration. Data is transferred between processes by explicit messages in MPI. However, the current MPI standard assumes a CPU-centric single-memory model for communication. The default MPI+GPU programming model employs a *hybrid* two-staged data movement model, where data copies are performed between main memory and the local GPU's device memory that are preceded and/or followed by MPI communication between the host CPUs (Figures 1a and 1b). This is the norm seen in most GPU-accelerated MPI applications today [9, 10, 12]. The basic approach (Figure 1a) has less complex code, but the blocking and staged data movement severely reduce performance because of the inefficient utilization of the communication channels. On the other hand, overlapped communication via pipelining efficiently utilizes all the communication channels but requires significant programmer effort, in other words, low productivity. Moreover, this approach leads to tight coupling between the high-level application logic and low-level data movement optimizations; hence, the application developer has to maintain several code variants for different GPU architectures and vendors. In addition, construction of such a sophisticated data movement scheme above the MPI runtime system incurs repeated protocol overheads and eliminates opportunities for low-level optimizations. Moreover, users who need high performance are faced with the complexity of leveraging a multitude of platform-specific optimizations that continue to evolve with the underlying technology (e.g, GPUDirect [3]).

2.2 Application Design Using GPU-Integrated MPI Frameworks

To bridge the gap between the disjointed MPI and GPU programming models, researchers have recently developed GPU-integrated MPI solutions such as our MPI-ACC [6] framework and MVAPICH-GPU [28] by Wang et al. These frameworks provide a unified MPI data transmission interface for both host and GPU memories; in other words, the programmer can use either the CPU buffer or the GPU buffer directly as the communication parameter in MPI routines. The goal of such GPU-integrated MPI platforms is to decouple the complex, low-level, GPU-specific data movement optimizations from the application logic, thus providing the following benefits: (1) portability: the application can be more portable across multiple accelerator platforms; and (2) forward compatibility: with the *same* code, the application can automatically achieve performance improvements from new GPU technologies (e.g., GPUDirect RDMA) if applicable and supported by the MPI implementation. In addition to enhanced programmability, transparent architecture specific and vendor specific performance optimizations can be provided within the MPI layer. For example, MPI-ACC enables automatic data pipelining for internode communication, NUMA affinity management, and direct GPU-to-GPU data movement (GPUDirect) for all applicable intranode CUDA communications [6, 19], thus providing a heavily optimized end-to-end communication platform.

Using GPU-integrated MPI, programmers only need to write GPU kernels and regular host CPU codes for computation and invoke the standard MPI functions for CPU-GPU data communication, without worrying about the aforementioned complex data movement optimizations of the diverse accelerator technologies (Figure 1c). In this paper, we design, analyze, and evaluate GPU-accelerated scientific applications by using MPI-ACC as the chosen GPU-integrated MPI platform. However, our findings on the efficacy of MPI-ACC can directly be applied to other GPU-integrated MPI solutions without loss of generality.

3. CASE STUDY: EPIDEMIOLOGY SIMULATION

GPU-EpiSimdemics [7, 9] is a high-performance, agent-based simulation program for studying the spread of epidemics through large-scale social contact networks and the coevolution of disease, human behavior, and the social contact network. The participating entities in GPU-EpiSimdemics are *persons* and *locations*, which

are represented as a bipartite graph (Figure 2a) and interact with each other iteratively over a predetermined number of iterations (or simulation days). The output of the simulation is the relevant disease statistics of the contagion diffusion, such as the total number of infected persons or an infection graph showing who infected whom and the time and location of the infection.

3.1 Phases

Each iteration of GPU-EpiSimdemics consists of two phases: *computeVisits* and *computeInteractions*. During the *computeVisits* phase, all the person objects of every processing element (or PE) first determine the schedules for the current day, namely, the locations to be visited and the duration of each visit. These *visit* messages are sent to the destination location's host PE (Figure 2a). Computation of the schedules is overlapped with communication of the corresponding visit messages.

In the *computeInteractions* phase, each PE first groups the received visit messages by their target locations. Next, each PE computes the probability of infection transmission between every pair of spatially and temporally colocated people in its local location objects (Figure 2b), which determines the overall disease spread information of that location. The infection transmission function depends on the current health states (e.g., susceptible, infectious, latent) of the people involved in the interaction (Figure 2c) and the transmissibility factor of the disease. These *infection* messages are sent back to the "home" PEs of the infected persons. Each PE, upon receiving its infection messages, updates the health states of the infected individuals, which will influence their schedules for the following simulation day. Thus, the messages that are computed as the output of one phase are transferred to the appropriate PEs as inputs of the next phase of the simulation. The system is synchronized by barriers after each simulation phase.

3.2 Computation-Communication Patterns and MPI-ACC-Driven Optimizations

In GPU-EpiSimdemics, each PE in the simulation is implemented as a separate MPI process. Also, the *computeInteractions* phase of GPU-EpiSimdemics is offloaded and accelerated on the GPU while the rest of the computations are executed on the CPU [9].[1] In accordance with the GPU-EpiSimdemics algorithm, the output data elements from the *computeVisits* phase (i.e., visit messages) are first received over the network, then merged, grouped, and preprocessed before the GPU can begin the *computeInteractions* phase of GPU-EpiSimdemics.

GPU-EpiSimdemics has two GPU computation modes: exclusive GPU computation, where all the visit messages are processed on the GPU, and cooperative CPU-GPU computation, where the visit messages are partitioned and concurrently processed on both the GPU and its host CPU. For each mode, we discuss the optimizations and tradeoffs. We also describe how MPI-ACC can be used to further optimize GPU-EpiSimdemics in both computation modes.

3.2.1 Exclusive GPU computation mode

In the exclusive GPU computation mode, all incoming visit messages are completely executed on the GPU during the *computeInteractions* phase. We present three optimizations with their tradeoffs.

---

[1]The current implementation of GPU-EpiSimdemics assumes one-to-one mapping of GPUs to MPI processes.

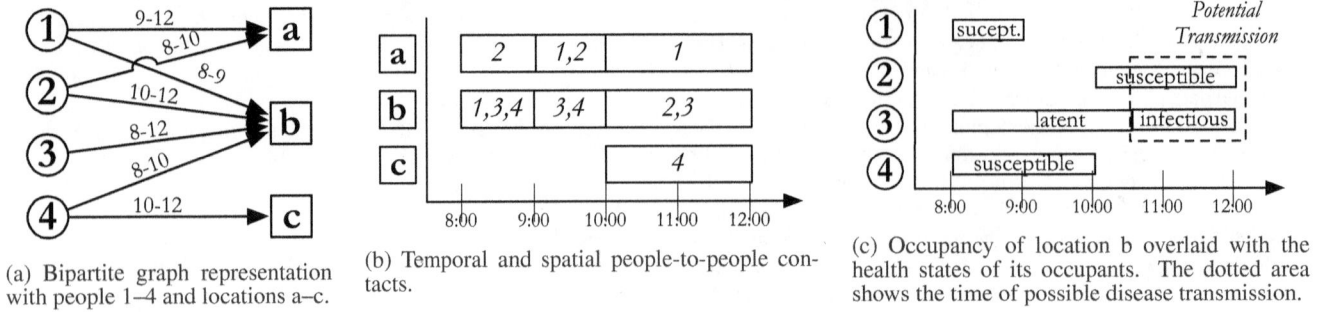

(a) Bipartite graph representation with people 1–4 and locations a–c.

(b) Temporal and spatial people-to-people contacts.

(c) Occupancy of location b overlaid with the health states of its occupants. The dotted area shows the time of possible disease transmission.

Figure 2: Computational epidemiology simulation model (figure adapted from [7]).

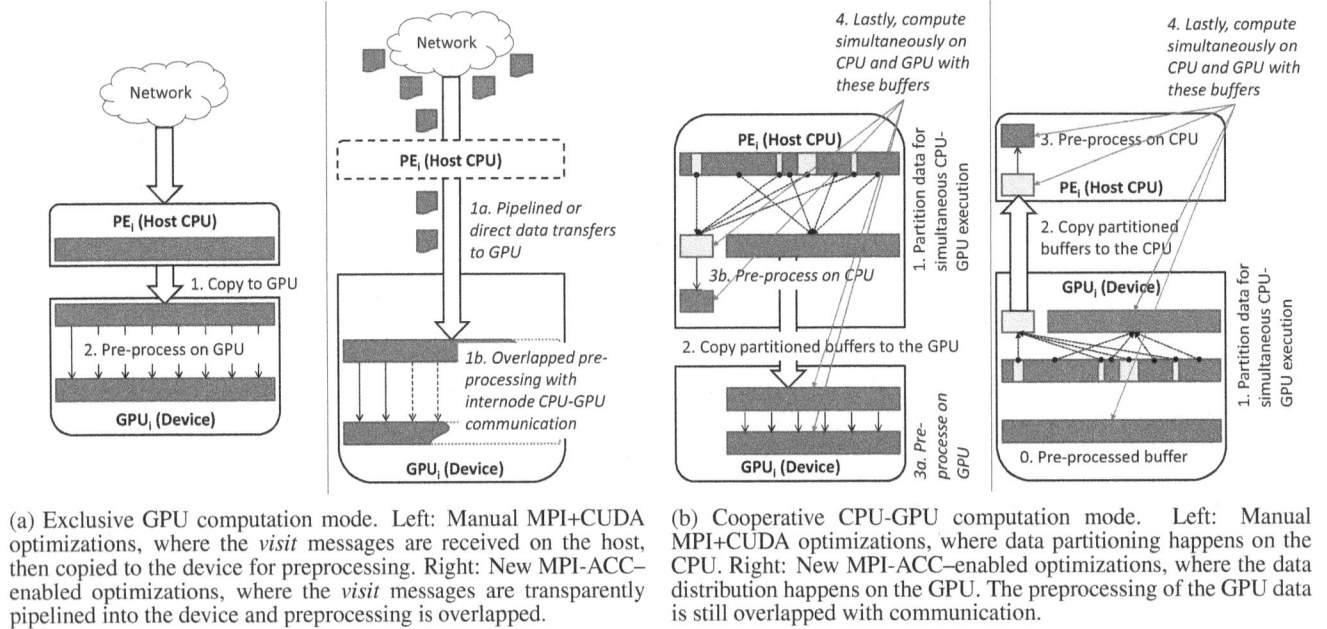

(a) Exclusive GPU computation mode. Left: Manual MPI+CUDA optimizations, where the *visit* messages are received on the host, then copied to the device for preprocessing. Right: New MPI-ACC–enabled optimizations, where the *visit* messages are transparently pipelined into the device and preprocessing is overlapped.

(b) Cooperative CPU-GPU computation mode. Left: Manual MPI+CUDA optimizations, where data partitioning happens on the CPU. Right: New MPI-ACC–enabled optimizations, where the data distribution happens on the GPU. The preprocessing of the GPU data is still overlapped with communication.

Figure 3: Creating new optimizations for GPU-EpiSimdemics using MPI-ACC.

Basic MPI+GPU communication-computation pattern.

Internode CPU-GPU data communication: In the naïve data movement approach, each PE first receives all the visit messages in the CPU's main memory during the *computeVisits* phase, then transfers the aggregate data to the local GPU (device) memory across the PCIe bus at the beginning of the *computeInteractions* phase. The typical all-to-all or scatter/gather type of operation is not feasible because the number of pairwise visit message exchanges is not known beforehand in GPU-EpiSimdemics. Thus, each PE preallocates and registers fixed-sized *persistent* buffer fragments with the `MPI_Recv_init` call and posts the receive requests by subsequently calling `MPI_Start_all`. Whenever a buffer fragment is received, it is copied into a contiguous visit vector in the CPU's main memory. The *computeInteractions* phase of the simulation first copies the aggregated visit vector to the GPU memory. While the CPU-CPU communication of visit messages is somewhat overlapped with their computation on the source CPUs, the GPU and the PCIe bus will remain idle until the visit messages are completely received, merged, and ready to be transferred to the GPU.

Preprocessing phase on the GPU: As a preprocessing step in the *computeInteractions* phase, we modify the data layout of the visit messages to be more amenable to the massive parallel architecture of the GPU [9]. Specifically, we unpack the visit message structures to a 2D time-bin matrix, where each row of the matrix represents a person-location pair and the cells in the row represents fixed time slots of the day: that is, each visit message corresponds to a single row in the person-timeline matrix. Depending on the start time and duration of a person's visit to a location, the corresponding row cells are marked as *visited*. The preprocessing logic of data unpacking is implemented as another GPU kernel at the beginning of the *computeInteractions* phase. The matrix data representation enables a much better SIMDization of the *computeInteractions* code execution, which significantly improves the GPU performance. However, we achieve the benefits at the cost of a larger memory footprint for the person-timeline matrix, as well as a computational overhead for the data unpacking.

MPI-ACC–enabled optimizations.

In the basic version of GPU-EpiSimdemics, the GPU remains idle during the internode data communication phase of *computeVisits*, whereas the CPU remains idle during the preprocessing of the *computeInteractions* phase on the GPU. We use the performance analysis tool HPCTOOLKIT to quantify the resource idleness and identify potential code regions for MPI-ACC optimization (Section 3.3: Figure 6a). With MPI-ACC, during the *computeVisits* phase, we transfer the visit message fragments from the source PE directly to the destination GPU's device memory. Internally, MPI-ACC may pipeline the internode CPU-GPU data transfers via the host CPU's memory or use direct GPU transfer techniques (e.g., GPUDirect RDMA), if possible, but these details are hidden from the programmer. The fixed-sized *persistent* buffer fragments are now preallocated *on the GPU* and registered with the `MPI_Recv_init` call, and the contiguous visit vector is not created in the GPU memory itself. Furthermore, as soon as a PE receives the visit buffer fragments on the GPU, we immediately launch small GPU kernels that preprocess on the received visit data, that is, unpack the partial visit messages to the 2D data matrix layout (Figure 3a). These preprocessing kernels execute asynchronously with respect to the CPU in a pipelined fashion and thus are completely overlapped by the visit data generation on the CPU and the internode CPU-GPU data transfers. In this way, the data layout transformation overhead is completely hidden and removed from the *computeInteractions* phase. Moreover, the CPU, GPU, and the interconnection networks are all kept busy, performing either data transfers or the preprocessing execution.

MPI-ACC's internal pipelined CPU-GPU data transfer largely hides the PCIe transfer latency during the *computeVisits* phase of GPU-EpiSimdemics. It still adds a non-negligible cost to the overall communication time when compared with the CPU-CPU data transfers of the default MPI+GPU implementation. However, our experimental results show that the gains achieved in the *computeInteractions* phase due to the preprocessing overlap outweigh the communication overheads of the *computeVisits* phase for most combinations of system configurations and input data sizes.

Advanced MPI+GPU optimizations without using MPI-ACC.

MPI-ACC enables efficient communication-computation overlap by pipelining the CPU-GPU data transfers with the preprocessing stages. However, the same optimizations can be implemented at the application level without using MPI-ACC, as follows. The fixed-sized *persistent* receive buffer fragments are preallocated on the CPU itself and registered with the `MPI_Recv_init` call, but the contiguous visit vector resides in GPU memory. Whenever a PE receives a visit buffer fragment on the CPU, we immediately enqueue an asynchronous CPU-GPU data transfer to the contiguous visit vector and also launch the small GPU preprocessing kernels. However, asynchronous CPU-GPU data transfers require the CPU receive buffer fragments to be nonpageable (pinned) memory. Without MPI-ACC, the pinned memory footprint increases with the number of processes, thus reducing the available pageable CPU memory and leading to poor CPU performance [26]. On the other hand, MPI-ACC internally creates and manages a *constant* pool of pinned memory for CPU-GPU transfers, which enables better scaling. Moreover, MPI-ACC exposes a natural interface to communicate with the target device, be it either the CPU or the GPU.

3.2.2 Cooperative CPU-GPU computation mode

The exclusive GPU computation mode achieved significant overlap of communication with computation during the preprocessing phase. When the infection calculation of the *computeInteractions* phase was executed on the GPU, however, the CPU remained idle. We again used HPCTOOLKIT to analyze the resource idleness and identified opportunities for optimizations. Consequently, in the cooperative computation mode, all the incoming visit messages are partitioned and processed concurrently on the GPU and its host CPU during the *computeInteractions* phase, an approach that gives

better parallel efficiency. Again, we present three optimizations with their tradeoffs.

Basic MPI+GPU with data partitioning on CPU.

In the MPI+GPU programming model, the incoming visit vector on the CPU is not transferred in its entirety to the GPU. Instead, the visit messages are first grouped by their target locations into buckets. Within each visit group, the amount of computation increases quadratically with the group size because it is an all-to-all person-person interaction computation within a location. Each visit group can be processed independently of the others but has to be processed by the same process or thread (CPU) or thread block (GPU). Therefore, data partitioning in GPU-EpiSimdemics is done at the granularity of *visit groups* and not individual visit messages.

At a high level, the threshold for data partitioning is chosen based on the computational capabilities of the target processors (e.g., GPUs get more populous visit groups for higher concurrency), so that the execution times on the CPU and the GPU remain approximately the same. The visit messages that are marked for GPU execution are then grouped and copied to the GPU device memory, while the CPU visit messages are grouped and remain on the host memory (Figure 3b).

Preprocessing and computation phases: In this computation mode, preprocessing, in other words, unpacking the visit structure layout to the person-timeline matrix layout, is concurrently executed on the CPU and GPU on their local visit messages (Figure 3b). Next, the CPU and GPU simultaneously execute *computeInteractions* and calculate the infections.

MPI-ACC–enabled optimizations with data partitioning on GPU.

In the MPI-ACC model, the computation of the *computeInteractions* phase is executed on the CPU and GPU concurrently. While this approach leads to better resource utilization, the data partitioning logic itself and the CPU-GPU data transfer of the partitioned data add nontrivial overheads that may offset the benefits of concurrent execution. However, our results in Section 3.3 indicate that executing the data partitioning logic *on the GPU* is about 53% faster than on the CPU because of the GPU's higher memory bandwidth. With MPI-ACC, the visit vector is directly received or pipelined into the GPU memory, and the data partitioning logic is executed on the GPU itself. Next, the CPU-specific partitioned visit groups are copied *to the CPU* (Figure 3b). As a general rule, if the GPU-driven data partitioning combined with the GPU-to-CPU data transfer performs better than the CPU-driven data partitioning combined with CPU-to-GPU data transfer, then GPU-driven data partitioning is a better option. Our experimental results (Section 3.3) indicate that for GPU-EpiSimdemics, the MPI-ACC enabled GPU-driven data partitioning performs better than the other data partitioning schemes.

The preprocessing phase *on the GPU* is still overlapped with the internode CPU-GPU communication by launching asynchronous GPU kernels, just like the exclusive GPU mode, thereby largely mitigating the preprocessing overhead. While this approach could lead to redundant computations for the CPU-specific visit groups on the GPU, the corresponding person-timeline matrix rows can be easily ignored in the subsequent execution phases. This approach will create some unnecessary memory footprint on the GPU; however, the benefits of overlapped preprocessing outweigh the issue of memory overuse. On the other hand, the preprocessing *on the CPU* is executed only after the data partitioning and GPU-to-CPU data transfer of CPU-specific visit groups. This step appears on the critical path and cannot be overlapped with any other step, but it causes negligible overhead for GPU-EpiSimdemics because of the smaller data sets for the CPU execution.

Advanced MPI+GPU with data partitioning on GPU.

GPU-driven data partitioning can also be implemented without using MPI-ACC, where the visits vector is created on the GPU and the preprocessing stage is overlapped by the local CPU-GPU data communication, similar to the advanced MPI+GPU optimization of the exclusive GPU computation mode. The data partitioning on the GPU and the remaining computations follow from the MPI-ACC–enabled optimizations. As in the GPU exclusive computation mode, however, the pinned memory footprint increases with the number of processes, which leads to poor CPU performance and scaling. Moreover, from our experience, the back-and-forth CPU-GPU data movement in the GPU-driven data partitioning optimization seems convoluted without a GPU-integrated MPI interface. On the other hand, MPI-ACC provides a natural interface for GPU communication, which encourages application developers to explore new optimization techniques such as GPU-driven data partitioning and to evaluate them against the default and more traditional CPU-driven data partitioning schemes.

3.3 Evaluation and Discussion

We conducted our experiments on *HokieSpeed*, a state-of-the-art, 212-teraflop hybrid CPU-GPU supercomputer housed at Virginia Tech. Each HokieSpeed node contains two hex-core Intel Xeon E5645 CPUs running at 2.40 GHz and two NVIDIA Tesla M2050 GPUs. The host memory capacity is 24 GB, and each GPU has a 3 GB device memory. The internode interconnect is QDR Infini-Band. We used up to 128 HokieSpeed nodes and both GPUs per node for our experiments. We used the GCC v4.4.7 compiler and CUDA v4.0 with driver version 270.41.34.

We compare the combined performance of all the phases of GPU-EpiSimdemics (*computeVisits* and *computeInteractions*), with and without the MPI-ACC–driven optimizations discussed earlier. We choose different-sized input data sets from synthetic populations from two U.S. states: Washington (WA) with a population of 5.7 million and California (CA) with a population of 33.1 million. We also vary the number of compute nodes from 8 to 128 and the number of GPU devices between 1 and 2. Each U.S. state begins its computation from the smallest node-GPU configuration that can fit the entire problem in the available GPU memory.

Our results in Figures 4a and 4b indicate that in the exclusive GPU computation mode, our MPI-ACC–driven optimizations perform better than the basic blocking MPI+GPU implementations by an average of 6.3% and by up to 14.6% for WA. Similarly, the new optimizations perform better by an average of 6.1% and by up to 17.9% for CA, where the gains come from the *computeInteractions* phase. The MPI-ACC–driven solution also outperforms the advanced pipelined MPI+GPU implementations by an average of 24.2% and up to 61.6% for WA and by an average of 13.1% and up to 32.5% for CA, but the gains come from the *computeVisits* phase. We also observe that the new optimizations are better than the basic MPI+GPU solution for smaller node configurations and are superior to the advanced MPI+GPU solution for larger nodes. For large number of nodes, however, the basic MPI+GPU solution can also outperform the MPI-ACC–enabled optimization by at most 5% for WA and only 0.1% for CA. Also, we find that the MPI-ACC–enabled solution is always better than or on par with the advanced MPI+GPU solution.

We see identical trends in the cooperative CPU-GPU computation mode (Figure 4c), where the MPI-ACC–driven GPU data-

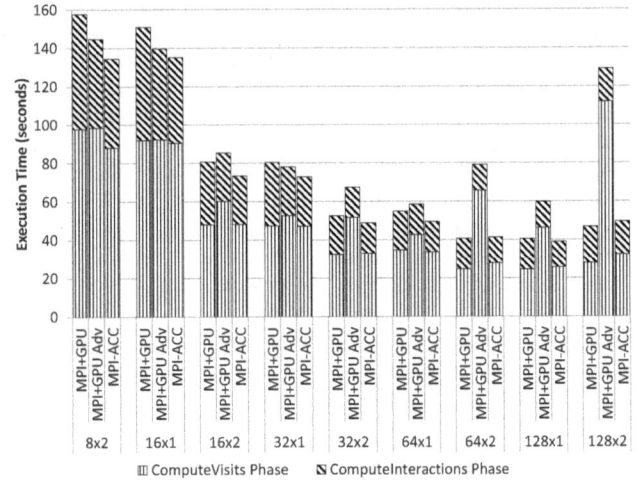

(a) Exclusive GPU mode for Washington.

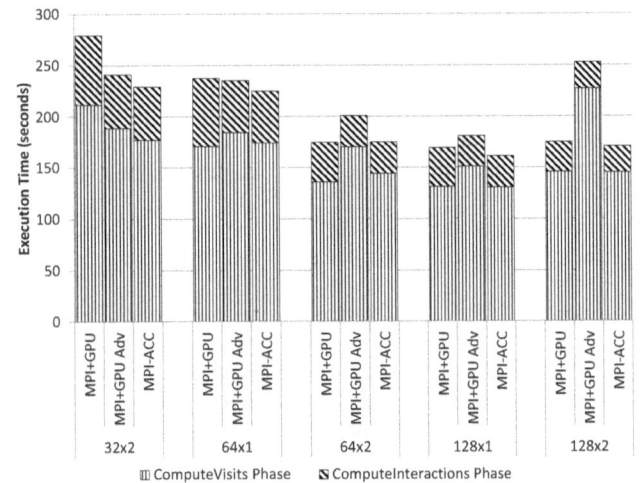

(b) Exclusive GPU mode for California.

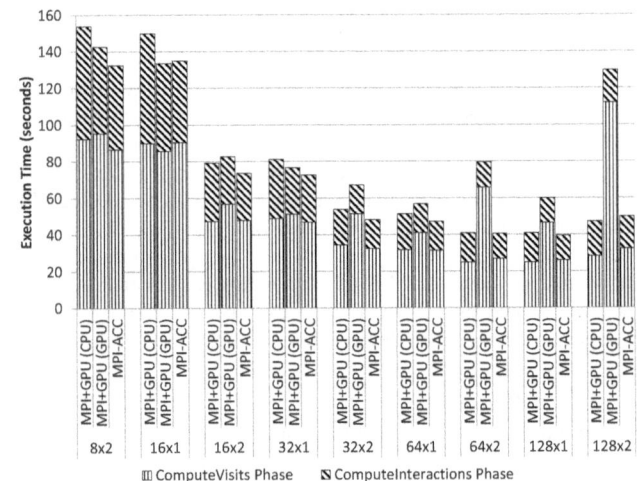

(c) Cooperative CPU-GPU mode for Washington.

Figure 4: Execution profile of GPU-EpiSimdemics over various node configurations. The x-axis increases with the total number of MPI processes P, where $P = $ Nodes * GPUs.

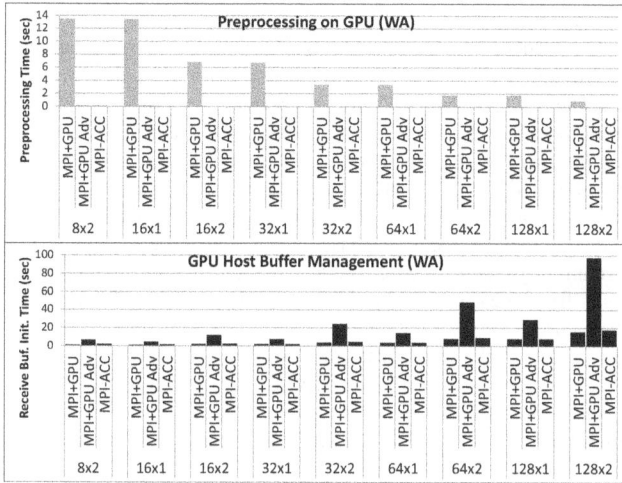

Figure 5: Analysis of MPI-ACC–enabled performance optimizations. The x-axis indicates the MPI process count P, where P = Nodes * GPUs.

partitioning strategy usually performs better than both the MPI+GPU implementations of CPU-driven and GPU-driven data-partitioning schemes. MPI-ACC is better than the CPU-driven MPI+GPU solution for smaller number of nodes, while it heavily outperforms the GPU-driven MPI+GPU solution for larger node configurations. The data-partitioning logic, by itself, performs about 53% faster on the GPU.

3.3.1 MPI-ACC–enabled optimization vs. basic MPI+GPU

The top portion of Figure 5 depicts an in-depth analysis of the benefits of overlapped preprocessing on the GPU in the exclusive GPU mode for the WA state. However, the following analysis holds good even for the CA state and the cooperative compute modes as well. We can see from the top portion of Figure 5 that for the MPI-ACC and advanced MPI+GPU implementations, the preprocessing step (data unpacking) of the *computeInteractions* phase is completely overlapped with the CPU to remote GPU communication. This is why the MPI-ACC solution outperforms the basic MPI+GPU solution for most node configurations.

Scalability analysis. For larger node configurations, however, the local operating data set in the *computeInteractions* phase becomes smaller, which means that the basic MPI+GPU solution takes less time to execute the preprocessing (data unpacking) stage. Thus, the gains over the basic MPI+GPU solution, achieved by overlapping the preprocessing step with GPU communication, also get diminished. Note that MPI-ACC or any other GPU-integrated MPI, by itself, does not impact the performance gains. In contrast, MPI-ACC enables the developer to create newer optimizations for better resource utilization, but the scalability of GPU-EpiSimdemics itself limits the scope for performance improvement. Thus, we see comparable performances of the basic MPI+GPU and the MPI-ACC–driven optimizations for larger number of nodes, but the threshold node configuration at which we see diminishing returns from the new optimization varies for different input data sets (states).

3.3.2 MPI-ACC–enabled optimization vs. advanced MPI+GPU

The bottom portion of Figure 5 shows that the receive buffer management time in the advanced MPI+GPU case increases rapidly

for larger numbers of nodes. The reason is that the pinned memory footprint is an increasing function of the number of MPI processes, which largely reduces the available pageable CPU memory and leads to poor performance [26]. This is why the MPI-ACC–enabled solution outperforms the advanced MPI+GPU solution for most node configurations, especially for larger node configurations. We can also observe that for the same number of MPI processes, the node configuration with two MPI processes (or GPUs) per node performs worse than the node with a single MPI process (e.g. 64×2 vs. 128×1). This result is expected because both MPI processes on each node create pinned memory buffers, thus leading to even lesser pageable memory and poorer performance. On the other hand, MPI-ACC provides a more scalable solution by (1) managing a fixed-size pinned buffer pool for pipelining and (2) creating them at `MPI_Init` and destroying them at `MPI_Finalize`. Note that the pipelined data movement optimization, by itself, does not significantly improve performance in the application's context. Instead, MPI-ACC's efficient buffer pool management for pipelining provides huge benefits for the application.

The basic MPI+GPU solution has the preprocessing overhead but does not suffer from any memory management issues. While the advanced MPI+GPU implementation gains from hiding the preprocessing overhead, it loses from nonscalable pinned memory management. Also, for the advanced MPI+GPU implementation, it turns out that the performance loss due to the inefficient pinned memory management is in general much more severe than the gains achieved by hiding the preprocessing overhead (figure 5). On the other hand, MPI-ACC gains from both hiding the preprocessing overhead and efficient pinned memory management. It is possible to create and manage an efficient pinned memory pool at the application level in the advanced MPI+GPU case, but doing so increases the complexity of the simulation and leads to poor programmer productivity. Ideally, the lower-level memory management logic should be decoupled from the high-level simulation implementation, as is made possible by MPI-ACC.

3.3.3 Analysis of resource utilization using HPCToolkit

HPCTOOLKIT [5] is a sampling based performance analysis toolkit capable of quantifying scalability bottlenecks in parallel programs. In this paper, we use an extension of HPCTOOLKIT that works on hybrid (CPU-GPU) codes; the extension uses a combination of sampling and instrumentation of CUDA code to accurately identify regions of low CPU/GPU utilization. HPCTOOLKIT presents program execution information through two interfaces: `hpcviewer` and `hpctraceviewer`. Hpcviewer associates performance metrics with source code regions including lines, loops, procedures, and calling contexts. Hpctraceviewer renders hierarchical, timeline-based visualizations of parallel program executions.

In Figure 6, we present snapshots of the detailed execution profile of GPU-EpiSimdemics from the `hpctraceviewer` tool of HPCTOOLKIT. Figure 6a depicts the application without the MPI-ACC-driven optimizations. The `hpctraceviewer` tool presents the timeline information of all CPU processes and their corresponding CUDA streams. The *call path* pane on the right represents the call stack of the process/stream at the current crosshair position. Although we study a 32-process execution, we zoom in and show only the 0th and 1st processes and their associated CUDA streams, because the other processes exhibit identical behavior.

The figure depicts two iterations of the application, where a couple of *computeInteractions* phases, with the corresponding GPU activity, are surrounding a *computeVisits* phase, where there is no

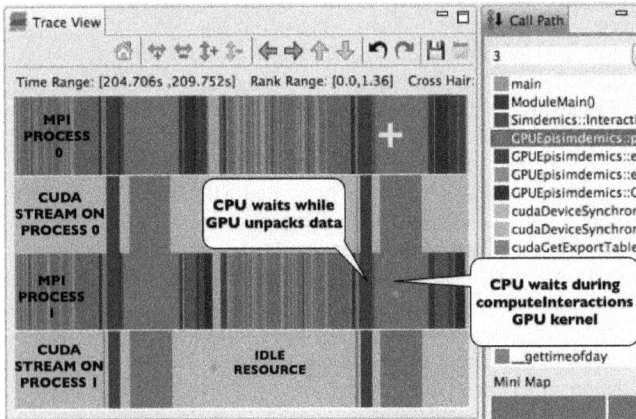

(a) Manual MPI+CUDA optimizations. The *visit* messages are first received on the CPU and copied to the device; then the preprocessing (unpacking) takes place on the GPU.

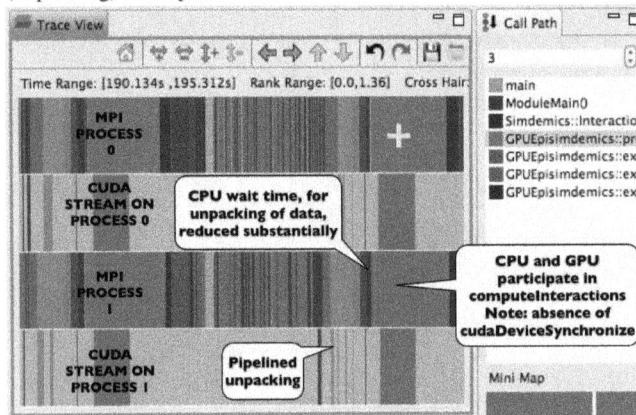

(b) MPI-ACC optimizations. The *visit* messages are received directly in the device. Preprocessing (unpacking) on the GPU is pipelined and overlapped with data movement to the GPU. This leads to negligible CPU waiting while the GPU preprocesses/unpacks the data.

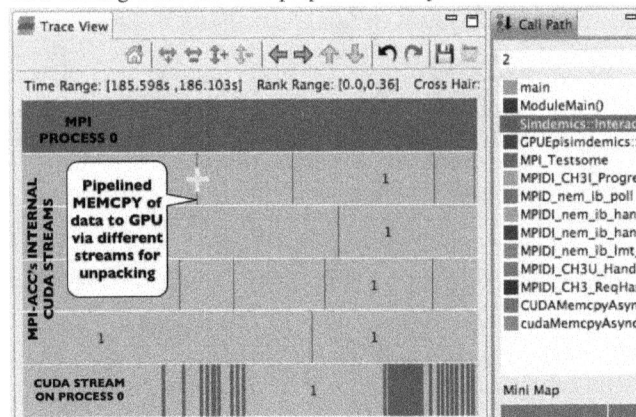

(c) MPI-ACC optimizations. This figure combines (b) with activity occurring on other streams. MPI-ACC employs multiple streams to push the data to the device asynchronously, while the application initiates the unpacking of data.

Figure 6: Analysis and evaluation of MPI-ACC–driven optimizations using HPCTOOLKIT. Application Case Study: GPU-EpiSimdemics.

GPU activity. The GPU idle time during the *computeVisits* phase can be reduced by offloading parts of the *computeVisits* computation to the GPU; but that is beyond the scope of this paper.

In the basic hybrid MPI+GPU programming model, the application launches kernels on the *default* CUDA stream for the *computeInteractions* phase, including the preprocessing (or data unpacking) and the main infection processing stages. In the figure, we can see a corresponding set of bars on the default CUDA stream in the *computeInteractions* phase, which denote the following: (1) a small, negligible sliver showing cudaMemcpy of the visit messages from the CPU to the GPU; (2) a medium-sized bar showing preprocessing (or data unpacking) on the GPU; and (3) a thick band showing the main infection computation kernel. The figure thus helps identify two distinct issues and opportunities for performance improvement in the *computeInteractions* phase of GPU-EpiSimdemics.

1. The thick band on the CUDA stream representing the main kernel of the *computeInteractions* phase has a corresponding thick cudaDeviceSynchronize band on the CPU side; that is, the CPU is idle while waiting for the GPU, thus indicating that some work from the GPU can be offloaded to the CPU.

2. The medium-sized bar on the CUDA stream representing the preprocessing (data unpacking) step has a corresponding cudaDeviceSynchronize bar on the CPU, which indicates that the CPU can start offloading the data to be unpacked to the GPU in stages, thus overlapping data transfers to the GPU with their unpacking on the GPU.

We resolve the first issue by using the cooperative CPU-GPU computation mode. The second issue is resolved in both the cooperative and the exclusive GPU modes, as discussed in Sections 3.2.1 and 3.2.2. We use MPI-ACC to pipeline the data unpacking before the *computeInteractions* phase by overlapping it with the *computeVisits* phase. We use a custom CUDA stream to execute the preprocessing kernel so that we can achieve an efficient overlap between the H-D data transfers within MPI-ACC and the preprocessing kernel of GPU-EpiSimdemics. Figure 6b, which represents HPCTOOLKIT's trace view on applying these optimizations, shows that the time wasted by the CPU in cudaDeviceSynchronize while the GPU unpacked the data has disappeared (compared with Figure 6a). This reduction in the CPU idle time characterizes the success of the MPI-ACC–driven optimizations.

Figure 6c shows a zoomed-in version of Figure 6b, where we can see the internal helper streams that are created within MPI-ACC along with the custom CUDA stream of one of the processes (only a subset of MPI-ACC's internal streams is shown here for brevity). While the GPU kernels of the *computeInteractions* phase are executed on the application's custom stream, the staggered bars in the MPI-ACC's internal streams represent the pipelined data transfers before the unpacking stage, thus showing efficient use of concurrency via multiple GPU streams.

Summary.

In summary, MPI-ACC helps achieve the following for both the GPU computation modes of GPU-EpiSimdemics:

- Provides a natural way of moving data to the desired computational resource (CPU or GPU), which encourages application developers to explore new optimization techniques such as GPU-driven data partitioning and to evaluate them against the more traditional optimization schemes

- Enables receiving and preprocessing the data on the GPU concurrently with the data generation on the CPU, thus enhancing the utilization of all the computation and communication resources of the system

- Efficiently manages pinned buffer pool to help pipeline the GPU data quickly via the host CPU

4. CASE STUDY: SEISMOLOGY MODELING

FDM-Seismology is our MPI+GPU hybrid implementation of an application that models the propagation of seismological waves using the finite-difference method by taking the Earth's velocity structures and seismic source models as input [23]. The application implements a parallel velocity-stress, staggered-grid finite-difference method [11, 14, 24] for propagation of waves in a layered medium. In this method, the domain is divided into a three-dimensional grid, and a one-point-integration scheme [23] is used for each grid cell. Since the computational domain is truncated in order to keep the computation tractable, absorbing boundary conditions (ABCs) are placed around the region of interest so as to keep the reflections minimal when boundaries are impinged by the outgoing waves [23]. This strategy helps simulate unbounded domains. In our application, PML (perfectly matched layers) absorbers [8] are being used as ABCs for their superior efficiency and minimal reflection coefficient. The use of a one-point integration scheme leads to an easy and efficient implementation of the PML absorbing boundaries and allows the use of irregular elements in the PML region [23].

4.1 Computation-Communication Patterns

The simulation operates on the input finite-difference (FD) model and generates a three-dimensional grid as a first step. Our MPI-based parallel version of the application divides the input FD model into submodels along different axes such that each submodel can be computed on different CPUs (or nodes). This technique, also known as domain decomposition, allows the computation in the application to scale to a large number of nodes. Each processor computes the velocity and stress wavefields in its own subdomain and then exchanges the wavefields with the nodes operating on neighbor subdomains, after each set of velocity or stress computation (Figure 7a). These exchanges help each processor update its own wavefields after receiving wavefields generated at the neighbors.

These computations are run for a large number of iterations for better accuracy and convergence of results. In every iteration, each node computes the velocity components followed by the stress components of the seismic wave propagation. The wavefield exchanges with neighbors take place after each set of velocity and stress computations. This MPI communication takes place in multiple stages wherein each communication is followed by an update of local wavefields and a small postcommunication computation on local wavefields. At the end of each iteration, the updated local wavefields are written to a file.

The velocity and stress wavefields are stored as large multidimensional arrays on each node. In order to optimize the MPI computation between neighbors of the FD domain grid, only a few elements of the wavefields, those needed by the neighboring node for its own local update, are communicated to the neighbor, rather than whole arrays. Hence, each MPI communication is surrounded by data marshaling steps, where the required elements are packed into a smaller array at the source, communicated, then unpacked at the receiver to update its local data.

4.2 GPU Acceleration of FDM-Seismology

MPI+GPU with data marshaling on CPU (MPI+GPU): Our GPU-accelerated version of the application performs the velocity and stress computations as kernels on the GPU. In order to transfer the wavefields to other nodes, it first copies the bulk data from the GPU buffers to CPU memory over the PCIe bus and then transfers the individual wavefields over MPI to the neighboring nodes (Figure 7a). All the data-marshaling operations and small postcommunication computations are performed on the CPU itself. The newly updated local wavefields that are received over MPI are then bulk transferred back to the GPU before the start of the next stress or velocity computation on the GPU.

MPI+GPU with data marshaling on GPU (MPI+GPU Adv): A much faster GDDR5 memory module is available on the GPU. If the memory accesses are coalesced, the data-marshaling module performs much better than the CPU, which has the slower DDR3 memory. Also, the packing and unpacking operations of the data-marshaling stages can benefit from the highly multithreaded SIMT execution nature of GPU. Hence, it is a natural optimization to move the data-marshaling operations to the GPU (Figure 7b). Moreover, the CPU-GPU bulk data transfers that used to happen before and after each velocity-stress computation kernel are avoided. The need to explicitly bulk transfer data from the GPU to the CPU arises only at the end of the iteration, when the results are transferred to the CPU to be written to a file.

However, such an optimization has the following disadvantage in the absence of GPU-integrated MPI. All data-marshaling steps are separated by MPI communication, and each data-marshaling step depends on the preceding marshaling step *and* the received MPI data from the neighbors. In other words, after each data-marshaling step, data has to be explicitly moved from the GPU to the CPU only for MPI communication. Similarly, the received MPI data has to be explicitly moved back to the GPU before the next marshaling step. In this scenario, the application uses the CPU only as a communication relay. If the GPU communication technology changes (e.g., GPU-Direct RDMA), we will have to largely rewrite the FDM-Seismology communication code to achieve the expected performance.

4.3 MPI-ACC–Enabled Optimizations

Since the MPI-ACC library enables MPI communication directly from the GPU buffer, the new version of the application retains the velocity and stress computation results on the GPU itself, performs the packing and unpacking operations using multiple threads on the GPU, and communicates the packed arrays directly from the GPU. Similar to the MPI+GPU Adv case, the bulk transfer of data happens only once at the end of each iteration, when results are written to a file.

The MPI-ACC–driven design of FDM-Seismology with data marshaling on the GPU greatly benefits from the reduction in the number of expensive synchronous bulk data transfer steps between the CPU and GPU. Also, since the data-marshaling step happens multiple times during a single iteration, the application needs to launch a series of marshaling kernels on the GPU. While consecutive kernel launches entail some kernel launch and synchronization overhead per kernel invocation, the benefits of faster data marshaling on the GPU and optimized MPI communication make the kernel synchronization overhead insignificant.

GPU-driven data marshaling provides the following benefits to MPI+GPU Adv and MPI-ACC–based designs of FDM-Seismology: (1) it removes the need for the expensive bulk `cudaMemcpy` data transfers that were used to copy the results from the GPU to the CPU after each set of velocity and stress computations; and (2)

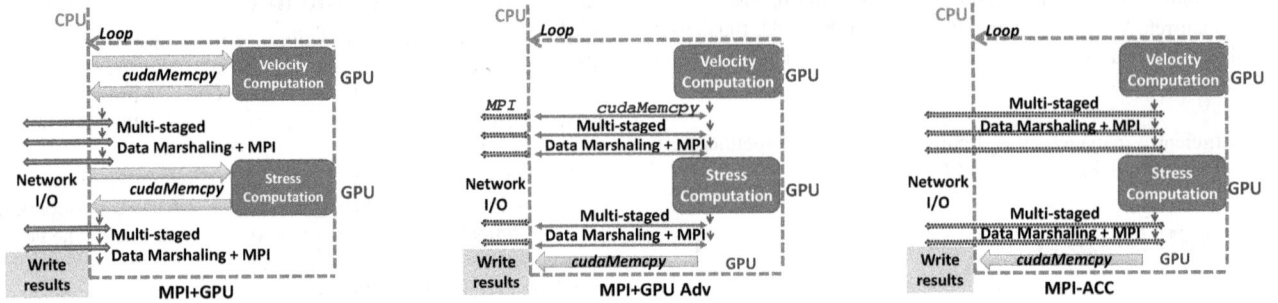

(a) Basic MPI+GPU FDM-Seismology application with data marshaling on CPU.

(b) MPI+GPU FDM-Seismology application with data marshaling on GPU.

(c) MPI-ACC–driven FDM-Seismology application with data marshaling on GPU.

Figure 7: Communication-computation pattern in the FDM-Seismology application.

the application benefits from the multiple threads performing the data packing and unpacking operations in parallel, and on the faster GDDR5 device memory.

Other than the benefits resulting from GPU-driven data marshaling, a GPU-integrated MPI library benefits the FDM-Seismology application in the following ways: (1) it significantly enhances the productivity of the programmer, who is no longer constrained by the fixed CPU-only MPI communication and can easily choose the appropriate device as the communication target end-point; (2) the pipelined data transfers within MPI-ACC further improve the communication performance over the network; and (3) regardless of the GPU communication technology that may become available in the future, our MPI-ACC–driven FDM-Seismology code will not change and will automatically enjoy the performance upgrades that are made available by the subsequent GPU-integrated MPI implementations (e.g., support for GPU-Direct RDMA).

4.4 Evaluation and Discussion

In this section, we analyze the performance of the different phases of the FDM-Seismology application and evaluate the effect of MPI-ACC optimizations on the application. The platform for evaluation is the HokieSpeed cluster, whose details were specified in Section 3.3. We use strong scaling to understand the variation in the application's performance when the number of nodes increases and the internode data transfer size decreases. We vary the nodes from 2 to 128 with 1 GPU per node and use two different sized datasets, Dataset-1 and Dataset-2, as input. Our scalability experiments begin from the smallest number of nodes required to fit the given data in the GPU memory. For the larger input data (i.e., Dataset-2), the size of the MPI transfers increases by 2× while the size of data to be marshaled increases by 4× when compared with the smaller Dataset-1.

4.4.1 MPI-ACC–enabled optimizations vs. basic and advanced MPI+GPU

Figure 8 shows the performance of the FDM-Seismology application, with nodes varying from 16 to 128, when used with and without the MPI-ACC–enabled designs. In the figure, we report the average computation time across all the nodes, because the computation-communication costs vary largely, depending on the location of the node in the structured grid problem representation of FDM-Seismology. In the MPI+GPU case, we perform both data-marshaling operations and MPI communication on the CPU. In the MPI+GPU Adv case, we perform the data-marshaling operations

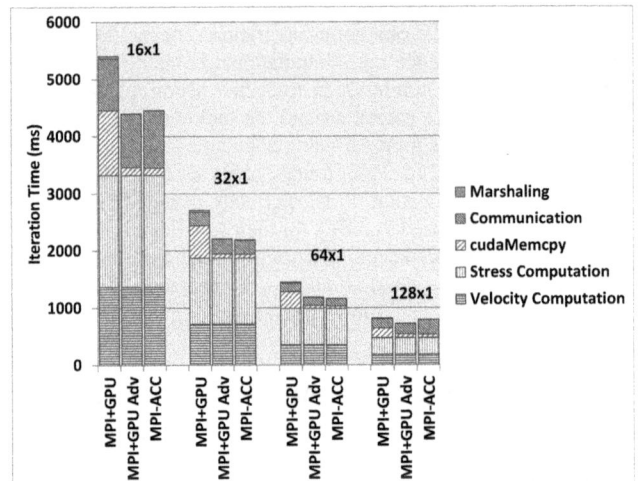

Figure 8: Analysis of the FDM-Seismology application when strongly scaled. The larger dataset, Dataset-2, is used for these results. Note: MPI Communication represents CPU-CPU data transfer time for the MPI+GPU and MPI+GPU Adv cases and GPU-GPU (pipelined) data transfer time for the MPI-ACC case.

on the GPU, while the MPI communication still takes place explicitly from the CPU.

One can see that although the velocity and stress computations take most of the application's computation time (>60%), the MPI-GPU Adv and MPI-ACC–driven design of the application see large performance improvements over the MPI+GPU case, primarily because of the reduction in expensive explicit bulk data transfer operations between the CPU and GPU (Figure 7c). In the MPI+GPU case, the application needs to move large wavefield data between the CPU and the GPU for the data-marshaling computation and MPI communication. On the other hand, when used with MPI-ACC, the application performs all the data-marshaling computation and MPI communication directly from the GPU, and it needs to transfer smaller-sized wavefield data from GPU to CPU only once at the end of the iteration for writing the result to the output file.

In the MPI+GPU Adv case, since the marshaling steps are performed on the GPU and much smaller-sized data arrays are moved between the CPU and GPU for MPI communication, we still benefit from avoiding the bulk data transfer steps. However, these small wavefield data movements have to be invoked many times and result in reduced programmer productivity. With MPI-ACC, the pro-

200

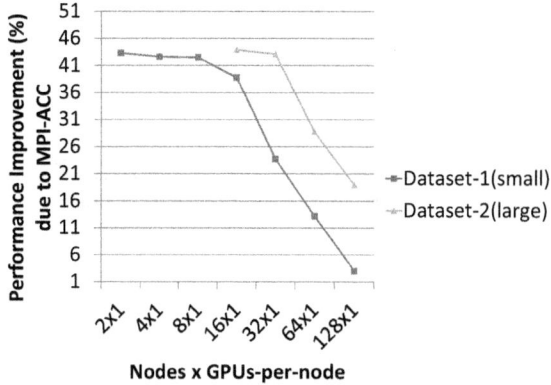

Figure 9: Scalability analysis of FDM-Seismology application with two datasets of different sizes. The baseline for speedup is the naïve MPI+GPU programming model with CPU data marshaling.

grammer enjoys productivity gain as well as the performance improvements as a result of pipelined data transfers via the CPU.

We also analyzed the FDM-Seismology application with HPC-TOOLKIT and observed CUDA stream activity similar to that in Figure 6c, where multiple internal CUDA streams asynchronously transfer the data over MPI while the application's stream is busy doing marshaling computations. This approach helps the application performance by increasing the resource utilization.

4.4.2 Scalability analysis

Figure 9 shows the performance improvement due to the MPI-ACC–enabled GPU data marshaling strategy over the basic hybrid MPI+GPU implementation with CPU data marshaling. We see that the performance benefits due to the GPU data marshaling design decrease with increasing number of nodes. The reason for this behavior is twofold:

- For a given dataset, the per-node data size decreases with increasing number of nodes. This reduces the costly CPU-to-GPU and GPU-to-CPU bulk data transfers (Figure 8) and thus minimizes the overall benefits of performing data marshaling on the GPU itself.

- As the number of nodes increase, the application's MPI communication cost becomes significant when compared with the computation and data marshaling costs. In such a scenario, the CPU-to-CPU communication of the traditional hybrid MPI+GPU implementations will have less overhead than will the pipelined GPU-to-GPU communication of the MPI-ACC–enabled design.

While the pipelined data transfer optimization within MPI-ACC improves the communication performance to a certain degree, it has negligible impact on the performance gains of the application. If newer technologies such as GPUDirect-RDMA are integrated into MPI, we can expect the GPU-to-GPU communication overhead to be reduced, but the overall benefits of GPU data marshaling itself will still be limited because of the reduced per-process working set.

5. RELATED WORK

GPUs have been used to accelerate many HPC applications across a range of fields in recent years. For large-scale applications that go beyond the capability of one node, manually mixing GPU data movement with MPI communication routines is still the status quo, and its optimization usually requires expertise [10, 16]. In this work, our experience with MPI-ACC [6], our GPU-integrated MPI implementation, shows that the manual hybrid programming model can be replaced with extended MPI support, with additional optimizations automatically made available to developers.

Several research groups have worked on designing and optimizing GPU-integrated data communication libraries. The cudaMPI library studies providing wrapper API functions by mixing CUDA and MPI data movement [21]. Similarly to MPI-ACC, Wang et al. propose to add CUDA [2] support to MVAPICH2 [22] and optimize the internode communication for InfiniBand networks [28]. All-to-all communication [27] and noncontiguous datatype communication [17, 29] have also been studied in the context of GPU-aware MPI. With a focus on intranode communication, our previous work [18, 19] extends transparent GPU buffers support for MPICH [1] and optimizes the cross-PCIe data movement by using shared memory data structures and interprocess communication (IPC) mechanisms. In contrast to those efforts, here we study the synergistic effect between GPU-accelerated MPI applications and a GPU-integrated MPI implementation.

6. CONCLUSION

In this paper, we studied the interactions of GPU-integrated MPI on the complex execution patterns of scientific applications from the domains of epidemiology (GPU-EpiSimdemics) and seismology (FDM-Seismology) on hybrid CPU-GPU clusters, and we presented the lessons learned. By using MPI-ACC as an example implementation, we created new optimization techniques, such as overlapped internode GPU communication with concurrent computations on the CPUs and GPUs and discussed their benefits and tradeoffs. We found that while MPI-ACC's internal pipeline optimization helped improve the end-to-end communication performance to a certain degree, its benefit was less in the context of the entire application. We also showed how MPI-ACC helped in naturally expressing the communication targets that were chosen based on the execution profiles of the tasks at hand. MPI-ACC decoupled the application logic from the low-level GPU communication optimizations, thereby significantly improving scalability and application portability across multiple GPU platforms and generations. Thus, GPU-integrated MPI helps move the GPUs toward being "first-class citizens" in the hybrid clusters. Our results on HokieSpeed, a state-of-the-art CPU-GPU cluster, showed that MPI-ACC can help improve the performance of GPU-EpiSimdemics and FDM-Seismology over the default MPI+GPU implementations by enhancing the CPU-GPU and network utilization. Using the HPCToolkit performance tools, we were able to measure, visualize, and quantify the benefits of MPI-ACC–driven optimizations in our application case studies.

Acknowledgments

This work was supported in part by the DOE grant DE-SC0001770, contracts DE-AC02-06CH11357, DE-AC05-00OR22725, and DE-ACO6-76RL01830, by the DOE Office of Science under cooperative agreement number DE-FC02-07ER25800, by the DOE GTO via grant EE0002758 from Fugro Consultants, by the DTRA CN-IMS contract HDTRA1-11-D-0016-0001, the NSF PetaApps grant OCI-0904844, the NSF Blue Waters grant OCI-0832603, and by the NSF grants CNS-0960081, CNS-0546301 and CNS-0958311, as well as an NVIDIA Graduate Fellowship, NVIDIA Professor Partnership, and CUDA Research Center at Virginia Tech. This research used the HokieSpeed heterogeneous computing resource at Virginia Tech, which is supported by the National Science Foundation under contract CNS-0960081.

7. REFERENCES

[1] MPICH2. http://www.mcs.anl.gov/research/projects/mpich2/.

[2] NVIDIA CUDA toolkit 4.1. http://developer.nvidia.com/cuda-toolkit-41.

[3] NVIDIA GPUDirect. http://developer.nvidia.com/gpudirect.

[4] TOP500. http://www.top500.org/lists/2012/06/highlights.

[5] ADHIANTO, L., BANERJEE, S., FAGAN, M., KRENTEL, M., MARIN, G., MELLOR-CRUMMEY, J., AND TALLENT, N. R. HPCToolkit: Tools for performance analysis of optimized parallel programs. *Concurrency Computation: Practice and Experience 22* (April 2010), 685–701.

[6] AJI, A. M., DINAN, J., BUNTINAS, D., BALAJI, P., FENG, W.-C., BISSET, K. R., AND THAKUR, R. MPI-ACC: An Integrated and Extensible Approach to Data Movement in Accelerator-Based Systems. In *14th IEEE International Conference on High Performance Computing and Communications* (Liverpool, UK, June 2012).

[7] BARRETT, C. L., BISSET, K. R., EUBANK, S. G., FENG, X., AND MARATHE, M. V. EpiSimdemics: an efficient algorithm for simulating the spread of infectious disease over large realistic social networks. In *Proceedings of the 2008 ACM/IEEE conference on Supercomputing* (2008), SC '08.

[8] BERENGER, J. A perfectly matched layer for the absorption of electromagnetic waves. *Journal of Computational Physics 114*, 2 (1994), 185–200.

[9] BISSET, K., AJI, A., MARATHE, M., AND CHUN FENG, W. High-performance biocomputing for simulating the spread of contagion over large contact networks. In *IEEE 1st International Conference on Computational Advances in Bio and Medical Sciences (ICCABS)* (Feb. 2011), pp. 26–32.

[10] BROWN, W. M., WANG, P., PLIMPTON, S. J., AND THARRINGTON, A. N. Implementing molecular dynamics on hybrid high performance computers – short range forces. *Computer Physics Communications 182*, 4 (2011), 898–911.

[11] COLLINO, F., AND TSOGKA, C. Application of the perfectly matched absorbing layer model to the linear elastodynamic problem in anisotropic heterogeneous media. *Geophysics 66*, 1 (2001), 294–307.

[12] ENDO, T., NUKADA, A., MATSUOKA, S., AND MARUYAMA, N. Linpack evaluation on a supercomputer with heterogeneous accelerators. In *Parallel Distributed Processing (IPDPS), 2010 IEEE International Symposium on* (April 2010), pp. 1–8.

[13] FENG, W.-C., CAO, Y., PATNAIK, D., AND RAMAKRISHNAN, N. Temporal Data Mining for Neuroscience. In *GPU Computing Gems*, W. mei W. Hwu, Ed. Morgan Kaufmann, February 2011. Emerald Edition.

[14] FESTA, G., AND NIELSEN, S. PML absorbing boundaries. *Bulletin of the Seismological Society of America 93*, 2 (2003), 891–903.

[15] GROUP, K. OpenCL 1.2. http://www.khronos.org/opencl/.

[16] HAMADA, T., NARUMI, T., YOKOTA, R., YASUOKA, K., NITADORI, K., AND TAIJI, M. 42 TFlops hierarchical N-body simulations on GPUs with applications in both astrophysics and turbulence. In *Proceedings of the Conference on High Performance Computing Networking, Storage and Analysis* (2009), ACM.

[17] JENKINS, J., DINAN, J., BALAJI, P., SAMATOVA, N. F., AND THAKUR, R. Enabling Fast, Noncontiguous GPU Data Movement in Hybrid MPI+GPU Environments. In *IEEE International Conference on Cluster Computing (Cluster)* (September 2012).

[18] JI, F., AJI, A., DINAN, J., BUNTINAS, D., BALAJI, P., FENG, W.-C., AND MA, X. Efficient Intranode Communication in GPU-Accelerated Systems. In *The 2nd Intl. Workshop on Accelerators and Hybrid Exascale Systems* (May 2012).

[19] JI, F., AJI, A. M., DINAN, J., BUNTINAS, D., BALAJI, P., THAKUR, R., FENG, W.-C., AND MA, X. DMA-Assisted, Intranode Communication in GPU Accelerated Systems. In *14th IEEE International Conference on High Performance Computing and Communications* (Liverpool, UK, June 2012).

[20] JOSEPH, R., RAVUNNIKUTTY, G., RANKA, S., D'AZEVEDO, E., AND KLASKY, S. Efficient GPU Implementation for Particle in Cell Algorithm. In *IEEE International Parallel Distributed Processing Symposium (IPDPS)* (May 2011), pp. 395–406.

[21] LAWLOR, O. Message passing for GPGPU clusters: CudaMPI. In *IEEE International Conference on Cluster Computing and Workshops, 2009. CLUSTER '09.* (Sept. 2009), pp. 1–8.

[22] LIU, J., JIANG, W., WYCKOFF, P., PANDA, D., ASHTON, D., BUNTINAS, D., GROPP, W., AND TOONEN, B. Design and implementation of MPICH2 over InfiniBand with RDMA support. In *Parallel and Distributed Processing Symposium, 2004. Proceedings. 18th International* (April 2004), p. 16.

[23] MA, S., AND LIU, P. Modeling of the perfectly matched layer absorbing boundaries and intrinsic attenuation in explicit finite-element methods. *Bulletin of the Seismological Society of America 96*, 5 (2006), 1779–1794.

[24] MARCINKOVICH, C., AND OLSEN, K. On the implementation of perfectly matched layers in a three-dimensional fourth-order velocity-stress finite difference scheme. *J. Geophys. Res. 108*, B5 (2003), 2276.

[25] NERE, A., HASHMI, A., AND LIPASTI, M. Profiling Heterogeneous Multi-GPU Systems to Accelerate Cortically Inspired Learning Algorithms. In *IEEE International Parallel Distributed Processing Symposium (IPDPS)*, (May 2011), pp. 906–920.

[26] NVIDIA. NVIDIA CUDA C Programming Guide version 4.0.

[27] SINGH, A. K., POTLURI, S., WANG, H., KANDALLA, K., SUR, S., AND PANDA, D. K. MPI alltoall personalized exchange on GPGPU clusters: Design alternatives and benefit. In *Workshop on Parallel Programming on Accelerator Clusters (PPAC '11), held in conjunction with Cluster '11* (Sept. 2011).

[28] WANG, H., POTLURI, S., LUO, M., SINGH, A., SUR, S., AND PANDA, D. MVAPICH2-GPU: Optimized GPU to GPU communication for InfiniBand clusters. *International Supercomputing Conference (ISC) '11* (2011).

[29] WANG, H., POTLURI, S., LUO, M., SINGH, A. K., OUYANG, X., SUR, S., AND PANDA, D. K. Optimized non-contiguous MPI datatype communication for GPU clusters: Design, implementation and evaluation with MVAPICH2. In *Proceedings of CLUSTER* (2011), IEEE.

[30] WEIGUO, L., SCHMIDT, B., VOSS, G., AND MULLER-WITTIG, W. Streaming Algorithms for Biological Sequence Alignment on GPUs. *IEEE Transactions on Parallel and Distributed Systems 18*, 9 (Sept. 2007), 1270–1281.

VGRIS: Virtualized GPU Resource Isolation and Scheduling in Cloud Gaming

Miao Yu [*], Chao Zhang, Zhengwei Qi, Jianguo Yao
School of Software, Shanghai Jiao Tong University, Shanghai, China
{superymk, kevin_zhang, qizhwei, jianguo.yao}@sjtu.edu.cn

Yin Wang
HP Labs, Palo Alto, USA
yin.wang@hp.com

Haibing Guan
Shanghai Key Laboratory of Scalable Computing and Systems, Shanghai Jiao Tong University, Shanghai, China
hbguan@sjtu.edu.cn

ABSTRACT

Fueled by the maturity of virtualization technology for Graphics Processing Unit (GPU), there is an increasing number of data centers dedicated to GPU-related computation tasks in cloud gaming. However, GPU resource sharing in these applications is usually poor. This stems from the fact that the typical cloud gaming service providers often allocate one GPU exclusively for one game. To achieve the efficiency of computational resource management, there is a demand for cloud computing to employ the multi-task scheduling technologies to improve the utilization of GPU.

In this paper, we propose VGRIS, a resource management framework for **V**irtualized **GPU** **R**esource **I**solation and **S**cheduling in cloud gaming. By leveraging the mature GPU paravirtualization architecture, VGRIS resides in the host through library API interception, while the guest OS and the GPU computing applications remain unmodified. In the proposed framework, we implemented three scheduling algorithms in VGRIS for different objectives, i.e., Service Level Agreement (SLA)-aware scheduling, proportional-share scheduling, and hybrid scheduling that mixes the former two. By designing such a scheduling framework, it is possible to handle different kinds of GPU computation tasks for different purposes in cloud gaming. Our experimental results show that each scheduling algorithm can achieve its goals under various workloads.

Categories and Subject Descriptors

C.4 [**PERFORMANCE OF SYSTEMS**]: Modeling techniques, measuring techniques

---

[*] The first author's current affiliation is Cylab, Carnegie Mellon University. The contact email is superymk@cmu.edu

Keywords

GPU, Resource management, Scheduling, Cloud gaming

1. INTRODUCTION

The cloud computing significantly reduces cost of capital and equipment maintenance by allowing users to host their softwares on the cloud under a simple pay-as-you-go. As a cloud service, cloud gaming is a game service that executes the game programs and renders the graphics on the server side, while players stream the video through broadband connection using thin clients. This gaming model has several advantages. It allows easy access to games without owning a console or high-end graphics cards or Graphics Processing Unit (GPU)s. Game distribution and maintenance become much easier.

Concurrently, virtualization technology is making a significant impact on how resources are used and managed in a cloud data center. Several virtualization solutions (VMware products, Xen [1], VirtualBox) are getting more and more mature in constructing a huge cloud computing center. As virtualization technology has been successfully applied to a variety of devices, GPU virtualization technology has developed dramatically in the past a few years. Due to the powerful performance on floating-pointing arithmetic as well as cost-efficiency, GPU virtualization has been widely studied, especially in the High Performance Computing (HPC) domain. Several research work [29, 28, 13, 30, 9] leverages GPU virtualization for general purpose computing on GPU (GPGPU). Based on the interception of vendor specific library such as Nvidia CUDA, AMD Accelerated Parallel Processing and OpenCL, the GPU resources are efficiently shared in the virtualization environment. Besides, HPC applications running on systems including GViM [13], vCUD-A [30], rCUDA [9], etc. has a competitive performance with those running in a native, non-virtualized environment.

In addition to GPGPU, the other main application scenario of the GPU is for graphics processing including gaming, 3D rendering and so on. Techniques of GPU virtualization for graphics processing such as VGA-passthrough [25] and GPU paravirtualization [20, 7] are reaching their maturity. For example, VMware player 4.0 achieves 95.6% of the native performance using paravirtualization (3DMark06 with Windows 7 as both the guest and host), while VMware Player 3.0 released four years ago achieved only 52.4%. Due to these technological advances, there is an increasing number of data centers dedicated to GPU computing tasks such as cloud gaming and video rendering. Taking cloud gaming for instance, the platform renders games remotely and streams the result over the network so that clients can play high-end games without owning the latest hardware. Many cloud gaming service providers such as OnLive [1] became publicly known in the past four years. OnLive is currently partnering with more than 90 publishers and servicing close to 300 games online.

However, how a graphics card is shared among games running on top of the Virtual Machines (VM)s is not well studied. Resource sharing in existing virtualization solutions is often poor. For example, while OnLive runs multiple instances of a game that requires very little or no GPU computation, it allocates one GPU per instance for other games [15]. Proprietary motherboards are also used to host more GPU adapters in one machine. On the other hand, game developers heavily optimize their products to meet the capacity of mid-range hardware. Hence allocating a whole graphics card to some game causes the waste of hardware resources.

This paper proposes VGRIS, a scheduling framework for **V**irtualized **G**PU **R**esource **I**solation and **S**cheduling. VGRIS transparently enables different VMs in the cloud to share a single GPU efficiently. Leveraging GPU paravirtualization technology, VGRIS is a lightweight resource scheduler in the host. A challenge of resources management on GPU is that graphics processing such as frame rendering is executed in an asynchronous and non-preemptive manner. Specifically, VGRIS adopts *library API interception* so as not to care about the underlying scheduling. Different from GViM, vCUDA and rCUDA, VGRIS intercepts the library for graphics processing such as DirectX and OpenGL, instead of the one for GPU programming. One major benefit of the library API interception is that we only need to modify a few binary within the intercepted library. No other part of the software stack on top of the physical machine needs to be changed to embrace VGRIS. Moreover, VGRIS does not need any source code or design information of the library in order to perform such modification.

Similar as our previous storage scheduling system does [32], we implement two scheduling policies which address the trade-off between the Service Level Agreement (SLA) and the throughput, based on VGRIS framework. More specifically, SLA-aware scheduling strives to achieve SLA requirements for each VM, which can benefit cloud gaming platforms. However, the GPU may not be fully utilized under this scheduling policy. Another policy, Proportional-share scheduling, allocates GPU resources to each VM in proportion to its given weight, which can benefit job prioritization in rendering farms and the total throughput at the cost of SLA. Furthermore, VGRIS introduces the hybrid scheduling that guarantees minimum resources for SLA while proportionally shares surplus resources among all VMs. This third policy has better resource utilization than SLA-aware scheduling and it prevents starvation that may occur with proportional sharing.

Our experimental results show that all the three scheduling policies satisfy their design goals under various workloads. For example, applying SLA-aware scheduling, the average Frames Per Second (FPS) of workloads increases by 65%. The percentage of frames with excessive latency drops to 3.19%. In the meanwhile, the GPU performance overhead incurred by VGRIS is limited to 3.66%.

The contributions of this paper are summarized as follows.

- We propose a GPU scheduling framework based on the GPU paravirtualization architecture, which can be applied to servers for various GPU computing tasks for efficient resource management. Benefited from library API interception, VGRIS is lightweight and requires no source code level changes in the guest OS, the guest game and the host graphic drivers.

- We implement three scheduling policies in the proposed framework for different typical performance needs: high performance of SLA, proportional resource sharing and performance and fairness trade-offs.

- We implement the VGRIS through real games and benchmark programs to demonstrate the effectiveness of our framework and scheduling policies.

- We conduct several experiments with various types of workloads. The overhead of our framework is limited to 3.66%.

The rest of the paper is organized as follows. Section 2 describes motivating experiments to show the poor performance of the default scheduling mechanism for GPU. Section 3 introduces the framework of VGRIS as well as the design and implementation of the three scheduling policies we integrate in VGRIS. Section 4 presents the experimental results of the proposed VGRIS with real games and benchmark programs. Section 5 is the related work, and Section 6 concludes the paper with a discussion.

2. MOTIVATION

This section mainly describes some motivating experiments to show the poor performance and low utilization of the default GPU resource scheduling as well as the analysis of the problem. We conducted the experiments on the machine with mid-range CPU and an ATI HD6750 graphics card. Before analyzing the poor performance and low utilization of running multiple VMs on a single graphics card, we first briefly describe the standard 3D rendering and programming model and then discuss how the original graphics library schedules GPU resource.

2.1 GPU Computation Model

One of our objectives is to control the FPS of workloads, and hence the GPU resources can be scheduled. However, the real world games such as DiRT3, in fact, seem not run at the same or a close FPS during the process of gaming. The FPS may continuously vary with the change of game scenes. Basically, the GPU processing as well as the CPU computation determines the FPS. As shown in Figure 1, GPU computation for various applications, e.g., gaming, rendering, stream processing, is usually processed in an infinite loop [27]. Each loop determines exactly one frame.

First `UploadComputeKernel` uploads the computation program to the GPU, and `DeclareThreadGrid` specifies the

---

[1]OnLive, Inc. OnLive. http://www.onlive.com/.

```
UploadComputeKernel();
DeclareThreadGrid(&Threads);

While(1) {
  CPUComputation();
  // copy data from memory to GPU buffer
  UploadData(&VGA_Buf, &Input_Buf);
  // GPU computation
  DispatchComputation(&Threads);
  // send results back to memory
  DownloadData(&VGA_Buf, &Output_Buf);
}
```

Figure 1: GPU Computation model.

Table 1: Game performance on iCore7 2600K + HD6750.

Game	FPS	GPU Usage	CPU Usage
DiRT 3	67.14	56.14%	39.61%
Portal 2	212.70	94.77%	85.42%
Shogun 2	64.76	84.33%	29.48%
Call Of Duty 7	68.97	73.48%	69.09%
NBA 2012	104.57	69.50%	86.45%

number of threads for the computation. After the initial setup, each iteration of the loop performs some tasks, e.g., drawing a frame for gaming and rendering arithmetic calculations for general-purpose computation. There are four stages. First some CPU computation prepares the data for GPU, e.g., calculating objects in the upcoming frame according to the game logic. The data is uploaded to the GPU buffer next, and then the GPU performs the computation, e.g., rendering, using its buffer contents. Finally, the calculation result is sent back to the main memory for the next iteration or output to the screen. The GPU computation library depends on the application, e.g., Direct3D or OpenGL for gaming and rendering, DirectCompute, OpenCL, or CUDA for general-purpose GPU computation. The detailed API calls vary too, e.g., `glutSwapBuffers()` for OpenGL and `IDirect3DSwapChain9::Present()` for Direct3D 9. Since we mainly focus on the graphics processing of a specified GPU, we evaluate VGRIS framework using Direct3D library which is the most popular graphics processing library among game vendors on the planet. The design principle applies to other libraries and platforms as well.

Under the Direct3D architecture, graphics API calls are asynchronous. Each application has its own Direct3D command queue, and a command is non-blocking unless the queue is full. Direct3D runtime decides when to submit the queue to the device driver. Using library API interception, such Direct3D API invocation will firstly notify VGRIS framework before executing the API. Under the framework, we implement various policies for GPU resource isolation and scheduling among multiple VMs. Since all Direct3D APIs are processed at the host, Paravirtualization greatly facilitates our design and implementation. The paravirtualization technology will be further discussed in Section 3.1. Therefore we implement VGRIS in the host and in the meanwhile, neither the guest application, the guest OS nor the host graphics drivers need to be changed.

2.2 Inefficiency of Default GPU Sharing

We now present the experiments to show the potential improvements of throughput in a shared GPU environment while guaranteeing SLA of each workload. To illustrate the potential improvements of throughput, we first evaluate the performance of the individual workloads on the platform with windows 7 as the host OS. We choose five popular games listed on GameSpot [2] on November the 10th, 2011. The version of the graphics library is Direct3D 9. Table 1 shows the performance results, in which the GPU usage is

[2]GameSpot. http://www.gamespot.com/.

calculated based on hardware counters. Usually, cloud gaming requires the FPS rate in the range of 30 to 60 for smooth user experience. The lower rate will make the game unplayable while higher rate does not make a difference for human eye. As we can see in the figure, all the workloads are able to provide a smooth user experience. But running these workloads individually results in waste of GPU and CPU resources though the corresponding FPS is fast enough to provide a smooth user experience. For instance, the workload of DiRT3 only occupies about half of the GPU utilization and 39.61% CPU utilization when providing a smooth FPS. The rest of the GPU and CPU resources are sufficient enough to play another game, even on our mid-range ATI HD6750 graphics card. Since cloud gaming service providers like OnLive upgrade their CPUs and GPUs to the latest every six months [15], running these games with dedicated GPUs will inevitably cause unnecessary low GPU utilization.

Based on this observation, we then show the performance results of running multiple VMs on the single ATI HD6750 graphics card, as shown in Figure 2. The experiment involves in three workloads: DiRT3, 3DMarks05 and NBA2012. DiRT3 and NBA2012 are two popular games while 3DMarks05 is a 3D benchmark that renders several game scenes and measures the FPS. Each workload concurrently runs in a separate VM which is configured with Windows 7 as the guest OS supporting the Direct3D graphics library. In Figure 2a, DiRT3 has an average FPS of 31 while NBA2012 runs at around 90 FPS. Compared to their original performance with the same game configuration, their FPS reduce a little due to the GPU resources contention. However, from 115th sec. to 180th sec., the second game test of 3DMarks05 runs at a FPS below 30 FPS, which offers a rough user experience. Except for FPS, the user experience also depends on the frame latency which defines the cost time of one frame. Figure 2b illustrates the corresponding frame latency of the second game test scene in 3DMark05 in Figure 2a. As we can see, the latencies of more than 6.22% frames are beyond 33 ms. The maximum latency is 388.82 ms. The larger frame latency is, the more difficult the user can play the game.

One likely reason of the default poor resource scheduling mechanism is the asynchronous and non-preemptive nature of GPU process. For instance, the default GPU scheduling mechanism in Direct3D runtime library tends to allocate resources on a first-come first-serve manner, which results in excessive FPS for low-end games and unplayable FPS for GPU demanding games when they are running concurrently on separate VMs. Graphics APIs also typically work in an asynchronous way to maximize hardware performance. APIs such as `Present` in Direct3D immediately return when they issue a GPU command and submit to the GPU. The GPU maintains a command buffer for the coming request

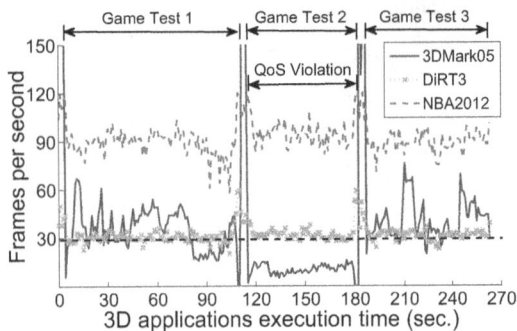

(a) FPS of Three Workloads

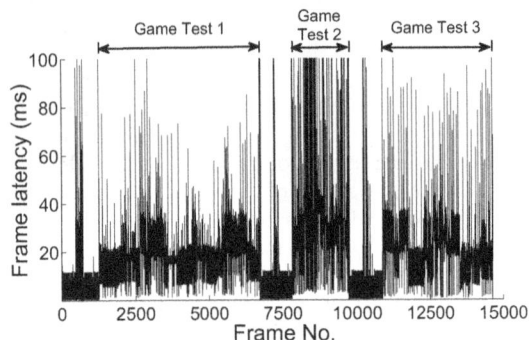

(b) Frame Latency of 3DMark05

Figure 2: Default scheduling results in poor performance under heavy contention.

from the user space. Therefore, if the underlying command buffer is full, the 3D application has to be blocked for some time. Take Direct3D applications for example. In a typical 3D application development, every 3D application creates a unique Direct3D device to represent its own graphics context. The Direct3D calls issued by an application is usually converted into device-independent commands, batched in a command queue within the application's context. When the command queue is full or at any appropriate time, the Direct3D runtime submits the current device's command queue to the underlying GPU driver. The driver stores the coming queue into its local command buffer for the GPU cores to process asynchronously. There are commands still kept by Direct3D runtime for a period of time until available room is found in the command buffer at the driver side. Thus, if two or more 3D applications run concurrently on a single graphics card, the resources contention inevitably occurs. If one 3D application runs a little fast and submits its command queue frequently to the underlying layer, it probably gets more GPU resources. Meanwhile, another 3D application hence suffers from severe starvation, causing its FPS low as it is running. Besides, it is noteworthy that a 3D application needs to recreate resources after its windows has been updated. Hence, it is common that only one GPU-accelerated 3D application occupies the whole GPU for a period of time regardless of how many cores or threads the GPU has.

Based on the aforementioned analysis, we focus on the graphics runtime library. If we can intercept DirectX APIs, especially the ones related to GPU rendering, we are able to do some scheduling for all the running 3D applications. It

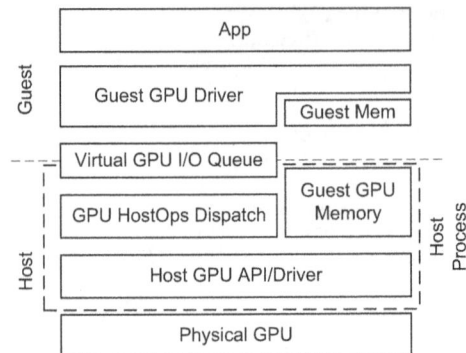

Figure 3: GPU Paravirtualization Architecture.

also brings an additional benefit that no modification is required for the 3D application, the underlying driver and the hypervisor. For instance, if a 3D application runs a little fast, we can make it slower so that other 3D applications get more change to access the GPU and will not starve any more. We are also able to assign each 3D application a priority and hence a 3D application with high priority is capable of getting more resources and responsive on the GPU. Currently, we integrate three scheduling policies into our VGRIS framework. One is for guaranteeing SLA, one is for high throughput and the other mixes the former two to balance the trade-off between SLA and throughput. Other scheduling policies are applicable to the VGRIS framework as well.

3. VGRIS ARCHITECTURE

This section mainly discusses the design and the implementation of the VGRIS as well as the three algorithms we have incorporated in it. Before introducing VGRIS architecture, we first present the necessary background of GPU paravirtualization since VGRIS leverages the technology. The three algorithms address different requirements for different GPU computing applications.

3.1 GPU Paravirtualization and VGRIS Framework

Paravirtualization provides virtual machines a software interface different from the underlying hardware. This interface significantly reduces the overhead of operations which are substantially more difficult to run in a virtual environment. The guest operating system must be explicitly ported to exploit the new interfaces for better performance. For commercial operating systems that cannot be modified, this is often achieved by paravirtualization-aware device drivers. Due to the complexity of GPU device drivers, hypervisors that support GPU paravirtualization achieve near-native efficiency only recently.

Figure 3 shows the typical GPU paravirtualization architecture for type 2 (hosted) hypervisor [7]. Typically a GPU rendering task issued by a guest Operating Systems (OS) application is executed as follows. After the guest application invokes a standard GPU rendering API, the guest GPU computation library, e.g., OpenGL, Direct3D, DirectCompute, CUDA, prepares the corresponding GPU buffer contents in main memory and issues the GPU command packets. These packets are pushed into the virtual GPU I/O queue, which are subsequently processed by the HostOps Dispatch in the host. Finally, this dispatch layer sends the commands to the device driver in an asynchronous manner. Buffer contents in guest OS memory are transferred to the GPU buffer using Direct Memory Access (DMA) through this process. We choose Windows 7 x64 as the guest OS running on VMware player 4.0 since it is most compatible with commercial games, especially high-end ones. Running 3Dmark06 on guest OS with both Windows 7 x64 and Ubuntu 11.04 x64 hosts, the FPS are 95.5% and 62.9% of the native performance, respectively. Therefore we use Windows 7 x64 as the host for all our experiments.

Figure 4 is the architecture of VGRIS within the paravirtualization framework shown in Figure 3, where modules introduced by VGRIS are highlighted in grey. These modules are all inside the host. There is one *agent* for each VM, which schedules GPU computation tasks and monitors the performance. In addition, there is a centralized scheduling controller that serves two purposes. First, it receives commands from the administrator to decide which scheduling algorithm to use. Second, under the hybrid scheduling policy, it automatically selects between the SLA-aware and proportional-share policy based on the performance feedback received from all agents. The content and frequency of the performance report from each agent are specified by the central controller too. Some scheduling algorithm does not require any feedback at all. In our prototype implementation, each agent simply intercepts Direct3D API invocations from GPU HostOps Dispatch for rescheduling. Its performance monitoring function utilizes GPU performance instrumentation methods. The centralized scheduling server is implemented as an independent process.

Similar to our previous design [32], we implement three representative scheduling policies for different optimization goals. The brief introductions of the three policies are as follows.

- **SLA-aware scheduling** allocates just enough GPU resource to each VM to fulfill its SLA requirement. However, the GPU resources may be not fully used under this policy.

- **Proportional-share scheduling** allocates all GPU resources to all running VMs in proportion to their weights assigned by the administrator. Due to the mistake or thoughtlessness of the administrator, some VM may not fulfill the SLA requirement.

- **Hybrid scheduling with a compromise** mixes the above two schemes. It first allocates minimal amount of resource to each VM so its SLA is satisfied, surplus resource is then proportionally allocated to all VMs to maximize GPU utilization.

3.2 Scheduling Policies

Currently, VGRIS mainly integrate three scheduling policies. Other scheduling algorithms are applicable to VGRIS architecture as well.

SLA-aware Scheduling SLA requirements in cloud gaming service providers try to guarantee a minimum FPS and a maximum latency for smooth user experience. As Figure 2a illustrates, the default GPU scheduling algorithm allocates resources fairly under contention. As a result, even if the SLA requirement is the same for all VMs, less GPU demand-

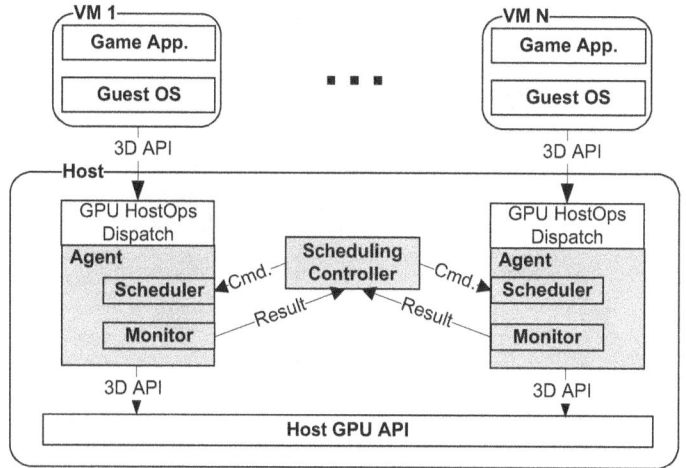

Figure 4: VGRIS Architecture.

ing ones may get more resources than necessary while GPU demanding ones cannot meet the requirement. SLA-aware scheduling is designed to address this issue. It allocates just enough resource for each VM to guarantee its SLA. To achieve this goal, we slow down less demanding applications to free extra resources for more demanding applications. We use the application of cloud gaming to illustrate this idea. The solution can be extended to other applications.

For smooth and responsive gaming experience, the latency of each frame must be in the range. Maximum latency is always implied by cloud providers' SLA. Therefore we consider the latency requirement as our SLA objective.

Computer games follow the same GPU computation model in Figure 1, where each iteration calculates and displays exactly one frame. For example, Figure 5a is the pseudocode using Direct3D. Methods `ComputeObjectsInFrame`, `DrawPrimitive`, and `Present` correspond to `CPUComputation`, `UploadData`, and `DispatchComputation` in Figure 1, respectively. In computer gaming, there is no need to send the result back to main memory. Instead, the GPU outputs the calculated frame through its external interfaces either to a screen or the network (after hardware compression). After the `Present` call returns, we have no direct control over when the frame becomes visible. However, the extra delay is negligible in the case with a local display. If the frame is displayed remotely, we assume a fixed amount of network delay. Therefore, we consider a frame latency as the time duration in-between the returns of two consecutive `Present` calls, illustrated in Figure 5b.

To stabilize the frame latency according to a given SLA, we extend each frame by delaying its last call, `Present`. This is achieved via inserting a `Sleep` call before `Present`. The amount of delay should be equal to the desirable latency subtracted by the computation time of `ComputeObjectsInFrame`, `DrawPrimitive`, and `Present` altogether. While VGRIS measures the computation time of the former two operations, the computation time of `Present` can only be predicted.

Fortunately we observe that the computation time of `Present` is very stable for each game application running in a VM, because it is mostly affected by the complexity of the scene, which changes only gradually. Furthermore, since each agent predicts the computation time based on its own historical

```
While(1) {
  ComputeObjectsInFrame();
  DrawPrimitive(&VGA_Buffer);
  Sleep(calculated_sleep_time);
  Present(&VGA_Buffer);
}
```

(a) Pseudocode under Direct3D

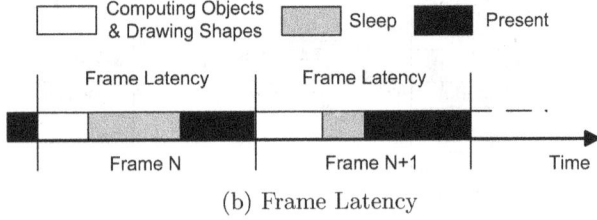

(b) Frame Latency

Figure 5: SLA-aware Scheduling Approach.

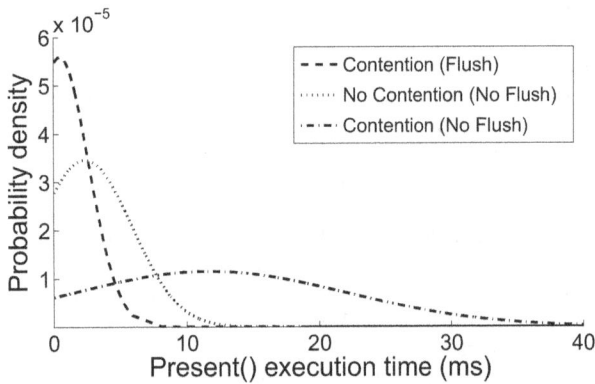

Figure 6: Probability distribution of present time cost.

information only, GPU context switch [18] has little impact on prediction accuracy of an individual agent. Therefore our prototype implementation simply uses the average time of the past twenty Present calls as the prediction for the upcoming one.

We also observe that the computation time of Present varies. When there is heavy contention, the average execution time of Present raises from 2.37 ms to 11.70 ms, as shown in Figure 6. This is because the DirectX runtime batches Direct3D commands for better efficiency. Hence, heavy contention increases the possibility of full command buffer, resulting in the execution time of Present less predictable. The Flush command can mitigate the problem significantly. Figure 6 shows that the average computation time of Present is reduced from 11.70 ms to 0.48 ms under heavy contention. The Flush command induces extra CPU computation cost. Since we mainly consider GPU bound VMs, it is reasonable to spend a little extra CPU time for more accurate prediction, and therefore more stable latency of each frame. We insert Flush in each iteration immediately before Sleep so we can measure, instead of estimate, its computation time.

Proportional-share Scheduling The SLA-aware scheduling strives to meet SLA requirements, which may result in low resource utilization when there are insufficient numbers of VMs. For applications such as offline rendering and general-purpose computation on the GPU, we may want to fully utilize the resources while ensuring each VM gets a fair amount of shares. Proportional sharing is a scheduling mechanism that is very well suited for these application scenarios.

Our proportional-share scheduling algorithm adopts the *Posterior Enforcement Reservation* policy used in Time-Graph [18], which queues and dispatches GPU commands based on task priorities. First each VM i is assigned a share s_i that represents the percentage of GPU resource it can use in each period t. The shares of all VMs add up to one. Budget e_i is the amount of GPU time that VM i is entitled for execution. This budget is decreased by the amount of time consumed on the GPU, and is replenished by at most ts_i once every period t as follows

$$e_i = \min(ts_i, e_i + ts_i). \tag{1}$$

The proportional-share scheduling dispatches Present API invocation if the budget for the corresponding VM is greater than zero, otherwise it postpones the dispatch. We set $t = 1$ ms in our implementation, which is sufficiently small to prevent long lags.

Hybrid Scheduling SLA-aware scheduling may result in low GPU utilization with an insufficient number of VMs. On the other hand, proportional-share scheduling can maximize utilization but inappropriate weights can lead to starvation of some VM. Our hybrid scheduling mechanism combines the benefits of the two by automatically choosing the appropriate algorithm with calculated parameters. In order to achieve this, we introduce a centralized scheduling controller that monitors the performance of each VM and coordinates all agents.

Algorithm 1 Hybrid scheduling algorithm. *FPSthres* is the minimal acceptable FPS; *GPUthres* is the preferred minimal overall GPU usage; *Time* is the maximum bearable duration for unsatisfied feedbacks.

1: **while** each second **do**
2:    **if** $CurrentAlgo = PropShare$ **and**
      $FPS < FPSthres$ for $Time$ sec **then**
3:      $CurrentAlgo \leftarrow SLAAware$
4:    **else if** $CurrentAlgo = SLAAware$ **and**
      $GPUTotalUsage < GPUthres$ for $Time$ sec **then**
5:      $CurrentAlgo \leftarrow PropShare$
6:      CalcShareForAllVMs()
7:    **end if**
8: **end while**

The scheduling controller collects the performance information from each VM every second. It determines the appropriate scheduling algorithm for all VMs based on user pre-defined criteria settings. When initialized, hybrid scheduling algorithm retrieves the threshold values from user settings and employs proportional-share scheduling with a fair share as the default algorithm. During runtime, any reported status below the criteria for the wait duration will lead to changing the scheduling algorithm among all agents. For example, the administrator may indicate the wait duration is 5 seconds. If proportional-share scheduling is leveraged as the current scheduling algorithm for all VMs, hybrid scheduling uses SLA-aware scheduling algorithm if and only if some VM has a low FPS for five seconds. On the contrary, the proportional-share scheduling algorithm is selected if the current scheduling method is SLA-aware scheduling and the physical GPU usage is below a certain criteria for 5 seconds.

The hybrid scheduling algorithm needs to determine the proper share for each VM when switching to proportional-share scheduling algorithm, as illustrated in Line 6 in Algorithm 1. The proportional share for the i-th VM (s_i) is achieved as follows:

$$s_i = u_i + \frac{(1 - \sum_{i=1}^{n} u_i)}{n}. \tag{2}$$

This formula approaches proportional sharing while guaranteeing SLA for each VM. u_i means the GPU usage of the i-th VM. It represents the minimum share of GPU resource needed when switching to proportional-share scheduling. Meanwhile, $(1 - \sum_{i=1}^{n} u_i)/n$ represents the fairness division of the abundant GPU resource to each VM. This fairly division permits that every VM owns more GPU resource than required to fulfill the SLA requirement in the current situation.

4. EXPERIMENTAL EVALUATIONS

We now provide a detailed quantitative evaluation of V-GRIS. All the experiments are conducted with the same workloads for the three scheduling policies. First, we evaluate SLA-aware scheduling in case of under-provision GPU resource. Then, we evaluate proportional-share scheduling's ability in maximizing GPU resource usage. Thirdly, we evaluate the effectiveness of hybrid scheduling. At last, we provide the micro- and macro-analysis to evaluate VGRIS's performance impact to guest legacy software.

The configurations of the testbed and VMs are derived from the top 5 most popular games listed in Table 1. The testbed is configured with i7-2600k 3.4GHz CPU, 16GB RAM, and an ATI HD6750 graphics card. Each hosted VM owns dual Cores and 2GB RAM. Windows 7 x64 is used as both the host OS and guest OSes. All the games are running under high graphic quality with 1280×720 resolution. To simplify performance comparison, swap space and GPU-accelerated windowing system are disabled on the host side.

We use two different types of workload and one benchmark in the following experiments. The first workload group, named *Ideal Model Games*, has almost fixed objects and views and hence a stable FPS is maintained. Many strategy games belong to this type. We choose PostProcess, ShadowVolume, Parallax and LocalDeformablePRT from DirectX 9.0 SDK samples as the representations of this kind of workload. The other workload group is the *Reality Model Games*, whose FPS keeps constant for a short time but varies from minute to minute. Games of First Person Shooter genre and Sports genre mainly constitute this group of games. We pick DiRT 3, Portal 2, and NBA2012 as the representative games. The 3DMark benchmarks (including 3DMark05 and 3DMark06) are also employed as the Reality Model Games because they satisfy the features mentioned above. 3DMark05 doesn't fully employ GPU resource. It sequentially runs three Game Tests (GT), in which GT1 doesn't consume all the GPU resources to produce a high FPS. GT2 and GT3 consume all the GPU resources, but the GT2 produces below 55 FPS for more than 30% of running time while the FPS of GT3 is below 70 FPS only within 5% of running time. 3DMark06 maximizes the GPU resource usage in all two game tests and two High Dynamic Range Tests (HDRT).

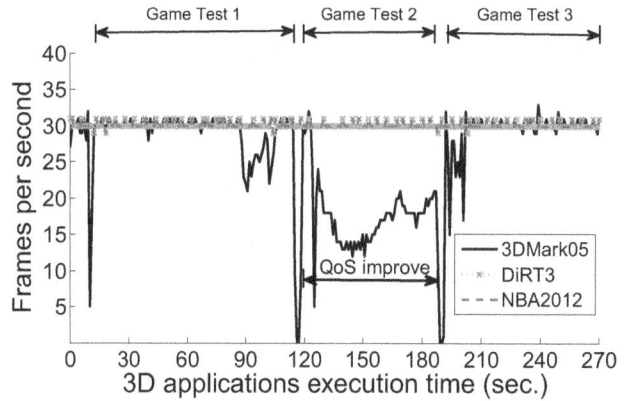

(a) FPS of Three Workloads

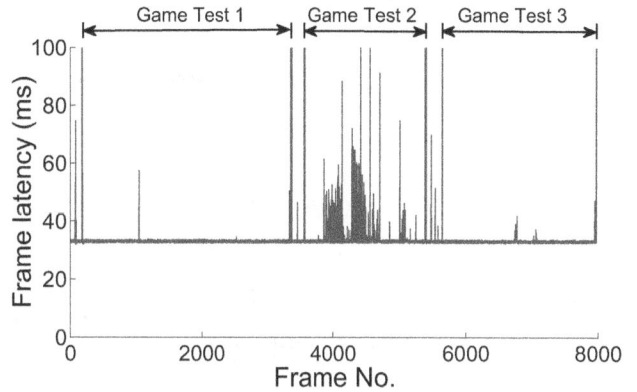

(b) Latency of 3DMark05

Figure 7: SLA-aware scheduling improves performance.

4.1 SLA-aware Scheduling Evaluation

We first evaluate SLA-aware scheduling provided by V-GRIS. We evaluate the policy with three workloads concurrently running in separate VMs and sharing one single graphics card. Using the same configurations with the experiments in Section 2, Figure 7 shows result improvements, compared with Figure 2. In Figure 7a, the average FPS of the GT2 rises 65.05% after SLA-aware scheduling. Also, the percentage of frames of excessive latency drops to 3.19% in Figure 7b, with the maximum value decreasing to 131.27 ms. Insufficient GPU hardware capability indicates that it cannot meet the FPS criteria ($\geq$30 FPS) for all three games at the same time in Figure 7a.

Next, we evaluate SLA-aware scheduling's effectiveness in controlling the FPS and GPU resource usage of the only VM. PostProcess application is used in this experiment and consumes 100% of GPU resource without control. The initially complete GPU resource usage is achieved by setting the resolution at 1920 × 1200 as well as enabling the Bloom effect specifically in the PostProcess application. An initial sleep time per frame of 300 ms is set by VGRIS which then decreases the sleep time by 1 ms in each second. Figure 8a depicts that sleep time (x) is approximately reciprocal with FPS (y_1) and GPU usage (y_2), similar to frame latency. The correlation result of the sleep time (x) and FPS (y_1) is $y_1 = 646.11x^{-0.927}$ with the correlation coefficient (R^2)

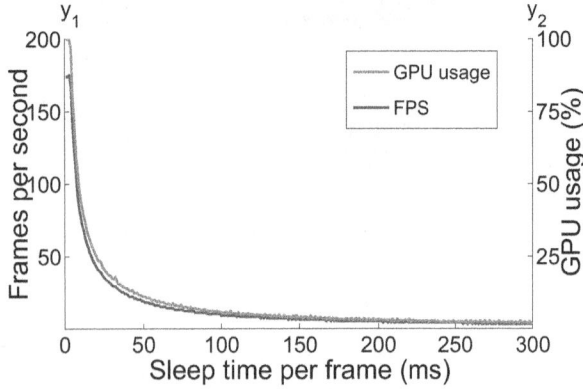

(a) FPS and GPU usage result for one VM

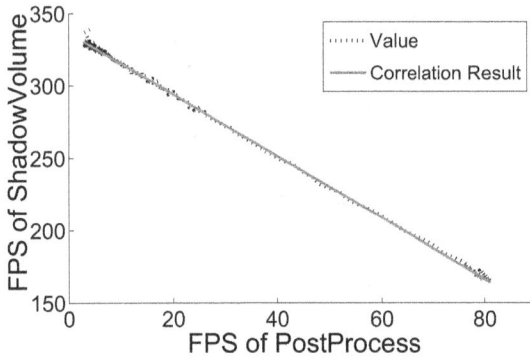

(b) FPS result for two VMs

Figure 8: Scheduling effectiveness on Ideal Model Games.

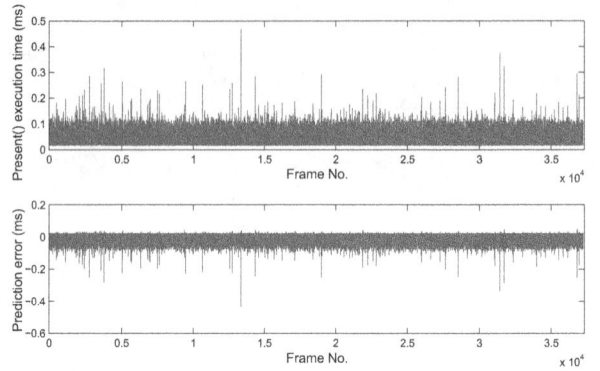

(a) LocalDeformablePRT - No GPU Contention

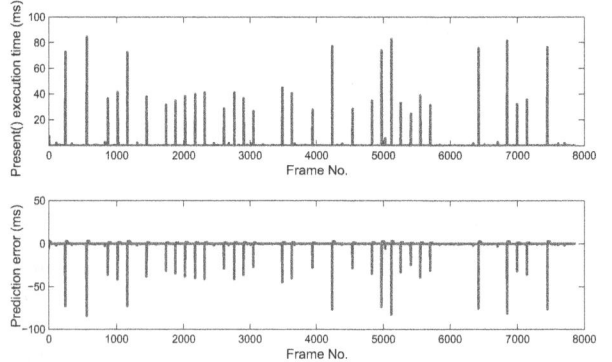

(b) LocalDeformablePRT - With GPU Contention

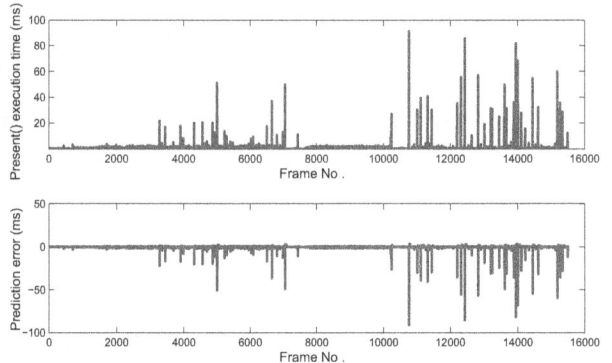

(c) 3DMark05 - With GPU Contention

Figure 9: Errors of **Present** API execution cost prediction.

to be 0.9828. Meanwhile, the correlation result of the sleep time (x) and GPU usage (y_2) is $y_2 = 332.33x^{-0.887}$ with R^2 to be 0.9838. The reason is straightforward according to the definition of FPS. Also, the loop-based GPU rendering model results that GPU resource usage shares the same trend with FPS.

In order to evaluate the impact to other VMs' FPS when controlling one VM only, we execute multiple VMs concurrently. Based on the same configuration in the last experiment, a new VM running ShadowVolume is introduced in. Its resolution is also set at 1920×1200 to fully consume GPU resource individually. As shown in Figure 8b, when the FPS of PostProcess increases, the FPS of ShadowVolume decreases in an approximately linear way. The correlation result of FPS value satisfies $y = -2.13x + 336.8$ and R^2 equals 0.9981. This experiment proves that the amount of GPU and CPU resource stripped from one VM can be acquired by other VMs and hence VGRIS can effectively control the GPU resource on multiple VMs.

Figure 9 depicts both actual and prediction of **Present** API execution cost in two game models: Ideal Model Games and Reality Model Games. The GPU resource is fully consumed and we record the result for a 60-second period. Figure 9a shows that the proposed prediction approach achieves 0.4 ms error margin. When GPU resource competition occurs, though the prediction error increases to -84.17 ms at most, only 4.12% of the frames have the predicted **Present**

API execution costs more than 2 ms error margin (Prediction Failures), as shown in Figure 9b. Meanwhile, even for the Reality Model Games in contention case, the percentage of prediction failures is 1.95% and the maximum prediction error is -91.32 ms, as presented in Figure 9c. It is noteworthy that a 2 ms prediction error only results in an instant decrease from 30 to 28.30 FPS or from 60 to 53.57 FPS. This is acceptable in the frequent long-time gaming experience.

4.2 Proportional-share Scheduling Evaluation

We next demonstrate the effectiveness of proportional-share scheduling in regulating GPU resource usage according to user settings. Figure 10 shows the GPU resource usage of Reality Model Games using different initial GPU shares: (1) NBA2012 is set to use 30% GPU resource while requiring 44.48% GPU resource individually. (2) Looped

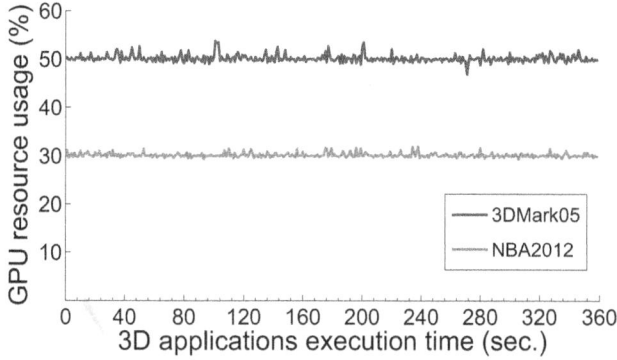

Figure 10: Proportional-share scheduling evaluation result.

Table 2: Performance comparison of proportional-share scheduling and SLA-aware scheduling.

	SLA-Aware Scheduling		Proportional-Share Scheduling	
	FPS	GPU Usage	FPS	GPU Usage
NBA2012	30.12	12.41%	79.16	30.12%
3DMark05	30.30	26.95%	61.76	50.30%

GT 1 in 3DMark05 is set to use 50% GPU resource while requiring 70.82% GPU resource individually. Especially, we measure the GPU usage discrepancy within each instance in Figure 10 to evaluate the control accuracy. The results show that the range is 13.75% to the average GPU usage value for 3DMark05 and 8.31% for NBA2012. This result proves that proportional-share scheduling successfully provides user specified GPU resource share. It even works for Reality Model Games which owns the inherently dynamic nature of complex scene switches and abruptly changing in visible objects.

Furthermore, we compare the GPU resource usage of the proportional-share and SLA-aware scheduling to evaluate proportional-share policy's ability in maximizing hardware performance. Proportional-share scheduling uses the same resource allocation with the former experiment while the FPS criteria of SLA-aware scheduling is set to be 30 FPS. Table 2 depicts that proportional-share scheduling employs more available GPU resource than SLA-aware scheduling does. This is because SLA-aware scheduling limits FPS according to the user indicated FPS criteria. Meanwhile, GPU resource usage is direct proportion to the FPS for the same game. Hence, SLA-aware scheduling doesn't use GPU resource effectively due to its criteria based FPS limitation.

4.3 Hybrid Scheduling Evaluation

We now evaluate hybrid scheduling's automatic determination of scheduling algorithms with proper parameters. Three Reality Model Games are used to evaluate hybrid scheduling's effectiveness, including NBA2012, DiRT3, and 3DMark05. First, we run the NBA2012 and DiRT3 games concurrently. After 28 seconds, we start 3DMark05's GT3 which will finish its execution in 87 seconds. Figure 11 illustrates the selection of algorithms and the impacts to the FPS of running VMs. In this figure, α represents proportional-share

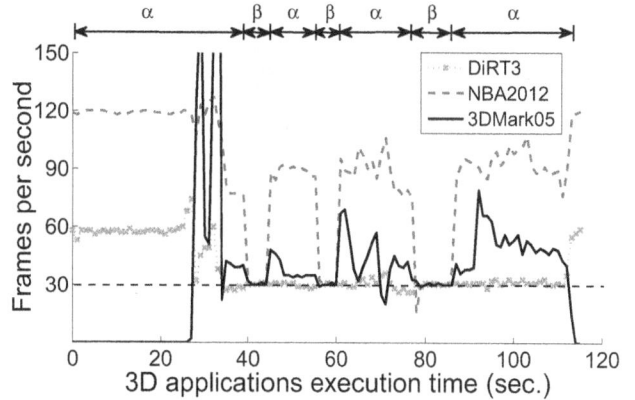

Figure 11: Hybrid Scheduling Results.

scheduling and β stands for SLA-aware scheduling. Firstly, hybrid scheduling employs proportional-share scheduling algorithm and assigns full GPU resource for each VM since both of their FPS satisfy the FPS criteria. At the time of 40 second, the VM running DiRT3 has not got sufficient GPU resource to maintain its SLA for the most recent time which is 5 seconds according to the administrator's setting. Hence, hybrid scheduling employs SLA-aware scheduling to release the excessive GPU resources in other VMs. However, this results in a low overall GPU usage and hybrid scheduling switches back to proportional-share scheduling after duration. Because hybrid scheduling always fairly divides the abundant GPU resource and assigns them to each VM, it can be observed that VM's FPS increases when switching back to the proportional-share scheduling algorithm. In the rest of Figure 11, the algorithm selection always follows the above mechanism.

4.4 Performance Discussions

In order to evaluate VGRIS's performance impact to legacy applications and OSes, we first perform micro analysis to illustrate the potential hot spot. PostProcess and 3DMark06 GT1 are leveraged to fully utilize available GPU resource. We only evaluate the execution cost of each part in SLA-aware scheduling and proportional-share scheduling. The hybrid scheduling is not included because there are only trivial changes based on the other two scheduling methods and the performance impact can be ignored. Figure 12 shows the microbenchmark results. The execution time of SLA-aware scheduling constitutes four parts, in which the GPU command flush operations contribute the main performance overhead. This is due to the design of current Direct3D library and the implemented flush strategy in VGRIS prototype. It's possible to achieve a better result by adopting different flush strategies in the future.

Having no GPU Command `Flush` operation, proportional-share scheduling contains three parts in its execution time. For the same reason, the `Present` API execution time unsurprisingly becomes the most expensive operation. It is noteworthy that no aggressive flush of Direct3D command buffer is added in proportional-share scheduling, because proportional-share scheduling always assumes the existence of over-provision GPU resource. In total, SLA-aware scheduling algorithm incurs 6.74% overhead for PostProcess while

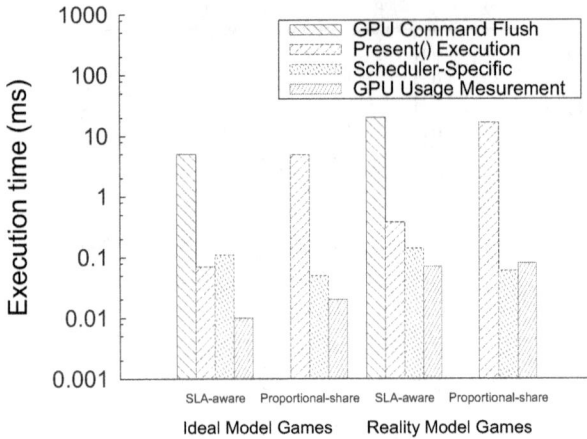

Figure 12: Microbenchmark Results.

Table 3: Macrobenchmark Results.

	Native	SLA-aware Scheduling		Proportional-share Scheduling	
	FPS	FPS	Overhead	FPS	Overhead
GT1	43.023	42.044	2.28%	42.221	1.86%
GT2	48.686	45.996	5.53%	48.284	0.83%
HDRT1	59.062	57.923	1.93%	57.700	2.31%
HDRT2	65.808	62.854	4.90%	65.984	-0.27%

24.01% for 3DMark06. The results for proportional-share scheduling are 1.56% and 0.11%.

When considering the infrequent invocation of **Present** API, the performance overhead is significantly decreased. 3DMark06 with default settings is used to evaluate VGRIS's performance overhead in application level. Table 3 shows the evaluation results, proving VGRIS brings in 3.66% performance overhead in average for SLA-aware scheduling while 1.18% for proportional-share scheduling. Thus, the scheduling methods provided by VGRIS are demonstrated to incur slight performance overhead. Moreover, VGRIS is even able to provide the same SLA with that provided by commercial cloud gaming services (e.g., OnLive). Our evaluation result shows that VGRIS is able to run one DiRT3 and two Portal 2 instances concurrently with the FPS criteria set to be 60. As a result, VGRIS is able to execute multiple game VMs concurrently while ensuring acceptable SLA individually.

5. RELATED WORK

Virtualized resource management is an active area of research over the past decade. Based on the general trend of all related research works, we can broadly classify them into three groups: 1)scheduling in virtualization, 2) GPU scheduling, and 3) applications of GPU virtualization.

Scheduling in Virtualization: Previous works focus on CPU and I/O scheduling including disk and network resources. Credit, Simple Earliest Deadline First (SEDF), Borrowed Virtual Time (BVT) [10] and vSlicer [34] are available CPU schedulers [6] for general purpose hypervisor like Xen [1]. Achieving the ability of scheduling processor resource according to the indicated proportions, these method-

s can also be employed in the proportional-share scheduling in VGRIS. BVT is optimized for latency sensitive applications by decreasing the corresponding job's next schedule time and borrowing time slices from its future processor usage. Credit scheduling achieves the same optimization by boosting corresponding virtual CPU in the block state when an external event arrives [6]. Besides, CPU schedulers for real time guest OS control the expected latency by arranging virtual CPU run queue in certain order [21, 35]. However, these scheduling methods cannot be applied to manage GPU resources to fulfill the SLA requirement. The reason is that all of these scheduling approaches treat VM to be black box and hence ignore guest applications' SLA-related measurements. In contrast, by effective library API interception on host side, VGRIS can perform SLA-aware scheduling algorithm without modifying guest software.

For the I/O resource scheduling in virtualization, prior works mainly analyzed the scheduling methods of disk and network resources. Similar to our approach, AVATAR [36] is implemented to ensure the proportional-share scheduling of storage resources and fulfill the service level objectives. However, the dynamic change in GPU resource usage in certain kinds of GPU applications results that AVATAR possibly dissatisfies the SLA of GPU computation tasks. This issue is identified to be one important problem and solved by hybrid scheduling in VGRIS.

DVT [19] is primarily designed for network resource scheduling. It provides differential resource scheduling and gradual latency variation in case of workload capacity's change to support performance isolation for guest OS's resource management mechanisms. Stillwell et al. [31] focus on scheduling algorithms on distributed platforms. The algorithms can allocate resources to competing services. Based on workload data supplied by Google, the algorithms provide good performance. Compared with them, VGRIS provides both proportional-share and SLA-aware scheduling by obtaining guest application's SLA measurements.

GPU Scheduling: Previous GPU resource scheduling approaches mainly target native systems. For example, Phull et al. [28] present a framework to predict and handle interference and schedule GPU resources in a time-share model. Kato et al. [17] address the priority inversion problems of user GPU tasks in GPU-accelerated windowing systems. Elliott et al. [12] have presented two methods for integrating GPUs into soft real-time multiprocessor systems to improve total system performance. Maeda et al. [23] develop an automatic resource scheduling to accelerate stencil applications on GPGPU Clusters. A task-based dynamic load-balancing scheduling [4] is proposed for single- and multi-GPU systems. Ravi et al. [29] propose a framework that enable applications running within VMs to transparently share one or more GPUs. Compared with them, VGRIS mainly focuses on graphics processing including 3D rendering and gaming. Both SLA of the 3D applications in the VMs and the overall throughput are taken into account. TimeGraph [18] implements a real-time GPU scheduler to isolate performance for important GPU workloads. To achieve its design goal, TimeGraph queues GPU command groups in the driver layer and submits them according to user predefined settings as well as GPU hardware measurements. TimeGraph cannot guarantee SLA for all the VMs, especially for less important workloads. Instead, our hybrid scheduling algorithm is used to effectively provide both SLA and maximized the GPU resource usage. Becchi *et al.* [3] add two features to improve the sharing of GPUs: dynamic application-to-GPU binding and virtual memory for GPUs. Aimed at different goals, VGRIS can further employ this work to support load balancing and solve GPU memory constraint for applications.

GERM [2, 11] aims at providing fair GPU resource allocation. Besides, fixed frame rate approaches like Vertical Synchronization (V-Sync) [3] are designed for games to avoid excessively use of hardware resource. Unfortunately, GERM fails to consider SLA requirements while fixed frame rate approaches fail to consider using hardware resource effectively. Due to fixed frame rate, both approaches are inflexible to adjust resource utility on-the-fly.

Applications of GPU Virtualization: The rapid development of GPU virtualization accelerates many new applications, especially in cloud gaming and general-purpose GPU computing.

In cloud gaming, previous studies on cloud gaming platform focus on streaming graphical content and decreasing the required network bandwidth [5, 33, 26, 16]. Li *et al.* [22] take cryo-electron microscopy 3D reconstruction as an example to present how to exploit parallelism on both CPU and GPU in a heterogeneous system. Different from them, our approach is able to run multiple game VMs sharing with GPU resource based on GPU Para-Virtualization (PV) technique.

In general-purpose GPU computing, vCUDA [30] introduces GPU computing into virtualization execution environment. It motivates our research in scheduling resources for GPU computing. rCUDA [9] and Duato's work [8] try to decrease the power-consuming GPUs from high performance clusters while preserving their 3D-acceleration capability to remote nodes. Gupta *et al.* [14] propose Pegasus that uses NVIDIA GPGPUs coupled with x86-based general purpose host cores to manage combined platform resources. Based on Pegasus, Merritt *et al.* [24] propose Shadowfax, a prototype of GPGPU Assemblies, improves GPGPU application scalability as well as increases application throughput. However, none of these approaches has studied the management of virtualized GPU resource isolation and scheduling to achieve the computational efficiency in cloud gaming which is the main focus of this paper. Comparing with them, our approach tries to improve the SLA of GPU computation on cloud platform and maximize the overall resource usage. Additionally, VGRIS provides three representative scheduling algorithms to meet multiple optimization goals in case of under- and over-provisioned GPU resource.

6. CONCLUSION

We presented VGRIS, a Virtualized GPU Resource Isolation and Scheduling framework for GPU-related computation tasks. By introducing an agent per VM and a centralized scheduling controller to the paravirtualization framework, VGRIS achieves in-VM GPU resource measurements and regulates the GPU resource usage. Moreover, we propose three representative scheduling algorithms: SLA-aware scheduling allocates just enough GPU resources to fulfill the SLA requirement; Proportional-share scheduling allocates all GPU resources to all running VMs in proportion to their weights; Hybrid scheduling provides a mixed solution to meeting the SLA requirement while maximizing

---

[3] V-Sync. http://en.wikipedia.org/wiki/Vertical_synchronization/.

the overall GPU resource usage. Using the cloud gaming scenario as a case study, our evaluation demonstrates that each scheduling algorithm enforces its goals under various workloads. We plan to extend VGRIS to multiple physical GPUs and multiple physical machine systems for data center resource scheduling as our future work.

7. ACKNOWLEDGMENTS

Thanks for Jiewei Wu and Xi Chen's contribution to this project. We also thank for Yueqiang Cheng's and Zheng Zhang's suggestions. Also, we appreciate the valuable comments come from the reviewers. They help us in revising our work one step further. This work is supported by the Program for PCSIRT and NCET of MOE, NSFC (No. 61073151, 61272101), 863 Program (No. 2011AA01A202, 2012AA010905), 973 Program (No. 2012CB723401), the key program (No. 313035) of MOE, and International Cooperation Program (No. 11530700500, 2011DFA10850), and Shanghai Natural Science Foundation (No.12ZR1445700).

8. REFERENCES

[1] P. Barham, B. Dragovic, K. Fraser, S. Hand, T. L. Harris, A. Ho, R. Neugebauer, I. Pratt, and A. Warfield. Xen and the art of virtualization. In *Proceedings of ACM Symposium on Operating Systems Principles*, SOSP, 2003.

[2] M. Bautin, A. Dwarakinath, and T. cker Chiueh. Graphic engine resource management. In *Proceedings of Multimedia Computing and Networking*, MMCN, 2008.

[3] M. Becchi, K. Sajjapongse, I. Graves, A. Procter, V. Ravi, and S. Chakradhar. A virtual memory based runtime to support multi-tenancy in clusters with GPUs. In *Proceedings of international symposium on High-Performance Parallel and Distributed Computing*, HPDC, 2012.

[4] L. Chen, O. Villa, S. Krishnamoorthy, and G. R. Gao. Dynamic load balancing on single- and multi-gpu systems. In *Proceedinigs of IEEE International Symposium on Parallel Distributed Processing*, IPDPS, 2010.

[5] L. Cheng, A. Bhushan, R. Pajarola, and M. E. Zarki. Realtime 3D graphics streaming using MPEG-4. In *Proceedings of the nineteenth ACM symposium on Operating systems principles*, BroadWise, 2004.

[6] L. Cherkasova, D. Gupta, and A. Vahdat. Comparison of the three CPU schedulers in Xen. *SIGMETRICS Performance Evaluation Review*, 35(2):42–51, 2007.

[7] M. Dowty and J. Sugerman. GPU virtualization on VMware's hosted I/O architecture. *SIGOPS Operating Systems Review*, 43:73–82, 2009.

[8] J. Duato, F. D. Igual, R. Mayo, A. J. Peña, E. S. Quintana-Ortí, and F. Silla. An efficient implementation of GPU virtualization in high performance clusters. In *Proceedings of European Conference on Parallel Processing*, Euro-Par Workshops, 2009.

[9] J. Duato, A. J. Peña, F. Silla, R. Mayo, and E. S. Quintana-Ortí. rCUDA: Reducing the number of GPU-based accelerators in high performance clusters. In *Proceedings of the International Conference on High Performance Computing and Simulation*, HPCS, 2010.

[10] K. J. Duda and D. R. Cheriton. Borrowed-virtual-time (BVT) scheduling: supporting latency-sensitive threads in a general-purpose scheduler. In *Proceedings of the ACM Symposium on Operating Systems Principles*, SOSP, 1999.

[11] A. Dwarakinath. A fair-share scheduler for the graphics processing unit. *Master Thesis*, 2008.

[12] G. A. Elliott and J. H. Anderson. Globally scheduled real-time multiprocessor systems with GPUs. *Real-Time Systems*, 48(1):34–74, 2012.

[13] V. Gupta, A. Gavrilovska, K. Schwan, H. Kharche, N. Tolia, V. Talwar, and P. Ranganathan. GViM: Gpu-accelerated virtual machines. In *Proceedings of the ACM Workshop on System-level Virtualization for High Performance Computing*, HPCVirt, 2009.

[14] V. Gupta, K. Schwan, N. Tolia, V. Talwar, and P. Ranganathan. Pegasus: Coordinated scheduling for virtualized accelerator-based systems. In *Proceedings of the 2011 USENIX conference on USENIX annual technical conference*, ATC, 2011.

[15] Joystiq. GDC09 interview: OnLive founder Steve Perlman, continued. `http://www.joystiq.com/2009/04/02/gdc09-interview-onlive-founder-steve-perlman-continued/`.

[16] A. Jurgelionis, P. Fechteler, P. Eisert, F. Bellotti, H. David, J.-P. Laulajainen, R. Carmichael, V. Poulopoulos, A. Laikari, P. H. J. Perälä, A. D. Gloria, and C. Bouras. Platform for distributed 3D gaming. *Int. J. Computer Games Technology*, 2009.

[17] S. Kato, K. Lakshmanan, Y. Ishikawa, and R. R. Rajkumar. Resource sharing in GPU-accelerated windowing systems. In *Proceedings of the 2011 17th IEEE Real-Time and Embedded Technology and Applications Symposium*, RTAS, 2011.

[18] S. Kato, K. Lakshmanan, R. Rajkumar, and Y. Ishikawa. TimeGraph: GPU scheduling for real-time multi-tasking environments. In *Proceedings of the 2011 USENIX conference on USENIX annual technical conference*, ATC, 2011.

[19] M. Kesavan, A. Gavrilovska, and K. Schwan. Differential virtual time (DVT): rethinking I/O service differentiation for virtual machines. In *Proceedings of the 1st ACM symposium on Cloud computing*, SoCC, 2010.

[20] H. A. Lagar-Cavilla, N. Tolia, M. Satyanarayanan, and E. de Lara. VMM-independent graphics acceleration. In *Proceedings of the International Conference on Virtual Execution Environments*, VEE, 2007.

[21] M. Lee, A. S. Krishnakumar, P. Krishnan, N. Singh, and S. Yajnik. Supporting soft real-time tasks in the Xen hypervisor. In *Proceedings of the 6th ACM SIGPLAN/SIGOPS international conference on Virtual execution environments*, VEE, 2010.

[22] L. Li, X. Li, G. Tan, M. Chen, and P. Zhang. Experience of parallelizing cryo-em 3D reconstruction on a CPU-GPU heterogeneous system. In *Proceedings of the ACM International Symposium on High Performance Distributed Computing*, HPDC, 2011.

[23] K. Maeda, M. Murase, M. Doi, H. Komatsu, S. Noda, and R. Himeno. Automatic resource scheduling with latency hiding for parallel stencil applications on GPGPU clusters. In *Proceedinigs of IEEE International Symposium on Parallel Distributed Processing*, IPDPS, 2012.

[24] A. M. Merritt, V. Gupta, A. Verma, A. Gavrilovska, and K. Schwan. Shadowfax: scaling in heterogeneous cluster systems via GPGPU assemblies. In *Proceedings of the 5th international workshop on Virtualization technologies in distributed computing*, VTDC, 2011.

[25] B. H. Ng, B. Lau, and A. Parkash. Direct access to graphics card leveraging VT-d. Technical report, University of Michigan, 2009.

[26] Y. Noimark and D. Cohen-Or. Streaming scenes to MPEG-4 video-enabled devices. *IEEE Computer Graphics and Applications*, 23(1):58–64, 2003.

[27] J. Owens, M. Houston, D. Luebke, S. Green, J. Stone, and J. Phillips. GPU computing. *Proceedings of the IEEE*, 96(5):879 –899, 2008.

[28] R. Phull, C.-H. Li, K. Rao, S. Cadambi, and S. T. Chakradhar. Interference-driven resource management for GPU-based heterogeneous clusters. In *Proceedings of the ACM International Symposium on High Performance Distributed Computing*, HPDC, 2012.

[29] V. T. Ravi, M. Becchi, G. Agrawal, and S. T. Chakradhar. Supporting GPU sharing in cloud environments with a transparent runtime consolidation framework. In *Proceedings of the ACM International Symposium on High Performance Distributed Computing*, HPDC, 2011.

[30] L. Shi, H. Chen, and J. Sun. vCUDA: GPU accelerated high performance computing in virtual machines. In *Proceedinigs of IEEE International Symposium on Parallel Distributed Processing*, IPDPS, 2009.

[31] M. Stillwell, F. Vivien, and H. Casanova. Virtual machine resource allocation for service hosting on heterogeneous distributed platforms. In *Proceedinigs of IEEE International Symposium on Parallel Distributed Processing*, IPDPS, 2012.

[32] Y. Wang and A. Merchant. Proportional-share scheduling for distributed storage systems. In *Proccedings of the 5th conference on File and storage technologies*, FAST, 2007.

[33] D. D. Winter, P. Simoens, L. Deboosere, F. D. Turck, J. Moreau, B. Dhoedt, and P. Demeester. A hybrid thin-client protocol for multimedia streaming and interactive gaming applications. In *Proceedings of the International Workshop on Network and Operating Systems Support for Digital Audio and Video*, NOSSDAV, 2006.

[34] C. Xu, S. Gamage, P. N. Rao, A. Kangarlou, R. R. Kompella, and D. Xu. vSlicer: latency-aware virtual machine scheduling via differentiated-frequency CPU slicing. In *Proceedings of the ACM International Symposium on High Performance Distributed Computing*, HPDC, 2012.

[35] P. Yu, M. Xia, Q. Lin, M. Zhu, S. Gao, Z. Qi, K. Chen, and H. Guan. Real-time enhancement for Xen hypervisor. In *Proceedings of Embedded and Ubiquitous Computing*, EUC, 2010.

[36] J. Zhang, A. Sivasubramaniam, Q. Wang, A. Riska, and E. Riedel. Storage performance virtualization via throughput and latency control. *Trans. Storage*, 2:283–308, 2006.

COSMIC: Middleware for High Performance and Reliable Multiprocessing on Xeon Phi Coprocessors

Srihari Cadambi, Giuseppe Coviello, Cheng-Hong Li, Rajat Phull,
Kunal Rao, Murugan Sankaradass and Srimat Chakradhar

Computing Systems Architecture Department
NEC Laboratories America, Inc.
Princeton, NJ, USA.

ABSTRACT

It is remarkably easy to offload processing to Intel's newest manycore coprocessor, the Xeon-Phi: it supports a popular ISA (x86-based), a popular OS (Linux) and a popular programming model (OpenMP). Easy portability is attracting programmer efforts to achieve high performance for many applications. But Linux makes it easy for different users to share the Xeon Phi coprocessor, and multiprocessing inefficiencies can easily offset gains made by individual programmers. Our experiments on a production, high-performance Xeon server with multiple Xeon Phi coprocessors show that coprocessor multiprocessing not only slows down the processes but also introduces unreliability (some processes crash unexpectedly).

We propose a new, user-level middleware called COSMIC that improves performance and reliability of multiprocessing on coprocessors like the Xeon Phi. COSMIC seamlessly fits in the existing Xeon Phi software stack and is transparent to programmers. It manages Xeon Phi processes that execute parallel regions offloaded to the coprocessors. Offloads typically have programmer-driven performance directives like thread and affinity requirements. COSMIC does fair scheduling of *both processes and offloads*, and takes into account conflicting requirements of offloads belonging to different processes. By doing so, it has two benefits. First, it improves multiprocessing performance by preventing thread and memory oversubscription, by avoiding inter-offload interference and by reducing load imbalance on coprocessors and cores. Second, it increases multiprocessing reliability by exploiting programmer-specified per-process coprocessor memory requirements to completely avoid memory oversubscription and crashes. Our experiments on several representative Xeon Phi workloads show that, in a multiprocessing environment, COSMIC improves average core utilization by up to 3 times, reduces make-span by up to 52%, reduces average process latency (turn-around-time) by 70%, and completely eliminates process crashes.

Categories and Subject Descriptors

D.4.1 [**Process Management**]: Process Management – *multiprocessing/multiprogramming/multitasking, scheduling.*

Keywords

Middleware, Xeon Phi, Manycore, Servers, System Software.

1. INTRODUCTION

The Intel Xeon Phi manycore processor is a PCIe device with 60 cores and 240 hardware threads. Unlike the GPU and other manycores, several design choices make the Xeon Phi easier to program. First, its cores are x86 compatible. Second, it runs the Linux operating system, enabling easy multiprocessing with services such as virtual memory and context switching. Third, it supports OpenMP, a popular parallel programming model. Intel also provides middleware to manage data transfers between the host and coprocessor. Consequently, the Xeon Phi is widely perceived to be more programmable for a range of parallel applications, especially when compared to other manycore offerings in the recent past [1], [2]. Many OEM vendors are releasing Xeon Phi-based high-performance servers and several application kernels have achieved a speedup on these systems [3].

1.1 Portability, Speed and Reliability

In order to use the Xeon Phi, a programmer uses pragmas to indicate code regions that can be "offloaded" to the coprocessor, for which the Intel compiler automatically generates coprocessor instructions and the glue code to manage transfer of data. This is the "offload programming model" where the main trunk of the code runs on the host processor while regions identified by pragmas are offloaded to the Xeon Phi coprocessor. Thus, if portions of a program are already parallelized using OpenMP, offloading them to the Xeon Phi is easy.

Unfortunately, quick and easy portability rarely results in a high performance implementation on the Xeon Phi. Rather, additional programmer effort such as carefully selecting the number of threads, mapping them to cores, ensuring that no thread or memory oversubscription occurs, and load balancing the application across multiple coprocessors is necessary.

Such application tuning may work well when individual applications exclusively "own" the coprocessor, but not in a multiprocessing environment. The Xeon Phi coprocessor runs Linux, which allows multiple processes to easily share the coprocessor. Multiprocessing is common not only in cluster and cloud deployments, but it is also indispensable for good hardware utilization in individual servers. As we show in Section 3, most applications neither scale to 240 hardware threads nor fully utilize all the hardware resources in the Xeon Phi. Further, our experiments in Section 3 on a production Xeon Phi server also show that when multiple applications compete for coprocessor resources and programmers are unaware of each other's intentions, Xeon Phi processes nearly always slow down, and often crash. Thus, *coprocessor multiprocessing may improve utilization, but it does so at the cost of performance degradation and unreliable execution.*

1.2 Multiprocessing Challenges on Coprocessors

Our experiments on a production, high-performance Xeon server with multiple Xeon Phi coprocessors, which we report in Section 3, suggest that processes must adhere to several guidelines in order to benefit from multiprocessing on a manycore coprocessor.

First, *they must not oversubscribe the coprocessor hardware threads* since context switching on a manycore is more expensive than it is on a multicore. Context switching overhead depends on the amount of state in a context, and on the available cache and memory bandwidth. Each Xeon Phi core contains more register state than a core in a multicore processor: it has 32 vector registers of 512 bits each making up at least 2KB of vector register state [4], while a regular Xeon core contains sixteen 128-bit XMM registers that make up a total of 256B of vector state [5]. Although the Xeon Phi has a larger overall cache and off-chip memory bandwidth than multicores, *it has a smaller cache per core, and a smaller off-chip memory bandwidth per core*. On Xeon Phi of 60 cores, the cache per core is about 0.5MB, and with a total aggregate off-chip memory bandwidth of 352GB/s, bandwidth per core is about 5.87GB/s. By comparison, a host processor like the Xeon E5-2630 has 6 cores per socket, a 15MB cache (2.5MB per core) and an off-chip memory bandwidth of 42.6GB/s or 7.1 GB/s per core.

Second, *processes must not oversubscribe the limited coprocessor main memory*. The Xeon Phi has up to 8GB of GDDR5 memory (similar to GPUs), while a multicore can have 100s of GB. Augmenting coprocessor memory by mapping a portion of the host memory as swap space is possible. However, as described in Section 3.4, swapping *introduces unreliability and performance loss*. Therefore, avoiding memory oversubscription *and* swap to ensure reliable and high-performance multiprocessing on Xeon Phi processors is a big challenge.

Third, *processes must carefully map threads to cores, as well as load balance across multiple coprocessor devices*. Manycore programmers often specify thread-to-core and offload-to-device mappings. In a multiprocessing environment, these specifications can conflict with each other, resulting in poor workload distribution and lower performance.

1.3 Multiprocessing on Xeon Phi

The Xeon Phi software stack, called the MPSS (Many Integrated Core Platform Software Stack), consists of a portion that executes on the host, and a portion that executes on the coprocessor. The host portion includes stock Linux running along with PCI and card drivers. A Symmetric Communication Interface (SCIF) is provided by Intel for communicating between Xeon Phi devices or between the host and a Xeon Phi processor. SCIF provides a set of APIs for communication and abstracts the details of communicating over the PCIe bus. On top of SCIF, the Coprocessor Offload Infrastructure (COI) [6] is a higher-level framework developed by Intel. It provides a set of APIs to simplify development of applications using the offload model. COI includes APIs for launching device code, asynchronous execution and data transfer between the host and Xeon Phi.

The other part of the stack executes on the coprocessor, and it includes a modified Linux kernel and drivers, the standard Linux "/proc" file system that can be used to query device state (for example, the load average), and the coprocessor side of the SCIF driver and the COI library.

For every host process that offloads work to the coprocessor, the COI middleware creates a process on the Xeon Phi that will execute offloaded code sections sent from the host process. We refer to such processes on the Xeon Phi as *COI processes*. Linux on the coprocessor is only aware of processes, but MPSS is aware of offloads within a COI process. However, while scheduling offloads, MPSS does not take into account or reason about the often conflicting programmer specified, offload specific performance directives associated with offloads in different COI processes. Our experiments described in Section 3 show that the current MPSS software stack adversely affects multiprocessing performance.

First, we observe a disproportionate increase in execution times when COI processes oversubscribe threads. Second, when the combined memory usage of COI processes exceeds the coprocessor physical memory, we observe that, in addition to performance loss, *some COI processes are killed or the coprocessor OS crashes*. Third, COI processes are unaware of each other, and their offload specific performance directives often conflict, leading to suboptimal workload distribution on cores within a coprocessor, and across coprocessors. In particular, under multi-processing, the existing software stack does *not* protect against thread and memory oversubscription, isolate the execution of offloads, manage cores to take advantage of data affinity, or balance COI processes across coprocessors and cores.

1.4 Our Contributions

First, we perform a comprehensive evaluation of multiprocessing on a production Xeon Phi server. We assemble and port a representative set of coprocessor workloads to the Xeon Phi. We use these workloads to quantify Xeon Phi hardware utilization and observe the need for multiprocessing on manycores like Xeon Phi. Then, we extensively quantify performance and reliability impact caused by thread and memory oversubscription, as well as load imbalance due to multiprocessing on Xeon Phi.

Second, to overcome the limitations of multiprocessing on Xeon Phi coprocessors, we propose a new, user-level middleware to automatically manage coprocessor resources by taking into consideration all concurrently running Xeon Phi processes *and* their offloads, in order to deliver high performance and reliable multiprocessing. Our middleware component is called COSMIC (Coprocessor Offload System for Many Integrated Core). COSMIC is not only completely transparent to programmers but it also requires no changes to the existing Xeon Phi software stack. It uses novel mechanisms, policies and algorithms to concurrently schedule COI processes and their offloads. It avoids thread and memory oversubscription, maps offloads to Xeon Phi cores to avoid inter-offload interference, and balances load on multiple Xeon Phi coprocessors. It also avoids crashing the coprocessor due to reasons like memory oversubscription, thus making the system more reliable. *To our knowledge, this is the first effort that improves both performance and reliability of multiprocessing on Linux-based manycore processors like the Xeon Phi.*

1.5 Organization of the Paper

After a brief background on the Xeon Phi and its programming model in Section 2, we evaluate multiprocessing on the Xeon Phi in Section 3. We describe the representative set of workloads that we put together and use throughout the paper, and show detailed data quantifying the benefits and adverse effects of multiprocessing on the Xeon Phi. In Section 4, we describe the software architecture of the proposed COSMIC system. In Section 5, we discuss COSMIC's mechanisms and policies. We evaluate COSMIC in Section 6, discuss related work in Section 7 and conclude in Section 8.

2. BACKGROUND

The Xeon Phi has more than 50 cores connected via a 512-bit bidirectional ring interconnect. It is packaged as a separate PCIe device, external to the host processor. Each Xeon Phi device has 8 GB of RAM that serves as the memory and file system storage for user processes, the Linux operating system, and ancillary daemon processes.

Each Xeon Phi core is dual-issue, in-order, and includes sixteen 32-bit vector lanes. The single thread performance of each core is considerably slower than a core in multicore processors. However, every Xeon Phi core supports 4 hardware threads, resulting in good aggregate performance for highly parallelized and vectorized kernels. This makes the offload model, where sequential code runs on the host processor and parallelizable kernels are offloaded to the Xeon Phi, an effective programming model.

Offload programming model. A programmer annotates code with "offload pragmas" [7] to identify regions to be offloaded to the Xeon Phi. An offload pragma can be placed before any statement, including compound statements such as loop nests or an OpenMP parallel block.

```
#pragma offload target(mic:1)          \
    in(a: length(SIZE))                 \
    in(b: length(SIZE))                 \
    inout(c: length(SIZE))
    for (int i = 0; i < SIZE; i++)
        c[i] = a[i] + b[i];
```

Figure 1: Offload pragma example.

Figure 1 shows the use of an offload pragma to offload a "for loop" to the coprocessor. The pragma specifies the keyword "mic" followed by an optional integer to indicate a target Xeon Phi. The compiler builds the offload block (in this case, the "for loop") to run on both the host and the coprocessor. The variables used by the code block are specified in the pragma statement as inputs ("in"), outputs ("out") or inouts. Inputs are copied from the host to the coprocessor. Outputs are copied only from the coprocessor to the host. Inouts are copied both to and from the coprocessor. Lengths of pointer variables, such as the arrays a, b and c in Figure 1, must be specified.

3. MULTIPROCESSING ON XEON PHI

We describe our experience with multiprocessing on a production high-performance server that has multiple Xeon Phi coprocessors. Using a representative set of coprocessor workloads, we systematically identify and quantify the adverse effects of multiprocessing on the Xeon Phi.

3.1 Coprocessor Workloads

Table 1 shows our coprocessor workloads, their descriptions and problem sizes. All workloads have been ported to the Xeon Phi using the offload programming model. We use the same workloads and problem sizes for all results in this paper. The table also shows the programmer specified thread-to-core affinity for each workload. Thread-to-core affinities can vary from COMPACT (assign each physical core its maximum of 4 hardware threads) to SCATTER (use as few hardware threads as possible per physical core).

3.2 Our Xeon Phi Server

Our commercial high-performance server consists of two 6-core Xeon CPU sockets and 2 Xeon Phi (Knights Corner) cards. Table 2 lists the hardware and software configuration of our server. For all the experiments reported in this section (Section 3) we only used 1 CPU socket (6 cores, 12 threads) and 1 Xeon Phi device. In Section 6, where we evaluate COSMIC, we use both 8GB coprocessors, and also another configuration with 2 3GB coprocessors.

Table 1: Xeon Phi offload workloads.

Name	Affinity	Description	Problem Size
KM	COMPACT	Computing K-means using Lloyd clustering algorithm	4M points/3 dimensions/32 means
MC	BALANCED	Monte Carlo simulation of N paths and T time steps	N = 32M, T = 1000
MD	BALANCED	Molecular dynamics simulation	25000 particles, 5 time steps
SG	COMPACT	A series of matrix-matrix multiplications (SGEMM)	8Kx8K matrices, 10 iterations
SS	COMPACT	Supervised semantic search indexing computing top K for each of the Q queries [8]	256K documents, K=32, Q=512
BT	SCATTER	Computation fluid dynamics (CFD) using block tri-diagonal solver [9]	Grid: 162x162x162, 200 iterations
SP	SCATTER	A CFD application using scalar penta-diagonal solver [9]	Grid: 162x162x162, 400 iterations
LU	SCATTER	A CFD application using lower-upper Gauss-Seidel solver [9]	Grid: 162x162x162, 250 iterations

Table 2: Characteristics of our Xeon Phi-based server.

	Host Processor	Coprocessor
CPU	Xeon E5-2630	Xeon Phi ES2-P1750
Cores	6 physical cores (12 threads) per socket	60 physical cores (240 threads) per coprocessor
Memory	16 GB	8 GB per coprocessor
OS	Linux RHEL 6.2, kernel 2.6.32-220	Linux kernel 2.6.38.8 MPSS 2.1.4982-15
Number	2 CPU sockets	2 coprocessors

3.3 Multiprocessing on Xeon Phi: Why?

Here we present our findings on workload utilization on the Xeon Phi, and make the case for multiprocessing.

3.3.1 Thread Scalability

Many applications cannot make use of a large number of threads due to lack of parallelism in the application and architectural constraints in the processor. In practice, performance either saturates or increases with diminishing returns after a certain point. Figure 2 shows the thread scalability of our workloads on the Xeon Phi. The x-axis shows the number of threads used for each offload, while the y-axis shows the speedup over an equivalent parallelized version running on our 6-core, 12-thread host CPU. The figure illustrates two aspects related to the Xeon Phi performance. First, it shows a speedup when using the Xeon Phi. Second, it shows that the speedup saturates around 120 threads with some workloads *even slowing down* after. Even Monte Carlo Simulation, where we observe an increase in speedup all the way up to 240 threads, shows diminishing gains after 120 threads. Lack of thread scalability reduces coprocessor utilization, thus providing an opportunity for multiprocessing.

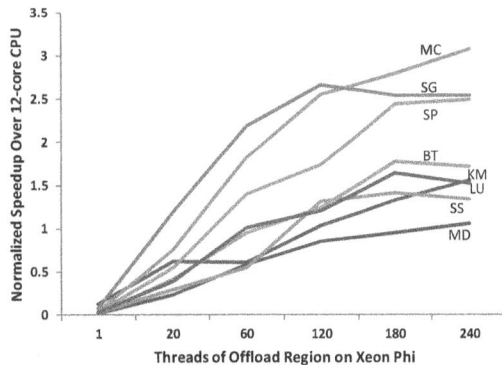

Figure 2: Thread scalability on Xeon Phi

3.3.2 Utilization

A host process only periodically offloads work to the coprocessor, and each offload does not typically use all the 240 hardware threads of the Xeon Phi. Thus, in a single host process situation, the coprocessor not only idles most of the time, but even during offloads, it is seldom that all of its cores are used. Figure 3 shows the time spent on the Xeon Phi coprocessor as a fraction of the total execution time of the host process, as well as the average core utilization across all offloads. Note that only 28% of the total execution time of the SS workload is on the Xeon Phi. For the other workloads, it varies from 69%-96%. These workloads used anywhere between 40%-91% of the

coprocessor cores, on average, and the overall utilization (product of time spent on the Xeon Phi and core utilization) ranges from 11%-88%, suggesting that many workloads do leave considerable room for resource sharing.

In addition to lack of thread scalability and poor utilization, "bag of tasks" [10] and similar throughput-oriented workflows can have multiple small, heterogeneous tasks on the coprocessor, necessitating multiprocessing.

3.4 Consequences of Xeon Phi Multiprocessing

We now identify and quantify the performance and reliability challenges due to multiprocessing on Xeon Phi servers.

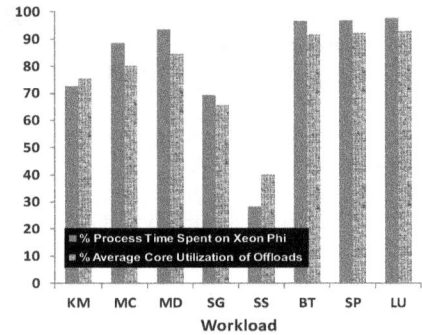

Figure 3: Xeon Phi utilization statistics.

3.4.1 Thread Oversubscription Effect

Thread oversubscription occurs when the total number of threads required by all processes running on a Xeon Phi device exceeds the number of hardware threads the device can support.

Table 3: Thread oversubscription: coprocessor vs host.

Application Pair	Xeon Phi			Xeon
	NTO (s)	TO (s)	% Overhead (TO/NTO)	% Overhead (TO/NTO)
KM, KM	49	458	+835%	-33.8%
MC, MC	47.5	46.5	-2.1%	+0.8%
MD, MD	59	55	-6.8%	+0.34%
SG, SG	53.5	453	+747%	-6.67%
SS, SS	34	91.5	+169%	-1%
BT, BT	235.5	266	+12%	-2.97%
SP, SP	280	349	+24%	-2.6%
LU, LU	346	2947	+752%	+107%

Table 3 shows the performance of our workloads, with and without thread oversubscription, on the Xeon Phi coprocessor and the Xeon host processor. Every offload is parallelized into the maximum available hardware threads: 240 for the Xeon Phi and 12 for the hyper-threaded 6-core Xeon host. The "NTO" column corresponds to the case where no thread oversubscription occurs because we run the pair of applications one after another. The "TO" column corresponds to the case with thread oversubscription where we run the pair of workloads concurrently to oversubscribe threads. The "% Overhead" column corresponds to the increase in execution time under thread oversubscription compared to the case without thread oversubscription (i.e., TO divided by NTO).

We observe that thread oversubscription on the Xeon Phi can lead to severe degradation in performance. For instance, K-means, Linear Algebra and Semantic Search degrade by as much as 169% to 835%. However, on the Xeon, the effect of thread oversubscription on performance is relatively less, and in some cases oversubscribing threads even improves performance. We also note that two of our Xeon Phi workload-pairs benefit marginally by thread oversubscription.

3.4.2 Memory Oversubscription and Reliability

Memory oversubscription occurs when the total memory usage exceeds the amount of physical memory on the coprocessor. To avoid oversubscription, Linux on the Xeon Phi can swap to the main memory or disk of the host. However, only a partial swap of COI processes is possible: MPSS uses buffers on the Xeon Phi to hold data that has been transferred from the host, and these buffers cannot be swapped as they are pinned. Therefore, a COI process can run out of coprocessor memory and crash, which is especially an issue on coprocessors since their physical memory (8-16GB) is much lesser than the typical physical memory of host processors.

To quantify the effect of memory oversubscription on the performance of multiprocessing on the Xeon Phi, we enabled swap of COI processes. We used 12 instances each of the Linear Algebra and K-means workloads. Both the workloads allocate Xeon Phi memory within offloads. We ensured that the total coprocessor memory used by the two workloads exceeds the physical memory on the coprocessor. After a pre-set threshold of coprocessor memory usage, the Linux OS starts swapping COI processes to the host. We also had to configure Linux's out-of-memory (OOM) killer so that it did not randomly kill COI processes to reclaim coprocessor memory.

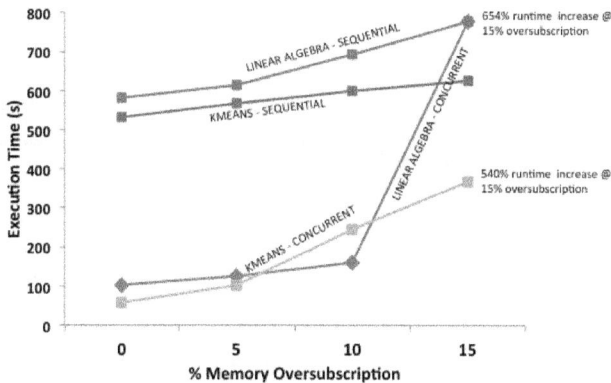

Figure 4: Memory oversubscription on Xeon Phi.

Figure 4 shows the execution times for the 12 instances each of K-means and Linear Algebra. We report execution times of a completely sequential schedule and a fully concurrent one for different amounts (0%, 5%, 10% and 15%) of memory oversubscription. A p% memory oversubscription means that the total memory of all 12 instances of a workload is p% more than the total physical memory of the Xeon Phi device.

We make two observations. First, memory oversubscription can be avoided by running the 12 instances of a workload sequentially, i.e., without multiprocessing. However, its execution times are worse than the execution times of a concurrent schedule with memory oversubscription. Second, there is a steep increase in execution times of a concurrent schedule even for small amounts of memory oversubscription.

Specifically, K-means degrades by 540%, and Linear Algebra by 654% with only a modest 15% oversubscription of the physical memory.

In Section 6.3, we report the result of using COSMIC for these two workloads. Instead of prescribing a fully concurrent or a completely sequential schedule, COSMIC comes up with another better schedule that avoids memory oversubscription, and also completes earlier.

Table 4: Effect of load imbalance on Xeon Phi.

Application Pair	Sequential Run (s)	Concurrent Run (s)	% Overhead (Concurrent / Sequential)
LU, KM	168.5	827	+391%
BT, KM	131.5	287	+118%
SP, MC	170.5	182.5	+7%
MC, MD	75	72	-4%
SG, MC	84	84	0%
SS, MD	62	98.5	+58.9%
SS, MC	54	71	+31.5%
KM, MD	72	129	+79.2%

3.4.3 Effect of Load Imbalance

Programmer directives to map threads can conflict, creating a load imbalance across COI processes. To quantify the performance impact of this, we concurrently ran several pairs of workloads. Table 4 shows the results. We see that when offloads from the two processes compete for the same cores, due to conflicting programmer-specified core requirement directives, an average performance loss of 74.7% (and a maximum of 391%) is seen. However, it can be beneficial to have offloads of a process use the same set of cores to take advantage of the data affinity among the offloads in the COI process.

4. THE COSMIC SYSTEM

A missing piece that can address the drawbacks of the current Xeon Phi software stack is a user-level middleware with a global view of all COI processes and their offloads, and detailed knowledge of the state of every coprocessor. Figure 5 shows a high-level, functional view of the COSMIC system. It manages offloads from host processes to several different coprocessors.

The figure shows three coprocessors each with a different number of cores and memory. A host process contains several offload blocks that are executed *sequentially*. Every offload can have its unique thread and affinity requirement. In the figure, user process 1 has two offloads, and the programmer has requested that offloads 1 and 2 should use 64 and 128 threads, respectively. To simplify memory management, COSMIC requires a COI process to specify its maximum coprocessor memory usage (this is described in Section 5.2). For example, user process 1 does not expect to use more than 2GB of coprocessor memory. This requirement is similar to job submission requirements in cluster schedulers such as Torque. Note offloads from the same process often share data in order to reduce unnecessary data movement between the host and Xeon Phi (data persistence). Therefore, as long as the COI process is alive, it will continue to use coprocessor memory.

However, unlike cluster schedulers, COSMIC does not require the process to specify the number of cores or devices. Rather, it automatically infers such information from the number of threads requested by the offload. Unlike coprocessor memory that is reserved for the life of a process, threads (and cores) are only allocated to an offload when the offload starts executing and they are released when the offload completes.

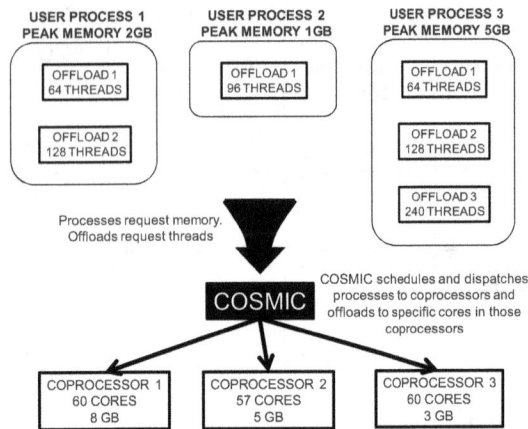

Figure 5: Functional view of the COSMIC system.

A COI process first requests COSMIC for coprocessor memory, and then every offload in the process requests COSMIC for threads. COSMIC arbitrates requests taking into consideration the different available coprocessors, the available cores within each coprocessor and the available coprocessor memory. It then allocates and schedules resources for the offloads to avoid oversubscription and imbalance.

4.1 COSMIC in the Xeon Phi Stack

Figure 6 shows MPSS (indicated by the dashed box) - the existing software stack of a Xeon Phi system - as well as COSMIC. The left half of the figure shows the stack on the host processor, while the right half of the figure is the stack running on the coprocessor. The top half of the figure represents user space, while the bottom half represents kernel space.

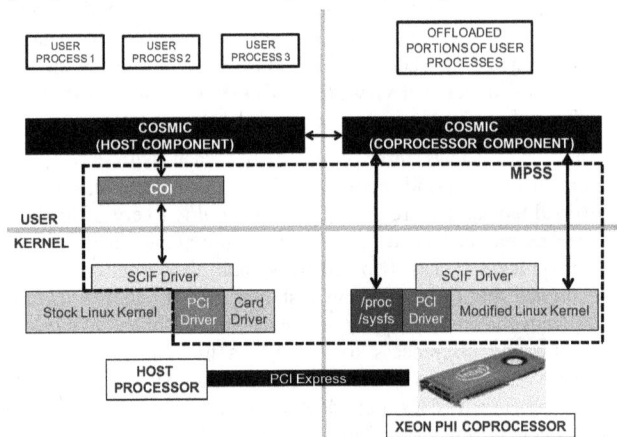

Figure 6: The Xeon Phi software stack and COSMIC.

COSMIC is a user-level middleware and it is architected to be lightweight and completely transparent to users of the Xeon Phi system. It interacts closely with both user processes and other kernel-level components. It controls offload scheduling and

dispatch by intercepting COI API calls. This is a key mechanism in COSMIC that enables us to transparently gain control of how offloads are managed. Every offload is converted by the Xeon Phi compiler into a series of COI calls, which are part of a standard API supported by Intel. These COI calls are used to move data between the host and coprocessor, and launch COI processes and offloads on the Xeon Phi. By intercepting these calls, COSMIC transparently controls how offloads are scheduled and dispatched.

4.2 COSMIC Software Architecture

Figure 7 shows the three main components of COSMIC each of which executes as a separate process: the client and the scheduler that execute only on the host, and the monitor that executes on the host and coprocessor. These processes communicate using explicit messages.

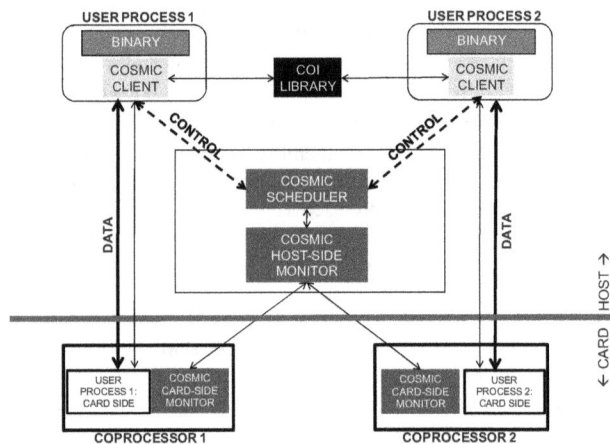

Figure 7: COSMIC architecture and its main components.

4.3 The COSMIC Client

The client intercepts COI calls and communicates with the scheduler for coprocessor resources. It consists of a host process that links with the Intel COI shared library, and intercepts and redefines every COI API function. The redefined COI functions first perform COSMIC-specific tasks, such as communicating with the COSMIC scheduler, and then invoke the original COI function. For the redefined functions, COSMIC creates its own shared library that is pre-loaded (using either LD_PRELOAD or by redefining LD_LIBRARY_PATH). The pre-loading ensures that the redefined COI functions in COSMIC are used instead of the COI functions defined in the Intel COI library. This is a fairly standard technique for interposing library calls.

Based on the intercepted COI call, the client sends different messages to the COSMIC scheduler:

- *NewProcess*: Sent when the first offload of a COI process is intercepted. The scheduler can now account for and keep track of the COI process and its coprocessor memory requirement.
- *NewOffload*: Sent when a new offload is intercepted. This message includes the COI process that the offload belongs to, the number of threads that the offload is requesting, and any affinity information.
- *OffloadComplete*: Sent when an offload completes. This allows the scheduler to account for recently freed resources such as coprocessor cores and threads.
- *ProcessComplete*: Sent when a process completes so the scheduler can update the available memory on the Xeon Phi due to the COI process completion.

4.4 The COSMIC Scheduler

The COSMIC scheduler is a key component of the COSMIC system. It manages multiple user processes, offloads and several coprocessor devices, and arbitrates access to all coprocessor resources. It runs completely on the host but unlike MPSS, it has global visibility into every coprocessor in the system. While scheduling offloads and allocating resources, it ensures that no thread or memory oversubscription occurs, inter-offload interference is avoided, and that the coprocessor cores and devices are balanced.

A key distinction between the COSMIC scheduler and traditional operating system schedulers is that COSMIC concurrently schedules processes *and* offloads. Note that coprocessors in the Xeon Phi server may have different memory and thread availabilities depending on ongoing multiprocessing. The COSMIC scheduler not only takes into account these dynamically varying availabilities, but it *also ensures fairness*, i.e., it makes sure that all COI processes and offloads eventually get access to coprocessor resources.

The scheduler is event-based. A scheduling cycle is triggered by a *new event* that can be the arrival of a new process, the arrival of a new offload in an existing process, the dispatching of an offload to a Xeon Phi device, the completion of an offload or the completion of a process. We maintain a queue of pending processes and multiple queues of pending offloads, one for each coprocessor in the system.

COSMIC keeps track of the total amount of available physical memory on each Xeon Phi device. We launch a COI process only if there is a Xeon Phi device with enough free memory to meet the COI process memory requirement. Whenever a COI process is launched or terminated, COSMIC updates its tally of free memory on each Xeon Phi device.

```
while (new event) {
  if (there is a process to be scheduled) {
    /* Process scheduler: schedule a process in Process queue */
    schedule(Process_Queue,
             firstFit(Memory Resource Limit),
             aging_threshold);
  }
  For each Phi card {
    if (there is an offload to be scheduled) {
      /* Offload scheduler: schedule an offload in Offload queue */
      schedule(Offload_Queue,
               firstFit(Thread Resource Limit),
               aging_threshold);
    }
  }
}
```

Figure 8: COSMIC scheduling procedure.

Figure 8 describes our scheduling algorithm. When a new event occurs, a pending process is selected and scheduled to a coprocessor that has enough free memory. Then, offload queues corresponding to each Xeon Phi are examined, and the scheduler dispatches an offload to a coprocessor that has enough free threads. For fairness, both processes and offloads are selected based on an aging-based first-fit heuristic. A COI process is granted resources when its age exceeds a configurable threshold.

The process selection algorithm is shown in Figure 9. At the start of a scheduling cycle, let P be the process at the head of the pending process queue. The scheduler maintains a circular list of the Xeon Phi coprocessors in the system. Let D be the next coprocessor in the list. The scheduler checks to see if the memory required by P fits in the available memory on D. If it does, then P is removed from the queue and dispatched to D.

Otherwise, the next coprocessor in the circular list is examined. If P does not fit in any coprocessor, then its age is incremented, and the next pending process is examined. When the age of a process reaches a threshold, all scheduling is blocked until that process is scheduled. This ensures fairness since every process will eventually get scheduled.

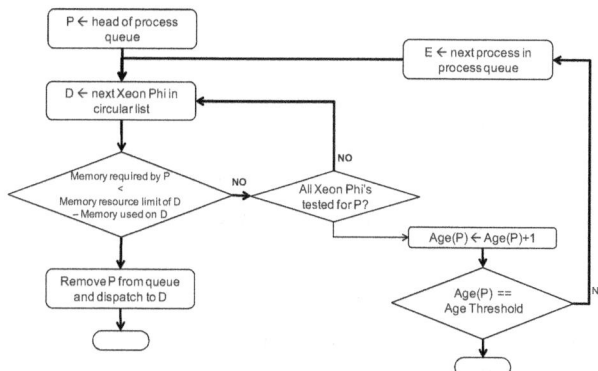

Figure 9: First-fit aging algorithm for process scheduling.

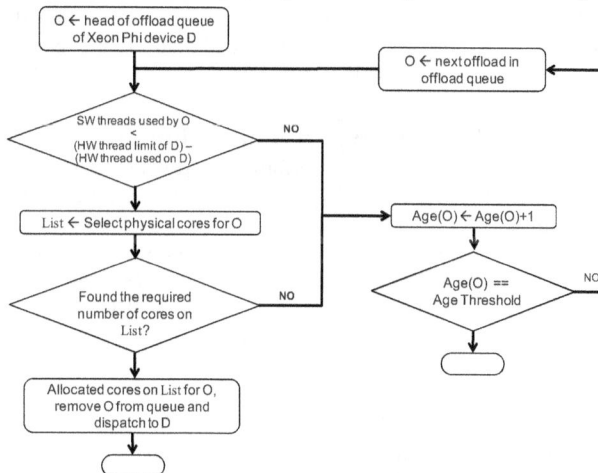

Figure 10: Algorithm for offload scheduling.

Figure 10 shows COSMIC's offload scheduling algorithm. Scheduling an offload is similar to scheduling a process but with one important difference. Instead of having a memory requirement, an offload has a thread and core requirement. COSMIC checks if adequate threads are available on the same coprocessor where the offload's COI process has been scheduled. If threads are available, COSMIC tries to select physical cores for the offload. If both thread and core requirements are satisfied, the offload is dispatched. Otherwise, we increment the age of the offload, and examine the next offload in the queue. Again, aging ensures fairness: no offload is denied resources when its age exceeds a configurable threshold. The core selection algorithm will be discussed in Section 0.

4.5 The COSMIC Monitor

The COSMIC monitor collects data about the state of the coprocessors. It has a host-side component that communicates with several coprocessor-side components. The host-side component also communicates with the scheduler. The coprocessor-side components monitor the load on each coprocessor, the number of threads requested by each offload and the health (i.e. whether the COI process is alive or not) of each COI process. If a COI process dies, the monitor reports the reason for possible use by the user or administrator.

In addition to COI API interception on the host, COSMIC also intercepts some programmer directives on the Xeon Phi. The coprocessor component of the monitor does this. Currently, we intercept `omp_set_num_threads` to determine the number of threads requested by each offload. Upon interception, the monitor blocks the offload, and communicates with the scheduler using these messages:

- *OffloadPause*: Sent to inform the scheduler that the offload has been paused.
- *OffloadResume*: Inform the monitor that the paused offload can resume with the new thread requirement.

5. MECHANISMS AND POLICIES

5.1 Avoiding Thread Oversubscription

COSMIC limits the total number of *actively* running software threads to avoid thread oversubscription. When an offload region is running, all threads spawned by the COI process are considered active. Otherwise the threads are considered dormant. COSMIC keeps track of the number of active threads spawned by offloads on a Xeon Phi device. COSMIC clears an offload to run only if the ratio of the sum of the *active* threads and the thread requirement of the offload, and the number of physical cores is no more than an integer N ($N = 4$ in COSMIC's default configuration). We refer to N as the thread-to-core ratio.

5.2 Avoiding Memory Oversubscription

To avoid process crashes and performance loss due to memory oversubscription, COSMIC adopts a new approach: the programmer or administrator specifies the worst-case coprocessor memory usage of a COI process, and Linux's memory containers are used to enforce the memory limit. If the memory footprint of a COI process exceeds the specified limit, then the memory resource controller invokes the OOM killer to terminate the offending COI process. Performance overhead associated with the use of memory resource controller ranges from almost negligible to up to 5%.

Such programmer input is necessary because it is difficult to *accurately* measure physical memory usage of a COI process using user-level middleware. We briefly review the main reasons behind this difficulty. COI processes make requests for virtual memory, and the Linux OS allocates virtual memory without verifying whether the total virtual memory allocated to all the COI processes has already exceeded the device physical memory. A virtual page is associated with a physical memory page only when the COI process actually starts using the virtual page. This is usually not a problem because the COI processes may not use all of the virtual memory they have requested. The Linux OS explicitly allows for over-allocation of virtual memory to increase the degree of multiprocessing (i.e., to increase the number of processes that are executing concurrently), leading to much higher multiprocessing performance. However, the virtual memory management mechanism and the aggressive multiprocessing approach of the Linux OS on the Xeon Phi, prevent *timely and accurate* measurement of the real physical memory usage of a COI process by using only user-level middleware.

5.3 Core Management

For every offload, COSMIC first allocates physical cores and then bind threads to these cores as per the programmer-specified thread affinity scheme. Since the best thread-to-core affinity depends on the application, COSMIC allocates cores but requires the programmer to specify the thread-to-core mapping.

Like Intel's OMP library, COSMIC also supports three types of thread affinity: *compact*, *scatter* and *balanced*.

COSMIC uses thread affinity and the number of threads to determine the number of physical cores for the offload. For compact affinity (the default setting), as few physical cores as necessary are used to host all threads without violating the thread-to-core ratio. For scatter affinity, we use as many physical cores as possible so that each physical core has at least 1 thread. For balanced affinity, we use as many physical cores as necessary to be in compliance with another new, configurable but pre-specified thread-to-physical-core ratio that is used only for the balanced affinity case (usually between 1 and 4). For example, consider an offload that requires 120 threads. For compact affinity, COSMIC allocates 30 physical cores so that every physical core executes 4 threads (assuming a thread-to-core ratio of 4). Alternatively, for scatter affinity, COSMIC allocates 60 physical cores. For the balanced affinity, assuming a separate thread-to-core ratio of 3, COSMIC will allocate 40 physical cores.

COSMIC schedules an offload only if there are as many free physical cores as required by the offload. A physical core is free if there is no active thread that is currently running on the core. COSMIC's core selection algorithm first attempts to allocate cores that were assigned to earlier offloads of the same COI process. If more physical cores are needed, then COSMIC picks cores that are both free and not currently assigned to any other COI process. If still more cores are needed, then physical cores that are free but have already been assigned to other COI processes, are chosen.

5.4 Configuration Parameters of COSMIC

COSMIC has several parameters that affect its policies and behavior. An administrator configures the aging threshold and the scheduling policy such as first-fit. Users are required to provide peak memory limits for their COI processes, as well as preferred thread affinity settings. The administrator can set default affinities used within COSMIC, as well as other default values such as the number of threads. A detailed exploration of the effect of these parameters is outside the scope of this paper.

6. EVALUATION OF COSMIC

Using the workloads and server described in Section 3, we first show how COSMIC helps MPSS improve latency, utilization and makespan. Then we describe controlled experiments showing thread and memory oversubscription, and load imbalance. All numbers are averaged across 3 runs.

6.1 Overall COSMIC Performance

In this section, we evaluate the beneficial effects of COSMIC on latency and makespan in a realistic multiprocessing situation. We create traces of job instances from our workloads and measure (i) average latency or turn-around-time (comprising the time a job has to wait plus the time the job takes to execute), (ii) makespan (the time between when the first job is issued and the last job completes execution) and (iii) average core utilization. MPSS without COSMIC must process jobs sequentially (FCFS) to avoid oversubscription and crashes, while MPSS with COSMIC does not have this restriction.

The first four experiments use a trace of 32 jobs on our server with 8GB Xeon Phi coprocessors. The next four use a longer trace of 64 jobs on the same hardware platform, while the final four experiments run the 64-job trace on a machine with the 8GB Xeon Phi coprocessors replaced by 3GB coprocessors.

Table 5 shows results for the first four experiments with the 32-job trace on our server with 8GB coprocessors. COSMIC improves average latency by 16% to 70% because it reduces job wait time by 39% to 94%. Another significant result is that COSMIC improves average core utilization by up to 3 times by suitably load balancing cores of the Xeon Phi across processes. COSMIC also improves average makespan by 8% to 52%.

When the trace of job instances is increased from 32 to 64 jobs, COSMIC's performance advantage over MPSS further improves. As Table 6 shows, the drop in latency for a 64-job trace ranges from 26% to nearly 90%. Makespan improves nearly 60%, while the core utilization improves by nearly 3.5x, reaching 70% for 3 of the 4 experiments. Thus, as the length of the job trace increases, COSMIC finds more opportunities to share resources and improve performance by avoiding thread and memory oversubscription.

Finally, we investigate COSMIC's performance with increasing resource constraints. Specifically, we substitute 3GB Xeon Phi coprocessors for the 8GB coprocessors in our hardware platform. This increases resource constraints, but also reduces concurrency. Therefore, as COSMIC tries to avoid thread and memory oversubscription, it ends up reducing concurrency or the number of processes and offloads that simultaneously share the coprocessor. Table 7 shows the latency, makespan and utilization results for the 64-job trace on a server with 3GB coprocessors. Latency improvements continue to be high at 16%-84%, and makespan falls by 2.5x. However, utilization does not exceed 60%, but this still surpasses MPSS whose average utilization is at most 45%.

Table 5: COSMIC under static and dynamic multiprocessing situations for 32 jobs on 8GB Xeon Phi cards.

Experiment	# Xeon Phi's	Average Latency (s)		Makespan (s)		Average Core Utilization	
		MPSS	COSMIC+ MPSS	MPSS	COSMIC+ MPSS	MPSS	COSMIC+ MPSS
All jobs issued at once	1	787	663	1483	1198	42.6%	65.8%
Jobs issued with random delays	1	558.3	333.7	1482	1359	42%	65.3%
All jobs issued at once	2	810.5	324.3	1553	741	20.4%	58.5%
Jobs issued with random delays	2	568.8	167.8	1531	802.7	20.3%	51%

Table 6: COSMIC under static and dynamic multiprocessing situations for 64 jobs on 8GB Xeon Phi cards.

Experiment	# Xeon Phi's	Average Latency (s)		Makespan (s)		Average Core Utilization	
		MPSS	COSMIC+ MPSS	MPSS	COSMIC+ MPSS	MPSS	COSMIC+ MPSS
All jobs issued at once	1	1509	1118	2941	1996	42.2%	70.6%
Jobs issued with random delays	1	1476	411	2883	2007	41.7%	70.6%
All jobs issued at once	2	1587.5	582.5	2089	995	19.9%	70.3%
Jobs issued with random delays	2	1099	119	3144	1238	19.9%	56.9%

Table 7: COSMIC under static and dynamic multiprocessing situations for 64 jobs on 3GB Xeon Phi cards.

Experiment	# Xeon Phi's	Average Latency (s)		Makespan (s)		Average Core Utilization	
		MPSS	COSMIC+ MPSS	MPSS	COSMIC+ MPSS	MPSS	COSMIC+ MPSS
All jobs issued at once	1	1556	1300	3036	2756	44.8%	54%
Jobs issued with random delays	1	1040.3	643.5	2998	2493	45%	59.9%
All jobs issued at once	2	1625.9	633.2	3187	1352	21.3%	55.8%
Jobs issued with random delays	2	1109.2	173.1	3195	1387	21.5%	54.4%

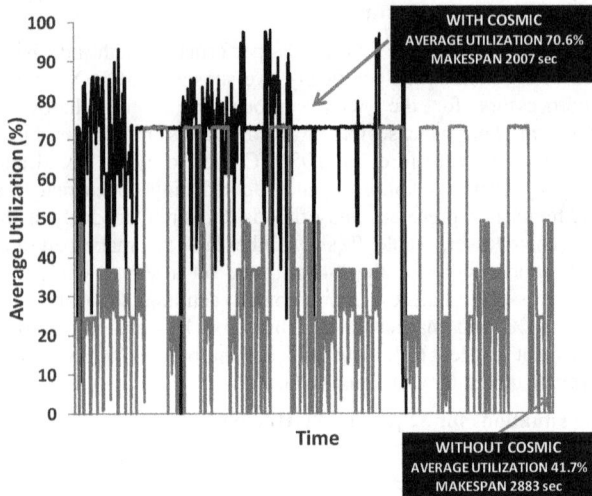

Figure 11: 8GB coprocessor utilization using COSMIC

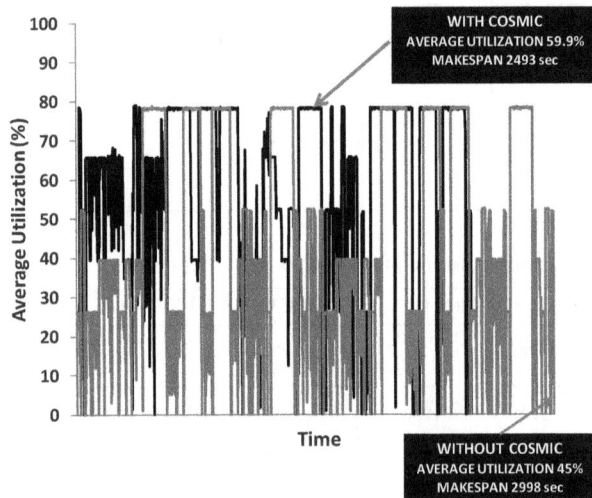

Figure 12: 3GB coprocessor utilization using COSMIC

Figure 11 shows detailed Xeon Phi core utilization over time for the 64-job trace where the jobs are issued dynamically at random time intervals on a single 8GB coprocessor server. Figure 12 shows the utilization for the same job trace on a single 3GB coprocessor server. From the utilization profile, it is clear that when using COSMIC, cores are better utilized on average, and the trace of jobs finishes sooner (i.e., shorter makespan) than when using MPSS.

6.2 Avoiding Thread Oversubscription

In Section 3.4.1, we showed how thread oversubscription adversely affects performance for 8 pairs of concurrently running applications. Here, we use the same workloads, and run them concurrently using 1 Xeon Phi card. Table 8 shows the execution times when the workload pairs are run without thread oversubscription (i.e., sequentially), and with thread oversubscription (concurrently) using MPSS and MPSS with COSMIC. We see that under multiprocessing and thread oversubscription, using MPSS with COSMIC outperforms using just MPSS by up to 90.1% (10.1x), and an average of 43.4%.

Table 8: Thread oversubscription with COSMIC.

| Workload Pair | No TO (sec) | With TO (sec) | | No TO / TO with MPSS | No TO / TO with MPSS + COSMIC |
		MPSS	COSMIC + MPSS		
KM, KM	49	458	67	0.11	0.73
MC, MC	47.5	46.5	45.5	1.02	1.04
MD, MD	59	55	58.5	1.07	1.01
SG, SG	53.5	453	45	0.12	1.19
SS, SS	34	91.5	42	0.37	0.81
BT, BT	235.5	266	233	0.89	1.01
SP, SP	279.5	349	276	0.80	1.01
LU, LU	346	2947	341	0.12	1.01

6.3 Avoiding Memory Oversubscription

In Section 3.4.2, we showed that at 15% memory oversubscription, concurrent runs of 12 instances of K-means and Linear Algebra degraded by 540% and 654% respectively. Table 9 shows the performance when these workloads are run (i) with no memory oversubscription (column labeled "NMO"), (ii) concurrently using MPSS with swap (memory is oversubscribed and the Linux OOM killer is disabled to avoid COI process crashes) and (iii) concurrently using COSMIC and MPSS. COSMIC+MPSS is 3-5x faster than the run using just MPSS.

Table 9: Memory oversubscription with COSMIC.

| | K-Means (sec) | | | Linear Algebra (sec) | | |
| | NMO | With MO | | NMO | With MO | |
		MPSS	COSMIC + MPSS		MPSS	COSMIC + MPSS
0%	531	58	60	580	103	100
5%	567	103	91	615	127	121
10%	598	244	99	694	160	133
15%	627	369	108	777	779	144

6.4 Balancing Core Usage

In Section 3.4.3, we quantified the adverse effects of load imbalance on the Xeon Phi. For the same workloads, Table 10 shows that MPSS with COSMIC is better than the no imbalance case (column labeled "SEQ: NO IMB") by an average of 26%, and outperforms a concurrent execution using just MPSS by an average of 42%, and up to 76% (4.18x).

Table 10: Balancing core usage with COSMIC.

| Workload Pair | SEQ: NO IMB (s) | CONC: with IMB (s) | | NO IMB/ IMB with MPSS | No IMB/ IMB with COSMIC + MPSS |
		MPSS	COSMIC+ MPSS		
LU, KM	485	777	448.7	0.62	1.09
BT, KM	390.3	543	369.7	0.72	1.06
SP, MC	471	537.6	420	0.88	1.12
MC, MD	75	72	54.5	1.04	1.38
SG, MC	84	84	44	1.00	1.91
SS, MD	62	98.5	53.5	0.63	1.16
SS, MC	54	71	48.5	0.71	1.11
KM, MD	72	129	54.5	0.56	1.32

6.5 Reliability

Using 36 workload instances, we measured how often MPSS without COSMIC crashed at different levels of concurrency. At each level of concurrency, a fixed number of workload instances were simultaneously issued to the system. Table 11 shows that at high concurrency levels, all runs consistently crash. Even at low concurrency levels, the number of crashes is too high (16.7% with 2 concurrent workloads) for the system to be considered reliable. In contrast, multiprocessing using MPSS and COSMIC completely avoids all crashes. In oversubscription cases that did not lead to crashes, the execution time steeply increased when not using COSMIC. Crashes and execution time degradation depend not only on concurrency but also on memory used. COSMIC takes into account these factors and is able to prevent crashes by avoiding memory oversubscription.

Table 11: Crashes prevented by COSMIC

# concurrent workloads	% runs that crashed	
	MPSS	COSMIC + MPSS
36, 18, 12, 9, 6	100 %	0%
4	66.7%	0%
3	50%	0%
2	16.7%	0%

6.6 COSMIC's Overhead

COSMIC has been carefully architected to be a lightweight add-on to the Xeon Phi software stack. To examine the overhead introduced by COSMIC itself, we ran each workload from our suite independently on MPSS and then COSMIC, with no oversubscription. COSMIC's maximum overhead was around 1.5%, but nearly zero in most cases.

7. RELATED WORK

To the best of our knowledge, COSMIC is the first middleware targeting high-performance and reliable multiprocessing on Intel Xeon Phi manycore processors. The idea of multiprocessing on Intel Xeon Phi is consistent with the recent trend of multiprocessing on homogeneous [11] or GPU-based heterogeneous clusters [12]–[14]. Although COSMIC faces several issues that were encountered in prior coprocessor sharing efforts, it also addresses several challenges that are unique to manycore processors that natively support multiprocessing.

Most of the past work on coprocessor sharing focused on sharing GPUs between multiple user processes or virtual machines (VMs) [12], [13], [15]–[18]. TimeGraph by Kato *et. al.* is a device driver-level scheduler for GPU sharing between multiple real-time (graphics rendering) tasks [18]. Other work specifically addressed the problem of sharing GPUs that are used as coprocessors for general-purpose computing (GPGPUs) between different VMs [12], [15]–[18] or multiple user processes in the same OS space [12], [13]. Since GPGPU's runtime libraries and device drivers are proprietary and, until recently, did not allow multiple processes to share the GPGPUs concurrently, these approaches apply the *API remoting* technique to the user-space GPGPU runtime library: the function calls issued by a user process to the GPGPU runtime library are intercepted by an interposer library and rerouted to a management process. The management process then re-issues these function calls to the real GPGPU runtime. Although Xeon Phi's runtime does not prohibit concurrent accesses from multiple user processes, COSMIC still adopts this API remoting

technique in user-space to implement advanced scheduling and resource management policies.

There is extensive research that focused on the effects of resource sharing and contention on a multicore or manycore processor [19]–[23]. It has been shown that the context switch and the contention of the shared resources, like the last-level cache, the memory channels, and the bus bandwidth, between concurrent processes and threads can lead to significant performance degradation. Unlike the previous work that attempts to find out the best combinations of processes or threads sharing a physical core on a multicore system [20], [21], [23], COSMIC enforces physical-core containers to prevent physical-core sharing and thus provide performance isolation between coscheduled COI processes. COSMIC's container-based approach is in line with the memory channel partitioning proposed by Muralidhara *et. al.* [22], but is applied to the physical cores and memory.

Researchers have proposed various types of resource containers to achieve design goals like performance isolation and robustness [24]–[28], both of which COSMIC also aims for. Banga *et. al.* designed resource containers to keep track of CPU usage associated with an independent computation activity for better scheduling [24]. COSMIC adopts Linux's stock memory resource controller to police memory usage of COI processors to guarantee system robustness. Like Tessellation OS [28], COSMIC also provides space-time partitioning of physical cores for performance isolation. As Tessellation, COSMIC also uses purely software-based scheduling and thread-to-core binding mechanisms to provide core partitioning. However, due to the overhead of page swapping, COSMIC only provides space partitioning of memory resources. Instead of constructing a new OS like Tessellation, COSMIC is a user-space middleware and relies on scheduling and the standard Xeon Phi OS's containers, and is completely transparent to user applications.

COSMIC's scheduler uses the classic aging-based algorithm to ensure fairness across processes and offloads [29]. Unlike OS scheduling algorithms, COSMIC schedules user processes and offloads, and considers their memory and core requirements. The problem of selecting a Xeon Phi that is able to meet the resource requirements of an offload is computationally hard (bin packing) [30]. COSMICS adopts the first-fit heuristics [30], which is very efficient and gives satisfactory results.

Several studies address the problem of scheduling coprocessor tasks originating from different user processes [13], [16], [18]. In [13] the runtime allows the scheduling policy to be configurable. In GViM, Pegasus, and TimeGraph credit-based scheduling techniques are used to provide fairness and performance isolation between different processes requesting coprocessor accesses. In addition, TimeGraph allows prioritization of different user processes to avoid priority inversion [18]. Pegasus combines credit-based scheduling and co-scheduling between CPU and GPU tasks, and dynamically ranks GPU devices for task assignment based on computation power and resource availability of GPU devices. COSMIC adopts an aging-based first-fit scheduling policy to achieve process-level fairness, load balance, and avoidance of resource oversubscription across multiple Xeon Phi devices.

The management of limited memory is critical to using coprocessors. Sundaram *et. al.* proposed a framework allowing a single application to process data that cannot fit into the available physical memory on a GPU device [31]. Some past work on GPU sharing requires or assumes the cumulative memory footprint of concurrent GPU tasks fits in the available GPU memory. Such a requirement is lifted in the recent work in [13], in which Becchi *et. al.* designed and implemented a GPU virtual memory system.. In COSMIC we choose to avoid memory oversubscription due to performance and reliability issues. COSMIC relies on Xeon Phi OS's memory controller to enforce user-specified memory usage on Xeon Phi devices.

8. CONCLUSIONS

In this paper, we study the effects of multiprocessing on the Xeon Phi manycore coprocessors, and propose a novel and transparent middleware called COSMIC to alleviate the adverse effects of such multiprocessing. Multiprocessing on manycores is necessary to improve hardware utilization, but reduces performance and reliability as workloads compete for manycore resources. COSMIC employs novel mechanisms and policies to concurrently schedule multiple Xeon Phi processes and offloads while avoiding oversubscription of resources and balancing core and coprocessor usage. Using a set of workloads put together for this work, we show that on a Xeon Phi server, COSMIC improves average core utilization on the Xeon Phi by up to 3 times, makespan by up to 52%, average process latency by 70% and average process waiting time by 94%.

REFERENCES

[1] E. Lindholm, J. Nickolls, S. Oberman, and J. Montrym, "NVIDIA Tesla: A Unified Graphics and Computing Architecture," *Micro, IEEE*, vol. 28, no. 2, pp. 39–55, 2008.

[2] S. Bell, B. Edwards, J. Amann, R. Conlin, K. Joyce, V. Leung, J. MacKay, M. Reif, L. Bao, J. Brown, M. Mattina, C.-C. Miao, C. Ramey, D. Wentzlaff, W. Anderson, E. Berger, N. Fairbanks, D. Khan, F. Montenegro, J. Stickney, and J. Zook, "TILE64 - Processor: A 64-Core SoC with Mesh Interconnect," in *Solid-State Circuits Conf., 2008*, pp. 88 –598.

[3] L. Koesterke, J. Boisseau, J. Cazes, K. Milfeld, and D. Stanzione, "Early experiences with the intel many integrated cores accelerated computing technology," in *Proc. of the TeraGrid Conf.: Extreme Digital Discovery*, 2011, p. 21.

[4] "Optimization and Performance Tuning for Intel Xeon Phi Coprocessors - Part 1: Optimization Essentials." [Online]. Available: http://software.intel.com/en-us/articles/optimization-and-performance-tuning-for-intel-xeon-phi-coprocessors-part-1-optimization.

[5] S. (Ticky) Thakkar and T. Huff, "Internet Streaming SIMD Extensions," *Computer*, vol. 32, no. 12, pp. 26–34, Dec. 1999.

[6] C. Newburn, R. Deodhar, S. Dmitriev, R. Murty, R. Narayanaswamy, J. Wiegert, F. Chinchilla, and R. McGuire, "Offload Compiler Runtime for the Intel Xeon Phi Coprocessor", to appear at *Intl. Supercomputing Conf.* 2013.

[7] N. Ravi, Y. Yang, T. Bao, and S. Chakradhar, "Apricot: an optimizing compiler and productivity tool for x86-compatible many-core coprocessors," in *Proc. of the Intl. Conf. on Supercomputing*, 2012, pp. 47–58.

[8] B. Bai, J. Weston, D. Grangier, R. Collobert, K. Sadamasa, Y. Qi, O. Chapelle, and K. Weinberger, "Learning to rank with (a lot of) word features," *Information Retrieval*, vol. 13, no. 3, pp. 291–314, 2010.

[9] H. Jin, M. Frumkin, and J. Yan, "The OpenMP implementation of NAS parallel benchmarks and its performance," Technical Report NAS-99-011, NASA Ames Research Center, 1999.

[10] A. Benoit, L. Marchal, J. F. Pineau, Y. Robert, and F. Vivien, "Scheduling concurrent bag-of-tasks applications on heterogeneous platforms," vol. 59, no. 2, pp. 202–217, 2010.

[11] M. Stillwell, F. Vivien, and H. Casanova, "Dynamic Fractional Resource Scheduling versus Batch Scheduling," *IEEE Trans. on Parallel and Distributed Syst.*, vol. 23, no. 3, pp. 521 –529, Mar. 2012.

[12] V. T. Ravi, M. Becchi, G. Agrawal, and S. Chakradhar, "Supporting GPU sharing in cloud environments with a transparent runtime consolidation framework," in *Proc. of HPDC*, 2011, pp. 217–228.

[13] M. Becchi, K. Sajjapongse, I. Graves, A. Procter, V. Ravi, and S. Chakradhar, "A virtual memory based runtime to support multi-tenancy in clusters with GPUs," in *Proc. of HPDC*, 2012, pp. 97–108.

[14] R. Phull, C.-H. Li, K. Rao, H. Cadambi, and S. Chakradhar, "Interference-driven resource management for GPU-based heterogeneous clusters," in *Proc. of HPDC*, 2012, pp. 109–120.

[15] G. Giunta, R. Montella, G. Agrillo, and G. Coviello, "A GPGPU Transparent Virtualization Component for High Performance Computing Clouds," in *Euro-Par-Parallel Processing*, vol. 6271, 2010, pp. 379–391.

[16] V. Gupta, A. Gavrilovska, K. Schwan, H. Kharche, N. Tolia, V. Talwar, and P. Ranganathan, "GViM: GPU-accelerated virtual machines," in *Proc. of ACM Workshop on Syst.-Level Virtlization for High Perf. Computing*, 2009, pp. 17–24.

[17] L. Shi, H. Chen, J. Sun, and K. Li, "vCUDA: GPU-Accelerated High-Performance Computing in Virtual Machines," *IEEE Trans. on Computers*, vol. 61, no. 6, pp. 804 –816, Jun. 2012.

[18] S. Kato, K. Lakshmanan, R. R. Rajkumar, and Y. Ishikawa, "TimeGraph: GPU scheduling for real-time multi-tasking environments," in *SENIX Annual Technical Conf.*, 2011.

[19] A. Agarwal, J. Hennessy, and M. Horowitz, "Cache performance of operating system and multiprogramming workloads," *ACM Trans. Comput. Syst.*, vol. 6, no. 4, pp. 393–431, Nov. 1988.

[20] S. Zhuravlev, S. Blagodurov, and A. Fedorova, "Addressing shared resource contention in multicore processors via scheduling," in *Proc. of ASPLOS.*, 2010, pp. 129–142.

[21] L. Tang, J. Mars, N. Vachharajani, R. Hundt, and M. L. Soffa, "The impact of memory subsystem resource sharing on datacenter applications," in *Intrl. Symposium on Computer Architecture, 2011*, pp. 283–294.

[22] S. P. Muralidhara, L. Subramanian, O. Mutlu, M. Kandemir, and T. Moscibroda, "Reducing memory interference in multicore systems via application-aware memory channel partitioning," in *Proc. of the IEEE/ACM Intl. Symposium on Microarchitecture*, 2011, pp. 374–385.

[23] J. Mars, L. Tang, R. Hundt, K. Skadron, and M. L. Soffa, "Bubble-Up: increasing utilization in modern warehouse scale computers via sensible co-locations," in *Proc. of the IEEE/ACM Intl. Symposium on Microarchitecture*, 2011, pp. 248–259.

[24] G. Banga, P. Druschel, and J. C. Mogul, "Resource containers: A new facility for resource management in server systems," *Operating Systems Review*, vol. 33, pp. 45–58, 1998.

[25] "Memory Resource Controller," [Online] Available: https://www.kernel.org/doc/Documentation/cgroups/memcg_test.txt

[26] B. Singh and V. Srinivasan, "Containers: Challenges with the memory resource controller and its performance," in *Linux Symposium*, 2007, p. 209.

[27] S. Soltesz, H. Pötzl, M. E. Fiuczynski, A. Bavier, and L. Peterson, "Container-based operating system virtualization: a scalable, high-performance alternative to hypervisors," *SIGOPS Oper. Syst. Rev.*, vol. 41, no. 3, pp. 275–287, Mar. 2007.

[28] R. Liu, K. Klues, S. Bird, S. Hofmeyr, K. Asanovic, and J. Kubiatowicz, "Tessellation: Space-time partitioning in a manycore client OS," *HotPar09*, vol. 3, p. 2009, 2009.

[29] A. Silberschatz, P. B. Galvin, and G. Gagne, *Operating System Concepts with Java*, 8th ed. Wiley, 2009.

[30] R. L. Graham, E. L. Lawler, J. K. Lenstra, and A. H. G. R. Kan, "Optimization and approximation in deterministic sequencing and scheduling: a survey," *Annals of Discrete Mathematics*, vol. 5, no. 2, pp. 287–326, 1979.

[31] N. Sundaram, A. Raghunathan, and S. T. Chakradhar, "A framework for efficient and scalable execution of domain-specific templates on GPUs," in *IEEE Intl. Symposium on Parallel Distributed Processing*, 2009, pp. 1 –12.

Interference and Locality-Aware Task Scheduling for MapReduce Applications in Virtual Clusters

Xiangping Bu
Department of Electrical &
Computer Engineering
Wayne State University
Detroit, Michigan 48202
xpbu@wayne.edu

Jia Rao
Department of Computer
Science
University of Colorado at
Colorado Springs, Colorado
jrao@uccs.edu

Cheng-Zhong Xu
Department of Electrical &
Computer Engineering
Wayne State University
Detroit, Michigan 48202
czxu@wayne.edu

ABSTRACT

MapReduce emerges as an important distributed programming paradigm for large-scale applications. Running MapReduce applications in clouds presents an attractive usage model for enterprises. In a virtual MapReduce cluster, the interference between virtual machines (VMs) causes performance degradation of map and reduce tasks and renders existing data locality-aware task scheduling policy, like delay scheduling, no longer effective. On the other hand, virtualization offers an extra opportunity of data locality for co-hosted VMs. In this paper, we present a task scheduling strategy to mitigate interference and meanwhile preserving task data locality for MapReduce applications. The strategy includes an interference-aware scheduling policy, based on a task performance prediction model, and an adaptive delay scheduling algorithm for data locality improvement. We implement the interference and locality-aware (ILA) scheduling strategy in a virtual MapReduce framework. We evaluated its effectiveness and efficiency on a 72-node Xen-based virtual cluster. Experimental results with 10 representative CPU and IO-intensive applications show that ILA is able to achieve a speedup of 1.5 to 6.5 times for individual jobs and yield an improvement of up to 1.9 times in system throughput in comparison with four other MapReduce schedulers.

Categories and Subject Descriptors

D.4.1 [**Operating Systems**]: Process Management—*Scheduling*; D.4.8 [**Operating Systems**]: Performance—*Modeling and prediction*

Keywords

MapReduce; Cloud computing; Task scheduling

1. INTRODUCTION

MapReduce has become an important distributed parallel programming paradigm for applications with various

computational characteristics in large-scale clusters [13]. It forms the core of technologies powering big IT businesses like Google, IBM, Yahoo and Facebook. Providing MapReduce frameworks as a service in clouds becomes an attractive usage model for enterprises [2]. A MapReduce cloud service allows users to cost-effectively access a large amount of computing resources without creating MapReduce frameworks of their own. Users are able to flexibly adjust the scale of MapReduce clusters in response to the change of the resource demand of their applications.

MapReduce services in clouds typically run in virtual clusters. This usage model raises two new challenges. First, interferences between co-hosted virtual machines (VMs) can significantly affect the performance of MapReduce applications. Although virtualization provides performance isolation to a certain extent, there is still significant interference between VMs running on a shared hardware infrastructure. A MapReduce cloud service has to deal with the interference coming from contentions in various hardware components, including CPU, memory, I/O bandwidth, and their joint effects.

In a virtual MapReduce cluster, the interference may cause variation in VM capacity and uncertainty in task performance [32], and ultimately impairs the correctness and effectiveness of the MapReduce key components, such as the task scheduler, fault tolerance mechanism, and configuration strategy. Our experimental results show that interference could slow down a job by 1.5 to 7 times. Performance degradation of MapReduce jobs due to VM interference was also observed in Amazon EC2 [1, 32]. There were studies on mitigating VM interference in virtual clusters through dynamic resource allocation, interference-aware task scheduling or application parameter tuning [23, 11, 20, 27, 26, 9, 10]. However, the MapReduce framework further complicates the interference problem on virtual clusters. MapReduce cloud service requires mitigating VM interference while maintaining the framework's features, such as job fairness and task data locality.

The second challenge for MapReduce cloud services is preserving good data locality for tasks of each job. In a MapReduce framework, the task scheduler assigns each task to an available node "closest" to its input data to leverage the data locality. To achieve good data locality while preserving job fairness in shared MapReduce clusters, Zaharia *et al.* proposed a delay scheduling algorithm to postpone a scheduled job for a few seconds if it can not launch a local task [31]. Such locality-aware task schedulers largely assume that the tasks are short lived. Unexpected task slowdown caused by interference in virtual clusters may render them no longer effective.

The MapReduce framework running on a distributed file system offers several levels of data locality. A task and its input data can locate in the same server node (*node locality*), in the same rack (*rack locality*) or in different racks (*off-rack*). Server virtualization adds one more layer of locality: tasks and their data being placed on the co-hosted VMs of the same physical server. We refer to this as *server locality*. Data exchange between co-hosted VMs is often as efficient as local data access because inter-VM communication within one physical server is optimized by Hypervisor and does not consume any network bandwidth. *Server locality is much easier to achieve than node locality, although they are expected to deliver similar level of performance.* When applied to virtual MapReduce clusters, existing task schedulers designed for physical clusters are not able to leverage this extra layer of data locality and lose the opportunity for achieving better performance.

In this paper, we present an interference and locality-aware (ILA) task scheduler to address the challenges in the provisioning of fair share MapReduce cloud services. There are recent studies on improving the performance of MapReduce applications in the cloud through resource allocation [25] or data and VM placement [21, 24]. In contrast, ILA focuses on task scheduling optimization in a virtual MapReduce cluster. ILA relies on an application-level task scheduling strategy to adapt to changes of data and VM deployment and cloud resource allocation. It requires no modification for the underlying resource management. We summarize the contributions of this paper as follows:

1. We develop an exponential interference prediction model to estimate task slowdown caused by interference in the virtual MapReduce cluster. We also introduce a Dynamic Threshold policy to schedule tasks based on the prediction model.

2. We develop an Adaptive Delay Scheduling algorithm, which improves the Delay Scheduling algorithm [31] by adjusting delay intervals of ready-to-run jobs in proportion to their input size. The algorithm also takes into account data locality in all layers including the *server locality*.

3. We develop a meta scheduling strategy to integrate the interference-aware scheduling and locality-aware scheduling algorithms and implement the algorithm in an interference and locality-aware (ILA) scheduling framework. We evaluated the efficiency of the framework on a 72-node Xen-based virtual MapReduce cluster. Experimental results with representative CPU and I/O-intensive applications demonstrate that the ILA scheduler can achieve a speedup of 1.5-6.5 times for individual jobs and yield an improvement of up to 1.9 times in system throughput compared with four recently proposed task schedulers. It improves data locality among map tasks by up to 65%.

The rest of this paper is organized as follows. Section 2 introduces the background and motivation of ILA scheduling. Section 3 presents the system architecture. Section 4 shows the design of our ILA Scheduler. Evaluation setting and results are given in Section 5. Related work is discussed in Section 6. Section 7 concludes the paper with remarks on limitation and possible future work.

2. BACKGROUND AND MOTIVATION

2.1 Hadoop in Virtualized Environments

In this paper, we use Hadoop implementation of MapReduce framework as an example to illustrate the concepts of VM interference and data locality [3]. Hadoop partitions each job into a number of map and reduce tasks. Each map task runs map functions on one data block (64MB by default) of an input file. A reduce task receives intermediate results from data dependent map tasks and generates final results. A MapReduce framework consists of a *master* and multiple *slaves*. The *master* is responsible for management of the framework, including user interaction, job queue organization and task scheduling. Each *slave* has a fixed number of map and reduce slots to perform tasks. The job scheduler located in the *master* assigns tasks according to the number of free task slots reported by each *slave* through a heartbeat protocol.

Hadoop running on a distributed file system HDFS assumes that the data storage is co-located within the compute cluster. MapReduce framework can exploit task locality without incurring extra management overhead. In the ILA framework, each *slave* is deployed on one VM with attached local disk image. It acts as both compute and data node. The HDFS was built across all the VMs. There exist other storage architectures in cloud environments. Amazon used distinct infrastructures for storage and compute. It is not suitable for MapReduce applications due to the requirement of loading data from a storage server to HDFS before the job execution and keeping large duplicated datasets during the execution. Recent works proposed several storage infrastructures to enable local data access for compute cluster and enhance the performance of MapReduce applications [21, 24]. ILA framework is able to deal with the interference and locality challenges under different storage architectures.

2.2 Virtual Machine Interference

Virtual cluster is the most common platform for cloud computing services. When multiple VMs are sharing hardware resources, the performance of their hosted applications may degrade due to imperfect VM isolation. We illustrate this problem using 5 Xen VMs deployed on a physical server for the execution of a benchmark of 10 representative CPU- and I/O-intensive applications; see Table 3 in Section 5 for their computation and I/O characteristics. Each *slave* VM was configured with 3 VCPUs, 2GB memory and with 3 map slots and 1 reduce slot. The VMs competed for 10 physical cores and one shared disk. One of the VMs executed the benchmark applications one by one and profiled the execution time for each application task. The other co-hosted VMs ran randomly selected applications from the benchmark as background jobs. Figure 1 and Figure 2 show the task completion time of each job, which is normalized to that of the task running alone on a dedicated VM. In Figure 1, the total CPU demand of co-hosted VMs is represented in the percentage of one physical core. We can see that, for CPU-intensive applications, there is no significant slowdown until the background demand reaches the capacity of 800 (8 cores). It is expected that I/O-intensive applications were insensitive to the total amount of CPU demands. Similarly, Figure 2 shows an exponential increase of the completion time of I/O intensive applications with the

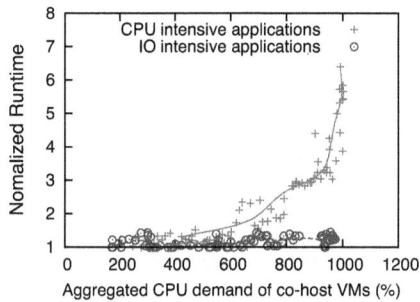

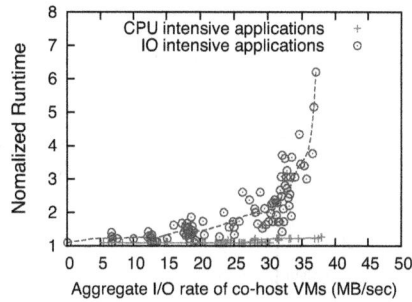

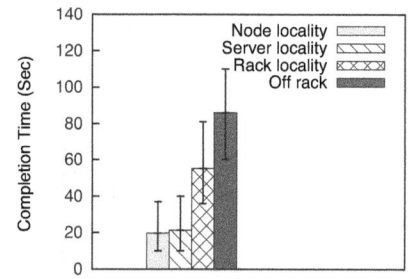

Figure 1: Effect of CPU interference. Figure 2: Effect of I/O interference. Figure 3: Effect of data locality.

aggregated I/O traffic from co-hosted VMs. Previous works mitigated VM interference through dynamic resource allocation or interference-aware scheduling [11, 20, 23]. But applying their approaches in virtual MapReduce clusters may degrade system performance greatly due to the unawareness of MapReduce's features, like job fairness and data locality.

2.3 Data Locality

Recall that a virtual MapReduce cluster defines data locality in four layers: *node locality*, *server locality*, *rack locality*, and *off rack*. We show their respective effect on performance using 24 VMs deployed on 12 physical machines with 2 VMs on each. Each VM was allocated sufficient resource to eliminate interference effect. The physical machines were installed on 2 racks, connected by a 100 Mbps ethernet switch (for the purpose of creating network contention scenarios). We ran TeraSort application in the benchmark with 120 map tasks over 12GB input data. From Figure 3 we can see that tasks with *server locality* would finishe in approximately the same time as those with *node locality*. However, tasks with *rack local* and *off rack* data access could take as long as 3x and 4x time to complete, respectively. The non-local data access dramatically degraded the performance.

There are many task scheduling algorithms designed to preserve task data locality for MapReduce applications in physical clusters. When they are applied to virtual clusters, the data locality can not be maintained effectively due to the presence of VM interference. Most of the existing approaches assume that the tasks are largely short lived and the task slots are not occupied for too long by any job. Thus, for a given task to be run, even the target nodes with local data are not available, they are assumed to be free up soon. The scheduler can always launch local tasks for each job with a few seconds delay. In a virtual MapReduce cluster, VM interference could prolong short-lived tasks and render the data locality policy ineffective. To demonstrate this issue, we built a virtual cluster with 24 VMs on 6 physical servers, each with 4 VMs deployed. For comparison, we also built a physical cluster with 24 physical machines. The clusters were run with a Hadoop framework, which deployed the delay scheduling algorithm [31] to enhance data locality. Table 1 shows that for the physical cluster, the approach can achieve 98.4% *node locality* for a total of 120 tasks. In contrast, in the virtual cluster, the most beneficial *node* and *server locality* are reduced to 72.3% and 2%, respectively. As a result, we observed 100% slowdown in job completion time. Thus it requires a specifically designed task scheduler for virtual MapReduce clusters.

Table 1: Degrees of data locality in different clusters

Locality	Node	Server	Rack	Off Rack	Time
Physical	98.4%	N/A	1.6%	0.0%	170 sec
Virtual	72.3%	2%	18.3%	7.2%	342 sec

3. SYSTEM ARCHITECTURE

The ILA scheduler works in a Hadoop virtual cluster. Figure 4 illustrates the architecture of the target system. The cluster consists of a number of physical servers, each of which has the same virtualized environment. Multiple VMs are allocated onto each physical server hosting running applications, supported by Hadoop HDFS. Hadoop framework is deployed on top of the virtual cluster with a single *master* and multiple *slaves*. Each *slave* is configured to run within one VM and the *master* is deployed on a dedicated physical machine with secondary backup.

The core of ILA-based task management is located in the *master*, consisting of four major components: 1) the *Interference-Aware Scheduling Module* (IASM) to mitigate the interference between tasks running on co-hosted VMs with the help of an interference prediction model; 2) the *Locality-Aware Scheduling Module* (LASM) maintains good data locality for map tasks by using Adaptive Delay Scheduling algorithm; 3) the Task Profiler estimates the task's demand of each job and feeds task information to IASM and LASM modules; 4) the ILA scheduler instructs IASM and LASM modules to conduct interference-free high-locality task management. To collect the running status of the servers, we deployed a VM resource monitor in each VM and a physical resource monitor in each physical server. They send resource consumption status to ILA scheduler periodically.

4. ILA SCHEDULER DESIGN

4.1 Interference Prediction Model

In this section, we present a model to characterize the impact of the interference. We focus on the CPU and I/O bandwidth resources. The CPU-bound and I/O-bound workloads are the most common workloads for MapReduce clusters.

Nonlinear Prediction Model. On the application level, the interference can be perceived as the performance variation, including job runtime [33] and I/O throughput [11]. For generality, instead of using the absolute completion time, we considered the task slowdown rate (S) as the prediction target, which is defined on the task's real completion time (T_{real}) over the run time without interference (T),

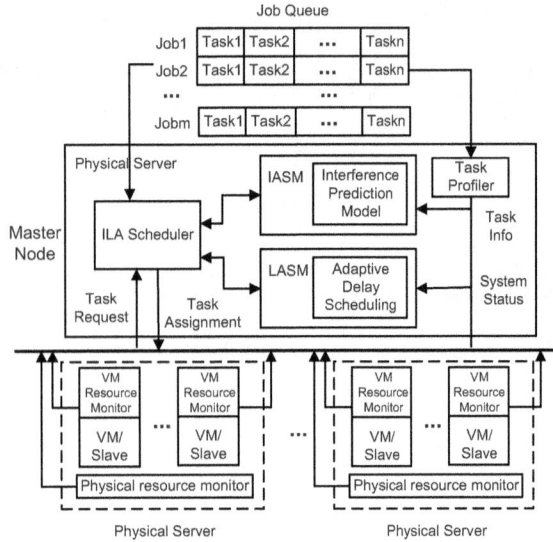

Figure 4: System Architecture.

Table 2: System metrics

	Parameters
System CPU	c_u: Local CPU usage in DomU c_a: Aggregated CPU usage of co-hosted VMs c_0: CPU usage in Dom0
System I/O	r_u: Local read rate in DomU w_u: Local write rate in DomU r_a: Aggregated read rate of co-hosted VMs w_a: Aggregated write rate of co-hosted VMs io_u: I/O utilization of physical server
Task	t_c: Average CPU demand t_r: Average read rate t_w: Average write rate

$S = T_{real}/T$. Such normalization helps the model deal with applications with different magnitudes in completion time.

The interference comes from two main sources : co-existed tasks in the same scheduled VM and the co-hosted VMs on the same physical server. Their impact on performance also varies with the application's demand. The prediction result should depend on the characteristics of the scheduled tasks as well as the resource consumption status of the target VM and co-hosted VMs on the same physical server. In an Xen-based environment, the privileged domain (Dom0) has direct access to hardwares. It is in charge of resource management of all guest domains (DomU). All of the effects should be included in the model. We selected CPU usage, disk Read/Write rate and I/O utilization to represent task demand and system status. These parameters are selected through covariance ranking and statistical hypothesis testing in order to keep the model simple and accurate. These eleven performance-critical parameters are listed in Table 2.

We first constructed separate interference prediction models for pure CPU-bound and I/O-bound applications. As shown in Figure 1, the characteristic of the data points is fit for an exponential curve. We constructed an exponential interference model for pure CPU-intensive application as follows:

$$\hat{S}_{cpu} = \alpha_{cpu} \exp\left(\gamma_t t_c + \sum_{i=1}^{3} \gamma_i CPU_i + C_{cpu}\right) + C_1, \quad (1)$$

where the task performance depends on its own CPU de-

mand as well as all the CPU relative metrics listed in Table 2, represented as CPU_i, including the CPU usage of the scheduled VM, co-hosted VMs and Dom0. γ and C represent the coefficient and constant in the model.

Similarly, as shown in Figure 2, the slowdown rate of I/O-bound applications demonstrate an exponential relationship with background I/O rate. We constructed a non-linear exponential model for pure I/O-bound applications as follows:

$$\hat{S}_{io} = \beta_{io} \exp\left(\tau_{tr}t_r + \tau_{tw}t_w + \sum_{i=1}^{5} \tau_i IO_i + \tau_0 c_0 + C_{io}\right) + C_2, \quad (2)$$

where task performance is estimated based on its read and write I/O demands as well as all the I/O relative metrics listed in Table 2, represented as IO_i, including Read/Write I/O throughout of the scheduled VM, the co-hosted VMs and the physical I/O utilization. τ and C represent the coefficient and constant in the model. Notice that the CPU usage of Dom0 was also introduced into the model. This is crucial because all the requests from guest VMs are routed through Dom0. Handling a large number of I/O requests on behalf of guest domain will consume substantial CPU resources in Dom0.

For general applications, both of the CPU and I/O resource can affect their performance. We introduced the final general interference prediction model based on the two special models above. We constructed a linear model to quantify the joint impact of CPU and I/O resource on performance, as follows:

$$\hat{S} = \alpha\hat{S}_{cpu} + \beta\hat{S}_{io} + C_3, \quad (3)$$

The experiments in Section 5.4 show that the general model can achieve as high as 90% prediction accuracy. It brings 10%-15% improvement over the linear and quadratic models used in previous works [11].

Model Training. The model was initially constructed through offline training. For generality, we selected 10 applications shown in Table 3 for interference profile. Each application was running on one VM with various workloads on the same VM and co-hosted VMs. There were 6 VMs deployed on the same physical server. We developed two kinds of workload generators to generate CPU and I/O-bound workloads. The CPU workload generator conducts a set of arithmetic operations in a loop with variable time intervals. The I/O workload generator repeatedly reads from or writes to a file, which is much larger than the allocated memory to avoid OS caching effect. Both generators are able to issue workloads with any level of intensities by adjusting the length of sleep interval between each iteration. We also created 200 workload combinations by randomly selecting real applications in Table 3 as the background applications in profiling the interference. All the required metrics were collected during the experiments and used as the input data for modeling process.

In the nonlinear modeling process, we used the *Gauss-Newton* algorithm [12] to generate the coefficients that minimize sum of squared errors (SSE). The *Gauss-Newton* method is an interactive process that gradually updates the parameters to obtain the optimal solution. We also employed a stepwise algorithm [14] to simplify the model as much as possible. This stepwise process repeatedly adds or removes possible variables from the equation and evaluates the new re-fitting models.

Online Model Adaptation. Although the proposed

prediction model is general for all kinds of applications, it keeps updating in order to achieve more accuracy for current applications. The time for modeling process is less than 2 seconds on a 3.0 GHz Inter Xeon processor. It can be dynamically re-calibrated when the accuracy is not acceptable with negligible overhead. The *Guass-Newton* method will be triggered whenever there are k new observations, k is set to 100 in this work. Thus the model can be easily adapted to a new cloud platform with different applications, virtual machines, operation systems and cloud infrastructures.

4.2 Data Locality Improvement

The impact of data locality on performance is difficult to predict because it involves the status of multiple levels of network nodes, including VMs, physical servers and switches. Instead of using explicit models, we propose an heuristic approach, namely Adaptive Delay Scheduling, to improve data locality. Compared with Delay Scheduling, the new approach is much more efficient and suitable for the virtualized environment.

Fair and Delay Scheduling. In practice, sharing a cluster between multiple users is more common and highly beneficial than dedicated clusters due to low building cost and data consolidation. We build our new scheduler on top of the existing fair scheduler. Briefly, at each scheduling interval, the fair scheduler sorts all the jobs according to their running tasks. It always assign available compute node to the job that is farthest below its fair share [31]. However, such strict scheduling order may conflict the data locality. The scheduled job may not be able to find a free node to launch a local task.

Delay scheduling is a simple but effective approach to improve locality by temporarily relaxing fairness [31]. The key idea is when the scheduled job can not launch a local task on the available node, the scheduler will delay this job and skip to process the next one, until the delayed job find a free node to run local tasks or the accumulated delay time exceeds predefined intervals. There are multiple wait time thresholds for different levels of data locality. For example, in the latest version of Hadoop, the default maximum wait time for a *node local* task (T_{node}) is 5 seconds, after which the scheduler will try to launch a *rack local* task. The default extra wait time for a *rack local* task (T_{rack}) is also 5 seconds. When the wait time goes beyond $T_{rack}+T_{node}$, the scheduler will launch any task of the delayed job without considering the data locality.

Adaptive Delay Interval. The Delay Scheduling approach delays all the jobs for the same amount of time as long as they do not have local data access. However, the impact of data locality varies with the task's input file size. For jobs with small input file, their performance are insensitive to data locality, as shown in Section 5.3. But the scheduler forces them to take unnecessary delay to achieve high data locality. In practice, CPU-intensive applications, such as machine learning applications, usually have small input file. Even for data intensive applications, their tasks' input file size could also be changed through specific job configuration. We propose an adaptive delay scheduling algorithm with the delay interval proportional to the task input file size, defined as follows. Note that the HDFS block size is the largest unit for each map task, which is treated as the upper bound for task input file size.

$$\hat{T}_{ij} = \begin{cases} 0 & If \ \ F_j/F_b \leq 0.01; \\ F_j * T_i/F_b & Otherwise, \end{cases} \quad (4)$$

where T_i is the maximum wait time for locality level i and $\hat{T}_{ij}$ is the actual wait time for job j. F_j represents the input file size of the tasks in job j and F_b represents the HDFS block size. When the input size less than 1% of the block size, the scheduler will launch the task without any delay.

Server Locality-Aware Scheduling. The virtualized environment adds one more layer in network topology: the co-hosted VMs. We defined it as "*server local* " if the data is not on the compute VM but on the same physical server. The inter-VM communication within one physical machine is more efficient than the cross-machine communication. It will not be affected by the outside network traffic because the communication is optimized by Hypervisor. As shown in Section 2.3, the *server local* task performs closely to the *node local* task. Thus we set a small delay interval for *server locality*, 0.5 second in this work. After failing to find a *node local* task, the scheduler will quickly search for a *server local* task instead of searching for a *rack local* one.

The *server locality* information is usually unavailable in virtual cluster. We designed several methods to detect the VM's physical location. Users can input the VM deployment information through XML configuration file. The framework can also automatically generate the information by using *traceroute* from each VM to locate their physical hosts. The first hop is always the *Dom0* or Hypervisor process for the physical server. The information may also be provided by specially desinged management system, as used in [21].

4.3 System Monitoring and Task Profiling

The scheduling decision is based on system resource consumption status and task resource demands. We deployed one VM resource monitor in each VM and one physical resource monitor in each physical server. We used the standard Xen tool *Xentop* to monitor the CPU usage of *Dom0* and each guest domain. Physical server I/O utilization and Read/Write I/O rate of each VM were measured via Linux *iostat* tool. We modified the *TaskTracker* in each *slave* (VM) to collect the resource consumption status. The information was sent to the *JobTracker* located in *master* node through periodical heartbeat operations. The resource information of physical servers was sent to *JobTracker* via TCP connections.

There is no standard tool to directly estimate the resource demand of an incoming task. We estimated the information through task profiling. For a MapReduce job, it usually consists of many small tasks. The tasks mostly have the same resource demand because they are often run in a data partition model for the same problem. We can estimate the task demand of job j $\hat{D}_j$ based on the measured demand of the finished ones D_j, as follows:

$$\hat{D}_{tj} = \begin{cases} init & If \ \ t = 0; \\ D_{0j} & If \ \ t = 1; \\ \alpha * D_{(t-1)j} + (1-\alpha) * \hat{D}_{(t-1)j} & Otherwise. \end{cases} \quad (5)$$

The value $\hat{D}_j$ is used to estimate the demand before the task running and the actual demand D_j measured after the completion is used to update the estimation for subsequent tasks. The index t represents the update time interval. Thus $\hat{D}_{tj}$ represents the estimated demand of all the tasks in job j scheduled during the interval t. Initially, when there is no finished task, i.e. $t = 0$, we set the *init* demand to a high value to avoid interference. We used a decayed model to estimate the task demand, which makes the new observations more relevant in prediction than old ones. We set α to 0.8 in this work. In this paper, we modified *JobTracker* to collect the task demand information. The consumed CPU time and the read/written file size of each task were obtained using MapReduce *CPU* and *FileSystem* Counter, respectively.

4.4 ILA Scheduling

ILA scheduler performs the interference and locality-aware scheduling operations on top of the fair scheduling. At each interval, it selects a job from a wait queue sorted according to the job's fairness. However, occasionally, the goal of mitigating interference and maintaining data locality may conflict with each other. ILA scheduler always considers the interference mitigation first due to the following two reasons: 1) VM interference causes much more performance degradation than remote data access. Scheduling a non-local task only affect the individual task. In contrast, VM interference may affect not only the scheduled task but also all the tasks running on the same VM and physical server. 2) No interference is a precondition for achieving good data locality. Any unexpected task slowdown would make the data locality policy ineffective.

Interference-Aware Scheduling. Whenever ILA scheduler receives a task request from one VM, it collects the VM's resource status as well as the information of its co-hosted VMs and its physical host. Then it searches down the sorted job list and gets the task's profile of the first job. Taking those as inputs, the prediction model returns a quantitative value to evaluate the interference. Previous works employed a Min-Min heuristics [11] to schedule the tasks based on the interference prediction. The scheduler always assign the "least-interference" task to available VMs. However, such tasks may still lead to the severe contention if all the tasks are resource intensive.

In this paper, we propose a scheduling strategy based on slowdown rate thresholds, as shown in Algorithm 1. We set a static threshold H to 1 by default, which means no task slowdown due to interference. When a free node $Node_i$ requests a task, ILA scheduler collects the system information and evaluates the tasks $Tasks_j$ of each job on the sorted list. ILA only evaluates a job once using its current estimated task demand $\hat{D}_t$ instead of testing all individual tasks in the job, since all the tasks in a job have similar demand. If the predicted slowdown rate $\hat{S}_j$ is not higher than H, ILA scheduler accepts job j and stops searching. Otherwise it refuses the job and processes the next one. If eventually no job satisfies the condition, the scheduler rejects $Node_i$ and lets it wait for resource releasing. Such static threshold method could lead to many idle slots and degrade the performance. For example, if current H is 1 and the number of running slots Z_R on the sever is 2, we assume that the completion time slowdown rate of all the running tasks in the same server is no higher than current H. Then the server's throughput is $Z_R/H = 2$. If we increase H to 2, which makes Z_R to go up to 6, we have the throughput $6/2 = 3$. Although all the tasks are slowed down, the throughput is improved. There is a tradeoff between individual task performance and the job's degree of parallelism.

We introduced a dynamic threshold H_d to deal with the

problem. ILA scheduler tries to increase the parallelism if the number of idle slots Z_I becomes more than one for k seconds (20 seconds in our experiments). Within one physical server, the scheduler compares the current throughput Z_R/H_d with the predicted throughput if adding one more task $(Z_R + 1)/\hat{S}_j$. If the latter is larger, ILA schedules the task in and updates H_d as $\hat{S}_j$. H_d should not be increased endlessly. It will be decreased gradually if $\hat{S}_j$ is no larger than H_d, which means H_d has become over set.

Algorithm 1 Interference-Aware Scheduling

1: **When** a hearbeat is received from a free node n:
2: Collect system information N_{info};
3: Given a job j
4: Fetch task's profile $Tasks_j$;
5: Predict the slow down rate $\hat{S}_j = Model(N_{info}, Tasks_j)$;
6: Get the number of running slots Z_R and idle slots Z_I
7: **if** $Z_I > 1$ for k seconds **then**
8:      // use dynamic threshold
9:      **if** $(Z_R + 1)/\hat{S}_j > Z_R/H_d$ **and** $\hat{S}_j > H_d$ **then**
10:         update $H_d = \hat{S}$ and return the accepted job j;
11:      **else**
12:         **if** $\hat{S}_j <= H_d$ **then**
13:            update $H_d = min(H_d - 1, \hat{S}_j)$ and return the accepted job j;
14:         **else**
15:            reject job j
16:         **end if**
17:      **end if**
18: **else**
19:      $H_d = H$; //use the predefined threshold
20:      **if** $\hat{S} <= H$ **then**
21:         return the accepted job j
22:      **else**
23:         reject job j;
24:      **end if**
25: **end if**

Locality-Aware Scheduling. The job that has passed through interference check is sent to LASM. The module searches all the tasks in the job and selects one whose input data is deployed closest to the requesting VM. We define the level of data locality according to the corresponding network hierarchy: L_0, L_1, L_2 and L_3 represent *node local*, *server local*, *rack local* and *off rack*, respectively. L_j denotes the maximum allowed locality level for job j. L_{jmin} denotes the minimal achievable locality level among all the tasks in job j given the requesting VM. If L_{jmin} is no higher than L_j, ILA scheduler accepts the task. Otherwise, ILA skips the job's scheduling unless its accumulated wait time W_j becomes lager than delay thresholds. $\hat{T}_{ij}$ denotes the wait time for locality level i for job j, $i \in [0, 2]$. No delay is needed in L_3. The locality-aware scheduling algorithm is shown in Algorithm 2.

In this algorithm, each job's maximum allowed locality level L_j is initialized to 0, i.e. the *node locality*. At each scheduling interval, L_j is reset to the locality level of the last accepted task in job j. If the scheduler can not find a sufficiently "close" task, the job only needs to wait for the cumulative delay interval, which is calculated from L_j to the minimal achievable level L_{jmin}, instead of from level 0. For example, if $L_j = 1$ and $L_{jmin} = 2$, the job only needs to wait for the time of T_{1j}, instead of $T_{0j} + T_{1j}$. This strategy tends to reduce the unnecessary delay for the jobs, for which the low locality levels are really difficult to achieve. We set

Algorithm 2 Locality-Aware Scheduling

1: System maintains four variables for each the job j:
2: maximum allowed level L_j; accumulated wait time W_j;
3: task input file size F_j;
4: the delay interval $\hat{T}_{ij}$ of each level i;
5: Get job j from Interference-aware scheduling module;
6: The free VM is vm_n;
7: **if** $F_j/F_b <= 0.01$ **then**
8:     return any unlaunched task t in job j ;
9: **else**
10:     In job j, find the task t with the minimal locality level L_{jmin} for vm_n;
11:     // the task whose input file located "closest" to vm_n
12:     **if** $L_{jmin} <= L_j$ **or** $W_j >= \sum_{l=L_j}^{(L_{jmin}-1)} \hat{T}_{lj}$ **then**
13:         set $W_j = 0$
14:         $L_j = L_{jmin}$; // reset L_j as the recently accepted level
15:         return the accepted task t in job j;
16:     **else**
17:         reject job j and update W_j
18:     **end if**
19: **end if**

the *level 0* delay to a very small value, 0.5 second. The delay intervals of other levels were all set to 5 seconds.

ILA Scheduling. The ILA scheduling algorithm is shown in Algorithm 3. At each scheduling interval, the scheduler sorts all the jobs according to their fair shares. The job that is farthest below its fair share obtains the free node first. Whenever a task request comes, ILA scheduler searches the sorted list and select the first job whose tasks do not cause interference. Then it searches the job's task list and pick a task that has "sufficiently close" data access. If failing to find a satisfactory task, the scheduler rejects the node and lets it wait for the next scheduling interval.

Algorithm 3 ILA Scheduling

1: System maintains the job queue Q;
2: **When** a hearbeat is received from a free node n:
3: Collect system information N_{info};
4: Sort jobs in Q according to the fairness policy;
5: **for** each job j in Q **do**
6:     $job = IASM(job_j, N_{info})$;
7:     **if** $job ==$ null **then**
8:         skip current job j, process the next one;
9:     **else**
10:         $task = LASM(job, n)$;
11:         **if** $task ==$ null **then**
12:             skip current job j, process the next one;
13:         **else**
14:             assign $task$ to the node n;
15:             **break** the loop;
16:         **end if**
17:     **end if**
18: **end for**
19: **if** $task ==$ null **then**
20:     reject node n;
21: **end if**

---

5. EVALUATION

5.1 Experimental Setup

We evaluated the ILA scheduling framework in a 72-node Xen-based private virtual cluster, which consisted of 12 physical servers, each was configured with 12 CPU cores, 32GB memory and one 500GB disk. Each server hosted 6 VMs and

Table 3: A summary of MapReduce benchmarks

Name	Type	Introduction
TeraSort	I/O	Sort the input data into a total order
TeraGen	I/O	Generate and write data into system
Grep	I/O	Extract matching regular expression
RWrite	I/O	Random write words into log file
WCount	I/O	Count words in the input file
PiEst	CPU	Estimate Pi using Monte Carlo method
Bayes	CPU	Contruct Bayes Classifier on input data
Kmean	CPU	Cluster analysis using K-mean method
Canopy	CPU	Cluster analysis using Canopy method
Matrix	CPU	Matrix add and multiplication

each VM was configured with 2 VCPUs and 2GB memory. The 6 VMs were configured to compete for 10 cores and one shared disk. The virtual cluster spanned 2 racks and was connected by a 1Gbps Ethernet.

We installed a modified version of Hadoop 0.20.205 equipped with ILA scheduler, system resource monitors and task profilers. Based on hardware capacity, we configured each *slave* with 2 map slots and 1 reduce slot, for a total of 144 map slots and 72 reduce slots in the cluster. The HDFS block size was set to 128 MB to improved performance according to a Facebook's report [31]. All other parameters were set to their default configurations.

We evaluated ILA scheduler using 10 MapReduce applications, most of which were widely used in evaluations of MapReduce framework by previous works [24, 17, 7, 32, 31, 8]. Table 3 shows their main characteristics. The machine learning applications were from mahout project [4]. In the experiments, we compared the performance of ILA scheduler with 4 other main competitors in practical use: 1) *PureFair scheduler* conducts fair scheduling using greedy method to maintain data locality, i.e. always selecting the "closest" task from the scheduled job without any delay [13, 31]; 2) *Delay scheduler* uses delay scheduling algorithm to achieve good data locality by slightly compromising fairness restriction [31]; 3) *Longest Approximate Time to End (LATE) scheduler* improves MapReduce applications' performance in heterogenous environment, like virtualized environment, through accurate speculative execution [32]; 4) *Capacity scheduler*, introduced by Yahoo, supports multiple queues for shared users and guarantees each queue a fraction of the capacity of the cluster [6]; We also compared two variants of ILA: 1)*Interference-Aware Only (IAO) scheduler* only conducts interference-free scheduling with the help of IASM, but uses greedy method to maintain data locality; 2) *Locality-Aware Only (LAO) scheduler* only uses LASM to conduct Adaptive Delay Scheduling to improve data locality without considering VM interference.

5.2 Performance of ILA Scheduler

We evaluated ILA scheduler through a set of macro benchmarks based on the workload trace from Facebook reported in [31], according to which, the job size, in terms of number of map tasks, presents the distribution as shown in the first two columns of Table 4. We adjusted the total number of jobs based on our cluster's scale and generated a job submission schedule for 25 jobs. According to the trace, the distribution of inter-arrival times between jobs was roughly exponential with a mean of 14 seconds. It makes our submission schedule 253 seconds long. The tested applications

Table 4: Job type and job size distribution

JobSize	%	#	# of I/O(size)	# of CPU(size)
1-2	54%	14	6 TeraSort(2)	8 Kmean(1)
3-20	14%	4	2 TeraSort(10)	2 Bayes(20)
21-150	14%	3	1 RWrite(40)	
			2 Grep(120)	
151-300	6%	1	1 WCount(250)	
301-500	4%	1		1 PiEst(480)
> 500	8%	2	1 TeraGen(600)	1 PiEst(1000)

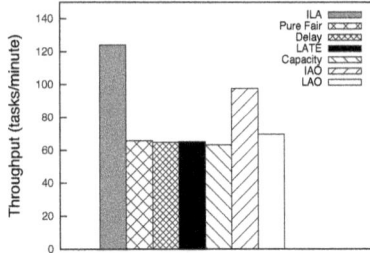

Figure 5: Throughput due to different schedulers.

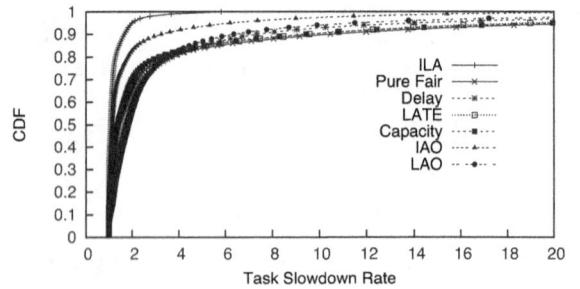

Figure 8: CDF of task completion time.

are listed in Table 4 with the columns representing the job size, the percentage of the total jobs, the actual number of running jobs, the number of I/O-bound jobs and the number CPU-bound jobs, respectively.

Figure 5 shows the system throughput due to different schedulers. ILA scheduler yielded an improvement of up to 1.9 time in throughput over interference-oblivious schedulers, including PureFair, Delay, LATE, Capacity and LAO schedulers, and led to an improvement of 1.3 times over IAO scheduler. Figure 6 shows the average completion time of each type of jobs due to different task schedulers. The results are normalized with respect to the performance due to ILA scheduler. Compared with interference-oblivious schedulers, ILA scheduler could speed up individual jobs by 1.5-6.5 times. It led to an improvement of 1.1-2.0 times in job completion time in comparison with IAO scheduler. The interference-oblivious schedulers had similar performance. The delay-based scheduling algorithm in Delay and LAO schedulers could not speed up the jobs because the tasks were significantly slowed down due to resource contention no matter how they access the data. Capacity scheduler also lost its effectiveness in such virtualized environments because it was unable to guarantee each job queue's resource portion in the presence of VM interference. LATE scheduler could not maintain its efficiency due to severe resource contention. IAO scheduler only considers the effect of interference. The greedy data locality policy is attributed to its performance degradation.

Figure 7 shows the percentage of tasks in the jobs with local data access. Since *node local* tasks and *server local* tasks have similar performance, the calculated local data access includes both *node local* access and *server local* access. Jobs are demonstrated in two groups: I/O-bound jobs and CPU-bound jobs. Recall that the Adaptive Delay Scheduling algorithm manages to achieve good data locality for tasks with sufficiently large input file. Thus, for CPU-bound jobs with small input files, ILA and LAO scheduler used default greedy locality policy. (*TeraGen* and *RWrite* are not shown because they have no input files). From Figure 7, we can see that

for I/O-bound jobs, ILA brought the average local data access up to 90%. It gained 65% improvement over PureFair, LATE, Capacity and IAO schedulers, and 20% improvement over Delay schedulers. As expected, schedulers using greedy locality policy, such as PureFair, LATE, Capacity and IAO schedulers, achieved the lowest local data access. For Delay scheduler, three major factors are attributed to its worse performance compared with ILA scheduler: first, it introduces much longer delay after failing to find a *node local* task. Second, launching premature *rack local* tasks instead of *server local* ones due to the unawareness of *server locality*. Third, many unexpected long tasks caused by interference make the delay scheduling less efficient. For CPU-bound jobs, their performance are insensitive to data locality. ILA scheduler generated 60% local task without any delay. Although Delay scheduler achieved the highest percentage, it may cause unnecessary long time delay and harm the performance.

ILA scheduler improved jobs' performance by accelerating each individual task. Figure 8 plots the cumulative distribution of completion time of individual tasks under different schedulers. The completion time is normalized with respect to that of the task running with *node local* data access and without any interference. We can see that under ILA scheduling, 70% of the tasks (2440 tasks in total) proceed without any slowdown, 90% run with less than 1.5x slowdown and 99% run with less than 2.5x slowdown. IAO performed slightly worse with 83% of tasks runnig less than 2x slower and 99% running less than 10x slower. The task slowdown rate significantly rised under the interference-oblivious scheduling. For PureFair, Delay, LATE, Capacity and LAO schedulers, only 15% of the tasks could run without any interference and up to 60% run with more than 2x slowdown. The completion times of 10% tasks were increased by more than 10 times.

From the results, we can make several observations. First, small jobs tend to be improved more by ILA scheduler than large jobs, as shown in Figure 6. One of the reasons is that small jobs are easily affected by interference. If one task of a small job is slowed down greatly, the whole job's completion time is very likely increased due to waiting for the slow task. However, for a large job, the task slowdown can be amortized by other concurrent normal running tasks as long as the delayed tasks are not in the last batch. Moreover, for a large job, the performance degradation in individual tasks may be compromised by the increased parallel degree. But for small jobs, the degree of parallelism is limited by the number of tasks. Another reason for small jobs gaining more improvement is that launching *node local* tasks is

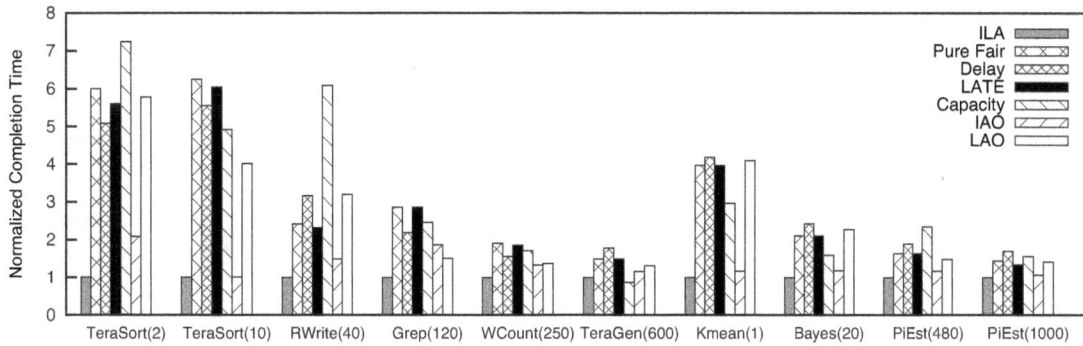

Figure 6: Job completion time due to different schedulers.

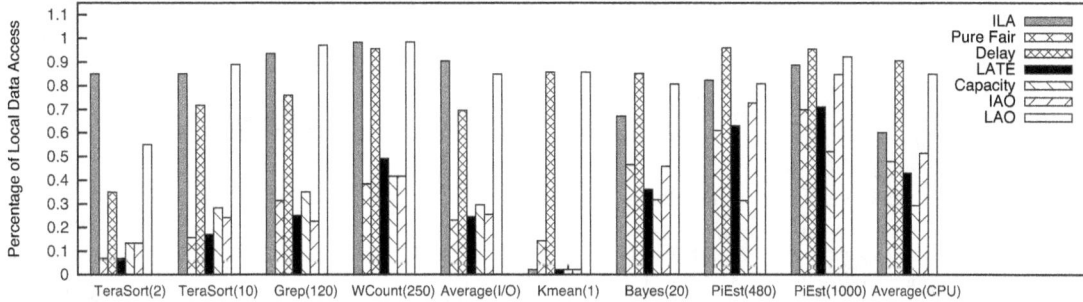

Figure 7: Data locality due to different schedulers.

much more difficult for them. Compared with large jobs, small jobs have much fewer input file blocks, which makes them having much less nodes with local data. Therefore, achieving the *server locality* could significantly increase the number of local nodes without degrading the performance. As shown in Figure 7, for the small job $TeraSort(2)$, the schedulers which are unaware of the *server locality* could only achieve less than 35% local access. ILA was able to improve it to 85%.

The second observation is that interference could cause much more severe performance degradation than remote data access. Remote data access could only affect individual tasks but interference may impose impact on the scheduled task and all of the co-hosted tasks. As shown in Figure 6 and Figure 8, LAO scheduler led to more job and task slowdown than IAO scheduler. This observation explains why ILA scheduler mitigates interference before improving data locality if there is a conflict between these two aspects.

5.3 Benefits of Interference and Locality Aware Scheduling

In this section, we demonstrate effectiveness of IASM and LASM modules with the specifically designed experiments.

Benefit from IASM. IASM is the component in ILA conducting the interference-aware scheduling. To isolate the effect from data locality, we selected the *Matrix* and *TeraGen* applications in evaluation because neither of them requires input data. Each *Matrix* job was comprised of 150 map tasks and each *TeraGen* job contained 400 map tasks. We submitted 3 *Matrix* jobs and 3 *TeraGen* jobs to the cluster alternatively with 15 seconds time interval.

Figure 9 shows the normalized completion time of each type of jobs due to different schedulers. Since there is no data locality effect, ILA and IAO were reduced to the same

scheduler, which speeded up the jobs by 2.0-3.0 times compared with the interference-oblivious schedulers. Delay and LAO schedulers became equivalent to PureFair scheduler without the data locality effect. There was also no obvious improvement achieved by either LATE or Capacity scheduler. Their performance were mainly limited by the side effect of interference. From Figure 9, we can also see that job's completion time only varied within 18% due to ILA scheduling. In contrast, under the interference-oblivious scheduling, job's performance fluctuated in a much wider range from 10% to 70%. The reason is that interference seldom evenly affects all the tasks in one job. Task's performance heavily depends on the current system status of the host VM, the physical server and its own characteristics. Thus only the interference aware scheduling could provide a stable and predictable system.

Benefit from LASM. LASM module is in charge of the locality aware scheduling. To demonstrate its effectiveness, we eliminated the influence from VM interference by designing a micro-benchmark with a set of elaborately modified applications. We carefully adjusted the resource demand of $PiEst$ and $Grep$ applications by injecting idle loops into the programs. These modified applications, noted as $MPiEst$ and $MGrep$, still consume sufficient resources to maintain their characteristics but will not cause resource contention even running on co-hosted VMs. Each $MPiEst$ job contained 100 map tasks and each $MGrep$ contained 350 tasks. We submitted 3 $MPiEst$ jobs and 3 $MGrep$ jobs and also run some independent applications to mimic background network traffic without interfering with the scheduling.

Figure 10 shows the normalized completion time and the percentage of local tasks due to different schedulers. For the I/O-bound job $MGrep$, the schedulers with LASM modules (ILA and LAO) brought the percentage of local tasks

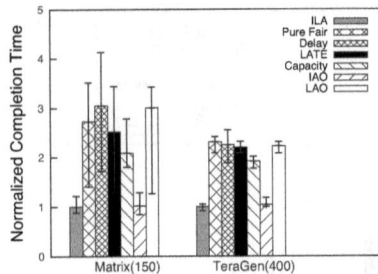

Figure 9: Benefits of interference-aware scheduling.

(a) Job data locality

(b) Job completion time

Figure 10: Benefits of locality-aware scheduling.

to nearly 100%. In contrast, the schedulers using the default greedy locality policy (PureFair, LATE, Capacity and IAO) only achieved less than 58% locality. As a result, these schedulers slowed down the jobs by nearly 1.8 times. The Delay Scheduling demonstrated its advantage over the greedy locality policy. It yielded 90% local tasks. However, due to the awareness of the *server locality*, ILA scheduler achieved a 10% improvement in data locality and a 23% improvement in completion time over Delay scheduler.

For CPU-bound job *MPiEst*, without any delay, LASM-based schedulers launched 80% local tasks and the schedulers with greedy locality policy launched 50%. Only Delay scheduler postponed tasks in order to improve data locality. Since *MPiEst* is insensitive to data access, although having achieved 95% locality, Delay scheduler was still the worst one due to unnecessary delay for each task. It slowed down *MPiEst* job by 1.3 times compared with ILA. This result shows that LASM could speed up jobs through dynamically setting delay intervals according to their input file sizes.

5.4 Interference Prediction Model Analysis

In this section, we evaluate the accuracy of the exponential interference prediction model. For comparison purpose, we also designed and implemented two other models: linear model and quadratic model, which are used in previous work [11]. These two models require the same performance critical parameters for interference prediction, as shown in Table 2. They estimate that the job's performance and the system resource consumption presents a linear and a quadratic relationship, receptively,

To assess the prediction accuracy of the interference model, we selected the coefficient of determination (R^2) as one of the measurement. R^2 is widely used in the context of statistical models whose purpose is the prediction of future outcomes on the basis of related information. It is defined as $R^2 = 1 - (\sum_{i=0}^{K}(y_i - \hat{y}_i)^2 / \sum_{i=0}^{K}(y_i - \bar{y}_i)^2)$, where K is the total number of samples. y, $\hat{y}$ and $\bar{y}$ denote the actual value, predicted value and the mean of actual values, receptively. Table 5 shows the R^2 value for each type of jobs due to different models. The evaluated job set includes all the 10 applications listed in Table 3. We can see that, compared with the other two models, the exponential model led to higher R^2 values for both types of jobs, which means higher accuracy. It brought overall R^2 value to 0.887. In contrast, linear model and quadratic model only achieve 0.657 and 0.714 for overall R^2 value, receptively.

We also evaluated the exponential model using a more direct metric, the *prediction error*, which is defined as $|y - \hat{y}|/y$. Figure 11 shows the yielded *prediction errors* for

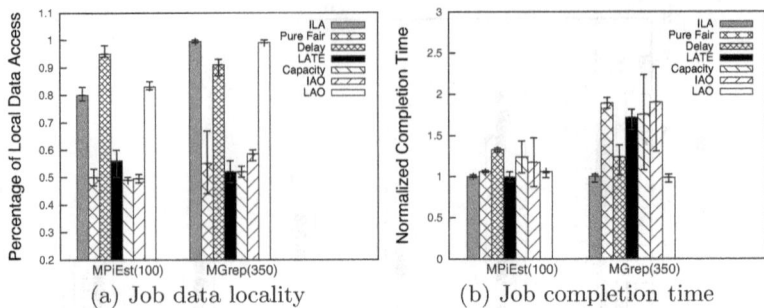

Table 5: R^2 due to different models.

Model	I/O-bound	CPU-bound	Overall
Linear	0.676	0.611	0.657
Quadratic	0.722	0.672	0.714
Exponential	0.895	0.879	0.887

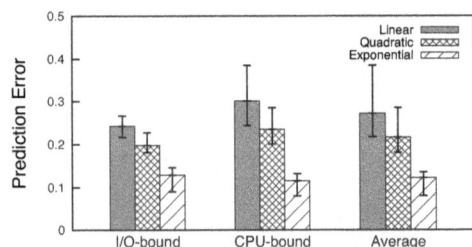

Figure 11: Prediction error due to different models.

each type of jobs due to different models. The box heights represent the average prediction errors and the error bars represent the prediction accuracy deviations among all of the evaluated jobs. We can see that the exponential model could reduce the average prediction error by 15% compared with the linear model and by 10% compared with the quadratic model. The exponential model led to an average of 12% error rate. It was able to keep the prediction error below 14% for all kinds of jobs. According to the experimental results in Section 5.2 , such accuracy of the interference prediction model is acceptable for ILA scheduling. It could efficiently mitigate the interference and make most of the tasks running without being slowed down.

5.5 Effectiveness of Dynamic Threshold

As discussed in Section 4.4, we introduced a dynamic threshold policy to deal with the tradeoff between the individual task performance and the degree of the job's parallelism during interference-aware scheduling. In this section, we evaluate the effectiveness of the dynamic threshold policy by comparising with the static ones.

We generated three types of workloads including mixed, pure CPU and pure I/O applications. The compared polices included static policies with the threshold H set as 1, 2, 4, 6 and 8, and the policy with no threshold. Figure 12 shows the system throughputs due to different polices. We observed that dynamic threshold policy always achieved the highest throughput for all kinds of workloads. In contrast, the no-threshold policy, i.e. the interference-oblivious pol-

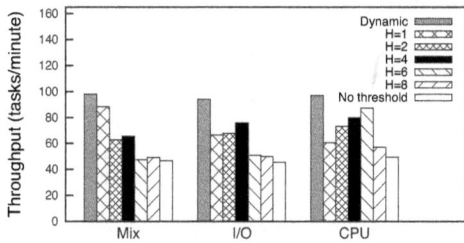

Figure 12: Performance improvement due to dynamic threshold policy.

icy, always performed worst. The static policies could not yield consistent performance. For example, when H is 1, the scheduler achieved nearly highest throughput under Mix workload, but caused 40% performance degradation under CPU-bound workload. That is because under the mixed workload, the scheduler is easy to find a task without any interference due to the diversity in task demands. However, under a pure CPU or I/O-bound workload, increasing the tasks' parallelism with a little compromising individual task performance may be more beneficial to the whole job. Thus, there is no single optimal static threshold for all kinds of workloads. We can see that dynamic threshold policy was able to improve the throughput by up to 40%-100% over static policies.

6. RELATED WORK

There have been many studies devoted to improving system performance of cluster applications, especially MapReduce applications via task scheduling optimization, adaptive resource management or data locality improvement.

Task Scheduling for Cluster Applications. Following on the MapReduce seminar work [13], many researches focused on improving task scheduling algorithms for this framework. Yahoo's Capacity scheduler supports multiple queues for shared users and guarantees each queue a fair share of the capacity of the cluster [6]. Facebook's fairness scheduler uses delay scheduling algorithm to achieve good data locality by slightly compromising fairness restriction [31]. In [32], Zaharia, *et al.* proposed Longest Approximate Time to End (LATE) scheduling algorithm to improve MapReduce applications' performance in heterogenous environment through accurate speculative execution. However, none of them could maintain its effectiveness in virtualized cloud environments due to VM interference.

A large body of work has studied the task scheduling algorithm in other distributed frameworks. For example, in [16], Isard *et al.* introduced a scheduler *Quincy* for Microsoft's *Dryad* computing environment [5] to achieve good data locality while maintaining fairness through an optimization process; In [29], the *Condor* scheduler was extended to grid to improve performance within locality constraints. However, these approaches are designed for physical clusters. Their performance may be compromised by the virtualization overhead and interference when moving to the cloud.

Resource Management and Interference Mitigation. As MapReduce cloud service becomes an attractive usage model, virtual resource management for MapReduce applications has draw more and more attentions. In [28, 19], resource management frameworks were proposed to dynam-

ically adjusts resource allocations to MapReduce jobs. Park *et al.* introduced a locality-aware dynamic VM reconfiguration technique to improve MapReduce's performance [25]. In [24], a resource management framework *Purlieus* was proposed to enhance the performance of MapReduce jobs by coupling data and VM placement. In [21], Li *et al.* proposed, CAM, a topology aware resource manager for MapReduce applications in clouds using a minimum cost flow method. CAM focused on optimizing data and VM placement with considerations of task data locality as well as resource utilization, including both computational and storage resources. In contrast, ILA addresses the management issue from a different perspective. It improves the performance of MapReduce applications via application-level task scheduling optimization. ILA is able to adapt to any data/VM deployment and resource allocation policy. It requires no modification for the underlying resource management. Moreover, ILA can not only avoid server overload due to inappropriate VM deployment or resource allocations, but also mitigate interference between co-hosted VMs.

Overcoming the interference between co-hosted VMs is one of the essential challenges in cloud management. Hardware or operating system solutions have been extensively studied in previous works, including dynamical cache partition [30], intelligent memory management [22] and improved operating system scheduling [34]. Our approach deals with the interference problem without any modification of existing hardware platforms or operating systems. In [23], *Q-Clouds* suggested to mitigate the interference by dynamically tuning resource allocation to VMs using an online feedback control method. Most recently, TRACON, an interference-aware task scheduler was proposed for data-intensive applications in virtual environment [11]. It is able to effectively mitigate I/O interference with the help of a prediction model. As shown in Section 5.4, their model is less accurate than ILA's exponential prediction model. Also TRACON focused on mitigating interference with no consideration of data locality.

Locality Improvement for Cluster Applications. A lot of works are devoted to improving data locality for data-intensive cluster applications. In [7], a system that replicated blocks based on their popularity was presented to alleviate data hotspots and speed up jobs. In [17], Jin *et al.* proposed an availability-aware MapReduce data placement policy for non-dedicated distributed computing environment. These approaches were mainly designed for physical environment. However, in cloud environments, the predictions on popularity [7] or availability [17] may lose their effectiveness due to the unawareness of the presence of two levels of topology: physical server and VM level. Hotspots may still exist on the physical server level when the data placement is optimized for the VM level. Moreover, in cloud, data locality optimization does not necessarily lead to performance improvement due to the resource contention. ILA scheduler considers both interference and task data locality.

Performance Optimization for MapReduce. The growing popularity of MapReduce has spurred many works on improving the MapReduce performance from system to application level. Kang *et al.* improved the performance of MapReduce virtual cluster by modifying the context-switching mechanism of the Xen credit scheduler [18]. Herodotou *et al.* proposed StarFish to improve MapReduce performance by automatically configuring Hadoop parameters [15]. In [8], an "outlier-control" framework *Mantri* was presented, which could detect the abnormal tasks and proactively take corrective action. These works are orthogonal to our ILA work.

7. CONCLUSION

This paper presents an interference and locality-aware scheduler for virtual MapReduce clusters. It relies on two scheduling modules: IASM and LASM. The former performs the interference-free scheduling with the assistance of a performance prediction model and the latter improves task data locality by using Adaptive Delay Scheduling algorithm. Experimental results show that ILA scheduler could achieve a speedup of 1.5-6.5 times for individual jobs and yield an improvement of up to 1.9 times in system throughput compared with 4 other schedulers. It improves data locality of map tasks by up to 65%. Although ILA scheduling algorithm is designed for MapReduce framework, it could be applicable to other virtual cluster schedulers.

In MapReduce clusters, besides locally running tasks, HDFS may also issue I/O requests for a remote data access. ILA considers this I/O flow as the background traffic and manages to mitigate the interference through task scheduling. In the future, we would like to extend ILA scheduler to mitigate the interference from HDFS through intelligent data placement and data node selection. In a MapReduce framework, the data transfer between map and reduce tasks consumes substantial network resource. ILA scheduler assumes the mappers evenly distributed across the cluster and the locality of reducers would not greatly affect the performance. Another direction of the future work is minimizing the communication overhead between map and reduce tasks by improving reducer's locality when the distribution of map tasks is skewed.

8. ACKNOWLEDGMENTS

This research was supported in part by U.S. NSF grants CCF-1016966 and CNS-0914330.

9. REFERENCES

[1] Amazon ec2. http://aws.amazon.com/ec2/.
[2] Amazon elastic mapreduce. http://aws.amazon.com/elasticmapreduce/.
[3] Apache hadoop. http://hadoop.apache.org.
[4] The apache mahout project. http://mahout.apache.org/.
[5] Microsoft dryad project. http://research.microsoft.com/en-us/projects/dryad/.
[6] Yahoo! inc. capacity scheduler. http://hadoop.apache.org/docs/stable/capacity_scheduler.html.
[7] G. Ananthanarayanan, S. Agarwal, S. Kandula, A. G. Greenberg, I. Stoica, D. Harlan, and E. Harris. Scarlett: coping with skewed content popularity in mapreduce clusters. In *EuroSys*, pages 287–300, 2011.
[8] G. Ananthanarayanan, S. Kandula, A. G. Greenberg, I. Stoica, Y. Lu, B. Saha, and E. Harris. Reining in the outliers in map-reduce clusters using mantri. In *OSDI*, 2010.
[9] X. Bu, J. Rao, and C.-Z. Xu. A reinforcement learning approach to online web systems auto-configuration. In *ICDCS*, 2009.
[10] X. Bu, J. Rao, and C.-Z. Xu. A model-free learning approach for coordinated configuration of virtual machines and appliances. In *MASCOTS*, 2011.
[11] R. C.-L. Chiang and H. H. Huang. Tracon: interference-aware scheduling for data-intensive applications in virtualized environments. In *SC*, page 47, 2011.
[12] E. K. P. Chong and S. H. Zak. *An Introduction to Optimization, 3rd Edition.* Wiley Press, 2008.

[13] J. Dean and S. Ghemawat. Mapreduce: Simplified data processing on large clusters. In *OSDI*, 2004.
[14] N. R. Draper and H. Smith. *Applied Regression Analysis.* John Wiley and Sons, 1981.
[15] H. Herodotou, H. Lim, G. Luo, N. Borisov, L. Dong, F. B. Cetin, and S. Babu. Starfish: A self-tuning system for big data analytics. In *CIDR*, pages 261–272, 2011.
[16] M. Isard, V. Prabhakaran, J. Currey, U. Wieder, K. Talwar, and A. Goldberg. Quincy: fair scheduling for distributed computing clusters. In *SOSP*, pages 261–276, 2009.
[17] H. Jin, X. Yang, X.-H. Sun, and I. Raicu. Adapt: Availability-aware mapreduce data placement for non-dedicated distributed computing. In *ICDCS*, pages 516–525, 2012.
[18] H. Kang, Y. Chen, J. L. Wong, R. Sion, and J. Wu. Enhancement of xen's scheduler for mapreduce workloads. In *HPDC*, pages 251–262, 2011.
[19] P. Lama and X. Zhou. AROMA: Automated resource allocation and configuration of mapreduce environment in the cloud. In *Proc. ACM International Conference on Autonomic Computing (ICAC)*, pages 63–72, 2012.
[20] P. Lama and X. Zhou. Ninepin: Non-invasive and energy efficient performance isolation in virtualized servers. In *DSN*, pages 1–12, 2012.
[21] M. Li, D. Subhraveti, A. R. Butt, A. Khasymski, and P. Sarkar. Cam: a topology aware minimum cost flow based resource manager for mapreduce applications in the cloud. In *HPDC*, pages 211–222, 2012.
[22] T. Moscibroda and O. Mutlu. Memory performance attacks: Denial of memory service in multi-core systems. In *16th USENIX Security Symposium*, 2007.
[23] R. Nathuji, A. Kansal, and A. Ghaffarkhah. Q-clouds: managing performance interference effects for qos-aware clouds. In *EuroSys*, pages 237–250, 2010.
[24] B. Palanisamy, A. Singh, L. Liu, and B. Jain. Purlieus: locality-aware resource allocation for mapreduce in a cloud. In *SC*, page 58, 2011.
[25] J. Park, D. Lee, B. Kim, J. Huh, and S. Maeng. Locality-aware dynamic vm reconfiguration on mapreduce clouds. In *HPDC*, pages 27–36, 2012.
[26] J. Rao, X. Bu, and C.-Z. Xu. A distributed self-learning approach for elastic provisioning of virtualized cloud resources. In *MASCOTS*, 2011.
[27] J. Rao, X. Bu, C.-Z. Xu, L. Wang, and G. Yin. Vconf: a reinforcement learning approach to virtual machines auto-configuration. In *Proceedings of the 6th international conference on Autonomic computing*, ICAC '09, pages 137–146, New York, NY, USA, 2009. ACM.
[28] T. Sandholm and K. Lai. Mapreduce optimization using regulated dynamic prioritization. In *SIGMETRICS/Performance*, pages 299–310, 2009.
[29] D. Thain, T. Tannenbaum, and M. Livny. Distributed computing in practice: the condor experience. *Concurrency - Practice and Experience*, 17(2-4):323–356, 2005.
[30] Y. Xie and G. H. Loh. Pipp: promotion/insertion pseudo-partitioning of multi-core shared caches. In *ISCA*, 2009.
[31] M. Zaharia, D. Borthakur, J. S. Sarma, K. Elmeleegy, S. Shenker, and I. Stoica. Delay scheduling: a simple technique for achieving locality and fairness in cluster scheduling. In *EuroSys*, pages 265–278, 2010.
[32] M. Zaharia, A. Konwinski, A. D. Joseph, R. H. Katz, and I. Stoica. Improving mapreduce performance in heterogeneous environments. In *OSDI*, 2008.
[33] Y. Zhang, W. Sun, and Y. Inoguchi. Predicting running time of grid tasks based on cpu load predictions. In *GRID*, 2006.
[34] S. Zhuravlev, S. Blagodurov, and A. Fedorova. Addressing shared resource contention in multicore processors via scheduling. In *ASPLOS*, pages 129–142, 2010.

A Comparative Study of High-Performance Computing on the Cloud

Aniruddha Marathe
Rachel Harris
David K. Lowenthal
Dept. of Computer Science
The University of Arizona

Bronis R. de Supinski
Barry Rountree
Martin Schulz
Lawrence Livermore
National Laboratory

Xin Yuan
Dept. of Computer Science
Florida State University

ABSTRACT

The popularity of Amazon's EC2 cloud platform has increased in recent years. However, many high-performance computing (HPC) users consider dedicated high-performance clusters, typically found in large compute centers such as those in national laboratories, to be far superior to EC2 because of significant communication overhead of the latter. Our view is that this is quite narrow and the proper metrics for comparing high-performance clusters to EC2 is *turnaround time* and *cost*.

In this paper, we compare the top-of-the-line EC2 cluster to HPC clusters at Lawrence Livermore National Laboratory (LLNL) based on turnaround time and total cost of execution. When measuring turnaround time, we include expected queue wait time on HPC clusters. Our results show that although as expected, standard HPC clusters are superior in raw performance, EC2 clusters may produce better turnaround times. To estimate cost, we developed a pricing model—relative to EC2's node-hour prices—to set node-hour prices for (currently free) LLNL clusters. We observe that the cost-effectiveness of running an application on a cluster depends on raw performance *and* application scalability.

Categories and Subject Descriptors

C.4 [**Computer Systems Organization**]: Performance of Systems

General Terms

Measurement, Performance

Keywords

Cloud; Cost; High-Performance Computing; Turnaround Time

1. INTRODUCTION

In recent years, Amazon's Elastic Compute Cloud (EC2) platform has had significant success in the commercial arena, but the story for high-performance computing (HPC) has been mixed. While "success" stories appear in the popular press periodically, most of them feature an embarrassingly parallel program being run on tens of thousands of cloud machines [8]. A more complicated issue is how well EC2 performs on more tightly-coupled applications, which are more representative of applications HPC users typically execute on HPC clusters (e.g., those at national laboratories or other supercomputing centers). The prevailing opinion is that EC2 is essentially useless for such applications [19, 34].

There are reasons to justify skepticism of EC2 for tightly-coupled, more traditional HPC applications. First, the latency and bandwidth of the network used by EC2 are usually inferior to that of a typical, dedicated HPC cluster (e.g., Ethernet vs. Infiniband, although Infiniband cloud offerings seem likely in the near future [33]). Second, compute nodes are virtualized, which causes concerns in terms of virtualization overhead as well as virtual machine co-location.

However, to compare EC2, which provides a fee-for-service model in which access is essentially available 24/7, to traditional HPC clusters on only the axis of execution time is unfair. This comparison ignores, for example, the sometimes significant queue wait time that occurs on HPC clusters, which typically use batch scheduling. Of course, it also ignores factors such as cost, where HPC clusters have a significant advantage. After all, HPC clusters in supercomputing centers such as Livermore Computing (LC) at Lawrence Livermore National Laboratory (LLNL) are free to the user, even though this is only an artifact of government funding.

In this paper, we take a novel look at these differences and we contrast high-end Amazon EC2 clusters against traditional HPC clusters, *but with a more general evaluation scheme.* First, we compare EC2 to five LLNL HPC clusters based on total turnaround time for a typical set of HPC benchmarks at different scales; for queue wait time on the HPC clusters, we use a distribution developed from simulations with actual traces. Second, to enable a comparison on total cost of execution, we develop an economic model to price LLNL clusters assuming that they are offered as cloud resources at node-hour prices. Because at reasonable scales, cloud computing platforms guarantee zero queuing delay, we disregard waiting time while modeling prices. Using well-known methods in economics on commodity resource pricing, the model achieves profit maximization from the perspective of the cloud provider. Using these node-hour prices, we then compare EC2 with the LLNL HPC clusters and argue that from a cost effectiveness perspective, applications should be mapped to the most appropriate cluster, which is not necessarily the highest performing one.

We make the following contributions in this paper.

- We evaluate EC2 and HPC clusters along the traditional axis of execution time at reasonable scales (over 1000 cores).

- We develop a pricing model to evaluate HPC clusters in node-hour prices based on system performance, resource availability, and user bias.

- We evaluate EC2 and HPC clusters along more general axes, including total turnaround time and total cost. This provides to the best of our knowledge the first comparison of EC2 and HPC clusters from a *user perspective* (as opposed to a data center perspective [34, 36]).

Our results show that the decision of whether to choose EC2 or HPC clusters is complicated. First, EC2 nodes are high-end and, thus, performance is comparable to HPC clusters on EC2 for some applications that incur modest communication. However, we confirm prior results showing that communication intensive applications are typically inefficient on EC2 [34]. Second and more importantly, while HPC clusters usually provide the best execution time, queue wait time on these frequently oversubscribed resources can lead to much larger turnaround times. For example, when median wait time is exceeded, total turnaround time on the LLNL machines is often larger than that on EC2 (sometimes by more than a factor of 4) even though execution time on LLNL machines (once the application starts) can be several times faster. Finally, using the modeled node-hour prices, we show that the choice of most cost-effective cluster for an application is non-trivial and depends on application scalability as well as user bias of cost versus turnaround time. For example, for a cost bound of $5000 per hour, the optimal cluster choice for LAMMPS is EC2, leading to a 51% lower turnaround time than the fastest cluster. On the other hand, given a 90 second time bound, it is 8.2% cheaper to run LU on Hera (an LLNL machine) than the fastest cluster.

The rest of this paper is organized as follows. Section 2 provides background of EC2 and motivates our comparison of EC2 to HPC clusters. Section 3 describes the machines and provides our experimental setup. Section 4 provides comparison of raw system performance. Section 5 provides an evaluation based on queue wait times and turnaround times, and Section 6 compares based on our pricing model. Section 7 discusses the implication of our results. We provide related work and our conclusions in Sections 8 and 9.

2. BACKGROUND AND MOTIVATION

The term *cloud computing* is somewhat difficult to define precisely. A traditional definition is that it provides, at an actual monetary cost to the end-user, computation, software, data access, and storage that requires no end-user knowledge about physical location and system configuration [32]. From a high-performance computing (HPC) perspective, the cloud provides a choice of different clusters.

Each cluster potentially provides different resources: number and type of cores, amount of memory, storage, and network latency and bandwidth. In this paper, we assume homogeneous computing, though we realize that certain cloud providers may not always make this guarantee for all of their clusters.

2.1 EC2 Basics

We focus on the most popular cloud platform, which is Amazon EC2 [6]. Amazon sells several kinds of *virtual machine* instances (VMs), which comprise cluster nodes. A virtual machine is an isolated, guest operating system that exists within a host system. There can be many virtual machines in one physical machine, and consequently a virtual machine has *resources*, as defined by an instance, that can be up to, but not exceeding, the resources on the physical machine.

Amazon EC2 markets several different instances, which are distinguished by different computational and network capabilities. In this paper we focus on the highest-end instance, called "cluster compute eight extra large", because it is the instance intended for HPC applications. EC2 also markets several kinds of ways of purchasing time on their systems; in this paper we use *on-demand* pricing, in which the user pays money for each VM instance and receives access to the purchased node immediately. We leave consideration of *reserved* and *spot-market* pricing for future work.

By default EC2 does not provide any guarantees of physical node proximity [15]. However, EC2 does allow physical proximity through a *placement group* on Cluster Compute. It is unclear how many nodes in a placement group a user can acquire without wait times similar to batch systems. In our experiments, we observed no delay due to placement groups, but we used at most 128 nodes. Compared with HPC systems, though, batch systems cannot guarantee physically proximate nodes either (they perform best effort [22]).

We emphasize that the cloud notion of having *no wait time* has limits. Executions on tens of thousands of cloud nodes [8], for one-time capability or hero type program executions, likely require some wait time or pre-arrangement with the cloud provider. These kind of runs are clearly better suited for resources as large compute centers, where control and scheduling is local and machines can be used for dedicated application times (note that such jobs will also not be handled by batch queuing systems any more and do require manual intervention or scheduling). In this paper, however, we focus on job sizes that are below that threshold and occur frequently, as those make up a vast majority of HPC workloads, in particular production workloads. Those jobs can be easily handled by the pooled resources of cloud providers and therefore require no wait time.

2.2 Comparing EC2 to HPC Clusters

As mentioned above, this paper compares EC2 and HPC clusters using turnaround time and cost; the latter necessitates developing a pricing model for HPC clusters. Even if HPC clusters are "free", the user may consider a cloud cluster for the following reasons[1]. First, the application may be compute intensive, and some of the nodes offered by EC2 may execute such applications faster than HPC nodes, as cloud providers typically can afford a faster upgrade/refresh

---

[1] In this paper, we do not consider the trivializing case where a user does not have access to an HPC cluster.

240

cycle for their machine park. Second, the application may execute faster from actual start time to finish on an HPC cluster, but the total turnaround time on the cloud may be less because of wait queue delay on the HPC clusters.

The second point above must be tempered by cost. That is, if we expand our notion of execution time to a less traditional metric such as total turnaround time, we cannot ignore the cost difference between an EC2 node (significant) and an HPC node ("free"). On the other hand, the HPC node is not really "free", and for a fair cost comparison, we need to create a pricing model.

Thus, there is a trade-off if one evaluates an EC2 cluster versus an HPC cluster on the basis of cost and performance. It depends on many factors, including the application, the current cluster utilization, and the cost per node. The goal of this paper is to try to characterize these factors and to better understand in which situations using EC2 for traditional HPC applications makes sense. Note that in this paper, we do not make any judgments about the relative importance of turnaround time and cost.

3. EXPERIMENTAL SETUP

This section describes our experimental setup and test platforms. First, we provide a description of all test systems and benchmarks used in our evaluation. Second, we describe configurations used by the benchmarks.

3.1 Machine and Benchmark Description

Table 1 shows configurations for our test systems. Five of our systems reside at Lawrence Livermore National Laboratory (LLNL), which we refer to as "LLNL clusters" or "HPC clusters" interchangeably in the rest of the paper. Sierra and Cab are newer clusters at LLNL. Sierra consists of 1849 Intel Xeon 5660 with 12 cores per node, a clock speed of 2.8 GHz, 12 MB cache, and a memory size of 24 GB/node. Cab has 1296 Intel Xeon 2670 nodes with 16 cores per node, a clock speed of 2.6 GHz, 20 MB cache, and a memory size of 32 GB/node. Both Sierra and Cab have Infiniband QDR inter-node connectivity. Hyperion runs 1152 nodes with 8 cores per node, a clock speed of 2.5 GHz, 6MB cache, 12 GB/node system memory and Infiniband DDR inter-node connectivity. Currently, the largest partition available on Hyperion contains 304 nodes. Hera is a somewhat older system; it has 800 Opteron nodes with 16 cores per node, clock speed of 2.3 GHz, 512 KB cache, a memory size of 32 GB/node, and Infiniband DDR inter-node connectivity. LLNL also hosts uDawn, a BlueGene/P systems. It has 2048 nodes running IBM PowerPC processors with a clock speed of 850 MHz, 4 cores per node, 2 KB caches and a memory size of 2 GB/node.It is connected internally by a 3D torus network for point-to-point communication.

Amazon EC2 offers two HPC-oriented virtual machines: Cluster Compute Quadruple Extra Large "CC1" and Cluster Compute Eight Extra Large "CC2". In this paper we focus on the more powerful instance, CC2, which consists of Xeon Sandy Bridge processors with two oct-cores, a clock speed of 2.59 GHz, 20 MB cache, a memory size of 60.5 GB/node, and 10 Gb Ethernet inter-node connectivity. CC2 has hardware-assisted virtualization support to reduce overhead. For convenience we most often refer to this as simply "EC2" in the rest of the paper.

We use benchmarks from the NAS Parallel [7], ASC Sequoia [5], and ASC Purple [1] benchmark suites. Specifi-

cally, we run CG, EP, BT, LU and SP from the NAS suite; Sweep3D and LAMMPS from ASC Sequoia, and SMG2000 from ASC Purple. We did not execute all of the programs from a given suite because we wanted some diversity, and executing all of the benchmarks from each suite would have taken several extra hours of compute. The cost per hour at scale (128 nodes/1024 tasks) on EC2 is over $300.

3.2 Program Setup

We used MVAPICH-1.7 (for the LLNL clusters) and MPICH2 (for the EC2 clusters). We compile all benchmarks using the -O2 option. All experiments avoid execution on core 0. This is because EC2 currently pins all interrupts on to core 0. For communication intensive programs, this causes severe load imbalance on core 0 and significant performance degradation, a problem first reported by Petrini [27]; and, we borrow their solution of leaving core 0 unused. We executed separate experiments that show that using core 0 leads to as much as a 500% overhead on our benchmarks. Personal communication with Amazon indicates that in the near future interrupt handling will be spread throughout the cores [29], and we expect that this problem will then cease to exist.

However, we go further and, in fact, use only *half* of the available cores on a node (except on Sierra, where we use 8 out of the 12 available cores because of the power-of-two nature of the benchmarks). We use only half of the cores because to use 15 out of the 16 cores on a node would lead to an uneven core distribution (e.g., 64 cores spread over 6 nodes with 15 utilized cores each and one node with 4 cores). This can cause additional communication and imbalances in the applications due to the particular topology mapping chosen by individual MPI implementations (which are different between the LLNL clusters and the EC2 clusters). Our experiments show that on a core-to-node mapping that is a power-of-two, this additional communication is minimized. We also disabled hyperthreading on the EC2 cluster, because our experiments showed that hyperthreading most often degrades performance.

We use strong scaling, so in each set of results, all of the benchmark sizes are identical across different MPI task counts, and we configure the benchmarks to run for between 30 and 170 seconds on EC2 across all scales. For the NAS programs, we edited npbparams.h directly; the benchmark sizes were close to class C (sometimes smaller, sometimes larger). For SMG2000, we use a size of 65x65x65 at 1024 tasks, and then adjusted sizes accordingly at lower scales to convert it to a strongly scaled application. For Sweep3d, we use the makeinput utility and modified the sizes. For LAMMPS, we use the Lennard-Jones input deck.

Our benchmarks cover a wide variety of message characteristics. Many are communication intensive (BT, CG, LU, and SP), sending, per MPI rank, at least 100K messages totaling at least 1 GB (SP sends over 2 GB per rank). SMG2000 sends about 400 MB per rank. LAMMPS sends about 200 MB per rank, but did so over far fewer messages (only about 1000 per rank), and has far less time spent in MPI communication than BT, CG, LU, SMG2000, or SP. Finally, EP is computation intensive, sending only about 1 KB per rank.

4. COMPARING RAW PERFORMANCE

This section describes our base performance evaluation of clusters at LLNL and EC2. First, we measure point-to-point

Cluster	CPU speed (GHz)	Cache size (MB)	Memory size (GB)	Cores/Node	Interconnect Technology	Cost ($/Hour)
Sierra	2.8	12	24	12	Infiniband QDR	—
Hera	2.3	0.5	32	16	Infiniband DDR	—
Cab	2.6	20	32	16	Infiniband QDR	—
Hyperion	2.4	6.0	12	8	Infiniband DDR	—
uDawn	0.85	0.02	2	4	3D Torus	—
EC2	2.59	20	23	16	10 GigE	2.4

Table 1: System specification for our test systems

	Cab	Hera	Sierra	Hyperion	uDawn	EC2
Latency	1.61 μs	2.23 μs	1.58 μs	1.91 μs	2.92 μs	55.15 μs
Bandwidth	22.6 Gb/s	9.3 Gb/s	23.1 Gb/s	16.9 Gb/s	3.1 Gb/s	3.7 Gb/s

Table 2: Network latency and bandwidth for Cab, Hera, Sierra, Hyperion, uDawn and EC2

latency and bandwidth between physical nodes. Second, we analyze computation performance of a single node on each cluster with single-task configurations of standard HPC benchmarks. Third, we evaluate execution times at scales of up to 1024 tasks with standard HPC benchmarks.

4.1 Raw Computation and Communication Performance Evaluation

We use a set of simple microbenchmarks to measure performance of individual system parameters. Our tests cover network latency and bandwidth between nodes as well as relative single node computation performance.

First, we present the results of network latency and bandwidth, using a standard ping-pong benchmark, in Table 2. The experiments show that Sierra has the least inter-node latency and the fastest bandwidth. This is due to the Infiniband QDR technology used for communication. uDawn employs a 3-D Torus network for MPI point-to-point communication with about 5 times higher latency and 3 times lower bandwidth compared to Infiniband QDR in Sierra. EC2 shows low variance in network bandwidth, confirming previous work [13]; however, the latency is at least 50 times higher than Sierra. These times are consistent with results reported elsewhere [36, 34].

To understand the computation power of the systems, we executed the benchmarks with a single MPI task. Table 3 shows the result of executing all of our benchmarks on one MPI task. Each machine is expressed in terms of average speedup over uDawn, which is the cluster with worst single-node performance. The highest performing node is Cab, and the next fastest is EC2; both are the same architecture with different processor speeds. We used the Stream benchmark [24] to measure the memory bandwidth and latency on both Cab and EC2 nodes. We found that Cab has 40% higher memory bandwidth and about 30% lower memory latency than EC2. This affected performance of some memory-bound benchmarks such as BT and CG by as much as 30%. Also, our EC2 cluster does not co-locate virtual machines [29] and, because as stated above we avoid core 0, there is no significant noise overhead.

We did not specifically perform tests to try to characterize the virtualization overhead, because we do not have identical, non-virtualized nodes with which to compare. However, as shown earlier, sequential performance on EC2 nodes is quite good, even if virtualization overhead exists (plus, there

is hardware support to reduce it). Others have studied the impact of virtualization on HPC applications [35, 18].

4.2 Execution Time at Scale

In this section, we first present results of our MPI benchmarks that allow us to compare EC2, Cab, Sierra, Hyperion, Hera and uDawn. We use 128 nodes and a total of 1024 MPI tasks. Second, we provide scaling results from 256 tasks to 1024 tasks.

We first consider the difference in execution time for the various systems, i.e., the elapsed time from program start to program end. Figure 1 shows the median values collected during at least three runs on the systems (normalized to EC2 times, with a breakdown of relative computation and communication time shown also). For the most part, our results here are similar to execution time measurements collected by others [36, 19], in the sense that communication-intensive applications have significant overhead on the cloud due to the use of 10 Gb/s Ethernet instead of Infiniband[2]. LU performs 1.3-2.6 times worse on EC2 than LLNL clusters, except uDawn, due to communication time dominating program execution. Due to their similarity to LU in relative performance on EC2 and HPC clusters, we do not show numbers for BT, CG and SP (space considerations prohibit it later in the paper, so we omit them everywhere for uniformity). SMG2000 performs 1.9-4.6 times worse on EC2 than Cab, Sierra and Hyperion, and about 28% slower than Hera.

For EP, EC2 is slower than Cab by 12% and faster than other clusters. For Sweep3D, EC2 is the fastest cluster. Somewhat surprisingly, EC2 outperforms both Hyperion and Hera on LAMMPS, but is 68% and 29% slower than Cab and Sierra, respectively. While these three codes do have non-trivial communication at 1024 tasks, the superiority of the EC2 nodes compensates somewhat for its inferior communication infrastructure.

Out of all LLNL clusters, uDawn shows slowest performance for most of the benchmarks. This is because uDawn uses slower, more power efficient processors and employs slower interconnects than Infiniband; its strength is that the BlueGene design scales to large node counts. In case of compute-bound applications, uDawn performs 4.2-4.7 times

---

[2] As mentioned earlier, Microsoft Azure has announced its intention to offer an Infiniband-based cluster [33], which will presumably have competitive performance with HPC clusters.

uDawn	Cab	Sierra	Hyperion	Hera	EC2
1.00	9.55	7.30	7.22	3.62	8.22

Table 3: Relative sequential performance (normalized to uDawn) for Cab, Sierra, Hyperion, Hera and EC2.

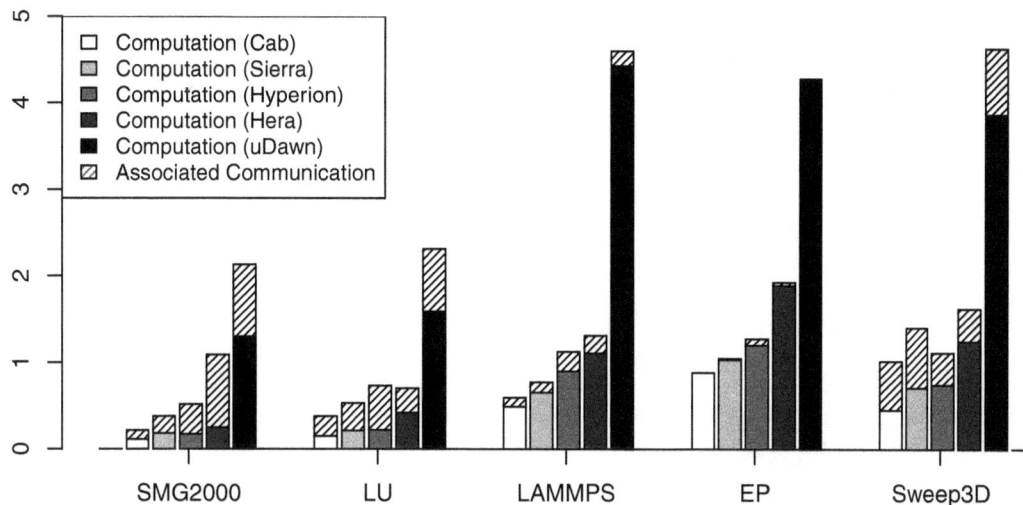

Figure 1: Comparison of execution times on Cab, Sierra, Hyperion, Hera, uDawn and EC2 clusters (128 nodes/1024 tasks). Times are normalized to those of EC2, and the relative percentage spent in computation and communication is shown.

slower than EC2 with 1K tasks, even though uDawn has negligible system noise.

5. TURNAROUND TIME COMPARISON

This section compares job turnaround times on HPC and EC2 clusters on a variety of job sizes and core/node counts. Turnaround time is the sum of execution time and job queuing delay. We evaluate execution time using standard HPC benchmarks at large scales. We evaluate job queuing delay by both real and simulated experiments at different task scales and sizes that represent real-world jobs.

5.1 Queue Wait Times

This section is concerned with comparing total turnaround times, which is the time between submission of the job and completion of the program. LLNL clusters use batch submission and are optimized for execution time. On the other hand, EC2 optimizes for turnaround time [29].

To measure turnaround time, we need to know queue wait time, which varies with HPC cluster, job size, and maximum run time. On EC2, using on-demand instances with non-excessively-sized requests, we observed low queue wait times. However, HPC clusters are well utilized by a large number of users and hence can have significant queue wait time.

Estimating wait time is particularly tricky because (1) the batch submission algorithm used is opaque, and (2) queue wait time may not be linear in the number of nodes or time requested. To estimate the wait time, we therefore simulate job execution times using the Alea-3 simulator [21]. Job scheduling on LLNL clusters is performed by the Simple Linux Utility for Resource Management (SLURM) job

scheduler, which employs First-Come First-Serve and Backfilling algorithms [4]. We configure Alea-3 to match the SLURM properties using the Easy Backfilling algorithm, which is optimized for throughput, provided the maximum job execution time is specified at submission. Additionally, we modify the simulator to handle node-level allocations and output queue wait times. We use job logs for ANL's Intrepid cluster from the Parallel Workloads Archive [3] collected during January 2009 to September 2009. We chose Intrepid logs since it provided similar volume of workload compared to LLNL's Sierra, Hera, Cab, Hyperion and uDawn clusters. To estimate the wait times on each cluster, we configure the simulator separately with the machine specification for each LLNL cluster. For each cluster, we manually add jobs with a unique identifier at 12 hour intervals to probe for queue wait times in the simulation. These probe jobs were configured to measure wait times at task counts from 32 up to 1024 in steps of powers of 2. We set the maximum job time (the time at which, the program, if still executing, is killed) to (separately) 2 minutes and 5 hours (somewhat arbitrarily).

To validate our numbers, we also collect job wait times on Sierra and Hera at similar job sizes. The maximum job time was set to 2 minutes and 5 hours, and we submitted the jobs at 10 A.M. and 10 P.M. every day for two months. We would have liked to execute these experiments with a larger variety of maximum job execution times. However, we did not, as we wanted to minimize our consumption of LLNL resources.

The results are shown in Figure 2 as a series of boxplots, which show the median in addition to the ranges of each quartile. For real experiments, queue wait times increase with an increase in maximum job execution time, as long as a

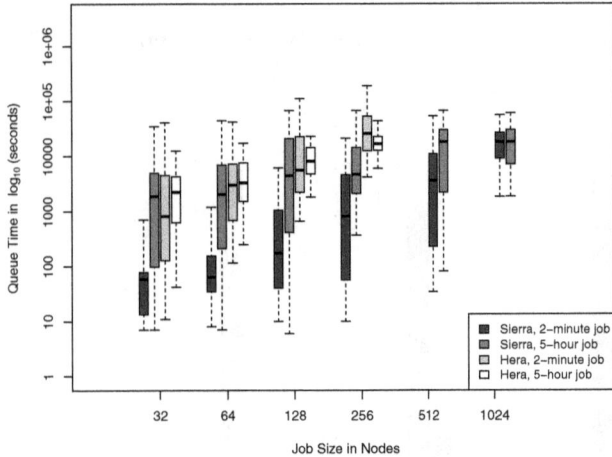

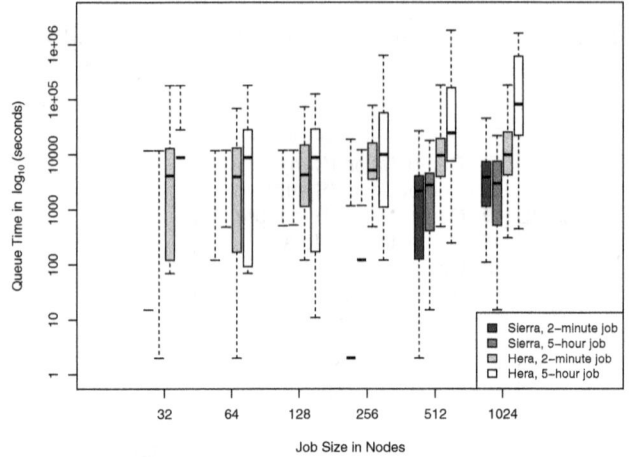

Figure 2: Boxplots showing comparison of (a) real queue wait times and (b) simulated queue wait times at different node counts on Sierra and Hera

node request is below a significant percentage of the available nodes (which is roughly 64 nodes on Hera and between 512 and 1024 nodes on Sierra). In addition, the data shows that even for the two-minute jobs, there are potentially significant wait times.

Although the real clusters can have different workloads than the one used in our simulation, simulated runs show similar trends for queue wait times at increasing scales and job limits. For example, median values for simulated and real queue wait times for Sierra at 512 and 1024 tasks fall in the same range. Similarly, median simulated queue wait times for Hera at 128 and 256 tasks follow corresponding numbers in real experiments. Also, Sierra shows lower queue wait times than Hera in both simulated and real experiments, typically at higher scales, due to higher resource availability. Thus, the real queue wait times validate simulated queue wait times at relevant scales. Hence, we use simulated numbers for other clusters for the analysis of total turnaround times.

On EC2, we measured queue wait time as the time from request submission to MPI hostfile setup on all nodes, because that is when an MPI program can be initiated. We measured wait times of 146 seconds, 189 seconds and 244 seconds to acquire 16, 32 and 64 EC2 nodes, respectively. Due to limited funds (each experiment to measure startup time on 64 nodes costs $150), we iterated our experiments few times, and our measurements are not statistically significant. However, because the wait times on EC2 are clearly orders of magnitude lower than those on LLNL clusters, this does not affect the validity of our overall findings.

5.2 Turnaround Time

In this section, we focus on the same six machines (EC2, Cab, Sierra, Hyperion, Hera and uDawn), but turn our attention to total turnaround time. Figure 3 presents a statistical representation of total turnaround time on all machines at three different MPI task counts: 256, 512, and 1024. The data is presented as follows. We scale the execution times

on each LLNL cluster for an application on a 5-hour scale relative to execution times on EC2. The lower edge of the boxplot represents normalized execution time. Note that the fourth quartile of the boxplot is not visible because of the queue wait time distribution and normalization. We then add queue wait times on the respective clusters to get total turnaround times. Thus the combined plot shows the factor of total turnaround time for each application compared to EC2 total turnaround time. Because queue wait time is a distribution, we use a boxplot to represent it; here, we use the results we collected for the 5-hour wait times.

The results show two general trends: First, in many cases, the EC2 execution time is better at lower scales. For example, EP and LAMMPS on most clusters have higher execution times than EC2, especially at 256 tasks. In such situations, of course, total turnaround time will be much better on EC2, as queue wait time is an additive penalty on higher-end LLNL clusters. However, as we increase the number of MPI tasks, higher-end LLNL clusters scale better than EC2; again, this is not surprising as (1) we are using strong scaling, and (2) higher-end LLNL clusters use Infiniband, and EC2 uses 10 Gb Ethernet.

Second, at higher task counts, demand for more resources generally causes longer turnaround times. For example, consider applications LU and SMG2000 at 1024 MPI tasks. Clearly, the queue wait time governs turnaround time for most of the clusters (except uDawn, which consistently shows higher execution times than EC2). That is, for these applications, if the queue wait times fall within the first quartile, LLNL clusters are superior. On the other hand, if the queue wait times fall in the fourth quartile, then EC2 is clearly better. If the queue wait time falls in the second or third quartile, which system is better depends on (1) where in the quartile the wait time falls, along with (2) the relative superiority of the execution time on HPC clusters.

The effect of wait queue times is more pronounced for applications with overall higher computation times at higher scales, due to better execution times on EC2. For example,

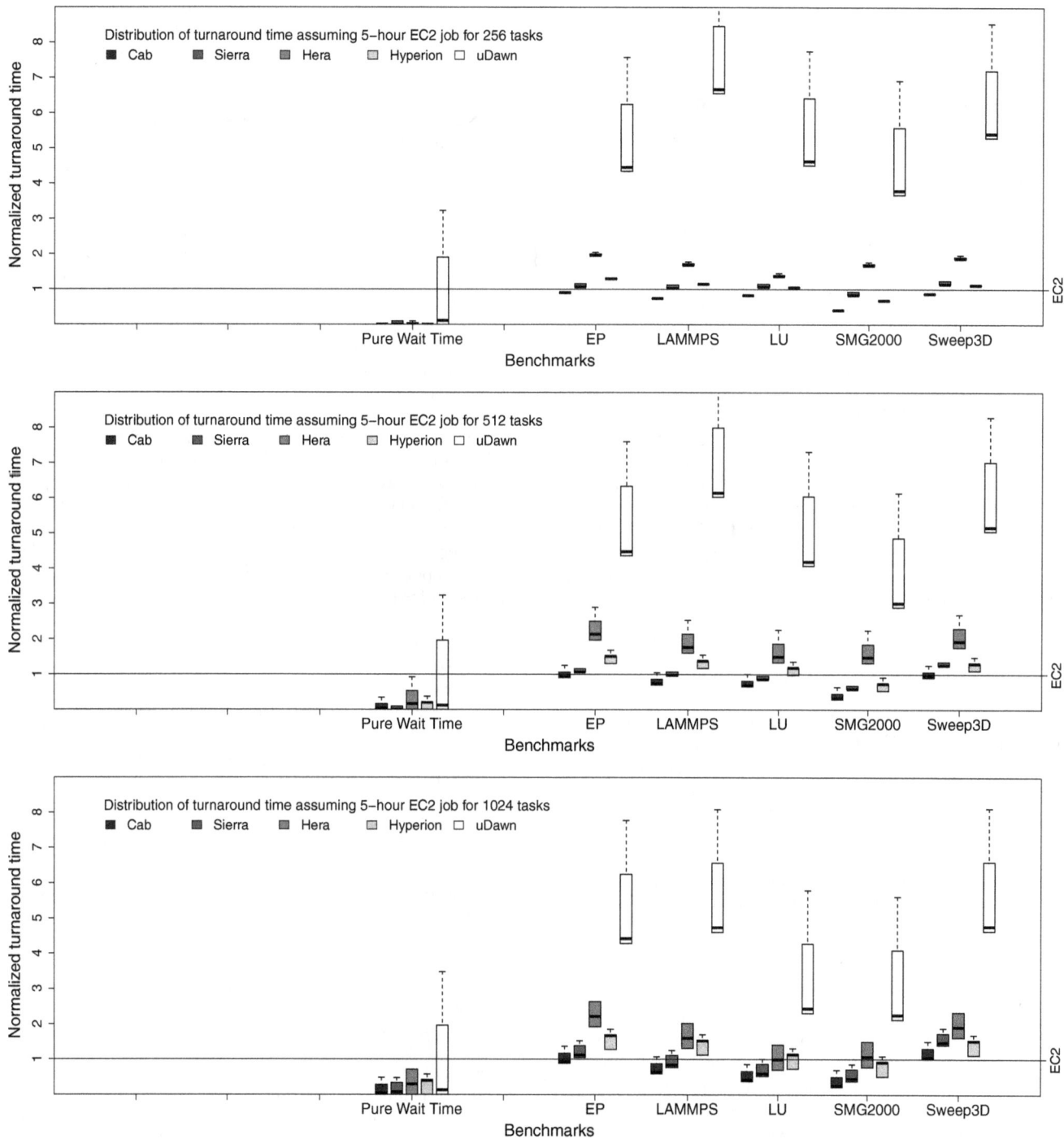

Figure 3: Comparison of total turnaround times on EC2 and LLNL clusters on 256, 512, and 1024 tasks. The figure shows turnaround times on LLNL clusters normalized to the EC2 turnaround times assuming 5-hour jobs on EC2. The y-axis represents multiples of EC2 turnaround time.

Application	Cab	Sierra	Hyperion	Hera	uDawn
EP	25%	0%	0%	0%	0%
Sweep3D	0%	0%	0%	0%	0%
LU	40%	35%	15%	25%	0%
SMG2000	35%	0%	0%	0%	0%
LAMMPS	35%	25%	0%	0%	0%

Table 4: Percentage of time that LLNL clusters are expected to have lower turnaround time than EC2 for a 1024 tasks job.

consider Sweep3D, EP and LAMMPS on LLNL clusters and EC2 at 1024 MPI tasks. In most cases, EC2 turnaround time (horizontal line) falls below HPC cluster execution times.

We can also view the expected wait time using existing methods such as QBETS[26]. With QBETS, a binomial is used to determine a confidence level that a given percentage of jobs will have lower wait time than one of the values from the pool of measured wait time samples. Prediction accuracy of the binomial method in QBETS has been shown to be quite good (close to the actual time on average). We use a confidence level of 95%, and we find, for each application, the percentage of time that LLNL clusters are expected to have lower turnaround time than EC2 at 1024 tasks. The results are shown in Table 4 (page eight). In the table, for the 0% case, such as Sweep3D, the applications run faster on EC2 than the other clusters. For other cases, the table shows that even on the fastest machine, Cab, the expectation ranges from 25% to 40%. This shows that the queue wait time can be a dominating factor on many clusters.

6. COST COMPARISON

In this section, we compare the EC2 and HPC clusters based on total cost of execution. Because clusters at LLNL are free to end users, we derive node-hour prices relative the market price of the EC2 CC2 cluster ($2.40 per node hour). We expect that clusters similar to the HPC clusters we are using in this paper will be available shortly (but we have no pricing information yet) [33]. Other factors in influencing node-hour prices include system performance, scalability and availability of resources.

This section is organized as follows. First, we present our methodology, which draws on economic theory, to price LLNL clusters. Second, using the generated node-hour prices, we present a cost-performance analysis.

6.1 Pricing Methodology

To compare clusters on the cost axis, we need to generate reasonable prices for currently un-priced clusters. One approach might be to view computation as a public utility and base prices only on the cost of ownership for the cluster operator. Cost data is not publicly available, however, and would not be publishable if we were able to obtain it; this necessitates an alternate model.

The approach we take is to assume the LLNL clusters are operated as a competitor in a market for computation. This results in generated prices that are naturally comparable to Amazon's EC2 cluster and provides for the future possibility of additional types of analysis (e.g. optimizing future machine acquisition based on the market value of individual components' effects on performance). To be clear, we are *not* implying that publicly procured computational re-

sources should be priced this way (or priced at all). Instead, we are studying how a competitively priced situation would inform a cost-time performance analysis.

Our competitive model is developed with economic theory by nesting a model of users making optimal execution choices, given pricing and timing information, inside a model of a profit-maximizing cluster operator. Amazon's EC2 cluster is included as an outside option with a fixed price, and the operator chooses prices relative to Amazon's.

Users are assumed to have a fixed problem size. That is, they are not choosing the size of the problem to execute, only which cluster and how many nodes to split the work over. There are four user types, defined by the type of application they are running, each modeled by the speedup properties of LU, CG, BT and SP, where we took care to balance computation and communication so as not to bias the HPC or EC2 clusters. As explained later, our user model requires that we develop a continuous performance prediction function, and we use linear regression to do this. On HPC clusters, we use job scales of up to 2048 tasks to obtain sufficient data for regression, while on on EC2 we had to limit ourselves to job scales of up to 128 tasks due to limited funds. To gather enough data points to obtain sufficient significance in the linear regression, we run benchmarks 8 times at each task count. We adjust input sizes by modifying the `npb-params.h` file so that each benchmark has a total execution time of 30-500 seconds, which is large enough to compensate for variance introduced by system noise and virtualization overhead. For each cluster/application pair, execution time is modeled by a execution time function derived using a standard Ordinary Least Squares regression. Using a continuous timing model allows the user model to optimize over all possible choices of node counts, instead of restricting choices only to the set of benchmark experimental runs.

The user must choose among the available computational clusters, each with hourly price p, then decide how many nodes n to purchase. The optimal choice is defined to be that which minimizes the combined implicit and explicit costs of execution [20], $C = (p \times n \times t(n)) + (a \times t(n))$. The explicit cost, $p \times n \times t(n)$, is the actual expenditure incurred by purchasing the nodes for the time required to execute the application. The implicit cost, $a \times t(n)$, may have different interpretations depending on the context. In a business or scientific environment, this may be a literal cost incurred by waiting longer for execution to finish, for example, from giving to delay a cost-saving decision dependent on the results. In this case, parameter a is the hourly cost of waiting. Alternatively, for an individual user, a would represent the individual's personal relative valuation of time. In this case, a large a may be due to a looming deadline, or other behavioral influences that cause a person to prefer shorter execution times.

A cluster operator can then use this model of user choice to predict purchase decisions, given a candidate set of hourly node prices for each cluster. These predictions can in turn be used to achieve a particular operational objective. Here, we assume that the operator wishes to maximize profit, though achieving target utilization rates for each cluster might be a plausible alternative.

To predict the user's choice, first, for each (cluster i, user type u) pair and candidate set of prices, we solve for the optimal (cost-minimizing) number of nodes $n_{ui}(p)$. This function (evaluated for all possible prices) represents the

CC2	Hera	Sierra	Hyperion	uDawn	Cab
2.40	2.36	3.83	2.13	0.25	5.49

Table 5: Node-hour prices (in dollars) for LLNL and EC2 clusters

user's classical demand function for nodes on this cluster. In our case, the functional form of $t(n)$ means that there is no closed-form solution for $n_{ui}(p)$, so n must be found with an optimization algorithm.

Next, for each user type, we calculate the probability that the user will choose each cluster using the Logit Random Utility model [30]. In short, this model states that there are unobservable factors that cause some noise to be added to the user's cost function C, and models this noise with a Logit distribution. This results in the following formula:

$$s_{ui} = e^{-C_{ui}} / \sum_{j} (e^{-C_{uj}})$$

s_{ui} can be interpreted in two ways: for an individual user, it is the probability that a user of type u chooses cluster i; for a population of users, it is the market share for cluster i among users of type u. That is, it is the proportion of users of type u that choose cluster i. The operator can then choose the set of prices that results in the desired objective. Here we assume that (1) the operator is profit-maximizing over the short run, such that only hourly operational costs, and not acquisition costs, are relevant, and (2) the hourly costs of operation are effectively the same for all clusters. These assumptions mean that profit maximization is equivalent to revenue maximization. Clearly, these assumptions may not hold in the real world, but they do not substantively change the way the model works and are therefore acceptable abstractions given the absence of available cost data. Using this model, the expected profit/revenue is then calculated as the sum over the clusters and users of the expected revenue, or:

$$R = \sum_{i} (\sum_{u} (s_{ui} \times p \times n_{ui}(p) \times t(n_{ui}(p))))$$

Table 5 shows the results obtained by our model by choosing prices p to maximize R. At each iteration of the maximization algorithm, user choice as a function of price $n_{ui}(p)$ is obtained by the user's cost-minimization problem as described above.

6.2 Cost vs Performance Comparison

In this section we present cost-performance trade-offs for our MPI benchmark set using the prices obtained in the previous section. We consider pure execution times for comparison (that is, zero wait times), as we assume equal distribution of jobs across all clusters. The purpose of this section is to answer the following questions. First, what is the trade-off between execution time and cost at various scales? Second, if the user has a turnaround time bound (e.g., "finish the weather prediction for tomorrow before the evening newscast at 7pm"), is the most cost-effective way to do that always to use the fastest cluster (Cab), or might using a less powerful cluster be better?

Figure 4 shows the trade-off between cost and turnaround time. The figure is displayed as a scatterplot of turnaround time (x-axis) and cost (y-axis), with the points representing the same cluster connected to show scalability of each cluster. In general, computational scientists execute large programs for large amounts of time. For practical reasons (again, our cost on EC2), we execute short programs. Because this does not map well to the hour billing granularity used by EC2, we compensate by pro-rating the hourly rate for the given execution time. The pro-rated hourly rate is obtained by dividing the per-hour node price by 3600 (seconds per hour) and multiplying the result by the execution time and number of nodes. (Essentially, we are assuming the billing function is continuous instead of discrete.) In Figure 4, points closer to origin show superior configuration choice in terms of both cost and performance over other configurations. Points higher in the plot imply higher total cost of execution, while the points towards the right indicate higher execution time. Plots with smaller slopes indicate good application scalability where as larger slopes indicate poor scalability. If addition of nodes to a configuration decreases the slope, it shows better scalability, and hence adding more nodes to the configuration is cost-effective.

There are several interesting cases. First, for different applications, different clusters minimize total cost of execution. For example, the total cost of execution of running EP, Sweep3D, LAMMPS and LU is least on EC2. Except with EP, EC2 is cheapest at 256 tasks. This is because the price of EC2 is optimized for computation bound applications. This is confirmed by the nature of EC2 plot from EP to LU, with slope decreasing in proportion of computation in overall application execution. On the other hand, it is cheapest to run SMG2000 on Cab, even though the Cab nodes are most expensive. This is because the node-hour price of Cab is optimized for applications with significant communication overhead, which characterizes SMG2000 (recall Figure 1).

Second, different clusters optimize performance for certain classes of application characteristics. For example, SMG2000, EP, LU and LAMMPS are fastest on Cab, whereas Sweep3D performs best on EC2. The application characteristics for which the individual clusters are optimized include communication overhead, communication topology and cache pressure. From the architectural specifications, we can see that clusters with fast interconnects, certain cores per node and larger L2 cache per processor show better performance with applications characterized to use these resources. For example, Sierra and Cab are optimized for communication performance (with Infiniband QDR), which is well suited for SMG2000 and LU. Also, Cab, Hera, EC2 and Hyperion have cores per node in powers of two, which provides optimal communication topology for BT benchmark. Finally, EC2 and Cab are optimized for applications with high cache pressure, such as CG, as Cab has 20 MB of cache per processor.

Third, if a turnaround time bound exists, then optimizing cost may require using one of the less-powerful or more expensive clusters. For example, on LU with a turnaround time bound of 90 seconds (shown with a grey vertical line), Hera is the cheapest option at 1024 tasks. Recall that EC2, which runs more cores per node, is the cheapest option without a time bound at 256 tasks. Likewise, with a turnaround time bound of 8 seconds with EP, the cheapest choice of cluster is Cab at 1024 tasks, because both cost about the same. Without a time bound, EC2 is the cheapest option at 512 tasks. A similar situation can occur if a cost bound

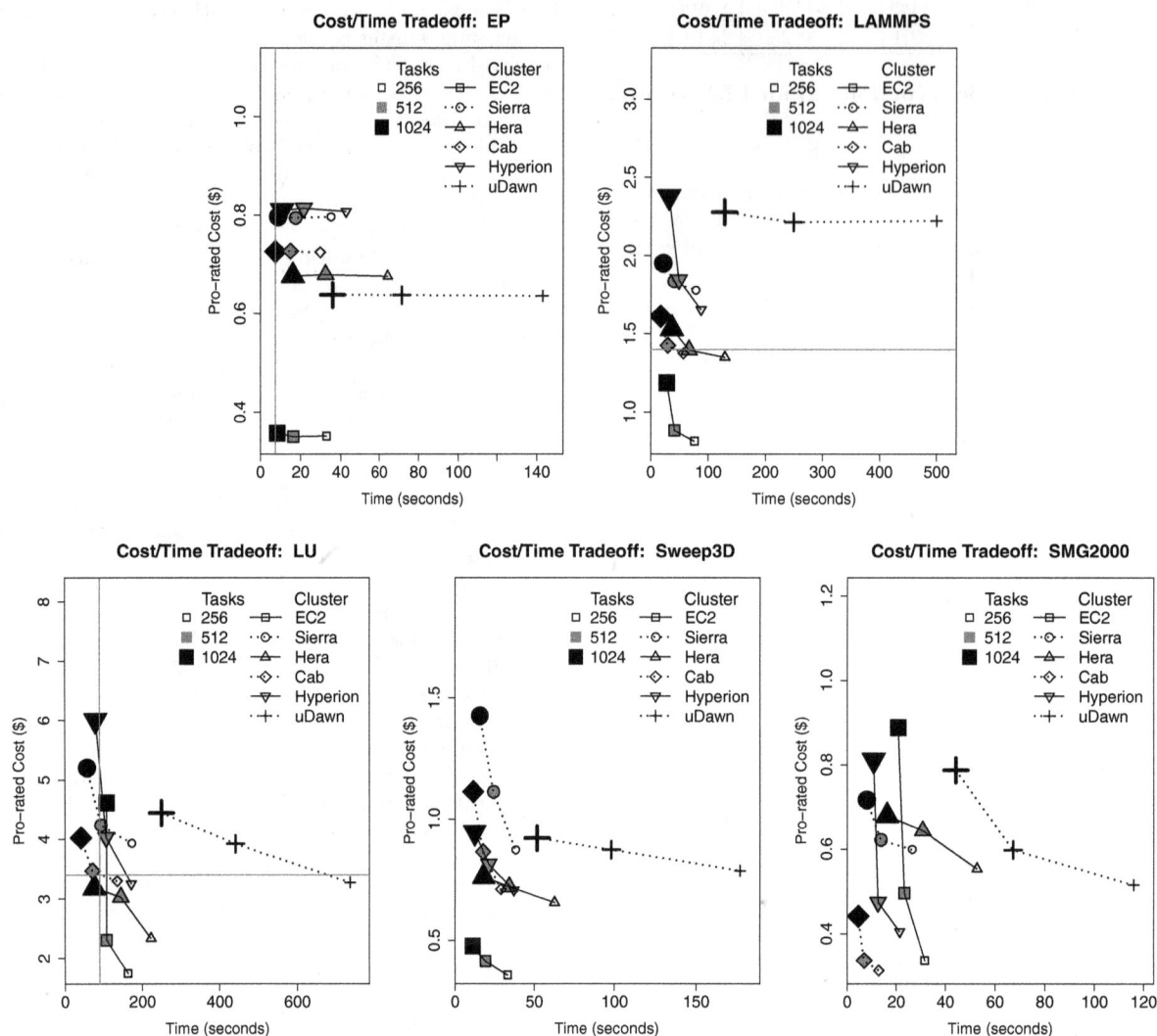

Figure 4: Cost versus turnaround time comparison for LLNL and CC2 clusters. Increasing sizes and darker shades indicate higher task counts. Different scales are used for each plot for readability. Vertical and horizontal lines indicate user cost and turnaround time constraints.

exists. For example, for a cost bound of $5000 per hour ($1.39 per second) with LAMMPS, EC2 is the fastest choice at 1024 tasks. Similarly, with a cost bound of $12000 per hour ($3.33 per second) with LU, Hera is the fastest choice at 1024 tasks. Without a cost bound, LAMMPS and LU run fastest on Cab at 1024 tasks. Thus, for either a time or a cost bound, we observe that the optimal choice of cluster is non-trivial.

7. DISCUSSION AND FUTURE WORK

Our evaluation reveals several interesting items. First, we establish that the choice of which cluster to use is dependent on the application, queue wait time, price, and the user's bias towards either turnaround time or total cost. Obviously, the user does not have the luxury of exhaustively trying all clusters and then deciding which was best after the fact. In our opinion, this motivates designing software

systems that perform cluster selection automatically, which has also been discussed by Li et al. [23]. While this is certainly not a simple task, an effective software system could save users a significant amount of time and money.

Second, in order to develop systems that decide between HPC clusters such as those at LLNL and EC2, it is necessary for the HPC systems to provide wait queue data—likely both historical and current. This would allow analysis to determine the expected wait time on the HPC clusters, which is clearly a critical factor in which cluster to choose. However, there are clear security concerns. These can probably be alleviated by anonymizing some queue data. On the positive side, there should be an incentive for organizations like LLNL to provide this data, as it could reduce demand.

Finally, our pricing model could be useful to the cloud provider in various ways. For example, the user's time preference parameter could be adjusted to improve prices over time depending upon real-world demands. This could be extended to obtain prices at different times of day, week or month, considering that workloads on the cloud spike up due to external known or unknown events. (For example, cloud providers could provision high-throughput resources by asking the question, "What is the time preference on the Black Friday sale?") Conversely, the pricing model could be used to incentivize use of certain resources and avoid oversubscription of other resources. The model could also indicate, based on real-world workload type and demand, which resources to upgrade. For example, if the workload consists primarily of communication-intensive applications, the pricing model would suggest an upgrade of interconnect technology. This would be indicated by low count on optimal number of nodes suggested by the pricing model.

8. RELATED WORK

There is a large body of work related to this paper. We focus on two areas in public clouds (e.g., Amazon EC2 [6], FutureGrid [2], and OpenCirrus [9]): (1) performance analysis of standard HPC benchmarks and comparative usability and (2) cost analysis of running real scientific codes on small, medium and large scale HPC-style clusters.

Amazon EC2 has become increasingly popular with scientific HPC users due to high availability of computational resources at large scale. Several researchers have benchmarked EC2 using MPI programs. Previous work [25, 16, 28, 17, 19, 12, 11, 14, 13] has focused on extensively benchmarking currently available EC2 cluster types with standard MPI benchmarking suites such as NAS [7] and Sequoia [5]. Our work uses both large task counts and takes a user perspective, which has not been studied simultaneously. Also, we investigate the cost/performance tradeoff at different scales on EC2, which to our knowledge has not been investigated.

Several attempts have been made to formalize and compare the cost of running standard HPC benchmarks as well as real applications on Amazon EC2 and standard cluster systems. Formalizing the cost of a standard HPC cluster is not straightforward due to the manner in which the computational resources are charged per user. Walker et al. [31] attempt to formalize the cost of leasing CPU in HPC clusters. Work on comparing the cost of resources on medium-scale university-owned cluster with Amazon EC2 Cluster Compute (CC) instance has been carried out [10]. Cost estimation of a large-scale cluster presented by Yelick et al. [34] involves a detailed modeling of cost of ownership, support, and hardware and software upgrades. The work showed that other factors in total cost include amortized cost of a cluster, utilization rate and job execution times and input sizes. Because resources are charged on an hourly basis, attempts have been made to execute applications cost-effectively. Li et al. [23] present a comparative study of public cloud providers for different real HPC applications. Again, our work differs in the use of turnaround time and cost/performance analysis at scale.

The work most closely related to our work compares the cost of renting virtual machines in the cloud against hosting a cluster [36]. The authors present a detailed analysis of MPI applications on CC1. Also, a cost comparison between CC1 and an HPC cluster is presented with amortized cost calculations.

Our work differs from that above in several ways. Most importantly, our work studies turnaround time and cost; i.e., the perspective of the user, as opposed to the cost of

running a supercomputer center. From the point of view of the owner of the center, operating an HPC cluster is always better as long as the system is reasonably well utilized, and supercomputer centers easily fit that characteristic, as they tend to be oversubscribed.

Other differences also exist with our work. First, the scale at which benchmarks were studied is typically quite small in number of cores/nodes and problem sizes. Second, most of the work employed small and medium instance types provided by Amazon EC2 that are not specifically intended for HPC applications. We present benchmarking results on the recently introduced CC2. Third, most conclusions present network latency and bandwidth, and virtualization overhead as the factors causing application performance degradation. We show that system noise is not significant compared to HPC clusters, so long as core 0 is not utilized.

9. CONCLUSION

This paper evaluated the cloud against traditional high-performance clusters along two axes–turnaround time and cost. We first confirmed prior results that high-end traditional HPC clusters are superior to the cloud in raw performance. However, we also found that queue wait times can potentially increase total turnaround times. Finally, we developed a pricing model for HPC clusters that are currently unpriced. We used the pricing model as a tool to make a fair comparison of traditional HPC and cloud resources in terms of total cost of execution. Our pricing model can be used from the perspective of the user and the provider; in this paper we focused on the user perspective. From that perspective, we found that there are multiple considerations in choosing a cluster, including the expected queue wait time along with the actual cost.

Based on this evaluation, we believe that choosing the optimal cluster is a task that should be abstracted from the typical user. Our goal in our future work is to utilize turnaround time and cost to develop tools and techniques for directing users of diverse sets of applications, given particular constraints, to the most appropriate cluster.

Acknowledgments

Part of this work was performed under the auspices of the U.S. Department of Energy by Lawrence Livermore National Laboratory under Contract DE-AC52-07NA27344 (LLNL-CONF-634532). We also thank Amazon for a grant for time on EC2. Finally, we thank our shepherd, Thilo Kielmann, as well as the anonymous reviewers for comments that improved the quality of this paper.

10. REFERENCES

[1] ASC purple benchmarks. https://asc.llnl.gov/computing_resources/purple/archive/benchmarks/.

[2] Futuregrid project. https://portal.futuregrid.org/.

[3] Parallel workloads archive. http://www.cs.h-uji.ac.il/labs/parallel/workload/.

[4] Simple linux utility for resource management, faq. https://computing.llnl.gov/linux/slurm/faq.html#backfill.

[5] ASC sequoia benchmarks. http://asc.llnl.gov/sequoia/benchmarks/, 2009.

[6] Amazon. Amazon web service elastic compute cloud (EC2). http://aws.amazon.com/ec2.

[7] D. H. Bailey, E. Barszcz, J. T. Barton, D. S. Browning, R. L. Carter, L. Dagum, R. Fatoohi, P. O. Frederickson, T. A. Lasinski, R. Schreiber, H. D. Simon, V. Venkatakrishnan, and S. Weeratunga. The NAS parallel benchmarks–summary and preliminary results. In *Supercomputing*, Nov. 1991.

[8] J. Brodkin. $1,279-per-hour, 30,000 core cluster built on Amazon EC2 cloud. `http://arstechnica.com/business/news/2011/09/30000-core-cluster-built-on-amazon-ec2-cloud.ars`, 2011.

[9] R. Campbell, I. Gupta, M. Heath, S. Y. Ko, M. Kozuch, M. Kunze, T. Kwan, K. Lai, H. Y. Lee, M. Lyons, D. Milojicic, D. O'Hallaron, and Y. C. Soh. Open cirrus cloud computing testbed: federated data centers for open source systems and services research. In *Hot Topics in Cloud Computing*, 2009.

[10] A. G. Carlyle, S. L. Harrell, and P. M. Smith. Cost-effective HPC: The community or the cloud? In *IEEE International Conference on Cloud Computing Technology and Science*, 2010.

[11] J. Ekanayake and G. Fox. High performance parallel computing with clouds and cloud technologies. In *Cloud Computing*, pages 20–38. 2010.

[12] Y. El-Khamra, H. Kim, S. Jha, and M. Parashar. Exploring the performance fluctuations of HPC workloads on clouds. In *IEEE CloudCom*, Nov. 2010.

[13] R. R. Expósito, G. L. Taboada, S. Ramos, J. Touriño, and R. Doallo. Performance analysis of HPC applications in the cloud. *Future Generation Computer Systems*, pages 218–229, 2013.

[14] M. Fenn, J. Holmes, and J. Nucciarone. A performance and cost analysis of the Amazon elastic compute cluster compute instance. `http://rcc.its.psu.edu/education/white_papers/cloud_report.pdf`, 2011.

[15] Y. Gong, B. He, and J. Zhong. An overview of CMPI: network performance aware MPI in the cloud. In *ACM PPOPP*, Feb 2012.

[16] Q. He, S. Zhou, B. Kobler, D. Duffy, and T. McGlynn. Case study for running HPC applications in public clouds. In *ACM HPDC*, 2010.

[17] Z. Hill and M. Humphrey. A quantitative analysis of high performance computing with Amazon's EC2 infrastructure: the death of the local cluster? In *International Conf. on Grid Computing*, Oct. 2009.

[18] K. Z. Ibrahim, S. Hofmeyr, and C. Iancu. Characterizing the performance of parallel applications on multi-socket virtual machines. In *IEEE/ACM CCGrid*, 2011.

[19] K. R. Jackson, L. Ramakrishnan, K. Muriki, S. Canon, S. Cholia, J. Shalf, H. J. Wasserman, and N. J. Wright. Performance analysis of high performance computing applications on the Amazon web services cloud. In *IEEE CloudCom*, Nov. 2010.

[20] G. A. Jehle and P. J. Reny. *Advanced Microeconomic Theory*. Prentice Hall, 2000.

[21] D. Klusáček and H. Rudová. Alea 2 – job scheduling simulator. In *SIMUTools*, 2010.

[22] S. H. Langer, B. Still, P.-T. Bremer, D. Hinkel, B. Langdon, J. Leviney, and E. Williams. Cielo full-system simulations of multi-beam laser-plasma interaction in NIF experiments. In *Cray Users Group Meeting*, May 2011.

[23] A. Li, X. Yang, S. Kandula, and M. Zhang. CloudCmp: comparing public cloud providers. In *IEEE Conference on Internet Measurement*, 2010.

[24] J. D. McCalpin. The STREAM benchmark. `http://www.cs.virginia.edu/~mccalpin/STREAM_Benchmark_2005-01-25.pdf`.

[25] P. Mehrotra, J. Djomehri, S. Heistand, R. Hood, H. Jin, A. Lazanoff, S. Saini, and R. Biswas. Performance evaluation of Amazon EC2 for NASA HPC applications. In *Workshop on Scientific Cloud Computing*, 2012.

[26] D. Nurmi, J. Brevik, and R. Wolski. Qbets: Queue bounds estimation from time series. In *Wkshp on Job Scheduling Strategies for Parallel Processing*, Jun 2007.

[27] F. Petrini, D. J. Kerbyson, and S. Pakin. The case of the missing supercomputer performance: Achieving optimal performance on the 8,192 processors of ASCI Q. In *Supercomputing*, 2003.

[28] F. Schatz, S. Koschnicke, N. Paulsen, C. Starke, and M. Schimmler. MPI performance analysis of Amazon EC2 cloud services for high performance computing. In *Advances in Computing and Communications*, pages 371–381. 2011.

[29] D. Singh. personal communication, Mar. 2012.

[30] K. E. Train. *Discrete Choice Methods with Simulation*. Cambridge University Press, 2009.

[31] E. Walker. The real cost of a CPU hour. *Computer*, 42(4):35–41, 2009.

[32] Wikipedia. Cloud computing. `http://en.wikipedia.org/wiki/Cloud_computing`.

[33] Windows Azure Big Compute. `http://www.windowsazure.com/en-us/home/features/big-compute/`.

[34] K. Yelick, S. Coghlan, B. Draney, and R. S. Canon. The magellan report on cloud computing for science. `science.energy.gov/~/media/ascr/pdf/program-documents/docs/Magellan_Final_Report.pdf`, December 2011.

[35] L. Youseff, R. Wolski, B. Gorda, and C. Krintz. Evaluating the performance impact of Xen on MPI and process execution for HPC systems. In *International Workshop on Virtualization Technology in Distributed Computing*, 2006.

[36] Y. Zhai, M. Liu, J. Zhai, X. Ma, and W. Chen. Cloud versus in-house cluster: evaluating amazon cluster compute instances for running MPI applications. In *Supercomputing*, Nov. 2011.

kMemvisor: Flexible System Wide Memory Mirroring in Virtual Environments

Bin Wang[†], Zhengwei Qi[‡], Haibing Guan[†], Haoliang Dong[‡], Wei Sun[‡], Yaozu Dong[§]

[†]Shanghai Key Laboratory of Scalable Computing and Systems
Shanghai Jiao Tong University, Shanghai, China
{binqbu2002, hbguan}@sjtu.edu.cn

[‡]School of Software, Shanghai Jiao Tong University, Shanghai, China
{qizhwei, daodaoliang, zmsw2008129}@sjtu.edu.cn

[§]Intel China Software Center, Shanghai, China
eddie.dong@intel.com

ABSTRACT

Today's commercial cloud service providers require the availability with an annual uptime percentage at least . 5%. While memory errors become norms instead of exceptions with the increasing memory's density and capacity in cloud applications. Thus, uncorrected errors from DRAM can be a significant source of system downtime. To address this increasingly important concern, both hardware and software memory mirroring technologies are studied nowadays to provide memory high availability. However, hardware solutions like mirror memory, which uses doubled chip, need dedicated and costly peripheral hardware. While existing software approaches, i.e., virtual machine's checkpoint technology, reduce the expense but incur the high overhead in practical usage.

In this paper, we present a novel system called kMemvisor to provide system-wide high availability memory mirroring. It is a software approach achieving exible multi-granularity memory mirroring via virtualization and binary translation technology. Specifically, kMemvisor first creates backup space of the same size of the specified memory for applications or virtual machines. We can exibly set memory areas to be mirrored or not mirrored from application level to system-wide. Then, all memory write instructions in the native memory space are captured and instrumented by mirror memory write instructions to synchronize the data in backup space. Furthermore, this instruction level memory synchronization reduces backup overhead and lowers the probability of data loss compared with traditional software approaches. So kMemvisor could use data from the backup space to recover when memory failures happen. The results show that kMemvisor causes 55% overhead in the worst case of system-

wide high availability and 30% average for the real world applications, which outperforms the state-of-the-art software approaches even in the worst case.

Categories and Subject Descriptors

D.4.5 [**Reliability**]: Fault-tolerance; C.4 [**PERFORMANCE OF SYSTEMS**]: [Reliability, availability, and serviceability]

Keywords

exible memory mirroring; system-wide high availability; virtualization

1. INTRODUCTION

Many mission-critical applications in cloud are designed to enable maximum system uptime, which typically rely on redundant components and functionality to achieve fault detection, isolation and recovery. Unfortunately, the memory component gradually becomes error-prone with the increasing density and capacity [27] thus fails to guarantee high availability for such applications. Moreover, uncorrected errors from DRAM, detected by the hardware but cannot be corrected, can be a significant source of system downtime [42]. For instance, Google's latest research shows memory (DRAM) errors are common in modern compute clusters, and more than % of DIMMs affected by errors per year [6]. This rate is unacceptable for today's commercial cloud service providers (CSP) such as Google App Engine [23] and Amazon EC2 [2], because they require availability with an annual uptime percentage at least . 5%. In cloud era, with larger deployment of virtualization technology, one server's memory is sometimes shared with thousands of virtual machine (VM) instances. If the executing instances access the error block of the memory, the data corruption and system crashes will happen in cloud services [5].

Memory errors can be characterized as soft errors (e.g., a bit ipped by cosmic rays) and hard errors (memory damaged physically and permanently) [6]. Accordingly, the existing mirroring solutions can be cataloged as hardware and software. In hardware solution, dedicated and cost-ineffective facilities are employed for fault-tolerance. The bit retrieving approach is the most direct way to enhance memory availability. It sets additional bits to detect and store single bit error in native memory. Bit retrieving happens if the checking bits represent different results with the native bits. The typical prototypes are parity [10] check and ECC [31]. For example, the parity check memory uses parity check code [20] while ECC memory uses Hamming Code [36]. One benefit of bit retrieving is that it can repair errors rapidly without CPU's involvement, but it can only repair restricted errors at bit-granularity rather than block failure. Sometimes, ECC-based memory has more risk tendency than the native one with the increasing of the ECC bits [31] due to the higher accessing-intensive in memory. The other way of hardware solution is mirror memory [27] which uses doubled chip to backup the data on the y. But sometimes, mirror memory generates too much overhead and is more expensive than the native memory. Both approaches have low compatibility and exibility. For instance, only few enterprise server motherboards can customize ECC recovery strategies. And the memory manufacturers such as HP and IBM design their proprietary memory mirror hardware which fails to support other mainboards.

In software solution, one approach is to use software to simulate hardware checking. For instance, Software ECC [15] works like the hardware ECC, which provides a library for developers to enhance the availability of specific blocks of memory. However it can only correct soft errors. The second approach is to attempt duo-backup at application level. It can be re ected in the special HA in Google and Amazon. Google File System [37] and Amazon Dynamo [22] have high fault-tolerance architectures with well-defined properties. Data is duplicated in two or more end hosts. Although duo-backup represents low latency and little interrupts, it only considers the application's tolerance which cannot provide HA for operating systems. Some VM based solutions can conquer this shortage [25]. For example, Remus [ ] is a system using virtualization technology to backup the whole VM by checkpoint. But VM's checkpoint technology does not backup the system on the y (data between two checkpoints will lose if failure happens), and the overhead of Remus is more than 100%. To support content-based page duplication, Singleton [40] considers the sharing memory characteristic of VM instances in cloud computing and attempts to manage the physical memory by both hypervisor and guest OS. Thus, it resolves the double page-cache overhead in KVM [1] by an exclusive-cache mechanism.

Based on the existing solutions as listed above, we argue that a good mirroring strategy would have the following considerations:

Low cost: The proposed redundancy should be cost-effective so that it can be widely used for massive machines in the cluster.

Efficiency & compatibility: The redundancy in memory should leverage the compatibility and the efficiency. For instance, The limited mainboard support of ECC sometimes leads to poor efficiency in hybrid distributed systems, in which some are related to ECC while others are not.

Low maintaining: The redundancy in memory should take up circumstance (e.g., bandwidth utilization in distributed system) with low consumption. For example, duo-backup approach sometimes reduces the bandwidth utilization. A topology designer has to consider the number of redundancies and their positions in the cluster [7].

Cloud requirement: In cloud era, the communicating entity is VM. VM should have its own software redundancy in memory rather than external mirroring because the latter involves the networking situation. For example, VM checkpoints in VLAN are affected by the link congestion and the hop distance, and some migrations even happen with inter-DNS resolutions.

All the above issues are considered in our design. Our design has three advantages. Firstly, our strategy is fast and efficient for retrieving because it does not need any I/O operation from external device. Secondly, a hypervisor in the physical host does not need to launch new VMs for the backup of native VMs. Finally, we narrow the redundancy in one general machine or single server, which does not involve the networking resilience and migration maintaining. The large-scale deployment of our strategy will minimally affect bandwidth utilization.

Memvisor is presented in our previous work[26], which is a cost-effective software memory mirroring approach on application level. Memvisor uses binary translation modifying applications to replicate the data to mirror memory so when a memory failure happens, the data could be restored from the replica. Since Memvisor focuses on application level memory mirroring, it could not cover system wide memory including kernel space in machine without the full support of virtualization.

In this paper, we extend it to support exible and multi-granularity memory mirroring and propose a more powerful software approach called kMemvisor. The characters of kMemvisor are as follows:

- kMemvisor is a hypervisor providing system-wide memory mirroring based on hardware virtualization. It instruments mirror instructions not only for user mode code but also kernel mode code to backup the data. Only low-cost memory is required to recover the data when the memory corrupts.

- kMemvisor is a more exible and low-priced approach than the hardware solutions. The virtualization technology assists it with the ability of supporting VMs with or without mirror memory feature on a same physical machine. The binary translation technology offers the choice of application level or system-wide level high availability. Also the mirror memory could easily be set to support $NModularRedundancy$ for some special mission critical applications.

- kMemvisor is also more efficient than other software approaches. The results show that the performance of CPU intensive tasks is unaffected, and even in the worst situation, our stressful memory write benchmark shows that the backup overhead is 55%. In real world applications the overhead is from 10% (thttpd) to 50% (sqlite), much less than 100% of Remus and other software approaches.

The rest of the paper is organized as follows. The overall architecture and the process of kMemvisor are introduced in Section II. Section III gives detailed implementation and Section IV evaluates performance and overheads. Section V discusses some engineering issues to support practical mirroring and recovery. Section VI covers related work and Section VII concludes the paper.

2. DESIGN

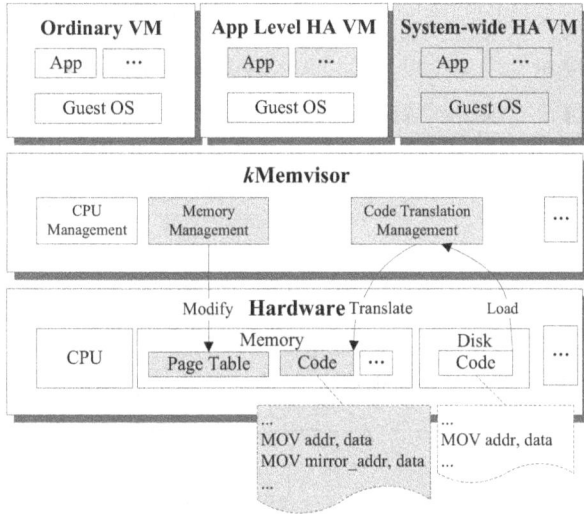

Figure 1: The high-level architecture of kMemvisor. The gray blocks indicate the difference between kMemvisor and a typical hypervisor. The VMs can be classified as three categories: ordinary VM, application level HA VM, and system-wide HA VM.

kMemvisor is a modified hypervisor which provides system-wide high available memory features. kMemvisor creates redundant virtual space via virtualization technology, then it inserts instructions (mirror instructions) through binary translation technology and replicates data to this space. Data can be recovered from the replica when errors happen. In this section, we will introduce the architecture and the process of the data replication and recovery.

2.1 Architecture

Figure 1 illustrates the high-level architecture of kMemvisor. As we mentioned in the last section, virtual machines can be configured as native or HA VMs, i.e., application level or system-wide level high availability VM, where different types of VMs can be run on the same physical machine. The application level HA VM has been implemented in Memvisor [26], and we will mainly introduce system-wide HA VM in this paper.

kMemvisor can be divided into two parts. The first is the Memory management module, and the second is the Code translation module.

Memory management module monitors the page table related operations to create mirror page tables. Page table maps virtual addresses to physical addresses. Since kMemvisor maintains mirror memory together with native memory, two sets of page tables are needed. One is native page table which deals with native addresses mapping. The other is mirror page table that handles the mirror addresses mapping. The memory allocation strategy is controlled by memory management module in hypervisor, which should be modified to satisfy the requirement of kMemvisor.

We choose the hypervisor instead of the operating system (OS) for two reasons. First, the memory can be replicated at VM granularity. That means kMemvisor can guarantee VMs using high available memory together with VMs using native memory both working correctly on a same physical machine. And it is very flexible to switch VMs between high available memory and native memory depending on the OS critical level. Second, if the data of an OS are corrupted, the OS will crash and become unable to recover the data by itself. But using the hypervisor overcomes this difficulty. Although the data of the hypervisor can also be corrupted, the probability is much less than that for the OS given that the hypervisor uses far less memory.

Code translation management module [26] takes charge of inserting mirror instructions. It identifies all memory writing instructions and replicates them. The difference between original instruction and replicated instruction is the destination address. Replicated instructions will write the same data to "mirror virtual address". Mirror virtual address is a virtual address mapped to an additional physical area. This physical area is created by kMemvisor to store the redundant data. The relationship of mirror virtual address (mva) and native virtual address (nva) has been designed in Memvisor:

$$mva = \mathbf{mirror}(nva) \; [26] \qquad (1)$$

2.2 Replication and Recovery

We will introduce two processes here to illustrate how data are replicated and recovered.

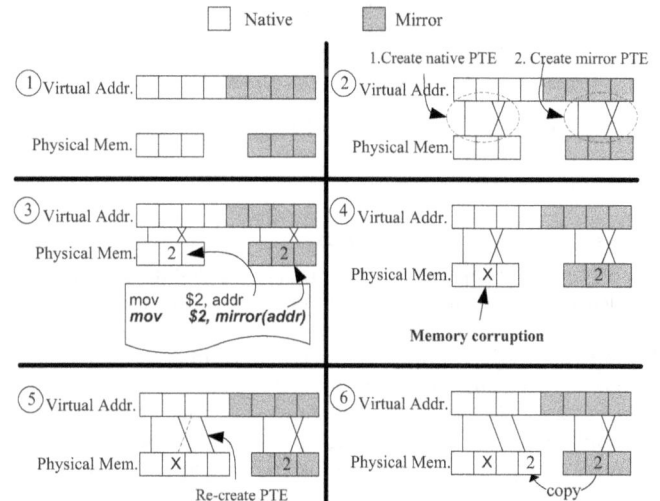

Figure 2: The process of memory recovery: 1. A block of physical memory will be reserved when a VM startups. 2. When native PTEs are updated, the related mirror PTEs will also be created. 3. Native instructions and mirror instructions will write the same data in different address. 4. If a page is corrupted, a new page will be allocated to the VM. 5. Map the virtual address to the new page. 6. Copy data from the mirror address.

The process of data replication is similar to Memvisor in the application level, but we extend it to VM level, and it also can be divided into three steps. Furthermore kMemvisor supports native VMs and HA VMs run on a same physical machine. So the process of data replication needs to be slightly changed (Figure 2, part 1 to part3):

1. **Reserve physical memory:** When a VM startups, kMemvisor will check the configuration. If the VM is configured as HA type. A block of physical memory

will be reserved as mirror area. The size of this area is as same as the memory size configured in this VM.

2. **Create mirror page table:** *k*Memvisor will intercept the page table related operations of VM. When a PTE is updated and the VM is configured as HA type, the related mirror page table will be also be created.

3. **Write redundant data:** If a VM is configured as HA type, it should be processed by instruction management module which will be introduced in the next section. After that each memory write instruction will be replicated, and the redundant data will be written by the mirror instruction.

When a memory failure happens, a hardware detection mechanism (e.g., parity check [10] or ECC) will notify the *k*Memvisor by invoking machine check exception (MCE). Traditionally, OS will simply restart the machine if a memory related MCE is invoked [3]. But in *k*Memvisor, the system will quickly and effectively retrieve the corrupted data by the following steps (Figure 2, part 4 to part 6):

1. **Allocate a new page:** In some cases, memory errors are caused by physical damage (e.g., aging equipments) rather than bit- ipping caused by cosmic rays. The data should be recovered in another physical block, so we should allocate a new page to recover the data.

2. **Map to the new page:** Rewrite corrupted PTE and map it to the new page just allocated.

3. **Retrieve the corrupted data:** Copy data from *mva* to *nva*. After error recovery, the program will continue to execute.

2.3 Binary Translation

Memvisor [26] uses binary translation technology to duplicate memory write instructions. The translation can be static or dynamic. Static translation means that the redundant instructions are added at compile time which reduces performance impact at run time; dynamic translation translates the instructions at run time which does not need an application's source code. Figure 1 shows the process of dynamic translation; the mirror instructions are inserted when OS loads the program from the disk.

Since *k*Memvisor may run in kernel mode, interruptions may incur some side effects after the mirrored instructions are inserted. One is that if an interrupt happens between one native instruction and the following mirror instruction, the data will not be replicated for a relatively long time. Another side effect may happen in a multi-core environment. If two cores write to the same address through atomic instructions (the lock-prefix instructions in x 6 [2]) instead of using other forms of locking, then a data race will occur because the mirror instructions destroy the atomicity. We will discuss this issue in Section 5.

3. IMPLEMENTATION

We have implemented *k*Memvisor in Xen-3.4.2 with 3 lines of code. Those modifications include three parts: First, at the time virtual machine initializes its memory, a block of physical memory should be allocated as mirrored physical memory. Second, a mirror PTE should be created when the

native PTE is created. Third, mirror instructions should be instrumented at compile time. The details will be described in this section. We choose Linux 2.6.30 and XV6 [44] as the Guest OS whose memory management strategy needs to be changed slightly. Finally we will introduce how to add mirror instructions to duplicate data to mirror memory.

3.1 Create Mirror Page Table

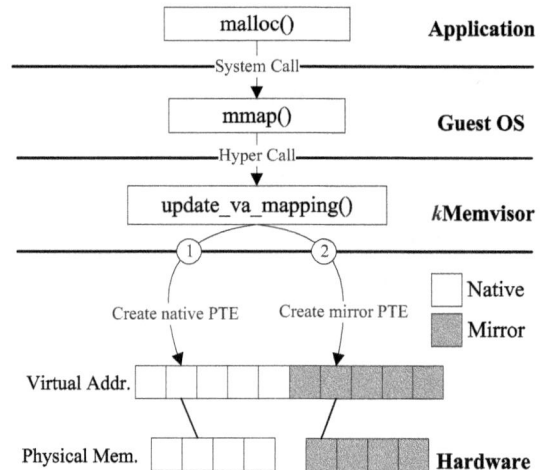

Figure 3: The process of memory allocation in *k*Memvisor. During the hypercall processing, the native page table and then the mirror page table are created.

The mirror PTE should be created before the mirror instructions write to the mirror memory address; otherwise it would cause a page fault. Although we can fill in the mirror PTE in the page fault process, it will result in low performance because of the overhead of intercepting frequent page faults.

Since XV6 is a lightweight OS, the memory management mechanism of it is very simple. In the implementation for XV6, we modified the Guest OS to create mirror PTE directly. But the implementation for Linux, the page table related operations are complicated. So we need to modify the hypervisor memory management to ensure that the mirror PTE and native PTE are created simultaneously.

There are three memory virtualization technologies in today's virtualization management: direct page table (DPT), shadow page table (SPT) [14] and extended page table (EPT) [21]. EPT needs hardware support and the mechanism cannot be modified by software. DPT and SPT are the software implementations which can be employed in *k*Memvisor. We will introduce both technologies brie y:

- **Direct page table:** In this mechanism, the guest OS must write the page table using a hypercall. *k*Memvisor intercepts the hypercall and fills in the PTE if the operation is legal. The mirror PTE can be filled in after the native PTE is created (Figure 3).

- **Shadow page table:** Once the guest OS modifies *cr3*, a control register that contains the base address of the page table, *k*Memvisor will translate the native page table to a new table and reset *cr3* to point to the new page table. In the process of the translation, kMemvisor can create mirror PTEs in the new page table.

In this paper, we finally choose the DPT technology to create mirror page table in order to improve performance and reduce engineering effort.

3.2 Modify Guest OS

Memory management in Linux is implemented with some complicated mechanisms. One of them is the *vm_struct* which records a lot of page table information including the map between virtual addresses and physical addresses [32]. When a process is killed, the virtual address is also eliminated, and the related physical address should be released. In this process, Linux will iterate through the page table with the help of *vm_struct*. However, we modify the page table through kMemvisor, and the guest OS has no awareness of this modification. An error will occur because there is no *vm_struct* for the mirrored page table. To address this issue, we add a special flag in a PTE for mirrored memory, and we modify the guest OS (Linux) slightly. The flag can be used to tell a native PTE from a mirror PTE. When the guest OS finds that a PTE needs to be processed during the iteration, it checks the flag. If the PTE is mirror PTE, the guest OS ignores it.

3.3 Modified Memory Layout

In this paper we employ a straightforward but efficient way to present **mirror** function, that is:

$$mva \quad \mathbf{mirror}(nva) \quad nva \quad offset \quad (2)$$

offset stands for a relatively large integer constant, and the value of it will be discussed later. This approach needs little effort to realize and is much faster than others. Since the plus operation does not need additional instructions on the x 6 platform, it can be integrated into assembly instructions.

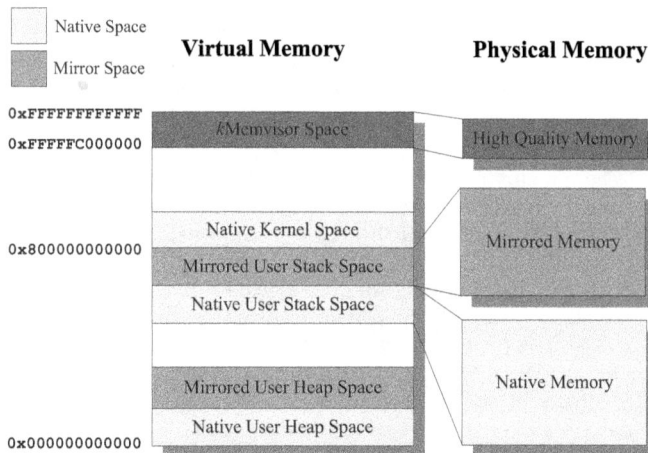

Figure 4: A overview memory layout of a kMemvisor implementation. The light gray area means native area while deep gray means mirror area. kMemvisor area lies in the highest part. Virtual addresses are mapped to physical addresses by the page table.

Figure 4 shows a memory layout in kMemvisor implementation. The virtual addresses are divided into three parts as kMemvisor space, kernel space, and user space. Memvisor

offers mirror memory only for user space [26]. In kMemvisor, we cover not only user space but also kernel space. Each part of memory and its related mirror memory reside in different physical memory so that the data are replicated physically. This figure is a simple layout, the actual memory layout will be more complicated, e.g., a multi-threaded program has more stack areas, and the dynamic link area is also not shown in this figure.

3.4 Memory Synchronization through System-wide Instrumentation

kMemvisor must guarantee data synchronization between native and mirror memory when the system is running. As is shown in Figure 5, when an instruction changes the data in native memory, kMemvisor should capture it then an identical instruction (mirror instruction) must be instrumented to update the corresponding data in mirror memory. We employ the static binary translation technology to implement this feature. kMemvisor modifies the procedure of GCC to perform static binary translation. It analyzes the assembly source files before the assembler (GAS) handles them. All work starts from finding out memory write instructions from the native instructions according to various addressing modes. The referenced native memory addresses can be retrieved from the native instructions. Then kMemvisor calculates the mirror memory addresses finding the place to replicate the data. At last mirror instructions are instrumented into source files which would be processed by assembler as executable files.

These instructions would not lead to problems for indirect branches and indirect jumps because in the assembly files created by GCC the target addresses are represented as labels. After the executable files are generated, they are born with the ability to write data to both native memory and mirror memory. So when the programs are running, data are replicated on the fly.

User mode code can be easily dealt with since most instructions are simple which usually change data in memory directly. These instructions that modify data in memory can be classified into two types. One is *e plicit* write instructions that are usually data transfer and arithmetic instructions (e.g., *mov*, *add*, etc.). The memory address that instructions manipulate on can be seen according to the addressing mode. For this type of instructions, mirror addresses and instructions could be easily instrumented. Another type is *implicit* write instructions which are usually stack related (e.g., *push*, etc.). These instructions update the data whose address are related to the *esp* register. But the *esp* register can not be seen explicitly from the instructions themselves. Hence, to cope with these instructions needs special efforts.

Explicit and implicit instructions differ in processing memory addresses operated on while the mirror instructions can both instrumented just after native instructions. But some instructions can change the instruction execution sequence like the *call* instruction. It saves procedure linking information on the stack and branches to the called procedure. If mirror instructions were inserted right after native ones, they will not be executed until the called procedure returns. That will end in a long time data inconsistency between native and mirror memory. So kMemvisor employs a special way, called *copy-on-call*, to replicate the linking information by inserting the mirror instructions at the very start of the called procedure, as shown in Figure 6. It also reduces the

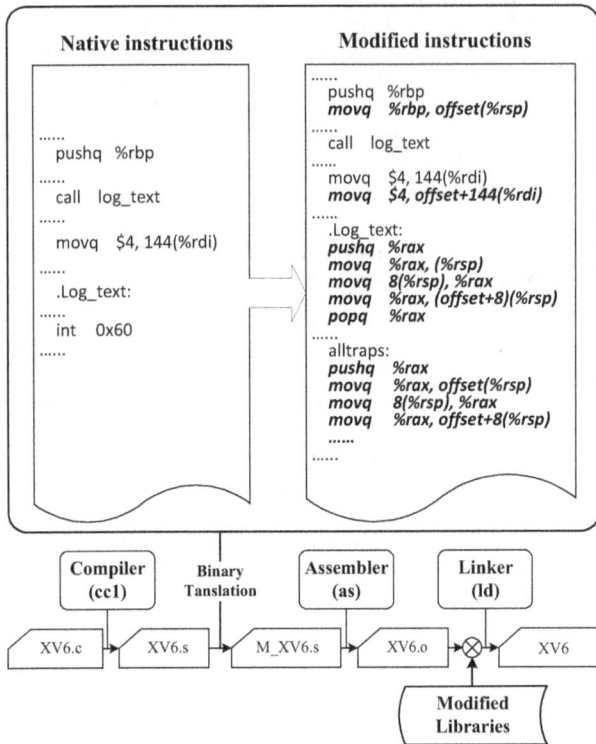

Figure 5: The overall architecture of binary translation.

number of mirror instructions since a called procedure may be called several times but need to be instrumented only once.

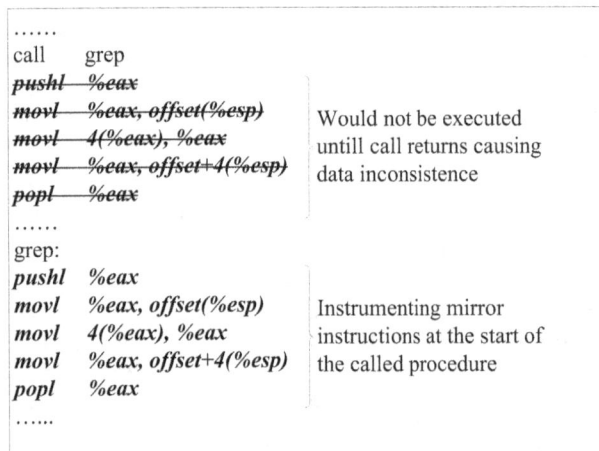

Figure 6: The approach for *call* instruction processing.

The code of kernel is much more complicated than those of user-mode programs since instructions have to cope with atomic operations and privilege change. While some parts of them could be dealt with via the same way as user-mode code, special cases must be taken care of through unique approaches. For example, kernel handles all interrupts. An interrupt stops the normal processor loop and starts executing a new sequence called interrupt handler. Before that,

the processor saves several registers such as *eip* and *esp* and so on. So that the operating system can restore them when it returns from the interrupt. This procedure consists of several memory related operations and should be instrumented carefully. To explain this, the following paragraphs will detail the procedure of instrumenting system call.

To make a system call on x 6, a program invokes a special instruction such as *int*. It will save different registers according to the privilege check. If a privilege change is detected, say from user mode to kernel mode, two more registers *ss* and *esp* should be saved onto the kernel stack. These two registers are not necessary if the privilege stays the same. Figure 7 shows the stack after an *int* instruction completes. *k*Memvisor has to save the data newly pushed on kernel stack during the *int* instructions. We should address two challenges: how to copy registers consistently whether changing privilege or not, and where to instrument the mirror instructions.

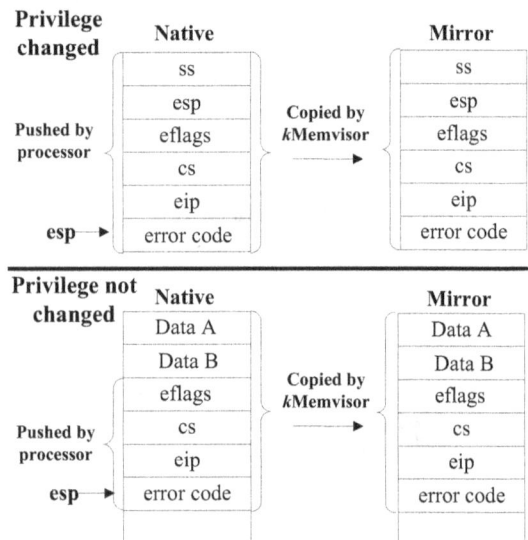

Figure 7: The processor will save 6 registers when the privilege is changed while save 4 registers when privilege stays the same. *k*Memvisor copies a fixed memory region of 6 registers every time independent of the privilege state.

For the first challenge, the difference brought by privilege change only lies in the number of registers pushed into kernel stack. After the hardware saves the registers, *k*Memvisor copies the data in stack as if a privilege change happens. So if the privilege actually changed, the data *k*Memvisor copied are all necessary. If the privilege stays the same, *k*Memvisor will still copy two existing registers' data (shown in Figure 7 as Data A and Data B) in the current stack to obtain a consistent way with privilege's changing. Because these data are overwritten with the same value, this copy does not change the value. Therefore, *k*Memvisor keeps the same stack frame with native one to assure the correctness of mirroring. This approach sacrifices little data copying performance while saves the privilege change's detection overhead every time an interrupt happens.

For the second challenge, an operating system can use the *iret* instruction to return from an *int* instruction. It pops the saved values during the *int* instruction from the stack, and resumes execution at the saved *eip* register. So instrumenting mirror write instructions just after *int* instruction is not right in that it will not be executed until the *int* instruction returns and the stack may be wrong. Similar to *copy-on-call*, *k*Memvisor interferes the process when the hardware saves the registers and calls the interrupt handler, instrumenting mirror instructions lazily at the very start of the interrupt handler to synchronize the data in stack to mirror memory.

4. EVALUATION

*k*Memvisor has been designed to support system-wide high availability for different VMs exibly and its overhead should be acceptable so that it could be deployed on today's commodity hardware. In this section, we will quantify the impact on performance brought by *k*Memvisor to find out the possibility to use this system in practice. Before we measure the performance, we will verify the correctness of *k*Memvisor. Then, we will give a primary case study to emulate the memory error in VM and to observe how to recover this error. After that, a micro-benchmark will test the memory related operations. Finally, we test some practical applications, thttpd [1] (represent for IO-intensive tasks) and SQLite [41] (represent for memory-intensive tasks), to evaluate the performance and concurrency impact in real world applications. We test the overhead in compilation and runtime separately and also count the inserted instructions to see the relationship between overhead and mirror instructions.

4.1 Test Environment

Our tests are run on a Dell PowerEdge T610 server with a 6-core 2.67GHz Intel Xeon CPU with 12MB L3 cache. There are two Samsung GB DDR3 RAMs with ECC and a 14 GB SATA Disk. As we described in the previous section, *k*Memvisor is implemented on Xen-3.4.2. We choose Linux as the guest OS, the kernel version is 2.6.30, and we also deploy a lightweight system, Busybox-1.1 .2 [17]. Each VM is allocated two virtual CPUs and 64MB memory. We choose XV6 [44] to do the system-wide high availability correctness test, thttpd and SQLite to represent real world applications with application level high availability.

4.2 Correctness Verification

We added a hypercall and code in Memvisor to compare the native memory and the mirror memory bit-by-bit [26]. The same way is employed to test the correctness of *k*Memvisor. Unlike Memvisor, the entire virtual addresses have been verified. We choose a unix-like system called XV6 to do the test [44]. It is simple but enough to test the *k*Memvisor's system-wide high availability feature. XV6 has a micro benchmark itself which is used for the test. After the benchmark tests some memory related operations we add the hypercall to verify the data in native memory and the data in mirror memory. About 5MB data in user space are verified and we have successfully improved the correctness rate to 100%. While the correctness rate of kernel space data is now .6% as approximately total 100MB data tested with 0.4MB different. There are some really small areas of kernel data that cannot be replicated may lead to this result, which will be detailed in section 5.

4.3 Primary Case Study: Error Recovery

Although memory errors are common in clusters, they are scarcely happening in a single machine at a short period time. To validate the availability of *k*Memvisor, we design

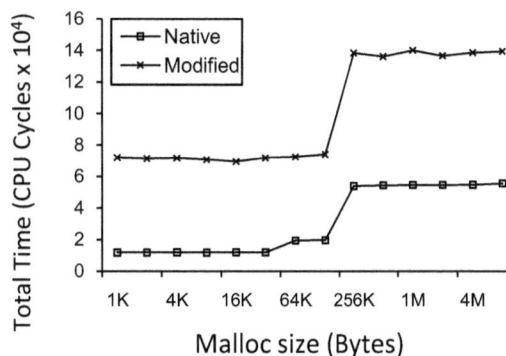

Figure : Malloc micro-test with different block size.

a primary case study to emulate the memory error in VM and observe the impact on it.

Actually, Linux uses hwpoison [1] to recover some memory errors, which needs a large engineering effort to integrate *k*Memvisor into this architecture. To simply our case study, we implement a hypercall to pollute a specific block of memory area with garbage data, then it will invoke the recovery process of *k*Memvisor to restore data. This case study had been tested both on user mode and kernel mode. We invoke the hypercall when an application or the kernel is running. As we expected, the correctness of the application or even the whole VM are unaffected. It takes about 24000 CPU cycles to restore each page. That means if the size of error memory is less than 500KB, it can be fixed in 1ms. Both user and application will not be aware of the failure due to such short recovery time.

4.4 Micro-benchmark

*k*Memvisor modifies the hypervisor memory management module to create the mirrored space which may lead to some performance impact when creating the page table. For a user application that means the *malloc()* function may take more time. The additional mirrored instructions may also double the time for a memory write. We therefore design a study case to measure those operations. Memory tests are divided into two types as average sequential write cost and average sequential read cost.

In *malloc()* operation, the OS will mark the related memory area and create the page table on demand. To incur the page table creation, we will write one byte to each page after invoking the *malloc()* function. The overhead is mainly ascribed to the creation of additional PTE and the cost of TLB ush. Figure depicts the overhead of the *malloc()* function with different size. The impact on performance is somewhat large when the allocated memory is less than 256KB but much more limited when the size is larger. The overhead is amortized over the larger allocation so the overall effect is small.

Figure shows the performance result of sequential memory write and sequential memory read. We vary the size of memory from 1KB to 1MB and the overhead of *k*Memvisor is stable at about 33%. And for the sequential memory read test, the overhead can be ignored as expected. It shows that *k*Memvisor is a scalable solution with a relatively small performance impact on memory operations.

---

[1]http://www.kernel.org/doc/Documentation/vm/hwpoison.txt

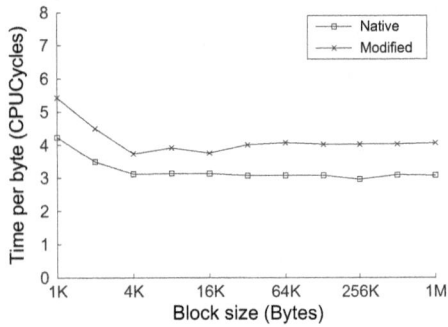
(a) Overhead for sequential memory read

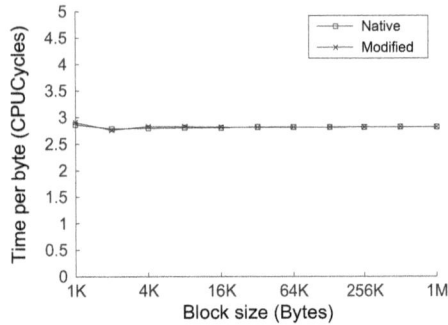
(b) Overhead for sequential memory write

Figure : (a) Average overhead for sequential memory write is small at about 33%. (b) Overhead for sequential memory read is almost none.

4.5 XV6 Benchmark

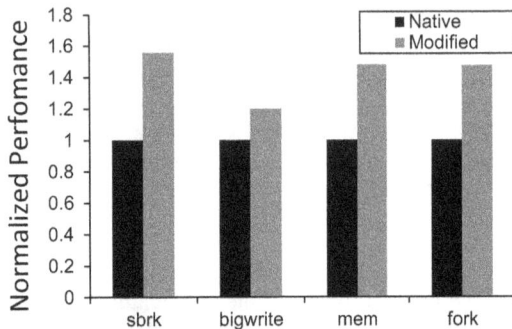
Figure 10: Normalized difference of usertests performance between native system and modified system.

In order to test the system-wide high availability performance, we leverage the applications and benchmark of XV6 again. Figure 10 shows the results of XV6 benchmark named usertests. It contains several memory tests and the result shows that the largest overhead is still less than 60% and the average overhead is only 43%. The expected overhead is about 100% since memory write instructions are doubled and the test shows a much better result. We have also tested several most useful Unix commands to evaluate the impact on system common features and the results are shown as Figure 11. The largest overhead is 7.2% and the average overhead is less than 5%. We analyze each command source file to find the number of inserted mirror instructions and the result is shown in Figure 11. The more mirror instructions

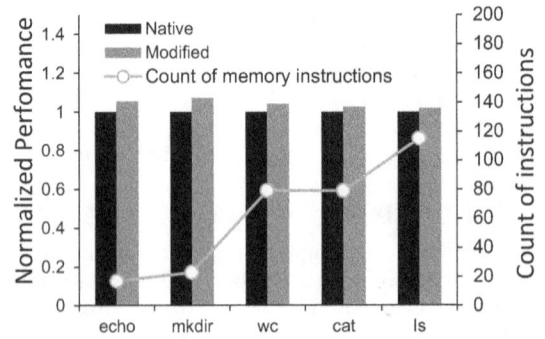
Figure 11: Normalized difference of command performance between native system and modified system.

instrumented the higher overhead it will cost. The number sometimes does not match the overhead because some complex instructions need special care like *call* instructions.

4.6 Web Server

To measure the impact on a real world web server, we choose thttpd-2.25b as a representative IO-intensive application, and evaluate the performance and concurrency difference between kMemvisor and the native hypervisor. We deploy thttpd in the guest OS, and start up another VM running with Apache Bench [4] to send 100,000 requests to thttpd. These requests are sent at different concurrency pressure, then we observe the throughput and the latency. Figure 12 shows the result.

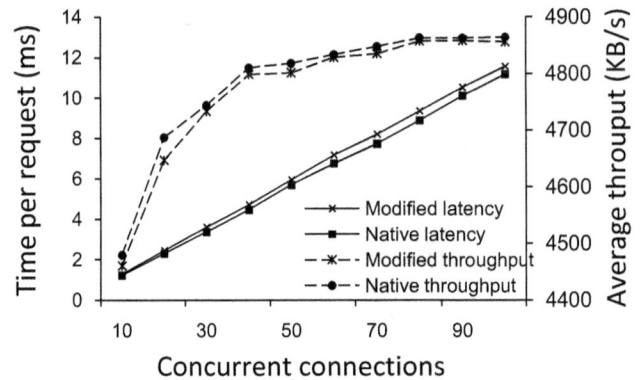
Figure 12: Performance of thttpd with different concurrent pressures.

There is less than 10% overhead in kMemvisor, which is reasonable given that the performance impact is mainly ascribed to the lock operation in multi-threaded applications. Memory write operations are relatively fewer in a web server, so their impact is limited. Memory read operations are frequent, but from the previous micro-benchmark, we know that they will not cause much overhead. This means the impact of kMemvisor is acceptable in a real-world web server.

4.7 Database

Databases are widely used in cloud services, which can be also used to represent memory-intensive applications. SQLite-3.7.11 is chosen to measure the performance impact. We write a test suite including five kinds of operations: *create, insert, select, update* and *delete*. Then, we measure the total time (including the time of resolving SQL statements) for each test. Figure 13 shows the results.

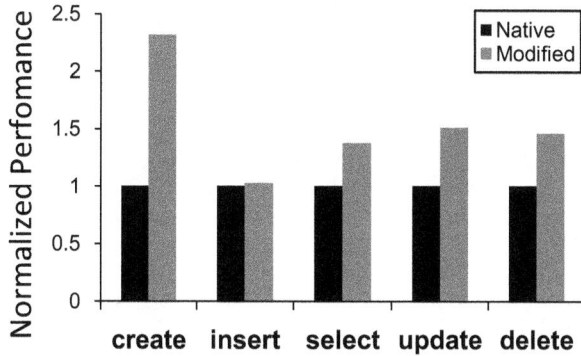

Figure 13: The performance impact for *create*, *insert*, *select*, *update*, and *delete* in SQLite.

The results indicate that different operations present different overheads in *k*Memvisor. The *insert* operation causes only little overhead while the *create* operation needs double time to finish the same thing. This difference depends on the implementation of SQLite, e.g., the cache mechanism will cause frequent memory writing operations. Luckily, the *create* operation is scarcely used in a real world server, and the other four operations are used frequently but cause a little performance impact. We can conclude that *k*Memvisor is also suitable for a database.

4.8 Compilation Time

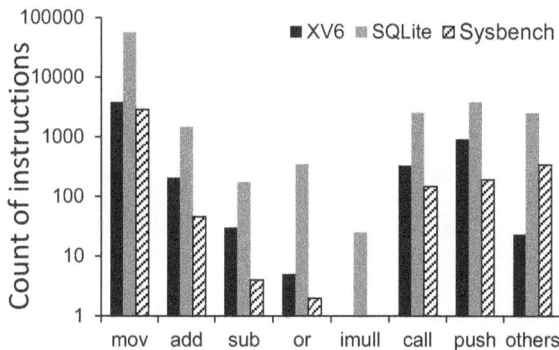

Figure 14: Mirror instructions detail information.

*k*Memvisor instruments mirror instructions via static binary translation technology, which does all the work in programs compilation. To evaluate the impact brought by the *k*Memvisor due to inserting mirror instructions, we test the compilation time of native and modified programs separately. Figure 15 shows the result of XV6, Sysbench, and SQLite compilation test. Native compile time stands for the original GCC while the modified compile time is for *k*Memvisor. We can see that instrumenting mirror instructions at compile time only costs a little. We also count the number of mirror instructions instrumented by *k*Memvisor. XV6 and Sysbench are lightweight with only about 5 thousand instructions inserted while SQLite is instrumented with almost 70 thousand instructions. The more mirror instructions inserted the longer time it will cost in compilation.

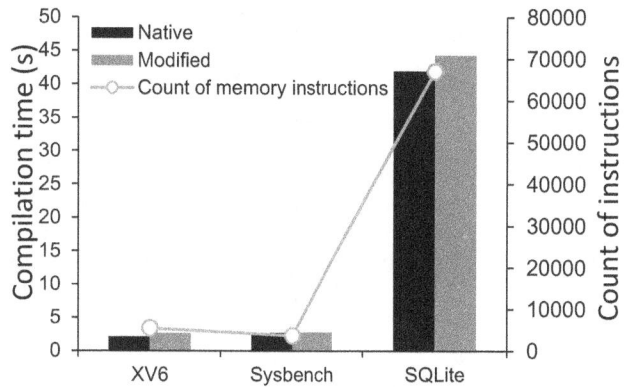

Figure 15: Compilation time overhead brought by *k*Memvisor.

SQLite only suffers 5.64% overhead while the average overhead of the three programs is just 6%. *k*Memvisor supports extra interface to analyze the mirror instructions as shown in Figure 15. As mirror instructions are relative to native ones, we can tell the detail information of native programs. Among all the memory write instructions, the explicit write instructions are the majority. Just *mov* instruction alone makes up about 0 percent. The implicit write instructions are less but usually more complicated themselves which would cost extra overhead.

5. DISCUSSION

Generally, the current *k*Memvisor can almost support exible multi-granularity memory redundancy, i.e., process-level, application-level, and VM level. However, the following issues need more engineering efforts to be addressed. First, some memory areas cannot be made redundant or cannot be recovered if an error happens, e.g., *k*Memvisor area, page table area, etc. Second is that the native virtual address and the mirror virtual address may con ict. Thirdly, we will introduce some challenges in binary translation. At last, we will discuss a solution for the problem in a multi-threaded and multi-core environment which have been mentioned in Section 2.

5.1 Special Memory Areas

There are several memory areas which cannot be made redundant. First is the page table memory, because in the x 6 platform the page table is located in physical memory. The problem is that replicating a mirrored page table would need to write a new mirrored page table, and that would cause an infinite loop. The second is *k*Memvisor memory area. Replicating this area is futile although mirrored instructions could be added to *k*Memvisor statically. If the data of *k*Memvisor is corrupted, it will crash and cannot recover the data all by itself.

To relieve these problems, we suggest using high quality physical memory for those memory areas to reduce the error probability. Since those areas are relatively small, it will not increase cost too much.

Another problem lies in the IO mapping memory area. Currently, the binary translation module cannot know at translation time whether the instruction will write to the IO mapping area. Actually, since devices has cache, this area need not be redundant. Fortunately, it is not a big deal if we add the mirrored instructions in this area; they only in uence performance a little.

5.2 Other Device Memory Operations

In modern computer architecture, not only the CPU but also other devices can write the memory (e.g., via DMA). kMemvisor needs to intercept all memory modifications. The way to solve the problem is to modify the related driver. In the DMA case, after a DMA device finishes a memory operation, it will send an interrupt to the CPU and invoke the related driver. In the interrupt process, we can add code to copy the data from the DMA area to the related mirrored area.

5.3 Address Conflict

Address con ict means two or more memory areas are overlapping. The **mirror** function in kMemvisor's current implementation is a simple addition, mva nva $offset$. The offset is a constant and needs to be set properly. If the value is too small, the mirrored user space will overlap the native user space, if the value is too large, the mirrored stack space will overlap the native kernel space (shown in Figure 4).

We implement kMemvisor on a 64-bit machine to relieve this problem because of the large linear address space. But there is still a possibility to cause an address con ict, for example when the user applies for a large block of memory or uses too many dynamic link libraries. Moreover, in the implementation of VM of XV6, the problem has been solved permanently. We modified the memory layout to ensure the mirrored memory space will not be used by the guest OS.

5.4 Challenges in Binary Translation

Static binary translation cannot deal with self-modifying code. And some parts of the executable may be reachable only through indirect branches, whose value is known only at run time, so they are beyond static binary translation's scope. This challenge can be solved by combining dynamic binary translation together with static binary translation technology.

5.5 Multi-threads and Multi-cores

As described in the Section II, kMemvisor needs to overcome some challenges in multi-threaded and multi-core environments. In a multi-threaded environment, kMemvisor needs to check the instruction after an interrupt happens. If the next instruction is a mirrored instruction, kMemvisor should emulate this instruction before executing the interrupt handler. That ensures all the mirrored data is created immediately. In a multi-core environment, if the binary translation module finds a lock-prefix instruction, to assure the atomicity after the code is modified, an explicit mutex lock should be added for each lock-prefix instruction and its mirrored instruction.

6. RELATED WORK

Generally, the existing solutions of memory HA can be divided into two categories: hardware and software. The hardware solutions enhance the availability by special motherboards and/or memory chips; while software solutions are mostly based on checkpoint, VM replication, logging and replay techniques. Now, we will introduce these technologies and compare them with kMemvisor. Finally, memory error

prediction and algorithm-based recovery are also shown in this section, which may be complementary to kMemvisor.

Hardware redundance: Initially, hardware providers consider using extra bits to check and correct memory errors. A typical technology is parity [10] check which uses one extra bit to check data. Another solution is ECC [31], which uses Hamming Codes [36] to detect and correct the internal data corruption. Some machine providers promote ECC to support their motherboard services (e.g., HP Advanced ECC [27], Google ECC [2], and IBM Chipkill [43]). Another bit checking method for large area failures is ECP [3], which corrects a failed bit in a memory line by recording the position of the bit in the line and its correct value [34]. However, bit-based checking can only retrieve limited bit errors rather than massive block failures and more error check bits are needed with the increment of native data bits. Some approaches also focus on the promotion of the bit checking at the phase change memory (PCM) [35] because it suffers from limited write endurance. For instance, PAYG [34] requires 3 times lower storage overhead and yet provides 13% more lifetime. And SAFER [3] partitions a data block dynamically while ensuring that there is at most one fail bit per partition and uses single error correction techniques per partition for failure recovery.

To retrieve massive block failures, previous work focuses on hardware mirrored. HP mirrored channel [27] provides full protection against single-bit and multi-bit errors. The subsystem writes identical data to two channels simultaneously. It automatically retrieves the data from the mirrored when errors happen. Similar solution is re ected in Dell mirrored memory [33] on PowerEdge 1 50, 2 00, and 2 50 servers [16]. However, the high cost and strict environment requirement become problems for providers. The providers may possibly pay as much as 2 or 3 times money to guarantee their memory availability. Meanwhile, hardware solution also represents poor exibility in mission critical servers. If mission critical clients and non mission critical ones coexist in one cluster environment, extra work need be done to schedule mission critical clients only to such hardware mirrored servers. With kMemvisor, it supports multigranularity memory mirroring, and each VM only needs a configuration of whether to support memory HA or not. Compared to the hardware mirrored, kMemvisor is a cost-effective and exible solution.

Software duplication/checkpoint: Memory HA is also considered as a part of the whole system HA. To smooth the y tolerance, some distributed systems deploy redundancies based on network topologies and the relationships among nodes. For instance, Google File System [37] and Dynamo [22] are the most famous application level HA systems. They employ special algorithms to distribute data on two or more physical machines, and can recover the data immediately from the backup.

Another typical model of system HA is dual-machine VM replication [12, 24]. A backup server is used to get synchronized to the primary host. Remus [ ] is a notable case of such solution. In Remus, the state of the primary VM is frequently recorded and transmitted to the backup server during execution. In the evaluation of Remus, Linux kernel compilation time was doubled, and SPEC-web benchmarks suffer more slowdown when doing 40 checkpoints per second using a 1 Gbit/s network connection for transmitting changes in memory state. VMware has provided another replication model based on replaying [13], but it can be applied only to uniprocessor VMs and is highly architecture-specific.

To reduce the size of VM checkpoint, a live checkpoint mechanism is proposed by saving the memory image in a copy-on-write (COW) manner [25], which reduces the checkpoint file size by up to 7% and shorten the total checkpoint/restart time by a factor of up to 71%, in comparison with the Xen's default checkpoint mechanism. kMemvisor has better performance, which brings only about 55% overhead with the most affected memory-write-intensive workload. Moreover, without the limitation incurred by periodic checkpoints, kMemvisor replicates the data on the y. Moreover, kMemvisor is a solution based on local backup, so the network bandwidth is no longer a problem.

Algorithm-based recovery: Sometimes, checkpoint-based approaches cannot resolve the iterative methods because they generate large inherent redundant information which cannot be retrieved by checkpoints. So an algorithm-based recovery method [11] is proposed for such problem. For example, Kutlu Mucahid, *et al* [30] divided the dataset into smaller parts before replication and distribute the replicated data parts. Each processor normally processes only its own primary data and replicas for tolerance. This algorithm saves 13 % recovery time at most than checkpoint. The algorithm-based approach can reduce the overhead from frequent checkpoints. Our kMemvisor can combine this algorithm and consider the iterative applications on the guest OS in the future.

Lock retrieving: LIBSDC [1] establishes a library for memory's high reliability by trapping memory operations (read/write). It checks the errors and rolls back the data in page-granularity. If the page is the candidate for checking, it will be locked, otherwise it will be unlocked. LIBSDC usually marks the inactive pages as 'lock'. The FIFO [ ] mechanism will guarantee which pages are inactive. However, if error happens during the unlock period, the recovering process may not be completed.

Memory error prediction: Memory error prediction can also be used to reduce memory errors. Recent research provides a system to predict memory errors [45] which takes advantage of studies on the characteristics of hardware memory errors. It employs a cost-effective self-healing mechanism that diagnoses, predicts, and prevents memory errors to reduce their potential damage and loss at system level. It is used to protect the VM host reliability. This method can only decrease the risk rather than eliminate system failures and it needs specific hardware support. However, kMemvisor can integrate this prediction to improve the reliability of aging memory.

7. CONCLUSION

kMemvisor is a hypervisor providing system-wide memory mirroring based on hardware virtualization. It instruments mirror instructions not only for user mode code but also kernel mode code to backup the memory. kMemvisor could support high available VMs and native VMs simultaneously. VMs can easily choose to use application level or system-wide level high availability. kMemvisor also can increase memory copies on demand, which is more exible than hardware approaches. Moreover, kMemvisor leverages the binary translation technology to guarantee the data are replicated on the y, which is a large improvement over other software HA solutions.

Compared with current software HA systems, e.g., Remus incurs 103% overhead making 40 checkpoints per second, our instruction level rewriting gets a better result. The results show that the performance of CPU-intensive tasks is almost unaffected while the average overhead in real world applications with application level high availability is 30%. And even in the worst case, our stressful memory write benchmark shows that the overhead of backup is 55%.

The current kMemvisor is implemented with static binary translation and direct page table technology. In a near future, we will release kMemvisor as an open source project and devote much engineering efforts (as we mentioned in Section V) to develop a mechanism to support multi-granularity memory mirroring and recovery in cloud environments, from a specified memory area to a whole virtual machine.

8. ACKNOWLEDGMENTS

This work is supported by the Program for PCSIRT and NCET of MOE, International Cooperation Program (No. 11530700500, 2011DFA10 50), the key program (No. 313035) of MOE, 63 Program (No. 2011AA01A202, 2012AA010 05), NSFC (No. 61073151, 61272101), and 73 Program (No. 2012CB723401).

9. REFERENCES

[1] ACME Laboratories. thttpd - tiny/turbo/throttling HTTP server.
http://www.acme.com/software/thttpd/.

[2] Amazon. Amazon EC2 Service Level Agreement.
http://aws.amazon.com/ec2-sla/.

[3] Andi Kleen. Machine check handling on linux. In S SE abs, 2004.

[4] Apache Software Foundation. ab - Apache HTTP server benchmarking tool. http://httpd.apache.org/docs/2.0/programs/ab.html.

[5] Bernd Panzer-Steindel. Data integrity. E N/IT, 2007.

[6] Bianca Schroeder, Eduardo Pinheiro and Wolf-Dietrich Weber. Dram errors in the wild: a large-scale field study. ommun A M, 54(2):100–107, 2011.

[7] Bodik Peter, Menache Ishai, Chowdhury Mosharaf, Mani Pradeepkumar, Maltz David A., Stoica Ion. Surviving failures in bandwidth-constrained datacenters. SI OMM omput ommun ev, 42(4), Aug. 2012.

[ ] Brendan Cully, Geoffrey Lefebvre, Dutch T. Meyer, Mike Feeley, Norman C. Hutchinson and Andrew Warfield. Remus: High availability via asynchronous virtual machine replication. (best paper). In *NSDI*, pages 161–175, 200 .

[ ] Chang Cheng-Shang, Chen Yi-Ting, Lee Duan-Shin. Constructions of optical fifo queues. *IEEE/A M Trans Netw*, 14(SI), June 2006.

[10] Chen, C. L. Error-correcting codes for semiconductor memory applications: A state-of-the-art review. In *IBM Journal of esearch and Development*, 1 4.

[11] Chen izhong. Algorithm-based recovery for iterative methods without checkpointing. In PD , pages 73– 4, 2011.

[12] Christopher Clark, Keir Fraser, Steven H, Jakob Gorm Hansen, Eric Jul, Christian Limpach, Ian Pratt and Andrew Warfield. Live migration of virtual machines. In *NSDI*, pages 273–2 6, 2005.

[13] Daniel J. Scales, Mike Nelson and Ganesh Venkitachalam. The design of a practical system for fault-tolerant virtual machines. *Operating Systems eview*, 44(4):30–3 , 2010.

[14] David Chisnall. *The Definitive uide to the en ypervisor*. Prentice Hall, 1 edition, 2007.

[15] David Fiala, Kurt B. Ferreira, Frank Mueller and Christian Engelmann. A tunable, software-based dram error detection and correction library for hpc. *Euro-par 2011, PA A E P O ESSIN O KS OPS*, 7156:251–261, 2012.

[16] Dell. Dell PowerEdge 12th generation servers. http://www.dell.com/poweredge.

[17] Denys Vlasenko. BusyBox: The Swiss Army Knife of Embedded Linux. http://www.busybox.net/.

[1] Fenn Michael, Murphy Michael A., Goasguen Sebastien. A study of a kvm-based cluster for grid computing. In *A M-SE*, pages 34:1–34:6, 200 .

[1] Fiala David, Ferreira Kurt, Mueller Frank, Engelmann Christian. A tunable, software-based dram error detection and correction library for hpc. In *sc*, 2011.

[20] R. Gallager. Low-density parity-check codes. In *Information Theory, I E Transactions on*, pages 21 – 2 , 1 62.

[21] Gang Wu, Jian Gao, Huxing hang and Yaozu Dong. Improving pcm endurance with randomized address remapping in hybrid memory system. In *STE (poster)*, pages 503–507, 2011.

[22] Giuseppe DeCandia, Deniz Hastorun, Madan Jampani, Gunavardhan Kakulapati, Avinash Lakshman, Alex Pilchin, Swaminathan Sivasubramanian, Peter Vosshall and Werner Vogels. Dynamo: amazon's highly available key-value store. In *SOSP*, pages 205–220, 2007.

[23] Google. App Engine Service Level Agreement. https://developers.google.com/appengine/sla.

[24] Haikun Liu, Cheng- hong Xu, Hai Jin, Jiayu Gong, Xiaofei Liao. Performance and energy modeling for live migration of virtual machines. In *PD* , pages 171–1 2, 2011.

[25] Haikun Liu, Hai Jin, Xiaofei Liao, Bo Ma, Cheng- hong Xu. Vmckpt: lightweight and live virtual machine checkpointing. *S IEN E INA Information Sciences*, 55(12):2 65–2 0, 2012.

[26] Haoliang Dong, Wei Sun, Bin Wang, Haiyang Sun and hengwei Qi. Memvisor: Application level memory mirroring via binary translation. In *STE (poster)*, 2012.

[27] HP Corporation. HP advanced memory protection technologies. http://h18000.www1.hp.com/products/servers/technology/memoryprotection.html.

[2] Intel Corporation. IA-32 Intel Architecture Software Developer's Manual. http://www.intel.com/content/www/us/en/processors/architectures-software-developer-manuals.html.

[2] JM Deegan. High reliability memory subsystem using data error correcting code symbol sliced command repowering. *S Patent ,206,962, oogle Patents*.

[30] Kutlu Mucahid, Agrawal Gagan, Kurt Oguz. Fault tolerant parallel data-intensive algorithms. In *PD* , pages 133–134, 2012.

[31] Levien L, Meyers W. Special feature: Semiconductor memory reliability with error detecting and correcting codes. In *omputer*, pages 43–50, 1 76.

[32] Mel Gorman and Patrick Healy. Supporting superpage allocation without additional hardware support. In *ISMM*, pages 41–50, 200 .

[33] Qingsong Li, Utpal Patel. Enabling Memory Reliability, Availability, and Serviceability Features on Dell PowerEdge Servers. http://www.dell.com/downloads/global/power/ps3q05-20050176-patel-oe.pdf.

[34] Qureshi Moinuddin K. Pay-as-you-go: low-overhead hard-error correction for phase change memories. In *MI O-44*, pages 31 –32 , 2011.

[35] Qureshi Moinuddin K., Srinivasan Vijayalakshmi, Rivers Jude A. Scalable high performance main memory system using phase-change memory technology. In *IS A*, pages 24–33, 200 .

[36] RW Hamming. Error detecting and error correcting codes. *Bell System technical journal*, 1 50.

[37] Sanjay Ghemawat, Howard Gobioff and Shun-Tak Leung. The google file system. In *SOSP*, pages 2 –43, 2003.

[3] Schechter Stuart, Loh Gabriel H., Straus Karin, Burger Doug. Use ecp, not ecc, for hard failures in resistive memories. *SI A omput Archit News*, 3 (3), June 2010.

[3] Seong Nak Hee, Woo Dong Hyuk, Srinivasan Vijayalakshmi, Rivers Jude A., Lee Hsien-Hsin S. Safer: Stuck-at-fault error recovery for memories. In *MI O*, pages 115–124, 2010.

[40] Sharma Prateek, Kulkarni Purushottam. Singleton: system-wide page deduplication in virtual environments. In *PD* , pages 15–26, 2012.

[41] SQLite. SQLite Web Site. http://www.sqlite.org/.

[42] Sridharan Vilas, Liberty Dean. A study of dram failures in the field. In *S* , pages 76:1–76:11, 2012.

[43] Timothy J. Dell. Ecc-on-simm test challenges. In *IT* , pages 511–515, 1 4.

[44] XV6. XV6 Doc. http://pdos.csail.mit.edu/6.828/2011/xv6.html.

[45] Yuyang Du, Hongliang Yu, Yunhong Jiang, Yaozu Dong and Weimin heng. A rising tide lifts all boats: how memory error prediction and prevention can help with virtualized system longevity. In *otDep SENI Association Berkeley*, 2010.

262

Author Index